THE PAPERS OF

WOODROW WILSON

VOLUME 35
OCTOBER 1, 1915–JANUARY 27, 1916

SPONSORED BY THE WOODROW WILSON
FOUNDATION
AND PRINCETON UNIVERSITY

THE PAPERS OF

WOODROW WILSON

ARTHUR S. LINK, *EDITOR*

DAVID W. HIRST, *SENIOR ASSOCIATE EDITOR*

JOHN E. LITTLE, *ASSOCIATE EDITOR*

ANN DEXTER GORDON, *ASSISTANT EDITOR*

PHYLLIS MARCHAND AND MARGARET D. LINK,
EDITORIAL ASSISTANTS

Volume 35
October 1, 1915–January 27, 1916

PRINCETON, NEW JERSEY
PRINCETON UNIVERSITY PRESS
1980

Copyright © 1980 by Princeton University Press
All Rights Reserved
L.C. Card 66-10880
I.S.B.N. 0-691-04676-X

Note to scholars: Princeton University Press
subscribes to the Resolution on Permissions of
the Association of American University Presses,
defining what we regard as "fair use" of copyrighted works. This Resolution, intended to encourage scholarly use of university press publications and to avoid unnecessary applications
for permission, is obtainable from the Press or
from the A.A.U.P. central office. Note, however,
that the scholarly apparatus, transcripts of
shorthand, and the texts of Wilson documents
as they appear in this volume are copyrighted,
and the usual rules about the use of copyrighted materials apply.

Publication of this book has been aided by a
grant from the National Historical Publications
and Records Commission.

Printed in the United States of America
by Princeton University Press
Princeton, New Jersey

INTRODUCTION

WILSON is beset on all sides by difficult problems as this volume begins. The crisis over the *Arabic* case, which has seemingly been settled with Count von Bernstorff's pledge of September 1, 1915, erupts again when the German government claims that *Arabic* had tried to ram the submarine that sank her and refuses to assume any liability for the death of Americans aboard the liner. Germany and the United States are once again on the brink of war. Under heavy pressure from Wilson and Lansing, Bernstorff, on October 5, violates his instructions and disavows the act of the submarine commander. Officials in Berlin are furious at Bernstorff but dare not repudiate him openly.

A satisfactory settlement of the *Arabic* case thus achieved, Lansing now moves to obtain a settlement of the *Lusitania* case. Bernstorff and the German Foreign Office are dilatory. Wilson and Lansing press hard for an open avowal of the illegality of the sinking of *Lusitania*, and, as this volume ends, a break in diplomatic relations between the United States and Germany seems inevitable.

For the first time since early 1913, the situation in Mexico is relatively tranquil. Carranza has decisively beaten Villa and consolidated his power. Wilson extends *de facto* recognition to Carranza on October 19 and persuades the Latin American governments to follow his (Wilson's) lead. Thus relations between the *de facto* Mexican government and the United States are unusually friendly during the balance of the period covered by this volume.

With the submarine controversy seemingly settled by Bernstorff's letter of October 5, 1915, Wilson now moves against the British maritime system. In a note to Great Britain on October 21, Wilson and Lansing denounce the British blockade of the Central Powers as "illegal" and "indefensible." They also ringingly reaffirm American neutrality and, going further, announce that the United States has "unhesitatingly" assumed the task of defending neutral rights.

Meanwhile, a controversy over preparedness has virtually convulsed the country. Wilson and the War and Navy departments have been at work on an administration program. Wilson announces that program in a speech in New York on November 4. His plan for naval expansion meets with general approval. However, the linchpin of Wilson's army program—a Continental Army of 400,000 men—is mired in controversy in the House Committee on Military affairs as this volume ends.

Wilson's hopes for an opportunity to bring the war in Europe to an end through his own mediation are fired by receipt of a letter from Sir Edward Grey, the British Foreign Secretary, in which Grey intimates that Great Britain might consent to Wilson's mediation if the United States was prepared to enter a postwar league of nations with adequate power to preserve the peace. Wilson replies positively at once and then sends Colonel House to London to lay the groundwork for Anglo-American cooperation for peace. House, having talked to many British leaders, is about to leave for Berlin and France to take soundings about peace in those capitals. In Washington, Wilson and Lansing, on January 18, 1916, launch their *modus vivendi* suggesting that the Allies disarm their merchantmen in return for a German pledge that submarines would follow the rules of cruiser warfare in attacking merchant vessels.

Wilson's brief but warm courtship of Edith Bolling Galt comes to a triumphant conclusion when they announce their engagement on October 6 and are married on December 18.

"VERBATIM ET LITERATIM"

In earlier volumes of this series we have said something like the following: "All documents are reproduced *verbatim et literatim*, with typographical and spelling errors corrected in square brackets only when necessary for clarity and ease of reading." The following essay explains our textual methods and review procedures.

We have never printed and do not intend to print critical, or corrected, versions of documents. We print them exactly as they are, with a few exceptions which we always note. We never use the word *sic* except to denote the repetition of words in a document; in fact, we think that a succession of *sics* simply defaces a page.

We often repair words in square brackets when letters are missing. As we have said, we also repair words in square brackets for clarity and ease of reading. Our general rule is to do this when we ourselves cannot read the word without stopping to determine its meaning. Jumbled words and names misspelled beyond recognition of course have to be repaired. We are usually able to correct the misspelling of a name in the footnote identifying the person.

However, when an old man writes to Wilson saying that he is glad to hear that Wilson is "comming" to Newark, or a semiliterate farmer from Texas writes phonetically, we see no reason to correct spellings in square brackets when the words are perfectly understandable. We do not correct Wilson's misspellings unless they are unreadable, except to supply in square brackets letters missing in words. For example, for some reason he insisted upon spelling "belligerent" as "belligerant." Nothing would be gained by correcting "belligerant" in square brackets.

We think that it is very important for several reasons to follow the rule of *verbatim et literatim*. Most important, a document has its own integrity and power, particularly when it is not written in perfect literary form. There is something very moving in seeing a Texas dirt farmer struggling to express his feelings in words, or a semiliterate former slave doing the same thing. Second, in Wilson's case it is crucially important to reproduce his errors in letters that he typed himself, since he always typed badly when he was in an agitated state. Third, since style is the essence of the person, we would never correct grammar or make tenses consistent, as one correspondent has urged us to do. Fourth, we print exact transcripts of Charles L. Swem's copies of Wilson's letters. Swem made many mistakes (we correct them in footnotes from a reading of his shorthand books), and Wilson let them pass. We thus have to assume that Wilson did not read his letters before signing them, and this, we think, is a significant fact. Finally, printing letters and typed documents *verbatim et literatim* tells us a great deal about the educational level of the stenographical profession in the United States during Wilson's time.

We think that our series would be worthless if we produced unreliable texts, and we go to considerable effort to make certain that the texts are authentic.

Our typists are highly skilled and proofread their transcripts carefully as soon as they have been typed. The Editor sight proofreads documents once he has assembled a volume and is setting the annotation. The editors who write the notes read through documents several times and are careful to check any anomalies. Then, once the manuscript volume has been completed and all notes checked, the Editor and Senior Associate Editor orally proofread the documents against the copy. They read every comma, dash, and character. They note every absence of punctuation. They study every nearly illegible word in written documents.

Once this process of "establishing the text" is completed, the manuscript volume goes to our editor at Princeton University Press, who checks the volume carefully and sends it to the printing plant. The volume is set by linotype by two typographers who have been working on the Wilson volumes for years. The galley proofs go to the proofroom, where they are read orally against copy. And we must say that the proofreaders at the Press are extraordinarily skilled. Some years ago, before we found a way to ease their burden, they used to query every misspelled word, absence of punctuation, or other such anomalies. Now we write "O.K." above such words or spaces on the copy.

We read the galley proofs three times. Our copyeditor gives them a sight reading against copy to look for remaining typographical errors and to make sure that no line has been dropped. The Editor and the Senior Associate Editor sight read them against documents and copy. We then get the page proofs, which have been corrected at the Press. We check all the changes twice. In addition, we get revised pages and check them twice.

This is not the end. Our indexer of course reads the pages word by word. Before we return the pages to the Press, she comes in with a list of queries, all of which are answered by reference to the documents.

Our rule in the Wilson Papers is that our tolerance of error is zero. No system and no person can be perfect. We are sure that there are errors in our volumes. However, we believe that we have done everything humanly possible to avoid error; the chance is remote that what looks at first glance like a typographical error is indeed an error.

We are greatly indebted to Katharine E. Brand and to Professors John Milton Cooper, Jr., William H. Harbaugh, and Richard W. Leopold for reading the manuscript of this volume and making helpful suggestions. We continue to benefit from the careful work and oversight of Judith May, our editor at Princeton University Press.

It is with great sadness that we here record the death of Julie (Mrs. Paul M.) Herzog on May 14, 1980. Mrs. Herzog was for many years the executive director of the Woodrow Wilson Foundation. In that capacity, she served as financial manager of the Wilson Papers from 1958 to 1963. All the while, as a member of the Board of Directors of the Woodrow Wilson Foundation, she gave us constant and warm support. We have had no better friend than she, and we will miss her greatly.

THE EDITORS

Princeton, New Jersey
May 29, 1980

CONTENTS

ILLUSTRATIONS

Following page 264

A Medley of Cartoons by Rollin Kirby
(All appeared originally in the New York *World*, 1913-1916)

The Employment Agent

Ready for Business

Ripping It Out

Wiping Away His Tears

The Class in Reading and Writing

"Obstructing Traffic, Your Honor"

"The German Government believes that it was acting in justified self-defense."

"To Arms! To Arms!"

ABBREVIATIONS

AL	autograph letter
ALI	autograph letter initialed
ALS	autograph letter signed
CC	carbon copy
CCL	carbon copy of letter
CCLS	carbon copy of letter signed
CLS	Charles Lee Swem
CLSsh	Charles Lee Swem shorthand
EAW	Ellen Axson Wilson
EBG	Edith Bolling Galt
EBW	Edith Bolling Wilson
EBWhw	Edith Bolling Wilson handwriting, handwritten
EMH	Edward Mandell House
FR	*Papers Relating to the Foreign Relations of the United States*
FR-LP	*Papers Relating to the Foreign Relations of the United States, The Lansing Papers*
FR-WWS 1915	*Papers Relating to the Foreign Relations of the United States, 1915, Supplement, The World War*
FR-WWS 1916	*Papers Relating to the Foreign Relations of the United States, 1916, Supplement, The World War*
Hw	handwriting, handwritten
HwC	handwritten copy
HwCL	handwritten copy of letter
HwS	handwritten signed
JPT	Joseph Patrick Tumulty
LMG	Lindley Miller Garrison
MS	manuscript
MSS	manuscripts
PCL	printed copy of letter
RG	record group
RL	Robert Lansing
T	typed
T MS	typed manuscript
T MSS	typed manuscripts
TC	typed copy
TCL	typed copy of letter
TL	typed letter
TLS	typed letter signed
TS	typed signed
WGM	William Gibbs McAdoo
WHP	Walter Hines Page
WW	Woodrow Wilson
WWhw	Woodrow Wilson handwriting, handwritten
WWsh	Woodrow Wilson shorthand
WWT	Woodrow Wilson typed
WWTL	Woodrow Wilson typed letter
WWTLI	Woodrow Wilson typed letter initialed
WWTLS	Woodrow Wilson typed letter signed

ABBREVIATIONS FOR COLLECTIONS
AND REPOSITORIES
Following the National Union Catalog of the Library of Congress

Ar	Archives
BIA	Bureau of Insular Affairs
CSt	Stanford University
CSt-H	Stanford University, Hoover Institution on War, Revolution, and Peace
CtY	Yale University
DLC	Library of Congress
DNA	National Archives
EBR	Executive Branch Records
FFM-Ar	French Foreign Ministry Archives
FO	British Foreign Office
GFO-Ar	German Foreign Office Archives
MH	Harvard University
MH-Ar	Harvard University Archives
MH-BA	Harvard University, Graduate School of Business Administration
MHi	Massachusetts Historical Society
NcD	Duke University
NcU	University of North Carolina
NjHi	New Jersey Historical Society
NjP	Princeton University
NNC	Columbia University
OHi	Ohio State Historical Society
PRO	Public Record Office
PSC	Swarthmore College
PSC-Hi	Swarthmore College, Friends Historical Library
PSC-P	Swarthmore College, Peace Collection
RSB Coll., DLC	Ray Stannard Baker Collection of Wilsoniana, Library of Congress
ScCleU	Clemson University
SDR	State Department Records
ViU	University of Virginia
WC, NjP	Woodrow Wilson Collection, Princeton University
WDR	War Department Records
WHi	State Historical Society of Wisconsin
WP, DLC	Woodrow Wilson Papers, Library of Congress

SYMBOLS

[Oct. 11, 1915]	publication date of a published writing; also date of document when date is not part of text
[[Oct. 21, 1915]]	delivery date of speech if publication date differs

THE PAPERS OF
WOODROW WILSON

VOLUME 35
OCTOBER 1, 1915–JANUARY 27, 1916

THE PAPERS OF
WOODROW WILSON

To William Spry

My dear Governor Spry: [The White House] October 1, 1915

Of course, you understand that I sent you the message I did in the Hillstrom case[1] only because I thought it due to the representative of a foreign nation to give him the utmost benefit of any possible process in the case of a subject of his government sentenced to death. I shall communicate to the Swedish Minister, through the State Department, your wishes as expressed in your telegram of September thirtieth and have no doubt that he will do everything that is right in the circumstances.

Very sincerely yours,   Woodrow Wilson

TLS (Letterpress Books, WP, DLC).
[1] Wilson's message is printed at September 30, 1915, Vol. 34.

From Edward Mandell House, with Enclosures

Dear Governor: New York. October 1st, 1915.

I am enclosing you a copy of a letter which I have just received from Mr. Balfour, First Lord of the Admiralty, through Sir Horace Plunkett. I am also sending you Sir Horace's letter.

You can never know how deeply the English feel when any matter touching their Navy comes to the fore, and I would urge the greatest possible caution in changing any existing rules that might have a tendency to hurt their sensibilities.

Parts of Balfour's and Plunkett's letters were in code which I deciphered.

I am not sure how far our people would be willing to go in order to obtain a disavowal for the Arabic incident. I think the main thing now is that there should be no more accidents or happenings of that sort. If there are, if I were you, I would send Bernstorff home without any discussion whatsoever.

I shall try and see Lansing tomorrow and stir him up upon South American matters.

I am wondering whether this Government should not make some sort of protest over the Armenian massacres. That, I think, would appeal to our people, for the moment, more strongly then a rigid insistence upon a disavowal of the Arabic.

Your affectionate,   [E. M. House]

TCL (E. M. House Papers, CtY).

E N C L O S U R E   I

Sir Horace Plunkett to Edward Mandell House

No. 22.

My dear Colonel House,   Dublin. 17th September, 1915.

Yesterday I received the enclosed letter from Aftermath[1] which I have slightly mutilated for a reason you will understand. It has been approved by Affection[2] and I have been asked to transmit it and at the same time to advise you by cable of its transmission and, so far as our code permits, to indicate its gist. The cable, which was sent yesterday but was delayed by the Censor, who will still, I am afraid, insist on its going to your name and address in New York, was as follows: "Aftermath hearing contemplated change aura Municipal Law tending to facilitate Adder[3] methods sends an important note for Beverley.[4] Suggest Dado to-morrow."[5] If I get it off to-day it will end with the word "to-day" instead of "to-morrow."

I am sure you and Aaron[6] will both be pleased to get this very human document. What I particularly liked in it was the frank avowal of the case which, on purely technical grounds, might be made against us. I feel sure, however, that if the letter is not to override the spirit of the very undefined law which is supposed to govern nations at war, the broader view of the conduct of our sea captains when dealing with an adversary who knows no law but his own interests will appeal both to you and your great friend.

If I were to presume to add any considerations to those which seem to me to be so conclusive in Aftermath's letter, I think I should urge two points of view. An intimation of the change which Aaron was going to recommend to his own people and press upon other nations after the war might be preferable to raising an issue which would embarrass the Allies out of all proportion to any advantage it could bring to the United States in the interval between now and the time when the matter could be calmly discussed by all concerned. My second point is that if it be said that the occasion is too favourable to the establishment of a mercantile fleet in the United States to be missed, the answer may fairly be made that were such a fleet in existence the United States would never allow rightful self-defence to be tampered with.

I assume that, if the step which is apprehended over here is really likely to be taken, it will be on account of pressure from Altruist.[7] I hope, however, that Aaron will take the view that his influence in working for Fibre[8] later on would be immensely strengthened if he prevents action which would be particularly distasteful to Aptitude[9] and her allies.

Aftermath has not forgotten the promised letter upon Fibre. Indeed, he actually wrote it and it did not satisfy him so he is going to take another opportunity of sending you his considered view.   Yours very sincerely,   Organise.

You might perhaps cable receipt of this letter No 22

TL (E. M. House Papers, CtY).
  1 Balfour.
  2 Grey.
  3 Von Tirpitz.
  4 House.
  5 "Suspend action until you receive my letter."
  6 Wilson.
  7 The United States Congress.
  8 Freedom of the seas.
  9 Great Britain.

E N C L O S U R E   I I

Arthur James Balfour to Edward Mandell House

Private.

My dear Mr. House   [London] 12th September, 1915.

You were good enough to say that I might write to you privately on any matter of interest, and I would have done so long before this had I not been aware that others had kept you fully informed upon all that is going on here. A matter however has just come to my knowledge which may have a very important bearing, not only upon the interests of this country, but as I think upon the interests of the civilized world, whether neutral or belligerent. It will without doubt be the subject of official communication between the Foreign Office and the State Department; but what I am now writing to you is not between Department and Department, but between man and man.

It was only an hour ago that I heard from the Foreign Office that the State Department were considering whether they ought not to modify the rules laid down at Washington for the treatment of belligerent merchant ships armed for purely defensive purposes and carrying out purely commercial operations. The ground for this alteration is the alleged fact that such vessels, though armed only for defence, have in fact taken the offensive against German submarines. The position taken up by the State Department is (as I understand it) that the U. S. rules which were properly applicable to the old condition of things, require modification in the face of new developments; and into necessity and character of these modifications they are now examining.

I am, as you know, the last person to suggest that in the presence of ever-varying conditions of war, old rules can remain unmodified, and it is on much broader grounds than those which are based on precedent alone that I now base my appeal.

The German practice is to sink without notice any ship which they suppose to be trading with Britain. All neutrals admit that this is contrary both to the Law of Nations and the principles of humanity. But so far they have been powerless to stop it; and no one supposes that Germany is likely to listen to any appeal on the subject except an appeal to her self-interest. But neutrals who have got no effective weapon short of war which they can use against the Germans, possess a very powerful weapon in the shape of their Municipal Law which they can use against the Allies. If they can do little to paralyse the attack, they can do much to embarrass the defence; and I greatly fear that this unfortunate result would be achieved if the leading neutral of the world were to throw in its weight against the defensive armament of merchant ships.

The German arguments on this subject are, it seems to me, as cynical as the German practice is inhuman. They complain that merchant ships in submarine-infested seas adopt a zigzag course, which no doubt may occasionally make either their bow or their stern point in the direction of the submarine. This, they plead, is a proof of aggressive intention on the part of the merchant ship: if the bow is pointing towards the submarine the obvious intention is to run her down; if the stern is pointing in the direction of the submarine, the object is clearly to bring the merchantman's guns to bear upon it. In either case the submarine in self-defence is justified in torpedoing at sight. In other words, the Germans argue that the mere attempt of the victim to escape involves a threat of hostile action which justifies the extremest degree of brutality.

It may no doubt be urged that it is not always in this fashion that matters proceed. If the captain of a merchantman, armed or unarmed, saw a hostile submarine across his bows, I think it extremely likely that he would endeavour to ram her. I frankly admit that if I were the captain that is how I should proceed, although well aware that if my attempt failed the submarine would attempt to sink me. But this is what the submarine would do in any case; and I do not see how the merchant captain can be blamed. When maritime warfare was carried on under civilized rules it would have been in the highest degree blameworthy for any merchant ship to initiate hostile action. By so doing she would convert herself without notice into an armed cruiser and would have no claim to be treated as a peaceful trader when she called at neutral ports. But when we are dealing with an enemy who knows no law, and who not once nor twice and accidentally, but repeatedly and of set purpose, has sunk peaceful traders without notice, how is it possible for these to wait until they are summoned to surrender? No summons of surrender is ever uttered. A torpedo is discharged or guns are fired, and all is over. Cold-blooded butchery takes the place of the old procedure sanctioned and approved by International Law.

I cannot help thinking that if this question is looked at in a broad spirit, it will be seen that whatever are to be the laws of maritime warfare, and however they are to be enforced, it cannot be in the interests of international morals that the Municipal Law of any great neutral should be modified in the direction favourable to the perpetrator of outrages and hostile to his victims. Doubtless the problems which this war will leave behind it for peaceful solution are of extreme difficulty; but those difficulties would I venture to say be increased and not diminished if, while the weight of the best neutral opinion is hostile to the German misuse of submarines, neutral action was, however unintentional, employed in its favour.

Pray believe me,

Yours very sincerely,   (A J. Balfour)

P.S. I may perhaps remind you that on the 30th January of this year, before the "Wilhelmina" carrying food stuffs to Germany was stopped and before any pronouncement was made by Germany about her new submarine policy, the British steamers "Tokomaru" and "Ikaria" were deliberately torpedoed without warning off Havre, the submarine never coming to the surface or giving the slightest warning. This act took place before any British merchant vessels had been armed against submarine attack, and when the only defensively armed vessels were those which had been so armed as a protection against enemy cruisers on the trade routes.

This is a letter from A. J. Balfour. Sir Horace thought it best to mutilate it.   E.M.H.

TL (E. M. House Papers, CtY).

Sir Horace Plunkett to Edward Mandell House[1]

My dear Colonel House: Dublin. October 1, 1915.

I wanted in this letter to say a few things which I should not like to run any risk of being read by others so I have asked James Byrne,[2] whom I think you know, to send the letter to you by hand.

The week I spent in London has left certain impressions upon my mind which I will give to you for what they are worth. The chief of them is that the tide has at last turned and there ought no longer to be any grave fear of the defeat of the Allies. Had we gone into the winter with the Russians driven out of Poland, with the Dardanelles exploit having failed and the Balkans practically offering an open road to the Central Powers for their southern march, while Germany remained firmly rooted in Belgium and in the chief industrial portion of France, it is hard to say what internal trouble might not have arisen in Russia, France, and indeed in Britain, to make the effective resumption of hostilities in the spring somewhat problematical.

I know many soldiers who have been engaged in Flanders and who had come to the conclusion that it would be hopeless to attempt to break through the German trenches. It has, however, been demonstrated that when the Allies are adequately equipped with artillery and ammunition the strongest trenches with their barbed wire entanglements, can be blown to pieces and reduced to a condition where the attack quickly becomes as formidable as the defense. We have no full news yet but the wounded— the first batches of whom are already in the London hospitals— testify to the complete confidence of the British troops that they can break through the German lines whenever they have a proper equipment for the purpose.[3]

I hold more strongly than ever that, should the United States be drawn into the conflict, it would be a determining factor in bringing it to an early conclusion. But I am quite happy now about this eventuality because I feel confident that the President

[1] House sent this letter to Wilson on October 18.
[2] James Patrick Byrne, an old friend of Plunkett and a founder of the Irish Agricultural Organization Society.
[3] Wilson marked the entire following paragraph on the margin.

will not only take part in the war if he ought to do so and stay out if he ought not, but, if he does come in, he will bring the people so overwhelmingly with him that no domestic complications will impair the fighting efficiency of the Republic. My chief fear for the future, so far as your country is needed to help in the making of it, is that, in the misunderstanding by the belligerents of the attitude of the leading neutral, the opportunity may not come for the President's mediation.

While I was in London I took occasion to get to know Owen Seaman, the Editor of Punch. That paper, as you are aware, has an extraordinary influence upon public opinion and its influence has been steadily used in a most unfortunate manner to impugn the motives of the President. I think I cleared away some misapprehensions in the Editor's mind. He made one promise to me which I shall call upon him to fulfil if the occasion arises. If the United States does become a belligerent full justice will be done to the fine stand the President has made, not so much on behalf of your country but in the interests of civilization. I mention this as, although few newspapers have offended in the same way, I learned that public opinion in these islands towards the United States has decidedly not improved since the Arabic and Hesperian incidents seemed, to those who did not understand the President's difficulties, to throw doubt upon his determination to get a satisfactory answer to his third Lusitania Note. Those of us who would like to enlighten public opinion upon the real issues involved and upon the considerations, wholly unknown to Old World folk, which a President of the United States has to take into account, have hesitated to enter upon the discussion of a diplomatic situation which changes almost from day to day. But I shall try and organize a body of friendly opinion as soon as I see clearly the precise situation which will have to be explained. For the future peace of the world I feel it to be of real importance that throughout the British Empire there should be a sound and just appreciation of the President's motives either for becoming a belligerent or remaining neutral.

As I said in a hurried note from London (September 27), Arthur Balfour understands very clearly—and this understanding is the first fruits of your readily acquired intimacy with him— the importance of having the issues upon which the British Empire may appear to be insufficiently regardful for the interests of the United States, frankly faced and clearly explained.

In his confidential letter to you he admitted that in strict law Great Britain might not be able to establish a theoretically per-

fect justification and might have to rely upon the previous wrong
doing and the general disregard of international agreements on
the part of Germany.

Nothing but the broadest view of the whole situation will serve
to prove that, on the whole, it is better for England to help the
Allies in the most effective way at her command until the trouble
is over and then to try and find a means of obviating the necessity for resorting to these violent expedients in the future. Somehow or other this war must be brought to such an end that Germany will be willing to put aside the armament which forty
years of preparation had given her good reason to believe might
make her master of the Old World, if not of the New as well,
an ambition which I am inclined to think the events of the last
few days must have shown her to be impossible of realization.

I am afraid, however, there is a big body of opinion in the
United States which does not even now see that Prussian [militar-
ism] is, either in the abstract or in its practical working out, any
worse for the world than British navalism, and as long as that
impression widely prevails there seems to me to be no chance of
the United States having her rightful influence in the peace settlement.

Perhaps the gravest fact brought out in this war is that there
is hardly any limit to the application of science to the destruction
of human life. For instance, gases, as you know, are only just
beginning to be used and it is known that those which produced
such horrible results when the Germans introduced the practice
can be greatly improved upon by these diabolical chemists. If
the war were to end today, as far as I can judge of the feelings
of the average man in these islands, the threat of extermination
has not been realized to a point where the primal instinct of self-
preservation would make peoples compel their rulers to get together and find some means of preventing war. Most of the peace
talk is laughed at, and I am inclined to think that the pacificists
do not prepare the ground sufficiently for their proposals by first
making people realize what a war, say five years hence, might
mean. Curiously, my American correspondence and conversations with Americans I met over here shows that your people
have grasped the situation far better than, at any rate, the people
of these islands. This makes me rely more upon the United States
to save[4] disaster in the future than upon any Old World Power;
for, insular though you may think me, I believe that we are more
likely to solve the problem than any other belligerent.[5]

[4] Thus in the original of this letter in the House Papers. Presumably he
dictated "stave."

[5] Wilson marked the entire following paragraph on the margin.

I shall weary you if I go on so I will only tell you, in the strict confidence with which we write to each other, of one thing that Grey said to me and which I think you ought to know. I asked him to tell me straight whether he wished the United States to come in, whether he believed that their doing so would hasten the conclusion of the war and whether he had any fears that it would embarrass the British envoys in the peace congress that would follow. He seemed to realize the tremendous effect your intervention would have. He said that, in his private capacity, he hoped you would intervene but that, of course, he could never in his official capacity express any such hope or desire. As regards the attitude of the United States in negotiating for peace, he said that the mere fact that the whole world would know that, unlike any other belligerent, they had come in for the single purpose of warring against war would give them a tremendous influence in devising a scheme of peace. And, he added, Germany would have to accept any terms insisted upon by the United States as her economic life could not possibly be reconstructed without the good will of your country.

I have such mountainous arrears of work here after my week's absence that I fear I may not have dictated an adequate letter. I shall think of a lot of other things I ought to have said to you when today's mail has gone. The main thing I want you to feel is that I am extremely anxious to do my small part in guiding public opinion aright upon the motives which actuate the President in whatever course he decides to take. From what I have said I think you will understand the circumstances in which it might be well to give me early notice should any decision be imminent calling for the publicity activity we have discussed.

Believe me, Yours sincerely,   Horace Plunkett.

I think you will find this well worth reading. E.M.H.

TCL (WP, DLC).

From Edith Bolling Galt

Dearest: [Washington] Oct. 1st [1915], 8:45

What a perfectly awful day for you to have to go to Arlington.[1] I am so worried and do hope those old wretches will have sense enough to postpone the ceremony.

Please put on things to protect you and have some cover over your head. It was such fun seeing you yesterday, only I wanted so to stay and when we were talking about Tea this afternoon I forgot about Miss Woodrow's coming[2] and that Helen will have to be with her. I know you forgot this too so suppose *we* will have to wait until tomorrow after all. Does absence make the heart grow fonder? If it does no wonder Bishop Bones has such a time making us be sensible when we are together.

I am wondering what you did last night if you went to the Theatre? I have looked all through the paper and find no mention of anything you did but was cheered to see that 2 *ladies kissed your hand* yesterday,[3] which you failed to mention when I was there.

Oh! dear, I had thought I would stay in bed this morning (where I am now writing) but old Mr. W.[4] has just phoned he will be here at 9:30 so I must stop and get dressed.

I love you my precious Woodrow—and want so to see you.

Always your own,   Edith.

Your sisters letter[5] is sweet, and I appreciate all she said. E.

Extra Edition. 10:20 a.m.

As Mr. Wilson came before I sent this to you, I am adding a line more to tell you he is so anxious to see you and talk over things with you (I don't know clearly just what he does want to say) but he says if you could give him an appointment for a little interview it would be a comfort to him as well as a great pleasure. I told him you had said you were going to ask him to lunch with you some time. But he insisted that was quite unnecessary as it would consume so much of your time, and that he had better just come when you could talk uninterruptedly. Don't bother about it this week Dearest, for I know how much you have pressing—and this can wait. But I only told you because I know how interested you always are.

Let me know what Col. House says—about the question you asked him—and if you know what day the Smiths' will come? Forget my ill humor Wednesday night, and know that I am always your own.

Edith.

ALS (WP, DLC).

[1] Wilson was scheduled to lay the cornerstone for the Arlington Memorial Amphitheater. The event was postponed to October 13 on account of rain.

[2] Katherine Hamilton Woodrow, daughter of James Hamilton and Katherine McGregor McMaster Woodrow. Miss Woodrow, along with other guests, accompanied Wilson that evening to the Keith Theater.

[3] The two ladies had so greeted Wilson during a reception in the afternoon at the White House. He shook hands with some 4,404 persons attending the G.A.R. encampment.

[4] That is, Nathaniel Wilson, her old friend and adviser.

[5] Annie J. W. Howe to WW, Sept. 28, 1915, ALS (WP, DLC).

Count Johann Heinrich von Bernstorff
to Robert Lansing[1]

My dear Mr. Secretary: Cedarhurst, N. Y., October 2, 1915.

Prompted by the desire to reach a satisfactory agreement with regard to the Arabic incident my Government has given me the following instructions:

The orders issued by His Majesty the Emperor to the commanders of the German submarines—of which I notified you on a previous occasion—have been made so stringent that the recurrence of incidents similar to the Arabic case is considered out of the question.

According to the report of Commander Schneider of the submarine that sank the Arabic and his affidavit as well as those of his men, Commander Schneider was convinced that the Arabic intended to ram the submarine, ⟨and he evidently had every reason to be so convinced⟩. On the other hand, the Imperial Government does not doubt the good faith of the affidavits of the British officers of the Arabic, according to which the Arabic did not intend to ram the submarine. The attack of the submarine, therefore, was undertaken against the instructions issued to the commander. The Imperial Government *therefore* regrets ⟨this⟩ *and disavows the act* and has notified Commander Schneider accordingly.

⟨As you know, my Government does not recognize the liability of paying⟩ *In the circumstances my Govt is prepared to pay an* indemnity for the American lives, which to its deep regret have been lost on the Arabic. ⟨However, in a spirit of conciliation and friendship for the United States my Government will be prepared to pay an indemnity, about the amount of which⟩ I am authorized to negotiate with you *as to the amount of this indemnity.*

I am, my dear Mr. Lansing,

Very sincerely yours,   J. Bernstorff

TLS (SDR, RG 59, 841.857 Ar 1/105½, DNA).

[1] Bernstorff handed this letter to Lansing at a brief meeting at the Hotel Biltmore in New York in the morning of October 2. Lansing left for Washington and discussed the letter with Wilson during the evening of October 3. During or after this conversation, Lansing emended Bernstorff's letter in order to make it acceptable to Wilson and himself. See Lansing's memorandum printed at Oct. 5, 1915, and RL to EMH, Oct. 6, 1915. Lansing's suggested deletions are in angle brackets; his suggested new text is italicized.

Count Johann Heinrich von Bernstorff
to Robert Lansing, with Enclosure

My dear Mr. Secretary: Cedarhurst, N. Y., October 2, 1915.

With regard to our conversation about the Arabic incident this morning I beg to say that according to my instructions the report of Commander Schneider of our submarine and the German affidavits have been sent to you through the American Embassy in Berlin. If you should not have received them, I will be glad to send you a copy.

In this same envelope I have pleasure in sending you my tentative letter about the Lusitania incident.

I remain, my dear Mr. Lansing,

Yours very sincerely,   J. Bernstorff

TLS (SDR, RG 59, 763.72/2236½, DNA).

E N C L O S U R E

Strictly confidential.

My dear Mr. Secretary: Cedarhurst, N. Y., October 2, 1915.

Prompted by the desire to reach an amicable understanding about the Lusitania incident my Government has given me the following instructions:

The attack on the Lusitania formed part of the reprisals enacted by my Government against Great Britain on account of her unlawful starvation policy. In our opinion such reprisals were amply justified by the inhuman British warfare. At that time the Imperial Government had not yet issued the instructions which now regulate our submarine warfare and according to which the Arabic case was settled. Even then, however, it was not the intention of the Imperial Government that our reprisals should lead to the loss of the lives of noncombattants. My Government has, therefore, on previous occasions expressed its deep regret that American lives should have been lost on the Lusitania.

As you know, the Imperial government does not acknowledge any liability to grant an indemnity in the matter. However, in a spirit of friendship and concilation the Imperial Government is prepared to submit the question of liability to pay indemnity to the Hague Tribunal.

In your note of July 21st concerning the Lusitania incident the Government of the United States invited the practical cooperation of the Imperial German Government in contending for the principle of the freedom of the seas, and you added that this great object could in some way be accomplished before the present war ends. I am instructed to say that the Imperial Government will at all times gladly cooperate with the Government of the United States for the purpose of accomplishing this great common object.

I remain, my dear Mr. Lansing,

Very sincerely yours,   J. Bernstorff

TLS (SDR, RG 59, 763.72/2235½, DNA).

To Edith Bolling Galt, with Enclosure

My lovely, adorable Sweetheart,   [The White House] Saturday,
7.40 A.M. 2 Oct., 1915

Here is House's reply. It came over from the office last night while we were at the theatre. This answers one of your questions. You heard Helen answer the other yesterday: the Smiths are to come on Wednesday. What is my dear Lady's verdict? Are we to have our freedom next week, or must we wait until the fifteenth?

Ah, my precious One, how full my heart is of you, and how hard it is to fill the hours with any sort of contentment that I must spend away from you! Every time I am with you I seem to discover anew how *perfectly* you satisfy every need of my heart,—with what deep, deep delight you quicken me, and what bliss it is to know and feel your love: you are all the world to me, and my heart waits for to-night with an infinite longing! My precious Darling!

Your own   Woodrow

I am just starting out for golf.

ALS (WP, DLC).

E N C L O S U R E

From Edward Mandell House

Dear Governor,   [New York] October 1, 1915.

I do not believe there is anything to be gained by delaying the announcement of your engagement. For the first time I have taken Mrs. House into our confidence, and she agrees to this conclusion. I think it would be well to let it be known that Mrs. Galt and you met for the first time last spring. Please come to see me soon after the engagement is made public, and let us all have a good time together. I have a plan by which you may be able to see each other as much as you wished and without anyone being the wiser. There are some good plays here which we could enjoy, and I am sure both of you would have a happy time. If this plan meets with your approval, I will go into the details later. I am, with deep affection,

Your devoted friend,   E. M. House

ALS (WP, DLC).

A Draft of An Announcement by Stockton Axson[1]

[c. Oct. 2, 1915]

The engagement was announced to-day of Mrs. Norman Galt and President Woodrow Wilson.

Mrs. Norman Galt is the widow of a well known business man of Washington who died some eight years ago. She has lived in Washington since her marriage in 1896. She was Miss Edith Bolling and was born in Wytheville, Virginia, where her girlhood was spent and where her father, the Hon[ourable] William H. Bolling, a man of remarkable character and charm, won distinction as one of the ablest, most interesting and most individual lawyers of a State famous for its lawyers. In the circle of cultivated and interesting people who have had the privilege of knowing her Mrs. Galt has enjoyed an enviable distinction, not only because of her unusual beauty and natural charm, but also because of her very unusual character and gifts. She has always been sought out as a delightful friend, and her thoughtfulness and quick capacity for anything she chose to undertake have made her friendship invaluable to those who were fortunate enough to win it.

It was Miss Margaret Wilson and her cousin Miss Bones who drew Mrs. Galt into the White House circle. They met her first in the early part of the present year, and were so much attracted by her that they sought her out more and more frequently and the friendship among them quickly ripened into an affectionate intimacy. It was through this association with his daughter and cousin that the President had the opportunity to meet Mrs. Galt, who spent a month at Cornish this summer as Miss Wilson's guest. ⟨There she was thrown, too, with Mrs. Sayre, the President's second daughter, who promptly became as warm a friend and admirer as her sister and cousin already were.⟩[2] It is, indeed, the most interesting circumstance connected with the engagement just announced that the President's daughters should have picked Mrs. Galt out for their special admiration and friendship before their father did.

WWT MS (WP, DLC).
  1 See S. Axson to WW, Oct. 6, 1915.
  2 This sentence deleted by Wilson.

To Edith Bolling Galt

[The White House] Sunday,
My precious Darling,   9.10 A.M. 3 Oct., 1915

The more we are together the more I love you, the more I need to have you always with me, and the more inadequate *written* words become to speak my heart to you,—the more impatient I grow of the pen, the more eager to whisper the love that floods my heart into my Darling's lips as I hold her close in my arms. And yet the more necessary does it become to relieve my heart with *some* message of love, even if it be only written. Please go to ride with us this evening, precious little girl, so that I can whisper something in your ear—*some*thing of my happiness and love, and accept this, in the meantime, as a piece out of my very heart, which is all yours but cannot be sent as I wish to send it by letter. It has to be presented in person. I cannot express in written words, either, the happiness you gave me last night. How unspeakably lovely and delightful you are, and how altogether satisfying—and how empty and lonely the house is without you. You carry away its light and its home-likeness whenever you leave it. It seems to yearn for you as I do. I love, *love*, <u>love</u> you.

Your own   Woodrow

ALS (WP, DLC).

From Edith Bolling Galt

[Washington] Oct. 3rd, 1915
My precious One: Sunday, 10 a.m.

Altrude has just gone and I am waiting for Mr. Wilson, who will come before I have said anything, save the thing you know best already, and that is—I love you. Are you happy dear little Boy this radiant morning?

Some way, last night I thought you did not seem as bouyant as usual. I hope I was mistaken and that nothing, mental or physical, is disturbing you.

Altrude and I talked until after three this a.m. and I woke

before Seven, but I feel perfectly fresh and well—and so happy
—because you love me

Hope Mr. Lansing will bring good tidings from his interview,
and there will be an end of anxiety from that quarter. Did you
read your Sister's note to me? It is sweet and generous, and I
shall answer it at once. With all my love, I am

Your own,   Edith

ALS (WP, DLC).

To Edith Bolling Galt

[The White House] Sunday, 3 Oct. [1915]

Just a word, precious little girl, about something in your note
to-day. I never *felt* more bouyant in my life than I did last night,
for you were so radiantly lovely and happy and made me feel your
love so exquisitely. If I seemed quiet, it was for two reasons—
first and chiefly, because when happiness goes deepest with me
I am apt to find the feeling *too* deep for expression,—and I am
sure you must have seen that I was happy and beyond measure
enjoying my radiant and enchanting Darling—Second because I
have felt that I have very often failed to make you wholly happy
when you were with me and I was trying to take my cue wholly
from you and love you exactly as your mood made you wish me
to love you,—trying to *learn* and think wholly and all the while
of you—and it made me very happy to do so! And so nothing—
not the least thing—was the matter, my precious, thoughtful,
loving Darling, either mentally or physically: I was just studying
your pleasure and rejoiced to do it—and was myself too happy
to give adequate expression to it. I love you with all my heart
and life   Your own   Woodrow

ALS (WP, DLC).

Two Letters to Edward Mandell House

Dearest Friend,   The White House. 4 October, 1915.

The announcement will be made on Thursday morning next,
the seventh, and we plan (Mrs. Galt, her mother, Helen, and I)
to go over to New York on Friday, the eighth, if that will be a
convenient day for you on which to carry out the delightful plan
of a theatre party. The ladies will go to a hotel and I will come
to you, always provided the time is a convenient one for you;
and I know that you will frankly say whether it is or not. I have

never seen "Grumpy";[1] would that play suit you as well as another.

It was like you to plan such a pleasure for us, and I am sure we shall all be very happy together.

Would you think it an imposition if I were to ask you to have some diamond engagement rings sent up to your apartment for us to choose from? There is a man named Dreicher[2] who has unusual designs. Tiffany seems to have lost the artistic taste and originality that we formerly looked for. It would be great fun to make the choice Friday night.

I feel that I am asking a great deal, but it would be very embarrassing to go to the shop ourselves on such an errand, and it has not been possible to select a ring sooner, for reasons you will readily devine.

I am sending you a letter on business under another cover.

Affectionately Yours,   Woodrow Wilson

[1] *Grumpy*, a comedy by Horace Hodges and T. Wigney Percyval, then playing at the Empire Theater in New York. The star was Cyril Maude.
[2] Jacob Dreicer of Dreicer and Co., jewelers of Fifth Avenue.

Dearest Friend,   The White House. 4 October, 1915.

The idea about a main issue for the campaign next year seems to me a fine one: it is indeed the one that has been vaguely in my own mind for some time. I am to greet the D.A.R. within a week or so: what would you think of my using that occasion, when the natural theme would be patriotism, to develope the idea?

I read the letters from Plunket and Balfour with the greatest interest. The matter of armed merchantmen is not so simple as Balfour would make it. It is hardly fair to ask Submarine commanders to give warning by summons if, when they approach as near as they must for that purpose they are to be fired upon, as Balfour would evidently have them fired upon. It is a question of many sides and is giving Lansing and me some perplexed moments.   Affectionately Yours,   Woodrow Wilson

WWTLS (E. M. House Papers, CtY).

To Joseph Rucker Lamar

My dear Mr. Justice: [The White House] October 4, 1915

This is just a message of affectionate interest. I have been deeply distressed to learn that you did not more rapidly grow better and I want you to know with what deep and genuine sympathy I have sought to keep in touch with you.[1] My heart goes out to you in your illness and I wish with all my heart that there was something I could do to cheer you on the way to recovery.

Cordially and sincerely yours,   Woodrow Wilson

TLS (Letterpress Books, WP, DLC)
  [1] Justice Lamar, seriously ill for several months from high blood pressure, had suffered a slight stroke, followed by lung congestion, in early September.

From Edward Mandell House

Dear Governor: New York. October 4th, 1915.

I had a long talk with Lord Reading Saturday at the house of a friend and unknown to anyone.

He is anxious to pay his respects to you before leaving the country, but does not desire to do so until after all matters in regard to the loan have been settled.

I told him you had made it a rule not to see foreigners who came here on matters relating to the war, but that because of his position as Lord Chief Justice of England, an exception might be made.

I have a feeling that it would be well to see him for I think the circumstances are different from anything that has yet arisen. I promised Lord Reading to let him know whether or not to make the formal request through the British Ambassador.[1]

Your affectionate,   E. M. House

TLS (WP, DLC).
  [1] Wilson saw Lord Reading at the White House on October 13.

Benjamin Franklin Battin[1] to Pieter Wilhelm Adriaan Cort van der Linden[2] and Jonkheer John Loudon[3]

Gentlemen: [New York?] October 4th, 1915.

(1) I am taking advantage of the return of Dr. A. Jacobs from the United States to Holland to forward to you, by her, in person a confidential note, which I did not care to entrust to the mails; it seemed best not to write to you until after I had seen President Wilson. . . .[4]

(6) My interview with President Wilson occurred on September 20th. After a thorough discussion, he authorized me to make to both of you and to the Foreign Ministers at London, Berlin and Berne the following statement: "International Conditions are at present of such a nature as to preclude the United States Government from enunciating any position on the question of a conference of neutral powers." At present I shall send this statement

to you two gentlemen only—not to London, Berne and Berlin. In general the attitude of the United States Government is one of deliberate caution, considering that the time is not now opportune for such a conference; that the plan will be carefully studied and is well worth watching; that conditions might arise such as to make a belligerent of any of the neutrals proposed for the conference; that Spain is more important for such a plan than is generally credited.

(7) As no positive attitude has been taken by the United States Government, it seems to me that further unofficial inquiry should be made at once at Paris, Rome and other capitols.

(8) I should be glad to receive an intimation from you or Dr. Jacobs, whether further unofficial activity on my part now or in the immediate future would be of value; in this case I shall arrange to return to Europe for such time as may seem advisable.

With expressions of high respect,   Benjamin F. Battin

TLS (Netherlands Foreign Ministry-Ar).

1 Professor of German at Swarthmore College and a member of the conference that met at Bern in December, about which see n. 2 to the memorandum by L. P. Lochner printed at Nov. 12, 1915 (first of that date).

2 Foreign Minister of the Netherlands *ad interim* from August 29 to September 27, 1913; Prime Minister of the Netherlands since 1913.

3 Foreign Minister of the Netherlands from September 1913 to September 1918.

4 Here follows his report on his conversations with various English and French leaders about the prospects for neutral mediation.

To Edith Bolling Galt

[The White House] Monday,
My own precious Darling,   7.30 A.M. 4 Oct., 1915

Good morning! I hope you had a lovely, restful sleep and that you felt my arms about you, my heart close to yours. It is five months to-day, my Sweetheart since I told you of the great love for you that had come into my heart and asked you to be my wife,—only five months, and yet I seem to have known and loved you always. I cannot think of happiness apart from you. You fill my thoughts and my life. My spirits rise and fall with yours. Your thoughts and your love govern the whole day for me. And, as these crowded months have gone by, filled with experiences that seemed to search our hearts to their very depths—to depths to which no plummet had ever reached before—how steadily we have struggled towards the light—with what joy we have seen it broaden about us, until now we stand, hand in hand, where it shines warm and life-giving in all its full and vital splendour! We have not loved lightly, my Darling. With a great price we have bought this supreme happiness. It has been tested by fire, and has come out refined and purged. We know ourselves and we know one another better than it would have been possible to learn them by the experiences of any ordinary five years, or any commonplace lifetime; and we know that it was inevitable that we should love one another and utterly give our hearts up to one another. Out of the fire has come to me, little by little revealed and made perfect, the woman I perfectly love and adore, the lovely, lovely woman who, at each stage of the strange struggle, seemed to me to grow more lovely and more desirable. I loved you, my precious Edith, ah, how tenderly and deeply, that May evening when I first opened my heart to you; but I now know that that was but the beginning of my love. It has grown like a great tide of life and joy, until now I know that my whole destiny is centred in you, my sweet, sweet Love, my incomparable Darling!   Your own   Woodrow

ALS (WP, DLC).

From Edith Bolling Galt

Dearest One: [Washington] Oct. 4, 1915

Thank you for your precious note to mark this 5th anniversary of the great miracle your love has brought into my life. And all the tender things you say echo the thoughts that fill my own heart. My precious Woodrow, I want so to make your life radiant and bring months and years of happiness to make up for all the hours of loneliness and heartache you have suffered.

I am sending you the proofs of the small pictures   Select the one you want, please, but I think the most *obscure* one preferable.

Do you know I went for another ride last night—just 'round the Potomac Drive, the old part—with Dr. Ruffin[1] to try his new car, and I told him our wonderful secret. He was so glad for my happiness and said he knew of no one in the World whom he admired so much, or trusted so completely as he did you and that he could only say it seemed the most complete and *right* thing he had ever known. I want so to have you two really know each other. He is the best friend I have in the World and has been down in the Valley of Shadows with me and has never failed or faltered in doing all in his power to help me. Helen is here, so I must stop.

I am perfectly well and had nearly five hours sleep, and

promise to do better tonight. Do go this afternoon and play a game.   Always your own   Edith

ALS (WP, DLC).
  1 Sterling Ruffin, M.D., close friend of many years and the Bolling family's physician.

From Alice Gertrude Gordon

Richmond, Virginia. October the fourth.
My dear Mr. President,   Nineteen hundred and fifteen.

What you were kind enough to write me of Dr. Grayson made me very happy. The sweet welcome from you and Miss Bones and the wonderful, wonderful news which Mrs. Galt told me, have made my happiness complete.

She has added more sunshine in my life and been nearer and dearer to me than anyone else for many years. To know of her and your happiness brings more joy to my heart than I can express.

As to your good fortune, I think it just as great as mine—and what more can I say, when you take into consideration my prejudice in favor of your physician?

Please accept my heartfelt good wishes, and my appreciation of your friendship toward Dr. Grayson and me.

Believe me to be,
Most sincerely yours,   Alice Gertrude Gordon.

ALS (WP, DLC).

To Mary Allen Hulbert

Dear Friend,   Washington, 4 Oct., 1915.

Before the public announcement is made, I want you to [be] one of the first to know of the good fortune that has come to me. I have not been at liberty to speak of it sooner. I am engaged to be married to Mrs. Norman Galt of this city, a woman I am sure you would admire and love as every one does who knows her, and I feel that a blessing greater than I can measure in words has come to me.

I hope that the business continues to promise all that it did at first, and that you have been able to carry out your wish to join Allen in the actual work. My interest will follow every step of it. It is fine to see how your spirits have responded to the new life and

I wish with all my heart that I could see you both in your new surroundings.

I am writing in great haste, amidst a pressure of clamorous engagements that cannot be gainsaid, but you will know in what spirit. Helen joins me in affectionate messages. Margaret has not yet returned from N. H.

Your devoted friend   Woodrow Wilson

WWTLS (WP, DLC).

To Edith Gittings Reid

Dearest Friend,   The White House. 5 October, 1915.

Before others know it, I want you to know what has happened to me. I am engaged to be married to a lovely lady here whom I met last April and who compels everybody who knows her to love her by the sheer charm of her character and whole personality,— Mrs. Norman Galt. I will not tell you about her: I want you to find her out for yourself.

The last fourteen months have seemed for me, in a world upset, like fourteen years. It is not the same world in which my dear Ellen lived; and one of the very last things she said to me was that she hoped that what has happened now would happen. It seemed to me incredible then, and would, I think, have continued to seem so if I had not been brought into contact with Mrs. Galt. She seemed to come into our life here like a special gift from Heaven, and I have won a sweet companion who will soon make me forget the intolerable loneliness and isolation of the weary months since this terrible war began.

I hope that you will sympathize and approve.

My thoughts constantly seek you out. I wish that I could see you and have an old-fashioned talk. Things crowd upon me so every day that I hardly have time for any indulgencies of that sort; but I must find it or starve.

Your loving friend,   Woodrow Wilson

WWTLS (WC, NjP).

From Edward Mandell House

Dear Governor: New York. October 5th, 1915.

I am happy beyond measure to know that our party is to come off on Friday.

Chief Flynn of the Secret Service tells me that you will be here at three o'clock. That is fine.

I have made arrangements for "Grumpy" and will also attend to the commission you have given me. Unless I hear from you otherwise we shall expect you, Mrs. Galt, her mother, Miss Bones, and Doctor Grayson for dinner.

Why not have the ladies stop at the St Regis which is near by?

If there is anything else you can think of, please let me know.

Looking forward with much eagerness to your coming, I am,

Your devoted,   E. M. House

You can never know how happy I am that such great good fortune has come to you. I feel that a more splendid day has dawned, and that soon there will be no more lonely hours.

TLS with Hw P.S. (WP, DLC).

A Memorandum by Robert Lansing

INTERVIEW WITH THE GERMAN AMBASSADOR,
OCTOBER 5, 1915. 10.30 A.M.

The German Ambassador called at my request in regard to the note which he had submitted to me, dated October 2d, concerning the ARABIC case.

I informed the Ambassador that when he handed me the note in New York on the 2d that as I then told him I was not prepared to comment upon it, although I congratulated him on having influenced his Government to secure an amicable settlement of the controversy. I also told him that after digesting the note I had submitted it to the President, without comment, and that he had reached substantially the same conclusion as I—namely, that it was not satisfactory in its present form.

The Ambassador asked me in what particulars it was not satisfactory. I pointed out to him that in the third (3) paragraph the German Government appeared to support entirely the commander of the submarine in the conviction which he had reached as to the purpose of the ARABIC to ram the submarine. I told him that in view of the fact that the note stated that the attack of the submarine was against the instructions issued to the commander, this assertion appeared to be contradictory.

The Ambassador replied that he was willing to omit that from the note.

I also said that it was very unsatisfactory that the note failed to frankly disavow the act; that there was no question but that the language was open to the interpretation of the disavowal. The Ambassador said that that was his intention and I then asked him why he had not stated it in the note. He said he thought that he possibly could do so.

In regard to the last paragraph, relating to the payment of indemnity, I said to him that the note offered to pay an indemnity as an act of grace and that this Government could not accept it on that basis, for they considered there was a legal right to an indemnity. I suggested, however, that a controversy on this point could be avoided by a change of language.

The changes which I proposed I indicated on the note of October 2d, in lead pencil.

The Ambassador said that he was not sure whether his instructions would permit him to go as far as these changes, but that he would go back to the Embassy and examine the instructions, and if they were broad enough he would make the changes proposed and would send me a new note within an hour.

When he left I was convinced that he would meet the wishes of this Government as he assured me his instructions were of the broadest character. Robert Lansing.

TS memorandum (SDR, RG 59, 841.857 Ar 1/106½, DNA).

Count Johann Heinrich von Bernstorff to Robert Lansing

My dear Mr. Secretary,   Washington, D. C., October 5, 1915.

Prompted by the desire to reach a satisfactory agreement with regard to the Arabic incident my Government has given me the following instructions:

The orders issued by His Majesty the Emperor to the commanders of the German submarines—of which I notified you on a previous occasion—have been made so stringent that the recurrence of incidents similar to the Arabic case is considered out of the question.

According to the report of Commander Schneider of the submarine that sank the Arabic and his affidavit as well as those of his men, commander Schneider was convinced that the Arabic intended to ram the submarine. On the other hand, the Imperial Government does not doubt the good faith of the affidavits of the British officers of the Arabic, according to which the Arabic did not intend to ram the submarine. The attack of the submarine, therefore, was undertaken against the instructions issued to the commander. The Imperial Government regrets and disavows this act and has notified commander Schneider accordingly.

Under these circumstances my Government is prepared to pay

an indemnity for the American lives which to its deep regret have been lost on the Arabic. I am authorized to negotiate with you about the amount of this indemnity.

I remain, my dear Mr. Lansing,

Yours very sincerely,   J. Bernstorff[1]

TLS (SDR, RG 59, 841.857 Ar 1/92, DNA).

[1] This letter was published on the front page of the *New York Times*, Oct. 6, 1915.

To Edith Bolling Galt

[The White House] Tuesday,

My precious Edith,   1.30 P.M. 5 Oct., 1915

I slept late this morning and ever since I got up have been chased by tasks I could not elude,—so that this is the first moment I have had to send you a love message. Ah, how *full* my heart is of love for my precious Darling—and of happy love! It makes me sad that she must go through this picture business and all the rest that goes with it and that she dreads and hates so: but I know that she is a dead game sport, and it makes me *so* proud that she is willing to go through it all for my sake—for dear love's sake! And I am so eager (I must confess) to have everybody know how wonderful and beautiful she is.

It seems a long time till to-night. I long for you every moment—think of you all the hours through as the most wonderful and adorable Darling in all the world. Lansing came over at noon to tell me that Bernstorff had come to terms and given perfectly satisfactory assurances—so that my heart is light about that, too. And now we are free to be gay and happy! My heart is too full for words—full of joy and pride and love.

Your own   Woodrow

ALS (WP, DLC).

From Margaret Woodrow Wilson

Cornish, New Hampshire

My darling precious Father,   [Oct. 5, 1915]

I wish that I were going to be with you tomorrow. I know however that you understand perfectly why I did not go down with the Smiths, and that you know that only "business" has kept me away from you so long. I feel that I ought to do all in my power to make it possible for me to give of my best in these three recitals.[1]

I am so glad, oh so glad that you are going to announce the glad secret tomorrow for then you will be free to see much more of our sweet Edith. Give her my warmest love and tell her that I can hardly wait to see her again.

Dear Father I am so happy for you and have been ever since I knew what was going to happen, and I am sure you know that I am happy for myself too. It must be evident to you how much I love to be with Edith. Above all however, because I love you so much, I am glad that you are going to have her love and companionship constantly.

I long to see you dearest Father. What terrible times you have been going through! Your patience and poise are marvellous to me—but then everything about you is wonderful.

The Davids came back today and my work begins again, but after these days alone I shall go at it with more hope and joy than just before they left. I have been in the depths of discouragement, but now I feel brimful of courage and am looking forward to my concerts not only with hope, but with joyful eagerness.

I love you darling Father with all my heart and mind and soul.   Your devoted,   Margaret.

ALS (WC, NjP).
   [1] One of them was at Buffalo on October 12.

A Press Release

October 6, 1915

I intend to vote for woman suffrage in New Jersey[1] because I believe that the time has come to extend that privilege and responsibility to the women of the state; but I shall vote, not as the leader of my party in the nation, but only upon my private conviction as a citizen of New Jersey called upon by the legislature of the state to express his conviction at the polls. I think that New Jersey will be greatly benefited by the change. My position with regard to the way in which this great question should be handled is well known. I believe that it should be settled by the states and not by the national government, and that in no circumstances should it be made a party question; and my view has grown stronger at every turn of the agitation.[2]

T MS (WP, DLC).
   [1] The National American Woman Suffrage Association and its New Jersey affiliate had spearheaded the campaign for a special referendum on a constitutional amendment enfranchising women. It failed at the polls on October 19 by 46,278 votes.
   [2] There is a WWT draft of this statement in WP, DLC. Following "I think that New Jersey will be greatly benefited by the change," Wilson had added: "and my opinion in that matter has been very much strengthened by the character of the opposition to the measure." He then struck out this portion.

Remarks to the Naval Consulting Board[1]

October 6, 1915.

Gentlemen: There is very little that I can say to you except to give you a very cordial welcome and to express my very great pleasure in this association of laymen with the government. But I did want to say this:

I think the whole nation is convinced that we ought to be prepared, not for war, but for defense, and very adequately prepared; and that the preparation for defense is not merely a technical matter, it is not a matter that the army and navy alone can take care of, but a matter in which we must have the cooperation of the best brains and knowledge of the country outside the official service of the government as well as inside. For my part, I feel that it is only in the spirit of a true democracy that we get together to lend each other voluntary aid—the sort of aid that comes from interest, from a knowledge of the varied circumstances that are involved in handling a nation.

I want you to feel—those of you who are coming to the assistance of the professional officers of the government—that we have a very serious purpose, that we have not asked you to associate yourself with us except for a very definite and practical purpose—to get you to give us your best independent thought as to how we ought to make ready for any duty that may fall upon the nation. I do not have to expound it to you. You know as well as I do the spirit of America. The spirit of America is one of peace, but one of independence. It is a spirit that is profoundly concerned with peace, because it can express itself best only in peace. It is the spirit of peace and good will and of human freedom. But it is also the spirit of a nation that is self-conscious, that knows and loves its mission in the world, and that knows that it must command the respect of the world.

So it seems to me that we are not working as those who would change anything of America, but only as those who would safeguard everything in America. I know that you will enter into conference with the officers of the navy in that spirit and with that feeling, and it makes me proud, gentlemen, that the busy men of America, the men who stand at the front of their profession, should be willing, in this way, to associate themselves voluntarily with the government in the task in which it needs all sorts of expert and serious advice. Nothing ought to be done in this country by any single group of persons. Everything ought to be done by all of us united together, and I welcome this association in the most serious and grateful spirit.

T MS (WP, DLC).

[1] A newly constituted civilian advisory group on the development of naval weapons. It was composed of twenty-two representatives from the nation's eleven largest private engineering organizations. Thomas Alva Edison was president of the board.

From Anna Howard Shaw

Reading, Penna., October 6, 1915.

Permit me to express the sincere gratitude of the women of the United States who believe in Democracy and freedom for all citizens for your clear and helpful statement of your views and purpose to vote for the suffrage amendment to the New Jersey Constitution.   Anna H. Shaw, Pres't.
National Suffrage Ass'n.

T telegram (WP, DLC).

From Carrie Clinton Lane Chapman Catt

New York, October 6, 1915.

On behalf of a million women in New York State who have declared they want the ballot, please accept gratitude for your announcement that you will vote for the woman suffrage amendment in New Jersey.

Carrie Chapman Catt.
Chairman, Empire State Campaign Committee.

T telegram (WP, DLC).

From George Mason La Monte

Bound Brook New Jersey
My dear Mr. President Wilson,   Oct. 6, 1915.

I need not tell you how gratified I am with your statement in regard to woman's suffrage. I knew it would come in time. Mrs. La Monte[1] is delighted and sends her thanks.

Ever yours   Geo. M. La Monte

ALS (WP, DLC).
[1] Anna Isabel Vail La Monte.

From William Gibbs McAdoo

Strictly Personal.

Dear Mr. President: Washington October 6, 1915.

Merely to outline concretely, so that you may think over what I said to you the other day, I submit the following:

I am satisfied that it will be essential, in order to provide needed revenues for the Government,

1. To extend the emergency revenue measure, which expires by limitation December 1, 1915, for a reasonable length of time.

2. To postpone the time when the free sugar provisions of the present tariff law are to go into effect. I think it ought to be postponed until May 1, 1919 or 1920.

We get approximately $50,000,000 a year from the present duty of one cent a pound on sugar. It is a distinctively revenue measure, and is justified on that ground only. I do not know where we can get $50,000,000 of revenue so easily and acceptably as through this source. The tax is in existence and the people are accustomed to paying it.

In addition to these already established sources of revenue, we shall have to find new sources to meet the increasing expenditures of the Government, to say nothing of the requirements of the proposed preparedness program.

I am preparing my annual report, and I desire to recommend the extension of the emergency revenue measure and the postponement of free sugar, unless you see objection to them. If you see none, I think it would be very helpful, in the present circumstances, if we should announce the fact that I am going to make such recommendations. An early announcement about sugar is particularly desirable, because the Louisiana planters have to provide now the seed cane which is necessary for their next year's crop, and it would aid them very much to know promptly what the attitude of the Government is likely to be. Moreover, I think it is extremely important to take this action, if we are going to take it at all, before the sugar interests of the country can organize, as I am satisfied they are preparing to do, a campaign in the next Congress to retain the existing sugar duties. We are much better off, if we are going to take this action at all, to take it voluntarily and without the appearance of having submitted to pressure. We can shut off the entire agitation if we announce our position promptly.   Faithfully yours,   W G McAdoo

TLS (WP, DLC).

An Announcement

The White House October 6, 1915.

The announcement was made today of the engagement of Mrs. Norman Galt, of this city, and President Woodrow Wilson.[1]

✧

Mrs. Norman Galt is the widow of a well known business man of Washington who died some eight years ago.

She has lived in Washington since her marriage in 1896.

She was Miss Edith Bolling, and was born in Wytheville, Virginia, where her girlhood was spent and where her father, the Honorable William H. Bolling, acquired distinction as one of the State's ablest lawyers.

Mrs. Galt is a woman of charm and pleasing personality.

It was Miss Margaret Wilson and her cousin Miss Bones who drew Mrs. Galt into the White House circle.

They met her first in the early autumn of last year.

Their friendship ripened into intimacy.

Mrs. Galt spent a month this summer at Cornish as Miss Wilson's guest.

It was through this intimacy of his daughter and cousin with Mrs. Galt that the President had an opportunity to meet and know her.

T MS (WP, DLC).

[1] The text that follows was given to reporters for background information.

From Sir Cecil Arthur Spring Rice

Personal

Dear Mr President   Washington. 6 October 1915

I hope you will allow me to offer you my warmest congratulations on the news of your engagement. As a resident in your capital I claim the right to join with all American citizens in wishing you all possible happiness and that assistance in your great task which only a wife can give. As Ambassador of Great Britain I am expressing the warm personal feelings of sympathy which I know will be felt for you in all the world and in no place more than in the British Dominions.

With the assurance of my profound respect

Believe me to be dear Mr President

Your most obedient servant   Cecil Spring Rice

ALS (WP, DLC).

From Stockton Axson

My dear Brother Woodrow: Chicago Oct 5 [6], 1915

I spent a day with Meemee Brown[1] on my way west, and because she is among the most loyal of your friends (and had already heard the news from the Colonel)[2] I showed her something I had written.

She disapproved, said that the details made it sound like an apology. It was precisely that which I wanted to avoid, but Mrs. Brown thinks that *any* detailed statement will carry that impression—and I am afraid she is right.

She says, "The President has nothing to explain, and the best statement is that which he himself proposed, the brief dignified announcement of the fact."

She added that the next day's paper might very well carry a paragraph stating that notwithstanding the short acquaintance between Mrs. Galt and the family, the girls are already much attached to her. Such an item would cover two important points, and I should think that it ought to appear in the same issue with the original announcement, for otherwise it would seem like an afterthought, and no subsequent note will reach all who read the original announcement. I don't know that there will be any feasible way of getting this said in the newspapers—but it ought to be done if possible, I think.

So my suggestions come to very little, after all, for Meemee Brown convinced me of the faults in what I had written—I saw them when she pointed them out—and yet I don't believe I could "shade" a statement more delicately than that. I think she is right when she says that *any* statement (beyond the fact) will sound like an explanation.

Her profound interest in everything that touches your welfare and her deep affection for you personally, combined with a slightly more detached point of view than ours, make her "reactions" important, I think. Like me, she is fervently glad that the announcement is to be soon, and she believes that the best part of the country will understand without explanation. She adds that the papers will do their own talking, no matter what we say.

I have had some trouble getting a desirable lodging place, and only today am I leaving the hotel—for 5739 Kimbark Avenue (which will be my address for telegrams—but the post office address will be simply *University of Chicago*).

You have taken the wind out of Roosevelt's sail with the announcement of the way you are going to vote on Oct. 19! But it *is* funny, the way the suffrage "leaders" assume that you must now be for the Constitutional amendment.

With devoted love for each and all of you (in which I should like to include Mrs. Galt)

Yours affectionately always   Stockton Axson

ALS (WP, DLC).
¹ Mary Celestine Mitchell (Mrs. Edward T.) Brown.
² That is, her husband.

Robert Lansing to Edward Mandell House

PERSONAL:

My dear Colonel House: Washington October 6, 1915.

I am returning to you the letter from Mr. Vick which you were good enough to send me, in regard to J. T. Vance.¹ I shall bear in mind the information it contains when the question comes before me, which it has not done yet.

You will have seen by the morning papers the successful outcome of the negotiations regarding the ARABIC. Last Saturday, when I saw the German Ambassador, I felt a measure of discouragement on account of the note which he then handed me. I told him, however, I would take the matter up with the President. I did so and the President agreed with me that we could not accept a note of that sort. After reaching this decision I asked Count von Bernstorff to call upon me at the Department, which he did on Tuesday, and the published note is the result of our conference on that day.

I hope I can see you in a few days in regard to the South American matter, in which the President is so much interested, and concerning which I am not as familiar as I wish I was. I have no doubt that a talk with you would help very much.

With warm regards believe me,

Very sincerely yours,   Robert Lansing.

TLS (E. M. House Papers, CtY).
¹ W. W. Vick to EMH, Oct. 2, 1915, TLS (E. M. House Papers, CtY). See WJB to WW, May 19, 1915, n. 2, Vol. 33.

To Edith Bolling Galt

[The White House] Wednesday,

My precious Darling,   7.10 A.M. 6 Oct., 1915

I am afraid that your bad habits are catching. I did not get to bed until about midnight and waked at five and have not been really asleep since, though I lay and tried to coax sleep back again until half past six. I had plenty of delightful things to think about, but I really need more sleep than that, and must try to teach the loneliness that disturbs me to be a little less tormenting. I lay and sent many, many tender thoughts to find my Darling, about whom and whose happiness (for which I am now responsible) *all* my thoughts hovered; but I know that she does not wish to be disturbed, and ought not to be disturbed, at that time of the morning, even by her lover. I hope the loving solicitude with which the messenger thoughts were freighted only made you sleep the more peacefully and restfully, my precious pet!

I need not tell you what impression you made on the dear Smiths. You must have seen that you won their admiration and affection at once,—for you did. I did not need to hear it from them after you left to know that it had happened. They warmed my heart, though, and made me love them more than ever, by their enthusiastic appreciation of you, and it makes me very happy to see what friends you are going to be, for I know that they are friends worth having.

I shall follow you in my thoughts all day, my Darling, and only wish I had asked you to tell me what you were going to do each part of it till I see you again to-night. Even while business crowds upon me this forenoon I shall be following you around on the intensely interesting errands to the several members of the family (mine as well as yours, Dearest) telling them what a happy man I am and how you have blessed me and are going to crown my life. Please tell them that nothing fills me with such pride and strength and joy as that I am   Your own   Woodrow

ALS (WP, DLC).

From Edith Bolling Galt

My precious One: [Washington] Oct. 6th, 1915 8 a.m.

I waked at 6 after a very restful night and have just come for a little talk with you before going up to tell the rest of the family our secret.

It does give me a queer feeling to think that by this time tomorrow it will no longer be just our *own* secret, but blazen to the world, and I confess it costs much to give it up.

But you are worth anything it could ever cost, and I loved you more last night than ever before. But it was such a solemn, deep love that I seemed unlike myself.

But I came home and went straight to bed and read "War Lords"[1] until I felt sleepy and then I shut the light out and put my arms 'round your dear body and my head on your shoulder and went to sleep.

I think it was about one ock. and I did not move until six.

So, you see, I am quite refreshed and ready for the day.

I hope so that you are and that the German conquest is only the happy beginning of good fortune. I am so proud of you my precious Woodrow and so proud that the world will know you through big situations, such as this, for only in big things can you find your true interpretation.

Just here your note has come, and I feel so guilty, Dearest, to have caused you a sleepness night. I will kiss those splendid eyes tonight until they close in spite of themselves—and make you dream—instead of *think* of how I love you.

With all my love, Always your own,   Edith.

I did not keep the messenger until I read your enclosures but will enjoy them, as I always do. So happy the Smiths liked me. You know how I fell a victim to them at once. My love to them & to Col. B. & the Bishop.

ALS (WP, DLC).
    1 See EBG to WW, Sept. 15, 1915, n. 1, Vol. 34.

From Viscount Sutemi Chinda

My dear Mr. President   Washington Oct. 7th 1915

I take the liberty to respectfully offer you my most sincere congratulations on the occasion of your happy engagement. In so doing, I indulge in the hope that this short but non[e] the less cordial expression of felicitation may be accepted by you as a humble contribution to the general feelings of joy which, I am sure, reign over the whole land at the present moment for the auspicious event just announced

Yours Most Respectfully   S. Chinda.

ALS (WP, DLC).

From Albert Sidney Burleson

Personal

My dear Mr. President: Washington October seventh [1915].

Last night I heard of the new joy in store for you. I beg for Mrs. Burleson[1] and myself the privilege of tendering you and the fair lady our congratulations and sincerest good wishes

Faithfully yours   A. S. Burleson

ALS (WP, DLC).
    1 Adele Steiner Burleson.

From Claude Augustus Swanson

My dear Mr. President: Chatham, Virginia Oct 7th 1915

Mrs. Swanson[1] and myself desire to extend to you our hearty congratulations on your announced engagement to one of Virginia's most charming and accomplished daughters. We wish for you both great happiness. As soon as Mrs. Swanson read the announcement in the morning paper she exclaimed "the President is fortunate, he could have found nowhere a sweeter, dearer wife, nor one more worthy to be first lady of the land.["] We Virginians are much gratified and feel highly honored. If possible it has brought you closer to our people. Our wish is that all measure of happiness may come to you both.

I also wish to congratulate you upon the splendid manner in which you have handled our foreign affairs. Your patience, courage and tact won, under great difficulties, a most signal triumph. You are stronger than ever before in the esteem and affection of the American people. They will demand that you shall continue to guide them in these dangerous and troublous times. They admire how bravely you have borne your heavy burdens, how splendidly you have maintained a calm equipoise, amid much excitement and confusion. With kindest regards and best wishes I am,   Your friend,   Claude A. Swanson.

ALS (WP, DLC).
[1] Elizabeth Deane Lyons Swanson, M.D.

From Count Johann Heinrich von Bernstorff

New York, October 7, 1915.

I beg leave to extend to you my most sincere and best wishes for your happiness on the occasion of your engagement and to add the expression of my highest esteem and respect.
                                          J. Bernstorff.

T telegram (WP, DLC).

From Thomas Davies Jones

My dear Mr President   Lake Forest, Illinois Oct 7, 1915

I hesitate to take the word of the newspapers for anything; but (to parody Lord Justice Bowen)[1] truth will out occasionally even in the newspapers. And I joyfully accept as truth the interesting despatches of this morning. Allow me to tender my heartiest felicitations. I trust that the alliance which you have formed will bring to you all the added comfort and courage—all the enhancement of the vital energies which a happy marriage brings with it, and which you need to strengthen you for the heavy burdens which you have to carry.

Ever Faithfully Yours   Thomas D. Jones.

ALS (WP, DLC).
[1] Charles Synge Christopher Bowen (1835-94), the famous and oft-quoted British justice.

From Jean Jules Jusserand

Dear Mr. President,   Washington Oct. 7, 1915

Allow me, on this auspicious occasion, to offer you my sincerest compliments and good wishes.

May your happiness be as long as it is sure to be complete. I rejoice the more at the news that circumstances have caused your great task to be the heavier. It will continue as great. The load however will seem less heavy.

Believe me, dear Mr President

Very respectfully and sincerely yours   Jusserand

ALS (WP, DLC).

From Clarinda Pendleton Lamar

My dear Mr. President: Washington October seventh [1915].

Your kind letter, and the beautiful roses have just reached us; having traveled to the White Sulphur Springs and back again, without losing any of its good cheer, or their sweetness. It was so thoughtful of you to remember my dear Husband, and your affectionate message has brought so much strength and encouragement to his sick bed, that I must add my grateful appreciation to his, for your kindness.

We brought him back to Washington a day or two ago, and already he is much better for the change; though he is still so weak as to make his convalescence seem slow and tedious.

I hope it will not be an intrusion if I say how we both rejoice at the great happiness which is in store for you, and that none of your friends will be more glad than we over every blessing that Providence may send you.   .

I am, my dear Mr. President,

Very gratefully and sincerely yours,

Clarinda Pendleton Lamar

ALS (WP, DLC).

From Cleveland Hoadley Dodge

Dear Mr President   New York. October 7th 1915

Our hearts are very full of rejoicing today for the new joy which has come to you, and Mrs Dodge joins with me in heartiest congratulations and best wishes that you may enter on a new life of great happiness.

Now that engagements are being announced, you & Margaret will be interested to know that my daughter Elizabeth[1] has just become engaged to one of the Robert College professors—George H. Huntington.[2] He is a very fine man; a scholar and a gentleman —a little older than she. It is a bore to have another child go to the Turkish Empire but the hope is that by another year, when the marriage will probably take place, there may not be any Turkish Empire.

Early in the Summer you asked me to represent you & read your letter at a meeting for newly naturalized voters. This meeting was postponed & will be held Oct. 29th & unless I hear from you to the contrary, I will attend the meeting and read your letter as originally proposed[3]

Trusting that it may not be long before I have the pleasure of congratulating you in person and at the same time of felicitating Mrs. Galt

Believe me   Ever affectionately yours   C H Dodge

ALS (WP, DLC).

[1] Elizabeth Wainwright Dodge.

[2] The Rev. George Herbert Huntington, educated at Williams College, Hartford Theological Seminary, and Union Theological Seminary in New York. He later became vice-president of Robert College in Istanbul.

[3] WW to C. H. Dodge, June 16, 1915, TLS (WC, NjP). It read:

"It is a genuine disappointment to me that I cannot be present when the new citizens are welcomed to the privileges they are henceforth to enjoy, and I wish I knew some adequate greeting to send to them through you.

"Will you not say to them for me that I wish to join very heartily in the welcome and that I hope they will let me remind them of the great responsibilities they are assuming? They will be expected not only to exemplify the true spirit of American citizenship, but to infuse into it an enthusiasm for the things that make for right and for liberty which will assist to quicken the patriotism of every other man who thus voluntarily assumes the obligations of citizenship in this great country which we love and serve."

From Bernard Mannes Baruch

New York, Oct. 7, 1915.

Your diplomatic success with Germany has astonished the world. Your defense speech yesterday struck a sympathetic chord in the breast of every American citizen but the announcement of your engagement has pleased and gratified your real friends above even these two great achievements. I congratulate you and trust that the joy and happiness to which you are so justly entitled will come to you and the future Mrs. Wilson.

Bernard M. Baruch.

T telegram (WP, DLC).

To Edith Bolling Galt

[The White House] Thursday,

My own precious Darling,   7.30 A.M. 7 Oct., 1915

How my heart yearns for you this morning! What would I not give to be with you all through the day, to protect you from every kind of annoyance and try to make you feel only the deep, deep happiness that is in my heart and the love for you that wells up in it like the tide of life itself, and the pride that I should have won your love and its sweet acknowledgement to the whole world. To feel that to-day and for the rest of our lives you are identified with me,—*you*, who I know to be and all the world will presently know to be the loveliest and most adorable woman a man ever won,—with *me*, who have no claims except pure, unbounded love and my great need,—makes a new day for me, a day of strength and joy and confidence, and of zest in work and duty. The old shadows are gone, the old loneliness banished, the new joy let in like a great healing light. I feel, when I think of the wonderful happiness that your love has brought me, a new faith in everything that is fine and full of hope, a new confidence that God's in his Heaven and all's right with the world. Duty looks simple and the task of the day pleasant and easy. And with what unspeakable joy do my thoughts hover about the incomparable lady who has wrought this miracle by her love! It is so *delightful* to think about her,—and to know that she is mine is a sweet, sweet ecstacy! I love to think of her grace, her tenderness, her quick, comprehending sympathy, her wit, her instant grasp of whatever she is interested to know, her ineffable, unfailing, irresistible charm, and her deep, deep love, the tides of which she strangely checks sometimes, but can never resist, because they issue from the very springs of her being, where those deep, life-giving waters are which have revived and will always refresh and sustain

Her own   Woodrow

ALS (WP, DLC).

From Edith Bolling Galt

My precious Woodrow   [Washington] Oct. 7, 1915 8:15

How like you to be the first to send me a greeting this day of days, and what an infinitely tender message it is. I am keeping Mr. Hoover long enough to write a short answer, because it is so much nicer to address it to you, instead of even Helen. Thank you for all you put into these words, that leave so much for just my own interpretations. And I still feel your presence here in this room and reach out to find you, and long to kneel as I did before the fire last night and put my arms about you while I whisper I love you, and trust you and will never again hurt you, if I can help it.

I have seen the Post, and every thing is guided by that dear, strong hand I love and into whose keeping I have put my own in utter faith and trust.

Please be happy today Dearest and let the sunshine of our love keep out all clouds, and forget everything but the blessed fact that we belong to each other.   Your own,   Edith.

ALS (WP, DLC).

To Edward Mandell House

The White House October 8th, 1915.

Will arrive New York Penna Station three seventeen this afternoon.   Woodrow Wilson.

T telegram (E. M. House Papers, CtY).

From Edward Graham Elliott

Dear Mr President: Berkeley, California Oct. 8th 1915.

Allow me to join with Margaret in the heartiest congratulations upon your new and very wonderful happiness and in all good wishes for you both. We can but rejoice that you have been able to find one who will be the joy and comfort to you that so charming and delightful a woman as Mrs Galt is, must surely be.

I wrote you a note just before hearing from your letter of your engagement, expressing the hope that you might come to California.[1] May I renew it twofold?

With much love to all and with every good wish for your happiness and success.

          Always sincerely yours,   Edward Elliott

ALS (WP, DLC).
[1] E. G. Elliott to WW, Oct. 1, 1915, ALS (WP, DLC).

From Henry Burchard Fine

My dear Tommy,   Princeton, Oct. 8, 1915

My heartiest congratulations. I am very, very glad that this new and great happiness has come to you.

Mrs. Fine and the children join me in messages of love.

As ever,   Affectionately Yours,   Henry B. Fine

ALS (WP, DLC).

From the Diary of Colonel House

October 8, 1915.

Today started off with the usual bustle incident to a visit from the President. Telegrams, Telephone calls, secret service men, newspaper reporters notes, etc. etc. However, the confusion will cease the moment the President arrives, for I do not permit the telephone to ring and we are undisturbed by letters, notes, telegrams or visitors. When he is once here, everything appears as peaceful as if there were no such things as noise and confusion in the world.

Dudley Malone called for final arrangements. Dreicer, the jeweller, sent his Mr. Hull up with thirteen beautiful engagement rings from which the President and Mrs. Galt may make a selection. Mr. Hull wished to take one back to avoid the unluckly thirteen, but I vetoed this because the President considers thirteen his lucky number.

After lunch Dudley came again and I insisted upon his going to the station with me to meet the party. We did not have many minutes to spare and our ride down Fifth Avenue, where we were given the right of way, was rather an exciting one. There was a great crowd around the station awaiting the President and his bride-to-be. Chief Flynn of the Secret Service was there to meet me, and the station master took us to the platform where the train came in a moment later. There was a great cheer when we passed through the crowd and later, when we left the station, there was much enthusiasm. The police arrangements were perfect, the traffic having been stopped along the route we took, and police were everywhere. We drove first to the St Regis to see that the ladies were comfortably located in rooms which I had ordered through Dudley.

The President and I then went to our apartment at 115 East 53rd Street. The streets were lined with large crowds and they cheered him enthusiastically. We remained in the apartment a few minutes and then returned to the hotel to get Mrs. Galt, her mother, and Miss Bones, and rode for nearly two hours along the River.

Upon our return to the apartment it was almost time to dress for dinner, but there were a few things the President desired to discuss with me which we did expeditiously. He had in mind to send Bernstorff home, and said he did not see why we should send Dumba and not Bernstorff. I thought the two cases were not the same and that he had lost his opportunity to send Bernstorff. I thought Bernstorff was about the best of his tribe and had done more to bring about a solution of our differences with Germany than perhaps any one man. The President complained, however, of the increasing German intrigue and said we should not permit it. I agreed to this most heartily, but thought it should be suppressed in a different way and not by sending the Ambassador home. I suggested, therefore, that he tell the German Government, through Bernstorff, that this Government was very tired of their activities in America, which embraced not only activities in Mexico, but also in many South American countries, and that if they did not cease, he would sever diplomatic relations with the Imperial Government.

The President thought well of this and decided to act upon it. I expl[a]ined further that it was the German Government at fault and not Bernstorff, and it was unfair to hold him personally responsible rather than the Government. If Bernstorff was sent home he should be sent because of the Government's actions and not because of his own.

He asked what I thought of sending von Papen and Boy-Ed, the German Military and Naval Attaches, home.[1] I advised doing this and by intimation that their presence was no longer desired.

The President requested that I come to Washington next weel [week] and talk with Lansing and make him button up the South American proposal. I agreed to go Wednesday. He said he would see Lansing and make an appointment for Wednesday evening.

I outlined very briefly a plan which has occurred to me and which seems of much value. I thought we had lost our opportunity to break with Germany, and it looked as if she had a better chance than ever of winning, and if she did win, our turn would come next, and we were not only unprepared but there would be no one to help us stand the first shock. Therefore, we should do something decisive now—something that would either end the war in a way to abolish militarism or that would bring us in with the Allies to help them do it.

My suggestion is to ask the Allies, unofficially, to let me know whether or not it would be agreeable to them to have us demand that hostilities cease. We would put it upon the high ground that the neutral world was suffering along with the belligerents and that we had rights as well as they, and that peace parleys should begin upon the broad basis of both military and naval disarmament.

I suggested that no nation be mentioned, but let it be understood that the word "militarism" referred to the Continental Powers and the word "navalism" referred to Great Britain. If the Allies understood our purpose, we could be as severe in our language concerning them as we were with the Central Powers, the Allies, after some hesitation, could accept our offer or demand, and if the Central Powers accepted, we would then have accomplished a master stroke in diplomacy. If the Central Powers refused to acquiesce, we could then push our insistence to a point where diplomatic relations would first be broken off, and later the whole force of our Government, and perhaps the forst [force] of every neutral, might be brought against them.

The President was startled by this plan. He seemed to acquiesce by silence. I had no time to push it further, for our entire conversation did not last longer than twenty minutes.

We dressed hurriedly, went to the St Regis, brought the ladies to the apartment, looked at the rings and made a selection, dined, and went to the Empire Theater to see Cyril Maude in Grumpy. The dinner party consisted of the President, Mrs. Galt, Mrs. Bolling, Miss Bones, Dr. Grayson, Gordon, Janet, Loulie and myself. To these, Mr. and Mrs. Dudley Malone[2] were added at the theater. The audience arose when we entered and remained until the President took his seat. Our boxes were draped with American flags and a generous round of applause greeted him. After the play we returned to the hotel, and then to our apartment. It was so late that we did not linger, but went immediately to bed, around 12.30.

T MS (E. M. House Papers, CtY).

[1] Von Papen had been implicated in Ambassador Dumba's plots to foment strikes and walkouts in American munitions plants. Since the beginning of the war, both Von Papen and Boy-Ed, along with Bernstorff, had been surreptitiously involved in obtaining provisions for German cruisers at sea and counterfeiting passports for German soldiers bound for home via neutral European ports. Wilson had known about these intrigues since December 1914. For details see Arthur S. Link, *Wilson: The Struggle for Neutrality, 1914-1915* (Princeton, N. J., 1960), pp. 558-60 and 645-49, and Reinhard R. Doerries, *Washington-Berlin 1908/1917* (Düsseldorf, 1975), pp. 165-217.

[2] May O'Gorman Malone.

From Robert Lansing

PERSONAL AND PRIVATE:

My dear Mr. President: Washington October 9, 1915.

I am enclosing you the draft of the note to Great Britain upon which we have been working for so long a time.[1] It is unavoidably long, which, to my mind, takes away a certain measure of strength. At the same time I do not see how it can be well abbreviated. Possibly you will think it better to send it by mail, provided it meets with your approval, rather than by telegraph.

Faithfully yours,   Robert Lansing

TLS (SDR, RG 59, 763.72112/1851A, DNA).
  [1] See WW to RL, Oct. 21, 1915.

From Josephus Daniels, with Enclosure

My dear Mr. President: Washington. October 9, 1915.

I have a telegram from Bishop Warren A. Candler, of Atlanta, Ga., a copy of which I enclose herewith. Bishop Candler, as you know, was for a long time President of Emory College, in Georgia. He is a big-brained man, and has charge of all the Methodist Missions in Mexico. He has spent much of his time in that country. I should myself feel like giving great weight to his statement. He is a very close friend of mine, and this is the first time he has ever communicated with me in regard to Mexico. I know that he is much interested in the outcome.

Faithfully yours,   Josephus Daniels

TLS (WP, DLC).

E N C L O S U R E

Atlanta, Ga., October 7, 1915.

I have inside information from Mexico, which I feel the President should have and which I ask you to lay before him. From a high and very trustworthy source I am informed that Carranza has Mexico virtually in his hands and that he has an army of one hundred and fifty thousand men with ample arms and supplies. My informant [says] that the recognition of Carranza would crown with success the President's wise Mexican policy and end the Mexican problem. All this reaches me as the bishop having charge of our Mexican Missions and from a source with whom I have been well acquainted for ten years and whom I implicitly trust for both intelligence and integrity.

W. A. Candler

TC telegram (WP, DLC).

From the Diary of Colonel House

October 9, 1915.

We breakfasted at eight, had a few minutes conversation regarding the political situation in general and a few minor matters which needed attention, and went to the St Regis to take the ladies for a drive. I did not go, preferring to get at some of my pressing mail, since I was leaving for Tuxedo for the week-end.

At eleven o'clock I went to the station and bade the President and party goodbye.

I then went to the McAlpen[1] and got the Attorney General and we motored out to Tuxedo Park where Loulie and the Mezes met us to spend the week-end with Mrs. Minnie K. Young.[2]

I telephoned Lord Reading that the President would be glad to see him in Washington on Wednesday or Thursday and advised him to make a formal request through the British Ambassador.

[1] The McAlpin Hotel in New York.
[2] Minnie Knowlton (Mrs. William Henry) Young.

From Richard Heath Dabney

Dear Woodrow: Washington, D. C. 10 Oct., 1915.

According to the newspapers, a very avalanche of congratulatory telegrams & letters has been descending upon you since the announcement of your engagement, and I am not certain whether any more of them may not be a sort of nuisance to you. Yet even at the risk of surfeiting you, I do not feel that I can, in justice to myself, refrain from telling you how I rejoice in the prospect of renewed happiness that looms so auspiciously before your eyes. Knowing, as I do, how tenderly you loved your wife, and knowing from personal experience that, the more happily married a man is, the more intensely he craves feminine love and sympathy if he has the misfortune to lose his wife, I can appreciate not only the terrible loneliness of your situation since August, 1914, but also the deep joy that has come into your heart in these latter days. The cares of state weighing upon you have been so tremendous that the whole country must rejoice that the burden upon you will now be lightened by the exhilarating love of a charming and lovely woman.

Most heartily do I congratulate you and remain, as ever,
Faithfully & affectionately yours,   R. H. Dabney.

ALS (WP, DLC).

An Address to the Daughters of the American Revolution[1]

[Oct. 11, 1915]

Madam President and ladies and gentlemen: Again it is my very great privilege to welcome you to the City of Washington and to the hospitalities of the capital. May I admit a point of ignorance? I was surprised to learn that this association is so young, and that an association so young should devote itself wholly to memory I cannot believe. For, to me, the duties to which you are consecrated are more than the duties and the pride of memory.

There is a very great thrill to be had from the memories of the American Revolution, but the American Revolution was a beginning, not a consummation, and the duty laid upon us by that beginning is the duty of bringing the things then begun to a noble triumph of completion. For it seems to me that the peculiarity of patriotism in America is that it is not a mere sentiment. It is an active principle of conduct. It is something that was born into the world, not to please it, but to regenerate it. It is something that was born into the world to replace systems that had preceded it and to bring men out upon a new plane of privilege. The glory of the men whose memories you honor and perpetuate is that they saw this vision, and it was a vision of the future. It was a vision of great days to come, when a little handful of three million people upon the borders of a single sea should have become a great multitude of free men and women spreading across a great continent, dominating the shores of two oceans, and sending West, as well as East, the influences of individual freedom. These things were consciously in their minds as they framed the great government which was born out of the American Revolution. And every time we gather to perpetuate their memories, it is incumbent upon us that we should be worthy of recalling them, and that we should endeavor by every means in our power to emulate their example.

The American Revolution was the birth of a nation. It was

1 At Memorial Continental Hall, on the occasion of the twenty-fifth anniversary convocation of the Daughters of the American Revolution. Daisy Allen (Mrs. William Cumming) Story, president-general, presided at the meeting.

the creation of a great free republic based upon traditions of personal liberty, which theretofore had been confined to a single little island, but which it was purposed should spread to all mankind. And the singular fascination of American history is that it has been a process of constant recreation, of making over again, in each generation, the thing which was conceived at first. You know how peculiarly necessary that has been in our case, because America has not grown by the mere multiplication of the original stock. It is easy to preserve tradition with continuity of blood; it is easy in a single family to remember the origins of the race and the purposes of its augmentation. But it is not so easy when that race is constantly being renewed and augmented from other sources, from stocks that did not carry or originate the same principles.

So, from generation to generation, strangers have had to be indoctrinated with the principles of the American family, and the wonder and the beauty of it all has been that the infection has been so generously easy. For the principles of liberty are united with the principles of hope. Every individual, as well as every nation, wishes to realize the best thing that is in him, the best thing that can be conceived out of the materials of which his spirit is constructed. It has happened in a way that fascinates the imagination that we have not only been augmented by additions from outside, but that we have been greatly stimulated by those additions. Living in the easy prosperity of a free people, knowing that the sun had always been free to shine upon us and prosper our undertakings, we did not realize how hard the task of liberty is and how rare the privilege of liberty is. But men were drawn out of every climate and out of every race because of an irresistible attraction of their spirits to the American ideal. They thought of America as lifting, like that great statue in the harbor of New York, a torch to light the pathway of men to the things that they desire. And men of all sorts and conditions struggled toward that light and came to our shores with an eager desire to realize it and a hunger for it such as some of us no longer felt, for we were as if satiated and satisfied and were indulging ourselves after a fashion that did not belong to the ascetic devotion of the early devotees of those great principles. Strangers came to remind us of what we had promised ourselves and, through ourselves, had promised mankind. All men came to us and said, "Where is the bread of life with which you promised to feed us, and have you partaken of it yourselves?" For my part, I believe that the constant renewal of this people out of foreign stocks has been a constant source of reminder to this people of what the inducement was that was offered to men who would come and be of our number.

Now we have come to a time of special stress and test. There never was a time when we needed more clearly to conserve the principles of our own patriotism than this present time. The rest of the world, from which our polities were drawn, seems for the time in the crucible, and no man can predict what will come out of that crucible. We stand apart, unembroiled, conscious of our own principles, conscious of what we hope and purpose, so far as our power permits, for the world at large, and it is necessary that we should consolidate the American principle. Every political action, every social action, should have for its object in America at this time to challenge the spirit of America; to ask that every man and woman who thinks first of America should rally to the standards of our life. There have been some among us who have not thought first of America, who have thought to use the might of America in some matter not of America's origination. They have forgotten that the first duty of a nation is to express its own individual principles in the arena of the family of nations and not to seek to aid and abet any rival or contrary ideal.

Neutrality is a negative word. It is a word that does not express what America ought to feel. America has a heart, and that heart throbs with all sorts of intense sympathies. But America has schooled its heart to love the things that America believes in, and it ought to devote itself only to the things that America believes in; and, believing that America stands apart in its ideals, it ought not to allow itself to be drawn, so far as its heart is concerned, into anybody's quarrel. Not because it does not understand the quarrel, not because it does not in its head assess the merits of the controversy, but because America has promised the world to stand apart and maintain certain principles of action which are grounded in law and in justice. We are not trying to keep out of trouble; we are trying to preserve the foundations upon which peace can be rebuilt. Peace can be rebuilt only upon the ancient and accepted principles of international law, only upon those things which remind nations of their duties to each other, and, deeper than that, of their duties to mankind and to humanity.

America has a great cause which is not confined to the American continent. It is the cause of humanity itself. I do not mean in anything that I say even to imply a judgment upon any nation or upon any polity, for my object here this afternoon is not to sit in judgment upon anybody but ourselves, and to challenge you to assist all of us who are trying to make America more than ever conscious of her own principles and her own duty. I look forward to the necessity in every political agitation in the years which are immediately at hand of calling upon every man to declare himself where he stands. Is it America first or is it not?

We ought to be very careful about some of the impressions that we are forming just now. There is too general an impression, I fear, that very large numbers of our fellow citizens, born in other lands, have not entertained with sufficient intensity and affection the American ideal. But the number of such is, I am sure, not large. Those who would seek to represent them are very vocal, but they are not very influential. Some of the best stuff of America has come out of foreign lands, and some of the best stuff in America is in the men who are naturalized citizens of the United States. I would not be afraid, upon the test of "America first," to take a census of all the foreign-born citizens of the United States, for I know that the vast majority of them came here because they believed in America; and their belief in America has made them better citizens than some people who were born in America. They can say that they have bought this privilege with a great price. They have left their homes, they have left their kindred, they have broken all the nearest and dearest ties of human life in order to come to a new land, take a new rootage, begin a new life, and so, by self-sacrifice, express their confidence in a new principle; whereas, it cost us none of these things. We were born into this privilege; we were rocked and cradled in it; we did nothing to create it; and it is, therefore, the greater duty on our part to do a great deal to enhance it and preserve it. I am not deceived as to the balance of opinion among the foreign-born citizens of the United States. But I am in a hurry for an opportunity to have a line-up and let the men who are thinking first of other countries stand on one side—biblically it should be on the left—and all those that are for America first, last, and all the time on the other side.

Now, you can do a great deal in this direction. When I was a college officer, I used to be very much opposed to hazing, not because hazing is not wholesome, but because sophomores are poor judges. I remember a very dear friend of mine, a professor of ethics on the other side of the water, who was asked if he thought it was ever justifiable to tell a lie. He said yes, he thought it was sometimes justifiable to lie; "but," he said, "it is so difficult to judge of the justification that I usually tell the truth." I think that ought to be the motto of the sophomore. There are freshmen who need to be hazed, but the need is to be judged by such nice tests that a sophomore is hardly old enough to determine them. But the world can determine them. We are not freshmen at college, but we are constantly hazed. I would a great deal rather be obliged to draw pepper up my nose than to observe the hostile glances of my neighbors. I would a great deal rather be beaten than ostracized. I would a great deal rather endure any sort of physical hardship if I might have the affection of my fellow men. We constantly discipline our fellow citizens by having an opinion about them. That is the sort of discipline we ought now to administer to everybody who is not to the very core of his heart an American. Just have an opinion about him, and let him experience the atmospheric effects of that opinion! And I know of no body of persons comparable to a body of ladies for creating an atmosphere of opinion! I have myself in part yielded to the influences of that atmosphere, though it took me a long time to determine how I was going to vote in New Jersey.

So it has seemed to me that my privilege this afternoon was not merely a privilege of courtesy, but the real privilege of reminding you—for I am sure I am doing nothing more—of the great principles which we stand associated to promote. I, for my part, rejoice that we belong to a country in which the whole business of government is so difficult. We do not take orders from anybody; it is a universal communication of conviction—the most subtle, delicate, and difficult of processes. There is not a single individual's opinion that is not of some consequence in making up the grand total, and to be in this great cooperative effort is the most stimulating thing in the world. A man standing alone may well misdoubt his own judgment. He may mistrust his own intellectual processes; he may even wonder if his own heart leads him right in matters of public conduct. But if he finds his heart part of the great throb of a national life, there can be no doubt about it. If that is his happy circumstance, then he may know that he is part of one of the great forces of the world.

I would not feel any exhilaration in belonging to America if I did not feel that she was something more than a rich and powerful nation. I should not feel proud to be, in some respects and for a little while, her spokesman if I did not believe that there was something else than physical force behind her. I believe that the glory of America is that she is a great spiritual conception, and that in the spirit of her institutions dwells not only her distinction but her power. The one thing that the world cannot permanently resist is the moral force of great and triumphant convictions.[2]

T transcript (WC, NjP) of CLSsh (C. L. Swem Coll., NjP).
[2] There is a WWT outline of this address, dated Oct. 11, 1915, in WP, DLC.

To Francis Burton Harrison

My dear Governor Harrison:

[The White House]
October 11, 1915

I greatly appreciate your letter of August thirty-first[1] which sets forth so fully the matters with which my thought has been repeatedly and anxiously engaged.

I think I have every reason to be confident that the Jones Bill will pass substantially in its present form at the approaching session of Congress. Certainly I will put my full weight behind it and seek to secure its enactment at as early a date as possible. There are some particulars in which I would have written the bill differently, but it is on the whole so suitable to the present conditions in the Philippines, as I believe, that I can get behind it with a great deal of genuine conviction.

I am very much indebted to you for your judgment as to what the general line of Republican attack upon the Phillippine policy will be, but I really think that they will not make much headway. They have been very blundering recently and show no signs of increasing intelligence.

I hope that your health and the health of your family is withstanding the tropics successfully. I feel every day that I have reason to be very grateful to you for taking the responsible post which you are administering so admirably.

Cordially and sincerely yours,   Woodrow Wilson

TLS (Letterpress Books, WP, DLC).
[1] F. B. Harrison to JPT, Aug. 31, 1915, printed in Vol. 34.

From Louis Seibold[1]

My dear Mr. President: Atlantic City, N. J. October 11, 1915.

It was characteristic of you to steal a minute during the most exacting period of your Administration to drop a line to a fellow who was being separated from a very badly spoiled appendix.[2] You may take my word for it that the process is not one of the joys of life, however, it looks as if I will have the best of the bargain in the end and continue my activities to the annoyance of some of our very good friends.

It seems to me that you are rather working over time and not playing enough. You remember that I told you some months ago that you ought to collect at least one laugh every day. You certainly are entitled to two for one day's work last week. I hope that you will be happy as a consequence and that you will always have good luck for a great many other reasons.

I sincerely congratulate you.

Gratefully yours,   Louis Seibold

TLS (WP, DLC).
1 White House reporter for the New York *World*.
2 WW to L. Seibold, Oct. 6, 1915, TLS (Letterpress Books, WP, DLC).

From Mary Allen Hulbert

Dearest Friend,   [Los Angeles, c. Oct. 11, 1915]

I have kissed the cross. We are very very glad you have found happiness, and that you had time to think of us in the midst of it. I need not tell you again that you have been the greatest, most enobling influence in my life. You helped me to keep my soul alive, and I am grateful. I hope you will have all the happiness that I have missed. I can not wish you greater. We are well, and both working at the business that your friendly purchase of the mortgages made it possible for us to embark upon. Why can't you run away to California for a moment? It is hard to imagine a more perfect air than this, and it would please this great warm hearted, effusive young state.

She is very beautiful and some time perhaps I may meet her. I wish you had told me before, for your letter was only mailed the 4th, and the newspapers had already published the fact. The cold peace of utter renunciation is about me, and the shell that is M.A.H still functions. It is rather lonely, not even an acquaintance to make the air vibrate with the covering warmth, perhaps, of friendship. God alone knows—and, you, partly, the real woman Mary Hulbert—all her hopes and joys, and fears, and mistakes. I shall not write you again thus intimately, but must this once. It was good of you to think of the new work, and care to write of it. Allen is *splendid*. They call him the "busy man" in this apartment, as he leaves for the valley at four every morning. Of late he has come in to stay with me at night but I think he longs for his tent and the fresh air of the open. Now that I am better he will go back, save for the week ends. Write me sometimes, the brotherly letters that will make my pathway a bit brighter. And believe me to be

Your friend, Mary Allen Hulbert.

This is rather a whine, but is the best I can do, now. God bless you!

ALS (WP, DLC).

Edward Mandell House to Robert Lansing

Dear Mr. Secretary: New York. October 12th, 1915.

Sometime early in January of this year the President requested me to see the Ambassadors of the A.B.C. Powers and ascertain from them whether or not they would be willing to join the United States in a convention which would guarantee the political and territorial integrity of the North, Central and South American Republics under republican forms of government.

Also if they would be willing to agree that all manufacture of munitions of war should be owned by the governments of the respective countries.

The President wrote these two articles himself and I took them first to the Argentine Ambassador, whom we thought would perhaps be most sympathetic. The Ambassador received the proposal cordially, after I had outlined to him just what the President had in mind. I called his attention to the fact that there was a military party in the United States just as there was in other countries, and after President Wilson relinquished office, there was a possibility of a military policy being adopted. I said if this happened it was quite probable that instead of following the path laid down by President Wilson there might be a sentiment for expansion. I told him there was sure to be a large part of the people who would want to try out the military and naval machine. If this should happen, no one could tell the final outcome.

I told him, too, that the President thought the time had come when this nation should cease to assume a guardianship over its sister republics and to ask them to come into partnership. I explained it was the President's intention to approach the A.B.C. Powers first and later to approach the smaller republics, either directly or through the A.B.C.

The Ambassador was very much in favor of permitting the A.B.C. Powers [to] deal with the smaller republics, and it was tacitly agreed that this should be done. He spoke of writing to his government in regard to the proposal, to which I objected and asked him to cable it so we might hear in a few days.

He was filled with enthusiasm and declared that the proposal was almost epoch making, and that he was sure it would be cordially received by his people. He doubted, however, whether Chile would be agreeable because of her territorial aspirations. He told me in confidence that Chile wanted to go north practically to Panama, and that at one time she had made a proposal to Argentine to divide Bolivia.

The Ambassador begged me to give him the original draft which the President had written, saying he believed it would be an historic document of enormous interest. I gave it to him and he wrote with his own hand a copy for me to use with the other Ambassadors.

I had a similar reception by the Brazilian Ambassador, and I gave him practically the same argument. The discussion followed largely along the lines I have mentioned with Naon.

The Chilian Ambassador was somewhat less receptive and showed a disposition to delay. He brought up at once the question of their boundary conflict with Peru—a subject about which I had informed myself in advance so as to be able to discuss the matter with intelligence.

I told him the President had in mind that there should be an article in the convention which would permit a reasonable time for the settlement of such disputes and a mode of procedure. This seemed to satisfy him.

All three abassadors promised an answer within a few days. The one came first from Argentine and was entirely favorable. Then Brazil was heard from to the same effect. Chile, later gave an equivocal consent. This was a few days before my departure for Europe, and the President requested me to acquaint Mr. Bryan with what had been done and ask him to carry it to a conclusion.

Mr. Bryan was receptive, but suggested that his peace treaties shou[l]d be also concluded between them. He wanted to know if there was any objection to this. The President said there was not.

I heard nothing from the matter while abroad until sometime in April when the President cabled me that the Chilean Ambassador had said he was under the impression that I had agreed in my conversation with him that the convenant should not be binding unless all of the A.B.C. Powers concurred. I cabled the President that there was no such understanding, and that probably the Ambassador had in mind the tacit consent that the smaller republics should be approached by the A.B.C. powers rather than by us directly.

This, Mr. Secretary, is a record of what occurred through me. I do not know what Mr. Bryan did.

Of course you understand that the President's purpose is to broaden the Monroe Doctrine so that it may be upheld by all the American Republics instead of by the United States alone as now.

Sincerely yours,   E. M. House

TLS (SDR, RG 59, 710.11/206½, DNA).

To William Archibald Bolling[1]

My dear Doctor Bolling: [The White House] October 12, 1915

I am really touched by your generous letter of October eighth.[2] It has given me the greatest pride and pleasure.

I need not tell you how proud I am to have won the love of such a woman as your dear sister. My ambition is to make her life such that she will never regret the choice.

One of the things I am looking forward to with the greatest pleasure is meeting you and the other members of her family whom I have not yet had the privilege of knowing. She has told me so much about you I feel that it will be easy for us to know one another.

With affectionate regard,

Faithfully yours,   Woodrow Wilson

TLS (Letterpress Books, WP, DLC).
 [1] Edith Bolling Galt's brother, a physician, of Louisville, Ky.
 [2] W. A. Bolling to WW, Oct. 8, 1915, ALS (WP, DLC).

To Richard Heath Dabney

My dear Heath: The White House October 13, 1915

It was very thoughtful of you to send me your letter of October eighth and what you say has gone straight to my heart. I think of you very often and rejoice in the happiness that has come to you as much as you can rejoice in that which has now come to me. I hope that it will soon be possible for Mrs. Galt to know you as the delightful friend you are.

In haste   Affectionately yours,   Woodrow Wilson

TLS (Wilson-Dabney Corr., ViU).

To Hugh Lawson Rose and Mary Francesca Granville Delaney Rose

My dear Friends: [The White House] October 13, 1915

Thank you with all my heart for your message of congratulation.[1] I feel that I am indeed to be congratulated on the wonderful good fortune that has come to me and the certain prospect of happiness, but you must not think that I am stealing her away from any of her friends. Would it not be possible for you to come to Washington sometime early next year and see us at the White House? It would be very delightful if you could.

Cordially and sincerely yours,   Woodrow Wilson

TLS (Letterpress Books, WP, DLC).
1 H. L. and Mary F. G. D. Rose to WW, Oct. 7, 1915, T telegram (WP, DLC).

To Cleveland Hoadley Dodge

My dear Cleve: The White House October 13, 1915

Of course you thought of me in my renewed happiness, and your letter of October seventh brought me the greatest joy! I am very anxious that you should know Mrs. Galt. I am sure that you and she will take to one another instinctively. She has much of the open and generous and frank way with her that makes everybody that really knows you love you, besides having, like yourself, many deeper qualities that are lovable.

I am exceedingly interested to hear of Elizabeth's engagement. Will you not convey to Professor Huntington my warmest congratulations? He is certainly getting a wonderful woman. I wish with all my heart you could keep your children nearer to you, but they will be a comfort to you wherever they are.

Always   Affectionately yours,   Woodrow Wilson

TLS (received from Cleveland E. Dodge, Jr.).

To Thomas Davies Jones

My dear Friend: The White House October 13, 1915

I thank you with all my heart for your message of congratulation. I knew that you would be thinking about me and it is fine to feel the touch of your hand. I believe that tasks will grow easier for me now and every thought you give me helps.

Cordially and sincerely yours,   Woodrow Wilson

TLS (Mineral Point, Wisc., Public Library).

To Claude Augustus Swanson

My dear Senator: [The White House] October 13, 1915

I want to thank you most warmly and sincerely for your letter of congratulation. It warmed my heart. It is very delightful to have you think of me in such terms. I am very proud of what has happened to me and am sure that everybody who knows Mrs. Galt will think that I am the most fortunate of men.

Please present to Mrs. Swanson my warmest regards and my cordial thanks for her own thought of us.

Sincerely yours,   Woodrow Wilson

TLS (Letterpress Books, WP, DLC).

From Wilhelm August Ferdinand Ekengren

Washington, D. C.,
My dear Mr. President,   October 13, 1915.

As a result of your representation to the Governor of Utah, Joseph Hillstrom, who is under death sentence, was granted a respite until the next meeting of the Board of Pardons which convenes on the 16th instant, when, as I understand it, a new date will be fixed for the execution.

This delay has afforded me an opportunity to investigate carefully the facts in the case and the course of the trial. The result of that is that I am more firmly of the opinion that the evidence and course of the trial do not warrant the execution of a death sentence, nevertheless there seems now to be but one way to prevent this, i.e., to secure a commutation. I cannot see how it would be possible to obtain a new trial. The records show numerous instances where exceptions might have been noted that would have made a new trial almost emparative, at least easy to obtain, but they were not made; and now one cannot take advantage of errors and irregularities as a means to reopen the case. The legally trained men whom I have consulted are of the same opinion.

As the experience I have already had with the authorities of Utah leads me to fear that representations by me to the Board of Pardons will be unavailing and wishing to do all that possibly can be done I venture to once more address you, Mr. President, directly in this matter. This time I would most respectfully ask whether you could consistently recommend to the Board of Pardons of the State of Utah that the death sentence be commuted.

I am, my dear Mr. President,
Most respectfully yours,   W. A. F. Ekengren

TLS (WP, DLC).

From James Fairman Fielder

[Trenton, N. J.]
My dear Mr. President: October thirteenth 1915

I am glad to learn of the effort being made by citizens of our State to induce you to make your summer residence next year in this State.[1] This naturally brings to my mind the very auspicious circumstances which marked your last year of residence at Sea Girt, when the eyes of the Nation were centered upon you as the nominee for the great office you have so admirably filled. We hold you in the same affection as we then did and

as history does repeat itself, nothing would please the people of
New Jersey so much as to have you with them, so that the glad
tidings of your renomination might be brought you on New Jersey soil.

I earnestly join with those who are endeavoring to induce you
to establish your residence in New Jersey next summer.

Very cordially yours,   James F Fielder

TLS (WP, DLC).
  1 Representative Thomas J. Scully and a delegation of New Jersey citizens, on
October 15, invited the Wilsons to spend the summer at Shadow Lawn, a man-
sion at Long Branch, N. J. They delivered Fielder's letter at that time.

From the Diary of Colonel House

Washington. October 13, 1915.

I left for Washington at 11.08. . . .

Upon my arrival at the White House, Miss Bones met me and
told some of the troubles that have arisen since I was last here.
I reassured her to the best of my ability. The President was out
and did not return until just before dinner, when we had a few
minutes talk. After dinner we talked for nearly an hour. He
had arranged for Lansing to come at nine in order to discuss the
South American matter which was the primary cause of my
visit to Washington.

I talked to Lansing and explained to him in some detail what I
had done, and I looked over the papers he had on file in the State
Department concerning it, but they threw no great light upon the
subject. I found, however, that Mr. Bryan and the President
together had added something to the document as to the purposes
of the convention. I thought the additions weakened it and so told
Lansing. It was agreed that he should send copies of it to me in
the morning for the President and me to go over carefully, and
we would then get together again and compare views. I urged
him to expedite the matter and explained how essential it was to
have it done before the convening of Congress. He did not believe
this could be done, but said he would try.

I endeavored to point out ways in which he could do it best;
expressing my belief that it would be accomplished by the first
of December. I always have in mind that Lansing has the lawyer's
point of view which makes for delay.

I told him of my proposal to the President concerning intervention. He was much interested, and agreed with me absolutely.
I expressed it as my opinion that those of us who were temporarily charged with the direction of this country's affairs, ought

not to hesitate to do the things which we knew were best, no matter whether they met, at the moment, with popular approval; that it was clear it would not do to permit the Allies to go down in defeat, for if they did, we would follow in natural sequence. Lansing agreed and was willing to advise a strong course. He seems not to be afraid, and concurs in my opinion that Mr. Bryan did more to endanger the peace of this country than any other man, simply because of his "peace at any price" policy.

I continue to find Lansing satisfactory. He is not a great man, but he is level headed, has courage and has a fairly correct knowledge of diplomatic procedure. We discussed the note to Great Britain and I suggested that it would be advisable for me to see the British Ambassador and outline something of the contents of the note, and suggest that he advise his Government to make as many concessions as possible, leaving the rest to arbitration as provided by our peace treaty with them. Lansing approved of this, as did the President when I spoke to him about it later.

The President had already given me the note to Great Britain to read and criticize, saying that I knew better than he or Lansing the state of the British mind.

To David Benton Jones

My dear Friend: [The White House] October 14, 1915

I am sure you must know how I appreciate your thinking of me in this time of my renewed happiness.[1] I do not know any friends to whom my thought turns more frequently or with warmer affection than you and your brother, or any whose friendship and thought of me I value more. It sustains me and helps me through every sort of task to know that I have your confidence and support, and it is peculiarly delightful to me to know that you are thinking of me at this time.

Please give my warmest regards to your daughter and sons.[2]

Cordially and affectionately yours,   Woodrow Wilson

TLS (Letterpress Books, WP, DLC).
[1] D. B. Jones to WW, [c. Oct. 7, 1915], ALS (WP, DLC).
[2] That is, his oldest daughter Gwethalyn, and his two sons, Herbert and Owen Barton Jones.

To Edward Graham Elliott

My dear Ed: The White House October 14, 1915

Thank you with all my heart for your affectionate letter of October eighth. You and Madge are very sweet to me and you don't know how deeply I appreciate it. My love goes out to you both. I fear that it is going to be literally impossible for me to get to California, but sometime and somehow I must have you both know the dear lady who has promised to unite her fortunes with mine.

Warmest love to Madge, to whom I am also writing.

Affectionately yours,   Woodrow Wilson

TLS (WC, NjP).

To Margaret Randolph Axson Elliott

Dearest Madge: The White House October 14, 1915

I can't tell you how your letters to Mrs. Galt and me[1] delighted and touched me. I am sure you know, my dear girl, how entirely I love you and this message from you has given me peculiar pleasure and happiness.

I am very impatient for you to know Mrs. Galt. I am sure that you and she will take to one another at once, and the only trouble is to get footloose here and be able to move any distance from the base of operations.

I am writing in great haste but with the deepest love.

Affectionately yours,   Woodrow Wilson

TLS (WC, NjP).
[1] They are missing.

From the Diary of Colonel House

October 14, 1915.

The President and I had some conversation at breakfast and afterward. The Postmaster General came at 9.30 and remained for a half hour. When the President had finished his mail we had a longer discussion. My talk with Burleson was unimportant and dealt largely with party questions.

In my conference with the President we took up some routine matters and discussed the contents of some letters I had brought for his attention. I told of my talk with Lansing last night which, indeed, was held in his study at the White House while he was absent making a call on Mrs. Galt.

Lansing had not sent over the memoranda so we could not go into that, but we went into the general idea of the South American proposal and discussed how it could best be carried out. He was interested in Lansing's approval of my suggestion as to intervention. I was pleased to find the President cordially acquiescing in my views regarding intervention in Europe, and that it was only a question as to when and how it should be done. I now have the matter in my own hands, and it will probably be left to my judgment as to when and how to act.

I had arranged with the British Ambassador to meet him at Billy Phillips home. I dismissed the White House car a block from there and walked in order to avoid notice. I at once began to discuss the note, but found the Ambassador in one of his highly nervous states. He started to talk in a very disagreeable way of the United States. Among other things he said, he supposed I knew that the record would forever stand that when the laws of God and man were violated, there came no protest from us, but that when our oil and copper shipments were interfered with, a most vigorous protest came. And this was the record that would forever stand against us.

In discussing the contents of the Note, which we purpose sending to Great Britain, he said: "No matter how low our fortunes run, we will go to war before we will admit the principle of blockade as your Government wishes to interpret it. If we acquiesced, it would be all to the advantage of Germany whom you seem to favor; Germany has neutral ports like Malmo and Copenhagen which are just as much German as Bremen or Hamburg, but Great Britain has none, and the rule you wish to lay down would isolate us in the event our enemies could blockade our coasts. On the other hand, no amount of blockade which Great Britain could bring to bear would shut off Germany."

I made the suggestion of arbitration and asked him to make it to his Government. I did not like the tenor of his talk and as is my custom, became more and more silent. In the course of the conversation he said: "At one time this country was composed of pure rock, but now it is composed of mud, sand and some rock, and no one can predict how it will shift or in what direction."

I incidentally mentioned Bernstorff's name and spoke of the Germans. This put him in a fine rage and he said: "I would be glad if you would not mention Bernstorff's name in my presence again; I do not want to talk to anyone who has just come from talking him [with] him, or to Germans. At this moment I do not know how many of my relatives have been killed in England by the raid of the German Zeppelins last night."

At this point I lost my temper and told him I regarded his remarks as an insult, and I would not permit him to say such things to me. I denied that he represented either his Chief or his Government and declared that his views were not their views, and I knew of no official anywhere who was serving his country so badly as himself. He replied that if I felt that way, he had better relinquish his post and go home. I advised him to use his own discretion as to that, but as far as I was concerned, I did not intend to have any further discussion with him.

When the Ambassador saw the length to which I was willing to go in severing relations with him, he became apologetic and asked me to forgive him. His feelings, he said, were very much wrought up by the bad news he had received from home, and because of the anxiety he felt regarding last night's raid. I replied that he should be able to look at public affairs quite apart from his private interests. And as to my discussing Bernstorff with him, he must know how necessary it was in my work to see him, and that I intended to continue to do this no matter how much feeling he might have upon the subject.

He again asked me to forgive him and to continue our good relations. He insisted that he regarded me as a friend and very much appreciated my advice and help. He spoke of the President in the highest terms and said he wished to God Great Britain had such a man directing her destinies since there was no one in the world to compare with him. He said at no time had he ever felt anything but the kindest and greatest respect for both the President and me, and whatever criticism he had made was directed at an element in this country which he was sure we disapproved as thoroughly as he did himself. He said it was because of his affection for me that he spoke as he had done; that if he had not had the greatest respect and friendship for me, he would have been diplomatic and not given his real mind.[1]

The upshot of it was that while he said things derogatory to the United States and praised the President and me, I praised Great Britain and spoke in a derogative way of him. I accepted his apologies and we parted amicably. He went immediately to the State Department and told the incident to Phillips. Phillips

[1] Spring Rice's report, C. A. Spring Rice to E. Grey, Oct. 14, 1915, Hw telegram (FO 115/1921, p. 1, PRO), follows:

"I have just given your letter [see House Diary, Oct. 15, 1915, n. 1] to friend.

"He said note would be sent to you by post soon. It was moderate & technical. He hoped that your answer would contain some minor concessions and a suggestion to refer questions in dispute to commission of enquiry under the Bryan Treaty. He thought this would satisfy public opinion. I urged that we could not give up principles of continuous voyage sanctioned by Anglo-American law or consent to any compromise which would make blockade illusory.

"Friend then said he had seen Bernstorff. I declined at once to receive any communication whatever from this tainted source and said I could not listen to anything relative to relations with Germany without authority from you. He was greatly disappointed and vexed.

"I understand from Lord Reading friend has been empowered by some German authority to offer peace on basis of 'freedom of seas.'

"No doubt he has most friendly intentions but his main idea is intervention of President as mediator in European war."

came to see me and said the Ambassador was much disturbed and asked him to come and talk with me about it. I told Phillips to please reassure Sir Cecil and tell him I had forgotten it and was sorry it had happened, and that everything would continue between us as usual as far as I was concerned. He sent me a note later in the day about another matter, and took occasion to say he was afraid I had thought he had been very disagreeable. I replied to the note kindly though briefly.

It is due Sir Cecil to say in explanation of many of his moods and actions, that he was sent over as Ambassador in 1913 and was so ill when he came that he could not perform his duties at first.[2] He took a long rest at Dublin, New Hampshire, and Sir William Tyrrell was sent by the Foreign Office to help. In 1914 when the war burst forth Spring-Rice was in London and should have been kept there. Washington was no place for a nervous and delicate Ambassador. It was unfair to him and unfair to us. He is a cultivated, high-minded and scholarly gentleman and when normal, is of the very best type of British diplomat.

In talking with Phillips we discussed some changes in the Diplomatic Service. I had already talked with the President and Lansing about transferring Ambassador Fletcher from Chile to Mexico. Phillips was delighted with this contemplated change and we talked of the best man to go to Chile. I asked him to leave it open for the present, for there was a suggestion I might want to make later, but which I could not make at the moment. I had in mind offering the Chilean Ambassadorship to Adolph Miller of the Federal Reserve Board. This would get him off the Board and prevent friction between him and McAdoo which at any moment may become acute.

Paul Warburg had been trying to see me all day for "a two hour talk." I told him it was impossible for me to give him any such time and we would have to defer our conference until he came to New York, or until I returned to Washington. As a matter of fact, I do not want to see him for I know quite well what he desires to say, and I do not care to be mixed up in the controversy in which he is involved.

I related to the President my conversation with the British Ambassador. He thoroughly approved what I had done. In speaking of a possible successor of the Ambassador, the President thought that Lord Bryce would not do because of his recent activities as Chairman of the Belgian Atrocities Committee. I suggested Sir Horace Plunkett which met with his approval.

[2] Spring Rice suffered from Graves' disease, a disease of the thyroid gland which causes irritability, agitation, and so on.

Polk and I had a talk in the afternoon largely about departmental affairs. Senator Owen came to call by appointment. Our conversation touched upon legislative matters and upon party questions. The Attorney General drove with me but there is nothing of importance to record.

The Postmaster General told me this morning that Mr. Bryan was much hurt by the President's reception of him when he was last in Washington, and that Bryan said he would never darken the doors of the White House again as long as Wilson was in it. I asked Burleson if Mr. Bryan had any feeling as to me. He thought not, but did not know. My opinion was to the contrary and I asked him to develop the actual situation. He did so by telephone later in the day, telling Bryan he was thinking of getting me to drive out there and see him in the afternoon. Bryan asked him not to do so and that he would talk to him later. I shall be curious to learn just what he will say. I take it that my relations with the President are entirely too close for Bryan to dissociate me from him, even in his own mind, and after all the years of friendship between us. Then, too, the fact that the President and I shaped the Government's foreign policy while he was Secretary of State, and without bringing him into our plans, has made him resentful. My trip to Europe was the last straw.

The President and I dined with Mrs. Galt. I did not remain long after dinner but returned to the White House to write some letters and make memoranda for tomorrow's work.

Robert Lansing to Edward Mandell House, with Enclosures

PERSONAL AND PRIVATE:

My dear Colonel House: [Washington] October 14, 1915

I send herewith a draft of the four articles with certain changes which I would suggest, together with a note upon Article IV.

Words in parenthesis and underscored with a solid line, are those which I suggest omitting; while words underscored with a broken line are those which I would add.

I shall be at liberty this evening in case you would like to confer on this matter, and can come to the White House if you so desire.   Very sincerely yours,   Robert Lansing

CCL (SDR, RG 59, 710.11/211 B, DNA).

E N C L O S U R E   I

I.

That the high contracting parties to this solemn covenant and agreement hereby join in a common and mutual guarantee to one another of undisturbed and indisputed territorial integrity and of complete political independence (<u>under republican forms of government.</u>) <u>provided that such guarantee shall become inoperative and void as to any of the high contracting parties which abandons a republican form of government</u>.

II.

That, to this end, and as a condition precedent to the (<u>foregoing</u>) <u>guarantee set forth in Article I of this Convention</u> (<u>of territorial integrity</u>), it is covenanted and agree <u>by and</u> between (<u>them</u>) <u>the high contracting parties</u> that all disputes now pending and unconcluded between any two or more of them with regard to their boundaries or territories shall be brought to an early and final settlement in the following manner, unless some equally (<u>prompt</u>) <u>expeditious</u> and satisfactory method of settlement can be agreed upon and put into operation in each or any case within three months after the signing of this convention and brought to a decision within one year after its inception:

Each of the parties to the dispute shall select two arbiters and those thus selected and commissioned shall select an additional arbiter or umpire; to the tribunal thus constituted the question or questions at issue shall be submitted without reservation; and the decisions (<u>and findings</u>) of this tribunal shall be final and conclusive as between the parties to the dispute and under the terms of this convention as to the whole subject-matter submitted. The (<u>findings</u>) decisions of such tribunal or tribunals shall be (<u>arrived at</u>) made and officially announced and accepted within (<u>not more than</u>) one year after the formal constitution of the tribunal; and the tribunal shall be constituted (<u>not more than</u>) within three months after the (<u>signing and</u>) <u>deposit of</u> ratifications of (<u>the</u>) <u>this</u> convention <u>by the high contracting parties which are parties to the dispute</u>.

III.

That the high contracting parties severally pledge themselves to obtain and establish by law such control of the manufacture and sale of munitions of war within their respective jurisdictions as will enable them (<u>absolutely</u>) to control (<u>and make them responsible for</u>) the sale and shipment of such munitions to any other of the nations who are parties to this convention, and impose responsibility upon them for such sale or shipment.

IV.

That the high contracting parties further agree, First, that all questions, of whatever character, arising between any two or more of them which cannot be settled by the ordinary means of diplomatic correspondence shall, before any declaration of war or beginning of hostilities, be first submitted to a permanent international commission for investigation, one year being allowed for such investigation; and, Second, that, if the dispute is not settled by investigation, to submit the same to arbitration, provided the question in dispute does not affect the honour, independence, or vital interests of the nations concerned or the interests of third parties; and the high contracting parties hereby agree, where this has not already been done, to enter into treaty, each with all of the others severally, to carry our [out] the provisions of this Article.

T MS (SDR, RG 59, 710.11/211B, DNA).

ENCLOSURE II

NOTE ON ARTICLE IV

The vital principle in this convention is contained in the guarantees in Article I.

Those guarantees to be effective must have back of them the possible exercise of physical force to prevent invasion of the territory of a neighboring state. To postpone the exercise of force, which would be an act of war, for a period of a year would deprive the guarantee of its vitality.

From another point of view the invasion of foreign territory would be a violation of the convention, particularly of this very article, and might be considered as relieving the other parties from the operation of the article in enforcing the guarantee of territorial integrity.

There is another thing in connection with this Article and the guarantees under the proposed convention. With most of the Governments, which are expected to be parties to the convention, we have "peace treaties" which delay actual warfare for a year pending the action of a joint commission. Will not these treaties interfere with the enforcement on our part of the guarantees? Ought there not to be some definite provision making inoperative treaties of that sort in case it becomes necessary to employ force to maintain the guarantees and compel respect of the territory of a party to the convention?

T MS (SDR, RG 59, 710.11/211½, DNA).

To Joseph Patrick Tumulty

Dear Tumulty: [The White House] Oct 15/15

I am sorry to say that this incident is not true.[1] I wish that it were.   The President.

TL (WP, DLC).

[1] Wilson was responding to a request to confirm a report to the effect that he had led the cabinet in prayer "in a recent meeting" and asked for divine guidance. See R. Scott to JPT, Oct. 5, 1915, TLS (WP, DLC), enclosing clipping from the New York *Evening Post*, Oct. 2, 1915.

From Robert Lansing

My dear Mr. President: Washington October 15, 1915.

In accordance with your letter of September 24th to Mr. Phillips, the post of Minister to Liberia was offered to Bishop Alexander Walters, and a reply has been received asking me to thank you most heartily for the consideration of his name. He adds that in justice to Mr. James L. Curtis,[1] "an excellent young man" for whom he has made an active campaign, he must decline the honor.

Mr. Curtis has the support of Senators O'Gorman and Kern, and Bishop Walters himself speaks of him in the very highest terms. I shall be glad to know whether you desire to appoint Mr. Curtis.

Perhaps I should add that another applicant for this post is Mr. A. Llewellyn Bowman of Jacksonville, Florida,[2] who has been presented to the Department by Senator Fletcher.

With assurances of respect, etc., I am, my dear Mr. President,
                    Faithfully yours,   Robert Lansing

TLS (WP, DLC).

[1] A native of Raleigh, N. C., and a graduate of Lincoln University and the Northwestern University Law School, he was at this time an attorney in New York. He was appointed Minister Resident and Consul General to Liberia on October 25, 1915.

[2] An attorney.

From the White House Staff

The White House. October 15, 1915.

The Swedish Minister telephones that the Board of Pardons is to meet tomorrow and take up the Hillstrom case. If a request is not made of the Board of Pardons to commute Hillstrom's sentence he will be executed next week. The Minister says he is anxious to know whether the President will request that the sentence be commuted. If the President does not feel it is proper for him to make this request he, the Minister, following instructions from his Government, wishes to communicate with the Governor by wire and make a final request that the sentence be commuted.

T memorandum (WP, DLC).

From Oswald Garrison Villard

Dear Mr President,   Dobbs Ferry, N. Y. Oct. 15, 1915.

Mrs. Villard[1] & I have rejoiced for you in your great happiness. Surely you more than earned it by all you have done for the country this summer & I am grateful, indeed, as an on-looker that your burdens are now to be shared and by one so evidently charming.

For your Administration, too, I rejoice that the White House is to be open & gay. I don't believe you realize how much the men who are helping to make your government a success need you and what it would mean to them to have the inspiration of seeing and talking with you and how sorely they miss this. I am sure Mrs. Galt realizes this & will help. But in any event, our sincerest good wishes and the very earnest hope that you will know nothing but happiness in every relation of life, go out to you.

Faithfully & cordially yours,   Oswald Garrison Villard

ALS (WP, DLC).
[1] Julia Breckenridge Sandford Villard.

From the Diary of Colonel House

October 15, 1915.

At twelve o'clock the President, Secretary of State and I went into session in the study at the White House. Neither the President nor I had had any time to go over the documents we wished to discuss and re-write. However, it was not really needful on my part because my mind was quite clear as to what should be done. The President read the first article and laughed when he said, "I do not understand what I was thinking of when I wrote this. I do not believe I did it." I replied that we had it in his own hand-writing, meaning the typewriter which he uses individually and which we call his "hand-writing." He said it was not only not clear, but not good English and he thought at least he could write correctly. His original article was perfectly clear, and I did not see how he went so far afield in this, and suggested it might have been that Mr. Bryan was sitting at his elbow. We laughingly let it go at that.

In a moment, he had reduced the article to a clear and concise statement of his intentions.

The second article[1] in regard to the manufacture and shipment of munitions of war, I urged should be cut out entirely. I thought if it remained, we would be discussing the matter with our Congress and with South America for a year, and would never arrive at a conclusion. This argument prevailed and both the President and Lansing accepted it.

The third clause concerned Mr. Bryan's peace treaties which he insisted upon adding to the convention, but which, in my opinion, have no place there. I urged again that they be eliminated and that we allow the South American countries to adopt (or not) these peace treaties as they may see fit. Lansing was in favor of this and the President was too, except he thought if we did this, Mr. Bryan would consider it a mortal offence and would believe we so intended it. I could see the force of this argument and we accepted it, yet had I been President, I should have eliminated this clause.[2]

We discussed the note to Great Britain, but arrived at no definite conclusion further than if the British Government would consent to the smaller matters which caused the greatest amount of irritation, the larger ones could be deferred.

In going back to the South American proposal, I urged expediency. I should mention, too, that in the first article, Lansing did not see clearly why we should leabe [leave] in it the phrase "under republican forms of government." We argued this at some length. The President agreed with me in believing it was essential to retain it. Lansing's idea was that we might put a clause in lieu of it declaring that "any republic not continuing under a republican form of government should cease to be a party to the covenant."

The President and I both thought this would not meet the case at all. I cited the fact that Germany might colonize a particular South American country, let us say Brazil, until she con-

trolled it. She might then declare it a monarchy, and by doing
so the only penalty she would incur would be to eliminate herself
from the league, which in fact was the very thing she desired
to do. Lansing did not see how it would help matters, for if the
Germans controlled a state, it would make no difference whether
it was a monarchy or a republic. I differed strongly as to this. I
told him Germany today would be i[n]nocuous and a satisfactory
member of the society of nations if she were a republic, and
there were no objections whatever to the Germans going to South
America in great numbers and getting peaceful control of the
governments, and in continuing them under republican forms
of government. That it would probably be of benefit to the Americas rather than a detriment, for the German population would
be in every way preferable to the population now in the majority
of South American countries.

The President and I lunched alone. We arranged that he
should come to New York week after next to visit me.

I had just received a letter from Sir Edward Grey which,
strangely enough, is dated September 21st.[3] I do not see why
his letters should be so long in transit. It was handed me by
the British Ambassador at our memorable conference. The President thought it gave much ground for hope. I suggested that I
reply to it giving my suggestion to Sir Edward regarding intervention. I thought I could put it sufficiently in code to hide its
meaning. I suggested that I draft a letter and send it to him for
approval and criticism. He assented to this. I hope I can feel
out the situation in this way without having to go to Europe
just now.

[1] He meant the second article that was discussed.
[2] The draft of the treaty that Wilson, Lansing, and House agreed upon is
printed as Enclosure I with RL to WW, Oct. 26, 1915.
[3] E. Grey to EMH, Sept. 22, 1915, TLS (E. M. House Papers, CtY), which follows:
"You ask me, in your letter of the 3rd, whether I think that the President
could make peace proposals to the belligerents at this time, upon the broad basis
of the elimination of militarism and navalism and a return, as nearly as possible, to the 'status quo': by which I understand is meant the 'status quo' before
the war.
"That is a question I cannot answer without consulting the Cabinet here and
the Governments of the Allies. It would not be easy to do that, unless I was in a
position to say that the President really was prepared to make such a proposal.
"My personal impression is that neither side is ready for such a proposal.
"To me, the great object of securing the elimination of militarism and
navalism is to get security for the future against aggressive war. How much are
the United States prepared to do in this direction? Would the President propose
that there should be a League of Nations binding themselves to side against any
Power which broke a Treaty; which broke certain rules of warfare on sea or
land (such rules would of course have to be drawn up after this war); or which
refused, in case of dispute, to adopt some other method of settlement than that
of war? Only in some such agreement do I see a prospect of diminishing
militarism and navalism in future, so that no nation will build up armies or
navies for aggressive purposes.
"I cannot say which Governments would be prepared to accept such a pro-

posal, but I am sure that the Government of the United States is the only Government that could make it with effect. Unless something of the kind is proposed, I do not see how the elimination of militarism and navalism is to take a practical form.

"As you mention Mr. Howard Taylor, I enclose a copy of a memorandum concerning him. I was away from London, and could not see him.

"I do not attach importance to the various peace kites flown by Germany in this way. I think that the Germans are simply manoeuvring for position. If Germany really wishes to have peace, she will find some means of making it known unmistakably.

"As the war goes on, the horror of what the state of things after the war may be increases. For instance, the use of poisonous gas by Germany and the indiscriminate use of Zeppelins make it evident that, after the war, there will be no security in future against the use in war of the most horrible methods that science can devise. The whole world will be busy devising means of extermination and of protection against such. This is an abominable prospect, and the only thing that can avert it is such an awakening of the conscience of nations and of their instinct of self-preservation as will make them band together to treat the maker of war as an enemy of the human race.

"I liked very much your saying that your people are awakening slowly but surely to the issues involved in this war, and that you believe they will be found willing to go to limits heretofore unthinkable to bring about a just solution, whether you are finally involved in the war or not. England is bound to fight on with her Allies, as long as they will fight, to secure victory, and I do long to see the bullied provinces of Alsace and Lorraine restored to the freer Government of France & Russia ought to get her outlet to the sea. But the minimum to avoid disaster is the restoration of Belgium and the preservation of France in the terms of peace. Russia can hardly be in vital danger: even if we were all defeated now, her life and future would be safe; she would perhaps become all the greater for defeat; the adversity of the last four months is making her shake off some of the reactionary things that have stifled her; and there is a soul in her people. But for us and for France defeat would mean our disappearance as Powers that counted in the world; and for Belgium it would mean murder and absolute death; and for all Western Europe the subordination of democracies to Prussian autocracy."

To Francis Burton Harrison

[The White House] October 16, 1915.

Please transmit my congratulations to both houses of the Philippine Legislature, and express my earnest hope that the result of their deliberations may be for the welfare of the country and the Filipino people.   Woodrow Wilson.

T telegram (WDR, RG 350, BIA, No. 17073-141, DNA).

To James Fairman Fielder

My dear Governor: [The White House] October 16, 1915

It was very kind of you to send a letter with the delegation that came yesterday to invite me to spend next summer in New Jersey, and you may be sure that it gave me a great deal of pleasure to accept. I shall look forward with the greatest satisfaction to being back in the old state.

In haste, with warmest regard,

Cordially and faithfully yours,   Woodrow Wilson

TLS (Letterpress Books, WP, DLC).

To Louis Seibold

My dear Seibold: [The White House] October 16, 1915

It was fine to see your signature and to know that you were coming back to your strength, and certainly your letter shows that nothing has happened to you, that your appendix was not necessary to the vitality of either your heart or your mind.

You may be sure I appreciate your thought of me very warmly indeed and that my warmest best wishes go with this hurried message. Faithfully yours, Woodrow Wilson

TLS (Letterpress Books, WP, DLC).

To Cleveland Hoadley Dodge

My dear Cleve: The White House October 16, 1915

My mind was so much taken up with the other matter that your last letter was about that I forgot to speak of the business you mentioned. I am perfectly willing to have the letter about the immigrants published and I hope that you will use it in any way you please. I am mighty proud to have you represent me.

In haste Affectionately yours, Woodrow Wilson

TLS (WC, NjP).

From the White House Staff

The White House. October 16, 1915.

The State Department advises that Hillstrom's reprieve expires today.

The Department has been informed by Senator Smoot's office that Hillstrom probably will have to be re-sentenced, which would of course necessitate the fixing of another day for the execution. This, however, is not official.

I do not feel that I can do more than I have done. Even that was apparently resented. W.W.[1]

TL (WP, DLC).
[1] WWhw.

To Wilhelm August Ferdinand Ekengren

My dear Mr. Minister: [The White House] October 16, 1915

What I have learned of the Hillstrom case has given me a great deal of concern and I wish most unaffectedly that it had been possible for me to do more than I did but, as a matter of fact, my slight intervention in the matter to obtain a respite aroused resentment on the part of the authorities of Utah, I fear, and I feel that anything further I might have done would have been without effect. Of course, you understand that the case is entirely beyond my official jurisdiction.

Cordially and sincerely yours, Woodrow Wilson

TLS (Letterpress Books, WP, DLC).

From Walter Hines Page

Dear Mr. President: London, 16 Oct. 1915

(1) I have heard to-day that the German Chancellor lately sent, by a neutral private messenger,[1] a proposition to Sir Edward Grey looking towards peace, and one of the conditions that he laid down was that Great Britain should pay an indemnity! I hear that Sir Edward's astonishment when he read that was such as not visibly to bring peace any nearer.

(2) I hear also—for the tenth time or more—that the differences in the Cabinet are on the verge of causing Mr. Asquith's resignation and the incoming of Lloyd George as Prime Minister.

I have every reason to believe that (1) is true; (2) may or may not not [sic] be true. I hear the following story also wh. I know is true:

Several months ago the English caught a German spy and discovered his superior's address in Holland, the kind of invisible ink the spy used etc. They have ever since made the spy write letters to his chief wh. they (the English Intelligence officers) dictate. When the answers come of course the Intelligence officers open them. In this way they keep up a useful correspondence with the German head-spy. Well, a little while ago they made their captive spy write to the Germans that the English and French were about to land a big army at Antwerp. It was judiciously whispered in the clubs that a great force was going to Antwerp. For two days the boats to Holland were stopped—the passenger-boats, I mean. Every man whispered to his neighbor "Troops going to Antwerp, you know." The daily papers one morning contained a mysterious paragraph about an allied army landing "somewhere." The Germans, of course, got the story as it was meant they should and they withdrew a considerable body of troops from France and rushed them to Antwerp. Then the English and the French made their big "drive"! I suppose the next time an Antwerp story is told, the Germans won't believe it and then an English army may really go.

[1] That is, Howard Taylor.

I could fill a dozen pages with a crop of such stories gleaned almost any good day for gossip—most of them true, but what matter? The air is full of them, clean up to the moon. But most of them are gloomy, such *e.g.* as the report that the British have lost 100,000 in the Dardanelles and that the late "drive" in France cost the British between 50,000 and 75,000 men. When these facts are made public in Parliament, nobody knows what sort of a convulsion will follow. Perhaps then what is known as the Northcliffe-George conspiracy may come to a head. Certainly the Government is in deep water. There are a dozen suppressed criticisms any one of wh. might (and may) cause a change of Prime Ministers and perhaps other changes almost as important —the censorship, the Dardanelles crime, the Balkan situation, conscription, etc. Except for the encouragement given by the recent advance in France, every recent military event has deepened the gloom. True, Russia is coming back, but Italy is doing nothing—will she really help in the Balkans? The Germans *may* reach Constantinople—they won't, but many persons fear they will. If the English people knew of the slaughter of their armies in France and in the Dardanelles, they wd. rend the Government and accept peace on almost any terms—they wouldn't, of course, but the Government seem to think they wd.

In these gloomy times, you will not be surprised,—you have not been surprised—that the German "come-down" in the *Arabic* case provoked so little comment here; for the English have destroyed so many submarines, that the Germans are, in that matter, at the end of their rope and they are using us to save their face. It's a moral certainty that the submarine which sunk the *Arabic* was itself sunk on that very day and there were no survivors. "Commander Schneider" is as dead as Rip Van Winkle's dog. But the English are interested in the *Lusitania* case. They say, "She was sunk nearly six months ago, and no satisfactory answer has yet been given about her—how long can the Germans keep the President waiting?" "Remember the *Lusitania*" was one of the most successful recruiting circulars during the early summer, and it has more than once been the battle-cry of attacking British forces in France. We shall not get credit in English opinion for a decisive diplomatic victory over Germany until the *Lusitania* case is satisfactorily closed.

The truth is—the sad truth for the English—in their present depressed mood everything has been forgotten but the one great task that they have in hand, wh. has not been going well of late. I see and feel in a hundred ways and am reminded by a hundred incidents of a considerable drifting apart of our people and the

English—not unnatural at all, but in a degree delicate: I do not
think dangerous. But it must be handled with care. Here they
are on the border of a panic about the war—perhaps also on the
verge of a political upheaval. The task is too great for their
organization and they are not clever at organization as a rule,
nor quick. All day every day we work with their difficulties and
their sorrows—concrete cases of dead and wounded and prisoners; and we live in the atmosphere (for that matter, in the
very area) of war. All day we hear women who come to ask if we
can find their sons & husbands and all day we read letters making
the same request. Last night a Zeppelin bomb that struck the
street in the Strand—the very centre of London—made missiles
of the pavement and half a mutilated man lay on the sidewalk
and the other half of him was splashed against a wall. Every
man you meet tells of a new death—the death of somebody you
knew; an officer on leave describes the effect of shelling the
Germans who had made a breastwork of their own dead. Every
shell sent men's heads & legs & arms high into the air. The
barber makes me listen to an extract from his son's letter wher[e]in
he tells of stepping on dead Germans in the recent advance in
France, and "now and then one poor devil will wriggle under
your feet." In official life you hear a few ghastly and disquieting
secrets, and every man there is worked to death. Sir Edward
Grey hasn't slept more than a few hours for nearly a week—
dispatches at all hours from all the troublesome capitals, any
one of which may report another Government gone with the
enemy as Bulgaria went. On the outskirts of official life you hear
of this impending change and that—that Sir Edward has failed
and must go, that Lord Kitchener is a stuffed dummy, that Lloyd
George, though a wind bag, is the best man they have, and so
on *ad nauseam* and *ad infinitum*.

Out of this atmosphere I go to the Foreign Office to insist on
the immediate release of a cargo of toys waiting in Rotterdam.
I am patiently listened to; but the next day I learn (thro' the
back-door) that one of the under-secretaries when he was told
what I askd., remarked: "Last Christmas the Americans were
giving us all, including the Germans, a shipload of toys. Now
they are quarreling because they can't get a ship-load from Germany—odd Yankees, aren't they?" This afternoon's paper lectures
us on our imbecility in trying to save the Armenians—or (as it
puts it) in trying "by the most valiant use of words." They are
on the borderland of a panic. Old John Morley, who hadn't before been heard of since the war began, appeared in the House
of Lords yesterday and askd. questions that might cause half the
Cabinet to fall, if they were to be pressed home with sufficient

vigor. The British people for the moment and a considerable part of the Government don't care a fig what we say or do or think or whether we exist. This feeling is not directed against us in particular. Everything but the war and the comparative failure of those who conduct it is excluded from their minds.

And yet—in spite of their muddling and their approach to panic —there is no doubt in my mind of the final result. The undecided thing for the present is whether there is to be a new lease of life for the war given by the Germans' getting to Constantinople. Of course they *may* get there, wh. I doubt. If they do the struggle will be prolonged and complicated. If they do not, they will have made their last "grand-stand" play and the beginning of the end will appear in France—on the battle-line—where the Allies will sacrifice vast armies and end it all in time. For a part of the intervening time they will have the Bull-Run—Gettysburg depression; and their longing for sympathy is pathetic.

To descend to a much smaller aspect of the same subject, there is an indescribable strain on the nerves of all men here: nobody is built for this kind of thing. A few days ago a little group, chiefly of medical men but partly also of military men and civilians, gave a goodbye luncheon to the American physician who has for a year been at the head of the Red-Cross, American hospital in this Kingdom.[2] Apropos of nothing in particular, almost every man at the table began to weep. Osler wiped his eyes time and again, and the General who sat next me said in a weeping whisper: "I've got to get back to the War Office to my work—can't stand this sort of thing." The strain tells on my staff. One after another of these robust and faithful young fellows is ordered to bed for a few days by his doctor—influenza, or indigestion or whatnot: it's all the same thing—an unnatural strain on their vitality. Nobody fortunately has been seriously ill, but almost every one has been laid up for a brief period. Whitlock, over in Brussels, has taken to his bed. "Not a physical thing the matter," says his doctor. I insisted on his making me a visit—to change one depressing atmosphere for another. "No," writes he, "I can't leave: my duties, my duties." He has (luckily) fewer duties than he thinks. One of the marks of this war-malady is the delusion that the victim gets—that he is somehow necessary to hold a toppling world together. As for me, I try twice a week to take the risk of the world's falling apart & I go out for two hours of golf. Thus so far I have escaped the war-malady and its accompanying illusion and I am able, therefore, to remain

Your modest and faithful friend,   Walter H. Page

ALS (WP, DLC).
2 Howard Walter Beal, M.D., of Worcester, Mass., chief surgeon of the American Women's War Hospital at Paignton, England.

From Edward Mandell House, with Enclosure

Dear Governor: New York. October 17th, 1915.

Here is a cablegram that Sir Edward sends me through Spring-Rice. I do not understand it and I am curious to know what sort of message Sir Cecil sent to call it forth.

When he handed me Sir Edward's letter the other day, I placed it in my pocket intending to read it later, but he suggested that I read it then in order that I might send a reply if I desired. This led me to believe that Sir Cecil knew the contents and I passed it to him after I had finished reading it.

This is the only basis I can think of that he has. He sent this cable to me by Frank Polk and was indiscreet enough to show him the original, which Polk tells me was even more cordial in assurances of friendship than this paraphrase.

I am writing to Sir Cecil telling him there was no intention to give him a message, that Sir Edward and I were discussing some matters as between friend and friend, and that I think it better for us to do so without any official notice being taken of it.[1]

Frankly, I am afraid of Sir Cecil's discretion and in the future I shall guard this point.

A letter has come from Sir Horace Plunkett saying he will be over soon. This, I think, is fortunate.

Lord Reading breakfasted with me yesterday. We had a very satisfactory talk. He understands our difficulties and out [our] viewpoint perfectly and is sympathetic. He believes he can eliminate the smaller matters which have caused so much irritation. He believes, however, that England cannot submit to arbitration the question of blockade.

While there was no definite method thought out as to this issue, he believes something satisfactory to both countries can be arrived at.

I called his attention to the unjust criticism that some of the English papers were making of you and I told him it was causing considerable irritation in this country. That it did you no harm, but it did England infinite harm and if it continued they need not be surprised to find sentiment in America drifting away from them, for our people resented any form of criticism from a foreign source.

This is another matter he promised to take up immediately upon his arrival. I suggested to him the method by which I thought this could be done and to which he gave his assent. He goes back thoroughly satisfied with the attitude of the Administration and our people.

Your affectionate,   E. M. House

I have told Pinchot that you would make the address at Columbus Dec. 10.[2] I am sending you a *very* important letter under a separate cover.

TLS (WP, DLC).
[1] EMH to C. A. Spring Rice, Oct. 17, 1915, TL (FO 115/1921, pp. 8-9, PRO).
[2] The newly formed Commission on the Church and Country Life of the Federal Council of the Churches of Christ, headed by Gifford Pinchot, planned special sessions on rural churches in connection with the annual meeting of the Federal Council's executive committee, December 8-10, 1915, at Columbus, Ohio. Wilson's address is printed at Dec. 10, 1915.

ENCLOSURE[1]

October 15, 1915.

Sir Edward Grey has just wired thanking you warmly for your message and asking me to tell you that he has such entire confidence in you that he is always prepared to listen to anything you have to say and to discuss all questions with you. If you were here he says, he would be glad to enter into such a discussion and he hopes you will send him anything you like by letter.

As to my receiving alone any message of the sort suggested from a foreign source,[2] Sir Edward sees the greatest difficulty. He thinks it would be well that my French friend[3] should be associated with me directly in anything of the kind, otherwise the mere fact of the communication would give rise to suspicion.

If you have reason to believe that the power in question really wants peace on any terms that would be fair to us and our friends, it would be worth your while to come to see him over there, though as you know his personal opinion on any terms does not count until the Cabinet and the other parties concerned have been consulted. He wants me to tell you this at once.

T MS (E. M. House Papers, CtY).
[1] The following is a somewhat expanded version of E. Grey to C. A. Spring Rice, Oct. 15, 1915, T telegram (FO 115/1921, p. 4, PRO).
[2] "German Ambassador" in Grey's telegram.
[3] "French Ambassador" in Grey's telegram.

From Jessie Woodrow Wilson Sayre

Williamstown Massachusetts
Darling, darling Father,   Oct. 17, 1915

We are so glad that everything has gone off so well, and we are only sorry that we are not nearer to share your joy by seeing it near at hand. The pictures of you, poor as they are, look so happy, it rejoices us.

We have just written to Edith, suggesting that if international complications permit, you run off here and allow us to see you and have the fun of chaperoning you for a little space. You know how quiet you can be here. The country is at its loveliest, a vision of rose and gold, the weather is Indian summer, and the rides in all directions are superb. The Smiths can tell you about the trail, over the alps to Albany is another glorious ride, and you know something about the Pittsfield valley.

Couldn't you come up after voting, right away quick before Germany hears about it and prevents it? We want you both so much and it seems as if we could hardly wait to see you. There is plenty of room for both, and you wouldn't be bothered here, I'm sure.

Francis has a really truly tooth to show you, which came through today on his ninth month birthday, without any attendant ills, not even crossness!

So, you see, we all three want you.

Ever adoringly   Jessie.

ALS (WC, NjP).

From Edward Mandell House

Dear Governor: New York. October 17th, 1915.

I am enclosing you a draft of the letter. Please eliminate and add wherever you think desirable and return it to me, if you can, by Tuesday morning so that I may catch the Lapland which sails Wednesday morning.

Affectionately yours,   E. M. House

TLS (WP, DLC).

To Edward Mandell House, with Enclosure

Dearest Friend,   The White House 18 October 1915.

I have made one or two unimportant verbal changes in this, but they do not alter the sense of it. I do not want to make it inevitable quite that we should take part to force terms on Germany, because the exact circumstances of such a crisis are impossible to determine. The letter is altogether right. I pray God it may bring results.

Affectionately Yours,   [Woodrow Wilson]

WWTL (E. M. House Papers, CtY).

ENCLOSURE[1]

October 17th, 1915.

Your letter of September 21st was handed me by Sir Cecil when I was in Washington. He suggested that I read it then because there might be some answer he could transmit by cable. I took it from this that he knew of its contents and let him read it. We had no discussion upon the subject and I cannot quite understand what he cabled you that brought forth your message to me yesterday.

I have written Sir Cecil that I think it is better that he should know nothing of what you and I are, at the moment, discussing, that it is now merely between friend and friend and that if anything comes of it, it can be brought to his attention officially. Sir Cecil knows nothing excepting what he read in your letter and I will not discuss the matter with him further, or with anyone else.

It has occurred to me that the time may soon come when this Government should intervene between the belligerents and demand that peace parleys begin upon the broad basis of the elimination of militarism and navalism.

I would not want to suggest this to the President until I knew in advance that it would meet the approval of the Allies. This approval, of course, would have to be confidential and known only to me.

In my opinion, it would be a world-wide calamity if the war should continue to a point where the Allies could not with the aid of the United States bring about a peace along the lines you and I have so often discussed. What I want you to know is that whenever you consider the time is propitious for this intervention I will propose it to the President. He may then desire me to go to Europe in order that a more intimate understanding as to procedure may be had.

It is in my mind that after conferring with your Government, I ⟨would⟩ *should* proceed to Berlin and tell them that it was the President's purpose to intervene and stop this destructive war, provided the weight of the United States thrown on the side that accepted our proposal could do it.

I would not let Berlin know of course of any understanding had with the Allies, but would rather lead them to think that our proposal would be rejected by ⟨them⟩ *the Allies*. This might induce Berlin to accept the proposal, but if they did not do so it would nevertheless be the purpose to intervene. If the Central Powers were still obdurate, it would *probably* be necessary for us to join the Allies and force the issue.

I want to call your attention to the danger of postponing action too long. If the Allies should be unsuccessful and become unable to do their full share, it would be increasingly difficult, if not impossible, for us to intervene. I would have made this proposal to the President last Autumn, but you will remember that it was not agreeable to the Allies.

It might be well for you to cable me under the code we have between us, unless you prefer to send a letter. The understanding will be that the discussion is entirely between you and me until it is desired that it be broadened further.

Your letters seem strangely delayed for it has been nearly a month since your last was written, and it has happened so each time.

T MS (E. M. House Papers, CtY).
    1 Words in the following document in angle brackets deleted by Wilson; words in italics inserted by him.

To Edward Mandell House

Dearest Friend,   The White House. 18 October, 1915.

I do not understand this any more than you do. Sir Cecil is certainly most "unexpected" in his performances. He has gone off on his own hook, evidently. You make the right comment in your letter to Sir Edward.

Affectionately Yours,   [Woodrow Wilson]

WWTL (E. M. House Papers, CtY).

To Edward Mandell House, with Enclosure

Dearest Friend,   The White House. 18 October, 1915.

I would like very much to know what you think of this. Does it alter your view at all as to what we should do or when we should do it? It disturbs me a little that Page should be so constantly seeking to give us the unfavourable English view.

Affectionately Yours,   Woodrow Wilson

WWTLS (E. M. House Papers, CtY).

E N C L O S U R E

London October 15, 1915.

3025. Following in the Secretary's private code and is CON-FIDENTIAL for him and the President only.

The Government and public opinion here are in about the

same mood that Northern opinion and Lincoln's administration were in the week after Bull Run or after Lee crossed the Potomac on his way to Gettysburg. The Balkan situation and the Dardanelles tragedy threaten a political uphe[a]val and the public feeling is far more tense than at any *time* (?). Many of our best friends here fear that it is an unfortunate moment for our long note to be presented while the present crisis lasts. Bryce has this feeling strongly. Northcliffe who has always been most friendly and helpful in his newspapers is greatly excited lest a feeling be provoked not so much by the note itself as by its coming now. I send you these strong convictions by these men and many more like them for whatever they may be worth and without recommendation of my own. But it is certain that the note will receive no serious attention by the Government till the present tension is relaxed and its presentation at this moment is likely to result in a public reception that may tend to defeat its purpose.   American Ambassador,   London.

T telegram (E. M. House Papers, CtY).

To William Phillips

My dear Mr. Phillips: [The White House] October 18, 1915

If Mr. Hohler expresses a desire to pay his respects to me, I am of course willing to give him the opportunity.

I had a long talk with him once[1] and found that he had nothing but British prejudice in him, but since the Secretary of State feels that it might serve a useful purpose, I am willing to offer myself up.

Cordially and sincerely yours,   Woodrow Wilson

TLS (Letterpress Books, WP, DLC).
[1] See the memorandum by T. B. Hohler, Feb. 11, 1914, printed as Enclosure II with C. A. Spring Rice to E. Grey, Feb. 14, 1914, Vol. 29.

To Oswald Garrison Villard

My dear Mr. Villard: The White House October 18, 1915.

The message of congratulation from Mrs. Villard and yourself has given me the most genuine pleasure and I thank you particularly for the generous terms in which it is conveyed.

Cordially and sincerely yours,   Woodrow Wilson

TLS (O. G. Villard Papers, MH).

From the White House Staff

The White House. October 18, 1915.

The Swedish Minister called this afternoon to say that he had received the President's letter concerning the Hillstrom case. The Minister asked that an expression of his very hearty appreciation of the President's courtesy in this matter be conveyed to the President, together with his hope that he had not too much inconvenienced the President.

TL (WP, DLC).

From Richard Evelyn Byrd

My dear Mr President,   Washington Oct. 18, 1915

I have waited until the flood of congratulations must have spent some of its force in order to tell you of my delight in your new happiness. The fact that your fiancee is a Bolling adds to my pleasure. My wife is Elinor Bolling Byrd, my son is Thomas Bolling Byrd and my nephew Hal Flood's boy is Bolling Byrd Flood so you see that we are somewhat proud of the Bolling blood. I would be so glad to see you and yet I know of your immense preoccupations, after which however I am going to ask for a fifteen minutes interview on the general situation.

With kindest regards,

Your friend   Richard Evelyn Byrd

ALS (WP, DLC).

To Lillian Baynes Griffin[1]

My dear Mrs. Griffin: [The White House] October 19, 1915

I have your letter[2] asking the privilege of photographing Mrs. Galt in her wedding gown. I am sorry to say that it will not be possible for you to do anything of the kind. Both Mrs. Galt and I particularly object to having photographs made of the things most intimately associated with our private life.

Very truly yours,   Woodrow Wilson

TLS (Letterpress Books, WP, DLC).

[1] A popular commercial photographer who was a member of the Camera Club of New York and the Royal Photographic Society of Great Britain. One of her specialties was photographing women in the nude.

[2] Lillian B. Griffin to WW, c. Oct. 18, 1915, ALS (WP, DLC).

From Edward Mandell House

Dear Governor: New York. October 19th, 1915.

I should not pay much attention to Page's cable. I do not see how you can.

Would it not be well to be careful not to make the question of absolute blockade imperative? That is the main thing to which they object, and for reasons I gave you when in Washington.

When explaining the matter to Lord Reading the morning he sailed, he seemed to understand and promised to take up the discussion as soon as he reached London. I found myself differing so constantly with Page when I was in London that it was impossible to carry on discussions in conjunction with him.

Please read the letter from Sir Horace Plunkett which I sent you yesterday.[1] Plunkett has a good idea of the American point of view and a better knowledge than Page of the British point of view.

The letter mailed today to Sir Edward will minimize all chance of trouble, for he will sense the big things in your mind, and nothing in the note will unduly disturb him.

I think it is important that there should be no leakage as to its contents. Sir Cecil was particularly insistent upon this, and said that if a garbled report should be given to the press, as was done once before, it would create a very disagreeable situation. I believe it would be better not to publish any part of it, if indeed that is possible.

Towards the end of our controversy with Germany, Bernstorff told me that if a satisfactory conclusion was to be arrived at, no more notes should be made public. The tendancy to use these notes for political advantage should be restrained in this instance.

Your affectionate,   E. M. House

TLS (WP, DLC).
[1] H. Plunkett to EMH, Oct. 1, 1915.

Lindley Miller Garrison to Joseph Patrick Tumulty

My dear Mr. Tumulty: Washington. October 19, 1915.

The following cablegram from Governor General Harrison at Manila was received yesterday evening and I quote it for the information of the President.

"Following resolution adopted at joint session of the Philippine Legislature October 16th: 'Resolution of the Philippine Legislature expressing its profound gratitude to the President of the United States for the message sent through the Governor

General to the Filipino people on the 8th day of March of the present year, and reiterating the same requests for liberty and independence that have been formulated at various times by the elected representatives of the people. Whereas the President of the United States on the 8th day of March of this year addressed the following message to the Governor General—Secretary of War has already told you of the impossibility of passing Philippine Bill at the session of Congress just closed. It was constantly pressed by the Administration, loyally supported by the full force of the party, and will be pressed to passage when the next Congress meets in December. It failed only because blocked by the rules of the Senate as employed by the Republican leaders who were opposed to the legislation and who would yield only if we withdraw the assurance of ultimate independence contained in the preamble. That we would not do. The bill will have my support until it passes and I have no doubt of its passage at the next session of Congress. Please express to the people of the Philippine Islands my deep and abiding interest in their welfare and my purpose to serve them in every possible way. In this I am expressing the spirit and purpose of the majority of the Congress and of the whole government of the United States. Please accept my congratulations upon the success of your administration and my earnest assurance of belief in a happy and prosperous future for the Islands. The people of the Islands have already proved their quality and in nothing more than in the patience and self-control they have manifested in waiting for the fulfillment of our promises. Continuance in that admirable course of action will undoubtedly assure the result we all desire. Woodrow Wilson.[1] Whereas, the Governor General of the Philippine Islands on the first day of the fourth session of the Third Legislature officially communicated to the Philippine Legislature the message above mentioned, now therefore be it resolved by the Philippine Commission and the Philippine Assembly in Joint Session assembled in the Marble Hall of the Ayuntamiento Building in Manila that the Governor-General be and he is hereby requested to send the following message from the Philippine Legislature to the President of the United States: We express our deep gratitude for the unwavering interest shown by the President in behalf of the people of the Philippine Islands. This reiteration of intention to support the Filipino people in their petition for an independent government shows the sincerity and perseverance with which the administration proposes to carry out the plan for the independence of the Philippines, and that this intention is the same as that communicated to the people of the Philippine Islands in so solemn a manner on the 6th of October, 1913,[2] and afterwards ratified by the President in his subsequent message to Congress. For our part we again reiterate in the name of the Filipino people the national desire and purpose set forth on many former occasions. We have also made such substantial progress in local government that it has been deemed wise and desirable to give to the people the practical management of their affairs both municipal and provincial. The result of the reform extending popular control in provincial government has demonstrated that the hopes of success of those responsible for this measure adopted because of full confidence in the capacity of the people, has justified the action; the confidence of the Government of the United States has been also fully justified by the result of extending Filipino control in the Insular Government, notwithstanding that the tumult of the world's greatest war still continues and that everywhere the effect has been felt in financial and economic crises, yet in spite of the limited resources of our government and the continuing limitations of our commerce the Government of the Philippine Islands has successfully met its every necessary expenditure without resort to additional loans either from the United States or foreign governments; but living not alone for the present our foresight goes far beyond, and we wish to assure a stable future for our people. We desire an increase of the elements of our national life and progress; we are yet loyal and for that reason in reiterating as we hereby do reiterate our urgent petitions for the liberty and independence for the people of the Philippine Islands, we the elected representatives of the Filipino people express our confidence that the efforts of the President of the United States to secure the fulfillment of his promises and the realization of our hopes will obtain early and complete success.' Harrison."

Very sincerely,   Lindley M. Garrison

TLS (WP, DLC).
  [1] This telegram is printed at March 6, 1915, Vol. 32.
  [2] WW to F. B. Harrison, Sept. 25, 1913, Vol. 28.

To Richard Evelyn Byrd

My dear Byrd: [The White House] October 20, 1915

Your letter of congratulation gave me a great deal of pleasure. You may be sure that I am very proud to connect myself with the Bolling tradition, and it interests me very much indeed that the name should occur so often in your own family.

It will be a real pleasure to see you some time when you turn up here. I am, as you say, very much preoccupied with all sorts of business, but I am never too busy to see an old friend.

Cordially and faithfully yours,   Woodrow Wilson

TLS (Letterpress Books, WP, DLC).

To Ollie Murray James

My dear Senator: [The White House] October 20, 1915

I have been following with the greatest interest the progress of the campaign in Kentucky and am very much interested to observe what just grounds of confidence the party has of success in your great state. My own association with Mr. Stanley has given me an impression of strength, capacity, intelligence, and integrity, which makes me feel that his election as Governor of the state will constitute a triumph to which the party can look back with special pride, because it is always a matter of pride to serve a great state by putting the very best man at her disposal for public service.[1]

Will you not convey to Mr. Stanley my warmest good wishes and my confident hopes for his complete success?

Cordially and sincerely yours,   Woodrow Wilson

TLS (Letterpress Books, WP, DLC).
[1] Augustus Owsley Stanley was elected governor on November 2, 1915.

From Robert Lansing

Dear Mr. President: Washington October 20, 1915.

Knowing your interest in the case of the two French ladies, Jeanne de Belleville and Madame Thuilliez,[1] who, according to a recent telegram received from the Embassy at Paris,[2] were to have been executed on the 18th instant by the German authorities at Brussels, on a charge of aiding in the escape of their own countrymen, I take pleasure in informing you that a telegram under yesterday's date has been received from Ambassador Gerard in which he reports that he has placed the case of these ladies before the Emperor, with a statement as to your interest in the matter,[3] and that they will probably be reprieved.[4]

I shall be glad to advise you promptly of any further developments in this case.

I am, my dear Mr. President,

Very sincerely yours,   Robert Lansing

TLS (WP, DLC).
[1] Countess Jeanne de Belleville of Montignies-sur-Roc and Louise Thuliez, a schoolteacher of Lille.

2 W. G. Sharp to RL, Oct. 16, 1915, T telegram (SDR, RG 59, 355.51/8, DNA): "Much concern manifested here over report that two French ladies, Miss Thuilliez, teacher at college Liege, and Miss Jeanne de *Belleisle*, will be executed at Brussels next Monday, 18th instant, on charge of aiding escape of their own countrymen, no charge of spying being made. Their relatives, among them Madame Waldeck Rousseau, widow former distinguished French Premier, have earnestly besought Embassy to call their plight to the attention of the Department in hopes that American Government might feel moved to endeavor to have penalty mitigated. Understand that Pope has been approached to intervene."

3 RL to J. W. Gerard, Oct. 17, 1915, T telegram (SDR, RG 59, 355.51/8a, DNA): "French Ambassador has stated that Jeanne de Delleville at Brussels and Madame Thuilliez at Liege have been sentenced by German authorities to be executed Monday eighteenth. President hopes that it will be possible for you to use your good offices to have sentences commuted. You will use your discretion as to propriety of making request after learning nature of the cases."

4 J. W. Gerard to RL, Oct. 19, 1915, T telegram (SDR, RG 59, 355.51/10, DNA): "Jeanne de Delleville and Madame Thuilliez will probably be reprieved. Their case has been laid before the Emperor with statement of President's interest."

The Kaiser commuted their sentences to life imprisonment on October 21 upon the intercession of Benedict XV, Alfonso XIII, and Wilson, and the two women remained in jail throughout the war. Mlle. Thuliez joined the resistance in France in the Second World War and died the most decorated woman in her country. See Rowland Ryder, *Edith Cavell* (London, 1975).

From Sir Cecil Arthur Spring Rice

Dear Mr President   Washington October 20 1915

As I hear from Hohler that my letter of congratulation did not reach your hands I am sending a copy. I should very much regret it, if the British representative, of all others, were thought to be indifferent to so great an increase to your happiness as the occasion must bring.

I am very glad that Hohler was enabled by your kindness to see you.

Believe me with the highest respect, your obedient servant
Cecil Spring Rice

ALS (WP, DLC).

A Thanksgiving Proclamation

[[Oct. 21, 1915]]

It has long been the honored custom of our people to turn in the fruitful Autumn of the year in praise and thanksgiving to Almighty God for His many blessings and mercies to us as a nation. The year that is now drawing to a close since we last observed our day of national thanksgiving has been, while a year of discipline because of the mighty forces of war and of changes which have disturbed the world, also a year of special blessing for us.

Another year of peace has been vouchsafed us; another year

in which not only to take thought of our duty to ourselves and to mankind but also to adjust ourselves to the many responsibilities thrust upon us by a war which has involved almost the whole of Europe. We have been able to assert our rights and the rights of mankind without breach of friendship with the great nations with whom we have had to deal, and while we have asserted rights we have been able also to perform duties and exercise privileges of succor and helpfulness which should serve to demonstrate our desire to make the offices of friendship the means of truly disinterested and unselfish service.

Our ability to serve all who could avail themselves of our services in the midst of crises has been increased, by a gracious Providence, by more and more abundant crops; our ample financial resources have enabled us to steady the markets of the world and facilitate necessary movement of commerce which the war might otherwise have rendered impossible; and our people have come more and more to a sober realization of the part they have been called upon to play in a time when all the world is shaken by unparalleled distresses and disasters.

The extraordinary circumstances of such a time have done much to quicken our national consciousness and deepen and confirm our confidence in the principles of peace and freedom by which we have always sought to be guided. Out of darkness and perplexities have come firmer counsels of policy and clearer perceptions of the essential welfare of the nation. We have prospered while other peoples were at war, but our prosperity has been vouchsafed us, we believe, only that we might the better perform the functions which war rendered it impossible for them to perform.

Now, therefore, I, Woodrow Wilson, President of the United States of America, do hereby designate Thursday, the twenty-fifth of November next, as a day of thanksgiving and prayer, and invite the people throughout the land to cease from their wonted occupations and in their several homes and places of worship render thanks to Almighty God.

In witness whereof I have hereunto set my hand and caused the seal of the United States to be affixed.

Done at the City of Washington this twentieth day of October, in the year of our Lord one thousand nine hundred and fifteen, and of the independence of the United States of America one hundred and fortieth.

WOODROW WILSON

By the President: Robert Lansing, Secretary of State.[1]

Printed in the *New York Times*, Oct. 22, 1915.

¹ There is a WWT draft of the second, third, and fourth paragraphs of this proclamation in WP, DLC. For his first paragraph, Wilson repeated the first paragraph of his Thanksgiving proclamation of 1914.

To Robert Lansing

My dear Mr. Secretary,   The White House. 21 October, 1915.

I am returning the note to Great Britain. I have made a few verbal changes, but they do not alter the substance at all, as I think you will agree.¹

I hope that you will send it by post. It is very important that there should be no leakage at all as to its contents. I hope that you will be kind enough to keep your own eye on the whole handling of the note so as to render a leak impossible, confining the copying, sealing, and mailing to the fewest possible persons, and those only the ones that are in your most intimate confidence. When It has reached the Foreign Office we can publish it as a whole.

Any leakage, or any publication of a garbled version, as happened once before, would create a very disagreeable situation. I would suggest that you let no one know that the note had been sent until Page lets you know by cable that it has arrived and been delivered.   Faithfully Yours,   Woodrow Wilson

WWTLS (SDR, RG 59, 763.72112/1851½, DNA).
¹ Lansing's draft is a T MS dated October 8, 1915, and is in SDR, RG 59, 763.72112/1861a, DNA. The draft is thirty-four pages long, with thirty-three pages of appendices.
Wilson's changes were all "verbal." However, many of them had the effect of giving greater force to Lansing's language. For example, Wilson changed "can be made" to "can rightfully be made"; "if the rule was adopted, ignore neutral rights" to "if the rule were adopted, entirely ignore neutral rights," and so on. On the other hand, Wilson sometimes softened Lansing's language. For example, when Lansing wrote that the United States "had no other course but to resist seizures of vessels at sea upon vague suspicions," Wilson wrote "no other course but to contest seizures of vessels at sea upon conjectural suspicion." Wilson substituted "harassing" for "intolerable" and "it appears" for "it is evident."
The note and its appendices, sent on October 21, 1915, is printed in FR-WWS 1915, pp. 578-601, and summarized at length in Link, Struggle for Neutrality, pp. 683-85. Suffice it to say here that it was a clear and emphatic denunciation as illegal of the "so-called 'blockade' measures imposed by the order in council of March 11." It ended with a ringing declaration, as follows:
"I believe it has been conclusively shown that the methods sought to be employed by Great Britain to obtain and use evidence of enemy destination of cargoes bound for neutral ports, and to impose a contraband character upon such cargoes, are without justification; that the blockade, upon which such methods are partly founded, is ineffective, illegal, and indefensible; that the judicial procedure offered as a means of reparation for an international injury is inherently defective for the purposes; and that in many cases jurisdiction is asserted in violation of the law of nations. The United States, therefore, can not submit to the curtailment of its neutral rights by these measures, which are admittedly retaliatory, and therefore illegal, in conception and in nature, and intended to punish the enemies of Great Britain for alleged illegalities on their part. The United States might not be in a position to object to them if its interests and the interests of all neutrals were unaffected by them, but, being affected, it can not with complacence suffer further subordination of its rights

and interests to the plea that the exceptional geographic position of the enemies of Great Britain require or justify oppressive and illegal practices.

"The Government of the United States desires, therefore, to impress most earnestly upon His Majesty's Government that it must insist that the relations between it and His Majesty's Government be governed, not by a policy of expediency, but by those established rules of international conduct upon which Great Britain in the past has held the United States to account when the latter nation was a belligerent engaged in a struggle for national existence. It is of the highest importance to neutrals, not only of the present day, but of the future, that the principles of international right be maintained unimpaired.

"This task of championing the integrity of neutral rights, which have received the sanction of the civilized world, against the lawless conduct of belligerents arising out of the bitterness of the great conflict which is now wasting the countries of Europe, the United States unhesitatingly assumes, and to the accomplishment of that task it will devote its energies, exercising always that impartiality which from the outbreak of the war it has sought to exercise in its relations with the warring nations."

Two Letters from Robert Lansing

PERSONAL AND STRICTLY PRIVATE:

My dear Mr. President: Washington October 21, 1915.

I am in receipt of the note to Great Britain with your changes and also your letter in regard to it. I am very much gratified that the note meets your approval.

For several days I have felt that the note should go forward as promptly as possible to Great Britain. There has been considerable criticism that we have delayed for so many months to reply to the series of notes which Great Britain sent to us on the subject of neutral trade, although the excuse of our controversy with Germany over submarine warfare seemed to be generally accepted as a reasonable ground for delay. After the practical settlement of the ARABIC question however, unfavorable criticism was renewed and has been increasing in volume from day to day.

I have not felt it was wise to take up the case of the LUSITANIA and the cases of Von Papen, Boy-Ed and Albert until the note to Great Britain was forwarded. For these reasons it seems to me that we ought not to cause further delay by sending the note by mail. The next pouch to London does not leave the Department until the 30th of this month, so that in all probability the note would not be received by the Foreign Office before the 10th or 12th of November. During the next month the complaints and criticisms would increase very much in volume. The Department has hundreds of letters from American importers and exporters asking what we are doing to relieve the situation in which they find themselves. Furthermore, if you approve of my policy of delaying a consideration of the further questions with Germany until the note to Great Britain has been sent, these could not be taken up until about the middle of November.

In view of all the circumstances I therefore think that the note should be telegraphed immediately to London. Will you please advise me today if possible as to your wishes in the matter.

Everything will be done to preserve the secrecy of the note and only my confidential men will see it.

Faithfully yours,   Robert Lansing.

PERSONAL AND STRICTLY PRIVATE:

My dear Mr. President: Washington October 21, 1915.

In accordance with your views expressed by telephone to me this afternoon I have arranged that Mr. Kirk[1] of the diplomatic service, who came from London as a special messenger with documents for the Department, will return to London on Sunday the 24th by the White Star SS FINLAND. He will carry the documents to Mr. Page and should arrive on November 1st.

Faithfully yours,   Robert Lansing.

TLS (WP, DLC).
1 Alexander Comstock Kirk, assigned to the embassy in Berlin.

To Edith Bolling Galt, with Enclosures

[The White House] 21 Oct., 1915

Thought you would like to have these despatches about the recognition of Carranza. Belt is Silliman's temporary substitute. Silliman came up to Washington to report.   W.

ALI (WP, DLC).

E N C L O S U R E   I

J. Belt, Esquire,   October 19, 1915. 12 noon.
Care General Venustiano Carranza, Torreon, Mexico.

I have today sent the following letter to Mr. Arredondo, General Carranza's representative here: "It is my pleasure to inform you that the President of the United States takes this opportunity of extending recognition to the de facto government of Mexico, of which General Venustiano Carranza is the Chief Executive. Paragraph.

The Government of the United States will be pleased to receive formally in Washington a diplomatic representative of the de facto government as soon as it shall please General Carranza to designate and appoint such representative; and, reciprocally, the

Government of the United States will accredit to the de facto government a diplomatic representative. Paragraph.

I should appreciate it if you could find it possible to communicate this information to General Carranza at your earliest convenience."   Lansing.

E N C L O S U R E   I I

Torreon, Coahuila, Mex., October 19, 1915.

IMPORTANT RUSH. Yesterday again this morning I had private interview with First Chief. Late last night telegram arrived from Arredondo stating proposed method of recognition. There was immediate evidence of friendly feeling exhibited. Announced recognition expected to arrive here to-day. General Carranza does not desire that he be considered President stating that many men have been recipient this title which was merely assumed. Prefers title in charge of the Executive power of the Republic, the same he has always used. The title First Chief applies more to the interior, he does not know exact form recognition will be extended but expects same to be of *de facto* Government. States that he is only legal authority remaining from old regime still retaining Governorship of Coahuila   Responsibility for property and lives of foreigners will be assumed throughout the Republic. Those districts not yet in control will be somewhat difficult for time being. Such guarantees given in proclamation more generally known. During fighting in north will not endeavor to call general elections. First calling of municipal elections that these officials may then later supervise general elections in adopting decrees and reforms already promulgated. After these will come elections for governors of states. The so called pre-constitutional period will last a year more or less. Stated in interview with press to-day that there was no reason why he should not become a condidate for President. Has never had that character before only First Chief of constitutionalists army in charge of the executive power and Governor of Coahuila. Stated anyone a candidate. No law prohibiting his being candidate. When asked whether he would be candidate he replied did not know   Shortly might be in event he was called. Trust that foreigners will not in future intermeddle in politics. This will no doubt prevent much future trouble. Treating of religious question stated that only Catholics that have meddled in politics have been punished. All religious toleration in Mexico will prevail as in past. He was asked by one member of press if he had choice as to who should be the Ambassador, he replied that the Ambassador should have a thorough knowledge of Mexico and conditions as they are to-day.

John W. Belt.

ENCLOSURE III

Torreon, Mex., October 19, 1915.

At exactly six p.m., in the Hotel Salvador, this city, in a crowded room in the presence of officials of this Government and at General Carranza's request, I read message quoting letter to Mr. Arredondo extending recognition on behalf of the President of the United States to the *de facto* Government of Mexico. Later I formally presented this important message in its written communication to the Secretary of Foreign Relations Acuna. General Carranza received the message with evident satisfaction expressing his thanks for my personal congratulations. Secretary Acuna informed me that the work of the establishment of the new government would now be undertaken by the civilians everywhere. News of recognition is the cause of rejoicing.

Sincerely appreciate Department's instructions to present this historical note.   John W. Belt.

T telegrams (WP, DLC).

To Sir Cecil Arthur Spring Rice

[The White House]

My dear Mr. Ambassador: October 21, 1915

I am distressed that your letter of congratulation miscarried, but you may be sure that I did not doubt for a moment your feeling and I thank you most warmly for your letter of October nineteenth accompanying a copy of your letter of October sixth.

It gives me peculiar gratification to have Lady Spring-Rice and yourself think of me in such cordial terms at this time and I thank you both with all my heart. It is very delightful to feel that I have such friends.

Cordially and sincerely yours,   Woodrow Wilson

TLS (Letterpress Books, WP, DLC).

From Leroy Arthur Mullen[1]

Honored Sir: Davidson, N. C., October 21, 1915.

It has been the custom here at Davidson each year to dedicate the annual, or year book of the college to some individual for whom the students have a high regard, and who, on the other hand, has in some way been associated with the life of the college.

Because, mainly, the students here cherish that high regard for you, and doubly so because one year of your early college life was spent on this campus, it is the desire of the annual staff to dedicate the 1916 volume of "QUIPS and CRANKS" to you. I am writing to ascertain whether we might get your consent, and if so, be favored with a cabinet photo of yourself, autographed.

Trusting that this matter will be given your prompt and favorable attention, I am,

Most respectfully,   L. A. Mullen.
Editor-in-Chief.

TLS (WP, DLC).

[1] A member of the class of 1916 at Davidson College.

From Duncan Upshaw Fletcher

My dear Mr. President: [Washington] October 21st, 1915.

Please permit me to urge that in any program of legislation for the coming session of Congress Rural Credits be included.

The United States Commission appointed by you held a meeting yesterday, and unanimously reaffirmed its report embodied in Senate Document No. 380, Parts I, II and III, and expressed the view that the time had arrived for legislation.

The Commission Bill, known as the Moss Bill in the House, and the Fletcher Bill in the Senate, we were ordered to introduce at the beginning of the session, with only a few minor changes, mainly in verbiage, not interfering with the essential principles of the bill. The general features of this bill, and of our report, you have approved.

You have heretofore recommended to Congress legislation on this subject. In your last reference to it you stated that the legislation had not been perfected. This is still true, but there has been a thorough study of it by the United States Commission and a definite proposal in its bill. Since that bill was presented there have been some eighty bills introduced.

A Joint Committee, composed of members of the Banking and Currency Committees of the House and Senate, has held hearings on our bill, and reported out what is known as the Hollis-Bulkley Bill, which adopts the principles of our bill with a few additional features.

The Commission you appointed has blazed the way, and the

whole country is now expecting that a law relating to long-term, land mortgage credit will be passed and a system established.

Our Commission will make the further report on the subject reserved in Senate Document No. 380, that of short-term, personal credit, suggesting measures that would bring about advantages in that direction, but we believe still that phase will be best reached through State legislation or local organization.

The Agricultural Appropriation Bill of March 4th, 1915, continued our Commission until June 30th, 1916. It also provided for a Joint Committee of the Senate and the House, to consist of three members each of the Banking and Currency and Agricultural Committees, to prepare, after investigations, "and report to the Congress on or before January 1st, 1916, a bill, or bills, providing for the establishment of a system of Rural Credits adapted to American needs and conditions."

While it is still true the legislation has not been perfected, and while there still continues a difference of opinion on the question of direct Federal aid, everything is in condition where a conclusion is demanded and ought to be definitely reached early in the session.

We firmly believe that the subject ought to be included in the work of the next Congress and we hope you will lay emphasis on it.

Very respectfully and sincerely,   Duncan U. Fletcher

TLS (WP, DLC).

A Memorandum by Thomas Beaumont Hohler

MEMORANDUM.   Washington October twenty first 1915

I had an interview yesterday morning with the President. He referred to my previous interview with him in February of last year in which I said I regretted to think how true a prophet of evil I had been: he replied that many interests and many people were bound to suffer in the course of a revolution. I said that on the one hand His Majesty's Government attached the greatest importance to our collaboration with the United States Government in Mexico. I had been the British representative there now for almost two years and had never failed to give effect in every possible way I could think of to that policy as I trusted the President was aware. He said he was and that he was very grateful for certain assistance I had been able to lend Americans. On the other hand, I continued, we were now confronted by the fact that Carranza and his Government had, without our being in any way consulted, been recognised, and thus the heavy responsibility fell upon me of deciding whether or not to recommend His Majesty's Government to take similar action. There was nothing I desired so much as to have a recognised government with which it would be possible to deal, but it was useless if that government was not responsible and powerful enough to act up to its responsibilities: Mr. Wilson said he was well aware that the past had not been satisfactory with any of the rival candidates but it was impossible to allow things to go on as they were between Mexico and the United States. He had no intention of intervening for he strongly entertained the opinion that every country had a right to struggle after liberty in whatever way it liked. I suggested that in the present case it looked more like a small section of the country struggling after loot, but the President rejoined that a country was free to set its own home on fire if it chose, and in that case other people did well to come away from the flames.

These remarks were strongly reminiscent of Mr. Wilson's Indianapolis speech,[1] but he went on to say that he had consulted with the South American governments as to the best way in which it would be possible to help to restore greater order in Mexico. Undesirable as the Constitutionalist Administration had shown itself, nevertheless facts showed it to be the strongest in the country and to be indeed the only one from whom the establishment of a regular government could be hoped. The decision had therefore been taken to recognize it as the de facto government of the country in the hope that the weight of responsibility which would thus fall upon it would make it more prudent and its behaviour more correct. This policy might in a way be criticised as one of despair but what else was there to do? What had I to suggest?

I said that while I knew it was the desire of His Majesty's Government to collaborate in every possible way towards securing a just and stable government,—the only thing we desired, for our interests were purely financial and commercial and we sought for no political influence, nor privileges nor favours of any kind and not even for the ratification of any unjust or improper contracts or concession or claims—,it seemed to me too late now to offer any opinion, though some ten days ago I had told the Secretary of State that I thought it would be desirable to make recognition dependent on the fulfillment of certain conditions and the grant of certain assurances and guarantees. Mr. Wilson stated that he had obtained certain assurances which he believed were adequate, but he did not see what kind of guarantees could

---

[1] Printed at Jan. 8, 1915, Vol. 32.

be had. I explained that my meaning was rather whether they would be held to the execution of their assurances. Yes, he replied, it is my intention to hold them closely to them.

I returned to my first point and again pointed out the difficult responsibility which lay upon me, and asked him what he would advise even in a private way and could he not tell what his wishes were as regards the action of His Majesty's Government. He said he did not feel justified in offering advice to another government which should be guided by the recommendation of its own agents. That, I replied, was precisely my difficulty for I was that agent. I did not see how to reconcile the two considerations I had in mind, and, after my experience, as an honest man, I hesitated to recommend the adoption of any particular measure: Could he give me no assistance?

Mr. Wilson said that the action he had taken showed what was the course he thought the best to pursue. He was fully alive, he continued, to the deplorable state of things in Mexico, but with one faction officially recognised, there would be someone to call to account: he trusted there would also be an end to organised armed opposition from the other factions and that many from them would now rally to that which had been recognised. The latest reports he had received from Mexico were increasingly satisfactory. I said I was glad indeed to hear this for matters were at a deplorable pass at the moment when I left the city: the train before mine and the train after were both blown up and mine met one coming up from Vera Cruz which had been dynamited and was being totally consumed by fire: I quoted other instances such as the political murder after the veriest farce of a trial of Senor Garcia Granados and the recent invalidation of bills of the forced currency issue and said that the worst features of all were that both from my own limited observation as well as from all reports that had reached me, only a third of the normal area had this year been cultivated, and of this, owing to the failure of the rains, only one third would bear produce, so that, while I hoped I was wrong, I had the gravest fears of a general famine towards the beginning of the new year. That, the President said, may help towards a solution. By exhaustion, I suggested, to which he assented.

I enquired whether it was the intention of the United States Government to assist Carranza in a financial way. He replied that the government had no funds at its disposal for such an object and at present he did not feel justified in prompting anyone to make an advance.

Finally I said that I confidently trusted that, just as we had not failed to give assistance to Americans and their interests whenever desired and possible, the United States Government would not fail to treat British subjects similarly, protecting them with no less zeal and energy than if they were Americans. This, he assured me, would be done.

As I was leaving, I told Mr. Wilson there was one disagreeable point to which perhaps too much importance should not be attached: the new German Minister[2] had stated before certain of Carranza's ministers and generals that in case of trouble between them and the United States they might count on German support. The President sniffed disparagingly, but I said it was nevertheless a fact which it was well to bear in mind, although I had no special fear of German intrigues in Mexico.

I had just previously had a brief conversation with the Secretary of State who had used similar language as to a recognition being the only possible step at the present time.

I reported the gist of these conversations to His Majesty's Ambassador and it seemed to us, upon discussion, that the only course upon [open] to His Majesty's Government taking into consideration all the attendant circumstances, was for them to grant exactly the same measure of recognition as the United States Government, i.e. of a de facto government of which Carranza was the chief of the executive—the more so as this was in reality practically only what His Majesty's Government had already done though in a less formal manner.

I had another interview accordingly with Mr. Lansing this morning in which I informed him that we had sent a recommendation in this sense to London being impressed by the predominating importance over all other considerations of acting in harmony with the United States Government so as to avoid a repetition of the unfortunate complications which resulted in the case of Huerta, owing purely to an unfortunate misunderstanding, from a recognition by some but not by others. At the same time I could not conceal from him the serious apprehensions I felt at the recognition of a government which had given us so little satisfaction in the past, a fact of which no government probably was better aware than that of the United States. Only last night too we had received a report from the British Consul in Mexico of the execution, without trial, on political charges of an engineer and a priest. We had agreed to work together, I observed, and I thought I had given sufficient proofs of a loyal collaboration to be allowed to say that it seemed somewhar [somewhat] hard that when a point of great importance

2 Heinrich von Eckardt.

such as the present arose, we were given no word of warning but it was the South American countries who possessed absolutely no interests whatever in Mexico who were called into consultation, with the results that we were suddenly forced to choose between courses neither of which were wholly tasteful. The Secretary replied that the United States Government had been obliged for political reasons to call in the South American governments to whom the Pan American idea was very dear, and they had had even to give them assurances that they had not consulted even confidentially the European powers from one of which an attempt at domination might be feared. I interrupted him that His Majesty's Government had no idea of dominating nor even of forcing in any way their opinion, but he said it was not His Majesty's Government to which he referred but quite another Power. He continued his remarks saying that he recognised the justice of my appeal and that in future His Majesty's Government should receive due warning of any important measure it was proposed to take, and he believed, now that the main point was reached, it would not be necessary further to submit the details of proposed arrangements to Governments not materially interested in Mexico.

He even admitted that he to a considerable measure shared in my apprehensions though he hoped for the best: he had received certain assurances from Carranza of which at my request he gave me copies, which are enclosed herewith, as to his future conduct, and he handed a list of recommendations, so far as I could understand, to Senor Arredondo, Carranza's agent here dealing with all kinds of points,—guarantees for life and property, notarial acts, freedom of conscience, maintenance of existing rights, contracts and concessions etc., etc., etc., and especially finance. Arredondo had started this morning to meet Carranza and submit them to him and perhaps I might do well to wait here till be [he] returned with Carranza's reply. As to finance Carranza had been warned as to adventurers and it had been poijted [pointed] out to him very clearly that he absolutely must address himself to the big and reliable banks: the financial problem was a very great one and while the resources of Mexico were such as to provide easy giarantees [guarantees] for a loan it must be done by reputable people in a reputable manner, not by a reckless sale of concessions and so forth. The United States Government would in fact, he said, take steps through the Treasury Board to prevent any financial transactions of which they did not approve.

I said that this information gave me much pleasure, and it

only appeared regrettable that these recommendations had not been presented before and not after the recognition, keeping that prize before Carranza like the carrot before the donkey's nose. The Secretary replied that they had found Carranza very difficult to deal with, but especially on those lines and eventually they had found themselves obliged to give him the carrot first in the hope that he would then run properly. He renewed the assurance he had previously given me that the United States Government would not fail to use their best endeavours on behalf of any British persons or interests who might need their assistance.

He said it was their intention to appoint a representative to Mexico as soon as possible: he was aware of the shortcomings of the agents they had had heretofore, but their position being irregular was very difficult, and anything they obtained was to be regarded rather as a favour from the faction granting it than as an obligation upon it: this would now be changed.

I received the impression that neither the President nor the Secretary of State were entirely confident as to the result of the step they have taken, and are waiting with anxiety to see what the outcome is likely to be.

Nothing could have been more friendly and cordial than the reception they accorded me.

The question of the recognition of the de facto government appears to me one of the greatest difficulty. So far as Carranza's administration is concerned, experience of the past and of the present shews that nothing could be more unworthy of recognition. So long as no government had given this in any formal way whatever, a kind of solidarity existed among foreign governments. Now to withhold it after the United States Government and the South American powers have granted it might possibly expose our interests to hostile action. But above all it would appear important, in view of all the circumstances which surround us, of an importance which tops all other considerations, to continue to act in the closest union with the United States Government both in order to avoid a repetition of the Huerta affair, and inasmuch as it is from the United States Government alone that a solution is to be finally awaited. There is also, the fact that the measure of recognition which the United States Government are granting is only limited to a de facto government of which Carranza is the chief of the executive, and His Majesty's Government have already recognised him to this degree and such parts of the Republic as he dominated, and the main result is only to outlaw from the international point of view, all other factions, and to try to hold this one responsible for law and order.

The balance of weight would thus appear to be in favour of taking identical action with the United States Government, but while it would be possible to allow it to become publicly known that this was the course which His Majesty's Government proposed to take, I seel [feel] such doubts as to the result of recognition that I am strongly disposed to welcome any opportunity to delay carrying it into actual effect, and it appears to me from every point of view prudent to adopt the hint of the Secretary of State and to postpone my return to Mexico pending the return of Senor Arredondo with Carranza's reply to the recommendations which have been put forward by the United States Government.

CC MS (FO 115/1926, pp. 28-37, PRO).

To Winston Churchill

My dear Mr. Churchill: [The White House] October 22, 1915

To my great regret I find that it will not be possible for me to take Harlakenden House another season. The place is altogether suitable to my tastes and uses and I have become very much attached to it. I am going to stay away from it next summer only because I must take some part in the political campaign and it is imperative that I should be somewhere near headquarters and easily accessible to those who wish to consult me. I have, therefore, felt obliged to promise to take a house in New Jersey.

I want to tell you how much I have appreciated all your generous courtesies in connection with my leasing of the house at Cornish, and to express my pleasure in having been associated with you in any way. I only wish that my visits had been less brief and that I might have had the pleasure of seeing something of you. I hope that this is only a pleasure postponed.

With warm regards,
Cordially and sincerely yours,   Woodrow Wilson

TLS (Letterpress Books, WP, DLC).

From Robert Underwood Johnson

New York, October 22, 1915.

In God's name cannot something be done to show America's reprobation of the execution of Edith Cavell?[1] Can't Whitlock be thanked?[2]   Robert Underwood Johnson.

T telegram (WP, DLC).
    [1] Edith Louisa Cavell, the celebrated British nurse, who was executed by German military authorities in Brussels on October 12 for helping French,

English, and Belgian prisoners of war to escape from Belgium and German-occupied northern France. Her trial gained tremendous international publicity, largely because she was both a woman and a nurse; the furor over her execution was in part responsible for the commutation of the death sentences of her associates, Countess de Belleville and Mlle. Thuliez. See Ryder, *Edith Cavell*, and A. E. Clark-Kennedy, *Edith Cavell, Pioneer and Patriot* (London, 1965).

2 Whitlock had begun to act on Miss Cavell's behalf on August 31, shortly after her arrest, and maintained communication with the German Governor General in Belgium until her execution. He also kept Page apprised of his appeals and sent to him the series of correspondence (published in *FR-LP*, I, 48-67) which, because it reflected unfavorably upon the German authorities, the British Foreign Office promptly released to the press. About this matter, and Wilson's and Lansing's reactions, see RL to WW, Nov. 1, 1915.

From Haigazoun Hohannes Topakyan[1]

My dear Sir:　　　　　　　　　　　　New York October 22, 1915.

The great calamity of the European War in which the entire Continent of Europe is stricken has brought to the American people an opportunity of International succor unparalleled in the history of the world, and which has indeed been most nobly met.

But to the vast and dreadful human suffering resulting from this disasterous war has now been added the horrible destruction of one of the families of the human race at the hands of cruel fantica[1] Moslems throughout Asia Minor.

The records of the State Department already show, from authentic official sources, that over five hundred thousand Armenian men, women, and children have been deported from their homes and cruelly murdered with unnamable atrocities.

All civilized governments are appealed to in order that this stain on humanity and our civilization may be removed. At the same time a heartrending cry for help reaches America from many quarters for immediate help for the many hundred of thousands of helpless men, women, and children now left starving, either in Turkey or across the borders in Egypt and the Causasus [Caucasus]. These helpless people after passing through terrible sufferings are facing actual starvation. This appeal is unparalleled in that it is for the salvation of the remnant of a race who have been noted for their loyalty, industry and thrift, and as pioneers of Western civilization in the East. It is to save the lives of helpless human beings by hundred of thousands homeless and shelterless and facing starvation. This urgent appeal comes to the noble generosity of the great American Nation now blessed above all others with peace and prosperity.

We pray your Excellency will use your noble influence to help so dire a need in a colossal International calamity, in a cause even of simple humanity, were all other considerations set aside, and this one act will stand out alone in the pages of history for all times, a great luminous vision of human kindness and compassionate mercy. I am confident, that your Excellency's name will again stand as a brilliant inspiration in the list of those who reach out to save a dying nation with help commensurate with the vastness of the dire need.

We have the honor, your Excellency, with earnest prayers for your health and the fulfillment of the desire of your heart to remain.

Your most humble and obedient servants,

H. H. Topakyan

TLS (WP, DLC).

¹ Rug merchant and mine owner, with offices in New York, who had lived in the United States since 1887. He was the Consul-General of Persia in New York.

Wilbur Fisk Sadler, Jr., to Joseph Patrick Tumulty

Personal

Dear Joe: Trenton, October 23, 1915.

For God's sake don't let the President make the mistake of fully endorsing the Garrison program for greater land defence. If it goes through it will ruin and disrupt the National Guard, which at the present time has 119,000 enlisted men and nearly 8300 officers.

If the Pay Bill is passed, which provides for remuneration in a slight degree for the services rendered by the officers and men of the Guard, we would soon have a dependable force of 250,000 men which could be quickly raised to war strength, giving us a force of about 600,000.

The Continental Army scheme has been the hobby of the Regular Army for years. It will not work, it is not fair to the National Guard, and you will find that about all that it will do will be to provide additional berths for Army officers. We have enough of them now and the people are tired of paying them after they reach the age of sixty-four, when they retire and do nothing but draw checks.

Garrison's program has made the officers and men of the Guard furious, and the President, if he endorses the program, will make more determined enemies than you know. I would like to run down to talk with him about the matter but imagine that he is so busy that he does not care to hear from anyone but Garrison, who is surrounded by Army officers who want everything for themselves and who do not realize that they must depend upon the National Guard in case of trouble.

I have been able to go along with the President, as you know, in nearly everything that he has done, but if he adopts the Continental Army plan, I simply cannot follow him.

If you save him from this course you will be doing him the biggest favor imaginable. It is unnecessary for me to tell you that if you want me to come to Washington, or if you feel that I should write the President, that I will be only too glad to do so.

The Pay Bill, which was introduced by Senator Chamberlain during the last session, was prepared at Garrison's direction by officers of the War Department, officers of the War College and the officers of the various National Guard Associations, at a three days' conference. When the bill was drawn it received the O.K. of the Judge-Advocate General, and your friends forced its approval in the National Guard Convention.

I hope you appreciate the seriousness of the situation and would write you more fully about it, but I know that every minute of yours is taken and that letters to you should be as short as possible.   Very truly yours,   W. F. Sadler Jr.

TLS (WP, DLC).

From Winston Churchill

My dear Mr President,   Windsor, Vermont. Oct 24 1915

Many thanks for your kind letter, which I deeply appreciate. I quite understand the circumstances that impel you to go to New Jersey next summer. It has been a great pleasure as well as a great honour to have had you in my house, and we shall miss you and your family greatly. I shall look forward indeed to seeing you sometime when you shall be less occupied, as I look back with pleasure to the conversation we had on the terrace. With kind regard, and best wishes

Sincerely yours   Winston Churchill

ALS (WP, DLC).

To Duncan Upshaw Fletcher

My dear Senator: [The White House] October 25, 1915

I have your interesting letter of October twenty-first. You may be sure that my interest in rural credit legislation is as keen as ever and that I will do all I can to promote it at the next Congress.   Cordially and sincerely yours,   Woodrow Wilson

TLS (Letterpress Books, WP, DLC).

To Robert Lansing

My dear Mr. Secretary: [The White House] October 25, 1915

Thank you very warmly for your letter about the two French ladies and for the welcome news of their reprieve. It is delightful to have been of any service in so important a matter.
          Cordially and sincerely yours,   Woodrow Wilson

TLS (Letterpress Books, WP, DLC).

To Leroy Arthur Mullen

My dear Mr. Mullen: [The White House] October 25, 1915

I have your kind letter of October twenty-first and in reply would say that it would give me real pleasure to have you dedicate the 1916 volume of Quips and Cranks to me. I feel very much gratified that you should have thought of me in this way, for I look back with the greatest pleasure to my year at Davidson.

Under another cover I am sending you an autographed photograph of myself as you request.
          Cordially and sincerely yours,   Woodrow Wilson

TLS (Letterpress Books, WP, DLC).

To Carter Glass

My dear Mr. Glass: [The White House] October 25, 1915

I have just heard with the greatest regret that you were obliged to undergo an operation. I hope with all my heart that it has met every expectation of the surgeons and that you will have a quick recovery and return to more than your usual strength. My heart goes out to you in genuine sympathy. I wish I had known of it all [the][1] sooner so that I might have told you how my thoughts were following you. Do be careful and come back to us in fine shape!
          Cordially and sincerely yours,   Woodrow Wilson

TLS (Letterpress Books, WP, DLC).
[1] Wilson dictated "all the sooner."

A Memorandum by Joseph Patrick Tumulty

[c. Oct. 25, 1915]

NATIONAL DEFENSE SPEECH.[1]

We will take leave to be prepared,—on land and sea; but never for purposes of aggression or self-aggrandizement. "Some time war may be necessary to vindicate spiritual conceptions." America covets neither the land, power nor influence of any other nation. She wishes to live her own life free and separate from the entanglements of the old world. Regardless of present day controversies, we shall be ready to defend American rights wherever and whenever invaded.

1—The President should here state our policy (in general terms) with reference *to defense*. It should not be a policy of turning America into an armed camp. It should be a policy of preparedness that will be as reasonable as it is adequate and practical. A policy in keeping with the immemorial policy of the country.

2—PROGRAMME.

It should not be the work of a particular man or group. No one man or group are able to comprehend the need of the whole country in this matter. It should represent the best judgment of the experienced men of the Army and the Navy.

With the policy thus formulated, we shall ask for the judgment and support of the country,—a country united and enthusiastic for this programme of self-defense and protection.

NO DIVISION.

No man who cares for America in the terms of love and affection would seek to divide her people. At such a crisis as this when the security of everything dear and valuable to America depends upon a strict observance of those rights of America, of life, liberty and property on the high seas, what shall be thought of a certain class of men in America who are engaged in opposing every measure that is calculated to defend and preserve the nation's rights? abetting and aiding the views of other nations as opposed to our rights? preferring the spirit of another foreign nation? When the policy of preparedness is thus formulated, we hope for it the hearty support of the country. There should be no division on this program. No man loves his country who would seek to divide its people. "Let us observe justice and good faith toward all other nations. Have neither passionate hatreds nor passionate attachments to any; and be independent politically of all; be an American and be true to yourselves."

Hyphenated Americans.

We have marked out our course in this awful controversy and shall not, cost what it may, be turned away from it. For the results of that course, the country shall hold me responsible. I can say that as for myself, neither ambition nor interested motives shall influence my conduct in the least. As for me, such abuse as has been heaped upon me, I am unmindful of. I stand as the trustee of the rights of the Nation. I shall continue modestly to defend those rights. Neither ambition nor interested motives shall influence my conduct. No agitation, no matter how conducted or directed as it may be by foreign influences, shall cause me to digress from it. We shall in all these things strive to raise a standard to which the wise and honest may repair. The event is in the hands of God.

T MS (C. L. Swem Coll., NjP).
[1] Which Wilson was to deliver before the Manhattan Club of New York on November 4.

To Jessie Woodrow Wilson Sayre

My darling Jessie,   The White House. 25 October, 1915.

It was a delight to get your letter. You are constantly in our thoughts, and I would give anything if it were possible to act on your delightful suggestion that Edith and I come up to you before this lovely autumn has passed. Alas! my dear little girl, that is impossible. I not only must stay cl[o]se at my tasks, but I must, just now particularly, make it evident to the country that I am doing so, and not galavanting around and seeking my own pleasure. If I followed my heart, Williamstown is the first place I would make for.

I hope that Frank's visit to Montana had a successful outcome.[1] Did it? And is he as well and [as] little Frank seems to be? Now that Francis has begun to get his teeth I hope that he will hurry up and push the job through, bless his heart. How I should like to see him.

While Nell and Mac are in the West Little Ellen is staying with us. She is wonderfully well, and now weighs about thirteen pounds, for she is gaining steadily. She is as good as gold, a singularly serene person, and has now, I am glad to say, an excellent permanest [permanent] nurse.

Margaret really had a wonderful success in her recitals and has come back quite radiant. Mrs. David has turned out a much better, because much more sympathetic, accompanyist than Miss David and all is serene and full of encouragement for the dear little girl.

Edith is greatly distressed by the foolish (and lying) publicity of which she is being made the object, poor girl, but is fine about it, as about everything else. She is very well indeed, and seems (to me, at least) to grow more radiant and lovely every day. I am sure she would send deepest love if she knew that I was writing today.

Margaret and Helen are well, and unite with me in messages of dearest love. I love you very tenderly and very deeply, my darling little girl, and your happiness makes me very happy. I love Frank as if he were my own son, and Francis as if he belonged to me.

Your devoted Father,   Woodrow W

WWTLS (photostat in RSB Coll., DLC).
    [1] The Editors are unable to determine the purpose of this trip.

To Frederic Yates

My dear Fred: The White House October 25, 1915

I want you to know what a thrill of pleasure it gave me to see your handwriting and to get the generous message of your letter of October eleventh.[1] Our thoughts constantly turn back to the dear Lake region and to our dear, dear friends there, and a message like this of yours which lies before me now touches and delights me.

I hope with all my heart that when the skies clear again and the world is once more in a normal temper, I may have the pleasure of bringing my sweet new partner to see you all. I am sure that you will love her, as I am sure that she will love you.

Please give my regards to all my good friends, to Miss Arnold,[2] of whom I often think, to the postman, to my friend who works on the road, and to all who think of me.

We are all very well. Margaret has developed wonderfully in her singing and has just given three concerts at which she had a veritable artistic triumph. It is fine to see how the plucky little girl has developed, and her enthusiasm for her art is as sane as it is great. Neither Nellie nor Jessie is here just now but I am sure that if they were here, they would join with Margaret and me in sending no end of love to you all. May God keep and watch over you all!   Affectionately yours,   Woodrow Wilson

TLS (F. Yates Coll., NjP).
    [1] F. Yates to WW, Oct. 11, 1915, ALS (WP, DLC).
    [2] Frances Bunsen Trevenen Arnold. See EAW to Anna Harris, Dec. 1, 1906, n. 2, Vol. 16.

To Wilbur Fisk Sadler, Jr.

My dear General: [The White House] October 26, 1915

Tumulty has shown me your letter of October twenty-third and I hasten to assure you that you must be laboring under some misapprehension. There is nothing in the plans which I am contemplating for the development of our military strength which works in the least against the National Guard. On the contrary, I am sure you know how high a value I attach to the National Guard and I think that by the time our plans mature you will see that we intend to make use of the National Guard in the new development not only, but also to safeguard and develop its interest in every way. Pray do not form a judgment until you hear the whole story.

In haste

Cordially and sincerely yours,   Woodrow Wilson

TLS (Letterpress Books, WP, DLC).

From Robert Lansing, with Enclosures

PERSONAL AND STRICTLY CONFIDENTIAL:

My dear Mr. President: Washington October 26, 1915.

As I telephoned you yesterday I took up the matter of the general Pan-American treaty with the Argentine Ambassador on the 20th, handing him the revised form which we had agreed upon—a copy of which I enclose. At the time he said that there would be, he feared, considerable objection to the arbitration provision in the second article in that it placed a time limit upon the settlement of disputed territorial claims.[1]

The following day he sent me a counter-draft which I enclose for your consideration. I do not think that the terms of article two meet the essential feature of amicable settlement of disputes which the original draft covers by providing arbitral proceedings. I do think, however, that there is something to be said as to the removal of the time limit since it might prevent objection particularly from Chile.

I shall endeavor to see the Chilean Ambassador today or tomorrow in regard to this matter and would like your comments on the Argentine Ambassador's counter-draft as soon as you can conveniently give them to me.

Faithfully yours,   Robert Lansing.

TLS (SDR, RG 59, 710.11/211½, DNA).
[1] It was a reformulation of Wilson's draft printed at Oct. 15, 1915.

ENCLOSURE   I

Handed to Argentine Amb. Oct. 20/15 RL

I.

That the high contracting parties to this solemn covenant and agreement hereby join one another in a common and mutual guarantee of territorial integrity and of political independence under republican forms of government.

II.

That, to this end, and as a condition precedent to the guarantee set forth in Article I of this convention, it is covenanted and agreed by and between the high contracting parties that all disputes now pending and unconcluded between any two or more of them with regard to their boundaries or territories shall be brought to an early and final settlement in the following manner, unless some equally expeditious and satisfactory method of settlement can be agreed upon and put into operation in each or any case within one year after the ratification of this convention and brought to a decision within one year after its inception:

Each of the parties to the dispute shall select two arbiters and those thus selected and commissioned shall select an additional arbiter or umpire; to the tribunal thus constituted the question or questions at issue shall be submitted without reservation; and the decisions of this tribunal shall be final and conclusive as between the parties to the dispute and under the terms of this convention as to the whole subject-matter submitted. The decisions of such tribunal or tribunals shall be made and officially announced and accepted within one year after the formal constitution of the tribunal; and the tribunal shall be constituted within one year after the deposit of ratifications of this convention by the high contracting parties which are parties to the dispute.

III.

That the high contracting parties further agree, First, that all questions, of whatever character, arising between any two or more of them which cannot be settled by the ordinary means of diplomatic correspondence shall, before any declaration of war or beginnnig of hostilities, be first submitted to a permanent international commission for investigation, one year being allowed for such investigation; and, Second, that, if the dispute is not settled by investigation, to submit the same to arbitration, provided the question in dispute does not affect the honour, independence, or vital interests of the nations concerned or the interests of third parties; and the high contracting parties hereby agree, where this has not already been done, to enter into treaty, each with all of the others severally, to carry out the provisions of this Article.

T MS (SDR, RG 59, 710.11/211½, DNA).

ENCLOSURE II

Handed me by Argentine Amb. Oct. 21/15 RL

I.

That the high contracting parties to this solemn covenant and agreement hereby join one another in a common and mutual guarantee of territorial integrity and of political independence under republican forms of government.

II.

That to this end, and as a condition precedent to the guarantee set forth in Article I of this convention, it is covenanted and agreed by and between the high contracting parties that all disputes now pending and unconcluded between any two or more of them with regard to their boundaries or territories shall be brought to an early and final settlement, unless some other expeditious method of settlement can be agreed upon between the interested parties, in the following manner.

The guarantee of territorial integrity until the final settlement of those disputes shall only lie as to the territories out of dispute.

III.

That the high contracting parties further agree, First, that all questions, of whatever character, arising between any two or more of them which cannot be settled by the ordinary means of diplomatic correspondence shall, before any declaration of war or beginning of hostilities, be first submitted to a permanent international commission for investigation, one year being allowed for such investigation; and, Second, that, if the dispute is not settled by investigation, to submit the same to arbitration.

The particulars in regard to the organization of the tribunal and method of procedure before that tribunal to be agreed on in each case, and the high contracting parties hereby agree, where this has not already been done, each with all of the others severally, to carry out the provisions of this article.

T MS (SDR, RG 59, 710.11/211½, DNA).

To Robert Lansing

My dear Mr. Secretary   The White House. 27 October, 1915.

I agree with your judgment about this. I think the only concession we can afford to make, if these articles are indeed to serve as any sort of a model for the action of other nations at any time, is to remove the definite time limit in Article Two; and that Article

Three should stand is [as] in our original. The new Article Three proposed by the Argentine Ambassador seems to me distinctly inferior to the original. It does not include the necessary reservation of questions of national honour, etc., upon which our Senate would certainly insist, and it seems to end nowhere, but to leave the whole thing vague. Do you not think so?

Article Two should, I think, provide that disputed questions of territory should be settled as promptly as possible, i.e., diligently purhed [pushed] to a settlement.

Faithfully Yours,   Woodrow Wilson

WWTLS (SDR, RG 59, 710.11/212½, DNA).

To Champ Clark

My dear Friend: [The White House] October 27, 1915

I wonder if you are expecting to be in Washington or in this neighborhood before the assembling of Congress? I am very anxious to discuss with you the more important matters of legislation which will come before the next Congress, and particularly the question of preparation for national defense in which I know you are as deeply interested as I am. If you are coming this way soon, will you not be kind enough to let me know so that we may get together for a good talk?

Cordially and sincerely yours,   Woodrow Wilson

TLS (Letterpress Books, WP, DLC).

To Claude Kitchin

My dear Mr. Kitchin: [The White House] October 27, 1915

It was a great disappointment to me that you could not see me when you were in town yesterday and today.[1] I consider it of the utmost importance that I should discuss with you the question of preparation for national defense which will necessarily engage the attention of Congress immediately upon its assembling, and I write now to beg that you will give me the pleasure of consulting with you at the earliest possible date.

I am informed that you will return to Washington on the sixth of November. I shall be very glad to see you then or as soon thereafter as you can make it convenient.

Sincerely yours,   Woodrow Wilson

TLS (Letterpress Books, WP, DLC).
[1] The White House staff had sought an appointment with Kitchin, but he had left for North Carolina before he could be reached.

From Robert Lansing, with Enclosures

PERSONAL AND PRIVATE:

My dear Mr. President: Washington October 27, 1915.

I enclose to you two papers which were handed to me today by the Japanese Ambassador and the British Ambassador. They are in fact, if not in language, protests to the Chinese Government against the reestablishment of a monarchy.

To neither of the Ambassadors did I express any opinion as to what the attitude of this Government would be. I confess that I am at a loss to understand the purpose of Japan in this action which has been taken. Perhaps I am very suspicious and that it has the object of preserving the peace in the far east. My own view is that it is not an action on their part to which we should make an objection. In fact I believe if it accomplishes its purpose it will be beneficial. Our reports while varied tend to show that the proclamation of Yuan Shih Kai as Emperor would cause insurrections in various parts of China. He is, to all intents, Emperor at the present time and I can see no reason other than ambition for the continuance of his family in power for the assumption of the title.

I do not think it is necessary for us to take any action in the matter other than to acknowledge the receipt of these papers. As it is a matter, however, of considerable moment I would be obliged if you would give me your views on the subject.

Faithfully yours,   Robert Lansing.

TLS (SDR, RG 59, 893.01/73, DNA).

E N C L O S U R E   I

Handed me by Japanese Amb.
11:30 am Oct 27/15 RL.

PARAPHRASE OF A TELEGRAM FROM BARON ISHII[1] TO
VISCOUNT CHINDA.

As no doubt the Government to which you are accredited is well aware, a plan to inaugurate a monarchical government in China has recently made sudden and rapid developments. While the inadequate means of communication, coupled with the fact of manipulation of the press freely resorted to by the Chinese authorities, make it extremely difficult to learn the actual and true state of affairs in China, one thing seems certain that the feeling prevailing in the country against the monarchical movement is very much stronger than at first suspected. This is particularly the case in the Yangtze Valley and South China where the strong opposition sentiment is widely diffused.

No pains are, it seems, spared by the Chinese Government in the endeavor to put a peaceful face on the situation by resorting to various means such as causing the provincial authorities to frame and submit reports favorable to the execution of the monarchical plan, and giving publicity thereto, or directing these authorities to exercise weighty pressure directly and indirectly upon the opposition. But, in point of fact, the more it attempts to hasten the realization of a monarchy, the stronger grows the opposition sentiment. So long as the present political status is maintained in China, there would seem to be little fear of any intestine disturbances arising in the immediate future, and it is to the monarchical plan that the present state of disquietude is to be attributed. Should change of the polity be unfortunately followed by an upheaval and dissensions, the consequences thereof to be suffered by the countries having important interests in China would be beyond calculation.

At a time when, in view of the European situation, it is deemed desirable to avoid any event that may in the least tend to further prejudice the general peace of the world, the Imperial Government, particularly solicitous as it is of peace in the Far East, cannot but view with grave concern the situation in China as is pointed out above. It need scarcely be mentioned that the Imperial Government has not the remotest intention to intervene in the internal affairs of China, but, the situation in that country being as it is, it is desirous of preventing possible disaster in time. With this object in view, the Imperial Government purposes, at this juncture, to enquire of the Chinese Government whether it is counting upon a peaceful inauguration of the monarchical form of government unattended by any disturbances, and, at the same time, to offer to it an informal and friendly advice in the sense that, inasmuch as the furtherance of the monarchical plan involves, in the opinion of the Imperial Government, a danger of inviting disorder in China, it would be more in keeping with the interest of the general situation to defer its execution for some time.

If the Government to which you are accredited shares the solicitude of the Imperial Government in above respect, it is earnestly hoped that it will see its way to give to the Chinese Government similar advice, in the interest of general peace in the Far East.

T MS (SDR, RG 59, 893.01/72, DNA).

[1] Kikujiro Ishii, Foreign Minister of Japan from October 1915 to October 1916.

E N C L O S U R E   I I

Handed me by British Amb. 2:30 pm
Oct 27/15 RL

MEMORANDUM.

The Japanese Government have communicated to the British Government a draft of instructions to the Japanese representatives at Washington, Paris and Petrograd, copy of which is annexed,[1] inviting the Governments of the United States, France and Russia to participate in representations to the Chinese Government in that sense.

After careful consideration of the circumstances the British Government have instructed the British representatives at Washington, Paris and Petrograd to make to the above named governments a communication in the same sense.

Having received from many sources information as to the rapidity with which events are proceeding in China; they have agreed with the Japanese Government that no time should be lost in tendering advice to the Chinese Government in the sense of the above named communication. They have accordingly instructed their representative in Peking to proceed at once with the communication and to concert with his Japanese colleague as to the manner in which the advice suggested can best be tendered to the Chinese Government.

The British Government trust that the United States Government will appreciate the reason for proceeding at once with the communication without awaiting the reply of the United States and hope that the United States Government will deem it expedient to send similar instructions to the American representative at Peking, with as little delay as possible in view of the gravity of the danger which appears to threaten the internal peace of China.

British Embassy
Washington
October twenty seven 1915.

T MS (SDR, RG 59, 893.01/73, DNA).
[1] Not printed.

From Carter Glass

My dear Mr. President: Baltimore, Md. Octo. 27/15.

I cannot begin to tell you how gratified I am to receive your kind note of the 26th and how cheering it is. My trouble is not as bad as was feared, and is rapidly yielding to treatment without the necessity of an operation. Dr. Barker[1] says he will have me in shipshape for Congress.

May I venture to obtrude upon your personal affairs to say how much pleased all Virginians are that one of our most gracious and lovely daughters is to be mistress at the White House. We very confidently wish for both of you the greatest possible happiness.

Thanking you again, Mr. President, for your kind note, believe me   Faithfully yours,   Carter Glass.

ALS (WP, DLC).
[1] Lewellys Franklin Barker, M.D., Professor of Clinical Medicine at The Johns Hopkins University and visiting physician at The Johns Hopkins University Hospital.

From Edward Mandell House

Dear Governor: New York. October 27th, 1915.

The past week has been strangely quiet. There has been nothing of interest of which to write.

Janet was operated on Monday for appendicitis and is doing fairly well.

I am counting upon your coming over next week and staying several days. Will you not let me know as definitely as you can so I may arrange something for the pleasure of the party.

                    Your affectionate,   E. M. House

TLS (WP, DLC).

William Phillips to Joseph Patrick Tumulty

Dear Mr. Tumulty: Washington October 27, 1915.

The French Ambassador has received instructions to express to the President if he has a suitable opportunity the thanks of the French Government for the President's interest and intervention on behalf of Jeanne de Belleville and Madame Thuilliez which resulted in the lives of these two ladies being spared.

The Ambassador realizes that the President is very busy and he does not therefore press for an audience. At the same I know that he would be very appreciative if an opportunity could be afforded him to carry out the instructions of his Government. Mr. Lansing, to whom I have referred the matter, thinks it would be desirable if the President could arrange to receive Mr. Jusserand in this instance.

With kindest regards,

                    Sincerely yours,   William Phillips

TLS (WP, DLC).

Edward Mandell House to Robert Lansing

Dear Mr. Lansing: New York. October 27th, 1915.

I would appreciate it if you would send me a copy of the memorandum which was agreed upon at our conference with the President week before last. I would like to keep it with the other data I have on the subject.

I am wondering how things are progressing in that direction.

With warm regards and good wishes I am,

Sincerely yours,   E. M. House

TLS (SDR, RG 59, 710.11/213½, DNA).

To Haigazoun Hohannes Topakyan

[The White House]

My dear Mr. Consul General: October 28, 1915

May I not acknowledge the receipt through the Department of State of your letter of October twenty-second about the sufferings of the Armenian people in Turkey, and may I not assure you of my deep interest in the whole subject? The State Department has not been slack in using every endeavor to alter the attitude of the Turkish Government in this matter and to lighten the sufferings of the Armenian people, and you may be sure that this Government will continue to do everything that it is possible for it to do through diplomatic channels.

Cordially and sincerely yours,   Woodrow Wilson

TLS (Letterpress Books, WP, DLC).

To Henry Morgenthau

[The White House]

My dear Mr. Ambassador: October 28, 1915

This is just a line to let you know that I am thinking of you and that I deeply and sincerely admire the way in which you are fulfilling the very trying obligations and duties of your present post. I have nothing special to write about; this is only a personal message to let you know that we are thinking of you constantly and that your labors are not passing unnoticed, but that we are very grateful.

With warmest regards to Mrs. Morgenthau[1] and yourself,

Cordially and sincerely yours,   Woodrow Wilson

TLS (Letterpress Books, WP, DLC).
[1] Josephine Sykes Morgenthau.

To Oswald Garrison Villard

Personal.

My dear Mr. Villard: The White House October 28, 1915

Tumulty has handed me your letter of October twenty-sixth.[1] I am sorry to think from the general tone of your letter that you feel I am really not interested in the colored people and in the colored vote. If you do, you are very much mistaken, though perhaps you and I do not hold exactly the same views about the best way in which to promote the welfare of the colored people.

If I were free to undertake engagements of the sort, I would be very much attracted by your suggestion that I speak in Carnegie Hall on Lincoln's Birthday, but my impression is confirmed from day to day and from week to week that I ought really to confine myself as much as possible to my duties here and to speaking upon pressing national questions chiefly of a nonpartisan sort, for the present at any rate. I am sure that you sympathize with this general position on my part and that you will believe that it is from no lack of interest either in the occasion or the subject that I feel I cannot speak on the occasion you describe in so attractive a way.

Cordially and sincerely yours,   Woodrow Wilson

TLS (O. G. Villard Papers, MH).
[1] O. G. Villard to JPT, Oct. 26, 1915, CCL (O. G. Villard Papers, MH), inviting Wilson to speak to the annual meeting of the National Association for the Advancement of Colored People in Carnegie Hall, New York, on Lincoln's birthday in 1916.

To William Howard Taft

My dear Mr. Taft: The White House October 28, 1915

I am writing to ask if you will not do the country and the American Red Cross the great service of accepting the chairmanship of the Central Committee of the American Red Cross. I know how active and how deep your interest in the Red Cross has been and it would be of the utmost advantage to the association if you could find the time and energy to serve in that capacity, and I am sure that we should all feel it a privilege to be associated with you.[1]   Cordially and sincerely yours,   Woodrow Wilson

TLS (W. H. Taft Papers, DLC).
[1] Taft accepted. See W. H. Taft to WW, Nov. 17, 1915, TLS (WP, DLC), and WW to W. H. Taft, Nov. 10, 1915, TLS (W. H. Taft Papers, DLC).

A Draft of the Manhattan Club Address[1]

[Oct. 28, 1915]

Mr. Toastmaster and Gentlemen: I warmly felicitate the club upon the completion of fifty years of successful and interesting life. Club life may be made to mean a great deal to those who know how to use it, and I have no doubt that to a great many of you has come genuine stimulation in the associations of this place and that as the years have multiplied you have seen more and more the useful ends which may be served by associations of this sort.

But I have not come to speak wholly of that, for there are others of your own members who can speak of the club with a knowledge and an intelligence which no one can have who has not intimately associated with it. Men band themselves together for the sake of the association no doubt, but also for something greater and deeper than that, because they are conscious of common interests lying outside their business occupations, because they are members of the same community and in intercourse find mutual stimulation and their real maximum of vitality and power. And I shall assume that here around the dinner table on this occasion our talk should naturally turn to the wide and common interests which are most in our thoughts, whether they be the interests of the community or of the nation.

A year and a half ago our thought would have been almost altogether of great domestic questions. They are many and of vital consequence. We must and shall address ourselves to their solution with all diligence, firmness, and self-possession, notwithstanding we find ourselves in the midst of a world disturbed by great disaster and ablaze with terrible war; but our thought is inevitably of new things about which formerly we gave ourselves little concern. We are thinking now chiefly of our relations with the rest of the world, ⟨—not our commercial relations, —⟩ about those we have thought and planned always,—but about our political relations, our duties as an individual and independent force in the world to ourselves, our neighbors, and the world itself.

Our principles are well known. It is not necessary to avow them again. We believe in political liberty and founded our great government to obtain it, the liberty of men and of peoples,—of men to choose their own lives and of peoples to choose their own allegiance. Our ambition, also, all the world has knowledge of. It

[1] Words in angle brackets in the following document deleted by Tumulty; words in italics added by him.

is not only to be free and prosperous ourselves, but also to be the friend and thoughtful partisan of those who are free or who desire freedom the world over. If we have had aggressive purposes and covetous ambitions, they were the fruit of our thoughtless youth as a nation and we have put them aside. We shall, I confidently believe, never again take another foot of territory by conquest. We shall never in any circumstances seek to make an independent people subject to our dominion, because we believe, we passionately believe, in the right of every people to choose their own allegiance and be free of masters altogether. For ourselves we wish nothing but the full liberty of self-development, and with ourselves in this great matter we associate all the peoples of our own hemisphere. We wish not only for the United States but for them the fullest freedom of independent growth and of action, for we know that throughout this hemisphere the same aspirations are everywhere being worked out under diverse conditions but with the same impulse and ultimate object.

All this is very clear to us and will, I confidently predict, become more and more clear to the whole world as the great processes of the future unfold themselves. It is with a full consciousness of such principles and such ambitions that we are asking ourselves at the present time what our duty is with regard to the armed force of the nation. (1)[2] The influences of a great war are everywhere in the air. All Europe is embattled. Force everywhere speaks out with a loud and imperious voice in a struggle of nations, and from one end of our own dear country to the other men are asking one another what our own force is, how far we are prepared to maintain ourselves against any ⟨possible⟩ interference with our national action or development.

In no man's mind, I am sure, is the question of the wilful use of force on our part against any nation or any people. No matter what military or naval force the United States might develop, statesmen throughout the whole world might rest assured that we were gathering force, not for attack in any quarter, not for aggression of any kind, not for the satisfaction of any political or international ambition, but merely to make sure of our own security. We have it in mind to be prepared, but not for war, only for defense, and with the thought constantly in our minds that the principles we hold most dear can be achieved in the slow processes of history only in the kindly and wholesome atmosphere of peace and not by the use of hostile force. The mission of America in the world is essentially a mission of peace

2 Here Tumulty refers to additions that he suggested in his memorandum printed at Oct. 29, 1915.

and good will among men. She has become the home and asylum
of men of all creeds and races. Within her hospitable borders
they have found homes and congenial associations and freedom
and a wide and cordial welcome, and they have become part of
the bone and sinew and spirit of America itself. America is made
up of the nations of the world and is the friend of the nations
of the world.

But we feel justified in preparing ourselves to vindicate our
right to independent and unmolested action by making the force
that is in us ready for assertion.

And we know that we can do this in a way that will be itself   X[3]
an illustration of the American spirit. ⟨We do not want a great
standing Army and we do not need one.⟩ *In accord with our
American traditions* We want only an Army adequate to the
constant and legitimate uses of times of international peace.
But we do want to feel that there is a great body of citizens who
have received at least the most rudimentary and necessary forms
of military training, that they will be ready to form themselves
into a fighting force at the call of the nation, and that the nation
has the munitions and supplies with which to equip them without delay should it be necessary to call them into action. We wish
to supply them with the training they need, and we think we
can do so without calling them at any time too long away from
their civilian pursuits.

It is with this idea, with this conception, in mind that the
plans have been made which it will be my privilege to lay before
the Congress at its next session. That plan calls for only such an
increase in the regular Army of the United States as experience
has proved to be necessary for the performance of the necessary
duties of the Army in the Philippines, in Hawaii, in Porto Rico,
upon the borders of the United States, at the coast fortifications,
and at the military posts of the interior. For the rest, it calls for
the training within the next three years of a force of 400,000
citizen soldiers to be raised in annual contingents of 133,000,
who would be asked to enlist for three years with the colors and
three years on furlough, but who during their three years of
enlistment with the colors would not be organized as a standing
force but would be expected merely to undergo intensive training
for a very brief period of each year. Their training would take
place in immediate association with the organized units of the
regular Army. It would have no touch of the amateur about it,
neither would it exact of the volunteers more than they could
give in any one year from their civilian pursuits. And none of

3 *Ibid.*

this would be done in such a way as in the slightest degree to supersede or subordinate our present serviceable and efficient National Guard. On the contrary, the National Guard itself would be used as part of the instrumentality by which training would be given the citizens who enlisted under the new conditions, and I should hope and expect the legislation by which all this would be accomplished would put the National Guard itself upon a better and more permanent footing than it has ever been before, giving it not only the recognition which it deserves, but a more definite support from the national government and a more definite connection with the military organization of the nation.

What we all wish to accomplish is that the forces of the nation should indeed be part of the nation and not a separate professional force, and the chief cost of the system would not be in the enlistment or in the training of the men, but in the providing of ample equipment in case it should be necessary to call all forces into the field.

Moreover, it has been American policy time out of mind to look to the Navy as the first and chief line of defense. The Navy of the United States is already a very great and efficient force. Not rapidly, but slowly, with careful attention, our naval force has been developed until the Navy of the United States stands recognized as one of the most ⟨respectable⟩ *efficient* and notable of the modern time. All that is needed in order to bring the Navy to a point of extraordinary force and efficiency as compared with the other navies of the world is that we should hasten our pace ⟨a little⟩ in the policy we have long been pursuing, and that chief of all we should have a definite policy of development, not made from year to year, but looking well into the future and planning for a definite consummation. (4)[4] It is not merely a matter of building battleships and cruisers and submarines, but also a matter of making sure that we shall have the adequate equipment of men and munitions and supplies for the vessels we build and intend to build. Part of our problem is the problem of what I may call the mobilization of the resources of the nation at the proper time if it should ever be necessary to mobilize them for national defense. We shall study efficiency and adequate equipment as carefully as we shall study the number and size of our ships, and I believe that the plans already in part made public by the Navy Department are plans which the whole nation can approve with calm enthusiasm.

For I think no thoughtful man feels any panic haste in this

[4] *Ibid.*

matter. ⟨No thoughtful man should feel any such haste.⟩ The country is not threatened from any quarter. She stands in friendly relations with all the world. Her resources are known and her self-respect and her capacity to care for her own citizens and her own rights. There is no fear amongst us. (6)[5] *Under these new world conditions* We have ⟨only⟩ become thoughtful of things which ⟨in any case we should have given thought to, and are setting ourselves to do what any nation should do which is⟩ *all reasonable men consider necessary and we are therefore formulating and intend to carry out these means of self-defense which every great nation which is* confronted with the great enterprise of liberty and independence.[6]

Trustees.[7]

The only thing which has given us grave concern in recent months has been that voices have been raised in America professing to be the voices of Americans which were not indeed and in truth American but which spoke alien sympathies, which came from men who loved other countries better than they loved America, who were partisans of other causes than that of America and had forgotten that their chief and only allegiance was to the great government under which they live. These voices have not been many though they have been very loud and very clamorous. They have proceeded from a few who were bitter and who were grievously misled. America has not opened its doors in vain to men and women out of other nations, and the vast majority of those who have come to take advantage of her hospitality have united their spirits with hers as well as their fortunes, and these men who speak alien sympathies are not their spokesmen but are the spokesmen of small groups whom it is high time that the nation should call to a reckoning. The chief thing necessary in America in order that she should let all the world know that she is prepared to maintain her own great position in the world is that the real voice of the nation should sound forth in its majestic volume and in the deep unison of a common, unhesitating national feeling. And I do not doubt that upon the first occasion, upon the first opportunity, upon the first definite challenge, that voice will speak forth in tones which no man can doubt and with commands which no man can gainsay or resist.

May I not say, while I am speaking of this, that there is another danger that we should guard against? We should rebuke not only manifestations of national feeling here in America where there should be none, but also every manifestation of religious and sectarian antagonism. It does not become America that within her borders, where every man is free to follow the dictates of his conscience and worship God as he pleases, men should raise the cry of church against church. To do that is to strike at the very spirit *and heart* of America. We are a God-fearing people. We agree to differ about methods of worship, but we are united in believing in Divine Providence and in worshipping the God of Nations. We are the champions of religious right here and everywhere that it may be our privilege to give our countenance and support. The government is conscious of the obligation and the nation is conscious of the obligation that no man create divisions where there are none.[8]

T MS (WP, DLC).
[8] There is a WWsh draft of this draft, dated Oct. 25, 1915, in the C. L. Swem Coll., NjP.

Robert Lansing to Edward Mandell House

CONFIDENTIAL:

My dear Colonel House: Washington October 28, 1915.

I enclose to you a copy of a memorandum which was agreed upon in our conversation the other day with the President. I gave a copy to the Argentine Ambassador who doubted the advisability of having a fixed time set for the setttlement of boundary disputes. With him I am more or less in agreement but I do not approve of his counter-draft of which a copy is enclosed.

I finally saw the Chilean Ambassador yesterday in regard to the matter and he is agreeable to have the matter taken up directly with his Government through our Ambassador, which I believe will be the better way. I think I overcame his objection to the guarantee of political independence but I think there will be opposition to the submission to arbitration of disputed territory between Chile and Peru on account of the importance of the territory to Chile in its relation to the nitrate deposits. He asked me to delay two or three days before taking the matter up with his Government, in order that he could communicate with them in regard to it. I of course had no option but to agree to this.

I wrote the President the other day in regard to the Argentine Ambassador's conversation with me and his objection to a time limit in the matter of the settlement of boundary disputes, and he is agreeable to leaving it indefinite, with the understanding that they shall be settled as soon as possible.

I hope that I can push matters more rapidly now. The difficulty has been to get in touch with the Chilean Ambassador.

Is there any prospect of your being in Washington again soon? With warm regards I am,

Very sincerely yours,   Robert Lansing.

TLS (E. M. House Papers, CtY).

To Edward Mandell House

Dearest Friend: The White House October 29, 1915

Thank you for your letter of October twenty-seventh. The week has been very quiet here, too.

I was startled to hear that your daughter was operated on and hope that you do not mean by saying that she is doing "fairly well" that she is not doing as well as you expected. Please give her my most affectionate regards and tell her how sincerely I sympathize.

On thinking the matter over I have come to the conclusion that it would be wise if I did not undertake any pleasures when I come to New York next week. I think it would make a better impression if I merely arrived some time early in the afternoon, went quietly to you, and then return home the next morning after the dinner at the Manhattan Club. Mrs. Galt and Helen will be in New York busy shopping and tiring themselves so with their shopping that it would not be wise for them to undertake much else, and it is my present plan to bring them back by the Jersey shore so that we can have a glimpse of the house we expect to occupy next summer. Don't you think, on the whole, that that is the wisest and most prudent programme?

I need not tell you how we all appreciate your constant thought of our pleasure as well as of our welfare.

Affectionately yours,   Woodrow Wilson

TLS (E. M. House Papers, CtY).

To William Phillips

My dear Mr. Phillips: The White House October 29, 1915

I have your letter of October twenty-seventh about the desire of the French Ambassador to thank me in person for what we were fortunately able to accomplish in the matter of the two French ladies, Jeanne de Belleville and Madame Thuilliez, and in reply would say that I shall be very happy to receive the Ambassador at two o'clock on Wednesday, the third.

Cordially and sincerely yours,   Woodrow Wilson

TLS (SDR, RG 59, 355.51/11, DNA).

From Robert Lansing, with Enclosure

PERSONAL AND PRIVATE:

My dear Mr. President: Washington October 29, 1915.

I enclose a memorandum which the Chinese Minister[1] read to me today stating it to be a confidential and personal communication from his Government.

It would appear from this that the Chinese Government had decided to establish a monarchical form of Government. Whether this determination was reached prior to the protest by Japan and the *entente* powers it is impossible to say, but in view of the usual delay of the Chinese in presenting communications of this sort I assume that this telegram came through before Japan and the other powers had acted.

I declined to give the Minister any opinion upon the matter, saying that I would take it under consideration. I assume that you have seen Minister Reinsch's telegram of midnight yesterday which deals with this subject.[2]

Faithfully yours,   Robert Lansing.

TLS (SDR, RG 59, 893.01/74, DNA).
[1] Kai Fu Shah.
[2] P. S. Reinsch to RL, Oct. 28, 1915, T telegram (SDR, RG 59, 893.01/41, DNA). Reinsch reported that Chinese ministers had expressed to him their great concern about an alleged Japanese move to block the monarchist movement in China and to obtain the cooperation of the United States and the Entente powers in doing so. Chinese officials feared that Japan was trying to strike a bargain by which Japan would supervise the contemplated change of the Chinese government in return for Japan's promise to guard all foreign interests in the Far East. Reinsch counseled against any participation by the United States in the plan.

E N C L O S U R E

MEMORANDUM

Our country has a territory immense in extent, and a population of five main groups different in customs and manners. In a republic the Chief Executive of the nation is frequently changed, and this cannot but cause great disturbances, not only endangering life and property in this country, but also injecting an element of uncertainty into the business affairs of foreign residents. The Republic has now been established for four years, but the business of the country is at a standstill owing to a lack of permanence in the occupation of the people and the acts of officials. In this unsettled state of affairs it is difficult to secure order. Our people, therefore, have been contemplating a change in the form of government from a Republic to a Monarchy. This movement has long been gaining ground in secret. The Government, in its endeavor to maintain the present form of government, has made repeated attempts to discourage it. But growing stronger with every opposition it now numbers among its adherents a great many influential persons. If the Government tries to put it down it is greatly to be feared that the peace of the country may be affected.

The Government, therefore, hesitates to take this great responsibility. But, in accordance with the general trend of public opinion, the Government has proclaimed the adoption of the recommendation of the legislative body by calling a National Convention of Representatives of the People to determine the form of government. Of late the officials of the different provinces have reported that this step has met with the approval of the people. All indications now point to a desire on the part of the people to adopt a constitutional monarchy. The Government will be powerless to oppose the will of the people inasmuch as in accordance with the republican principles all political powers rest finally with the people of the country. The will of the people, thus publicly expressed, must be obeyed. Since it is the people of the whole country that desire this change and demand the Government to act in accordance with their wishes there will certainly be no disorder. The provincial authorities, both civil and military, have given assurances that order will be maintained within their respective jurisdictions. It is the hope of the people of the whole country that they will thus secure permanent peace and prosperity.

There is no doubt that this hope is shared by the governments of all friendly nations, and that this step will be looked upon with favor by the governments of all friendly nations. Although this is a matter that concerns our domestic affairs, in view of the friendly relations between the two countries, this is communicated confidentially to the American Government before the act is officially promulgated, in order to avoid any misunderstanding.

Read to me by Chinese Minister as confidential and personal communication from his Govt. RL. Oct 29/15

T MS (SDR, RG 59, 893.01/74, DNA).

From Robert Lansing

PRIVATE AND CONFIDENTIAL:

My dear Mr. President: Washington October 29, 1915.

I have just had an interview with the Cuban Minister[1] who called here this afternoon to impart to me in the most confidential way a communication which he had received from his Government.

He tells me that the Spanish Minister at Habana[2] stated to the Minister of Foreign Affairs[3] that his Government had reason to believe that the King of Spain might be asked to mediate between the belligerents in the European war and that the Spanish Government desired to know whether the Latin-American Republics would lend their moral aid and support in case the King should become mediator.

The Cuban Minister said to me that his Government, in view of the very intimate relations between the two countries, desired to know what our views would be in regard to the matter. He said that he did not know whether any other of the Latin-American Governments had been approached on the subject, and that possibly Spain, knowing the relations between the United States and Cuba, desired to obtain through Cuba information as to how this Government would view such a step. He further said that he believed there must be some substantial ground for this action by the Spanish Government as they were unusually cautious in all matters of this sort. He added that he believed the suggestion emanated from Germany in view of her recent military successes and the apparent discouragement of the Allies at the present time.

I am at a loss to understand exactly what this means, and why the moral support which Spain seeks should be confined to the Latin-American Republics unless there is some influence being exerted in behalf of the Papal See. It would indicate, apparently a desire to eliminate this Government, if possible, in the final determination of the terms of peace.

The Cuban Minister was evidently much exercised over the matter and desired me as soon as possible to discuss the matter with him further in order that he might advise his Government. I think, therefore, that we should convey to him our views as soon as they can be formulated.

Faithfully yours,   Robert Lansing.

TLS (R. Lansing Papers, NjP).
[1] Carlos Manuel de Céspedes y Quesada.
[2] Alfredo de Mariatequi y Carratalá.
[3] Pablo Desvernine y Galdós.

From Edward Mandell House, with Enclosure

Dear Governor,   [New York] Oct. 29 [1915].

I think you will find this letter worth reading. Capt. Gherardi is our naval attaché at Berlin and is a man of good sense.

Affectionately yours   E. M. House

ALS (WP, DLC).

ENCLOSURE

Walter Rockwell Gherardi to Edward Mandell House

My dear Colonel House: Berlin, Oct. 11, 1915.

Since you were here last winter a good deal of water has run under the bridges, but the lake has not yet been drained. Nevertheless the attitude of mind of the people has undergone and is undergoing great changes. Such changes must necessarily be of slow development. The people are tired of the war and this I gather not from the governing, or even well to do classes, but from the soldier and the sailor, the country man, and more than all from the changed attitude of the women.

This change has been brought about by the moral factor of suffering and the material one of economic pressure. The two great factors in the war have been the German Army and the British Navy and the economic effects of the latter are being increasingly felt in every house and every peasant's hut in Central Europe.

More than the German, are the Austrian people desperately tired of the war. The Austrian Government has not the ascendancy over the spirit and intellect of its subjects, nor have the people the national vigor which sustains Germany. In Austria the preventive measures in economic matters have been carried out only by half way methods and the conditions for living there are much worse than in Germany. It is to be expected that this will be a hard black winter for Germany and a worse one for Austria.

In spite of the incomparable work of the German army, the slow, steady pressure brought by the British sea power is having its effect, just as our Civil War blockade strangled the resources of the Confederacy. The British "Grand Fleet" without an engagement holds the sea with all that it means.

Only one nation, our own, is in a position to initiate the movement for an understanding between the nations, and it appears possible that before the spring comes the sentiment amongst the German people will have so far progressed that their government will be ready to seriously see the necessity for coming to terms. Whether their opponents will feel ready to meet the proposition is another matter.

The Admiralty Staff has had a good cleaning out since the "Arabic" affair and a fine old sailor, Admiral von Holtzendorff,[1] now presides there. Our friend Behncke[2] is amongst those ousted. It marks (for the present at any rate) the end of the von Tirpitz control. Von Tirpitz never had any legal right to control the Admiralty Staff and its conduct of the war at sea, but in his eighteen years as Secretary of the Navy, he has built up an influence which seemed to be unshakable.

With best regards to Mrs. House in which Mrs. Gherardi[3] joins.

Sincerely yours,   W. R. Gherardi.

TCL (WP, DLC).
    [1] Henning von Holtzendorff, who had succeeded Admiral Gustav Bachmann as head of the German Admiralty on September 3, 1915.
    [2] Rear Admiral Paul L. Gustav Behncke, former deputy head of the Admiralty.
    [3] Neville S. Taylor Gherardi.

From Claude Kitchin

Dear Mr. President: Scotland Neck, N. C. Oct. 29/15

Permit me to acknowledge receipt of your letter of the 27th which is just received. I was very sorry that it was not possible for me to remain over till Wednesday last to see you. I was only in Washington a night & half a day Tuesday. Most urgent matters at home compelled my return.

I will go to Washington the night of the 7th November & will be there the *8th & 9th November*. On either of these days at such time as best suits your convenience, I will be glad to call to see you.

With high respect, I am,

Sincerely yours,   Claude Kitchin

ALS (WP, DLC).

From Frederic Clemson Howe

Ellis Island, New York Harbor, N. Y.

My dear Mr. Wilson: October 29, 1915.

In conversation with Mr. Charles R. Crane and Mr. Louis D. Brandeis in Boston last evening, the talk drifted to Mexico, and I commented on the similarity of the French Revolution and the struggles of the Mexican people, as well as the peculiarly close relations of this country with France by reason of the personal contact established by Franklin and Jefferson at that time. Both Mr. Crane and Mr. Brandeis seemed interested in the idea, and I am taking the liberty of repeating to you some of the things I said.

The revolution through which Mexico is passing is not dissimilar to the French Revolution. It is primarily agrarian, economic and social. It is moved by the same kind of feudal abuses that prevailed in France under the old regime. The decrees and declarations of the Mexican leaders are suggestive of the philisophy [philosophy] of the French physiocrats, of Turgot, Quesnay, du Pont de Nemours, and the others.

When the nation has settled down important questions as to the rights of foreign investors will be up for solution, as will the payment of indemnities, the settlement of concessions for oil wells, mines, land, railroads, etc. The arbitrament of these disputes will probably be a cause of some conflict, in which our representative will play an important part. Moreover, by reason of the Monroe Doctrine the claims of foreign investors may result in our becoming the arbiter of the immediate destiny of Mexico, insofar as internal economic reforms are concerned. In these controversies our representative will be the eyes and ears of our country. If he is sympathetic with the Mexican government, if he has a really democratic knowledge of the wrongs from which they have suffered, of the land question, of the methods employed in securing these concessions, and if he is willing to be a little tolerant of delay and of Mexican methods, he may cement the relations of the two countries, and also wipe away the suspicions of the Central and South American states, which have been rather apprehensive of the activities of American promoters. In addition, if the Minister is possessed of a knowledge of our own experiences with privileged interests, and if he knows something about banking, credit, finance, taxation and labor matters, he may be of great service to the new government. Permanent peace when secured in the country, might be permanently promoted by the assistance of the right kind of man who had the confidence of the Mexican people in the working out of these problems. It is even conceivable that a Pan-American entente for the maintenance of the Monroe Doctrine might be one of the indirect results of the work of a Minister whose good offices inspired the proper sort of belief in our disinterestedness.

Finally it seems to me that a really democratic Democrat might give a new note to diplomacy, just as did Franklin and Jefferson; a new page might be written in our history as pleasant to contemplate as that of our relations with France one hundred years ago. It is also quite conceivable that the work of the Mexican revolution may influence the United States in agrarian reforms, in credit operations, in land tenure, etc.

For these and other reasons it seems to me that the Mexican embassy is one of the greatest opportunities of the present day, an opportunity of real historic importance to the international results of the entire western contenent.

I realize that I am writing this with a rather meager knowledge of Mexican affairs, gained from occasional meetings with liberal minded Mexicans who have consulted me on questions of municipal administration and land taxation; but they have impressed me with their sincerity, and have given me a real confidence in Carranza. This and a deep interest in the strivings of the Mexican people has emboldened me to write you on the subject of appointing a man [of] unquestioned democratic sympathies to the post of Minister to Mexico. I realize that the list of such Democrats as I have described is a rather short one. Mr. Newton D. Baker of Cleveland has the experience, the knowledge and the temperament; Mr. Brand Whitlock is of the same general caste of mind; while Mr. Lincoln Steffens has the most wonderful capacity for the diffusion of ideas by personal contact of any man I know. He has dropped the seeds of progressive ideas in the minds of more individual men in public life than any man of my acquaintance. In addition, he has a pretty intimate knowledge of Mexico, from many months of residence there, and has the confidence of Carranza and his advisers as well. He also has a sympathetic appreciation of the Mexican point of view that is rather extraordinary. It seems to me that Mr. Steffens might in some way be of valuable service to you, and might possibly be included in those whom you are considering for the post of Minister.

I have the honor to remain,

Very sincerely yours,   Frederic C. Howe

TLS (WP, DLC).

From Jane Addams and Others

Dear Mr. President: Chicago October 29, 1915.

Feeling sure that you wish to get from all sources the sense of the American people in regard to great national questions, officers of the Woman's Peace Party venture to call to your attention certain views which they have reason to believe are widespread, although finding no adequate expression in the press.

We believe in real defense against real dangers, but not in a preposterous "preparedness" against hypothetical dangers.

If an exhausted Europe could be an increased menace to our rich, resourceful republic, protected by two oceans, it must be a still greater menace to every other nation.

Whatever increase of war preparations we may make would compel poorer nations to imitate us. These preparations would create rivalry, suspicion and taxation in every country.

At this crisis of the world, to establish a "citizen soldiery" and enormously to increase our fighting equipment would inevitably make all other nations fear instead of trust us.

It has been the proud hope of American citizens who love their kind, a hope nobly expressed in several of your own messages, that to the United States might be granted the unique privilege not only of helping the war-worn world to a lasting peace, but of aiding toward a gradual and proportional lessening of that vast burden of armament which has crushed to poverty the peoples of the old world.

Most important of all, it is obvious that increased war preparations in the United States would tend to disqualify our National Executive from rendering the epochal service which this world crisis offers for the establishment of permanent peace.

Jane Addams.
Lucia Ames Mead.
Anna Garlin Spencer.
Alice Thacher Post
Sophonisba P. Breckinridge[1]

TLS (WP, DLC).

[1] Not heretofore identified in this series are Lucia True Ames (Mrs. Edwin Doak) Mead, lecturer on international arbitration and economic and social reform and secretary of the Woman's Peace party; the Rev. Anna Carpenter Garlin (Mrs. William Henry) Spencer, Professor of Sociology and Ethics at Meadville Theological School and vice-chairman of the Woman's Peace party; Alice Thacher (Mrs. Louis Freeland) Post, vice-chairman of the Woman's Peace party; and Sophonisba Preston Breckinridge, Assistant Professor of Household Administration at the University of Chicago and treasurer of the Woman's Peace party.

A Memorandum by Joseph Patrick Tumulty[1]

Oct 29 1915

PRESIDENT'S SPEECH, page three—
Insert at place marked 1, after the word "Nation" the following:

Within a year we have witnessed what we did not believe possible, a great European conflict involving all the great nations of the world. The influences of a great war are everywhere in the air. Europe is embattled, etc.

PRESIDENT'S SPEECH, page four—
Leave out the words, "We do not want a great standing army and we do not need one." Add, "In accordance with our American traditions we want and shall work for only an army adequate to the constant and legitimate uses of times of international peace."

PRESIDENT'S SPEECH, page six—
After the word "consummation" add ("profiting as we shall at the same time from) *We can and should profit in all that we do by*

the experience and example that ⟨face us growing out of the present struggle in Europe.”⟩ *are made obvious to us by the present military and naval events of the actual present.*
Same page, bottom, leave out the words, “No thoughtful man should feel any such haste.”
PRESIDENT'S SPEECH, page seven—
Line four, after the word “us” add, “Under the new world conditions we have become thoughtful of the things which all reasonable men consider necessary ⟨and we are therefore formulating and intend to carry out these means of⟩ *for security and* self-defense, ⟨which⟩ *on the part of* every ⟨great⟩ nation ⟨which is⟩ confronted with the great enterprise of human liberty and independence ⟨is bound to consider⟩.”
Same page, after word “independence” add the following:
“Is the plan we propose sane and reasonable and suited to the needs of the hour? Does it not conform to the ancient traditions of America? Has any better plan been proposed ⟨in⟩ *than* this programme that we now place before the country in which there is no pride of opinion? It represents the best expert opinion of the country. But I am not so much interested in programmes as I am in guarding at every cost the good faith and honor of the country. If men shall differ with me in this vital matter, I shall ask them if they are interested in safeguarding the interests of the country.”
Add the following before the paragraph about hyphenated Americans:
“In the fulfillment of this programme I shall ask for the hearty support of the country, of the rank and file of America, of men of all shades of political opinion, for my position in this important matter is different from that of the ordinary individual who is free to speak his own thoughts and to risk his own opinions in this matter. For in this matter we are dealing with the very things that are vital to the life of America itself.[2] In this I have tried to purge my heart of selfish motives. For the time being, I speak as the trustee and guardian of a Nation's rights, charged with the duty of speaking for that Nation in matters involving her sovereignty,—a Nation too big and generous to be exacting and yet courageous enough to defend its rights and the liberties of its people wherever assailed or invaded. I would not feel that I was discharging the solemn obligation I owe this Nation were I not to speak in the terms of the deepest solemnity of the urgency and necessity of preparing ourselves to guard and protect at every cost the rights and privileges of our people which are the heritage of the fathers who struggled to make us an independent Nation.”

SUGGESTED PERORATION—

SEE page 153 of the Democratic Text-book: 1914[3]

"Here is the Nation God has builded by our hands. What shall we do with it? Who is there who does not stand ready at all times to act in her behalf in the spirit of the day or the true spirit of patriotism. The day of our country's life has but broadened into morning. Let us lift our eyes to the great tracts of life yet to be conquered in the interests of peace. Come, let us renew our allegiance to America and strive yet to serve our fellow men in quiet counsel."

T MS (WP, DLC).
1 Text in angle brackets deleted by Wilson; text in italics added by him.
2 Tumulty italicized this sentence for emphasis.
3 Democratic Congressional Campaign and National Committees, *The Democratic Text-Book 1914* (Baltimore, 1914). The quotation was from Wilson's Gettysburg Address, printed at July 4, 1913, Vol. 28.

From Edward Mandell House, with Enclosure

Dear Governor: New York. October 30th, 1915.

For your information I am sending a copy of a letter which I have just written Lansing.

I am glad to tell you that Janet is doing finely and will soon be herself again. The doctors believe it is now merely a matter of building up.

We are hoping that you will come on Thursday and remain until Sunday afternoon. Cleve Dodge was delighted to hear that a lunch at his place was on the program.

Your affectionate, E. M. House

TLS (WP, DLC).

E N C L O S U R E

Edward Mandell House to Robert Lansing

Dear Mr. Lansing: New York. October 30th, 1915.

Bernstorff has just called. He says his Government believe that the concessions they made in regard to submarine warfare, were largely for the purpose of getting us to maintain the doctrine of the freedom of the seas, and he wonders if this is not a propitious time for something to be done, either by them or by us.

I told him that what we all wanted was success and not a mere agitation for political or other reasons. That it might be very inadvisable to discuss this doctrine at this time, or to openly advocate it. I strongly advised against his Government pushing it at all for the reason that it would probably harden public opinion in England against it and make it more difficult of accomplishment when the right moment comes.

He tells me that he hopes to see you on Monday or Tuesday of next week, and I thought it well for you to know of our conversation. Sincerely yours, [E. M. House]

CCL (WP, DLC).

From Wilbur Fisk Sadler, Jr.

My dear Mr. President: Washington, D. C., October 30, 1915.

Your note of the twenty-sixth of October was very much appreciated. I had no idea that the letter written to Joe would be shown to you; but I am glad that you saw what I believe is a fair statement of the way the National Guard of New Jersey regard Mr. Garrison's scheme two years since the reactionaries of the organized militia attempted to pass resolutions and start a newspaper campaign which would have been antagonistic to your Administration. As Secretary Garrison knows and as General Mills,[1] the Chief of the Division of Militia Affairs, can tell you, I at once led the fight against these measures. You have no idea of the size of the row or the number of enemies that I accumulated. After the scheduled programme was defeated, the Secretary of War suggested that the officers of the War College, the Chief of the Division of Militia Affairs, the Judge Advocate General of the Army and certain officers representing the various National Guard associations, should meet and agree upon the terms of a pay bill. This meeting was held and when it adjourned, a bill was laid on the desk of the Secretary of War which met with the approval of all who had attended the conference. This bill provided for pay in about one-quarter the amount received by the regular army with less than this proportion for colonels and lieutenant colonels, and nothing for brigade commanders and members of their staff. This draft was initialed by all of the parties to the conference and Mr. Garrison said that he would approve and try to pass the bill if the chairman of the Military Affairs Committee of the Senate and the chairman of the same Committee of the House would approve it; and provided it received your approval.

He suggested that we see Senator Chamberlain and Mr. Hay, which we did. Senator Chamberlain introduced a bill and with our assistance, had it reported favorably. Mr. Hay told us that

[1] Brigadier General Albert Leopold Mills, U.S.A.

he had decided that the Guard should be paid and that at the next session of Congress, he would assist in passing a pay bill, but he did not know whether or not he could subscribe to all of the terms of the bill that had been drawn which changed the militia law to conform to the ideas of the War Department. While there was no promise on the part of the Secretary of War to get your endorsement, his friends left feeling that he would do everything in his power to get your approval. From time to time for more than a year he has given the "rush of business" as an excuse for not being able to report your position and said he had been unable to discuss the subject with you.

On Thursday last I received a telegram from Mr. Garrison asking me to attend a conference which was to be held the next day and which was to be attended by the Executive Committee of the National Guard Association of the United States and the members of the National Militia Board.

When we met we were astounded to have him tell us in plain terms that his programme contemplated the extinguishment of the National Guard as a body; that he proposed to ask for an increase in the regular Army so that it could be brought up to 140,000 within the next two or three years; that he proposed to provide for a Continental Army of 400,000, and that he proposed to ask for an increase in the appropriation of the National Guard. He, much to the surprise of everyone, wanted those present to endorse his proposition which means the extinguishment of the National Guard. He says that all officers of the Guard with whom he has talked want the militia Federalized; and I say to you that they do want the militia to be under Federal control but not the kind of control that Mr. Garrison suggests. We want to be a state force, officered as we are at present. We want the War Department to say what the organization shall be, what officers can or cannot continue to serve. We want to feel that in case of trouble our services will be accepted by the Government and we want the Government to pay something for the services rendered.

When we ask Mr. Garrison about the details of his proposed scheme, we find that he has not worked them out; but we do find that the state is to be left without any Guard and that its armories are to be used by the Continental Army.

The officers of the Guard who were in conference yesterday have served anywhere from fifteen to thirty years, giving the best days of their life to the service; have expended their time and money without stint and to be coolly told that they are to be wiped out of existence is startling.

After six years of service as the Adjutant General of New Jersey, I am firmly of the opinion that the Continental Army as suggested will not be a success, that the scheme proposed for the Guard will destroy it. While you were Governor of New Jersey, you saw a number of changes in the Guard, but even more radical ones have taken place since you were elected President, and the officers now have to spend on an average of three nights a week in their armories besides giving two weeks of their time for field work in the summer. No other body of men that I know of make greater sacrifices of time, and because of the increased requirements, enlistments are few.

If the pay bill is passed we will have more applicants than we can care for. We would be able to enforce discipline which at present is impossible because the only punishment that we can inflict is a dishonorable discharge which the men laugh at. If pay was given to the officers, the War Department could supervise the entire organization of the militia and demand the proper kind of service. Personally, I want them to supervise and direct us in our efforts and I have bent every energy to comply with every wish they have expressed. If the pay bill is passed, the Guard can quickly be raised to 250,000 peace strength which would mean about 600,000 war strength. The Army officers know this but from my viewpoint, they do not seem to want the Guard to prosper.

The Continental Army as proposed is simply an increase in the regular establishment and the plan of giving men two months intensive training and then letting them go for a period of ten months without assembling in the meantime is in the opinion of the officers of the National Guard, a very poor scheme. After hours of discussion yesterday and as we were adjourning late last night, I put this question to Secretary Garrison: If the National Guard convention which meets in San Francisco on November ninth endorses your scheme for an increase of the regular Army to 140,000; if it passes resolutions insisting upon the passage of the pay bill; if it passes a resolution endorsing your Continental Army proposition, will you help the Guard to pass its pay bill? And his reply was that he would, provided you did not interfere,—again putting the proposition up to you.

In this hurried way I am afraid that I do not convey more than one-tenth of the points I would like to make but you know that you have nowhere a more loyal friend or well-wisher; and I feel that when I say to you that I honestly believe that if you back Mr. Garrison's scheme, you will destroy the Guard, you at least know that I am sincere in my belief.

When I return to New Jersey and tell the five thousand men

whom we have held together and who are ready to offer their lives, if need be, at a moment's notice, what Secretary Garrison has in his mind, there will be plenty of noise. I suppose that the Secretary of War can force his programme but I appeal to you to keep the Guard alive and maintain its organization. As I said before, it will be even in Secretary Garrison's opinion years before the Continental Army grows to the size it should be; while at present you have an organization which is efficient and could be greatly increased at comparatively small cost with little effort. I wish that I could show you the letters which I have received from the various Adjutants General, especially those from the South who feel that the Continental Army in their sections will be composed of negroes, the only men that can be gotten if the troops are apportioned as proposed.

This memorandum is dictated hurriedly and I am unable to see it before it is handed to you so that I may have repeated myself and not have touched on points that I would like to. Joe thought that I should dictate it and I have done the best I could in the few minutes at my disposal. I wish that it were possible for the Executive Committee of the National Guard Association to see you so that you could get an idea of the way they feel, although I have tried in this crude way to lay the facts before you.

Cordially yours,   Wilbur F. Sadler

TL (WP, DLC).

From Oswald Garrison Villard

My dear Mr. President: New York October 30, 1915.

I thank you for your cordial letter of October 28th. If at any time later it should seem to you fitting to speak out on this question, we could make room for you on our Carnegie Hall program at any time.

I hope you will not take it amiss that I at the same time express to you my most profound regret that you have decided to go on the side of the large armament people. I find it very difficult indeed to reconcile this with your utterances in your last message to the effect that "America should not be an armed camp." From my benighted standpoint, it seems to me that you have abandoned your slogan of "Humanity first" in Philadelphia, and fallen back on an even narrower one than "America first." I cannot at the present stage of the world crisis believe else than that our action in going in for large armaments will do infinite injury to the poor people of all of Europe, in that it will make it harder than ever for forces that are making for disarmament at the close of the war to achieve anything. Will not Kaiser and King have a ready answer for those who wish to relieve the world of this most grievous burden by pointing across the ocean to Woodrow Wilson, the head of the greatest fleet and the greatest army that the United States has ever known in peace times? You are aware, of course, that the growth of our fleet was cited in the Reichstag and in Parliament just before the outbreak of the great war as a most cogent reason for increasing the military burdens of poor German people and the British tax-payers as well?

Again, it is such a waste of the Nation's resources that it seems to me useless to discuss their conservation when we are to pour out four hundred millions or five hundred millions a year in non-productive military and naval expenditure.

I admit, of course, that the current of popular opinion here in the East runs strongly in the direction of greater preparedness, but the Woodrow Wilson whom I have admired so greatly could, if he had taken the simple stand that there should be no armament question until the close of the war, or, at least, until Congress had put an end to the terrible waste of money which gives us only an inefficient army today, have had the people with him just as they were led by his restraining and calming leadership in the Lusitania matter. Your greatest hold on the people has invariably come when you took the highest moral grounds and when you showed your profound interest in the people. The new departure seems to me directly in variance with this policy—it is anti-moral, anti-social and anti-democratic, and the burdens rest primarily on the already over-taxed and over-governed masses.

I frankly feel grieved, too, that two requests of mine for interviews to talk with you about these matters were denied me. The various organizations who have appealed for hearings on the other side feel aggrieved that they were not given a chance to state their side of the case before you made your decision on so vital a matter, one that may have most far-reaching consequences for this country. For you are sowing the seeds of militarism, raising up a military and naval caste, and the future alone can tell what the further growth will be and what the eventual blossoms. Every nation that has been drawn into the military maelstrom has begun this way and each was certain that they could avoid the pitfalls of militarism and that the way to peace lay through armaments.

My series of articles on preparedness,[1] of which I spoke to you and which you were good enough to say you would read, is now under way, and comes too late to be of any value, I am afraid, but Colonel House is so struck with some of the points I am making that he wishes to bring the matter personally to your attention. I enclose the one article which appears today.[2] The one of last Wednesday shows what is the matter with the army, and the unusual opportunity you have had to compel Congress to cut out the waste and extravagance and inefficiency before building any further on this rotten military foundation.[3]

Faithfully yours,   Oswald Garrison Villard.

TLS (WP, DLC).
[1] O. G. Villard, "The Question of Preparedness," New York *Evening Post*, Oct. 23, Oct. 27, Oct. 30, Nov. 3, Nov. 6, Nov. 10, Nov. 13, and Nov. 17, 1915.
[2] "The Question of Preparedness—No. 3: The Present Military Foundation," New York *Evening Post*, Oct. 30, 1915, clipping in WP, DLC.
[3] "The Question of Preparedness—No. 2: What Is the Matter With the Army?" New York *Evening Post*, Oct. 27, 1915.

Edward Mandell House to Robert Lansing

Dear Mr. Lansing: New York. October 30th, 1915.

Thank you for your letter of October 28th with enclosures.

I am delighted to know that things are moving along so rapidly. I agree with the Argentine Ambassador as to the inadvisability of having a fixed time for the settlement of boundary disputes.

It is not an essential part of our proposal and the amendment he suggests is sufficient. The first article is the essence of the covenant, and if we can cling to that in its entirety, the President will have succeeded in his purpose.

My going to Washington is uncertain, but I hope to be there week after next.

With all good wishes, I am,

Sincerely yours,   E. M. House

TLS (SDR, RG 59, 710.11/214½, DNA).

Two Letters to Robert Lansing

Dear Mr. Secretary,   The White House. 31 October, 1915.

I suggest this as a possible course of action in this delicate matter. I wish that this great change in China might have been postponed, for certainly this seems a most inopportune time to add such fundamental reversals to the general upset of the world.

Could we not give a very plain intimation to the Japanese government and the governments which seem to be acting with it in this matter that we agree with the Chinese in their position that a change in their form of government, however radical, is wholly a domestic question and that it would in our opinion be a serious breach of China's sovereignty to undertake any form of interference or even protest without such evidences as are now wholly lacking that foreign interests would be imperiled which it is our privilege to safeguard; and at the same time intimate to the Chinese government, in the most friendly manner, our feeling that this is a most critical time in the affairs of the whole world and that her own international and national interests are in danger of being seriously compromised unless the present changes there can be guided with a very firm and prudent hand.

I must say that it would seem from what Reinsch tells us that they are handling the whole thing remarkably well.

Faithfully Yours, W.W.

WWTLI (SDR, RG 59, 893.01/78½, DNA).

My dear Mr. Secretary,   The White House. 31 October, 1915.

I do not know that I can say that I am surprised by this. I have expected all along that Germany would, when she thought that the time had come to talk of peace, try to exclude us from a part in the settlement of terms.

Spain has no strength, the King of Spain no influence whatever. I do not think that the Allies would meet his advances in any way except with polite rejection. But in any case there is nothing that we can do; and I am willing to look on at such experiments. They will, I should think, gravely affect Germany's prestige.

With regard to the question of the Cuban Minister, perhaps it would be a bit beneath our dignity to give his government any advice. What would you think of saying to him that we deeply appreciate his calling our attention to this matter; that we do not feel that we [are] at liberty to stand in the way of any plans that give promise of peace in Europe; but that we would hope in all matters of world politics to see the Americas stand together as a unit, refusing to be in any way divided in action?

Cordially and faithfully, W.W.

WWTLI (R. Lansing Papers, NjP).

From Edward Mandell House, with Enclosure

Dear Governor: New York. October 31st, 1915.

I am enclosing you a copy of a despatch which Sir Cecil has sent to Sir Edward.

I am told that Sir Cecil is now more pro-American than the worst of us, which does not make me regret, as deeply as I might, the little difference we had some two weeks ago.[1]

Your affectionate,   E. M. House

TLS (WP, DLC).

[1] House wrote to Spring Rice on the same day: "I am glad you are advising Sir Edward so wisely. There can be no serious controversy between us, and what has been done and is to be done, will in the end be of more advantage to you than to us." EMH to C. A. Spring Rice, Oct. 31, 1915, TL (FO 115/1865, p. 74, PRO). Spring Rice conveyed this message to London in C. A. Spring Rice to E. Grey, Nov. 3, 1915, Hw telegram (FO 115/1865, p. 73, PRO).

E N C L O S U R E

Telegram about internal Situation

You may expect pretty strong communication. Until popular opinion is convinced of necessity of taking sides (which it is not) Government must be impartial. Policy of pin pricks against one or other party will only give people impression of prejudice and one sidedness. What is non-essential can be arranged by give and take; what is essential can be referred under existing treaties to arbitral decision.

Despatch sent by British Ambassador to Sir Edward Grey. October 1915.

TC telegram (WP, DLC).

From Norman Hapgood

Dear Mr. Wilson: Washington Oct. 31 [1915]

I have somewhat hesitated to write you about your marriage, because deep things are hard to express. I believe in happiness, for its own sake, and for the strength, light, and direction it gives, and I have rejoiced extremely that you, in your isolated and immeasurably important task, were to have color, understanding, and consolation in the nearest place. I have rejoiced from the beginning, and still more strongly since I have heard from those who know Mrs. Galt. It is a privilege, but a tragic one, to count for much in the destiny of mankind. I am one of millions who (if I may say it) love you for the service your character and mind are rendering; and that appreciation of ours, warmed into affection, has a lyric note now, that in your personal life providence has been good to you.

Yours sincerely,   Norman Hapgood

ALS (WP, DLC).

To Frederic Clemson Howe

Personal.

My dear Howe: [The White House] November 1, 1915

Thank you very warmly for your interesting letter of October twenty-ninth. I have several times noted the extraordinary similarity between the way things have been going in Mexico and the way they went in France a little over a hundred years ago, and I have noted with a great deal of interest your analysis of the matter.

My difficulty about an Ambassador is that we must not only have a man of the right principles but a man thoroughly versed in Latin-American affairs and accustomed to dealing with a sensitive people in a way they wish to be dealt with. Your suggestion of names interests me very much indeed.

Very cordially yours,   Woodrow Wilson

TLS (Letterpress Books, WP, DLC).

To Edward Mandell House

My dearest Friend,   The White House 1 November, 1915.

Thank you for your letters: for the interesting opinion of Gherhardi, for the despatch of Spring-rice to Sir Edward, and for all the little tips you are kind enough to hand along.

I am might[y] sorry to disappoint you and Cleve. Dodge (and myself) by cutting out all "sprees" and pleasure trips, but I am now fully convinced that it is wisest to do so. I shall come up on Thursday about three seventeen, I believe. I shall go first to the St. Regis, if I may, to see Mrs. Galt, and then I shall come to 115. The next morning we must all set out for home again. These are hard resolutions to take, but a peaceful mind is, after all, the best. Self-denial is a tough job, but self-indulgence is in the long run a tougher!   Affectionately Yours, Woodrow Wilson

WWTLS (E. M. House Papers, CtY).

To Frank Parker Stockbridge[1]

My dear Stockbridge: [The White House] November 1, 1915

I thank you sincerely for your letter of October twenty-eighth.[2] I was, of course, deeply hurt by the statements contained in the news article about which Tumulty telephoned you,[3] and I do not think I can with dignity even make a statement about it. I really think that the paper owes it to fairness to correct its statement which was made as a statement of fact that a prominent representative of the steel interests had called on me, because I received no such call at any time and it is only fair that it should withdraw the imputations of the article.

I realize as fully as you do the dangers that come from the material interests involved in the policy of preparedness, but I think that that ought not to hold us back from the right course, that our duty lies in the direction of safeguarding the Government at every point against the dangers to which you allude. Of course, if we buy materials, the men who sell materials are going to be interested. That cannot be avoided, but we can see that they are interested only in the most business-like way and without any touch of graft or unfair advantage. Our laws should and will take care of that.

At the same time, I realize the cogency of your argument about the way in which the whole thing should be handled and I am frank to say that it is worthy of the most serious consideration.

May I not thank you very warmly for your generous editorial, "Stand by the President?"[4] I am sure I know the generous and friendly motives by which you are actuated.

Always

Cordially and faithfully yours,   Woodrow Wilson

TLS (Letterpress Books, WP, DLC).

[1] Wilson's former publicity agent during the preconvention presidential campaign of 1912; he was at this time managing editor of the New York *Evening Mail.*

[2] F. P. Stockbridge to WW, Oct. 28, 1915, TLS (WP, DLC).

[3] "Big Steel Profits in Defense Plan," New York *Evening Mail,* Oct. 27, 1915. This article said that the chief beneficiaries of the preparedness program would be the big steel interests of the country. It asserted, moreover, that the steel magnates, who, until recently, had strongly opposed the Wilson administration, were so pleased with the prospects of increased profits that they had sent an emissary to the White House to pledge their support to Wilson in his campaign for re-election. Tumulty had called Stockbridge in the morning of October 28 and had denied the report.

[4] New York *Evening Mail,* Oct. 29, 1915. It in effect repudiated the editorial in the *Evening Mail* of October 27.

From Robert Lansing

PERSONAL AND PRIVATE:

My dear Mr. President: Washington November 1, 1915.

I call your attention to a telegram from Mr. Whitlock which was received yesterday by the Department,[1] and which you have doubtless read.

To that despatch I propose to send the enclosed instruction if it meets with your approval.[2] We cannot, of course, retain Maitre de Leval in our service at Brussels in view of the fact that he is *persona non grata* to the German authorities.

I consider that it was very unfortunate that Mr. Page in London saw fit to permit the publication of Mr. Whitlock's correspondence with the German Authorities at Brussels.[3] The Department has never been informed, officially, of what took place. The whole matter was handled directly by Mr. Page and Mr. Whitlock which, to my mind, is an inadvisable method of doing business, particularly in a case of this character.

In view of the recent confidential communications which have passed between Mr. Page and me I do not feel like rebuking him for what he has done. I think, however, that he should be advised of the consequences and, in order to do so I propose to enclose for his information a copy of Mr. Whitlock's telegram.[4] If you have other views as to the matter I should like to be advised at your earliest convenience.

Please return the green telegram as soon as possible in order that it may be sent to Brussels.

Faithfully yours,   Robert Lansing.

TLS (RSB Coll., DLC).

[1] B. Whitlock to RL, Oct. 30, 1915, T telegram (SDR, RG 59, 124.556/7, DNA); printed in *FR-LP*, I, 62-65. Whitlock reported on his conversations with Baron von der Lancken, chief of the political department of the German general government in Belgium, regarding the publication in London and America of reports and correspondence revealing Whitlock's efforts to save the life of Edith Cavell. This breach of diplomatic etiquette, the Baron argued, provided England with information damaging to Germany and consequently "affected" American neutrality. To this argument, Whitlock had replied that he had had nothing whatever to do with the decision to publish the documents. Von der Lancken also declared that Gaston de Leval, a distinguished international lawyer, a Belgian, and legal adviser to the American legation, was *persona non grata*, especially because his report to Whitlock about his conversations with Von der Lancken's deputy had left the impression that the Germans had broken their word with Whitlock in the Cavell case. Whitlock recommended that the State Department ask for safe conduct out of Belgium for De Leval and continue his salary for some time after his departure.

[2] RL to B. Whitlock, Nov. 2, 1915, T telegram (SDR, RG 59, 124.556/7, DNA); printed in *FR-LP*, I, 65-66. Lansing instructed Whitlock to ask German authorities for safe conduct for De Leval and agreed to pay his salary for three months. He added: "Please make it clear to the German authorities that the case of Miss Cavell was not brought to the attention of this Government, nor was the Department the medium of communication in this instance between Brussels and London. This government, therefore, had no knowledge of the documents in the case, which were made public by the British Foreign Office without consultation with this Department."

[3] Whitlock enclosed copies of this correspondence in B. Whitlock to RL, Oct. 19, 1915, TLS (SDR, RG 59, 362.412 C31/1, DNA), which reached the State Department on November 5. They are printed in *FR-LP*, I, 48-61. They revealed the legation's activities on Miss Cavell's behalf between August 31 and October 12, including requests to German authorities for a statement of the charges against her and efforts to provide a lawyer for her. Once Whitlock had learned that Miss Cavell had confessed, he planned to wait until after her trial and sentencing to plead for leniency. However, the Germans moved swiftly and secretly after her trial on October 9 and shot her three days later. Reports to Whitlock from Hugh Simons Gibson and Gaston de Leval, both of the legation, about their conversations with German authorities indicated that the

Americans would receive notice of each decision in the case in time to reply. Whitlock's reports to Page made it clear that no such notices were received.
⁴ RL to WHP, Nov. 2, 1915, CCL (SDR, RG 59, 124.556/7, DNA).

To Robert Lansing

My dear Mr. Secretary,   The White House. 1 November, 1915.

Yes, I had read Whitlock's despatch and was a good deal disturbed by it.

Your despatch to Whitlock, herewith returned, is the right thing, though I must say that I did not at all relish the attitude of the German authorities in Brussels as reported by Whitlock, and dislike having to sacrifice Laval to them.

Your purpose about informing Page in London has my entire approval. I doubt whether it will turn out that he had anything directly to do with supplying the documents to the British Foreign Office. I take it for granted that you will send him a copy of Whitlock's despatch at the same time that you send him a copy of your message to Whitlock—by pouch,—I suppose.

Faithfully Yours,   W.W.

WWTLI (RSB Coll., DLC).

From Joseph Patrick Tumulty, with Enclosure

Dear Governor: The White House. November 1, 1915.

Yesterday I read to the Secretary of War your speech for the Manhattan Club. This morning the Secretary sends me the attached letter.   J.P.T.

TL (WP, DLC).

E N C L O S U R E

Lindley Miller Garrison to Joseph Patrick Tumulty

Dear Joe: Washington. November 1, 1915.

It is very necessary that these two statements in the matter that you and I talked over yesterday should be changed so as to conform to facts.

In the first one, there should be no statement that the Continental Army is not to be organized. It is perfectly true that it is not constantly to be under arms, but it is absolutely incorrect to say that it is not to be organized. You could not train any military body without organization.

The other statement that needs correction is that the National Guard of the States is to aid in training the Continental Army. This could not be. We have no *command* whatever over the National Guard.

It is absolutely necessary that these two statements should be changed, as otherwise they would excite great comment and be shown to be contrary to the facts.

Please attend to this, and let me know that it has been attended to, because I would like to feel sure that we do not lay ourselves open to adverse comment in these respects.

I hope to have my statement over to you around noon, and suggest that you immediately take it up with the President, and agree with him as to when it should be released. In view of election Tuesday filling Wednesday's papers and the President's speech Thursday filling Friday's papers, I think it should be released for Thursday morning.[1]

This would have one good effect. It would cause the editorial comment on the President's speech to deal with the facts as set forth in the statement, and aid in understanding his speech and in intelligent consideration of the whole subject.

Sincerely yours,   Lindley M. Garrison

TLS (WP, DLC).

[1] The statement was released on Friday, November 5. It outlined the final version of the so-called "Garrison plan" for the expansion of the army. The plan provided for an increase of the regular army from 108,008 officers and men to 141,797. In addition, it created a new reserve Continental Army of 400,-000 men to be recruited over the next three years, its members to serve on active duty two months a year for three years and in a ready reserve for an additional three years. The plan also provided for a modest increase in federal assistance to the National Guard and for substantial new appropriations for coastal defense and supplies to be held in reserve for emergencies. The total cost of the plan was estimated at $1,034,399,234 over the five fiscal years from 1917 to 1921. *New York Times*, Nov. 6, 1915.

To Joseph Patrick Tumulty

Dear Tumulty,   The White House. 1 November, 1915

It is too late to change the speech. The two statements to which the Secretary refers are not likely to be misunderstood. The men referred to will of course *not* be organized as a standing force, and, while everybody knows that we do not and cannot *command* the national guard we can, and I think we should, call unpon [upon] them for voluntary services of any kind. The plan suggested by the Secretary is susceptible, fortunately, of adaptation.

W.W.

WWTLI (WP, DLC).

From Robert Latham Owen

Dear Mr. President: [Washington] November 1, 1915.

I again call your attention to the importance of a Department of Health.

The republican platform of 1908 stated:

"We commend the efforts made to secure greater efficiency in national public health agencies and favor such legislation as will effect this purpose."

The democratic platform, upon which you were elected, reaffirmed previous declarations advocating the union and strengthening of the various governmental agencies relating to pure foods, quarantine, vital statistics and human health.

For four years this has been an active issue on the floor of the Senate and has been awaiting the influence of the Chief Executive to bring legislative action.

There are nearly two hundred thousand physicians in the United States, who visit every house, and they are enthusiastically in favor of a Department of Health under a Secretary who shall be a Cabinet Member.

The French Cabinet has seventeen members, not to mention a number of lower rank than minister.

The annual public loss from preventable disease in the United States is over two thousand millions of dollars. The National Commission on Conservation, in its report on national vitality,[1] showed where human life might be increased on an average of fourteen years almost immediately in the United States by the control of known preventable diseases.

All the great insurance companies are deeply interested in this issue, and many of them, since it arose, have established health departments to promote longevity among policy holders.

The opposition to a Public Health Department will be found among the patent medicine dealers and manufacturers of fake remedies, assisted by the Christian Scientists who believe that all disease is a mental error.

I think it safe to say that ninety per cent of the people of the United States would receive with enthusiasm the establishment of a Department of Health.

I pray you to give this matter your consideration and make it a part of your program for the coming winter.

Yours, very respectfully,   Robt L. Owen

TLS (WP, DLC).
    [1] Irving Fisher, *Bulletin 30 of the Committee of One Hundred on National Health, Being a Report on National Vitality, Its Wastes and Conservation; Prepared for the National Conservation Commission* (Washington, 1909).

From Edward Mandell House

Dear Governor: New York. November 1st, 1915.

If the weather is good Friday I wish you would stay over for the day and motor up to Cleve Dodge's country place for lunch and a game of golf. He says there is a good course near there, and he seems to want you very badly as indeed, we all do.

We need not go to the theater that night unless you desire, although I see no good reason why we should not.

I hope it will be convenient for you to reach New York early Thursday so we may have some little time together on that day.

Janet is entirely out of the woods and is ready to sit up.

Your affectionate,   E. M. House

TLS (WP, DLC).

From Hamilton Fish Armstrong[1]

                                          Princeton, New Jersey
Dear President Wilson: November 1st. 1915.

I have succeeded in collecting from various sources a complete file of the *Princetonian* for 1878-79, during which time you were its Managing Editor. These the 1916 Board of the *Daily Princetonian* have had bound and are now taking the liberty of sending to you with their compliments.[2]

We have been awfully glad to see the editorials of that year, and it may be that you will be interested in again looking them over. Two of the numbers you will see were Dr. McCosh's copies. I have been amused trying to spot the editorials which came from your pen; I suppose that of course the majority of them were, but among them all I thought signs of your style were particularly notic[e]able in such as the third and farewell editorial in the last number, the third in number sixteen, and the sixth in number seventeen. I'm probably all wrong, but I can't help wanting to know how often I struck right.

The volume was mailed to you yesterday; hoping that you will receive it in good condition, and with kind regards, believe me,

Yours sincerely,   Hamilton Fish Armstrong

TLS (Wilson Library, DLC).
[1] Princeton 1916, editorial chairman of the *The Daily Princetonian*.
[2] This volume is in the Wilson Library, DLC.

To Edith Bolling Galt

Washington,

My precious Darling,   Monday evening 1 Nov., 1915

It is just a few minutes before dinner time. I will begin this little epistle now and finish it after dinner, before I go to work on a revision of the statement the Secretary of War wants to publish about our preparation for national defence. Grayson and I played eighteen holes of golf, at the Columbia course; (I won) I have had my bath and dressed; and have just had an interview with an ex-Senator from Nebraska.[1] I feel fine—not a bit too tired. Grayson examined the "whelp" on my back and makes nothing of it. The bone, he says, is certainly absolutely all right. One of the ligaments on one side of it seems to have slipped a little and can be felt over the vertebra but will come all right of itself. The back feels a little better every day and the inconvenience it gives me now is really negligible.

After dinner

We had a little adventure on the golf course. Before we had got out of range from the seventh tee a fool drove off from it and his ball (fortunately at the end of its flight and when most of its force was spent) hit Grayson on the fleshy part of his leg. It gave him only a painful bruise, but the extraordinary conduct of the player who was responsible made me so angry that I walked back to the tee and told him (I do not know what his name was) what I thought of it.

I've had a very busy day of work. Even at lunch I had to do business. Mrs. Kirk,[2] the wife of the preacher we heard in Baltimore,[3] wanted to see me about work in the southern mountains and so I asked her and her husband to come in to lunch. But they left soon and we got off to golf about half past two.

I found your telegram[4] awaiting me, my precious One, when I came in, and blessed you for it. I am *so* glad you got through to your hotel without annoyances and am grateful to House and Dudley Malone for meeting you at the station. I have purposely kept busy at something every minute of the day so as not to give myself time to stop and think; and fortunately there is still plenty to do till bedtime, after I hurry this little note off to catch the post; but, oh, my Darling, my Darling, how lonely I am without you! How empty the whole place is—how empty *every*thing is, without you! I seem to be doing things mechanically, as if with some old momentum left over from days that were vital and you were by my side. And yet every place is full of you,—everything reminds me of you; there is no turn either of what I do or what I think that I do not come upon you,—seem to see your dear, exquisite face before me, feel your dear hand on my arm or your dear, sweet lips on mine. My love for you seems to have become part, the informing and inspiring part, of all that I feel or purpose or do,—and it is *so* sweet to be *aware* of you and of all that you mean to me *all the time*, to feel how you have taken possession of my life; and what an infinitely sweet presence it is! Ah, my love, my precious One, how much richer and fuller our love and our happiness grow all the while! When I was writing out our little announcement about the wedding to day (I hope you like the way it was phrased) I was as thrilled as if I were writing a romance![5]

I must stop to get this off. My whole heart goes with it—goes before it—follows you and stays with you all the time. Love to dear Helen. Tell her I wrote to Miss Hagner[6] and that Margaret got a beautiful pin for Miss H. to-day. Margaret joins me in loving messages. I am well, and am so deeply in love with you that *that* seems the whole life of   Your own   Woodrow

ALS (WP, DLC).

[1] William Vincent Allen, senator from 1893 to 1899, and, by appointment, from December 1899 to March 1901.

[2] Helen O. McCormick (Mrs. Harris Elliott) Kirk. The Kirks were old friends of the Wilsons from Princeton days. Mrs. Kirk was a member of the fund-raising committee of the Ellen Wilson Memorial, a fund for the Christian education of mountain youth organized by women of the southern Presbyterian Church and managed by its Board of Home Missions. See WW to Sarah C. P. Hughes, Aug. 25, 1914, Vol. 30.

[3] Wilson and Mrs. Galt had spent Sunday, October 10, in Baltimore, where they visited Joseph R. Wilson, Jr., and his family and heard Dr. Kirk preach at the Franklin Street Presbyterian Church.

[4] It is missing.

[5] It read: "In order to quiet speculation, President Wilson and Mrs. Norman Galt today authorized the announcement that their marriage will take place near the close of December. Their plans are for a very simple ceremony. It will be quietly performed at Mrs. Galt's residence. No invitations will be issued, and it is expected that the only guests will be the members of the two families." *New York Times*, Nov. 2, 1915.

[6] It is missing. Isabella Louisa Hagner, former social secretary at the White House, who married Norman James of Baltimore on November 2. Wilson, on October 27, had appointed Edith Benham to succeed Miss Hagner.

From Edith Bolling Galt

My own precious One: New York Nov. 1st, 1915

What a long day this has been without you, and yet how near you have been in my thoughts and heart.

It is now a quarter of 8 and I am perceiving you in the study at work and long so to slip in and put my arms about you and pour out all my love and longing for you. How I did hate to leave you on the side walk this morning and sail away in your car. And ever since I have wished for you to share everything with.

Now I will begin where we left off and tell you all we have done. I found Helen & Dr. Grayson at the station & Brooks looked after everything for us, and we were most comfortable. The trip was uneventful and Mr. Jervis most attentive. When we got off the train there were Col. House and Mr. Malone and the car you ordered for us—you precious thing—and Mr. Malone had got rid of a lot of Reporters & apparently, no one followed us. They came to the Hotel and Mr. Malone asked us for a theatre party Wednesday night, which Helen seemed delighted at, so we accepted and oh! I wish you were going to be here.

Col. House asked if I knew what time you were coming on Thursday, and I said you told me you would write him. Then he said something about our going to New Jersey and I said after it was all in the paper I thought you had decided *not* to go. And then he said, your friend Mr. Dodge (is that right) wanted you to come there for lunch Friday, and he did hope you would stay over and do it. I said I thought you planned to go home Friday, but of course was not positive. That was about all of that. Here at the Hotel we were welcomed with open arms and have such nice rooms—with a little sitting room which is filled with your dear flowers.

Also 2 kinds of roses from Col. House and a hugh cluster of Beauty roses from the Hotel. We got brushed up and Altrude joined us at the door, and we decided we would walk down 5th ave and Mr. Jervis went with us.

He said there were a number of newspaper men here, but they had promised him not to do anything impertinent.

I found a note from Mrs. House with a list of names for shopping, so I called her up and had a nice little talk and their daughter is much better, & Mrs. H. offered to do anything she could for me. We went to 3 places for dresses and saw some lovly things but decided to look further before positively deciding.

Then we got back at 6 and went right in to dinner with our street things on.

And now we are in our own snug rooms and find about 20 boxes of things sent in by Mrs. Dare.[1] And so Helen and Altrude are unpacking them, and I hear shrieks of laughter, so I think they are having a good time.

Now, dear little Sweetheart being a perfectly consistent lady I am crazy to hear your speech Thursday night and am wondering if there is any chance for us to be tucked under or behind anything where we would not be seened but where I could hear your dear voice.

Of course I would not go, if it had to be known, but do you think it would be possible Precious? If so *please* let us.

Then another thing. Helen and I wondered if you had thought how lovely it would be if you motored up on Thursday—the country is perfectly beautiful now—and we could all go back together. It may too long for you to consider it feasable, but I thought I would suggest it anyway—and perhaps you would enjoy it more than another long train journey.

One more thing. Will you ask Margaret where she got her trunk. I suppose I am getting feeble minded, but I cant remember.

I will hold you in my arms all through the night Sweetheart— and love you—love you, love you—and go with you tomorrow—and watch over you from afar. I so hope you had a golf game this afternoon, and that it did not hurt the dear back.

Tell me just how you are Dearest. And this is perfect truth from me—that I am tired tonight but perfectly well and happy because you love me.

Thank you Precious for the flowers, the car, Mr. Jervis and Helen—and remember that I love you with all my heart.

                              Always your own   Edith

I am sharing honors here with his Excellency the Governor of N. York,[2] and it is great fun seeing who creates the greatest excitement.

ALS (WP, DLC).
[1] Susan Dare, a dressmaker of 41 E. 28th Street.
[2] Charles Seymour Whitman.

To Norman Hapgood

My dear Hapgood: [The White House] November 2, 1915

I do not know of any letter that has touched or pleased me more than yours of October thirty-first about my approaching marriage. I do not know how to answer such a letter, because the thing that it is hardest to express is the thing that goes to the very source of one's emotions. I can only say that I am deeply grateful and deeply happy that you should think of me in such a way.

                    Cordially and sincerely yours,   Woodrow Wilson

TLS (Letterpress Books, WP, DLC).

To Oswald Garrison Villard

My dear Mr. Villard: The White House November 2, 1915

I have your letter of October thirtieth and have read it with the most sincere interest, and you may be sure that if I have come to conclusions which you cannot endorse, I have not done so lightly or without very prolonged and serious consideration of the many sides of the great question about which you write, and that it always adds to my hesitation in coming to a definite conclusion in such matters when I find myself arrayed against men whose character and judgment I value as I do yours. These things search the heart and the judgment.

Cordially and sincerely yours,   Woodrow Wilson

TLS (O. G. Villard Papers, MH).

To Walter Hines Page

My dear Page: The White House November 2, 1915

You may be sure that among the many messages of congratulation we have received none gratified me more than your own little note of October twentieth.[1] It must be very hard indeed for you to think of such things on that side of the water, though you have just had a marriage in your own household,[2] and I am particularly obliged to Mrs. Page and you for your generous thought of me.

Cordially and sincerely yours,   Woodrow Wilson

TLS (W. H. Page Papers, MH).
    [1] WHP to WW, Oct. 20, 1915, ALS (WP, DLC).
    [2] That is, the wedding of Page's daughter, Katharine Alice Page, to Charles Greely Loring, about which see WW to WHP, July 22, 1915, Vol. 34.

To Claude Kitchin

My dear Mr. Kitchin: [The White House] November 2, 1915

Thank you sincerely for your letter of October twenty-ninth. May I not beg that you will give me the pleasure of seeing you on the eighth of November at noon if that hour is convenient for you?[1] I shall look forward with a great deal of pleasure to having an opportunity to discuss matters with you.

Cordially and sincerely yours,   Woodrow Wilson

TLS (Letterpress Books, WP, DLC).
    [1] Kitchin saw Wilson at the White House at the time stipulated. They discussed the administration's preparedness program for more than an hour, and Kitchin made it clear that, for reasons of conscience, he was opposed to a large

expansion of the navy. He told Wilson that he would express his opinion during the debate in the House but assured him that he would state his views as an individual member, not as the majority leader. *New York Times*, Nov. 9, 1915.

To Jane Addams

[The White House]
My dear Miss Addams: November 2, 1915

Allow me to acknowledge with sincere appreciation the receipt of the letter of October twenty-ninth signed by yourself, Mrs. Mead, Mrs. Post, Miss Spencer, and Miss Breckinridge. You are right in thinking that I value such expressions of opinion, and I hope with all my heart that I may be enabled to follow a wise and conservative course in the great matter about which you have spoken so candidly.

Cordially and sincerely yours,   Woodrow Wilson

TLS (Letterpress Books, WP, DLC).

From Robert Lansing

PERSONAL AND PRIVATE:

My dear Mr. President: Washington November 2, 1915.

I had a talk this morning with Ambassador Bernstorff in regard to the LUSITANIA matter. He is evidently far less hopeful of a settlement satisfactory to this Government of that case than of the ARABIC case. I think I can understand this attitude in view of the telegrams which we have received from Berlin, and which you have undoubtedly seen, as to the disapproval of his Government of his action in admitting as much as he did. I believe he has been told by his Government that his conduct of that matter was not satisfactory.[1] For that reason I did not feel that I could insist as strongly as I otherwise could that the German Government should admit the wrong and pay indemnity without the intervention of arbitration.

At the time that the Ambassador delivered to me the note which settled the ARABIC question he also handed me for consideration a draft of a note in regard to the LUSITANIA.[2] He again produced this draft and said that he felt sure that was as far as his Government could go in the matter. I told him that I would consider the draft further but that in its present form it would be unacceptable to this Government. I will, in a day or two, send you the draft with notes and suggestions as to what, it seems to me, would be satisfactory. The Ambassador said that any suggestions I might have he would have to refer to Berlin as he did not feel he was authorized to accept them without instructions.

I pointed out to him that in view of the fact that they had under their naval instructions ceased to attack passenger vessels I could see no practical reason why they should insist that the attack on the LUSITANIA was justifiable; that there might be a sentimental reason for this insistence in view of the natural dislike which a Government had to admit a wrongful act and that I realized the public opinion in Germany might criticize such an admission. I told him further that I was willing to go as far as possible to relieve that situation but that we also had to deal with public opinion in this country and that in the case of the LUSITANIA it was not a sentimental matter at all but a practical matter and that I thought his Government should admit liability for the loss of life. He said that he was convinced his Government would not make such an admission and that some other method would have to be found to determine liability. I also said to him that I thought the matter should be settled because we had already been extremely patient in the matter. He replied that if we insisted upon an admission of liability he did not believe it could be settled. I said that I regretted very much to have him say that as I felt that the question must be settled and very soon.

He left me with the understanding that I would go over the draft and communicate with him in a few days.[3]

Faithfully yours,   Robert Lansing

TLS (WP, DLC).
  [1] About the Foreign Office's reprimand of Bernstorff, see Link, *Struggle for Neutrality*, p. 587, n. 108.
  [2] It is printed as an Enclosure with J. H. von Bernstorff to RL, Oct. 2, 1915.
  [3] For Bernstorff's completely misleading report of this conversation, see J. H. von Bernstorff to T. von Bethmann Hollweg, Nov. 3, 1915, TCL (Der Weltkrieg, No. 18a, Unterseebootkrieg gegen England, ganz geheim, Vol. 14, pp. 108-109, GFO-Ar), summarized in Arthur S. Link, *Wilson: Confusions and Crises, 1915-1916* (Princeton, N. J., 1964), pp. 61-62.

To Edith Bolling Galt

Washington,
My own lovely Darling,   Tuesday eve., 2 Nov., 1915

We got back from Princeton[1] a little while before dinner time and the first thing I asked for and seized upon was your dear letter. What a blessing it was to get it and how eagerly my heart drank in every word of it—and how the exquisite messages of love in it did comfort me in my loneliness and longing! I have been crazy to write to you all day, during all the long hours I have spent thinking of you and trying to keep the blues at arm's length, but I simply cannot make the pen, or even a pencil, go straight while the train is in motion and I did not take my typewriter along. So I am obliged again to write in a hurry and rush my letter message down to the P. O. itself with a special delivery stamp on it to catch my darling before she goes out in the morning. The day has been absolutely uneventful—almost without incident of any kind. We simply travelled from eight this morning till half past six this evening with the interval of an hour in Princeton during which I voted and took a walk. I did not call on anybody and ran across only one or two old friends on the street. Both going up and coming down I took a long nap—to soften my loneliness, and I feel scarcely at all tired to-night. My back gets steadily better. I have had hardly more than a twinge or two to-day to remind me that there was anything the matter with it. So you need not give a single anxious thought to *that*, my precious One.

It was so sweet of you, my precious Darling, to write me a full chronicle of all you did yesterday. It was what my heart desired. I want to follow you with my thoughts at every step. I've answered Mr. House's questions in a letter—all of them, I'm sorry, for his and Dodge's sake, to say, in the negative; but I'm sure that is best, all things considered. Do you really want to motor back? I am perfectly willing if you think you would be up to it after four very fatiguing days. On the railway car you could lie down and relax and get a lot of the kinks out of your tired muscles. But I'm in for anything you wish. If you prefer that way, just send me a wire as soon as possible after getting this with the word *motor* in it and I will send a car up to-morrow to be ready for us on Friday morning. As for hearing the speech Thursday night, my sweet One, it is not possible to arrange that without its being known that you are there, and I am going, for prudence sake, to *read* the speech, which I fear will make it pretty dull, but just say the word (just say 'Yes' at the end of the telegram about the motor—for I ought to know at once in order to have a place reserved for you) and I will make the arrangement with a great joy at my heart that you are to be there—and you know I mean every word of it. I am so *happy* that you should wish to be near me, my darling Sweetheart!

Margaret's trunk is a Hartmann and one can be got either a[t] Macy's, where she got hers, or at Stearns, where, I believe, Nell got hers.

Ah, Sweetheart, Sweetheart, how I love you and how long and empty, how barren and all but intolerable the days are that I must get through without you! Just to think, if you were in Washington you would be here this very minute. Ive lighted my fire to give this uninteresting and lonely study a touch of cheer and colour, but it does not work! I can't fool myself. My Darling is away and nothing will make the house or the town feel like home till she comes back. I love her more than my life. She is all the world to me. She fills my heart and all my thoughts. To be with her is life and joy—to lack her like having the very breath of life taken out of me. My wonderful Darling! You are so full of everything that is lovely and delightful and adorable, and your love is so infinitely precious to me, so full of every kind of inspiration and joy. *Please* take good, *good* care of yourself—be *very* careful not to overdo. Remember that you are the very source of my life and that without you the world would mean nothing to

Your own   Woodrow

Dearest love to Helen and warm regards to Miss Gordon.

ALS (WP, DLC).
[1] Wilson had gone to Princeton to vote in local and state elections.

A Letter and a Telegram from Edith Bolling Galt

My precious One: New York Nov. 2, 1915 5:15 P.M.

The day *really* began when your precious letter came this morning just at 9 ock. when I was picturing you leaving for Princeton—and oh! I was so glad to get it. Thank you Dearest for telling me about your back and I can't help feeling worried over the ligament. *Please*, if there is anything that could be done for it, have it done and don't play golf if it hurts you.

How I wish I was home to welcome you when you get back tonight, but I hope you will go to the Theatre, and have something good to divert and entertain you.

I got the paper to see the announcement this morning and appreciate your doing this for me, as it really will be a relief, and I think it is quite dignified and just as it should be and will I trust relieve us both of further impertinence. We have had a pretty strenuous day up to two ock, when all the stores closed on account of its being election. So at three we went for a ride out in the Park, I mean Altrude & I, as Helen wanted to go to see Mrs. Brown.[1]

So we took her there first and left her & she insisted she wanted to walk home for the exercise. So she has not yet come in, and I am going to rest for a little while before dinner after finishing this and then we are going out in the car with Jervis to look after us and ride around to see the election crowds.

This morning I woke at 6:30 and lay there thinking of you until 7:30 when I got up & found Altrude was awake. So I ordered breakfast for 8 and did not disturb Helen until it came and found her fast sleep. We got through & almost dressed before Mrs. Dare came to try on dresses. This took until nearly 11, but she had some lovly things. Then we went to "Lucile's," or Lady Duff Gordon's,[3] where we found the most wonderful things, and they were untiring in their attentions.

I only ordered one dress however & am considering others. Mrs. Malone insisted to Helen on the phone that we should come to dinner tomorrow at 7 and go to the theatre afterwards. So I am afraid with this in the evening & Mrs. House's lunch at 1:30 I will accomplish very little tomorrow and I may have to come back for a day or so later, but I will do all I can to get things while here. So sorry to hear Dr. Grayson was hurt by the golf ball, and it certainly was an outrageous thing for any player to do. Give him my love and tell him I am so sorry.

I almost forgot to tell you I was asleep last night by eleven oclock and did not move until 6. So you see I *am* being good and trying to do what you want me to.

If I were not so tired I could write on and on—but I know you will understand. So I am going to kiss your dear eyes and say goodby until tomorrow. My tender love to that sweet Margaret, and I do hope her cold is much better.

I love you you precious One and thank you for all the lovly things your letter tells me. It is so hard to say goodbye even on paper, but I will go on thinking of and loving you, and I am always   Your own   Edith

ALS (WP, DLC).
    [1] That is, Mrs. Edward T. Brown.
    [2] Lucile Ltd., dressmaker at 37 W. 57th Street, headed by the designer Lady Duff-Gordon.

New York, Nov. 3, 1915.

Think it best to leave things as arranged. No motor.

E.B.G.

T telegram (WP, DLC).

From Robert Lansing

PERSONAL AND PRIVATE:

My dear Mr. President: Washington November 3, 1915.

The Chilean Ambassador called to see me yesterday and informed me that he had communicated with his Government and that the Under Secretary of Foreign Affairs had said something to Mr. Fletcher about the proposed propositions for a Pan-American treaty, but had not intended to indicate to him that the Government desired to transfer the negotiations to Santiago. I explained to the Ambassador that Mr. Fletcher had merely drawn that conclusion from having been approached on the subject and that of course it was in no way desired to have the negotiations conducted other than here in Washington if it was agreeable to his Government. I said this perceiving that his Government would, in all probability, direct him to handle the matter and that it was of no use to attempt to do so through Mr. Fletcher.

The attitude of the Chilean Ambassador toward me in this matter is one of the greatest friendliness and from a conversation I had with him a short time ago I believe that he can be persuaded to advise his Government in favor of the propositions as drafted. He told me that the first proposition, granting territorial and political integrity, had been presented to him by Mr. Bryan with practically no explanation as to the meaning. After talking it over with him he felt that it was far less objectionable then [than] he had supposed and he believed that his Government would not seriously object to it. Of course it is the first proposition which is the essence of the compact and if we can secure his adhesion to that we can, in all probability, remove anything objectionable in the other propositions.

I will at once redraft the propositions eliminating the matter of time in the settlement of boundary disputes, and submit to you.

Faithfully yours,   Robert Lansing

TLS (WP, DLC).

A Memorandum by Robert Lansing

[Washington] November 3, 1915.

MEMORANDUM OF CONVERSATION WITH JAPANESE AMBASSADOR.

The Japanese Ambassador called and asked me if we had determined what course should be taken in regard to their request to join with them in expressing our disapproval of a change in the form of government in China at the present time.

I answered him that we had not taken any steps in regard to the matter; that it appeared to this Government that while he must understand we naturally were sympathetic with republican forms of Government we felt that it would be more or less an interference with the internal affairs of China, which would be, improper.

The Ambassador said that he regretted that we should feel so in the matter but he readily understood why action might be considered as an interference. I said to him that I believed the matter was substantially determined and that China would return to a monarchical form of Government under a constitution, and that I did not believe an expression of views at this time would materially affect the situation; that I understood the army was loyal and approved the change and that there was no serious organized opposition. He said that he hoped such was the case because the only object Japan had was to prevent domestic disturbances in China at a time when the whole world was at war.   Robert Lansing

TS MS (SDR, RG 59, 893.01/71, DNA).

To Edith Bolling Galt

                                                               Washington,
My precious Darling,   Wednesday 3 November, 1915

I am going to see you to-morrow (what joy it gives me just to write the words!), but my heart would not be quiet if I did not send you a letter—and so I am stealing a few minutes from a very busy morning to at least begin it, and will finish it when I can later in the day. To-morrow I shall hold you in my arms and tell you how deeply and tenderly I love you and with what a passionate longing I have missed you these long drawn days in this empty town, but I cannot wait till then. The longing is too intense. I feel as if it might crack my heartstrings if I did not pour it all out to you in the tenderest words my heart can find. *No* words suffice. I love you with every thought and with every breath I breathe, and I like to think that it makes you as happy to hear me say so as it makes me to hear you confess your love for me, —and yet how *can* it? It is so exquisite a delight to be loved by you, my incomparable Darling, that I cannot believe that it *can* be as delightful to be loved by *any* man. But fortunately you have never loved yourself and do not know what you have missed,— have had no chance to make the comparison! Your love is beyond all comparison sweet and satisfying. It has made me rich in all the happiest thoughts and experiences a man can have. And in return, precious little girl, I love you with a love that is not only without limit but is also full of gladness and of the sort of devotion that makes everything in life seem fine and deeply worth while to me. You are my inspiration as well as my joy! Since I began your precious letter of yesterday has been handed to me by the faithful Hoover. How sweet to me every word of it is! I seem to hear the tones of your dear voice as I read, and the tender

love in it all thrills me so, my precious One. Even in my loneliness I am deeply, joyously happy because of your love for me—
which seems to me a very wonderful and beautiful thing. You
need not be anxious for even a moment, my Darling, about the
ligament. Grayson says that nothing need be done for it,—that
it will come right of itself,—and he thinks there is no risk at all in
my playing golf this afternoon. His own hurt has turned out to
be trifling, I am glad to say. It was merely a bruise. My back is so
nearly well that I am not aware there is anything the matter with
it unless something happens to touch the exact spot.

I am so sorry that you should be so much interrupted in your
shopping, my Pet. It makes my heart sink to think that you may
have to be away again. My most interesting interview to-day (I
am writing piecemeal, as I get a few minutes chance, amidst a
swirl of distracting interruptions—as I would at every interval run
in to see you, if you were here) has been with Mr. Herbert
Hoover, the chairman of the Belgian Relief Commission. I wish
you could meet him. He is a real man, and came to me for a
little help against a member of the committee in New York who
is seeking to make trouble for him—help which I gladly gave. He
is an American mining engineer living in London—one of the
very ablest men we have sent over there, and has devoted his
great organizing gifts and a large part of his fortune, too, to
keeping nine million people alive (at a cost of ten million dollars
a day!); so that he has become a great international figure. Such
men stir me deeply and make me in love with duty!

I shall reach New York, if my train is on time, at three seventeen, my Sweetheart, and could, no doubt, reach the St. Regis
by a quarter of four; but I am so anxious to play no part in interfering with your shopping and making it necessary for you to
go to New York again that I am going to propose this: I will go
directly from the train to your hotel, but, if it will inconvenience
you or hurry you too much to be there so early, just leave or telephone word when you will probably be back and I will go on to
House's apartment, dress for dinner, and come back at the time
you name. My dinner is set for 7:30, but I need not be on the dot.
I am beyond measure eager to see you, but I want to help, not
embarrass, your plans, my precious One.

Margaret left this afternoon at three for Milwaukee, to make
her address on social settlement work to the teachers there.

Mac. and Nell got back from their long trip this morning—in
fine shape except that Mac. has caught a beastly cold. (Grayson
has put him to bed). They are perfectly delighted with the progress the baby has made. She gained nearly a pound a week while

they were away. It was touching to see how wildly happy Nell was to get back to the dear little creature. I never saw Nell look better, or lovelier. Nell and Margaret and Mac. all send you their dearest love, my Darling.

And what shall I say of what *I* send? My heart is wholly yours, my precious Sweetheart, and longs for its mistress with an infinite longing which can be quieted only in your arms. Bless you for your dear letters, bless you for your incomparable love, bless you for being your own adorable self, and for letting me be, altogether and in all things.   Your own   Woodrow

Grayson and I dine in lonely state together to-night and afterwards will seek to forget our miserable bachelorhood at Keiths.

I hardly knew I *had* a back while I was playing golf this afternoon—and I feel *fine* now (6.55)

ALS (WP, DLC).

From Edith Bolling Galt

New York, Nov. 3, 1915.
We have been so busy to-day did not send letter, but we are all well and looking forward tomorrow. Have just come from a charming dinner and theatre party with the Malone's. Wish you could have been with us.   E.B.G.

T telegram (WP, DLC).

To Thomas Watt Gregory

My dear Gregory: [The White House] November 4, 1915

For fear I should not get a chance to send you a letter while I am in New York today and tomorrow, I am dropping you a line now to congratulate you on your birthday and to wish you many, many happy returns.

I hope that you have been conscious of how fully you have won not only my confidence but the confidence of all with whom you have been associated here, and I trust that it is a source of real happiness to you that you should have rendered the country already such faithful and disinterested and distinguished service. My heart is in these congratulations, my dear friend, and I hope that the years will bring you increasing happiness.

            Cordially and sincerely yours,   Woodrow Wilson

TLS (Letterpress Books, WP, DLC).

To Edward Mandell House

The White House [Nov.] 4, 1915

Please expect me three seventeen Penna this afternoon   looking forward with great pleasure to seeing you again

Woodrow Wilson.

T telegram (E. M. House Papers, CtY).

An Address on Preparedness to the Manhattan Club

[Nov. 4, 1915]

Mr. Toastmaster[1] and gentlemen: I warmly felicitate the club upon the completion of fifty years of successful and interesting life. Club life may be made to mean a great deal to those who know how to use it. I have no doubt that to a great many of you has come genuine stimulation in the associations of this place and that as the years have multiplied you have seen more and more the useful ends which may be served by organizations of this sort.

But I have not come to speak wholly of that, for there are others of your own members who can speak of the club with a knowledge and an intelligence which no one can have who has not been intimately associated with it. Men band themselves together for the sake of the association no doubt, but also for something greater and deeper than that—because they are conscious of common interests lying outside their business occupations, because they are members of the same community and in frequent intercourse find mutual stimulation and a real maximum of vitality and power. I shall assume that here around the dinner table on this memorial occasion our talk should properly turn to the wide and common interests which are most in our thoughts, whether they be the interests of the community or of the nation.

A year and a half ago our thought would have been almost altogether of great domestic questions. They are many and of vital consequence. We must and shall address ourselves to their solution with diligence, firmness, and self-possession, notwithstanding we find ourselves in the midst of a world disturbed by great disaster and ablaze with terrible war; but our thought is now inevitably of new things about which formerly we gave ourselves little concern. We are thinking now chiefly of our relations with the rest of the world—not our commercial relations—about those we have thought and planned always—but about our political relations, our duties, as an individual and independent

1 Philip J. Britt, New York lawyer and president of the Manhattan Club.

force in the world, to ourselves, our neighbors, and the world itself.

Our principles are well known. It is not necessary to avow them again. We believe in political liberty and founded our great government to obtain it, the liberty of men and of peoples—of men to choose their own lives and of peoples to choose their own allegiance. Our ambition, also, all the world has knowledge of. It is not only to be free and prosperous ourselves, but also to be the friend and thoughtful partisan of those who are free or who desire freedom the world over. If we have had aggressive purposes and covetous ambitions, they were the fruit of our thoughtless youth as a nation and we have put them aside. We shall, I confidently believe, never again take another foot of territory by conquest. We shall never in any circumstances seek to make an independent people subject to our dominion; because we believe, we passionately believe, in the right of every people to choose their own allegiance and be free of masters altogether. For ourselves we wish nothing but the full liberty of self-development; and with ourselves in this great matter we associate all the peoples of our own hemisphere. We wish not only for the United States but for them the fullest freedom of independent growth and of action, for we know that throughout this hemisphere the same aspirations are everywhere being worked out, under diverse conditions but with the same impulse and ultimate object.

All this is very clear to us and will, I confidently predict, become more and more clear to the whole world as the great processes of the future unfold themselves. It is with a full consciousness of such principles and such ambitions that we are asking ourselves at the present time what our duty is with regard to the armed force of the nation. Within a year we have witnessed what we did not believe possible, a great European conflict involving many of the greatest nations of the world. The influences of a great war are everywhere in the air. All Europe is embattled. Force everywhere speaks out with a loud and imperious voice in a titanic struggle of governments, and from one end of our own dear country to the other men are asking one another what our own force is, how far we are prepared to maintain ourselves against any interference with our national action or development.

In no man's mind, I am sure, is there even raised the question of the wilful use of force on our part against any nation or any people. No matter what military or naval force the United States might develop, statesmen throughout the whole world might rest assured that we were gathering that force, not for attack in any quarter, not for aggression of any kind, not for the satisfaction of any political or international ambition, but merely to make sure of our own security. We have it in mind to be prepared, but not for war, but only for defense; and with the thought constantly in our minds that the principles we hold most dear can be achieved by the slow processes of history only in the kindly and wholesome atmosphere of peace, and not by the use of hostile force. The mission of America in the world is essentially a mission of peace and good will among men. She has become the home and asylum of men of all creeds and races. Within her hospitable borders they have found homes and congenial associations and freedom and a wide and cordial welcome, and they have become part of the bone and sinew and spirit of America itself. America has been made up out of the nations of the world and is the friend of the nations of the world.

But we feel justified in preparing ourselves to vindicate our right to independent and unmolested action by making the force that is in us ready for assertion.

And we know that we can do this in a way that will be itself an illustration of the American spirit. In accordance with our American traditions we want and shall work for only an army adequate to the constant and legitimate uses of times of international peace. But we do want to feel that there is a great body of citizens who have received at least the most rudimentary and necessary forms of military training; that they will be ready to form themselves into a fighting force at the call of the nation; and that the nation has the munitions and supplies with which to equip them without delay should it be necessary to call them into action. We wish to supply them with the training they need, and we think we can do so without calling them at any time too long away from their civilian pursuits.

It is with this idea, with this conception, in mind that the plans have been made which it will be my privilege to lay before the Congress at its next session. That plan calls for only such an increase in the regular Army of the United States as experience has proved to be required for the performance of the necessary duties of the army in the Philippines, in Hawaii, in Porto Rico, upon the borders of the United States, at the coast fortifications, and at the military posts of the interior. For the rest, it calls for the training within the next three years of a force of 400,000 citizen soldiers to be raised in annual contingents of 133,000, who would be asked to enlist for three years with the colors and three years on furlough, but who during their three years of enlistment with the colors would not be organized as a standing force but would be expected merely to undergo intensive training for a very brief period of each year. Their training would take place in immediate association with the organized units of the regular army. It would have no touch of the amateur about it, neither would it exact of the volunteers more than they could give in any one year from their civilian pursuits.

And none of this would be done in such a way as in the slightest degree to supersede or subordinate our present serviceable and efficient National Guard. On the contrary, the National Guard itself would be used as part of the instrumentality by which training would be given the citizens who enlisted under the new conditions, and I should hope and expect that the legislation by which all this would be accomplished would put the National Guard itself upon a better and more permanent footing than it has ever been before, giving it not only the recognition which it deserves, but a more definite support from the national government and a more definite connection with the military organization of the nation.

What we all wish to accomplish is that the forces of the nation should indeed be part of the nation and not a separate professional force, and the chief cost of the system would not be in the enlistment or in the training of the men, but in the providing of ample equipment in case it should be necessary to call all forces into the field.

Moreover, it has been American policy time out of mind to look to the navy as the first and chief line of defense. The Navy of the United States is already a very great and efficient force. Not rapidly, but slowly, with careful attention, our naval force has been developed until the Navy of the United States stands recognized as one of the most efficient and notable of the modern time. All that is needed in order to bring it to a point of extraordinary force and efficiency as compared with the other navies of the world is that we should hasten our pace in the policy we have long been pursuing, and that chief of all we should have a definite policy of development, not made from year to year but looking well into the future and planning for a definite consummation. We can and should profit in all that we do by the experience and example that have been made obvious to us by the military and naval events of the actual present. It is not merely a matter of building battleships and cruisers and submarines, but also a matter of making sure that we shall have the adequate equipment of men and munitions and supplies for the vessels we build and intend to build. Part of our problem is the problem of what I may call the mobilization of the resources of the nation at the proper time if it should ever be necessary to mobilize them for national defense. We shall study efficiency and adequate equipment as carefully as we shall study the number and size of our ships, and I believe that the plans already in part made public by the Navy Department are plans which the whole nation can approve with rational enthusiasm.

No thoughtful man feels any panic haste in this matter. The country is not threatened from any quarter. She stands in friendly relations with all the world. Her resources are known and her self-respect and her capacity to care for her own citizens and her own rights. There is no fear amongst us. Under the new-world conditions we have become thoughtful of the things which all reasonable men consider necessary for security and self-defense on the part of every nation confronted with the great enterprise of human liberty and independence. That is all.

Is the plan we propose sane and reasonable and suited to the needs of the hour? Does it not conform to the ancient traditions of America? Has any better plan been proposed than this programme that we now place before the country? In it there is no pride of opinion. It represents the best professional and expert judgment of the country. But I am not so much interested in programmes as I am in safeguarding at every cost the good faith and honor of the country. If men differ with me in this vital matter, I shall ask them to make it clear how far and in what way they are interested in making the permanent interests of the country safe against disturbance.

In the fulfillment of the programme I propose I shall ask for the hearty support of the country, of the rank and file of America, of men of all shades of political opinion. For my position in this important matter is different from that of the private individual who is free to speak his own thoughts and to risk his own opinions in this matter. We are here dealing with things that are vital to the life of America itself. In doing this I have tried to purge my heart of all personal and selfish motives. For the time being, I speak as the trustee and guardian of a nation's rights, charged with the duty of speaking for that nation in matters involving her sovereignty—a nation too big and generous to be exacting and yet courageous enough to defend its rights and the liberties of its people wherever assailed or invaded. I would not feel that I was discharging the solemn obligation I owe the country were I not to speak in terms of the deepest solemnity of the urgency and necessity of preparing ourselves to guard and protect the rights and privileges of our people, our sacred heritage of the fathers who struggled to make us an independent nation.

The only thing within our own borders that has given us grave concern in recent months has been that voices have been raised in America professing to be the voices of Americans which were not indeed and in truth American, but which spoke alien sympathies, which came from men who loved other countries better than they loved America, men who were partisans of other causes than that of America and had forgotten that their chief and only allegiance was to the great government under which they live. These voices have not been many, but they have been very loud and very clamorous. They have proceeded from a few who were bitter and who were grievously misled. America has not opened its doors in vain to men and women out of other nations. The vast majority of those who have come to take advantage of her hospitality have united their spirits with hers as well as their fortunes. These men who speak alien sympathies are not their spokesmen but are the spokesmen of small groups whom it is high time that the nation should call to a reckoning. The chief thing necessary in America in order that she should let all the world know that she is prepared to maintain her own great position is that the real voice of the nation should sound forth unmistakably and in majestic volume, in the deep unison of a common, unhesitating national feeling. I do not doubt that upon the first occasion, upon the first opportunity, upon the first definite challenge, that voice will speak forth in tones which no man can doubt and with commands which no man dare gainsay or resist.

May I not say, while I am speaking of this, that there is another danger that we should guard against? We should rebuke not only manifestations of racial feeling here in America where there should be none, but also every manifestation of religious and sectarian antagonism. It does not become America that within her borders, where every man is free to follow the dictates of his conscience and worship God as he pleases, men should raise the cry of church against church. To do that is to strike at the very spirit and heart of America. We are a God-fearing people. We agree to differ about methods of worship, but we are united in believing in Divine Providence and in worshiping the God of Nations. We are the champions of religious right here and everywhere that it may be our privilege to give it our countenance and support. The government is conscious of the obligation and the nation is conscious of the obligation. Let no man create divisions where there are none.

Here is the nation God has builded by our hands. What shall we do with it? Who is there who does not stand ready at all times to act in her behalf in a spirit of devoted and disinterested patriotism? We are yet only in the youth and first consciousness of our power. The day of our country's life is still but in its fresh morning. Let us lift our eyes to the great tracts of life yet to be conquered in the interests of righteous peace. Come, let us renew our allegiance to America, conserve her strength in its purity, make her chief among those who serve mankind, self-reverenced, self-commanded, mistress of all forces of quiet counsel, strong above all others in good will and the might of invincible justice and right.

Printed reading copy (WP, DLC).

From James Hay

My dear Mr. President: Madison, Va. Nov. 4th, 1915.

I have just been informed that the Secretary of War will give to the Press on Saturday next the program for National Defense.

It seems to me that this will be unfortunate.

Criticism of the details of the plan will at once be made.

The extreme peace men on the one hand and the extreme big Army men on the other will oppose the plan.

All of the talk and criticism which will be indulged in between now and the meeting of Congress will make it more difficult for us to pass the measure.

Would it not be best to let the matter rest until the bill is prepared and introduced?

I hope you will not think I am officious about this, but I really think it important to let the matter stand until Congress meets.

Very sincerely yours,   James Hay

TLS (WP, DLC).

Robert Lansing to the Japanese Embassy

Washington, November 4, 1915.

MEMORANDUM.

The American Government appreciates the invitation extended to it by the Imperial Japanese Government to join in the tender of informal and friendly advice to the Republic of China to defer for a time in the interest of general peace in the Far East the change in its form of government which is reported to be under consideration.

The American Government is naturally in sympathy with republican institutions, but is of opinion that any change by the Chinese in the form of their government, however radical, is wholly a domestic question and that any sort of interference by the Government of the United States would be, therefore, an invasion of China's sovereignty and would be without justification unless convincing evidence, which is not now in the possession of the United States Government, should show that any foreign interests which it is the privilege of the United States to safeguard would be imperilled.

CC MS (SDR, RG 59, 893.01/72, DNA).

Jean Jules Jusserand to Aristide Briand

Washington, le 4 novembre 1915.

No 910 J'ai reçu avec une très vive satisfaction le télégramme du Département, No. 594, m'invitant à exprimer au Président Wilson les remerciements du Gouvernement de la République pour son intervention en faveur de Mlle de Belleville et de Mme Thuilliez, condamnées à mort par les Allemands.

J'ai tenu à m'acquitter en personne d'une aussi agréable mission. Le Président s'est montré très sensible à la démarche dont j'étais chargé et a dit que sa seule crainte avait été que, vu la brièveté du délai, son intervention se fût trouvée inutile.

J'ai profité de l'occasion que m'offrait cet entretien pour lui marquer que le changement de Cabinet[1] ne signifiait aucun changement dans la politique de la France qui, victime d'une agression, ne mettrait bas les armes qu'après la victoire. Le demain, la déclaration de Votre Excellence aux Chambres,[2] reproduite et commentée de la manière la plus favorable par tous les journaux, confirmait, pour l'ensemble du public américain, les assurances que j'avais cru pouvoir donner par avance au Président.   Jusserand

TLS (Guerre 1914-1918, États-Unis, Vol. 497, p. 6, FFM-Ar).
    [1] The cabinet of Prime Minister René Viviani had resigned on October 28 on account of mounting criticism of the French government's failure to prevent Bulgaria from joining the Central Powers. Briand had been called upon to form a new cabinet in which he became Prime Minister and Foreign Minister.
    [2] That is, Briand's declaration in the Chamber of Deputies on November 3, emphasizing the determination of the new French government to continue the war until victory was won and a durable peace assured. New York Times, Nov. 4, 1915.

T R A N S L A T I O N

Washington, November 4, 1915.

No 910   I received with very deep pleasure the Department's telegram No 594, asking me to express to President Wilson the thanks of the government of the Republic for his intervention on behalf of Miss de Belleville and Mrs. Thuilliez, condemned to death by the Germans.

I was eager to carry out such a pleasant mission in person. The President appeared very moved by the mission with which I had been charged, and said that his only fear had been that, given the brevity of the reprieve, his intervention would have been futile.

I took advantage of the opportunity which this meeting afforded to point out to him that the change of the cabinet did not signify any change in the policy of France, which, victim of aggression, would lay down its arms only after victory. The next day, Your Excellency's statement to the Chamber of Deputies, republished and commented upon most favorably by all the newspapers, confirmed for all the American public the assurances which I had believed I was empowered to give to the President in advance.   Jusserand

From the Diary of Colonel House

November 4, 1915.

This has been a quiet day considering the President is to arrive. I have received a few crank letters and a few telephone calls. I have seen secret service men and have quietly made what arrangements were necessary. . . .

After lunch I went to the Hotel St Regis to see Mrs. Galt and talk over the question of having her portrait painted as a wedding gift to the President. She was inclined not to do it because she does not believe portraits are usually satisfactory. She has the matter under consideration.

She said the President had shown her some of my European correspondence especially the cablegram I sent him regarding the Lusitania.[1] I was with her only a few minutes because it was necessary to go to the station to meet the President upon his arrival at 3.17 from Washington.

I never saw so many detectives, secret service men, police and newspaper correspondence [correspondents] as were there. Unusual precautions for his safety were taken. The train arrived on time and the President and I proceeded to the waiting motors and drove to the St Regis where I left him with Mrs. Galt. We had some conversation en route concerning the inadvisability of much pleasure-making at this time. He thought it would make a bad impression upon the people in the distant States and he thought the quieter he was the better it would be. He expressed a desire to come over some Sunday and hear Dr. Jowett preach. We will arrange for this later.

The afternoon was quiet for no one could reach the apartment by telephone or otherwise and the President has been with Mrs. Galt. He came back at half past six and we had a few minutes talk before we dressed for dinner. He handed me two communications from Secretary Lansing, one concerning the South American proposal,[2] which seems to be getting along fairly well, and the other in regard to the Lusitania incident which Lansing is taking up with Bernstorff.[3]

The President says that the Minister from Cuba told Lansing that he had been approached by the Spanish Minister who wished to know whether Cuba and other Latin American countries would cordially receive the idea of the King of Spain acting as mediator in the European war. The President said Lansing was concerned about it and thought it indicated that the Germans were trying to get South and Central America's support for Spain as a mediator as against the United States. He advised Lansing to tell the Cuban Minister that this country hoped that all the Americas would work in union regarding this matter, and for them not to give a direct answer. The President asked what I thought of this. My opinion was that in the last analysis this country would have to be reckoned with. I expressed the opinion that selfish motives would bring this about. In all my talks with Bernstorff I had repeatedly pointed out the benefit that we could be to Germany in a final settlement and Sir Edward Grey surely knew how important it was to have us take part in the peace conference since England's and France's views were so near akin to ours. I was positive that even if he, the President, did not act as mediator, it would be impossible to keep him from playing an important part.

I advised the President to be cautious in his domestic policies, telling him very much what I told Cleve Dodge last Sunday, and which is already record.[4] He thought it would be necessary to go through with the Philippines Bill, the Conservation program and the Shipping Bill. I demurred at the latter and told him, without going into the merits of that bill, I questioned the political expediency of taking it up before the elections.

He believed a change had come about in the sentiment of the country, outside the Eastern Seaboard, and he did not think we could hold that section anyway. I differ from him in this view. He seemed to look with equinimity upon losing Massachusetts, Connecticut, New York and perhaps, New Jersey. If he loses all these states, he will find it difficult to recoup sufficient votes from the balance of the country.

I asked how far he was willing to go toward creating a tariff commission. He replied only so far as one might be assembled from existing boards like the Trades Commission and the Bureau of Commerce. He expressed the belief that the tariff was a political question which one could not relegate out of active politics, and what ever party was in should express its views as to the tariff. I disagreed wholly from this view. I believe American business has suffered more from tariff agitation than from any reduction which has been made. Our whole industrial system lacks stability. No man can tell what to expect or what to build upon. That, I think, is the real grievance, and I believe the stupidity of the business world is only second to that of the political world, which keeps this question constantly to the fore. No American manufacturer feels secure and he never knows whether to increase or curtail his plant. His European competitor has no such handicap as a constantly rising and falling tariff.

1 EMH to WW, May 9, 1915, Vol. 33.
2 RL to WW, Nov. 3, 1915.
3 RL to WW, Nov. 2, 1915.
4 House argued that Wilson should slow down his domestic program and concentrate instead on international affairs, which were much more important at the moment. House Diary, Oct. 31, 1915, T MS (E. M. House Papers, CtY).

From Seth Low

Dear Mr. President: New York November 5, 1915.

I read with great pleasure your speech of last night. I am glad you have taken the attitude as to preparedness which you expressed so forcibly last night. I especially rejoiced also in what you said on the subject of the alien citizens and on the subject of the antagonism of sects. You struck what I conceive to be the true American note in a notable fashion, and, for one, I thank you heartily.

Speaking of preparedness, I have agreed to serve on the Committee appointed by Governor Whitman to co-operate with the National Security League.[1] I am too unfamiliar with the details of what is proposed in any quarter to commit myself as to details, but I hope that your definite program, when outlined, will be such that our Committee and all other committees can stand with you. I am very certain that in spirit the American people, by a very great majority, are with you.

I take advantage of this opportunity to mail you a copy of what I said at the meeting of the Chamber of Commerce on Thursday in regard to the restoration of an American mercantile marine.[2] I can assure you that I shall leave no stone unturned to find a common meeting ground so that the Government and the mercantile interests, as represented by the Chamber of Commerce, can work together. I want you certainly to understand that the wish of the Chamber is to be constructive in its suggestions, and not simply critical. If the Administration and the mercantile community will approach the study of the question with open minds, I am sure that a platform ought to be found on which we can all stand, for we all earnestly desire to enlarge and make stable an American merchant marine for international trade.   Respectfully and sincerely, yours, Seth Low

TLS (WP, DLC).

¹ The Governor had appointed this State Committee on National Defense, consisting of thirty-one notable citizens from across the State of New York, on October 7, 1915, at the request of the National Security League, the leading preparedness organization in the United States.

² Undated T MS (WP, DLC). In his speech before the New York State Chamber of Commerce on November 4, Low opposed the administration's ship purchase bill on the grounds that it would drive private enterprise from the seas and establish a governmental monopoly. The chamber, he continued, would submit alternative proposals for increasing the merchant marine to Congress in the next session and try to work out a compromise measure.

From the Diary of Colonel House

November 5, 1915.

Frank Cobb of the World and Justice Victor Dowling called last night at 7.30 to take the President to the Biltmore Hotel where the Manhattan Club Banquet was held.

I had my dinner quietly at Gordon's ¹ and he and I and David Miller ² motored down at half past nine. The Club had kindly reserved for me and my guests a table of eight places. My other guests were Mark Sullivan, Charles R. Crane and William Allen White, John Wilson, the President's cousin, and a friend of his from Pittsburg.³ The affair was rather badly managed and it was five minutes of twelve before the President began to speak. I will not go into details here for it is well reported in the papers. We did not get to bed until after one o'clock.

We arose however at the usual time and had breakfast shortly before eight. At breakfast we discussed current pending public affairs, but none of them were of much importance. We talked of the best time and place to hold the National Convention and some other matters relating to party affairs.

After breakfast we walked to the St Regis where I left him with Mrs. Galt. At twelve I returned to the hotel and the President, Mrs. Galt, Loulie, Cleve Dodge and I motored to Riverdale and lunched with the Dodges. The President was indiscreet in his talk at the table. He criticised Gerard unnecessarily severely saying his dispatches were of no value and his advice even less so. He cited one instance where Gerard advised the acceptance of Germany's proposal designating a certain number of passenger ships which should be immune from submarine attacks, and later when this Government declined it, Gerard cabled his warm approval of the position taken.[4] He said he knew Gerard had no sense when he appointed him, but there was no international complication in sight and being hard pressed by Gerard's friends, in a moment of abberation, he consented.

I told both the President and Mr. Dodge that I thought he was unnecessarily severe and unfair. I called attention to the fact that Gerard had the most difficult place to fill of any of the Ambassadors, and the mere fact that he had been able to remain at his post without having been sent home was a tribute to his ability. Loulie also spoke of the excellent work done by Mrs. Gerard. To this the President readily assented.

Another indiscretion was when the President spoke of reporters before the servants. He said the day he got out of office, the first thing he would like to do would be to go out and shoot a reporter or two.

In talking with the President about Senator Reed of Missouri, I told him of Folk's ambition to become Governor, but expressed the opinion that I might switch him onto the Senatorship. This met with his warm approval. He thought Folk an exceedingly light-weight statesman, but anything was better than Reed. He declared he would have nothing to do with Reed in the event Missouri returned him: that he was thoroughly untrustworthy, was not a democrat, and he would treat him as if he were a member of the opposition party. He said someone wanted to know the other day if he did not think a certain statesman was the most selfish man in America. He replied that he was sorry, but he was already committed to Senator Reed.

We motored from Riverdale directly to the Pennsylvania Station and came perilously near running down a little eight year old boy, just as we turned into the station. He was knocked down but not hurt. The Presidential party left at 3.30 and seemed pleased with their visit.

1 That is, Gordon Auchincloss.
2 David Hunter Miller, a lawyer in New York City.
3 He was probably Lawrence Crane Woods.
4 See WW to RL, July 7, 1915, n. 3, Vol. 33.

To James Hay

My dear Mr. Hay: [The White House] November 6, 1915

I am exceedingly sorry I did not get your letter of November fourth in time to suggest to the Secretary of War a postponement of the publication of the details of the plan we have been discussing.[1] As you may have seen in the newspapers, I was in New York to make a speech at the Manhattan Club and did not return until late last evening. There is a great deal of force in what you say and if I had known how definitely and strongly you felt about it, it would certainly have given me pause, but I hope that now the thing is done it will turn out that a good deal of the debate can be disposed of before we actually tackle the legislation, and perhaps we may get some good pointers from the debate. At any rate, I hope so.

          Cordially and sincerely yours,   [Woodrow Wilson]

CCL (WP, DLC).
    [1] Garrison's army program was published in the press on November 6, e.g., the *New York Times*, Nov. 6, 1915.

To Seth Low

My dear Mr. Low: [The White House] November 8, 1915

I thank you very warmly for your generous letter of the fifth of November and for your courtesy in letting me see a copy of your remarks on the merchant marine question.

I am particularly gratified that you should so fully concur in the position I took in my speech to the Manhattan Club. There is a quotation from Ezekiel which I have had very much in my mind recently in connection with these important matters. It is the second, third, fourth, fifth, and sixth verses of Chapter thirty-three:

"2 Son of man, speak to the children of thy people, and say unto them, When I bring the sword upon a land, if the people of the land take a man of their coasts, and set him for their watchman:

3 If, when he seeth the sword come upon the land he blow the trumpet, and warn the people;

4 Then whosoever heareth the sound of the trumpet, and taketh not warning; if the sword come, and take him away, his blood shall be upon his own head.

5 He heard the sound of the trumpet, and took not warning, his blood shall be upon him; but he that taketh warning shall deliver his soul.

6 But if the watchman see the sword come, and blow not the trumpet, and the people be not warned; if the sword come, and take *any* person from among them, he is taken away in his iniquity; but his blood will I require at the watchman's hand."

Cordially and sincerely yours,   Woodrow Wilson[1]

TLS (Letterpress Books, WP, DLC).
[1] The Low-Wilson exchange was published in the newspapers on November 9, 1915, e.g., the *New York Times*, Nov. 9, 1915.

To John Sharp Williams

My dear Senator: The White House November 8, 1915

I think you know already that there are few men whose opinion on public affairs I value as I do yours, and I am sincerely obliged to you for your full and important letter of October twenty-eighth.[1]

I do not think that we essentially differ in our view of the necessary preparation for national defense. I quite agree with you that an enormous increase of our land forces would be a wasteful mistake, but you may be sure I shall propose nothing of the kind. I feel that the proposals worked out by the War Department at my suggestion are really conservative in character, the chief expense being, not the men, but the materials which would undoubtedly be necessary in case we should ever be called upon to defend the country against a foreign enemy.

I find myself in accord with the principles you lay down and I hope very confidently that we can agree upon the method of realizing them.

I honor your principle of advising before the event and not afterwards.

With warm regard,

Cordially and sincerely yours,   Woodrow Wilson

TLS (J. S. Williams Papers, DLC).
[1] J. S. Williams to WW, Oct. 28, 1915, TLS (WP, DLC). Williams wrote that he had come to the "reluctant conclusion" that a large preparedness program was necessary. However, he went on, the security of the United States demanded a large increase of the navy only. In view of the possibility of an attack by Germany, the United States had to have a navy superior to that of the German Empire because a large army, alone, could never defeat Germany unless the United States controlled the seas. "In my opinion," he concluded, "every dollar deflected from expenditure upon an all-around, adequate and efficient navy and devoted to the increase of land forces would be a dollar as thoroughly wasted as if thrown into the sea—worse wasted, because it would subtract from our real defense." Moreover, Williams added, a large standing army was always a menace to free institutions, whereas civil liberties had never been threatened by an efficient navy.

To Hamilton Fish Armstrong

My dear Mr. Armstrong: [The White House] November 8, 1915

I am very deeply gratified by the thoughtful kindness of the 1915 Board of the Daily Princetonian in sending me a bound copy of the Princetonian for 1878-79. I shall look it through with the greatest interest and shall value it not only because I am delighted to have it but also because it is a token of thoughtful friendship.

I am afraid that I am not a sufficient expert in my own style to be sure which editorials were written by myself. I think, however, that you are right about the little farewell editorial in the last number,[1] the third in No. 16,[2] and the sixth in No. 17.[3]

I am particularly interested to notice that some of the numbers bound belonged to my beloved president, Doctor McCosh.

Cordially and sincerely yours, Woodrow Wilson

TLS (Letterpress Books, WP, DLC).

[1] *The Princetonian*, III (May 1, 1879), 231, printed at that date in Vol. 1.

[2] *The Princetonian*, III (Feb. 27, 1879), 183-84, printed at that date in *ibid.*

[3] *The Princetonian*, III (March 13, 1879), 196-97. It reads as follows: "Sincerely wishing to say nothing prejudicial to the best interests of religion among us, we question the advisability of four college prayer meetings per week. With all respect for those who inaugurated this system, and for those who still approve of it, we think that the effects would be in every way advantageous and satisfactory, if this number were lessened to two. The regular attendants upon these meetings are generally good students, and the serious interruptions which are thus occasioned in their work on three evenings of each week ought not to be overlooked. But even if we leave this out of consideration, there are good grounds for believing that the ends which prayer meetings are supposed to have in view would be better subserved by the change which we have suggested. The profit of a prayer meeting, it is usually said, (and reasonably enough too) is commensurate with its interest; and this interest depends almost entirely upon the number and zeal of those present. But plainly the quality of this zeal may be improved by concentration, and no one can doubt that a lessening of the number of meetings will serve materially to increase the attendance upon each of them. Our proposed change would therefore bid fair to quicken the interest of college prayer meetings. And, to judge from the present state of things, whatever can accomplish that has more than a theoretical value. In the meetings of the separate classes, especially, the exercises are often sadly monotonous. Address, prayer and hymn follow each other with unvarying regularity and a select (and very limited) few are forced, by the absence of their companions, to take an active part in each evening's proceedings until their listeners have come to look upon most of them as utterly 'talked out.' These meetings are certainly doing their minimum of good at present; if their number be decreased they can hardly do less, while we prophesy for them with that alteration a marked increase in efficiency. This is simply a question of 'weariness to the flesh.' "

In the same issue, Wilson wrote another editorial which is printed at March 13, 1879, Vol. 1.

From Thomas Watt Gregory

Dear Mr. President: Washington Nov. 8, 1915.

You can never know how much I appreciate your note of the fourth. I can not express my gratitude & so do not try.

My hope is that I may have & utilize opportunities of showing that I am worthy of such confidence.

Faithfully Yours,   T. W. Gregory

ALS (WP, DLC).

From Edward Mandell House

Dear Governor: New York. November 8th, 1915.

I had a talk with Governor Folk yesterday and with Walsh of Kansas City the day before.

Walsh, as you know, now controls the Kansas City Post which is perhaps the most influential paper in western Missouri since the Star has somewhat lost its influence now that Colonel Nelson is dead.

Walsh tells me that Folk can be elected Governor or Senator as he prefers. He also tells me that he, Walsh, is at your disposal at all times, and that he is eager for an opportunity to serve you.

Folk thinks he can beat Reed if you throw your weight on his side, or he thinks he can be elected Governor if Senator Stone keeps his hands off. For the moment, he believes he could serve the party better by running for Governor because it will probably bring about harmony. If he runs for Senator he fears it will cause a bitter factional fight that might lose Missouri. He thinks Stone and Reed are lined up together, but that they both would like to have him make the race for Governor.

He is to think about the matter for a day or two and then will let me know. He assures me that no matter what his personal preference or judgment might be, he is entirely willing to be governed by your wishes.

I did not quote you in any way, nor did I tell him that we had discussed the matter.   Your affectionate,   E. M. House

TLS (WP, DLC).

To Robert Latham Owen

My dear Senator: [The White House] November 9, 1915

Thank you for your letter of November first reminding me of the very important matter of a Department of Health. To tell the truth, I have been so preoccupied with what may be called the going business of the Government that I have not had time to form a final judgment about an actual cabinet department of health and my present fear is that in the approaching session of Congress there will be so much to do and so much to spend money for that it is hardly likely we could get the matter considered and settled on its merits, but I shall be very happy to discuss it with you again when we all get together and you may be sure that my mind is thoroughly open on the question of how we should fulfill our pledges in this important matter.

Cordially and sincerely yours,   Woodrow Wilson

TLS (Letterpress Books, WP, DLC).

From Henry Rogers Seager and Others[1]

Dear Mr. President: New York City, November Ninth 1915.

Knowing your interest in all measures calculated to promote the safety and welfare of American wage earners, we venture to hope that you will include among the subjects touched upon in your message to Congress the need for a more adequate compensation law for federal employees.

This is no new question. The defects in the present law are universally conceded. It is also generally agreed that the Federal Government should be a model employer, and that its obligation with reference to a just system of compensating the victims of industrial accidents in its service is especially great, because federal employees are not able to have recourse to damage suits against their employer.

Congress has shown its interest in the matter. Last winter the Kern-McGillicuddy Bill, supported by this Association, the American Federation of Labor, and many disinterested students of the question, was reported on favorably by the Judiciary Committee of the House. Pressure of public business prevented it from coming to a vote.

The increasing pressure of public business which prevented legislation last winter is the only serious obstacle in the way of definite action in the coming session. A few sentences in your message, bringing this need to the attention of Congress, would be an invaluable aid to those who wish to promote preparedness, not merely by the necessary military measures, but by providing for the masses of our citizens the legal protections necessary to their highest efficiency, and to the development of that enthusiastic patriotism which you so eloquently voiced in your address before the Manhattan Club the other day.

With highest respect,   Faithfully yours,
Henry R Seager
Royal Meeker
Samuel McCune Lindsay
Paul U. Kellogg
John B. Andrews

TLS (WP, DLC).
1 Seager was Professor of Political Economy at Columbia and president of the American Association for Labor Legislation, one of the most important social justice groups in the United States at this time. Among the other signers of this letter, only John Bertram Andrews, secretary of the association and editor of its organ, *American Labor Legislation Review*, has not been identified earlier in this series.

To Edward Mandell House

Dearest Friend,   The White House. 10 November, 1915.

We had a message from Morgenthau the other day[1] in which he said that the Turkish Secretary of War had sent for him to say that this was the time to move for peace, if we were ever going to move,—before Germany had broken through the Balkans, crushed the Allies at the Dardanelles and got in a position to dictate peace! I have not known just what interpretation to put upon his unusual action. It would look, however, as if it were possible that Germany were getting anxious to have some one say that the fight must stop. The Turk would quite certainly, I take it, not have spoken without the knowledge of his German mentors.

Your letter about Folk and Walsh interests me very much. I confess that I am at a loss just what to advise. Reed can never be counted on. He is false and reactionary and hates this Administration. And yet it is hard to oppose him while Stone, who has been so faithful a friend, is supporting him. What do you think yourself? Shall we let their programme go through, and encourage Folk to run for the governorship?

I am encouraged by what you say of Folk's view of Mr. Bryan's present course of action.[2]

We are all very well, and all very grateful to you for the good time you gave us. Mrs. House and you certainly know how to help and how to make everything delightful. Please give her our warm regards and heartfelt thanks. I need not try to tell you what I think of your constant and generous friendship.

Affectionately Yours,   Woodrow Wilson

WWTLS (E. M. House Papers, CtY).
1 H. Morgenthau to RL, Nov. 3, 1915 (received Nov. 6), T telegram (SDR, RG 59, 763.72119/87, DNA): "In my last interview with the Minister of War he asked me to submit the following to the President: That the moment was opportune for peace negotiations and that just now the Central Powers would agree to more favorable terms for the British than when Servia has been entirely crushed and the Turks have started the Egyptian expedition which is now being prepared. This is sent simply to comply with request of Minister of War."
2 They must have discussed this during their conversation on November 5. Bryan had embarked upon a nationwide campaign against the administration's preparedness program.

From Edward Mandell House, with Enclosure

Dear Governor: New York. November 10th, 1915.

I was told in confidence after I had mailed my letter on the Lapland that she did not go directly to England but went to Canada in order to transport troops, thus delaying her.

I am enclosing you a copy of a cable which came from Sir Edward yesterday in the code we have between us. I also enclose copy of paragraph four of his letter to which he refers fearing lest you may not have it convenient.

With your approval, I shall send him in cypher this answer: "Yes, the proposal contemplated is, broadly speaking, along the lines mentioned in fourth paragraph of your letter to me of September 21st."

It seems to me that we must throw the influence of this nation in behalf of a plan by which international obligations must be kept, and in behalf of some plan by which the peace of the world may be maintained. We should do this not only for the sake of civilization, but for our own welfare, for who may say when we may be involved in such a holocaust as is now devastating Europe.

Must we not be a party to the making of new and more humane rules of warfare, and must we not lend our influence towards the freedom of both the land and sea? This is the part I think you are destined to play in this world tragedy, and it is the noblest part that has ever come to a son of man. This country will follow you along such a path, no matter what the cost may be.   Your affectionate,   E. M. House

TLS (WP, DLC).

E N C L O S U R E

November 9th, 1915.

Split letter received. What is the proposal of the elimination of militarism and navalism that you contemplate? Is it that suggested in fourth paragraph of letter to you of September 22nd?

I am writing more fully in reply.   E. Grey.

Proposed answer to the above cable.

Yes, the proposal contemplated is broadly speaking along the lines mentioned in fourth paragraph of your letter to me of September 22nd.

Paragraph four of Sir Edward Grey's letter of September 22nd.

"To me, the great object of securing the elimination of militarism and navalism is to get security for the future against aggressive war. How much are the United States prepared to do in this direction? Would the President propose that there should be a League of Nations binding themselves to side against any Power which broke a Treaty; which broke certain rules of warfare on sea or land (such rules would of course have to be drawn up after this war); or which refused, in case of dispute, to adopt some other method of settlement than that of war? Only in some such agreement do I see a prospect of diminishing militarism in future, so that no nation will build up armies or navies for aggressive purposes."

T MS (WP, DLC).

To Mary Allen Hulbert

Dearest Friend,   The White House. 10 November, 1915.

You are always fine. I have never seen you do anything in which you did not show it. I appreciate your letter most deeply. It is fine to see the way in which you have entered into the new life and are making a go of it with Allen, and I am so glad, glad to the bottom of my heart, to have been in a position to help a little, though it was nothing more than any friend would have done and involved no sacrifice of any kind.

My thoughts follow you constantly. I have been long in writing only because of the constant pressure of things upon me that would not wait. I wrote about my engagement, however, the moment Mrs. Galt was willing I should announce it to anybody, —as early as I did announce it to anybody. This is just a hasty line, but you may always be sure that you have a sincere and constant friend in   Yours faithfully,   Woodrow Wilson

WWTLS (WP, DLC).

To Edward Mandell House

The White House Nov 11-15

Message approved   you might even omit words broadly speaking and say merely along the lines of   Woodrow Wilson.

T telegram (E. M. House Papers, CtY).

From Robert Lansing, with Enclosure

PERSONAL AND PRIVATE:

My dear Mr. President: Washington November 11, 1915.

I send you herewith a revise of the four propositions to form a basis of a Pan American Convention. I have drafted these after consultation with Ambassador Naón who is heartily in favor of the plan as you know, and who understands the objections which have been raised by the Chilean Ambassador in particular to the original form.

Article II, you will see, I have greatly abbreviated because if the time for settlement is eliminated it would be better for the negotiations in my opinion to take this shorter form and not enter into such details as the constitution of the arbitral tribunal whish [which] is to settle the disputes.

You will observe that I have added a new article (Article IV) in place of the one which covered the control of the manufacture and sale of arms and ammunition. In order to prevent hostile action between neighbors it is necessary, I think, to bind the parties not to assist insurgents or revolutionists in the country. Such aid is a source of constant irritation in Central American countries and as you know it is one of the causes of disorder in Haiti and the Dominican Republic. I think, too, it is not unusual in South America. I believe that the article would be received with general approval and I cannot conceive of any serious objection to it.

If these articles, as revised, meet with your approval I will at once take the matter up with Ambassador Suárez with the hope that I can secure his adhesion and willingness to make a favorable report to his Government.

Faithfully yours,   Robert Lansing.

TLS (R. Lansing Papers, DLC).

ENCLOSURE

ARTICLE I.

That the high contracting parties to this solemn covenant and agreement hereby join one another in a common and mutual guarantee of territorial integrity and of political independence under republican forms of government.

ARTICLE II.

To give definitive application to the guarantee set forth in

Article I, the high contracting parties severally covenant to endeavor forthwith to reach a settlement of all disputes as to boundaries or territory now pending between them by amicable agreement or by means of international arbitration.

ARTICLE III.

That the high contracting parties further agree, First, that all questions, of whatever character, arising between any two or more of them which cannot be settled by the ordinary means of diplomatic correspondence shall, before any declaration of war or beginning of hostilities, be first submitted to a permanent international commission for investigation, one year being allowed for such investigation; and, Second, that, if the dispute is not settled by investigation, to submit the same to arbitration, provided the question in dispute does not affect the honour, independence, or vital interests of the nations concerned or the interests of third parties.

ARTICLE IV.

To the end that domestic tranquility may prevail within their territories the high contracting parties further severally covenant and agree that they will not permit the departure from their respective jurisdictions of any military or naval expedition hostile to the established government of any of the high contracting parties, and that they will prevent the exportation from their respective jurisdictions of arms, ammunition or other munitions of war destined to or for the use of any person or persons notified to be in insurrection or revolt against the established government of any of the high contracting parties.

Handed copy to Chilean Amb. Thurs. Nov. 18/15
Mailed copy to Brazilian Amb.   ”   ”   ”   ”

CC MS (R. Lansing Papers, DLC).

From Robert Lansing, with Enclosure

PERSONAL AND PRIVATE:

My dear Mr. President: [Washington] November 11, 1915.

I submit for your consideration a proposed formula in the LUSITANIA case which, if it meets with your approval, I will discuss orally with the German Ambassador.

You will observe that I have not used the word "disavow" in the formula as I am convinced that the German Government will not be willing to use the word in view of the great dissatisfaction expressed in regard to its use in the settlement of the ARABIC case. I believe, however, that the last paragraph of the formula may be interpreted as a disavowal and if we can obtain the assent of the German Government to that paragraph it will be interpreted generally as a formal disavowal.

I would like your views in this matter at your earliest convenience as I wish to renew my conversations with the Ambassador as soon as possible.

Faithfully yours,   Robert Lansing

CCL (SDR, RG 59, 763.72/2269B, DNA).

E N C L O S U R E

November 11, 1915.

The sinking of the British Steamship LUSITANIA was in pursuance of a policy of retaliation against the enemies of Germany.

Retaliatory measures by a belligerent against an enemy are essentially acts in contravention of the recognized rules of warfare.

Citizens of the United States on the LUSITANIA were justified in the belief that the recognized rules of warfare would be applied in the event that the steamship was intercepted by a German war vessel.

The sinking of the LUSITANIA being in violation of the international rules of naval warfare the act was illegal and so far as the lives of citizens of the United States are concerned imposed upon the German Government liability therefor.

The German Government, having in its instructions to its naval officers issued subsequent to the event shown its recognition that the sinking of the LUSITANIA was contrary to the rules of naval warfare and to the principles of humanity, expresses profound regret that citizens of the United States suffered by reason of the act of its naval authorities in sinking the LUSITANIA, declares it to have been in contravention of international law, and offers to make reparation for the lives of citizens of the United States which were lost, by the payment of a suitable indemnity.

CC MS (SDR, RG 59, 763.72/2269 B, DNA).

Two Letters from Edward Mandell House

Dear Governor: New York. November 11th, 1915.

The Morganthau message is interesting. Anything coming from a Turkish Cabinet official is under the suspicion of being dictated by Germany, and I take it, we may so regard it.

I do not know how closely Bernstorff is in touch with his government. In some things he seems to be well informed. He was in for a moment this morning and he said that his government had heard that Villard was being thought of to replace Gerard. He wanted you to know that they did not consider the suggestion favorably, not that they care particularly for Gerard whom he said they regard as being "fussy" and as having gotten them in wrong in the Lusitania incident.

It seems that the suggestion as to certain ships being immune from submarine attacks was Gerard's, and that he persuaded them to let him cable it home as their offer. I am merely mentioning this in order to explain a feeling I have that when the Germans are really ready for peace, we will get a hint in some way, from Bernstorff. I gave him an opportunity this morning, but he did not rise to it.

I do not believe that much can be done at the moment, or that the time is propitious for more than an understanding that is being arrived at through Sir Edward. If we can get that end of it properly buttoned up we can afford to wait until they consider the time opportune.

If next year were not a Presidential one, I would be in favor of going vigorously after Reed, but under the circumstances, I believe it would be wise to let him win by default. Folk said if he were Governor, he would undertake to measurably keep Reed straight by building a back fire which he could not resist. He thinks of Reed very much as we do, but he believes that he has committed himself so deeply to you that if he, Folk, were Governor, he could be held to his commitments.

I will write you when Folk comes again which will be in a few days.   Your affectionate,   E. M. House

TLS (WP, DLC).

Dear Governor: New York. November 11th, 1915.

In a letter received from Sir Horace Plunkett he says:

["]I am going to send my respectful felicitations to the President with a little Irish contribution to his library. I shall beg him not to reply if my letter reaches him, and as I shall have left before I could get his reply he may well be saved the trouble."

I have a letter from Winslow of the Berlin Embassy and among other things he says:

"I hope you may hear something interesting from the Judge[1] very soon. By what channel I am not certain and just what it is I am not certain. This is a little indefinite, but it cannot be helped."

This in connection with your message from Morganthau, is somewhat significant.   Your affectionate, E. M. House

TLS (WP, DLC).
[1] That is, Gerard.

To Edward Mandell House

Dearest Friend,   The White House. 12 November, 1915.

I am sure that you understood the telegram I sent you about your message to Grey. I think the paragraph quoted from his letter of September twenty-second contains the *necessary* programme.

I note with a great deal of interest the message from Winslow of the Berlin Embassy. I do not see the service of a vague message like that but it at least fits in conjecturally with the message from Morgenthau, as you say.

Sir Horace is very kind and friendly, and I shall await with real interest the receipt of his "little Irish contribution" to my library.

You are right about the Folk-Reed business, though it goes hard to travel that road and make believe a man is your friend when you know he is not!

Where in the world can they have got the idea in Berlin that we meant to send Villard there instead of Gerard? Of course he would not do.

What you tell me about Gerard's having originated the idea of certain immune liners is extremely interesting and fully confirms my estimate of "Jimmie."!

We are all well and are awaiting with great anxiety the real facts about the ANCONA.[1] It looks like beginning at the bigining [beginning] with Austria. I wonder if they have not noticed at Vienna what was going on in the rest of the world?
                    Affectionately Yours,   Woodrow Wilson

WWTLS (E. M. House Papers, CtY).
[1] The Italian liner *Ancona*, 8,210 tons, bound from Naples to New York, was sunk with heavy loss of life in the northwestern part of the Sicilian Channel by the German submarine *U38* on November 7, 1915. As the submarine was flying the Austrian flag, the Austro-Hungarian government subsequently assumed full responsibility. See Link, *Confusions and Crises*, pp. 62-72.

To Newton Diehl Baker

Personal.

My dear Mr. Baker: [The White House] November 12, 1915

Thank you sincerely for your interesting letter of November fourth.[1] I had already had a talk with Senator Pomerene who had given me substantially the same analysis and assessment of the results of the recent elections in Ohio, and it is very interesting to have the thing so clearly set out.

It cheers me very much that you should have such a view of the significance of the result as a whole. Personally, I am very sorry to see you retiring from public life. Your services have certainly been very notable and distinguished. I congratulate you on a most unusual record. I think the whole country has learned to admire and trust you. No doubt your instinct about getting an outside view again is a correct one, but I hope that after you have got it you will come into the ranks again.

In haste, with warm regard,
          Cordially and sincerely yours,   Woodrow Wilson

TLS (Letterpress Books, WP, DLC).
[1] It is missing.

From Robert Lansing, with Enclosure

PERSONAL AND CONFIDENTIAL:

My dear Mr. President: [Washington] November 12, 1915.

I enclose a letter which I have just received from Mr. Gerard and in which I thought you would be interested. You will observe from its contents that it is of a most confidential nature, and I would be obliged if you would return it to me after reading.
          Faithfully yours,   Robert Lansing

CCL (SDR, RG 59, 763.72/2272½, DNA).

ENCLOSURE

James Watson Gerard to Robert Lansing

My dear Mr. Secretary: [Berlin] Oct. 25 [1915]

I was wrongly informed about Dumba—he was *not* ennobled.

I had a long interview (over one hour) today with the Kaiser alone. I am supposed by rule here not to inform anyone of what he said—otherwise he will not receive me again or talk confidentially. The audience took place at Potsdam—had a special car going down & Royal carriage at station. Several ministers went down also to present their letters of credence.

An article yesterday in Socialist paper "Vorwaerts" is rather bitter about a new news service organized by the Government with the avowed purpose of influenci[ng] elections *after* the war. The Vorwaerts complains that this is a violation of the "truce" between Socialists & Gov't for the period of the war.

Much rejoicing quietly over the Balkan situation—I think they have the King of Greece solidly on their side—here.

Having much trouble now to get British prisoners *clothed* in German camps. It is a delicate matter to handle. Visited one camp myself & had all prisoners about 1800 lined up with all the clothes & blankets they possessed for my inspection.

A Prince Münster[1] told me the Servians are to be exterminated —no prisoners—he is in the staff of a General operating in that vicinity.

Disturbances at Chemnitz[2] continue—stringent measures taken & military on guard. There seems more objection to high prices than to being killed in the war.

The Germans are very bitter against our Embassy in Petrograd. Also at the loan in America—& especially at the attendant banquets to the loan commissioners. Must say these banquets are not very neutral.

I hope we are getting ready for defence. If these people win we are next on the list—in some part of South or Central America which is the same thing.   Yours   J.W.G.

ALS (SDR, RG 59, 763.72/2272½, DNA).
    [1] Alexander Fürst zu Münster von Derneburg.
    [2] That is, the food riots in late October 1915, during which several municipal foodshops were wrecked. They were among the first in a series of widespread disturbances in late 1915 and 1916 caused by the growing shortage and the increasing prices of basic foodstuffs.

From Stephen Samuel Wise

My dear Mr. President: New York Nov. 12, 1915

From time to time during the last two years, it has been my privilege to write to you in order to express my agreement with the things you have said and done. I therefore regard it as my duty to tell you how deeply I deplore the necessity under which you have found yourself of accepting and advocating a preparedness program. Up to the last moment I had hoped that against the preparedness campaign you might throw the weight not only of your great office but of your equally great hold upon the respect of the whole people. I had felt, as had many others among your friends, that, if you had found it possible to stand out, the people, who have learned to trust your wise and just judgment, would have been ready to follow your leadership as they have done since the beginning of the war.

It is occasion for profound regret to some of us in any event that you have seen fit at this time to urge that so-called defensive preparedness, which at other times and in other hands than your own is not unlikely to be used in the interests of aggression. You will pardon my pointing out that your program, moderate though you believe it to be, will not and of necessity cannot satisfy those advocates of military preparedness who will for a time purport to assent thereto and withal soon demand more effective and thorough-going preparedness measures.

I should not, my dear Mr. President, have written in this way nor would I burden you with my thought on this question if I did not feel in conscience bound to dissent in pulpit and on platform from your position. I regret this not only on personal grounds but because I believe that issues of deepest moment are at stake touching which you will not expect that even the most revering of friends should remain silent.

I am, with deep respect,

Faithfully yours,   Stephen S. Wise

TLS (WP, DLC).

Two Memoranda by Louis Paul Lochner[1]

[Washington] November 12, 1915. 10:30 A.M.

Dr. Jordan presented the resolutions formally, and said that he would not take the time to read or discuss them in detail, as the President was no doubt already familiar with them. To this the President replied affirmatively.

Dr. Jordan also stated that he would make no statement to the press as to how the President seemed to receive the ideas advanced, but that he would leave it to Mr. Wilson to make any statements he saw fit.

Then Dr. Jordan presented the case for continuous mediation, laying stress upon the unofficial sources of information which we have. He described how he himself had knocked about in

[1] Secretary of the Chicago Peace Society, director for the Central West of the American Peace Society, and secretary of the National Peace Federation. The following document is a record of a meeting at the White House on November 12 between Wilson and David Starr Jordan and L. P. Lochner, representing the American Peace Society.

Europe and thus had many friends who now keep writing him; how Jane Addams and her co-workers had amassed a lot of information. (Here in response to inquiry Mr. Wilson said he had read the confidential statement of the envoys as to what each foreign minister, etc., had said); how Lochner had had an opportunity to get in touch with things; how the Dutch group was working (here the statement of the December Conference at Berne[2] was handed to Mr. Wilson, who carefully scanned the names of the men and women identified with the movement.)

During most of this time the President kept wiping his glasses with his handkerchief, never taking his eyes, however, off Dr. Jordan.

Dr. Jordan concluded by saying, "You no doubt know a great deal more than we do about the situation, but our information is from a different angle." He assured the President that the European neutrals were ready and anxious to call the conference, and that they would probably do it even if he refused to come in on it, but that that would be a great misfortune, as the voice of our great democracy might be added as that of the most influential neutral. He admitted that any plan had defects; that there were in any case great obstacles to overcome; but that in his estimation some such form of mediation was the only solution short of the annihilation of Europe. He also suggested Sweden as a possible country to initiate the conference.

The President replied: "I have been revolving this proposal in my mind dozens of times. I wish I might see my way clear to it. But there are these objections: (1) The neutrals in Europe in several cases have governments out of sympathy with their peoples; (2) one side (the Allies) might object to mediation as a partisan measure; (3) that therefore America might be out-voted by the other neutrals, and more harm than good be done."

To this we replied: (1) The United States would, because of its influence, naturally dominate in the selection of the commissioners to such a conference. Our Minister Egan in Copenhagen, for instance, might well invite Wallenberg of Sweden and Loudon

[2] A conference called by the Central Organization for a Durable Peace, a group of peace workers from both belligerent and neutral countries, which had been formed at The Hague in April 1915. The Central Organization planned a conference at Bern from December 14 to 18, 1915, to study and determine the bases for a permanent peace. As a foundation for discussion, the organization presented a "minimum program" which included provisions for the abolition of secret treaties; popular control of foreign policy; reduction of armaments; freedom of the seas; and guarantees of religious freedom and equality. It suggested, moreover, the establishment of an international association based on The Hague conferences, with a court of justice and a council of investigation and conciliation to which nations would submit their disputes. The papers and reports presented at the conference were published in *Organization Centrale pour une Paix durable, Recueil de Rapports, sur les différents Points du Programme-minimum*, 4 vols. (The Hague, 1916-18).

of Holland to a conference, broach the subject to them, and outline the types of persons wanted for such a conference,—men of
international horizon." As for mediation being a partisan measure, we reminded him that the conference would begin on a
higher plane than temporary military advantage. Lochner also
added that the President's administration was marked because
of *unconventional* things done,—reading the message in person to
Congress, inviting Latin-American cooperation in Mexico, etc.,
—and that the peoples of Europe were looking to this free republic to lead them out of darkness. Lochner described how the
Belgians in Holland were all the time asking whether Mr. Wilson
would not soon act. All this seemed visibly to impress the President, and he repeatedly nodded pensively.

Dr. Jordan next emphasized that the struggling liberal groups
within the warring countries would rally to the support of such a
conference; that these groups included some of the best minds in
Europe.

Lochner then brought up the confidential statement of Del-
bruck, Dernburg, and other men close to the Kaiser, showing that
these were against the annexation of Belgium. He also stated
that in his opinion the liberal factions in the warring countries
had as yet nothing as an objective towards which to direct their
governments; once such a conference were in session, they could
keep knocking at the doors of their governments and demand
that the solutions of such a conference be given a respectful
hearing. The President seemed to fear that this and similar
groups might only support the neutral conference if its program
accorded with their wishes. But we insisted that these were
honest men who would support any rational program, and that,
besides, a year of war had mellowed them all considerably.

Dr. Jordan also emphasized letters he was all the time receiving from people abroad who were tired of the war, especially
one from a German army officer, from which he quoted. This
gave Lochner a chance to describe from personal experience how
terrible were the tales related of last winter's campaign, how the
frozen legs and arms that simply broke off as the nurses touched
the poor soldiers seemed more dreadful even than shot and shell,
(here the President winced visibly), and he went on to state that
in his belief, the approach of the Christmas season, with all that
that implied, and the approach of the winter, with its horrors,
were two valid reasons for acting now.

Dr. Jordan further endorsed the idea of Christmas and spoke
of the intense religious fervor obtaining abroad which ought to
be led into constructive channels.

The Christmas idea—of trying to mediate between now and

then—seemed to appeal to the President. He nodded gravely repeatedly.

Lochner then added that further arguments were the threat of revolutions at home (and revolutions, he said, were a destructive thing; it would be a pity not to utilize the idealism that was so abundant in each country for constructive things); the inexorability of time and the pressure of economic necessity. He also illustrated from a Canadian friend of his, how the sufferings of the warring peoples made them understand how their enemies must be suffering.

Dr. Jordan next emphasized that it would be a pity if Sweden and Holland should go ahead without us, for then we Americans should lay ourselves open to the charge that we were getting rich at Europe's expense (even though it was only a few who were getting rich—here the President interrupted, "Only a few"); and that we had an interest in seeing the war continued. This again appeared to affect the President visibly. He said, "Yes, of course, by merely keeping out of the war we are getting relatively richer." This was, however, not said in a tone as though he approved of it.

The President who, it appeared absolutely clearly to us, has no alternative plan, next said that of course this whole matter might be easier if the press in the belligerent countries did not so misrepresent things. To which Dr. Jordan replied that the press would *have* to report at least the *fact* of such a conference meeting. "And probably its recommendations," the President added.

Lochner then illustrated from his experience how in Germany, despite the rigors of censorship, news keeps leaking out. He spoke of his address before the Bund Neues Vaterland,[3] and of the heroism of the people composing it. He added that he did not doubt for a moment but that editors in the belligerent countries would print the news even at the risk of their lives; that they would perhaps print the news and take their chances on what might happen afterward.

This led us again to speak of the idealism released in the warring countries that could be led into constructive channels. Again and again Dr. Jordan emphasized that he was now *sure* that only by some action by the neutrals could a tolerable solution be found. He said he was an unwilling convert to the idea, but now firmly believed in it.

Lochner then spoke of how Dr. Van Hise, too, had slowly come to see the idea of continuous mediation, but how, once his power-

---

[3] About this organization, see J. W. Gerard to RL, July 13, 1915, n. 6, printed as an Enclosure with WW to RL, July 31, 1915, Vol. 34.

ful mind was applied to it, he saw many possibilities. We spoke of how President Van Hise came home time and again from his strike arbitration in the railroad difficulties, utterly discouraged, but how finally the application of scientific truth solved the tangle. Lochner emphasized that in this situation, too, scientific truth would ultimately prevail. Dr. Jordan interjected that Van Hise was just the sort of type of mind necessary in this situation. The phrases about scientific application to the problem seemed to catch the President's imagination. Dr. Jordan also stated that the conference should consist of men, not of diplomatic or governmental power, but of scientific power.

The President then declared that the Cabinet meeting was approaching, and that he must now go. Dr. Jordan said that any of us—Miss Addams and the rest—were ready at any time to cooperate with the President in any manner he saw fit. The President then rose. He seized Dr. Jordan's hand quite firmly and said, "I assure you gentlemen that you have done me real good." He turned to Lochner, and looked him straight in the eyes as he shook hands. This encouraged Lochner to say, "Then I may take a message with me that you will act?"

To this the President would not commit himself. "No, that is for me to say when the right moment, in my judgment, arrives."

"At least you will not refuse, should Sweden or Holland or some other neutral country invite you," was Dr. Jordan's parting comment, at which suggestion the President merely smiled.

Lochner's parting comment was, "Only yesterday we met a man who has lived in Argentina for eighteen years, who says that your invitation to the A.B.C. to cooperate in Mexico has promoted a profound feeling of confidence in us. The European neutrals (and the belligerents as well) who now think we are hoping for selfish reasons that the war may continue, will feel similarly reassured of our intentions if we cooperate with them in this situation."

Thereupon the President once more shook hands with Dr. Jordan.

T MS (L. P. Lochner Papers, WHi).

Strictly private and confidential—by L.P.L.   [Washington,
Additional data regarding our interview.   Nov. 12, 1915]

It was very evident to me that Pres. Wilson has no plan outside of a fight to the finish, and secondly, that he is afraid of what England, which he evidently regards as fighting the battle of democracy, may say to the proposal.

Further, it seemed to me that he was decidedly interested in our presentation, and that there seemed to be more of a deferential attitude and a willingness to listen than seemed to be characteristic of his interview with Miss Addams or of previous interviews that Dr. Jordan has had.

Dr. Jordan said afterward: "I have known the President for 25 years, and never have I seen him so human, so deferential, and so ready to listen. Usually he was difficult to talk to, and rather haughty."

All this I interpret to mean that the President may yet be won, but to do so, we must organize the Nov. 8th demonstration[1] many times over.

My feeling also is that, if a European neutral were to invite the U. S., Wilson would hardly dare to refuse to come in, especially if we—the democracy—should happen to know about this move of a European neutral and should organize to bring pressure to bear on the White House.

The President's Lone Game.

The two days in Washington have further convinced me that the President is playing a lone hand, and that nobody really knows (unless it be Mr. Lansing, who is inscrutable) what the President has in mind. Indeed, Mr. Lane seemed very anxious to find out from us what the President thought; he said, "I have not talked about this matter to the President for months," a most amazing statement from a member of Cabinet. Also, Joseph E. Davies, chairman of the Federal Trade Commission and one of the President's close political advisers, said that the President had not chosen to speak to him about the European matter. Mr. Bryan was exceedingly anxious to know what hope there is of the Administration's taking some action. I believe the thing to do is to keep pounding away at the doors of the White House—if in no other manner, than by continued demonstrations.

Hw MS (L. P. Lochner Papers, WHi).

[1] Lochner referred to nationwide demonstrations called by the National Peace Federation to adopt resolutions urging Wilson to call a conference of neutral nations to act as a voluntary court of continuous mediation, to flood the White House with telegrams to that end, and to publicize the manifesto issued on October 15 by Jane Addams and other envoys of the International Congress of Women at The Hague to the governments of Europe and the United States. See L. P. Lochner to "Dear Madam" Oct. 29, 1915, TL, with printed enclosures (Woman's Peace Party Papers, PSC-P).

To Robert Lansing

My dear Mr. Secretary,   The White House. 13 Nov. 1915

Thank you for letting me see this letter of Gerard's. It's astonishing how little he can put into his communications. He seems always *about* to say something. But there is at least an intimation or two in this of what he *might* have said.

Faithfully Yours,   Woodrow Wilson

ALS (SDR, RG 59, 763.72/2273½, DNA).

From Robert Latham Owen

My dear Mr. President: [Washington] Nov. 13, 1915.

In advising the country on preparedness, it occurs to me that you might promote international peace by calling the attention of the country to this thought:

That the best way to keep the country out of war is to improve the structure of government and thereby minimize the frailty of human leadership.

If the people of Europe had had an opportunity through a referendum vote to determine whether they would make war on each other, I am very sure Europe would be at peace. But under a structure of government where a small group of men are charged with governing, or believe themselves charged with governing, instead of being the instrumentalities through which the people govern themselves, they may easily be led into ordering mobilization and entering upon war out of mere apprehension of danger from their neighbors.

If the American Republics are governed on the principle that the sovereignty is vested in the people, and that the leaders of the people are merely instrumentalities through which the people govern themselves, this conception would go far to stabilize and make effective the forces working for peace on the American continent.

I believe that you could put to work forces which would establish within the next year working agreements between the Governments of North and South America, stipulating, first, that no Nation, under any circumstances, should invade the territory of another Nation; second, that a violation of this pact will be regarded as an act of war against the other members to the agreement, to be punished by the immediate cutting off of commercial relations, imports and exports, and that such Nation might be coerced by the military and naval forces of the Nations, parties to this agreement, until the forces of the offending Na-

tion should retire within its own orders; that permitting the violation of the Monroe Doctrine within its borders by any one of the
Nations, party to the pact, would thereby automatically exclude
such Nation from the pact.

All I meant to suggest at this time was that in your message
you emphasize the importance of our structure of government,
whereby its officers are merely instrumentalities through which
the people govern themselves; that this principle is the best safeguard of contentment at home, and the best means of protecting
the Nation against hostility or rash action, and of establishing
peace throughout the world.   Respectfully,   R. L. Owen

TLS (WP, DLC).

A Memorandum by Robert Lansing

MEMORANDUM OF CONVERSATION WITH DANISH MINISTER.

[Washington] November 15, 1915.

The Danish Minister[1] called this morning to say that he had
received from his Government another dispatch in regard to the
suggested sale to the United States of the Danish West Indies. He
said that he was under a considerable embarrassment about a
question which his Government had asked but which he
had hesitated to present to me. It was this: Whether he thought
that in case the Danish Government did not agree to a sale of the
Islands whether the United States would feel it necessary to take
possession of them.

I told the Minister that while I had not had in mind such action at the present time, as I had hoped that some form of negotiations would result in the transfer of the sovereignty of the
Islands to this Government, that I could conceive of circumstances which would compel such an act on our part. He asked
me what those circumstances were, and I replied that the possible consequence of absorption of Denmark by a great power
would create a situation which it would be difficult to meet other
than by occupation of the Islands, and such action would undoubtedly cause serious consequences.

The other circumstance was that if Denmark voluntarily, or
under coercion, transferred title to the Danish West Indies to
another European power, which would seek to convert them into
a naval base.

He said that he appreciated our position and would communicate with his Government. I urged him to lay before his Government the possibility of preserving by special privilege all the

commercial opportunities which the ownership of the Islands
gave to Denmark, even if the sovereignty was ceded to the United
States and that I was convinced that such transfer would be
acceptable to this Government.   Robert Lansing.

TS memorandum (SDR, RG 59, 711.5914/47½, DNA).
  1 Constantin Brün.

To Edith Bolling Galt, with Enclosures

[The White House] 15 Nov. [1915]
Here is something interesting   W.

ALI (WP, DLC).

E N L O S U R E   I

Peking, China, November 9, 1915.
STRICTLY CONFIDENTIAL. In the most absolute confidence I
have been informed that Yuan and his three chief counsellors
are at present considering the possibility of checkmating the
Japanese onset through a declaration of war against Germany.
They believe that by this stroke they would force Japan either
to act in good faith as an ally and to desist from interference
in China or to declare herself openly as an enemy and side with
Germany. Doctor Morrison[1] has prepared a memorandum urging
this policy. The Chinese Government will take the action only
upon assurance from Great Britain, Russia, and France that
Japan will not be allowed to use the alliance as a means to interfere in China. I am informed that the Russian and French
Ministers[2] have already reported this possibility to their governments while the British Minister[3] is still formally holding back
on account of consideration for the Japanese alliance.
Reinsch.

  1 George Ernest Morrison, M.D., London *Times* correspondent in China from
1897 to 1912 and political adviser to Yuan Shih-k'ai.
  2 Basil N. Kroupensky and A. R. Conty.
  3 Sir John Newell Jordan.

E N C L O S U R E   I I

Peking, China, November 9, 1915.
STRICTLY CONFIDENTIAL. Referring my cable of November 1,
9:00 p.m.
On November fifth Japanese Chargé d'Affaires[1] called on the

Minister for Foreign Affairs[2] and asked for an elucidation of China's reply stating that the question of monarchy was a matter affecting the peace of the Far East and therefore that the Japanese Government is entitled to know whether or not the movement was to be carried out. A misunderstanding might have regrettable consequences. The Minister for Foreign Affairs replied evasively that the elections in progress could not be stopped but would also not be accelerated.

It is plain that the President finds himself in the dilemma of either losing authority at home through obeying Japanese advice or giving a pretext for outside interference by disregarding it.

To-day I was informed by a member of the Foreign Office that Baron Ishi[i] had personally suggested to Chinese Minister at Tokyo[3] that a delay in proclaiming monarchy was highly desirable: the British and Russian Ambassadors gave similar advice. The Chinese Government has answered Tokyo that the monarchical restoration is not to be consummated in the course of this year.

Chinese Government is informed that seven Japanese naval vessels have been despatched to different points along China's coast.

It is reported to-day that an engagement has taken place north of Jehol in which large bodies of the well armed Mongols defeated the Chinese troops. Five train loads reenforcements went forward from Peking to-day.   Reinsch.

1 Obata Torikichi.
2 Lu Cheng-hsiang.
3 Lu Tsung-yü.

ENCLOSURE III

Peking. November 13, 1915.

Strictly confidential. The matter reported in my November 9, 11 p.m. is still under consideration. It is unlikely that China would obtain any special assurances but if received as an ally would have to rely on the solidarity of the allies for her security. It is reported that Great Britain while still disinclined to take the initiative is beginning to follow the trail and that France and Russia are favorably disposed.

The shifting of power in the Far East which a long continuance of the war would inevitably bring about is a matter of deep concern to the European representatives here who consider that in such event great perils would arise to Europe and America. It appears not unlikely that the American Government may be sounded as to its attitude on the alternative eventualities in the Far Eastern situation. Reinsch.

T telegrams (WP, DLC).

To Robert Latham Owen

My dear Senator: [The White House] November 15, 1915

I have read your letter of November thirteenth with the greatest interest and most thorough agreement and thank you for it very sincerely. In writing my message I shall certainly try to find a way, if a natural one can be found, to bring in an intimation of the kind you suggest.

Cordially and sincerely yours, Woodrow Wilson

TLS (Letterpress Books, WP, DLC).

To Royal Meeker

My dear Meeker: The White House November 16, 1915

Thank you for your letter of November fifteenth enclosing a memorandum[1] setting forth the difficulties as they have disclosed themselves in the present federal workmen's compensation laws. I shall be very much interested to read the memorandum very carefully.

Cordially and sincerely yours, Woodrow Wilson

TLS (WP, DLC).

[1] R. Meeker to WW, Nov. 15, 1915, TLS (WP, DLC), enclosing "MEMORANDUM IN RE FEDERAL WORKMEN'S COMPENSATION LAWS," Nov. 15, 1915, TS MS (WP, DLC). Meeker reviewed the four distinct compensation laws which covered only one fourth of all federal employees—in the life saving service, the railway mail service, the Panama Canal Zone, and a limited number of hazardous jobs such as construction work at arsenals and navy yards. None of these laws offered adequate coverage; sums prescribed to compensate for serious injuries were very low; waiting periods of fifteen days before eligibility for compensation began caused serious hardship to most workers; and insufficient funds often delayed payments. Meeker proposed that all federal employees be included in one compensation plan with a special fund from which all claims could be paid.

Meeker had requested an interview with Wilson to present this information, but Wilson requested a memorandum to which he could refer again and again. See R. Meeker to WW, Nov. 11, 1915, TLS; WW to JPT, c. Nov. 11, 1915, TL; and JPT to R. Meeker, Nov. 12, 1915, TLS; all in WP, DLC.

To Charlotte Everett Wise Hopkins

My dear Mrs. Hopkins: [The White House] November 16, 1915

Thank you for your letter of November fourteenth.[1] I need not assure you that my interest in the plan for an Ellen Wilson

Memorial Building, to be constructed in pursuance of the plans which Mrs. Wilson had so much at heart with regard to the redemption of the slums of this city, has my deepest and my continuing approval and support, and I hope that you will feel free to call upon me for any sort of assistance in the matter which you may think I can render. I have been very much touched by the evidence of the continued interest in the work and by the association of her name with it.

Cordially and sincerely yours,   Woodrow Wilson

TLS (Letterpress Books, WP, DLC).
[1] Charlotte E. W. Hopkins to WW, Nov. 14, 1915, ALS (WP, DLC). Mrs. Hopkins had reminded Wilson of his promise to write a letter about the Ellen Wilson Memorial Homes which she could use in her efforts to raise money for the project.

From Helen Adams Keller[1]

Wrentham, Mass., November 16, 1915.

Your excellency: I believe that Joseph Hillstrom has not had a fair trial and the sentence passed upon him is unjust.[2] I appeal to you as official father of all the people to use your great power and influence to save one of the nation's helpless sons, the stay of execution will give time to investigate   new trial will give the man justice to which the laws of the land entitle him.

Helen Keller.

T telegram (WP, DLC).
[1] Author and lecturer, famous for educating herself despite her total blindness and deafness. She had joined the Socialist party and supported the Industrial Workers of the World.
[2] The Utah Board of Pardons had terminated the respite given Hillstrom, and the court had resentenced him to be shot on November 19.

From Samuel Gompers

San Francisco, California, November 16, 1915.

The Convention of the American Federation of Labor assembled here unanimously adopted the subjoined preambles and resolutions:

"To the Officers and Delegates of the Thirty Fifth Annual Convention of the American Federation of Labor: We, your Committee on Ways and Means, to whom were referred the appeal affecting Joseph Hillstrom, report as follows: That we have examined this case as thoroughly as time would permit and have listened to lengthy statements from persons who claim to be conversant with the facts and we beg leave to offer the following resolution for immediate consideration and action:

"WHEREAS Joseph Hillstrom, a workingman of the State of Utah, and active in the cause of labor, has been sentenced to death by shotting by a Utah court and the date of his execution has been fixed for the nineteenth day of November, nineteen fifteen, and

WHEREAS the circumstances surrounding the said conviction and sentence are such as to make the grounds for this conviction and sentence appear to be utterly inadequate and matters of the gravest doubt in that the evidence was of a purely circumstantial nature and highly improbable and rights of the said Joseph Hillstrom do not appear to have been sufficiently or at all safeguarded, but on the contrary seem to have been violated to such an extent that the said Joseph Hillstrom did not have a fair and impartial trial and

WHEREAS the feeling against the said Joseph Hillstrom as a labor agitator was such as to have militated against him with the jury greatly to his detriment and

WHEREAS we are of the opinion that the said Joseph Hillstrom did not have a fair and impartial trial, therefore be it

RESOLVED by the Thirty Fifth Annual Convention of the American Federation of Labor that we urge the governor of the State of Utah to exercise his prerogative of clemency in this case and to stop the execution of the said Joseph Hillstrom and that he be given a new and fair trial and be it further

RESOLVED that the President of the American Federation of Labor is hereby authorized to forward at once copies of these resolutions to the governor of Utah[,] to the Board of Pardons of the State of Utah, to the Swedish Ambassador and to the President of the United States and that they be published in the American Federationist and in the official publications of the affiliated unions."

May I not prevail upon you to exercise your great influence to at least help in saving the life of Joseph Hillstrom, particularly when there is so much doubt concerning his case.

Samuel Gompers, President,
American Federation of Labor.

T telegram (WP, DLC).

Two Letters to Robert Lansing

My dear Mr. Secretary,   The White House. 17 November, 1915.

I think this, on the whole, the most satisfactory formulation of this important matter that we can hope to get adopted by all the parties, and I hope that you will find the way opening promptly to the acquiescence of Chili and Brazil, as well as Argentina.   Cordially and faithfully,   W.W.

WWTLI (R. Lansing Papers, DLC).

My dear Mr. Secretary, The White House. 17 November, 1915.

I believe that neither you nor I are satisfied with this formula,[1] but I think that it is probably the best that can be drawn, and I hope that you will press it upon the German Imperial Government. I have kept it in the hope that I could suggest something more satisfactory, but I have not been able to formulate anything that pleased me at all.

Faithfully Yours,   W.W.

WWTLI (SDR, RG 59, 763.72/2269½, DNA).
  [1] The Enclosure printed with RL to WW, Nov. 11, 1915 (second letter of that date).

To Edith Bolling Galt, with Enclosures

[The White House] 17 Nov. [1915]

This is the first we have heard from Austria. You will see from Lansing's message to Penfield that he regards it as "important if true" and suspects it *may* have been a *German* submarine, rather than an Austrian. W.

ALI (WP, DLC).

E N L O S U R E   I

Vienna via Berne Nov. 16, 1915.

From Vienna: "986, November sixteenth. For Department's information. Following is summary official announcement appearing in local press November fourteenth relative sinking Italian steamer ANCONA: 'Submarine fired warning shot across bow of steamer, whereupon latter fled at full speed. She thus carried out instructions officially given all Italian steamers at beginning of war to attempt escape upon being held up by submarine or to ram according to position of latter. Escaping steamer pursued and fired on by submarine but did not stop until receiving several hits. Forty-five minutes given passengers and crew to leave ship on which greatest panic reigned. Only a portion of boats lowered which were occupied by members ship's crew who pulled hurriedly away. Great portion of boats which would apparently have sufficed for rescue all hands, not occupied. After about fifty minutes submarine submerged on account rapidly approaching vessel, torpedoed ANCONA, which did not sink until further lapse of forty-five minutes. If many passengers lost lives, blame rests entirely with crew because instead of stopping upon warning shots, fled and compelled submarine to fire and because crew endeavored save only themselves and not passengers for which there was ample time and means. Story that submarine fired upon loaded boats and people in water is malicious fabrication for reason ammunition much too valuable for submarine if for no other. No further shot fired after vessel stopped.'

Penfield."

E N C L O S U R E   I I

Amembassy, Vienna.   November 16, 1915.

987. The Embassy has transmitted a copy of the Austro-Hungarian Admiralty's official report regarding the sinking of the ANCONA. Please ascertain the size and character of the attacking vessel, its armament, the name of the commander and the flag flown during the attack. If possible also obtain a copy of the Commander's report.

CONFIDENTIAL: Please examine the list of Austro-Hungarian submarines and report whether the vessel attacking the ANCONA appears on the list. Paragraph.

Report promptly by telegraph.   Lansing.

T telegrams (WP, DLC).

To Edith Bolling Galt, with Enclosure

[The White House] 17 Nov. [1915]

Another brief chapter   W.

ALI (WP, DLC).

E N C L O S U R E

Peking November 16, 1915.

Strictly confidential.

My telegram of November 13, 10 p m.

It is reported to me that the European entente powers have

now submitted to the Japanese Government the proposals to accept China as an ally.   Reinsch

T telegram (WP, DLC).

To William Spry

The White House, November 17, 1915.
  With unaffected hesitation but with a very earnest conviction of the importance of the case, I again venture to urge upon your Excellency the justice and advisability, if it be possible, of a thorough reconsideration of the case of Joseph Hillstrom.
                                    Woodrow Wilson.

T telegram (WP, DLC).

To Helen Adams Keller

My dear Miss Keller: [The White House] November 17, 1915
  I was very much touched by your telegram of November sixteenth with regard to Joseph Hillstrom and wish most sincerely that it were within my power to do something, but, unhappily, there is nothing that I can do. The matter lies entirely beyond my jurisdiction and power. I have been deeply interested in the case but am balked of all opportunity.
  With sincere regard,
                    Very truly yours,   Woodrow Wilson

TLS (Letterpress Books, WP, DLC).

From Robert Lansing

PERSONAL AND PRIVATE:

My dear Mr. President: Washington November 17, 1915.
  I had a talk this morning with Mr. L. W. Nieman, editor of the Milwaukee JOURNAL, whose strong support of the administration and desire to be helpful give weight to his views.
  The part of his conversation which particularly interested me was the fact that he tells me that there has been a very decided change in public opinion in the middle west toward this country's participation in the war; that the war spirit is growing on account of the increased hostility toward the Germans, who are being ostracised not only socially but industrially.
  As you personally know Mr. Nieman, and the value to be

placed upon his judgment, I would suggest if it can be arranged that you see him for ten or fifteen minutes tomorrow or Friday as I think you would find it interesting to have his point of view, which I do not feel that I can adequately portray in a letter. I am not making this suggestion at Mr. Neiman's request or with his knowledge.

Mr. Nieman is staying at the New Willard, in case you desire to ask him to come and see you.[1]

Faithfully yours,   Robert Lansing

TLS (WP, DLC).
[1] Wilson saw Nieman at the White House on December 3.

Joseph Patrick Tumulty to Samuel Gompers

The White House, November 17, 1915.

The President has received your telegram embodying resolutions of the Convention of the American Federation of Labor concerning the case of Joseph Hillstrom, and has this morning again telegraphed the Governor of Utah urging the justice and advisability of a thorough reconsideration of the case.

J. P. Tumulty.

T telegram (WP, DLC).

To Lucy Marshall Smith

Dearest Cousin Lucy,   The White House. 17 November, 1915.

Your letter[1] was a great joy to me, and to us all. It is indeed fine how New Orleans has taken this fresh disaster,[2] and none has taken it in finer spirit than you and Cousin Mary have.

It pleased me very deeply that you should like the New York speech and the note to Great Britain so much. I had very little hand indeed in the preparation of the note. I merely touched up its phraseology here and there. Lansing wrote it, and it seems to me an unanswerable paper.

We are all very well indeed. The newspapers are saying less and less about Edith and me and dear Edith's spirits are rising accordingly. She is well and altogether lovely.

I am busy in the preparation of my message, or address, to Congress. It is hard to write an important paper amidst constant interruptions; it makes it seem to me, what it is, piecemeal and artificially jointed; but there is no use hoping for uninterrupted time, and I do the best I can, in the hope that few will see the seams. I am besieged by people who want this, that, and the other "just mentioned" in the message and my principal job is one of exclusion. It wowld [would] be a perfect scrap basket if I took all the advice given me.

Please write as often as you can. Your letters give us deep pleasure. We think of you both constantly and, as I am sure you know, with deep and abiding and intimate affection.

All join me in messages of love.

Affectionately Yours,   Woodrow Wilson

WWTLS (photostat in RSB Coll., DLC).
¹ Lucy M. Smith to WW, Nov. 9 [1915], ALS (WP, DLC).
² New Orleans had suffered severe flooding and property damage, as well as several deaths and many injuries, when the worst hurricane on record to that date hit the city in the evening of September 29.

To Stephen Samuel Wise

My dear Rabbi Wise: [The White House] November 18, 1915

I have your letter of November twelfth and I need not say that it distresses me very deeply. I always mistrust my own judgment when I find myself disagreeing with you, but in this case I fear the disagreement is inevitable. I want you to know, nevertheless, that it does not affect in the least my estimate of you or my personal feeling. It is painful to go different ways but we can thoroughly respect one another in doing so.

Cordially and sincerely yours,   Woodrow Wilson

TLS (Letterpress Books, WP, DLC).

To Joseph Green Butler, Jr.¹

My dear Mr. Butler: [The White House] November 18, 1915

I am sincerely sorry to be prevented from being present at Niles on Saturday next to take part in the interesting exercises which are planned for that day in memory of Mr. McKinley. I am sure I am expressing only the feeling of the whole country when I say that such a memorial as is being erected to him by your association expresses the deep admiration and affectionate esteem not only of the people of Ohio but of the whole nation for a President who did his duty with conscientious solicitude and who lost his life in its performance. I wish that I might be present to render my own personal tribute of respect and admiration.

Cordially and sincerely yours,   Woodrow Wilson

TLS (Letterpress Books, WP, DLC).
¹ Manufacturer of Youngstown, Ohio, and president of the National

McKinley Birthplace Memorial Association. Butler had asked Wilson to send Tumulty as his representative at the ceremonies at McKinley's birthplace. Tumulty refused the invitation, and Butler wrote again to ask for a statement from Wilson. J. G. Butler, Jr., to WW, Nov. 6, 1915, TLS (WP, DLC), and J. G. Butler, Jr., to JPT, Nov. 15, 1915, TLS (WP, DLC).

To James Robert Mann[1]

My dear Mr. Mann: [The White House] November 18, 1915

I hope that you are planning to be in Washington at least a little while before the opening of the session of Congress. I would greatly value a conference with you on one or two of the more important matters which are to come before the Congress, matters which are or should be entirely non-partisan in the treatment given them and in which I would very much value your advice and cooperation; such, for example, as the question of national defense.

Cordially and sincerely yours,   Woodrow Wilson[2]

TLS (Letterpress Books, WP, DLC).

[1] Congressman from Illinois and the Republican minority leader in the House.

[2] On the same day, Wilson sent this letter, *mutatis mutandis*, to Jacob Harold Gallinger of New Hampshire, Republican minority leader in the Senate.

From William Spry

Salt Lake, Utah, November 18, 1915.

In June 1914, Joseph Hillstrom was convicted of the murder of J. G. Morrison, the jury having failed to recommend life imprisonment under the statute he was sentenced by the Court to suffer death. In July 1915 the judgment of conviction was affirmed by the Supreme Court and Hillstrom resentenced to be shot October 1st. September eighteenth the Board of Pardons heard and denied his application for commutation. September thirtieth you requested a stay of execution of the sentence to give the Swedish Minister an opportunity to present his view of the case. Upon the same day at your request only on the assumption that you were in possession of facts not presented to the Board I granted a respite until October sixteenth, the date of the regular meeting of the Board of Pardons, especially requesting that the Swedish Minister personally investigate the case and appear before the Board. Under date October first you advised me that your only reason for interceding was the request of the representative of a foreign government. October sixteenth at the regular Board meeting an open hearing was had in further consideration of the case. Hillstrom's attorney advised the Board that there was nothing further to present and that Hillstrom declined to again appear before the Board. The only representation in the convict's behalf was a short telegram from the Swedish Minister requesting commutation of sentence not by reason of any new thing in relation to the case but as he expressed it "For the sake of humanity and comity usually practiced between friendly nations." Because of the absence of any showing the Board terminated the respite and again denied commutation. The convict thereupon was on the eighteenth day of October resentenced by the Court to be shot November nineteenth. Forty six days after the granting of the respite and at the eleventh hour you as the President without stating any reasons therefore again wire urging a thorough reconsideration of the case because of its importance and the justice and advisability of such a course. Your interference in the case may have elevated it to an undue importance and the receipt of thousands of threatening letters demanding the release of Hillstrom regardless of his guilt or innocence may attach a peculiar importance to it, but the case is important in Utah only as establishing after a fair and impartial trial the guilt of one of the perpetrators of one of the most atrocious murders ever committed in this State. It is also important by reason of the fact that this case has had more careful and painstaking consideration at the hands of the proper officials of Utah than any other like case in the history of the State. As to your suggestion that justice requires further consideration of the case, I earnestly submit that the imputation contained not only in your message to me but also in your message to the President of the American Federation of Labor that this convict has not had justice in the courts of this state, is not justified. Three groups of attorneys have represented Hillstrom in the proceedings had before the district court and the supreme court and the Board of Pardons. The first group was employed by Hilstrom to conduct his defense; the second was engaged during the progress of the trial, participated in the defense represented him before the Supreme Court on appeal and before the Board of Pardons; the third group I am informed was employed in Hillstrom's behalf by the Swedish Minister. No fair minded person acquainted with the record has any doubt of Hillstrom's guilt. The Board of Pardons with most painstaking care has investigated every rumor, every suggestion and every clue that might tend to establish the innocence of this man and has most earnestly pleaded with him to shed any light on his movements and whereabouts on the night of the homicide. During every day of the twenty three months since he was charged with the crime the

Board has and even now stands ready to make further investigation and give due consideration to any tangible fact or circumstance that would tend to establish Hillstrom's innocence. It is a significant fact that those only are appealed to who have no knowledge of the facts and those only demand clemency who are either prejudiced in Hillstrom's favor or who demand his release regardless of his guilt. I am fully convinced that your request must be based on a misconception of the facts or that there is some reason of an international nature that you have not disclosed. With a full knowledge of all the facts and circumstances submitted I feel that a further postponement at this time would be an unwarranted interference with the course of justice. Mindful of the obligations of my oath of office to see to it that the laws are enforced I cannot and will not lend myself or my office to such interference. Tangible facts must be presented before I will further inte[r]fere in this case.

William Spry,   Governor.

T telegram (WP, DLC).

From Robert Lansing

PERSONAL AND PRIVATE:

My dear Mr. President: Washington November 18, 1915.

This morning the Brazilian Ambassador called upon me and I submitted to him the four propositions for the joint Pan-American treaty. As his Government had assented to Articles I and III as they stand I called his attention to Articles II and IV. He approved of both of them and said that his instructions were wide enough to permit him to assent to them. He informed me that he much preferred the present form of the propositions.

I requested the Chilean Ambassador to come to the Department this afternoon to see me, which he did. I then presented to him the four propositions as revised. I found him at first disposed to oppose the whole matter, but after half an hour's conversation on the subject he changed his views and assured me that he could see no reason now why Chile could not accept the propositions and that he would communicate with his Government immediately. I told him, and in telling him perhaps exceeded the actual fact, that it would be most gratifying if the matter could be settled before the assembling of Congress, as it would be an interesting part of your annual message. He said to me that the present Cabinet of Chile was more or less a Cabinet *ad interim* and that the new Cabinet would not be constituted until

December 20th—at the time, as I understand it, of the inauguration of the new President—that he was convinced that the present
Cabinet would take no action in the matter but that he would
immediately send the propositions to Chile with the request that
the members of the new Cabinet, who are known, would consider the matter and be prepared to act immediately upon the
Cabinet assembling. I told him that in view of this fact I would
say to you that I thought it would be advisable to postpone submission of the matter to Congress until after the holiday recess,
and that he might advise his Government that I did so out of
regard for Chile and in the expectation that she would join in
the treaty; that of course if Chile did not feel able to accept the
terms of the treaty at that time we would have to proceed without her, which would be a matter of very considerable regret to
me. He replied that he would explain this to his Government and
urge them to act promptly in accordance with our wishes.

The Ambassador, throughout this conversation, was affable
and friendly, the affability and friendliness increasing as we
drew nearer together. He spoke to me of the embarrassment in
which his Government found itself on account of the dispute
over the territory with Peru. I told him that I realized this and
that I thought Article II of the propositions was decidely in favor
of Chile, in that it would compel a speedy settlement of the dispute and that if Chile signed the Convention it would be in a
position under that Article to at once ask Peru to settle the question without further delay. He said he had not thought of that
but that he could see that it was strategically advantageous to
Chile.

In every way the interview was satisfactory.

Faithfully yours,   Robert Lansing

TLS (WP, DLC).

From Henry Lee Higginson

Dear Mr. President: Boston. November 18, 1915.

May I say a few words more on several topics?

Thanksgiving is coming, and you are going to speak to the
nation. Many people all over the land are thinking of the sufferers in Europe—sufferers of all nations. The Red Cross people
and the surgeons and nurses sent out by the Rockefeller Foundation and by the college units tell us of the horrible conditions
existing in many countries. We all are begging right and left
for these sufferers. At the Princeton game last Saturday a voluntary collection was taken up for them, and on next Saturday a
voluntary collection will be taken up at the Yale-Harvard game

in Cambridge. Can you find a place in your Message to remind people forcibly of these terrible conditions, and to beg them to go without many things, and to save in every direction in order to help these people? If it were not that the gifts do the givers more good than the recipients, my feeling about it would not be so strong, although how it could be much less than the suffering demands is beyond me to guess. Has history ever before showed us such a state of affairs, and have we ever been called upon so urgently to soften the woes of every nation in Europe?

Another point: We, as citizens, ought to know whether a man is on our side or on the side of another nation. It is an outrage and a fraud that a man should be a citizen of the United States and a citizen of any other country at the same time, and therefore doubt to which country he owes his allegiance. It tempts a man to treason. Lately I ventured to stir up the subject at a meeting of business men, who were astonished to learn that such was the fact. Man after man has come to me about the matter, and a great Princeton professor whom I saw at President Lowell's house last night said a few words on the subject. I can see but one way to avoid this trouble, and that is to refuse citizenship to every man born in another country unless that other country gives up all claim on him when he becomes a citizen of the United States.

We are all more than glad that you have taken up the question of preparedness as regards the army and navy. If one considers the conditions in Belgium or Servia or France, and dreams that his house may be burned and his wife and children killed or even exposed to the suffering which the people in those countries have had to undergo, he will say to himself: "Let us prepare to prevent it. It does not mean war, but peace." We have seen that the Germans have prepared in every way—in civic matters, manufactures, finance, trade, and have thus showed their strength. We also need to prepare in every direction.

You have encouraged me to speak freely to you, and will forgive anything which is amiss.

With best wishes, I am

Very truly yours,   Henry L. Higginson

TLS (WP, DLC).

From the Diary of Colonel House

November 18, 1915.

Dudley Malone telephoned from Washington that he had had a very satisfactory talk with the President and along the lines he had outlined before leaving. The upshot of it was that the President is to ask me in all matters appertaining to New York politics, and no one excepting the President and myself is to know what advice I give, or if indeed, I have given any. I insisted upon this for I do not want it known to anyone that I am giving a directing hand to New York affairs. I wish I could get away from this entirely, but it seems hopeless.

David Starr Jordan called to tell of his interview with the President concerning peace prospects. He expressed himself as finding the President greatly interested and sym[p]athetic, but without committing himself by word of mouth to anything. Jordan said he was making speeches throughout the country and was trying to sustain the President as far as he could. He also told of his interview with Mr. Bryan, saying he had gotten a better impression of him than every [ever] before, since he had talked more reasonably and unselfishly. Bryan has given up the thought of going to Europe, unless the President should call upon him to go upon some particular mission.

From Robert Lansing

PRIVATE AND CONFIDENTIAL:

My dear Mr. President: [Washington] November 19, 1915.

I am afraid that we are coming to an *impasse* in the matter of the LUSITANIA. Day before yesterday I had a conversation with the German Ambassador and submitted to him the possible formula which his Government might employ. He said that he would send it to his Government as his instructions were not broad enough to assent or dissent, but that he was doubtful of his Government admitting any liability for the lives of Americans lost on board of a British vessel.[1]

Of course, if Germany takes this position and we do not recede from our position, which we cannot do, there is a deadlock which no further diplomatic exchanges would affect, exchanges which, in my opinion, it would be unwise and improper to continue.

From two or three sources, which have been heretofore reliable, I have reports that the German Ambassador has indicated that it is his plan or that of his Government to prolong discussion of the question until the American people had forgotten it and this Government had let it drop.

Whether these reports are true or not I think that delay would cause wide criticism of the Administration as being supine and ready to go any lengths in order to avoid a direct issue with Germany.

Assuming that Germany fails to act promptly on the formula which we have suggested or refuses to acknowledge liability for the loss of American lives on the LUSITANIA, I believe that a situation will arise which will call for definite and firm action on our part and that action should be taken without delay. In order to do this our policy should be determined in advance. It seems to me that we have two courses to pursue. *First.* To sever diplomatic relations by withdrawing Gerard and by handing Bernstorff his passports. *Second.* By laying the facts before Congress and stating that, as further negotiations will be useless, it will be necessary to act, and that, as the action which may be necessary may be of nature involving the question of war or peace, the matter is laid before the branch of the Government charged with power to declare war.

Probably the first method is the simplest and less liable to commit the Government to drastic action. On the other hand the second method would impress the public, I believe, with the fact that the Administration desired the representatives, supposed to be nearest the people, to determine a question which may precipitate war.

From the selfish standpoint of politics I think that the people generally are very much dissatisfied with a continuance of negotiations, that, if our demands are not acceded to, they desire action in asserting our rights, and that if there is further delay, they will turn against the Administration. I believe the pro-German vote in this country is irrevocably lost to us and that, no matter what we do now, we can never win back any part of it. If this view is correct, we ought not from the political standpoint lose the support of the Americans hostile to Germany. And I am afraid that we will do so if we are not rigid in our attitude on the LUSITANIA case. The people have, I think, been patient and considerate in view of the fact that nearly seven months have passed since the vessel was torpedoed. They do not reason out the causes which compelled delay and I doubt if it could be explained satisfactorily to them. At any rate I notice a growing spirit of complaint at what they consider inaction by the Government. The country newspapers as well as letters coming in voice this increasing dissatisfaction.

I should like, therefore, an indication of your views on this subject in order that I may regulate my conversations with Count von Bernstorff accordingly and may be prepared to act promptly if action becomes necessary.

Faithfully yours,   Robert Lansing

CCL (SDR, RG 59, 763.72/2270½A, DNA).
1 For Lansing's record of this conversation, see his "MEMORANDUM OF INTER-

VIEW WITH GERMAN AMBASSADOR," Nov. 17, 1915, TS memorandum (SDR, RG 59, 763.72/2270½, DNA), printed in *FR-LP*, I, 490-91.

Bernstorff did not report to Berlin on this conference until November 23, and he then sent the report by mail (it arrived in Berlin on December 16). Again, Bernstorff was completely misleading, saying that Wilson was willing to permit the negotiations to stretch out, even to the end of the war, and that Wilson and Lansing were acting now only out of fear of congressional and public opinion. J. H. von Bernstorff to T. von Bethmann Hollweg, Nov. 23, 1915, TCL (Der Weltkrieg, 18a, Unterseebootkrieg gegen England, ganz geheim, Vol. 15, pp. 57-60, GFO-Ar). For a summary, see Link, *Confusions and Crises*, pp. 63-64.

From Edward Mandell House

Dear Governor: New York. November 19th, 1915.

Bernstorff was in this morning. He came ostensibly to tell me of his conversation with Lansing about the Lusitania and to leave a memorandum embracing what he, himself, felt authorized to do, and another expressing what Lansing desires.

He said he was disturbed because of the efforts to connect the German Embassy with the charges of plots, etc. He declared that this could not be done because he had had no connection with them. But he let slip a remark which indicated that the German Government, through other agents, might be involved, though he did not admit this.

He frankly, but unofficially condemned the sinking of passenger vessels.

We then fell to talking about possible peace proposals. I reiterated my belief that nothing could be done until Germany, on the one hand, was willing to agree to discuss the elimination of militarism, and England to discuss the elimination of navalism. Those were the two questions, I told him, that the neutral world were most interested in. I thought this country would sustain you if you at any time undertook to intervene upon these broad lines. But I asserted that you would hardly do this unless you knew in advance that such intervention would be agreeable to either one side or the other.

I expressly said that I was talking for myself alone and without your knowledge.

He was intensely interested and suggested that it would be a good time for me to go to Europe and make such a proposal direct. In reply I thought that this could not be done without some intimation either from one side or the other, of a willingness to consider peace parleys upon these lines.

I suggested that I might write to Gerard. This brought a quick reply that he had better approach his government himself, and that he would send a letter by the next mail asking them if they would talk along these lines.

I pointed out to him that Germany and the continental powers would necessarily be compelled to eliminate militarism in the near future for economic reasons. The shortage of men alone would make it imperative that no large body be held idle when needed to revivify industry. Further, that the financial conditions of each of the countries would not permit a continuance of militarism.

On the other hand, England would not have to meet such conditions, because to maintain her supremacy at sea, it required a comparatively small force. Besides, the fact that she was an island and had such extensive colonies would make it seem to her imperative to have a dominating navy. He admitted this.

I wanted to convince him that we would really have more difficulty in bringing about a reduction of navalism than we should have in the reduction of militarism. He also admitted this.

I left the impression upon him without saying so that there was danger of the Allies conceding what we desired first, and getting the weight of our influence on their side. I put out a vague intimation that the American people would sustain you to any degree that you might think it necessary to go in order to bring about peace along such lines.[1]

Many of our people are becoming restive because of the continued exposures of the German propaganda, and it is becoming increasingly difficult to refrain from drastic action. This is a cause for much concern as it is clear that something should be done to put an end to it. Yet any rupture of diplomatic relations with Germany must necessarily defeat the general plan to bring about peace.   Affectionately yours,   E. M. House

TLS (WP, DLC).
[1] Bernstorff's report of this conversation is printed at Nov. 23, 1915.

From Joseph Patrick Tumulty

Dear Governor: [The White House] November 19, 1915.

I wish you could get an opportunity to read the two enclosed clippings I am sending you,—one from the New York Herald,[1] the other from the New York Globe.[2]

The Globe has been a supporter of the Administration throughout and has ably defended our attitude toward Mexico. I never fear editorial comment unless it agrees with the general opinion which reaches the White House every day from all parts of the country. I do not like to alarm you but there is no mistaking the fact that the country is dissatisfied with our seeming attitude of indifference toward the propaganda initiated by our hyphenated friends. The country every day reads of the efforts of these hy-phenated Americans to destroy manufacturing plants, to poison and control public opinion in every way, and is astounded at the seeming indifference of the Administration toward these efforts to undermine us and to injure our people.

The Lusitania affair is again referred to and the demand for speedy reparation is growing by the hour. The Ancona affair is another cause for irritation. In my opinion, it is all leading to one idea,—that this Administration, for some reason, is lacking in *aggressive assertiveness*. Congress will soon be in session and then the propaganda of our Republican friends to destroy us will be started anew.

It seems to me that the time has come for *action*, and ACTION and MORE ACTION all along the line.

I do not want you to feel that I am alarmed, but I am simply voicing the sentiments of those who are interested in everything that effects you and your future.

Your Message should be a clarion call to the Nation; a defi to those Americans who would challenge the very sovereignty of America and engage in movements and attacks which strike at her very heart.

When I spoke to you the other day about legislation to cover the acts of those men who are destroying manufacturing plants, you thought it would not be wise to include in your Message a recommendation for such legislation. I do not agree with you in this matter. There ought to be a ringing paragraph with reference to the necessity for legislation which will prevent things of this kind from happening in the future.

I hope I have not unduly burdened or worried you.

Tumulty

TLS (WP, DLC).

[1] " 'Shoot the President!' is Cry as 'Friends of Peace' Speaker calls Mr. Wilson 'Unneutral,' " and "A Public Call for the Assassination of the President!" New York *Herald*, Nov. 19, 1915, clippings (WP, DLC). The first, a lengthy article composed principally of quotations, described a meeting at Cooper Union addressed by John Brisben Walker. Walker's passionate condemnation of Wilson's failure to stop the arms trade, his ultimatums to Germany, his approval of loans to the Allies, and his occupation of Veracruz elicited cries of "Shoot the President!", to which no member of the audience objected. Walker also predicted that Wilson would become "a monument of failure because he lacked the courage to fight unjust accumulators of wealth."

The *Herald*'s editorial in the same issue called for stronger action against "the unchecked secret warfare which the Teutonic allies have waged here," of which the Cooper Union meeting was an example.

[2] "Dissatisfactions," New York *Globe*, Nov. 18, 1915, clipping (WP, DLC). The *Globe*'s editor said that "no one seems particularly proud of the behavior of the country during the last fifteen months," and that the administration had few enthusiastic supporters. Pro-Germans took offense at the administration's rejection of Germany's explanations of its war policies; pro-Allied sympathizers objected to America's failure to "aid the Allies by all means short of war" and its defense of "sordid dollar chasers"; adherents of "old-fashioned

American views" despaired when the administration failed to condemn German actions in Belgium; pacifists saw militarism looming ahead, "preparationists," weakness. "The only elements seemingly pleased are a few speculators who are affronting mankind's sense of decency by their efforts to get rich when tragedy so envelops the world."

From Walter Hines Page

Dear Mr. President: London, Nov. 19. 1915.

I have not written you by an earlier pouch about the reception of our Note by British opinion, because I wishd. to make sure that I read British opinion accurately. I am sure that the prevailing opinion here (among the men who count) is accurately expressed by a clipping that I append from *The New Statesman*.[1] This is Sidney Webb's[2] paper and on such a subject as this it speaks as accurately as any paper the feeling of the intelligent mass rather than of any particular class. *The Times* and *The Spectator* said substantially the same thing, less well, it seemed to me, viz: (1) that the Note was lacking in courtesy; and (2) that the British Gov't must give a polite answer but shd. not yield any important point, the feeling on all sides being that any irreconcilable difference shd. be referred to arbitration.

What several journals call the "bare" manner of the Note has had an ill effect out of all proportion to any fair appraisal of its tone, if it were unconnected in the British mind with other facts. I can explain the criticism of its harshness in no better way than this: Your statement of the Panama-tolls controversy was brief and human and it was your own statement and not a lawyer's brief. Your notes to Germany were brief and human and they were your statements and not lawyer's briefs. The British public had become accustomed to *that* tone from our Government, and, when a long, legal, de-humanized document came, they felt that the principals to the controversy had retired and that it wd. now

---

[1] "The American Note," *New Statesman*, VI (Nov. 13, 1915), 125-27. It said that the note might "fairly and accurately be termed pettifogging." The United States Government had cited the letter of international law, but in actual fact ships could not be searched at sea effectively or safely; railroads rendered obsolete the rules of blockade which protected neutral ports; and the Declaration of London did not bind England in this war. The American claim that British prize courts administered municipal rather than international law was illogical and tended to clog diplomatic channels with individual ship cases. England might concede the American point that port costs be dropped; otherwise the British government should rely upon the precedents set by the United States during the Civil War, extend the list of contraband, and declare a full blockade of Germany. Finally, the editorial objected strongly to the tone of the American note and insinuated that both its tone and content had been designed to enhance Wilson's chances for re-election.

[2] Also principal founder of the London School of Economics, active in the Fabian Society, and co-author with his wife, Beatrice, of numerous books on socialism, public administration, and trade unionism.

become a lawyers' wrangle. Perhaps this is the necessary penalty you have to pay for writing the German Notes yourself. If the Note as it stands had been sent as an inclosure with a courteous, brief, human letter, I think that this feeling wd. not have arisen.

Of course it is only fair to remember that public opinion here is not normal—it is excited, strained, tense. The war is telling even on British nerves. And popular feeling towards us is intensified by other reasons, notably by the British disapproval of our submarine controversy. When Bernstorff was permitted to begin his negotiations with the *Arabic* case instead of the *Lusitania*, the English concluded that the Germans had hoodwinked us and were playing for time to destroy munition works and such things. They expected us to dismiss Bernstorff, wh. they do not believe wd. cause war, but wh. they wd. interpret as an act to express what our Notes said. The English, therefore, regard us as having been taken in by the Germans as they themselves were taken in for years before the war.

As I wrote House the other day, as nearly as I can judge, your Panama tolls action brought the two peoples and the two governments nearer together than they had ever been in our whole history; and their view of our succumbing to German tactics and our "harsh" lawyers' Note have put the two peoples into the least sympathetic attitude since our civil war. Not an English person has mentioned the Note to me. They consciously avoid the subject not wishing to offend me by saying that they regret its tone. In fact they—I hope not exactly avoid me, but they certainly no longer seek me—a matter of no consequence except for what it implies. And this feeling is likely to grow. English public feeling rises slowly and lasts—the exact contrary of American public feeling.

Since it is the tone rather than the matter of the Note that has given public offence, I am reminded that there are many things the form of wh. is of their essence. The Parthenon differs from the marble Baptist Church at Uba Dam only in form.

This curious talk is going about London—that the Japanese are going to take advantage of the European war to begin war with the U. S.—we can get no munitions now nor any other kind of help from Europe, not even coal or colliers, and the Panama canal is closed: this, then, is their chance. This rumor has been heard in three different circles by two members of my staff and by me. Whether it has a common origin, or what that origin is, I haven't found out. It doesn't carry conviction on its face. Japan is not economically strong to enter a war on her own account; she is making munitions for Russia; and war on us wd. stop our munition supplies to the Allies and wd., therefore, directly help Germany. But such a rumor sets one to thinking. It might seem to Japan a favorable time to attack us as soon as the European war comes within sight of an end—before our navy is made appreciably bigger and while her alliance with England is still in force. *That* may be worth thinking about. I think that this is put about by Germany. The Germans have had a deliberate policy for years to stir up Japan against us.

Of course I know, of my own direct knowledge, nothing about Japan and her plans. But living in this diplomatic atmosphere two or three years gives one an insight into governmental methods and ambitions that a private citizen living in one country continuously never gets. European public men, in general, I shd. say, confidently expect Japan to attack us (or fear she will) at some early time. I have continually heard this expectation since I have lived here—before the war as well as since. Their reasoning is human and obvious: all great nations have risen to power by successful wars—wars to secure their independence or to enlarge their power or their territory. In its war with China Japan smelt blood and glory; in its war with Russia, it gained a place among the Powers and made an alliance with England: it tasted more blood and glory. Now, what next? A war that shd. humiliate the United States wd. put Japan among the Great Powers and perhaps gain the Philippines. And every government in Europe agrees with her that she cd. seize the Philippines, the Hiwaiian Islands, perhaps Alaska and begin an attack on California before we shd. get ready to fight. After we got ready—in 3 or 4 years or more—we wd. of course win if our fighting mood shd. last so long. But they all regard the U. S. as the home of the peace-at-any-price people, and they think our fighting mood wd. not last. I have come to the conclusion that there are just two opinions held about the U. S. in Europe. The minority—a small learned and philosophical minority who care for the peaceful advancement of mankind and who stand aloof from the governing and military classes—regard us as the hope of the world. By far the larger class—the ruling classes, the fighting classes and the masses that take their cue from these—regard us as a soft, undi[s]ciplined agglommeration of unwelded masses, without any definite aim or singleness of purpose—the easiest sort of a rich folk for a trained army to spoil—a mob and not a nation. You could have found before this war in Petrograd (remotely), Berlin, and Tokio this active feeling: Who will get the first chance at the United States? Less, of course, in Petrograd, but a most active feeling, eager and restless, in Berlin and in Tokio. Neither

France nor England had it or will have it; but both expected—and expect—us to have to prove our virility by fighting.

This attitude to the U. S. pervades the foreign atmosphere, and the diplomatic and military atmosphere of all real monarchies.

In diplomatic and military life on this side the world you will find that men regard nations on the map as they regard chess-men. On our side of the world diplomatists and soldiers are ornamental or superfluous: here they and their masters hold nations in their power and move the chess-men as they can. I have been told by representatives—diplomatic and military—of nations wholly friendly to us, dozens of times since the war began and no less than twice yesterday: "*Your* next move is to come in with the Allies. You will end the war more quickly and get the credit for ending it. Hence you will have the strongest voice in the peace councils that will follow; and you will checkmate both Germany and Japan for a long time to come, for you can command the British fleet—a beautiful move."

This world, my friend, is not the world it seemed to my innocent youth of four years ago. Nor is it the world that can be read about in any books, or speeches or public utterances of any sort whatsoever. I have an infinite pity for it but also a grave fear of it. I cannot for a hundred years sleep as securely as I slept for fifty. I often wish that the era of sailing ships had lasted a century longer so that we might have had that time more fully to work out our ideals in safe isolation. I don't know whether this is a proper mood or not, but at times it is irresistible.

Well aware as I am of my ignorance and of the fallibilaty of human judgments—even of mine—I am, nevertheless coming to have some ideas of my own about the war, to wit: Germany may (and probably will) overrun the Balkans and open the way to Constantinople and possibly beyond. There *may* even be a rising in Egypt, and the Suez canal may be put in danger. Of this last I cannot judge, and Kitchener has gone to try to prevent it. Thereafter it is conceivable that Germany may even overrun Italy—destroy Venice and take Rome and exact a huge indemnity. I find that few military men think highly of the Italian as a soldier. Be this as it may, there is a chance for a long struggle in the Southeast and the South, where Germany may win much more territory and keep the spirit of victory active among her people at home. But the war must be won and will be won on the Western front. It will not end until the Germans are driven back into Germany or till they realize that they will be. Then their resistance will collapse. By attrition this will take a year or two: many men here predict till 1918. I shd. say that men and nerves and ammunition material will not last so long. But, barring some unexpected and dramatic military event, the end can hardly come within a year. And surely that is a long-enough period of gloom for anybody to look forward to. I even hear predictions that the Scandinavian states will be drawn in—one or two of them on the German side—and that Holland will be forced in. These will still leave Spain, Portugal, and Switzerland as European neutrals. What these prophets have against Spain, Switzerland, and Portugal, to deny them participation, I can't imagine. I am reminded of what a wounded Hindoo in an English hospital said when a visitor askd. him what he thought of the war. He smiled and answered. "Oh, it a very go-o-d war—*very* go-od war." It is surely sending enough men to Nirvana to satisfy even his philosophy. The feeling grows on me that when this murderous lapse into barbarism comes to an end, Europe will have lost its human interest. It will serve for a long time as a warning, and that will be its sad chief use.

Always sincerely yours,   Walter H. Page

ALS (WP, DLC).

From Robert Lansing, with Enclosure

PRIVATE AND CONFIDENTIAL:

My dear Mr. President: Washington November 20, 1915.

There has been an unfortunate and probably an unavoidable lack of coordination between the different Departments of the Government charged with investigation of violations of law, growing out of the activity of agents of the belligerent Governments in this country. It seems to me that it would be advisable to have a central office to which results of investigations could be reported day by day and the proper steps taken to continue such investigations in the most efficient way. With this idea in view I submit to you a memorandum on the subject. This Department is not anxious to assume additional duties but, unavoidably, all these investigations—or at least the majority of them—have an international phase which should be not only considered but, I think, should control the action of other Departments.

The memorandum rests primarily on the idea that the Counsellor for this Department should be the clearing house for the secret reports of the various Departments, and he could—if it seems advisable, and I think it does—furnish duplicates of his information day by day to the Secretary of the Treasury and the Attorney-General, who are especially interested in these investigations.

I should be pleased to receive your views upon the subject, or any suggestion which you may have as to a better plan of coordination of work.

Faithfully yours,   Robert Lansing.

TLS (WP, DLC).

E N C L O S U R E

It is understood that the attached memorandum deals only with the preliminary collection of information and investigations for the purpose of determining the importance of the information received. As soon as it appears that any laws have been violated or apparently violated the case would be turned over to the Department of Justice in the regular and orderly way.

The intent of the plan proposed is to keep this preliminary investigation free from delays and centralized in such a way as to keep the scattered threads together. It is also intended to keep the President accurately informed from day to day and the State Department constantly in touch with what is going on. The daily reports as summarized for the Counselor for the State Department should be forwarded in duplicate to the Secretary of the Treasury and the Attorney General.

CONFIDENTIAL:

MEMORANDUM.

A great amount of information, some of it important, much of it trivial and a considerable part of it misleading or absolutely untrue, is coming to various departments of the Government regarding the activities of people throughout the United States, who are alleged to be endangering the friendly relations of this Government with other governments by undertaking unneutral enterprises, some of which are criminal and some of which are merely indiscreet. Almost all of the acts reported, if true, require careful consideration from the viewpoint of our relations with other nations before this Government's action in the matter is determined.

The information may be divided roughly into information as to acts violating a law and for which the offenders can be prosecuted in the courts, and acts which are not technical violations of law, but which are calculated to place the United States in the position of permitting violations of neutrality if they are not stopped. Under the latter may properly come certain acts of accredited representatives of foreign governments. Some of these matters can only be handled by confidential representations to the accredited heads of the foreign governments involved that such acts are distasteful to our Government and must be discontinued.

There is another class of acts committed by citizens of the United States, either entirely on their own initiative or through influences which cannot be definitely traced and which can only be stopped by publicity, and in some cases the matters involved would be of such a delicate nature as to make it inadvisable even to call attention to them in an official way.

This information is at present coming to the Department of State, the War Department, the Navy Department, the United States Secret Service and the Department of Justice. Doubtless other Departments, such as Commerce, Post Office, and even Interior, receive or could gather information as well. It is seldom that information received is sufficiently definite even to warrant investigation and it is only by piecing together information from a number of sources that any practical lead can be obtained. At present there is no assurance that the various scattered scraps of information which when put together make a clear case will go to the same place. For instance, one item may be sent in to Justice mentioning certain activities, another item may be received by the Secret Service, the Navy may receive other information—all of which, when put side by side, makes a fairly clear case, but none of which when scattered through the different Departments seems of importance. It is evident that a single office where all this information must be instantly transmitted without red tape is absolutely necessary to an effective organization.

In view of the diplomatic questions involved it seems obvious that the receiving office should be under the Department of State. Otherwise grave errors may be made by well meaning but misdirected efforts. After this information has been received there are at present three ways in which it may be taken care of: The Department of Justice, the Secret Service and the Post Office Inspectors. The Department of Justice is charged with the gathering of evidence by which the Attorney General may proceed to prosecute for a definite crime; the Secret Service is charged with the protection of the President and the protection against counterfeiting and customs frauds; the Post Office Department is charged with watching for violations of the United States mail. None of these Departments is legally or by organization fitted to handle these matters alone and efficient cooperation without a central directing force with authority to supervise their operations and to assign them their respective work cannot be accomplished practically. There is the further objection that a case turned over by the State Department to any one of these investigating departments or bureaus is lost sight of and its daily developments are unknown for weeks and sometimes months.

To cure this situation, it is suggested:

That an Executive Order be issued placing all these matters under the authority of the Department of State, directing all Government officials and Departments to transmit immediately to the Department of State any information received along these lines and to collect at the request of that Department any information asked for. The Order should also direct that the Post Office Department, the Secret Service and the Department of Justice place their men when requested at the disposal of the Department of State for the purpose of investigating these matters.

It is suggested that the Department of State should assign the Counselor, as being able to decide the legal questions which sometimes arise without waiting for reference, as the head of the system, acting, of course, always under the Secretary of State and, through him, under the President himself.

It is not thought that any additional force for the Department of State would be required beyond possibly a thoroughly trustworthy stenographer, and if the work is unusually heavy a filing clerk, as it will be absolutely necessary to maintain a card index and to keep each case separate and up to date.

T MS (WP, DLC).

From Robert Lansing

PERSONAL AND PRIVATE:

My dear Mr. President: Washington November 20, 1915.

While municipal law does not lie in my province unless it relates to neutrality or similar subjects pertaining to our international relations, it occurred to me that it might not be inopportune in connection with your message on national defense to include in it some suggestion as to legislation covering foreign intrigues in our internal affairs such as conspiracies to blow up factories, to encourage strikes, to interfere with industrial operations, to gather information of this government's secrets, etc., etc. In view of the wide interest and indignation manifested throughout the country at the recent disclosures of activities of agents of belligerents I think that notice of the subject in your message would be received with general satisfaction.

Faithfully yours,   Robert Lansing

TLS (WP, DLC).

From Edward Mandell House, with Enclosure

Dear Governor: New York. November 20th, 1915.

I am enclosing you a copy of some memoranda which Gifford Pinchot has sent me in regard to conservation and which he very much desires you to see.

Would it be possible for you to come over on Friday before the game[1] and let us go to the theater that night?

There are a number of things that have accumulated since you were here that I would like to discuss with you. I hope you will be able to stay over Sunday and hear Doctor Jowett.

Affectionately yours,   E. M. House

Pinchot tells me the meeting at Columbus Dec. 10 promises to be a notable one.

TLS (WP, DLC).
[1] The Army-Navy football game in New York on November 27.

ENCLOSURE

Gifford Pinchot to Edward Mandell House

My dear Col. House: [Milford, Pa.] November 18, 1915.

In accordance with your suggestion, I take great pleasure in putting on paper what I told you yesterday.

There is a ripe and practicable opportunity for a big constructive advance in conservation at the coming session of Congress. I greatly hope that President Wilson will see and use it. If he will, it goes without saying that I shall be thoroughly glad to help him in it all I can.

Before I mention the specific measures I have in mind, there is one fact I hope you will not forget. The conservation policy is not now and never has been responsible for checking legitimate development. It has checked theft and waste, but not development. Two examples will show what I mean:

In every Congress since the coal lands of Alaska became an issue, the friends of conservation have worked hard to have passed such a fair and sound law as President Wilson has signed.[1] The friends of the grabbers repeatedly defeated it. They preferred no law to a good one. They, not we, locked up the coal.

Again, every water-power on the public lands and National Forests, with negligible exceptions, has been continuously open to development under the laws passed for that purpose, but not to misappropriation under laws passed for lands of other character. So with the timber and other resources of the National Forests. The bank has been closed against burglars but never against citizens who do business by daylight. That the present water-power laws are not better is directly due to the refusal of the water-power interests to allow the public to share in the improvement.

Development has, in fact, been retarded little if at all behind the actual possible uses of the West, and for what delay has occurred the grabbers of natural resources are themselves responsible.

Now as to the great chance which lies before the President. The following bills are of the first importance and can be passed if the Administration will push them vigorously to a decision:

1. The Kent grazing bill, which will double the meat producing capacity of about 300 million acres of public grazing land, and by reducing the price of meat will reach the high cost of living in the most direct way. This bill has the militant support of the western cattle men through the National Livestock Association.

2. The Ferris water-power bill. By applying to the public lands the system devised upon the National Forests, the Ferris bill safeguards both the rights of the public and the opportunity to develop. It passed the House at the last session. Its weakness is that it takes the control of water-powers on the National Forests away from the Department of Agriculture which started the work and has done it well, and turns it over to the Interior Department, which has neither equipment nor experience for it. This should be changed.

3. The Adamson water-power bill, in the form in which it passed the House last year. This bill deals with water-power on navigable streams, which it is of peculiar importance to protect in view of the hydroelectric production of nitrates for national defence.

There are other bills, like the general leasing bill, which applies to the coal, oil, and phosphate lands of the United States, the principles adopted for coal lands in Alaska, and the Newlands bill for the development of our water-ways, which ought to be passed but are less immediately attainable.

In addition to the three bills whose passage would amount to a great constructive gain in conservation, there is another to which I desire to call your special attention, because it ought not to pass. This is the Pitman bill, which takes the natural resources of Alaska out from under the protection of the Federal Departments which have charge of them now and turns them over to a commission subordinate to the Secretary of the Interior.

A commission is always a clumsy and ineffective instrument for such work. In this case politics would inevitably creep in. The resources of Alaska would be more expensively and less skilfully handled than at present, with no corresponding gain in development, and what is vastly more important, they would not be safe. Furthermore, if the National Forests in Alaska were turned over to local control, powerful interests would demand that the National Forests in the Western States should be turned over to those States, and if the forests, then the other natural resources also. This is a bad and dangerous bill, flatly opposed to the conservation of natural resources in the public interest, and it should be killed.

Very sincerely yours,   Gifford Pinchot

CCLS (WP, DLC).

1 The coal leasing bill for Alaska, which Wilson had signed in October 1914. See Arthur S. Link, *Wilson: The New Freedom* (Princeton, N. J., 1956), pp. 127-28.

To Robert Lansing

My dear Mr. Secretary,   The White House. 21 November, 1915.

I am quite clear that the position we should take, in conversations with the German Ambassador and in all future dealings with his government in regard to the matters in controversy between us, is

First, that the matter of the *Lusitania* is just as important and just as acute now as it was the day the news of her sinking arrived, and that a failure to secure a satisfactory settlement will disclose the same questions of future action that then lay in the background;

Second, that we now know, as a result of the various communications that have passed between that government and this, that the commander of the submarine which sank the *Lusitania* acted contrary to the instructions which had been given by the Imperial German Admiralty; and

Third, that we should regard a failure to settle this question in the same frank way that the sinking of the ARABIC was settled would be little less than a repudiation of the assurances then given us and seem to lead back to the very crisis in our relations that was then so happily avoided.

I think the Ambassador cannot be too explicit with his government in this matter.

Is there anyone representing Austria here whom we could get to understand the seriousness of the ANCONA affair? Or do you feel that you know enough of the facts?

Faithfully Yours,   W.W.

WWTLI (SDR, RG 59, 763.72/2271½, DNA).

From Edward Mandell House

Dear Governor: New York. November 21st, 1915.

Would it not be possible to immediately let some of the obnoxious underlings of the offending Embassies go? And would it not be possible to sever diplomatic relations with Austria because of the Ancona?

I do not believe it would be well to go through the same process as was done with the Lusitania and Arabic. When you laid down the law, and Germany agreed to comply, you were laying down the law to all the belligerents, and her disavowal and renunciation of her submarine policy should have bound her allies as much as it bound her.

I believe you will find that the Central Powers will now do almost anything to keep from an open rupture.

I hope you will ask Congress to give the Government more power to deal with the crimes committed by the hyphenates. It seems to me that power is needed to deport undesirables just as it is given the Immigration authorities. The country is ready and waiting for action and I believe it would be a mistake to send further notes.

Sometime when you have the opportunity, I wish you would think well of rebuking those Americans who are beyond the army age limit and who are defaming America because she does not enter the war. They might be termed "alien Americans" who are more pro-foreign in their sympathies than they are American. These garrulous talkers and writers are doing nearly as much harm as the hyphenates and a rebuke, I think, is due them. It is not America first, but every other nation with whom their sympathies and associations are bound.

Affectionately yours,   E. M. House

TLS (WP, DLC).

To J. Edwin Murphy[1]

My dear Sir: [The White House] November 22, 1915

I would be very much obliged for some explanation of the enclosed silly and annoying lie.[2]

Very truly yours,   Woodrow Wilson

TLS (Letterpress Books, WP, DLC).

[1] Managing editor of the *Washington Times*.

[2] "President's Typewriter Wri!txs Likxe Th?is," *Washington Times*, Nov. 21, 1915. It read:

"When Presidnet Wixlson wriets a mexsagxe to congRezs it looks somethixng like thiX?s

"In addition to which the machine's alphabet is badly chewed as to legs and shoulders. The space bar suffers from intermittent paralysis. Some of the letters are virtually mute. Others have bold, black faces. The ribbon is about as fresh and whole as a battle flag in a museum. The mechanism generally is decrepit, and limps heavily through the affairs of state only under the severest Presidential goading. Mr. Wilson admits it is far from faultless, but he likes it, and he is very proud of the fact that it has no hyphen.

"You couldn't get a typewritten line out of the President on any machine but this one—not even with a dark-lantern and a jimmie. White House humorists say he has hand-raised the poor old thing so long he has developed a personal attachment for it. If so, that is the only valuable attachment it has.

"For years and years the ancient machine has endured professional, authorial and Presidential pecking. And pecking is right, for Mr. Wilson is a disciple of the Hunt system, or forefinger hesitation. Wherefore it may be said that this is the only typewriter that ever had the distinction of having hesitated with a President. It might be added that this couple is getting ready to lead Congress a merry dance this winter while the orchestra plays 'O You Preparedness.'

"The low, rakish form of this ancient, rusty friend of the President's reposes in his library. They understand each other's id[i]osyncracies and eccentricities and they stand ready together at any time to battle submarines, blockades of neutral ports, or—oh, any damned thing."

To Henry Lee Higginson

The White House
My dear Major Higginson: November 22, 1915

I am sincerely obliged to you for your letter of November eighteenth. It suggests two matters which I have very much at heart and upon which I shall try to speak wisely and emphatically.

In haste

Cordially and sincerely yours,   Woodrow Wilson

TLS (H. L. Higginson Coll., MH-BA).

From Robert Lansing, with Enclosure

PERSONAL AND PRIVATE:

My dear Mr. President: Washington November 22, 1915.

I enclose a memorandum of the information which we have in regard to the ANCONA case. It seems to me that it is very unsatisfactory as to detail and definit[e]ness. We have made other inquiries in regard to the case both at Vienna and Rome which I hope will throw more light on the subject.

The Austro-Hungarian affairs in this country are in the hands of the Chargé, Baron Zwiedinek,[1] and we can communicate with him whenever the time seems opportune.

I also enclose an editorial from the New York EVENING MAIL[2] which seems to me is very sensible and shows that some of the papers at least understand the difficulties which the Department has to face in a case of this sort.

Faithfully yours,   Robert Lansing

TLS (SDR, RG 59, 865.857 An 2/75 A, DNA).
  [1] Baron Erich Zwiedinek.
  [2] A clipping, stamped November 17, 1915, of an editorial saying that the State Department's reliance on firsthand accounts by American "agencies" to establish the facts in the *Ancona* case indicated "its determination to be guided . . . not by the passions or resentments of belligerents but by the facts independently authenticated and coolly considered."

ENCLOSURE

THE ANCONA CASE.

The Department has received no official report from the Austrian Government in regard to the sinking of the ANCONA. Ambassador Penfield telegraphed a summary of an official report appearing in the Vienna Press, November 14th and the Austrian Chargé here, without instruction, informally sent to Mr. Phillips in a letter of November 15th, a copy of the same report.

From the information at hand from other sources it appears that the submarine, flying no flag, opened fire at a distance of five miles, whereupon the ANCONA took flight. The submarine pursued the ANCONA, raising the Austrian flag. Upon being overhauled the ANCONA stopped. Three shells and a torpedo were fired while the Captain and forty (?) were still on board. No proof that the ship's boats were fired at. (Statement of French Ministry of Marine, received from Prefect of Bizerta—/29)

One American survivor (said to be the only one) Mrs. Dr. Greil,[1] said that she is not sure as to the effort of the ANCONA to escape because she was below deck at the time. She was certain, however, that the submarine bombardment lasted forty-five minutes and continued after the vessel had stopped. She saw a red and white flag on the submarine. (Report of Consul at Tunis—/24)

The Captain of the steamship FRANCE, sunk on the same day by a German submarine which he plainly saw while in the boats, heard at noon twenty-three shots and saw a steamer five or six miles away apparently the object of the cannonading. (Report of French Ministry of Marine—/21)

The Italian Foreign Office has not confirmed the report that the submarine was German rather than Austrian, but said that the flag "appeared" to be Austrian. (Report of Rome Amb.—/27)

It seems that 206 passengers are unaccounted for out of 480, but the number of Americans among them is in doubt; one report stating that there were 26 Americans lost, some of them supposedly naturalized. (Naples and Rome—/1, 16, 21)

PRESS REPORTS:

A report in the Rome Press stated that the Captain of the ANCONA swore that the submarine was of German nationality. (Rome Ambassador—/28)

The official report appearing in the press in Vienna stated that after the submarine fired a warning shot the ANCONA fled and was pursued under fire, only stopping after several shots. No further shots were fired and forty-five minutes were given to leave the ship. There was great panic on board. Only part of the boats being lowered which were occupied by the crew. The other boats were not lowered. After fifty minutes the submarine submerged on account of a rapidly approaching steamer and torpedoed the ANCONA. (Vienna Ambassador—/23)

T MS (SDR, RG 59, 865.857 An 2/75 A, DNA).
[1] Cecile L. Greil, M.D., of New York, who was returning from Italy, where she had served with the Red Cross since 1914.

From Mary Allen Hulbert

Dear Woodrow: Los Angeles, Cal. Nov. 22nd, 1915.

I want to call you that hereafter. And wish you would address me as "Mary," for there is no one left for whom I care that calls me so since my Mother died. I am glad you think me "fine." I do not feel so.

I am enclosing two letters[1] that will explain themselves and for the last time am asking you to give the necessary help if you can. Mr. Herbert H. Clark is the man who called upon you in W[ashington]. and who is selling the ranch land we have planted in avocados. We knew Mr. Clark in Pittsfield and, as you will see by Mr. Dickensons[2] letter, others will vouch for his integrity. *We know* we have a fine, clean, valuable business to offer and have staked our all upon it. We have $1800.00 left to live on. If we fail, it is the end. And I am going out in *some way* if it does.

I'm tired. I have not cashed the check H.B.[3] sent. And am afraid to return it. If sickness comes to either of us, it would be hard to manage financially. If this business prospers, all is well. Hence:—do all you can in vouching for the honesty of Mr. C. through us. And we are honest. You can not imagine the humiliation I feel in again asking help. The Mr. Philip Bayer, referred to in the letter, has stock (U. S. Steel) loaned to him by Allen to tide him over financial difficulties and now refuses to return it, offering $2000.00 instead of the $10000.00 due. My *foolish* boy! He is *splendid* now, though, and is persevering in his work as well as his good habits. The shell known as M.A.H. still functions. I could laugh if it were not all so tragic. Do your best for your old friend   Mary A. H.

Nov. 24th.

I am enclosing with this the prospectus, Mr. Dickensons letter, referring to any of the gentlemen in the Conn. Gen. Life Ins. Co., an envelope upon which is stamped the address of two men in Washington who are experts on the avocado question and hope I have thus completed the circle. No impatience that you can feel, no thought that you are being *used*, is unforseen by me, and I assure you it is only because I am fighting for Allen's *life* that forces me to do it. I know no one else. In the supreme friendship for you, no one else has counted. And I suddenly find myself alone on my life raft. Of what use to say more. Unless you are indifferent you will see the necessity for action, and hasty action. Please telegraph C.O.D. if you can attend to this *at once*. Messrs. Popenoe[4] can be seen in Washington to assure you of the value of this undertaking. *Please ask them.*

The San Fernando Avocado Co: is M. A. & A. S. Hulbert.
Mr. Clark is Sales Manager.
We wish a letter to assure the buyers of our integrity.
    You are *only* interested through *Mr*. A. S. Hulbert, for whom you have affection and interest. M. A. Hulbert is a *very* silent partner, and her name need not be mentioned. Forward letter to Mr. Clark at St. Nicholas Club, 7 W. 44th St. N. Y. City.
    I have the Nantucket cottage free from encumbrance and the $1800.00 cash. Allen can mortgage the cottage to carry him on, if I have to go in event of Mr. Clarks failure to sell the property and carry out our plans to the full. *Please send* Enclosures, unless you wish to keep Mr. Dickenson's letter *to Mr. Clark.*

ALS (WP, DLC).
    [1] Both enclosures are missing.
    [2] All that is known about him is that his name was George L. Dickinson. See JPT to H. H. Clark, Dec. 14, 1915.

3 Helen Bones. She had obviously sent Mrs. Hulbert a check after Wilson received her letter of October 11. The canceled check was destroyed.

4 Charles Holcomb Popenoe and Wilson Popenoe, both of the Department of Agriculture. Wilson Popenoe had published articles on the avocado industry of southern California.

From the Diary of Colonel House

November 22, 1915.

Dudley Malone came this morning to tell of his activities in Washington. I have mentioned before what he had to say concerning his interview with the President. We discussed the New York Postmastership and he is to send his friend Larkin[1] to see me this afternoon so I may look him over for that place. He reported that he dined with McAdoo and that they parted in good humor.

The Director of the Mint, Robert Woolley, came to lunch. We had two hours together. We talked of the coming campaign almost wholly and of his independent committee which is, as far as I can see, doing the only campaign work that is being done. McCombs is doing nothing, and even worse than nothing, for every now and then we find where he has given the Administration an underhand thrust. It is a question whether to have an open break and get rid of him on December 7th when the National Committee meets, or to let matters continue as they are until the National Convention in June.

Woolley told much of the Washington scandal mongers' talk of the President. He thinks something should be done to counteract it. There is a deliberate purpose to make the President appear before the country as a thoroughly immoral man. The most exaggerated stories are being told of him, none of them having the slightest foundation. It is this characteristic of the human race, for it is not confined to any particular country, that discourages one most and makes one feel less confident for the future of the race. I am always urging the President to strike at this vicious practice and he promises he will do so when he is relieved of the cares of office. That, I fear, will be too late. To-day, he speaks to the Nation, tomorrow, as a private citizen, he will speak to but few.

1 William P. Larkin, of P. F. Collier and Son, publishers, and supreme director of the Knights of Columbus.

To Joseph Patrick Tumulty

Dear Tumulty: [The White House, Nov. 23, 1915]

Please express my regret to Mr. Lyon that I did not get this
letter in time to reply for his issue of tomorrow,[1] and please say
that I have always regarded Washington's work as of the very
highest consequences to his race and to the country.

The President.

TL (WP, DLC).
[1] E. Lyon and A. L. Gaines to WW, Nov. 20, 1915, TLS, (WP, DLC). Lyon,
the editor, and Gaines, the business manager of the Baltimore *Commonwealth*,
requested a contribution from Wilson for their symposium on the character and
life work of Booker T. Washington, who had died on November 14.

Count Johann Heinrich von Bernstorff
to Theobald von Bethmann Hollweg

Washington, den 23. November 1915.

A. Nr. 556. In meiner letzten Unterredung mit Oberst House
entwickelte mir dieser Herrn Wilson's neuesten Plan, nach wel-
chem der Präsident wieder als Friedensstifter auftreten will. Das
einzige Greifbare an dem Plan ist bisher, daß eine zweite Mission
des Oberst House nach London und Berlin erfolgen soll, wenn
Euere Exzellenz damit einverstanden sind.

Alles übrige ist noch nebelhaft und beruht zum Teil auf amerikanischen Phrasen und Vorurteilen. Herr Wilson ist der Ansicht,
daß er sich nicht in Fragen wie territoriale Änderungen, Indem-
nität usw. einmischen dürfe. Solche Angelegenheiten gingen die
Amerikaner nichts an, und der Präsident würde daher die hiesige
öffentliche Meinung nicht hinter sich haben, wenn seine Friedensaktion auf derartige Fragen einginge. Woran aber die Amerikaner allein großes Interesse hätten, sei die Wiederherstellung
des Friedens, sowie die Beseitigung von "militarism" und "navalism." Deutschland werde England nur in dem Fall zwingen
können, die "Freiheit der See" anzuerkennen, daß die Vereinigten Staaten von Amerika dieses Verlangen unterstützen und daß
wir bereit seien, unseren angeblich bedrohlichen Militarismus zu
beseitigen. Die kriegführenden Mächte sollten sich also gewis-
sermaßen gegenseitig dagegen versichern, daß ein neuer Krieg
ausbricht.

Oberst House sagt mir, er habe obige Gedanken Euerer Exzellenz bereits mündlich vorgetragen, sodaß ich nicht weitläufig
auf dieselben einzugehen brauche. Die praktische Durchführung
des Planes hält Herr Wilson für möglich, weil alle Kriegsvor-
bereitungen heutzutage, wie aus den neuesten Erfahrungen er-

sichtlich, von der Anfertigung der Munition abhängig [seien]. Nach dieser Richtung hin könnten von beiden Seiten bindende Zusagen gegeben werden. Der Präsident meint, diese Vorschläge müßten sämtlichen beteiligten Mächten willkommen sein, weil diese nach Wiederherstellung des Friedens alle Männer für die Industrie brauchen werden, um die Geldmittel zu beschaffen, mit denen die Kriegsschulden bezahlt werden könnten. Herr Wilson glaubt ferner, daß alles andere sich leicht erledigen ließe, wenn seine Friedensbasis angenommen würde.

Ich kann von hier aus nicht ermessen, ob Euere Exzellenz jetzt irgend eine Friedensaktion erwünscht ist und ob die Bedingungen, welche wir stellen werden, schon greifbare Form angenommen haben. Immerhin scheint mir Herrn Wilson's Idee "der Freiheit der See" sehr beachtenswert, weil England im letzten Ende diesen Krieg herbeigeführt hat, um seine Seeherrschaft wieder auf Jahre hinaus zu sichern. Zu entscheiden wäre nur, ob wir hinsichtlich des sogenannten "Militarismus" Konzessionen machen können und wollen. Es wären ja schließlich nur Scheinko[n]zessionen, da unser "Militarismus" niemals jemand bedroht noch bedrückt hat.

Von hiesigem Standpunkt aus betrachtet, erscheint mir die Mission House wünschenswert, weil die Vereinigten Staaten in Berlin leider so schlecht vertreten sind. Oberst House ist zum mindesten völlig neutral, sehr diskret sowie vertrauenswürdig und steht inmitten der hiesigen politischen Verhältnisse. Er könnte viel beitragen, die gegenseitigen Beziehungen zu verbessern. Wenn Euere Exzellenz indessen bereits dahin entschieden haben, daß der sogenannte "Militarismus" bei den Friedensverhandlungen gänzlich ausgeschaltet werden soll und muß, so könnte die Mission House uns Verlegenheiten bereiten. Falls dieselbe aber erwünscht ist, erbitte ich ein Radiogramm mit dem einzigen Inhalt "Einverstanden." Daraufhin würde Herr House gleich abreisen und ich will ihn gegebenenfalls zu bereden suchen, erst nach Berlin und dann nach London zu fahren. Wenn ich nichts von Euerer Exzellenz höre, so werde ich Herrn House dilatorisch behandeln. Er hat sich mir bisher außerordentlich nützlich erwiesen.   Bernstorff.

TCL (Der Weltkrieg No. 2, Vermittlungsaktionen, geheim, vol. 14, pp. 112-13, GFO-Ar).

Washington, November 23, 1915

A[nswering] No. 556. During my last conversation with Colonel House, he set forth Mr. Wilson's latest plan, according to which the President desires again to act as peacemaker. So far, the only tangible thing about the plan is that a second mission of Colonel House to London and Berlin is to take place, if Your Excellency will agree to this.

Everything else is still very uncertain and is based partly on American rhetoric and prejudices. House said that the President believes that he must not interfere in questions involving, for example, territorial changes, indemnity, etc. Such matters are of no concern to the Americans. If his peace initiative should go into questions of this kind, the President would, therefore, not have the support of public opinion. The only point that the Americans are strongly interested in is the restoration of peace as well as the elimination of "militarism" and "navalism." Germany would be able to force England to recognize the "freedom of the seas" only if the United States of America should support this demand and we would be prepared to abandon our allegedly threatening militarism. The belligerent powers should, so to speak, mutually insure each other against the outbreak of a new war.

Colonel House told me that he had already expressed the above ideas to Your Excellency verbally, so that I need not elaborate them any further. Mr. Wilson thinks that a practical execution of the plan would be possible because, as the most recent experiences have shown, all preparations for war are contingent upon the manufacture of munitions. With regard to this question, both sides could give binding assurances. The President is of the opinion that these proposals ought to be welcomed by all the powers involved, since, after the restoration of peace, they would need all their available men for industrial purposes in order to find the money to pay off the war debts. Mr. Wilson further believes that everything else could be easily settled once his basis for peace had been accepted.

I cannot determine from here whether Your Excellency desires any kind of a peace move at this time and whether the conditions which we will submit have already taken concrete form. Still, Mr. Wilson's idea of "the freedom of the seas" seems to me to be very noteworthy. For, in the final analysis, England has brought about this war for the purpose of again securing her domination of the seas for years to come. The only question to decide is whether we either can or want to make any concessions with regard to our so-called militarism. After all, they would be concessions in form only, as our "militarism" has never menaced or oppressed anyone.

Looked at from this standpoint, it seems to me that House's

mission is desirable, because the United States is, unfortunately, so poorly represented in Berlin. Colonel House is at least absolutely neutral, very discreet as well as trustworthy, and stands in the center of the political situation here. He could contribute much to the improvement of mutual relations. However, if Your Excellency should have already decided that the so-called militarism shall be and must be entirely excluded from consideration during the peace negotiations, House's mission could prove an embarrassment to us. But if his mission is desired, I ask for a telegram containing the single word "agreed." Mr. House would then depart immediately, and, if necessary, I will try to persuade him to go first to Berlin, and then to London. If I do not hear anything from Your Excellency, I will deal with House dilatorily. So far, he has proved himself to be of extraordinary value to me.

Bernstorff.

An Appeal

24th November 1915.

The day is at hand on which we bend our thoughts toward a consideration of the blessings of peace and security. Inevitably, the contemplation of our own good fortune must bring sharply to mind the anguish and the loss which lie, an intolerable and crushing burden, upon the bodies and souls of our neighbors across the seas. Our country has poured out generously of its sympathy and its means in behalf of those who suffer because of the war. But the harvest of death and desolation is not ended and our sympathy must not yet withdraw its hand.

The American Red Cross, through whose instrumentality hundreds of thousands of our people have been enabled to give substantial expression to their pity for those who have fallen beneath the iron tread of war, is nearing the exhaustion of its resources. Into its war relief fund it has received, in round sum, $1,600,000. In the sending and maintaining of near four hundred surgeons, nurses and sanitarians, who have carried American skill into all the zones of war, in financial aid to hospitals and other Red Cross institutions, and in the purchase and transport of near 4,000,000 pounds of hospital and medical supplies and equipment, this sum has been reduced to less than $50,000 now available to meet the great demands of the approaching winter.

That the splendid work of this organization which, more than any other, represents the sympathy of us all shall be permitted to cease, is unthinkable. Therefore do I call upon the people of the United States once again, by their generosity, to assure the Red Cross against the curtailment or discontinuance of the large activities in which it is engaged. That this assurance is urgent is shown by the comparatively small sum remaining in its treasury, a sum which, closely as it may be husbanded, will suffice for but a few weeks.

Contributions may be forwarded to any state or local treasurer of the Red Cross or to the National Headquarters, Washington, D. C.   Woodrow Wilson.

T MS (WP, DLC).

Two Letters to Robert Lansing

My dear Mr. Secretary,   The White House. 24 November, 1915.

This information is, as you say, most unsatisfactorily incomplete and inconclusive.[1] I sincerely hope that we can get a complete account of the case from the two points of view of Rome and Vienna, through our Ambassadors, at an early date. I think the public are growing uneasy because of our apparent inaction in what seems a very aggravated case.

Faithfully Yours,   W.W.

WWTLI (SDR, RG 59, 865.857 An 2/75½, DNA).
[1] The Enclosure with RL to WW, Nov. 22, 1915.

My dear Mr. Secretary,   The White House. 24 November, 1915.

Here are two recent letters from Mr. House[1] which I am sure will interest you. Bernstorff evidently wants to use House as a channel of unofficial communication with us.

I would be very much obliged to you if you would return the letters with your comments on them.

Faithfully Yours,   W.W.

WWTLI (SDR, RG 59, 763.72/2322½, DNA).
[1] EMH to WW, Nov. 19 and 21, 1915.

From Robert Lansing

PERSONAL AND PRIVATE:

My dear Mr. President: Washington November 24, 1915.

Thank you for letting me see the two letters from Colonel House, which I herewith return.

I tried to impress upon Bernstorff when I saw him the necessity of a speedy settlement of the LUSITANIA case. I have heard nothing from him since that conversation and shall write him today urging him to act in the matter.[1] Something must be done before Congress assembles or else I am afraid we will have some embarrassing requests for the correspondence.

I think the time is very opportune for us to press compliance with our demands; with the success of the Teutonic arms in the Balkans and the wavering neutrality of Roumania and Greece the German Government could ill afford to have any sort of a break with this Government on account of the moral effect it would have.

In regard to the discussion relative to peace, I think that there is a possibility that it might work out along the lines suggested but there are so many problems connected with it—such as boundaries, colonial possessions and indemnities, that I hardly like to express an opinion until it takes more definite form.

In regard to the two questions which Colonel House asks in his second letter relative to the removal of certain persons connected with the Embassies and Consular Service of Germany and Austria-Hungary, I feel that the time is very near when some such step should be taken. As you know, we have been collecting and marshalling, as far as possible, the evidence which we have against the various individuals. While the proofs are not conclusive I think there is sufficient for action but I would prefer to submit to you the memorandum on the subject before any decision is reached.

In regard to severing diplomatic relations with Austria on account of the ANCONA, you know how incomplete our information is. I hope that we may shortly have something definite from Vienna and from Rome also.

I am attending the Army-Navy football game in New York on Saturday and will remain over Sunday. Colonel House has been good enough to invite Mrs. Lansing and myself to luncheon Sunday, so I will have an opportunity to discuss these questions with him at length.   Faithfully yours,   Robert Lansing.

TLS (WP, DLC).

[1] RL to J. H. von Bernstorff, Nov. 24, 1915, TCL (SDR, RG 59, 763.72/2322c, DNA), printed in FR-LP, I, 496. Bernstorff sent Lansing's letter to Bethmann Hollweg on November 25, adding that he had learned from a "strictly confidential source" (House) that the President would not push the Lusitania question seriously any more. (J. H. von Bernstorff to T. von Bethmann Hollweg, Nov. 25, 1915, TCL (Der Weltkrieg, No. 18a, Unterseebootkrieg gegen England, ganz geheim, Vol. 15, pp. 107-108, GFO-Ar.)

From Robert Lansing, with Enclosure

PERSONAL AND CONFIDENTIAL:

My dear Mr. President: Washington November 24, 1915.

I enclose a memorandum covering the subject of the Monroe Doctrine, its application, and the possible extension of the principle in a way to constitute a policy which may be termed a "Carribean Policy," since it is limited in application to the territory in and about the Carribean Sea.

Briefly, the memorandum is this:

The Monroe Doctrine is based on the theory that any extension by a European power of political control, beyond that which exists over any territory in this hemisphere, is a menace to the national safety of the United States. The means of extending political control, thus far recognized, has been by occupation of unattached territory, by conquest and by cession.

Recently the financing of revolutions and corruption of governments of the smaller republics by European capitalists have frequently thrown the control of these governments into the hands of a European power.

To avoid this danger of European political control by this means which may be as great a menace to the national safety of this country as occupation or cession, the only method seems to be to establish a stable and honest government and to prevent the revenues of the republic from becoming the prize of revolution and of the foreigners who finance it.

Stability and honesty of government depend on sufficient force to resist revolutions and on sufficient control over the revenues and over the development of the resources to prevent official graft and dishonest grants of privileges.

The possession of the Panama Canal and its defense have in a measure given to the territories in and about the Carribean Sea a new importance from the standpoint of our national safety. It is vital to the interests of this country that European political domination should in no way be extended over these regions. As it happens within this area lie the small republics of America which have been and to an extent still are the prey of revolutionists, of corrupt governments, and of predatory foreigners.

Because of this state of affairs our national safety, in my opinion, requires that the United States should intervene and aid in the establishment and maintenance of a stable and honest government, if no other way seems possible to attain that end.

I make no argument on the ground of the benefit which would result to the peoples of these republics by the adoption of this policy. That they would be the chief beneficiaries in that their public and private rights would be respected, and their prosperity and intellectual development insured, is manifest. Nevertheless the argument based on humanitarian purpose does not appeal to me, even though it might be justly urged, because too many international crimes have been committed in the name of Humanity.

It seems to me that the ground of national safety, the conservation of national interests, is the one which should be advanced in support of this policy. It is reasonable, practical, and in full accord with the principle of the Monroe Doctrine.

In considering this policy it should be borne in mind what has been done already in Cuba, Panama, Nicaragua, the Dominican Republic and Haiti, and what may have to be done in the small neighboring republics. The Danish West Indies and the colonial possessions of other European nations in the Carribean should not be forgotten in considering this policy as through a change of their sovereignty they might become a serious menace to the interests of the United States.

Faithfully yours,   Robert Lansing

TLS (SDR, RG 59, 710.11/1881½, DNA).

E N C L O S U R E

November 24, 1915.

PRESENT NATURE AND EXTENT OF THE MONROE DOCTRINE.

The Monroe Doctrine is in substance that the United States considers an extension of political control by a European power over any territory in this hemisphere, not already occupied by it, to be a menace to the national safety of the United States.

In 1823, when the doctrine was enunciated, the dangers of the extension of European political power on this continent lay in the possible occupation of unsettled regions and in the conquest of the territory of an independent American state.

Later, during the Polk Administration, another danger was recognized in the possibility of a voluntary cession of territory by an American state to a European power, and the Monroe Doctrine was shown to be broad enough to include this means of acquiring political dominion.

While the primary idea of the Monroe Doctrine is opposition by the United States to any extension of European control over American territory or institutions, the idea is subject to modification that the control must possess the element of permanency.

When the hostile occupation of the territory of an American state or the coercion by force of its government by a European power is intended to be temporary, and is employed solely as a means to compel the government of the state to meet a particular international obligation, which it has wilfully neglected or refused to perform, the territorial occupation or coercion would not appear to be in violation of the Monroe Doctrine. Nevertheless the intention of temporary control must be beyond question, and any indication of converting temporary control for a particular purpose into permanent control for general purposes would bring the case within the scope of the Doctrine and create a situation, in which the United States might be compelled to intervene.

Just how far a European government should be permitted to exercise control over American territory or over an American government as a means of obtaining redress for an international wrong is a question which must be decided in each case upon the facts. If it may be reasonably presumed from the circumstances surrounding the assumption of control or from the length of time it continues that the intention is to make it permanent, denial of such intention by the controlling power should in no way interfere with the assertion by the United States of its established policy or with its insistence that the European aggressor immediately withdraw from the territory or surrender its control.

In dealing with the cases as they arise the two essential elements of the Monroe Doctrine must be constantly borne in mind: first, that the doctrine is exclusively a *national* policy of the United States and relates to its national safety and vital interests; and second, that the European control, against which it is directed, must possess the element of *permanency*, or a reasonable possibility of permanency.

While occupation and conquest, as a means of obtaining political control over American territory by a European power, are acts of that power alone, voluntary cession, as a means, is the mutual act of the two governments which are parties to the transfer. As a consequence the inclusion of voluntary cession among the acts of acquisition, against which the Monroe Doctrine is directed, introduces the necessary corrolary that it may be invoked against an American government as well as against a European government. It is manifest from this that the Monroe Doctrine is, as has been said, a national policy of the United States and also that it is not a Pan-American policy. The opposition to European control over American territory is not primarily to preserve the integrity of any American state—that may be a result but not a purpose of the Doctrine. The essential idea is to prevent a condition which would menace the national interests of the United States.

In case it should become necessary to enforce the Monroe Doctrine against another American republic, which has ceded or apparently intends to cede any of its territorial rights to a European power, the preventive action of the United States would appear to be a direct interference with the sovereign authority of the American republic over its own territory. Logically such action, in case a cession is made or intended, amounts to an assertion of the primacy of the United States in the Western Hemisphere. The primacy of one nation, though possessing the superior physical might to maintain it, is out of harmony with the principle of the equality of nations which underlies Pan-Americanism, however just or altruistic the primate may be.

While, therefore, the Monroe Doctrine and Pan-Americanism may come into conflict, the Monroe Doctrine will in case of conflict prevail so long as the United States maintains the Doctrine and is the dominant power among the American nations. The equality of American republics and, in a measure, their independence are legal rather than actual, but it is necessary to acknowledge their legal existence, if the theory of Pan-Americanism is accepted. The Monroe Doctrine, on the contrary, is founded upon no assumptions of this character but upon a fact, namely, the superior power of the United States to compel submission to its will whenever condition arises involving European control over American territory, which, because of the permanent nature of the control, is considered to be a menace to the national safety of the United States.

The Monroe Doctrine, therefore, should not be confused with Pan-Americanism. It is purely a national policy of the United States, while Pan-Americanism is the joint policy of the American group of nations. The Pan-American policy may support and may probably be considered as invariably supporting the idea of the Monroe Doctrine in opposing the extension of European political control over any portion of this continent. The reason, however, for such support will not be the national safety of the United States, but the mutual protection of American nations from European attempts upon their independence. In its advocacy of the Monroe Doctrine the United States considers its own interests. The integrity of other American nations is an incident, not an end. While this may seem based on selfishness alone, the author of the Doctrine had no higher or more generous motive in its declaration. To assert for it a nobler purpose is to proclaim a new doctrine.

As stated, this traditional policy, as originally declared and subsequently defined, relates to European acquisition of political power in America by means of occupation, conquest or cession of territory. There is, nevertheless, another method by which such power may be acquired, a method, which today can be more easily and more successfully employed than those to which the Monroe Doctrine has been in the past applied. It is a mode of extending political power, which, in my opinion, has caused much of the confusion and uncertainty as to the scope of the Monroe Doctrine because of its gradual development and the failure to recognize it as practically defeating that policy, particularly in the smaller republics about the Carribean Sea.

NEED AND NATURE OF A CARRIBEAN POLICY BASED ON THE PRINCIPLE OF THE MONROE DOCTRINE

Within the past quarter of a century the rapid increase of wealth in the United States and the great nations of Europe has caused their people, in constantly increasing numbers, to seek investments in foreign lands. No richer field has been presented than the vast undeveloped resources of the republics south of the United States. Hundreds of millions of dollars have been expended in these lands by the capitalists of this country, Great Britain, France, Germany, and other European nations in the construction of railways, the establishment of steamship lines, the development of mines, the cultivation of cotton, fruits, and other agricultural products, and the operation of various industrial enterprises.

In the opening up of these countries and the development of their resources their governments, particularly those of the smaller countries, require financial aid, or seize the opportunity to replenish their treasuries. Eager investors, appreciating the natural riches of these regions and the possibilities of large returns to those who obtain the right to exploit them, lend their money readily in exchange for special privileges, concessions and excessive rates of interest.

The governments of many of these small republics, impoverished, improvident and frequently in the hands of unscrupulous and avaricious men, borrow beyond the limit of their capacity to repay, hypothecating every possible source of national revenue for years to come. As a result some of these republics, ruled by military dictators or oligarchies, who have enriched themselves at the expense of the people, have become bankrupt.

In some cases citizens of the United States, in others subjects of a European power, are the chief creditors, to whose favor the insolvent nation must look for the means to continue its political existence.

With the industrial activity, the scramble for markets, and the incessant search for new opportunities to produce wealth, which have been characteristic of economic life in recent years, commercial expansion and success are closely interwoven with political domination over the territory which is being exploited, and particularly so if the government is weak or corrupt.

The European power, whose subjects supply the capital to install and operate the principal industries of a small American republic and furnish the funds upon which its government is dependent, may, if it finds it expedient to do so, dominate the political action of the government. To state it in another way, a European power whose subjects own the public debt of an American state and have invested there large amounts of capital, would be able to control the government of the state almost as completely as if it had acquired sovereign rights over the territory through occupation, conquest or cession.

The method of obtaining political mastery by means of financial control has been an increasing menace to the independence of the republics situated in or about the Carribean Sea. Revolutions have been frequent, due in the majority of cases to the desire of a factional leader by becoming master of the nation's revenues to amass wealth for himself and his immediate friends. A revolutionary chief finds little difficulty in financing his venture among foreign speculators, who are willing to take the risk because of the large profits which will be theirs if the revolution is successful. As a result the people of these countries are the victims of constant strife between rival leaders, and their condition is little improved by the governments, which exist only a short time and which are used to enrich their rulers and those who have financed them.

The consequent instability of government in these small republics, the corrupt character of the rulers, and the powerful influence of foreign financiers who have aided the rulers in obtaining and will aid them in maintaining control, not only threaten the national independence but prevent the people from developing intellectually or from attaining any degree of prosperity.

The United States in any circumstances would be desirous as a friend of an American republic, which is suffering from this state of affairs, to aid it in removing the cause. But in the case of the Carribean republics self-interest as well as friendship appeals. Since the construction of the Panama Canal it is essential for its safety that the neighboring nations should not come under the political domination of any European power either by force or by cession or through the agency of financial control. While force and cession are not impossible means if the government of a republic is corrupt or weak, the greater danger lies in financial control.[1]

To meet this danger the surest if not the only means, is the establishment of a stable and honest government which will devote the revenues of the state to developing its resources, and to educating its people, and which will protect individuals in their rights of life, liberty and property, and in the enjoyment of their political rights.

In order to accomplish this the first thing to be done is to remove the prize of revolution, namely, the control of the public revenues. If this can be done there will be few revolutions about the Carribean. In the second place the government must not be dependent on foreign financiers for its continuance in power. In the third place it must possess a reliable and efficient military force sufficient to suppress any insurrection against the established authority.

If there could arise in all the Carribean republics men of strong character, patriotic and honest, as there have in some, who are able to carry out such a policy, it would be well for all concerned. Unfortunately this is not the case, and the United States is of necessity forced to choose between permitting these republics to continue to be the prey of unscrupulous adventurers native and foreign, or to undertake the task of aiding in the establishment of a stable and honest government, which will insure political independence and prevent any possibility of European control.

It would seem, therefore, that in the case of the republics about the Carribean Sea the United States should expand the Monroe Doctrine, and declare that, while it does not seek dominion over the territory of any of these republics, it is necessary for the national safety of the United States, in view of its interests in Panama, that it aid the prople [people] of those republics in establishing and maintaining responsible and honest governments to such extent as may be necessary in each particular case, and that it will not tolerate control over or interference with the political affairs of these republics by any European power or its nationals or permit the occupation, even temporarily, by a European power, of any territory of such republics.

T MS (SDR, RG 59, 710.11/1881½, DNA).

1 In fact, Wilson, in WW to J. H. von Bernstorff, Sept. 16, 1914, Vol. 31, pp. 34-36, had already enunciated such a corollary to the Monroe Doctrine. Curiously, it was never published and was unknown until discovered in the State Department files by Dana G. Munro. He mentions it briefly in his *Intervention and Dollar Diplomacy in the Caribbean, 1900-1921* (Princeton, N. J., 1964), p. 339.

A Memorandum by Joseph Patrick Tumulty

NATIONAL DEFENSE—   [c. Nov. 25, 1915]

I think the President in his Message or in his speech at Columbus, Ohio, should show why a policy of preparedness is necessary.

The Richmond Times-Dispatch asks the question, "Preparedness for what?" And then says, "Certainly, this nation is not to prepare for world conquest, for war is in no man's heart or at least in no man's public speech, and equally it is not designed to prepare against the armed assault of all the powers of the earth. The taxpayers are entitled to a frank discussion of what the object is."

I think in the speech the President ought to say that there is an additional reason for preparedness and it lies in this: No one can foresee what the outcome of the war in Europe may be as effecting our own nation, her acts and her diverse interests and institutions. Certainly, one of the inevitable results of the war as the experience of the world teaches is that there will be new adjustments, new alighments [alignments], possibly new efforts for colonial expansion. These new alliances and new alignments may eventually threaten our own sovereignty, our own rights and our own interests in this hemisphere. Would there not be a threat to America and her interests in this hemisphere in the very circumstances growing out of these new alignments?

The Monroe Doctrine is vital to our own institutions and in the minds of most Americans, preparedness involves capacity to uphold the Monroe Doctrine, *not singly perhaps, but in coöperation with the great nations to the south*. Most Americans regard that doctrine as vital to the perpetuity of free institutions on this continent, and would not countenance its surrender or the sacrifice of its integrity.

As the Richmond Times-Dispatch says, "It is as clear as anything of the future possibly can be that the present war will be followed by epoch-making shifts in territorial suzerainty. One or another of the great combatants will lose its colonies, and thereafter hunger for new outlets for its population. Hardly a European nation but will feel the loss of much of its best manhood, fleeing from the clutch of war taxes. Who can doubt that, under such circumstances the eyes of disappointed ambition and shattered hope will be turned toward South America, with its hundreds of thousands of square miles of fertility and promise? *Who can doubt either that anything less potent than a Monroe Doctrine vigorously proclaimed and backed by a nation's might would be capable or [of] restraining the threatened seizure?"*

I think the President in this speech ought to re-affirm the basic principles of the Monroe Doctrine. (See copy of excerpts from Annual Message of James Monroe, 1823, attached herewith.)[1] And then he should restate a new Pan-American Doctrine which would make the ABC powers, representing twenty nations of South and Central America, partners with the United States in the defense of American soil against European aggression.

For such a statement, the foundation was laid at the Niagara conference on conditions in Mexico, and strengthened by the more recent Pan-American conference that resulted in the recognition of Carranza.

In this way the Monroe Doctrine would be popularized in South American countries and at the same time it would be rendered more formidable throughout the world.

T MS (WP, DLC).
[1] Not printed.

From Edward Mandell House, with Enclosure

Dear Governor: New York. November 25th, 1915.

Here is a letter that has just come from Sir Edward.

Please remember that when he wrote it he had not received my cable telling him that we had in mind paragraph 4 of his letter.

I hope I shall have a chance to discuss this letter with you when you are here so you may advise as to its answer.

Affectionately yours,   E. M. House

TLS (WP, DLC).

E N C L O S U R E

Sir Edward Grey to Edward Mandell House

Dear Colonel House: London. 11 November 1915.

If I were to approach the Allies, or even the Cabinet, about the elimination of militarism and navalism, they would ask what was meant by it; and I should have to put some definite proposal before them. That is why I cabled to ask exactly what you meant. I do not see how they could commit themselves in advance to any proposition without knowing exactly what it was, and knowing that the United States of America were prepared to intervene and make it good if they accepted it.

The position at present is this: France and Russia and this country have made up their minds to a winter campaign. France thinks that she is quite secure in the West. Russia thinks that the worst is over on her line of battle, and that when she gets some more rifles her situation will improve. The unfavorable spot is the Balkans and the Mohammedan world, where developments may be increasingly unfavourable.

I see two possibilities: One is that the President should let it be known that he is prepared to mediate, and that, if either side desires it, he will state the conditions on which he will do so. The other is that he should wait until he gets an intimation from one side or the other that mediation would be acceptable, in which case he could then reply by stating the conditions on which he would be prepared to act.

I wish that you were here, so that I could talk things over; but the situation at the moment and the feelings here and among the Allies, and in Germany as far as I know, do not justify me in urging you to come on the ground that your presence would have any practical result at the moment.

I have sent my letters to you through the Embassy, because I thought that they would go as quickly that way as by post. I will ascertain why this is not the case. It is much the safest method by which I can send letters.

I had my last letter sealed up on purpose that Sir Cecil Spring Rice might not know its contents. I trust him implicitly, but I think that it would be embarrassing, both for you and for him, that he should know everything that passes.

I do not know what our reply will be to your Note about Blockade and Contraband. The Note is before our Legal Advisers.

My feeling in reading it was that, if we admitted all its contentions, it would be tantamount to admitting that, under modern conditions, we could not prevent Germany from trading, at any rate through neutral ports, as freely in time of war as in time of peace; and that we must either continue the difference of opinion with your Government, or give up definitely and openly any attempt to stop goods going to and from Germany through neutral ports.

The friction and trouble that we have over this matter are so great that I have often wished, in despair, to give it up: but that would go near to abdicating all chance of preventing Germany from being successful.

After fifteen months of practical experience of war under modern conditions, I am convinced that the real question is not one of legal niceties about Contraband and other things, but whether we are to do what we are doing, or nothing at all. The contentions of your Government would restrict our operations in such a way that Germany could evade them wholesale, and they would be mere paper rights, quite useless in practice.

I cannot help feeling that, if we had done all the things that Germany has done in the war, and if we had instigated, as Germans have apparently instigated, criminal plots on American soil, American opinion would have pushed resentment home against us more than it has done against Germany.

As it is, it looks as if the United States might now strike the weapon of sea power out of our hands, and thereby ensure a German victory.   Yours sincerely,   E. Grey.

TCL (WP, DLC).

From J. Edwin Murphy

Dear Mr. President: [Washington] November 25, 1915.

Responding to your pointed and readily understandable note of the 22nd instant asking for an explanation of an objectionable item printed in The Times of the 21st instant, I have to confess that I can explain, but not justify.

The matter to which you object came to The Times from its regular news service, the United Press. It was used in exactly the form it was received by us, except for the fact that through an unexplainable typographical mistake the word "darned" in the last sentence of the United Press copy appears in The Times as "damned."

The item reached our columns and presses because, unfortunately, it did not pass under the eye of the undersigned, or of any other responsible editor equipped with the discretion and good taste that should have dictated that it be not printed. The publication of the item was in violation of a very insistent rule of The Times against printing objectionable personal matter about anybody, and especially against printing such things as involve the personal sensibilities or the official dignity of the President.

We have been compelled of late to make this rule much more stringent because of the flood of foolish, frivolous and inexcusable stories pouring into this office or published in papers throughout the country, and I am sure that if you could know the measure of success of our efforts to avoid deserving the humiliation your rebuke entails, you would realize that the newspapers, and especially The Times, are not compounded exclusively of carelessness.

I am writing you in this way with no expectation or hope that it will be an excuse for this dereliction in this instance. I beg of you to believe that my own regrets are as keen as your disgust must be, and finally, I ask you to accept my very sincere and earnest apology.   Yours very respectfully,   J. E. Murphy

TLS (WP, DLC).

From the Diary of Colonel House

November 27, 1915.

When I returned I found Secretary McAdoo waiting, although I had no engagement with him. We talked largely of his personal affairs, but were hurried as he also intended to meet the President upon his arrival. We ate a hasty lunch and drove to the station to find the President had come in by special ten minutes ahead of the regular train.

The party was waiting for Loulie and me and we drove to the Polo Grounds and took seats on the Navy side. . . .

The President and I had a few minutes talk before dinner and during dinner as we were quite alone. Much to my surprise, he told me he had not read Sir Edward Grey's letter which I had sent him and which was of great importance. He brought it over with him so we might discuss it together. He also brought over my last two letters which he had shown to Lansing and to which Lansing had written a reply giving his opinion and explanation. These were letters relating to my last interview with Bernstorff and my suggestions to sever relations with Austria, and to send home the underlings connected with the German Embassy.

The President gave me his message to read while he dressed for dinner. I was pleased to find that it contained practically all the suggestions I had made from time to time. Preparedness, which of course, has been urged upon him by many others; a hint of the South American proposal; another and stronger slap at the hyphenates and also a rebuke to alienated Americans. He puts it all strongly and well—better I think than anyone else could possibly do it. I believe the message will be cordially received with the exception perhaps of the purchase of ships in connection with the increase of the Navy. I take it, he will be criticised there. He seemed pleased with my warm praise of the message and said he thought he had not done his best because he had not been well.

We touched upon the European situation and agreed to take it up more fully tomorrow. After dinner we were joined by Loulie and went to see Chin Chin[1] at the Globe Theater. When we left the theater a great crowd had gathered and he was enthusiastically cheered. We went to bed immediately upon reaching home and did not attempt further conversation.

[1] *Chin-Chin, or A Modern Aladdin*, a musical comedy by Anne Caldwell, R. H. Burnside, James O'Dea, and Ivan Caryll, starred the comedy team of David C. Montgomery and Fred Andrew Stone.

November 28, 1915.

We breakfasted at nine o'clock and discussed public matters during the meal. I had invited the Lansings and Mr. and Mrs. Brand Whitlock to lunch today. I thought the President should meet Whitlock and show him some attention. I could see he hesitated at the suggestion and I was not surprised when later in the evening he remembered an old engagement he had made for a family luncheon. He asked me to express to Whitlock his sincere appreciation for his great service abroad and that when he came to Washington he hoped to see me [him].

After breakfast we had but little time before church. We went to hear Dr. Jowett and the President was pleased with his very able sermon. He went to his luncheon engagement and we returned to our apartment to meet our guests. When I found the President would not be present we invited Mr. and Mrs. Sidney Brooks[1] and Mr. and Mrs. Montgomery Hare.[2] Secretary Lansing came in advance and we had a few minutes conversation regarding foreign affairs, covering my conversation with Bernstorff, the Ancona incident and the question of sending home the undesirables.

The conversation during and after lunch was unimportant. I excused myself from my other guests and went with Lansing to the Biltmore where he had some papers he desired to go over with me. We remained in conference for an hour or more.

I tried to impress upon him the necessity of the United States making it clear to the Allies that we considered their cause our cause, and that we had no intention of permitting a military autocracy [to] dominate the world if our strength could prevent

[1] Mrs. Brooks was Florence Fenn Brooks, daughter of the Anglo-American artist, Harry Fenn.

[2] Montgomery and Constance Parsons Hare. He was a lawyer of New York.

it. We believed this was a fight between democracy and autocracy and we would stand with democracy. I pointed out that it was impossible to maintain cordial relations with Germany, not only for the reason that her system of government was different in its conception to ours, but also because so much hate against us had been engendered that it would be perhaps a generation or two before it could die out. Germany was being taught that her lack of success could be directly attributed to us. It was evident that the Government there was looking for some excuse for failure and the easiest and best in their opinion, seemed to be the United States' "unneutral attitude in regard to the shipment of munitions of war, and the lending of money to her enemies." I thought also that unless we did have a complete and satisfactory understanding with the Allies, we would be wholly without friends when the war was ended and our position would be not only perilous, but might become hurtful from an economic viewpoint.

Lansing agreed to this and we discussed the best means of reaching an understanding. He thought they should recall the British Ambassador and send such a man as Lord Bryce, with whom we could talk understandingly. He thought Jusserand was the right man for France to have here, and if England could send such another, an understanding could be reached at Washington. I suggested that I might outline the situation to Sir Edward Grey and have Spring-Rice recalled. Lansing approved this, and it was understood between us that we should go at it this way provided the President consented.

He laid some memoranda before me concerning the Carrabean countries which he thought needed attention. He believes that we should give more intimate direction to their affairs than we would feel warranted in doing to other South American states. He puts them in the same category with Santo Domingo and Haiti and believes we should take the same measures to bring about order, both financial and civil, as we are taking in those countries. I approved this policy and promised to express this opinion to the President.

The President in his hurry was I think indiscreet in showing Lansing my recent letters. While Lansing does not show the slightest trace of jealousy, I am wondering how much of that kind of thing he will be able to stand. His office is new to him, but when it grows older, he will be less inclined to overlook such matters.

We have promised to see more of one another. He is to come to New York to be with us over Sunday and we are to go to them for the dinner they are to give the President in January.

I urged Lansing to find some excuse to send as many of the Germans and Austrians home as he reasonably could. I also urged upon him the necessary [necessity] of breaking off diplomatic relations with Austria if it could possibly be done, because of the Ancona, and to do it as quickly as possible. My idea is that we should hold to Bernstorff as long as possible. He is the best of the lost [lot] and we do not want to sever all diplomatic relations with Germany. It would not suit our plans, and yet we do want to make that connection as slender as possible and leave it with a single thread so Germany will be careful not to commit any other overt act. I have a feeling now that they do not want to sever relations with us and will become less inclined as the war goes on.

I have said all this to the President, both upon this visit and through letters, but I wanted to impress it upon Lansing so when I am not in Washington, we will all be working to the same end.

I returned to the apartment in order to read again the President's message. The President returned at five and we had an uninterrupted conversation of an hour and a half. I went very thoroughly into the matters I had discussed with Lansing and in much the same way. He feels that we should let the Allies know how our minds are running, but he did not seem to think it could be done by a change of Ambassadors. I offered to go to Europe and do it in person. He seemed grateful for the offer, but wondered if there was not too much danger or risk in my doing so. I replied that traveling in the war zone had ceased to be safe or pleasant but there was no reason why I should not go. He thought my going was the only way to properly accomplish what we had in mind. He suggested that I might say to the British Government that we could not deal with "the highly excitable invalid they had here to represent them."

He said, too, that he would very much prefer not putting our thoughts and intentions into writing. He would rather have them conveyed by word of mouth. I feel, myself, that it could not properly be done excepting in this way and, if it is done at all, it should be done well, otherwise a hopeless situation might come about. We are now in the most delicate situation that has yet arisen and such negotiations as we have under advisement need the best that we all have in us. It means the reversal of the foreign policy of this Government and no man can foresee the consequences.

The President suggests that we leave the matter open for twenty-four hours to think of it. I thought it might be left even longer, for I did not believe there was any immediate necessity for action. I was not altogether candid in this expression, for I do think the sooner it is done the better, although I cannot see that it makes a great deal of difference whether it is done now or within the month. It would suit my plans better to go at the end of the month which would enable me to finish up the matters that are pending here.

We discussed his message in detail. I made a few unimportant suggestions which he adopted. He asked my advice as to the incorporation of a tariff commission in the message. I advised against it and thought he should go into the matter fully in another message. We discussed this idea of a tariff commission in some detail, I urging it and he arguing against it. I said it was one of the few things that he and I differed upon. His reply was that he doubted whether we did differ about it, for what I had in mind was largely what he had in mind, only he thought the Government now had the necessary machinery for doing it. He was afraid of a tariff commission such as the republicans suggested for the reason if such a commission was organized, it would finally come to be a legislative body upon that subject which would not be good for the country. He cited the Interstate Commission as what he had in mind. That Commission had been in force so long and the people had accepted it so thoroughly, that he did not believe Congress now dared to radically change any decisions they laid down. He thought the same thing would happen with a tariff commission, therefore, no matter what the people's views upon the subject were, or how they expressed themselves in the election of a Congress, Congress would be more or less timid in changing the rulings of the commission.

When we had finished with the message I made some suggestions to him regarding some unimportant matters which will come to his attention in the near future.

I told him of Gifford Pinchot's complaint of Lane and the Reclamation Service. He made notes of it and promised to speak to Lane. I spoke to him again about the Polish Relief question. I explained what was in my mind which he had not understood before. It was merely to see whether some arrangement could not be made with Russia and the Central Powers to do for Poland, through an American Commission, what England and France were doing for Belgium. This could be done through the Ambassadors of those countries. He approved of this and thought I had better take it up with Lansing and have him approach the German and Russian Ambassadors. He also made a note of it.

It was now dinner time and we were joined by Loulie, Mrs. Galt and Miss Bones. The conversation during dinner ran along light and pleasant lines. After dinner the discussion was general and the President, Mrs. Galt and Miss Bones left at half past nine. The President expressed himself as having very much enjoyed his trip to New York and said he felt much refreshed.

From Edith Gittings Reid

My dearest Friend: [Baltimore] Nov. 28th [1915]

I want much to have a little talk with you at your earliest convenience. Oh, not about Francis[1] or anything of the order. I hate being mysterious but it is something I can't put down on paper. And, of course, I think it worth while. And so does Harry.

Any time you name I will go to you. I shall only want about a half hours' private talk. I feel sure that you will be glad that I came.

My love in advance to Mrs Galt

Your devoted friend   Edith G. Reid

ALS (WP, DLC).
[1] Her son.

From Edith Bolling Galt

[New York]

My own precious,   Sunday, 5:20 PM [Nov. 28, 1915]

You have just gone[1] and I stood at the window & watched you get in the car and just *ached* to go with you

I have put on my Wrapper & am on the bed covered up warm & wish so you were right here for me to put my arms around you & tell you how utterly I love you. But, Precious do you realize that three weeks from today (if all goes as we plan) we will be off together in a world that holds only each other?

Don't be lonely, or blue while I am gone—for in reality I will be there every minute my Sweetheart, and sharing with you every thought.

I am so glad you have your dinner[2] to look forward to   You & I hope the 7[3] will cheer you up & take you back to college days—where there were no responsibilities. Play hard and know that in so doing you are bringing me happiness.

Thank you again for the car & Jervis & the orchids & everything.

Now I must stop, for Helen & Mrs. Flournoy[4] are here

Goodby my Precious One

Always your own with all her heart   Edith

ALS (WP, DLC).

¹ Mrs. Galt was staying over with "Altrude" Gordon in her apartment at 12 W. 10th St. in order to do additional shopping.

² Wilson had invited seventy-seven members of the Class of 1879 to dinner at the White House on November 30.

³ Wilson had invited the "Witherspoon Gang" (about which see WW to R. Bridges, June 13, 1894, n. 2, Vol. 8, p. 587)—Robert Bridges, Robert Randolph Henderson, William Brewster Lee, Charles Wellman Mitchell, Charles Andrew Talcott, James Edwin Webster, and Hiram Woods, Jr.—to spend the night at the White House after the dinner.

⁴ Unidentified.

To Joseph Patrick Tumulty

Dear Tumulty,   [The White House] 29 Nov., 1915.

Here is the message.¹ I wish you would read it and give me your impression of it.

And please keep it very carefully from any eyes but your own. It is still in provisional shape only, and there are a number of points I am still keeping under advisement.

Faithfully,   W.W.

WWTLI (J. P. Tumulty Papers, DLC).
¹ That is, his Annual Message on the State of the Union. Wilson sent a WWT draft with the composition date of Nov. 29, 1915, WP, DLC.

To Edith Bolling Galt

The White House Nov 29   1915

Arrived safe and fit   shall fill the day with work and play weather fine   love and all sorts of luck.   W.

T telegram (WP, DLC).

To Robert Lansing

My dear Mr. Secretary,   The White House. 29 November, 1915.

The argument of this paper¹ seems to me unanswerable, and I thank you for setting it out so explicitly and fully.

This will serve us as a memorandum when the time comes, and the proper occasion, for making a public declaration of policy in this important particular. Just now, I take it for granted, it is only for the guidance and clarification of our own thought, and for informal discussion with our Latin American friends from time to time, semi-confidentially and for the sake of a frank understanding.   Faithfully Yours,   W.W.

WWTLI (SDR, RG 59, 710.11/189½, DNA).
¹ The Enclosure with RL to WW, Nov. 24, 1915.

From Robert Lansing

PERSONAL AND PRIVATE:

My dear Mr. President: Washington November 29, 1915.

I feel that we cannot wait much longer to act in the cases of Boy-Ed, von Papen, and von Nuber. I believe we have enough in regard to the activities of these men to warrant us to demand of the German Government the recall of the two first named and to cancel the exequatur of von Nuber, giving notice to the Austro-Hungarian Government that we have done so.

The increasing public indignation in regard to these men and the general criticism of the Government for allowing them to remain are not the chief reasons for suggesting action in these cases, although I do not think that such reasons should be ignored. We have been over-patient with these people on account of the greater controversies under consideration for several months and did not wish to add to the difficulties of the situation by injecting another cause of difference. In my opinion action now cannot seriously affect the pending negotiations, and it would be well to act as expeditiously as possible.

In case you agree with me as to the action which should be taken would you favor informing Bernstorff orally that his attachés are *personae non gratae* or make a formal written statement to that effect without telling him in advance?

In the von Nuber case I would suggest that the Austrian Chargé be told that we intend to cancel the *exequatur* of von Nuber.

As you know, I believe that we will soon have to go even higher up in removing from this country representatives of belligerents who are directing operations here. It would appear that these higher officials consider our patience to be cowardice. If this is so, the removal of subordinates would indicate our earnest purpose and would, I believe, help rather than hinder the progress of present negotiations.

I hope a decision can be reached speedily in this matter, as it should in my judgment be done, if at all, before Congress meets.

I enclose memoranda[1] on German and Austrian officials here, among which you will find statements regarding the three mentioned.   Faithfully yours,   Robert Lansing

TLS (SDR, RG 59, 701.6211/323½, DNA).
  [1] A long T memorandum with annexes (SDR, RG 59, 701.6211/323½, DNA). It went into detail about the illegal and inappropriate activities in violation of American neutrality perpetrated by Albert, Von Papen, Boy-Ed, Von Nuber, and German trade representatives and consuls in the United States.

The Employment Agent

Ready for Business

Ripping It Out

Wiping Away His Tears

The Class in Reading and Writing

"Obstructing Traffic, Your Honor"

"The German Government believes that it was acting in justified self-defense."

"To Arms! To Arms!"

To Robert Lansing

My dear Mr. Secretary,   The White House. 29 November, 1915.

There need be no further delay in this matter. I would be obliged if you would act at once in regard to it. May I advise that you act in the following manner?

1. That you inform the Austrian Chargé that von Nuber's exequatur will be cancelled at once, and that the exequatur be then recalled after a courteous interval, perhaps, in which to await the Chargé's reply;

2. That you informally inform the German Ambassador that Boy-Ed and von Papen are *personae non gratae*, but that we wish to afford him an opportunity to have them promptly withdrawn without forcing us to make the formal demand that they be replaced, as we shall be obliged to do if they are not voluntarily recalled. I think that he will appreciate the courtesy and that it may be well to avoid a public course of action just now, though we should not hesitate to take it if there is no voluntary action.

Cordially,   W.W.

WWTLI (SDR, RG 59, 701.6211/324½, DNA).

From Joseph Patrick Tumulty

Dear Governor: The White House   November 29, 1915.

The Message as a whole has filled me with inexpressible joy.[1] It is a real clarion call to the Nation and will win you not only the applause and commendation of the people of this country, but friends will be made for you wherever it is read.

With your permission I am making certain suggestions and criticisms, the most important of which has to do with the linking of the programme of national defense with the merchant marine. However, I will discuss this later in this letter to you.

On page 8, line 11, from the bottom, I think the word "quiet" should be omitted. It makes the sentence stronger.[2]

On page 9, line 10 from the bottom, I think that the phrase "which they covet" would be misunderstood in Latin American countries when translated. I think it should read thus: "They must be fitted to play a great role in the world, and particularly in this hemisphere,—a role which they are qualified by principle and by chastened ambition to play."[3]

[1] That is, Wilson's draft of his Annual Message.
[2] Wilson accepted this suggestion.
[3] Wilson deleted "which they covet" and accepted Tumulty's emended version of this sentence.

On page 10, line 6 from the bottom, I think you ought to drop out the word "minimum" because it is too limiting a word and rather "pussy-footed."[4]

On page 12, line 10 from the top, the same criticism would apply to the sentence, "And yet at present it does not seem necessary that we should do more." As reframed, I would suggest that it read as follows: ["]At least so much by way of preparation for defense seems to me to be absolutely imperative now. We cannot do less and feel secure." I have added "do less and feel secure."[5]

On page 12, line 14 from the top, I think you ought to drop out the sentence, "It involves no radical departure from plans already forecast and sanctioned by the Congress." This is liable to be disputed because it does involve a radical departure and it looks like an apology when we ought to be putting our programme forth in a positive way. It should read, I think, thus: "The programme which will be laid before you by the Secretary of the Navy is similarly conceived. It involves only a shortening of the time within which plans long matured shall be carried out, etc."[6]

As to linking together the subjects of national defense and merchant marine: It is obvious that the question of merchant marine is a debatable one and not, in the present circumstances, as important and vital a subject as the question of national defense. Why not let this be argued on the floor of the House and not linked with the defense programme as an auxiliary? I am heartily in favor of your expressing your attitude on this matter in the most vigorous language but only differ with you as to the means. And what I am afraid of is that the charge will be made, as it already has been, that in order to push through the shipping bill you linked it to the programme of national defense upon which public opinion in the country is thoroughly united. In linking these two subjects together, it is my firm opinion that we are playing into the hands of the enemy and it will lay you open to the charge of insincerity. It will be said that in your last Message, you said the question of national defense was purely an academic one; that you agreed with Mr. Bryan's views; that you were a pacifist, and that you are more interested in the merchant marine than you are in national defense; that national defense is but a mere pretext to induce the passage of a shipping bill. The Message will be immeasurably weakened by the linking of these two subjects. What you thus

[4] Wilson accepted this suggestion.
[5] Wilson deleted this sentence but did not add Tumulty's suggested substitute.
[6] Wilson accepted this suggestion.

hope to accomplish by thus linking them together, I cannot imagine. What you have to say about the necessity for a merchant marine is conclusive without dragging in the need of it as a naval auxiliary. I would have your message so far as it refers to the merchant marine, read as follows:

Page 15, leave out the whole paragraph beginning with the word "but" down to the words "naval programme," and begin your merchant marine programme as follows: "It is necessary for many weighty reasons of national efficiency and development that we should have a great merchant marine. And then eliminate on page 16, lines 2, 3, 4, 5, 6, 7, 8, 9, and 10, resuming with the words, "That great body of sturdy sailors who used to carry our flag into every sea, men who were the pride and often the bulwark of the nation, we have almost driven out of existence by inexcusable neglect and indifference and by a hopelessly blind and provincial policy of so-called economic protection. It is high time we repaired our mistake and resumed our commercial independence on the seas.

"For it is a question of *commercial & industrial* independence. ⟨The supplying for the navy of needed auxiliaries and of indispensable men is a great enough reason in itself to put us upon our mettle in this matter,⟩[7] but there is a deeper and bigger reason. If other nations go to war or seek to hamper each other's commerce, our merchants, it seems, are at their mercy, to do with as they please. We must use their ships, and use them as they determine. We have not ships enough of our own. We cannot handle our own commerce on the seas. Our independence is provincial, and is only on land and within our own borders. We are not likely to be permitted to use even the ships of other nations in rivalry of their own trade, and are without means to extend our commerce even where the doors are wide open and our goods desired. Such a situation is not to be endured. It is of capital importance not only that the United States should be its own carrier on the seas and enjoy the economic independence which only an adequate merchant marine would give it, but also that the American hemisphere as a whole should enjoy a like independence and self-sufficiency, if it is not to be drawn into the tangle of European affairs. Without such independence the whole question of our political unity and self-determination is very seriously clouded and complicated indeed.

"Moreover, we can develop no true or effective American policy without ships of our own,—not ships of war, but ships of peace, carrying goods and carrying much more: creating friendships

---

[7] Tumulty struck through this sentence in Wilson's text.

and rendering indispensable services to all interests on this side the water. They must move constantly back and forth between the Americas. They are the only shuttles that can weave the delicate fabric of sympathy, comprehension, confidence, and mutual dependence in which we wish to clothe our policy of America for Americans.

"The task of building up an adequate merchant marine for America, private capital must ultimately undertake and achieve, as it has undertaken and achieved every other like task amongst us in the past, with admirable enterprise, intelligence, and vigor; and it seems to me a manifest dictate of wisdom that we should promptly remove every legal obstacle that may stand in the way of this much to be desired revival of our old independence and should facilitate in every possible way the building, purchase, and American registration of ships. But capital cannot accomplish this great task of a sudden. It must embark upon it by degrees, as the opportunities of trade develop. Something must be done at once; done to open routes and develop opportunities where they are as yet undeveloped; done to open the arteries of trade where the currents have not yet learned to run,—especially between the two American continents, where they are, singularly enough, yet to be created and quickened; and it is evident that only the government can undertake such beginnings and assume the initial financial risks. When the risk has passed and private capital begins to find its way in sufficient abundance into these new channels, the government may withdraw. But it cannot omit to begin. It should take the first steps, and should take them at once. Our goods must not lie piled up at our ports and stored upon side tracks in freight cars which are daily needed on the roads; must not be left without means of transport to any foreign quarter. We must not await the permission of foreign shipowners and foreign governments to send them where we will."[8]

On page 19, line 7 from the top, I would suggest that you leave out the words "our navy" the line then reading as follows: "With a view to meeting these pressing necessities of our commerce and availing ourselves at the earliest possible moment of the present unparalleled opportunity of linking the two Americas together in bonds of mutual interest and service, an opportunity which may never return again if we miss it now, proposals will be made to the present Congress *for the development of a merchant marine*[9] to be owned and directed by the government (then

[8] Words italicized added by Tumulty. Wilson accepted Tumulty's suggestions for excisions; otherwise, he retained his original text.

[9] Tumulty substituted these words for Wilson's "for the purchase or construction of ships." Wilson retained his original text.

leave out the following words: 'similar to those made to the last Congress') but modified in some essential particulars (then leave out the words: 'and linked as the former proposals were not with the immediate needs of the navy, and restudied in view of the programme I have set forth for preparation for national defense.')" Then follows: "I earnestly recommend these proposals to you for your prompt acceptance with the more confidence because every month that has elapsed since the former proposals were made has made the necessity for such action more and more manifestly imperative. That need was then foreseen; it is now acutely felt and everywhere realized by those for whom trade is waiting but who can find no conveyance for their goods."[10]

Suggested sentence:

"I am not so much interested in the particulars *of this program* as I am to take advantage of the present ⟨unparalleled⟩ opportunity ⟨of extending our commerce where the doors are wide open and our goods desired.⟩ *which awaits us if we will but act in this emergency.* In this matter, *as in all matters* a spirit of common counsel should prevail and out of it, let us hope there may come a solution of this *great & pressing* problem."[11]

On page 33, line 7 from the bottom, I think you ought to eliminate this sentence: "We should undo nothing." Suggested sentence: "The question is whether there is anything else we ⟨could⟩ *can* do that would supply us with effective means, in the very process of regulation, for bettering the conditions under which the railroads are operated and for making them more useful servants of the communities and the people they serve. ⟨for you cannot injure one interest without depressing the other.⟩ The progress of communities and railroads go hand in hand."[12]

On page 34, line 8 from the top, after the word "efficiency" I think you might add "and national security."[13]

Suggested sentence, beginning line 8, page 34, "We serve a great nation. We should serve it in the spirit of its peculiar genius, which is the genius of the common man engaged in the great enterprise of human liberty. It is the genius for self-government, ⟨for force⟩ *industry* and *justice*, ⟨enthusiasm,⟩ *liberty* and peace."[14]

[10] Wilson substantially accepted this suggestion.

[11] Wilson accepted this suggestion with slight verbal changes. Words in angle brackets deleted by Tumulty; words in italics added by him. Wilson retyped this page and destroyed the old one.

[12] Wilson retyped this page and accepted Tumulty's suggestion for the elimination of the text in angle brackets.

[13] Wilson added "and security."

[14] Wilson substantially accepted this suggestion.

I think it is important to start this programme off with vigor and enthusiasm and apparent party solidarity back of it. To link national defense with the shipping bill will destroy that aim, and give the Republican party the chance to say that we are playing politics with national defense.　　　Tumulty

TLS (WP, DLC).

To Edith Bolling Galt

My precious Darling,

Washington, 5.25 P.M.
Monday, 29 Nov., 1915

Just twenty-four hours ago you were sitting on the side of your bed in your wrapper writing the little note Murphy handed me this morning just as we were walking away from the train. My Darling, how incomparably sweet and lovely you are! The little piece of paper thrilled me when I took it from Murphy as if it had been a touch of your own dear hand that wrote it—how intensly I loved you for the sweet thought and knowledge of my need that prompted you to write it! That little piece of paper in my pocket, its contents at my heart, has made the whole day different. It has been almost as if my Darling were here—and the work has gone finely! I finished the message by about noon, copying and all, and was free to attend to one or two points about the class dinner before lunch. I have now only to give the message a last consideration, for alterations, omissions, or additions, and then it may go to the printer. House read it, by the way, and liked and approved it as much as my precious Sweetheart did. Grayson and I had lunch together, I sent telegrams to 'The Seven,' inviting them to spend to-morrow night at the White House, and a little before two o'clock we started for Virginia. I won the match, as a man with that note in his pocket was bound to; and as soon as I had had my bath and dressed I came here to talk to my precious Darling. I am writing on the closed type-writer desk. The other one is so piled and covered with papers of many sorts that there is not a foot of free space on it. Fifty-eight of my classmates have accepted the invitation for to-morrow evening, seventeen have declined, and two have not answered. I am happy to say all of the Seven have accepted. It will be jolly to have them all together again.

I called North 2727 this morning and had a little talk with Bertha, telling her about you, and before I got through had promised to take lunch with them to-morrow unless prevented. I am anxious to see the dear folks. They are all as usual.

To-night I must catch up with the neglected contents of "the drawer"—and begin to-morrow with a clean slate and a clear con-science! Politics has begun to boil. The Democrats of the Senate are here working on their organization for the Senate, and men whom we will have to side-track are trying to get control. I've been interrupted twice since I began this note to give counsel as to what is to be done, and can see that things are from this time on going to grow hotter and hotter. But I am not made ner-vous by a fight—and I shall have you. Ah, little girl, how I love you—how different you have made the world for me—how empty every place and everything is that does not contain you—how I want you, how I miss you, how I depend on and delight in you! I meant to write you a real letter, but politics has stolen half the time I had and I must hurry to get this to the P. O. I'm fight-ing hard to keep off the blues—because I promised you I would and it is almost ungrateful when you love me so—so generously, so sweetly, so wonderfully, and so delightfully. But come *soon*,—come as soon as ever you can—things *can* be bought even after a wedding, and as things thicken more and more about me here I more and more need and long for you, my blessed, lovely Dar-ling. I am in every thought and wish and purpose

Your own   Woodrow

ALS (WP, DLC).

From Edith Bolling Galt

My precious One,   [New York] Nov. 30th [29th] 1915

We have just come in from a hard, but very satisfactory days work. It is 10 minutes of Seven and I expect you are in the study ready for dinner—and oh! how I wish I was there to put my arms round you and tell you how deeply how tenderly I love you.

Thank you so for sending me the telegram. Helen & I started out at 9, so I did not get the message until I came in to lunch at 1:30 but it brought me such peace of mind to know you were safe & fit and ready for work & play. Bless your precious heart, I am so glad you are going to have your friends tomorrow and do hope the dinner will be the greatest success. I only wish I was going to be there to help you—if you needed me.

Now to give an account of myself. My throat is really better than it has been for a week & I hardly feel it at all. We all had a comfortable night, getting to bed about one, when I thought of you so tenderly. And oh, "Presh," in the night I had been asleep and suddenly woke to find my self moving way over to the edge of the bed—with my arms held out—saying, "Oh, Sweet-heart, please come—there is lots of room," and I was so sure you were there I just could not believe you were not. Wasn't that strange? But to continue the account of the day. We went to Kurzmans[1] at 9, saw some very *lovely* things & I got my afternoon dress. A good many of the models were not up from the Custom House, so at 11 we left to return at 4. Then we went to Jackels,[2] the Fur Store and saw such really lovely furs. And I was recklessly extravagant in your gift of a coat. They will make it to order for me—of caracul[3] and a border of yukon (which is white fox) colored and the price would be nearly a thousand dollars but they would make it for *me*—for $475.00

Don't faint—or think I have gone crazy—but it was just so pretty I couldn't help it! Although my conscience hurts me dreadfully, and I want to come & sit in your lap and have you tell me you love me even if I am extravagant. I am to go for a fitting tomorrow morning & get the coat in 2 weeks. Then I got a set of yukon fox furs—which were $150—and when they discovered me they made it $80.00 so I suppose I will let Annie Fendall[4] give me those.

After getting the coat we came back to lunch at 1:30. We went to Luciles at 2:30 & Altrude & Mrs. F. went with us. The dress I ordered there is lovely, & from there we went to Tappé[5] for hats. Then called on the Wilsons (who were out) and then went to Kurzmans, where we met Margarets Dr. De Vool[6]—sitting looking miserable waiting for her. She & Mrs. Hity[7] were in a fitting room & Margaret came out & seemed sort of fussed at seeing us. I don't know whether it was "Hity or the Dr." that caused it. She was awfully sweet though and seemed glad to see us but said she was awfully busy & on the go every minute.

Now you see all we have done, and I hope to get through by Wednesday night. I think Margaret & Helen both want to stay until Thursday, but because of you, Sweetheart I am going to try & get back. Mrs. House has just phoned they want us to have their car tomorrow & to dismiss yours, & though I argued it did no good. So I suppose we will have to have theirs, and we are now trying to get Mr. Jervis on the phone to tell him. I have not had a bit of trouble with reporters and every thing is so nice & quiet & homelike here.

I hope you are not very lonely tonight Dearest, and across the space you will feel my infinite love.

Give Dr. Grayson my love and with all my heart can hold know that I am now and always   Your own   Edith.

ALS (WP, DLC).

[1] M. Kurzman's Sons, leading importers of Paris fashions, located at 385 Fifth Avenue. Julius Kurzman, of this firm, designed Mrs. Galt's wedding dress.

[2] A. Jaeckel and Co., at 384 Fifth Avenue.

3 Glossy black pelt of a karakul lamb after the curl begins to loosen.
4 Annie A. Galt Fendall, widow of Reginald Fendall, a Washington lawyer, and sister of Norman Galt.
5 Herman Patrick Tappé, located at 25 W. 57th St., leading milliner and, later, one of the first American designers to gain international acclaim.
6 Edmund Devol, M.D., of New York, Margaret's good friend. Devol has been mentioned, with variant spellings of his name, several times in recent volumes. He first appears in EAW to WW, Sept. 5, 1913, Vol. 28.
7 Unidentified, as are "the Wilsons" mentioned earlier.

To J. Edwin Murphy

[The White House]
My dear Mr. Murphy: November 30, 1915

Allow me to thank you for your very handsome and generous note of November twenty-fifth. It pleases me very much to find that you feel as I do about items such as I called your attention to. You can appreciate that it is very distressing to me to be represented as a fool and a sloven as such an item as that would necessarily imply, and my feeling is that such things are apt to creep into permanent records through those who do not scrutinize and understand, but I am sure you do understand and will generously cooperate in protecting me from things of this sort.

Sincerely yours,   Woodrow Wilson

TLS (Letterpress Books, WP, DLC).

To Joseph R. Wilson, Jr.

My dearest Brother: The White House November 30, 1915

I wish with all my heart that I had known that you could get free and go to the game.[1] I am very thoughtless in such matters. The fact is that I don't pay any attention to them at all until it is time for the train to start, and things just happen casually. I will remember next time, and feel mortified that I did not this.[2]

Of course, your suggestion about Alice was proper[3] and you may be sure that I shall try not to forget it. I say "try" because my head is the leakiest thing I know about matters which do not come within the day's work. Just at this moment I am keeping bachelors' hall, Margaret and Helen both being in New York, but I will pass the thing on to them for the custody of their minds when they get back.

I am delighted to hear that Kate is to be with you soon again. Please give her my love. You may be sure we will keep you advised of our final plans.

In haste, with warmest love,

Affectionately yours,   Woodrow Wilson

TLS (received from Alice Wilson McElroy).

¹ Wilson was replying to J. R. Wilson, Jr., to WW, Nov. 27, 1915, TLS (WP, DLC). His brother had written that he had hoped for "a Presidential summons" to join the President's train to New York for the Army-Navy football game.

² Wilson dictated "this time."

³ J. R. Wilson had proposed that his daughter, Alice, "be able to get a glimpse of some of the important social events at the White House during the coming season."

To Edith Bolling Galt

My precious Darling,   Washington, Tuesday, 30 Nov., 1915.

I have just read your letter and my heart is all aglow with its wonderful love and sweetness. I wish *I* could write such letters—letters carrying the very breath and exquisite flavour of what is in my heart! I love you with a depth and tenderness, my lovely One, that seems to run beyond words and to be a part of my very self, which I can express best in tender action, and my very longing for you when we are separated seems to stunt my efforts at adequate expression. But what a pleasure it is to try! You darling! How sweet you were to make room for me in the night—and how perfectly it responded to my infinite longing—to my conscious thought and wish. It is all infinitely sweet and very wonderful!

I wonder if you see the *seams* in these letters? I began this before ten this morning: it is now ten minutes after two. Perhaps I can get a sentence or two written before another set of interruptions begin! I have just come from the *Cordova*, where I lunched with mother and Bertha. They were sweet enough to let me come in *just* for lunch and see them for three quarters of an hour, while we were actually eating. I told them all about our doings in New York—or, at least as much about them as Bertha would give me an opportunity to tell,—and they were very sweet and dear. They both seemed very well indeed. Randolph, of course, was not there; but they said was very nearly rested from the New York trip.

I am *so* happy, my Sweetheart, about the fur coat. It sounds like a great bargain,—but I would have been delighted to pay the full price. You are *not* extravagant—you are only doing what I begged you to do! It is delightful that you have found something *really* beautiful and satisfactory. So many of the fur garments they are making now seem *freakish*, in shape and purpose both. Your success yesterday raises my hopes for Wednesday night. My, how eager and impatient I am to see my lovely Darling again!

I did succeed in catching up with my work last night—by eleven o'clock, when I had solved even the seating problem for the dinner—after a fashion. Mahlon Pitney will sit on my right—by rank (as if '79 cared anything about that!) and Bridges on my left. Halsey, the president of the class, will sit opposite me, with Dodge on his right and Dr Davis of Philadelphia on his left. The table will be a big crescent, opening towards the West (the Army and Navy building) and there will be fifty-eight of us. The table flowers will be yellow crysanthemums, the Princeton flower.

I did not play golf to-day because there were too many little things to do, and the morning was full of the cabinet and miscellaneous engagements. The town is filling up with members of Congress so fast that there are very few hours I can call my own.

The baby has another tooth. I believe that is the only really important piece of news. And the message went to the printer this morning. But what fills all my thought is that you love me and soon, *soon* now, are coming to me to share all my life; that I love you and am free to love you for the rest of my days as your lover, your chum, your playmate, your dearest and nearest counsellor, your husband. I *delight* to think of you and all that you are! This empty house already seems yours, it is so full of thoughts of you. It seems to wait for you, as my heart does! I love you, love you, love you—that's the theme my heart rings to all day long—and I am so proud of you and so *long* for you. It's nearly half past five now. The seven are beginning to arrive, and I *must* go to welcome them, but my heart will stay with you. Bridges and Lee will be in the pink rooms, Woods and Webster in the yellow room, Mitchell and Talcott in Helen's room, and Henderson in the Blue Mountain room. Good-night, blessed Sweetheart. Come soon to

Your own   Woodrow

ALS (WP, DLC).

From Edith Bolling Galt

My precious One: [New York] Nov. 30th, 1915

Lizzie brought me your blessed letter at 7:30 this morning and I am so glad you were feeling so well and the day had gone so smoothly, although full of work. Thank you for giving me such a full account of all you did and also for phoning 2727. I do hope you could go to lunch with Mother today and know how they will enjoy having you. Hurrah for the "seven" and for the dinner. I am so glad you are really having it.

We have just finished lunch & we have half an hour before we have to go so I am writing to tell you I am still trying to get off tomorrow afternoon. I think the train goes about 5 and arrives about 10:30. If I find I can't make it I will telegraph you, but if you dont hear you may expect me.

This morning Helen & I were out at 9:30 and everything is ordered and ready for fittings tomorrow. I will tell you about it when I come. The House's car is a beauty & they insist I shall keep it the rest of my stay. Thank you Precious for the great box of flowers that came by Express this a.m. There were so many I sent some over to Mrs. House. And then Helen & I went to see them, and I had a talk with him & he is more than enthusiastic about your message, as I knew he would be.

We went in the Study, and it made me so homesick for you.

This afternoon we are going to call on the Malones and Helen is taking us all to the Theatre tonight. So you see I had to write this note now or not send any.

Do wish I had time for a real letter but I must drop Mother a note & tell Susie when to expect me.

My warmest and tenderest love follows you everywhere & I will be with you every minute in my thoughts

Take very tender care of my precious Sweetheart for I will soon be there to do it for myself.   Always your own,   Edith.

ALS (WP, DLC).

From Robert Lansing, with Enclosure

PERSONAL AND CONFIDENTIAL:

My dear Mr. President: Washington December 1, 1915.

This morning, at ten-thirty, I saw the German Ambassador and I enclose a memorandum of the conversation which I had with him. I told him that I expected to make public announcement on Friday that we had requested the withdrawal of Boy-Ed and von Papen.

This afternoon, at two-thirty, I saw the Austrian Chargé and went over the von Nuber case. I told him that this Government felt that von Nuber was unacceptable and that it was our purpose to revoke his exequatur.

Baron Zwiedinek was very much distressed and showed great feeling. We discussed the case and he was most insistent that von Nuber in his publication of warnings to Austro-Hungarian subjects in regard to work in munition factories acted under instructions from the Embassy, which it had received from the Vienna Government. He told me that he considered the action of his Government in this matter unwise and had so informed the Foreign Office; and that they had subsequently advised those who proposed to participate in strikes to avoid doing so. He plead with me to reconsider the question, and while I gave him no hope that our views would be changed I told him that I would do so. The fact is that his presentation of the case has shaken my judgment as to the wisdom of cancelling the exequatur. It is possible that we are doing an injustice and I should very much dislike being unable to furnish substantial grounds for our action, although, in my own mind, I believe von Nuber has been very active in these matters. It is merely a question of evidence.

Of course we do not need to give our reasons, but in this particular case if we give no reasons the inevitable conclusion is that we have accepted the statements of Goricar, the renegade Austrian Consul, and others who have made unproven allegations against von Nuber.[1]

In any event I think it would be well to consider the matter a few days longer. If you approve of this course will you please advise me tomorrow morning, in order that I may notify Baron Zwiedinek that the exequatur will not be revoked tomorrow, as I told him that was the intention.

I enclose several papers which he left with me bearing on the question and which I would be obliged if you would return to me as soon as possible, in order that I may further study the case.[2]

Faithfully yours,   Robert Lansing

P.S. I think I should add that von Nuber sent a cipher report to his Government by Archibald so that we have that substantial ground for revoking his exequatur.   RL

TLS (SDR, RG 59, 701.6211/325½, DNA).
  [1] Dr. Josef Goricar, Austro-Hungarian consul at San Francisco from 1911 until 1914, had resigned from the consular service and, in November 1915, supplied information about the organization of sabotage against munitions factories through Austro-Hungarian consular offices to the *Providence Journal* and then to the Justice Department. According to Goricar, Von Nuber, Von Papen, and Boy-Ed were the directing heads of the spy system; Von Nuber had even continued to agitate among his countrymen who were employed in munitions plants since Dumba's departure. Von Nuber had also helped to prepare the documents carried by Archibald and confiscated by British authorities. See the *New York Times*, Nov. 12, 14, and 19, 1915.
  [2] These papers left by the Chargé not printed.

ENCLOSURE

December 1, 1915.

MEMORANDUM OF INTERVIEW WITH GERMAN AMBASSADOR.

I told the Ambassador that I had asked him to come to the Department and that I had an unpleasant duty to perform, which was to say that Captain Boy-Ed and Captain von Papen were both unacceptable to this Government, and we desired them to withdraw from the country.

The Ambassador seemed very much perturbed and asked me if I did not think his Government would desire the reasons for their recall. I said that was possibly so but that of course he appreciated it was only necessary for me to say that they were unacceptable to this Government, without giving any reasons.

However, I told him briefly that their activities in military and naval affairs were such here that they involved violations of our laws, and fraudulent practices, and that on that account they ought not be shielded under diplomatic privileges from being subject to our Courts.

He asked as to particulars and I mentioned Boy-Ed's securing of false affidavits in regard to the shipment of supplies to German war vessels from the port of New York; his being involved in a fraudulent passport case for one Stegler; and also that he had communicated with Huerta who was proposing to enter Mexico. The Ambassador seemed much surprised at the latter statement and said he knew nothing about it. I told him we had very good proofs and certainly were convinced that Captain Boy-Ed had seen Huerta several times, both at the Hotel Manhattan and Hotel Astoria.

We did not discuss the case of von Papen.

The Ambassador asked me just where he stood—was he involved in these matters. I said no, that so far as he was concerned these matters were of a military and naval character and that we had gone no further at present.

I then spoke to him about the LUSITANIA case. He said he was hopeless of securing an agreement along the line suggested by me; that he was convinced his Government would not, in view of public opinion in Germany, dare to do as we desired; that the whole question was one of liability to pay damages.

I said to him that he had informed me that he had sent the formula by mail to his Government and that it seemed to me that more prompt action was required; and I therefore offered to send a cipher message for him through the Department.[1]

He expressed his thanks and said he would avail himself of it; and that he would notify his Government of our wishes in regard to Captains Boy-Ed and von Papen by wireless, which was working very well.

I also told him that I should make public announcement this week probably on Friday, of our request for the recall of his Military and Naval Attachés. He asked me how they could be allowed to depart, and I told him that we would do all we could to secure safe conducts for them.

T MS (SDR, RG 59, 701.6211/325½, DNA).
[1] J. H. von Bernstorff to the Foreign Office, received Dec. 5, 1915, T telegram (Der Weltkrieg, No. 18a, Unterseebootkrieg gegen England, ganz geheim, vol. 15, p. 17, GFO-Ar).

From Edward Mandell House

Dear Governor: New York. December 1st, 1915.

I had Dudley Malone speak to Frederic Howe concerning the Ford trip.[1] He had no intention of going.

Mezes had a long talk with Miller of the Reserve Board the other day. Miller said he wanted to conform to your ideas as to the policy of the board and would do so whenever he could find what your policy was about any given matter.

This leads me to suggest, that if the friction gets acute you send for Miller and talk to him in person. Unless Mezes is mistaken you will find him eager and willing to carry out your views.

Regarding the proposed trip abroad, I think before we come to a decision we had better wait until Sir Horace Plunkett arrives on Friday and we can get some confidential information he will be able to give as coming directly from Sir Edward and Mr. Balfour. I can then go to Washington and discuss the matter with you and decide what is best to be done.

I am willing, of course, to go at any time, but I doubt the necessity for precipitate action.

I am still thinking of your message. It has heartened me more than anything you have written in a long time, for I am sure it will appeal to the Nation.

                    Affectionately yours,   E. M. House

TLS (WP, DLC).
  [1] The Ford peace expedition, financed and accompanied by Henry Ford, sailed for Europe on *Oscar II* on December 4 with fifty-five pacifists and reformers, forty-four journalists, twenty-five students, and forty-two staff and family members. They planned to hold meetings in the neutral capitals of Europe and to establish a Neutral Conference for Continuous Mediation to receive and transmit peace proposals from belligerent nations. Rosika Schwimmer and Louis Paul Lochner had conceived the plan, excited Ford about it, and extended invitations. Some former allies in the peace movement scorned the idea, and newspapers generally mocked it before the group set sail. See Barbara S. Kraft, *The Peace Ship: Henry Ford's Pacifist Adventure in the First World War* (New York and London, 1978).
  House recorded in his diary, on November 30, that he asked Malone to tell Howe not to go with the Ford group, but not to intimate that the directive came from Wilson.

From Abram Woodruff Halsey

My Dear Wilson,   New York City Dec 1, 1915

The dinner was a great success. All the fellows were delighted. I have heard nothing but expressions of joy and praise at the inspiring evening you gave us at the White House. The best of it all was your simple unaffected manners—the same Wilson we had known and esteemed through all these years. Permit me to thank you in behalf of all who were privileged to be your guests.

The memory of the evening at the White House will be a fragrant memory with us all through coming years. It was most kind in you to think of us in the midst of your many and onerous duties

We *did* and *do* appreciate it and you.

Always Yours   A. W. Halsey

ALS (WP, DLC).

From the Diary of Brand Whitlock

Wednesday 1 December 1915

To the White House at 10:30 and received by the President with whom I spent an hour. He was standing by his desk, as I entered, with the smile that illuminates his long and highly sensitive face, that reveals his large teeth, with some dentistry in evidence. He wore a lounging suit of gray and the scarf pin he has worn, I believe, ever since he came into office—it has the eagle, the coat of arms, or something official about it. He was looking exceedingly fit; no lines of care, but well filled cheeks, of good healthy color and a fine clear eye through the glistening pince-nez. His manner most frank and cordial, as he expressed his satisfaction with my course: "I'm glad I sent you over there," he said, simply. When I told him how the Belgians felt toward him he was deeply touched, turned away, with a mist in his eye. We talked an hour, of many things—golf, among others—and the Germans and culture and philosophy.[1] . . . Very interesting view of the duty of every man, as raised by F.N.'s course:[2] Related Col. Listoe's classic,[3] and he committed it to memory. Wished me to let him know when I was to sail, for when I spoke of being back in Washington he said significantly, "I'm afraid I shan't be here then." He was very cordial, very charming, and I was proud to be one of his followers.

Hw bound diary (A. Nevins Papers, NNC).

[1] For an account of what Wilson said about Germany, see O. von der Lancken Wakenitz to A. von Montgelas, Jan. 16, 1916.

[2] Francis Neilson, former M.P., English actor, director, playwright, and novelist; an old friend of Whitlock's. He migrated to the United States in September 1915 and resigned his seat in the House of Commons because he was a pacifist and could not vote for war appropriations.

[3] Soren Listoe, Danish-born United States Consul-General at Rotterdam since 1902. Listoe's "classic" was uttered at Whitlock's dinner table during a visit to Brussels in December 1914. Asked what he thought about the war, the Consul-General, in a determined effort to observe neutrality of thought as well as of action, replied: "Well, if this war ends in the way some hope that it will, the other side will have to pay a very large indemnity." Brand Whitlock, *Belgium: A Personal Narrative* (2 vols., New York, 1919), I, 410.

To Edith Bolling Galt

The White House Dec 1 1915

Dinner went off delightfully. Everybody a boy again. The seven were just their old selves throughout. You were unanimously elected an honorary member of the class amidst loud cheers. The seven left this morning very happy. Love to all and congratulations on success of shopping. Well and fit this morning.

Woodrow Wilson.

T telegram (WP, DLC).

From Edith Bolling Galt

New York, December 1, 1915.

Leaving on Congressional, arrive eight thirty.

Edith Bolling Galt.

T telegram (WP, DLC).

To Robert Lansing

My dear Mr. Secretary,   The White House. 2 December, 1915.

I do not think that we need accede to the representations and request of Baron Zwiedinek. Our knowledge of von Nuber's activities does not by any means rest wholly on what Goricar said, and I think we have abundant ground for the withdrawal of the *exequatur*. A little prompt action just at this time will be better in its effect than any amount of action later.

Why was Albert not included in the representation to the German Ambassador? He has been in many ways the head anf [and] front of the offending, and it is probable that even the Ambassador is obliged to accept his decisions.

I understand that von Papen has left the country, and that he will at an early opportunity be promoted bo [by] the admiring government he serves.   Faithfully,   W.W.

WWTLI (SDR, RG 59, 701.6211/326½, DNA).

From Robert Lansing

PERSONAL AND PRIVATE:

My dear Mr. President: Washington December 2, 1915.

I have your note of today in regard to the von Nuber case, and while I agree with you that we have ground for the revocation of his exequatur I cannot say that I think it is "abundant." I have had the officers of the Department of Justice give me further information on the subject and am asking them to hasten the digest of other material which they have. If they do not furnish me with further evidence tomorrow I will act in accordance with the plan adopted—that is, send notice of the revocation of von Nuber's exequatur. I hope though, for my own peace of mind, to have a little more convincing evidence on the subject.

In regard to Albert: My only hesitation in his case was that he has been a very valuable assistant to our people in obtaining from Germany certain articles of commerce—such as beet seed, potash, medicines, etc., which are absolutely necessary for this country, and which cannot be produced here. My own opinion is that he is a more dangerous man than either of the two whom we desire removed. At the same time, it is a question of policy whether he is not of sufficient value to our industries to allow him to remain a little longer. If you, however, think it well to act in his case at once I shall be pleased to do so.

I have not heard that von Papen had departed. It is possibly so and I have no doubt that his services will be amply rewarded —in case he reaches Germany.

Faithfully yours,　Robert Lansing

TLS (SDR, RG 59, 701.6211/326½, DNA).

Four Letters from Robert Lansing

PERSONAL AND PRIVATE:

My dear Mr. President:　　　　Washington December 3, 1915.

I enclose a draft for an instruction to Ambassador Penfield in regard to the ANCONA case.[1] We have no further information on the subject than that which I have already submitted to you. The essential fact, that the vessel was shelled and torpedoed while persons were still on board—one of whom, at least, is an American—is amply proven.

Faithfully yours,　Robert Lansing

TLS (SDR, RG 59, 865.857 AN 2/75½A, DNA).
[1] It is printed as an Enclosure with WW to RL, Dec. 5, 1915 (first letter of that date).

PERSONAL AND PRIVATE:

My dear Mr. President:　　　　Washington December 3, 1915.

I have again been over the material which we have about Herr Albert and I do not believe that we have sufficient grounds to ask for his recall. I am convinced that his are the directing brains of German activities and propaganda in this country and that he is the one who controls the large sums of money being expended here. He has, however, protected himself well. We are continuing our investigations and may find substantial proof of improper conduct, but we have not got it now.

The enclosed memorandum[1] covers all the evidence which we have on Albert and I believe that when you read it you will agree that at present there is insufficient grounds for requesting his recall.   Faithfully yours,   Robert Lansing

TLS (SDR, RG 59, 701.6211/327½, DNA).
[1] The enclosure is missing.

PERSONAL AND PRIVATE: Washington December 3, 1915

My dear Mr. President:

The White House is being deluged with resolutions of the sort enclosed.[1] I have been a little in doubt as to whether any reply should be made to them at all. I however enclose a sample letter which I think might be sent if it is necessary to acknowledge and answer the resolutions.[2]

I would call your particular attention to the last paragraph and would like your opinion, in case you approve a reply, as to whether that paragraph with the quotation included should be sent.   Faithfully yours,   Robert Lansing

TLS (RSB Coll., DLC).
[1] It was a resolution adopted by "the Swedish speaking people of Rockford, Ill. in mass meeting assembled," signed by Fred Melson as chairman and dated Nov. 14, 1915, TC MS (SDR, RG 59, 311.582 H55/35, DNA), protesting against Hillstrom's then impending execution. It ended: "RESOLVED that, should, contrary to our expectations, the sentence be carried out, we shall hold the whole American people responsible for such an outrage; and be it further
"RESOLVED that, in such a case American citizenship has no longer any value to us, and that we forsware the loyalty and allegiance to American laws, government and institutions, which has heretofore characterized our people. For where law and government cease to be the instruments of justice and are used for the murder of the innocent, loyalty ceases to be a virtue. And be it further
RESOLVED, that these resolutions be immediately communicated to the press, to the President of the United States, to the Governor of the State of Utah and to the Mayor of our City."
[2] The draft reply, which had been prepared on November 24 and which was sent to each person who signed the resolutions, is a TL (SDR, RG 59, 311.582 H55/35, DNA). It reviewed the action that Wilson and the State Department had taken on Hillstrom's behalf and included the following reprimand: "In this connection, the Department desires to express its disapproval of the intemperate language contained in the next to the last paragraph of the resolution which bears your signature, and to direct attention to the consequences possibly attending the use of such language."

My dear Mr. President: Washington December 4, 1915.

You will recall that I told you of the informal conversations I have had with the Danish Minister in regard to the purchase by this Government of the Danish West Indies. As doubtless the course of these negotiations have slipped your memory I will repeat what took place.

In October I spoke to the Danish Minister of the desire of this Government to consider the purchase of the Islands if agreeable to his Government, and that I would be pleased if he would communicate with the Danish Foreign Office in regard to this matter, keeping it of course entirely informal at present. Some days later he replied to my inquiry that his Government at the present time would not negotiate upon the subject as they had very large commercial interests which were vastly increased by the construction of the Panama Canal. I then suggested to him that we might, in case his Government would consider the purchase, incorporate certain commercial privileges in favor of Danish subjects, as our interest in the Islands was largely naval.

About the first of November he communicated this second proposition to his Government, adding what I had said in a general way that under certain conditions the United States might find it necessary to occupy the Islands in case Denmark should lose sovereignty over them.

On November 15th the Minister again called to see me about the matter and said he was under considerable embarrassment about a question which his Government had asked, but which he had hesitated to present to me. The question was this: "Whether he thought in case the Danish Government did not agree to a sale of the Islands the United States would feel it necessary to take possession of them."

In reply I told the Minister that while it had not been in my mind that action of this sort would be necessary, as I had hoped some formal negotiation would result in the transfer of the sovereignty, that I could conceive of circumstances which would compel such an act on our part. He asked me what these circumstances were and I replied that they were the ones to which I had previously called his attention, namely, the possible consequence of absorption of Denmark by one of the great powers of Europe. Such a loss of sovereignty would create a situation which it would be difficult to meet other than by occupation of the Islands, in view of the fact that Danish possessions would come under a different sovereignty in Europe and in case it did, the result might be very serious.

The other circumstance was that if Denmark voluntarily, or under coercion, transferred title to the Islands to another European power, which would seek to convert them into a naval base.

The Minister called upon me on the first and left a paraphrase of a cablegram received by him on the 25th ultimo from the Danish Minister of Foreign Affairs of which I enclose you a copy.[1]

I also enclose a telegram just received from our Minister at Copenhagen, which is in line with the paraphrase.[2]

I believe we are now in a position to enter into negotiations for the purchase of the Islands. You will observe that the question of Greenland is involved. I do not think it is of material importance, but propose to ask to what extent possession is intended, because much of the Island is still unexplored. I believe that Denmark will ask a very considerable sum for the Islands but we will know more when we begin negotiations.

If the reply to our inquiry in regard to Greenland is satisfactory I will, with your consent, proceed to the direct negotiations of a treaty of cession.

I think I should add that in my opinion the Danish Government very possibly considers the Islands a menace to their sovereignty in Europe in that if the Islands are coveted by another European power the easiest method, and possibly the only method by which they could obtain legal possession of the Islands, would be their absorption of the Danish sovereignty.

Faithfully yours,   Robert Lansing.

TLS (SDR, RG 59, 711.5914/48½A, DNA).
[1] "Paraphrase of cablegram received on November 25th from the Danish Minister of Foreign Affairs," received Dec. 1, 1915, T MS (SDR, RG 59, 711.5914/48½, DNA). Erik de Scavenius explained that Denmark would part with its West Indian islands "only under the pressure of necessity." He went on, however, to state that the possibility of American occupation of the islands, and the consequent risk that Denmark would "be drawn into an international conflict," placed his country in such a position that it would not be able to refuse to consider a proposition from the United States, if such a proposition should be made.
[2] It is missing, but the sense of the telegram is, no doubt, similar to the Minister's letter of the same date, M. F. Egan to RL, Dec. 3, 1915, TLS (SDR, RG 59, 711.5914/42, DNA). Egan reported on his meeting with Scavenius in which he had assured the Foreign Minister that the United States intended to respect Danish commercial interests in the West Indies and had asked that the purchase not be presented to the Danish people as "merely commercial or imperialistic." Scavenius in turn pointed out his country's need for money and its intention to keep a monopoly in Greenland; he would name a price soon.

From Edward Mandell House

Dear Governor: New York. December 4th, 1915.

Tumulty has just telephoned me concerning Vick's[1] request to see you.

I had no idea he had any feeling in the matter. He even went so far as to say that if Vick came to the White House, he would go out.

I am sorry I made the suggestion and merely did so for the sake of harmony. Vick is the one man that was connected with your preliminary campaign from its inception, and it seemed to me unwise to have his ill will when a ten minute interview would have brought him on your side as against McCombs'.

I told Tumulty that I had no interest in it. The opposition does not give me as much concern as some of our friends that are at odds with one another.

Affectionately yours,   E. M. House[2]

TLS (WP, DLC).
  [1] That is, Walker W. Vick.
  [2] See EMH to WW, Nov. 14, 1915, printed as an addendum in this volume.

To Robert Lansing, with Enclosure

My dear Mr. Secretary,   The White House. 5 December, 1915.

This is a peremptory note, but I see no other course open to us.

I understand that Penfield has asked for a fuller statement of the facts from the government at Vienna, but that so far they have not furnished him with any more than we already had. Can we say that we have the Austrian official version of what happened?   Faithfully Yours,   W.W.

WWTLI (SDR, RG 59, 865.857 AN 2/76½, DNA).

E N C L O S U R E[1]

Draft Note to Austria-Hungary in the ANCONA case.

December 3, 1915.

Reliable information obtained from American and other survivors who were passengers on the steamship ANCONA shows that on November 7th a submarine flying the Austro-Hungarian flag fired a solid shot toward the steamship; that thereupon the ANCONA attempted to escape but being overhauled by the submarine she stopped; that after a brief period and before the crew and passengers were all able to take to the boats the submarine fired a number of shells at the vessel and finally torpedoed and sank her while there were yet many persons on board; and that by the gun-fire and foundering of the vessel a large number of persons lost their lives or were seriously injured, among whom were citizens of the United States.

The public statement of the Austro-Hungarian Admiralty has been brought to the attention of the Government of the United States and received careful consideration. This statement substantially confirms the principal declaration of the survivors, as it admits that the ANCONA after being shelled was torpedoed and sunk while persons were still on board.

The Austro-Hungarian Government has been advised, through the correspondence which has passed between the United States and Germany, of the attitude of the Government of the United States as to the use of submarines in attacking vessels of commerce, yet with full knowledge on the part of the Austro-Hungarian Government of the views of the Government of the United States as expressed in no uncertain terms to the ally of Austria-Hungary, the commander of the submarine which attacked the ANCONA failed to put in a place of safety the crew and passengers of the vessel, which they purposed to destroy because, it is presumed, of the impossibility of taking it into port as a prize of war.

The Government of the United States considers that the commander violated the principles of international law and of humanity by shelling and torpedoing the ANCONA before the persons on board had been put in a place of safety or even given sufficient time to leave the vessel. The conduct of the commander can only be characterized as wanton slaughter of defenseless non-combatants since at the time when the vessel was shelled and torpedoed she was not, *it appears*, resisting or attempting to escape, and no other reason is sufficient to excuse such an attack, not even the possibility of rescue.

The Government of the United States is forced, therefore, to conclude either that the commander of the submarine acted in violation of his instructions or that the Imperial and Royal Government failed to issue instructions to the commanders of its submarines in accordance with the law of nations and the principles of humanity. The Government of the United States is unwilling to believe the latter alternative and to credit the Austro-Hungarian Government with an intention to permit its submarines to destroy the lives of helpless men, women and children. It prefers to believe that the commander of the submarine committed this outrage without authority and contrary to the general or special instructions which he had received.

(The Government of the United States, therefore, demands) that the Imperial and Royal Government denounce the sinking of the ANCONA as an illegal and indefensible act, that the officer who perpetrated the deed be punished, and that reparation by the payment of an indemnity be made for the citizens of the United States who were killed or injured by the attack on the vessel.

The Government of the United States expects that the Austro-Hungarian Government, appreciating the gravity of the case, will accede to its demand ⟨unconditionally and⟩ promptly; and it rests this expectation on the belief that the Austro-Hungarian Government will not sanction or defend an act which ⟨the world⟩ *is* condemn⟨s⟩*ed by the world* as inhumane and barbarous, ⟨and⟩ which is abhorrent to all civilized nations.[2]

T MS (SDR, RG 59, 865.857 AN 2/75½A, DNA).

[1] Words in angle brackets deleted by Wilson; words in italics added by him.

[2] The note sent to Vienna on December 6, 1915 (SDR, RG 59, 865.857 An 2/76a, DNA), after Wilson and Lansing had conferred about it, reads as follows:

"Please deliver a note to Minister of Foreign Affairs, textually as follows:

"Quote: Reliable information obtained from American and other survivors who were passengers on the steamship ANCONA shows that on November seventh a submarine flying the Austro-Hungarian flag fired a solid shot toward the steamship; that thereupon the ANCONA attempted to escape but being overhauled by the submarine she stopped; that after a brief period and before the crew and passengers were all able to take to the boats the submarine fired a number of shells at the vessel and finally torpedoed and sank her while there were yet many persons on board; and that by gun-fire and foundering of the vessel a large number of persons lost their lives or were seriously injured, among whom were citizens of the United States.

"The public statement of the Austro-Hungarian Admiralty has been brought to the attention of the Government of the United States and received careful consideration. This statement substantially confirms the principal declaration of the survivors, as it admits that the ANCONA after being shelled was torpedoed and sunk while persons were still on board.

"The Austro-Hungarian Government has been advised, through the correspondence which has passed between the United States and Germany, of the attitude of the Government of the United States as to the use of submarines in attacking vessels of commerce and the acquiescence of Germany in that attitude, yet with full knowledge on the part of the Austro-Hungarian Government of the views of the Government of the United States as expressed in no uncertain terms to the ally of Austria-Hungary, the commander of the submarine which attacked the ANCONA failed to put in a place of safety the crew and passengers of the vessel, which they purposed to destroy because, it is presumed, of the impossibility of taking it into port as a prize of war.

"The Government of the United States considers that the commander violated the principles of international law and of humanity by shelling and torpedoing the ANCONA before the persons on board had been put in a place of safety or even given sufficient time to leave the vessel. The conduct of the commander can only be characterized as wanton slaughter of defenseless noncombatants since at the time when the vessel was shelled and torpedoed she was not, it appears, resisting or attempting to escape, and no other reason is sufficient to excuse such an attack, not even the possibility of rescue.

"The Government of the United States is forced, therefore, to conclude either that the commander of the submarine acted in violation of his instructions or that the Imperial and Royal Government failed to issue instructions to the commanders of its submarines in accordance with the law of nations and the principles of humanity. The Government of the United States is unwilling to believe the latter alternative and to credit the Austro-Hungarian Government with an intention to permit its submarines to destroy the lives of helpless men, women and children. It prefers to believe that the commander of the submarine committed this outrage without authority and contrary to the general or special instructions which he had received.

"As the good relations of the two countries must rest upon a common regard for law and humanity the Government of the United States can not be expected to do otherwise than to demand that the Imperial and Royal Government denounce the sinking of the ANCONA as an illegal and indefensible act, that the officer who perpetrated the deed be punished, and that reparation by the payment of an indemnity be made for the citizens of the United States who were killed or injured by the attack on the vessel.

"The Government of the United States expects that the Austro-Hungarian Government, appreciating the gravity of the case, will accede to its demand promptly; and it rests this expectation on the belief that the Austro-Hungarian Government will not sanction or defend an act which is condemned by the world as inhumane and barbarous, which is abhorrent to all civilized nations, and which has caused the death of innocent American citizens. Unquote.

"Please cable whether or not the Foreign Office has any objection to the United States making this note public on Friday the tenth. Lansing."

To Robert Lansing, with Enclosure

My dear Mr. Secretary,   The White House. 5 December, 1915.

Commenting on the enclosed, do you not think it would be well for you to have a very serious conversation with the Japanese Ambassador about the Chinese situation? It seems to me clear that the interests and the treaty rights of the United States would be very directly and unfavourably affected by the foreshadowed change of political suzereignty in China, and that this is the time to let Japan understand, in all friendly frankness, how we should look upon efforts on her part to gain further control of China. Is not this your opinion?   Faithfully Yours,   W.W.

WWTLI (SDR, RG 59, 793.94/488½, DNA).

ENCLOSURE

Peking, China, December 4, 1915.

STRICTLY CONFIDENTIAL. Referring to my cable of November 27, 10 p.m.

Situation still uncertain, but there are some indications that Great Britain is not receiving strong support from Russia in the endeavor to hold Japan to strictly joint action in Far Eastern Affairs, since Russia appears to feel only a moderate interest in China proper as long as her position in the north is safe. This isolation of British influence, which was accentuated by the premature publication of the Entente plan, is believed to have encouraged Japan to make counter proposals involving complete freedom of action in China and the consequent tacit recognition of her practical suzerainty over China, which the Japanese press is already loudly asserting. The preoccupation of Great Britain in Europe, the fact that Japan could easily become dangerous to her in Asia, the indifference of Russia, the endeavors of Germany further to weaken British influence in China and to keep China from joining the Allies, leave growing material power of Japan the one positive factor in the situation, foreshadowing irretrievable loss of European influence in China should the war continue. American interests would suffer together with European and the question arises whether it is, under the circumstances possible to give sufficient backing to the European Entente powers enabling them to preserve the status of International Rights in China and of Chinese sovereignty itself intact until the end of the war.   Reinsch.

T telegram (SDR, RG 59, 793.94/488, DNA).

Four Letters to Robert Lansing

My dear Mr. Secretary,   The White House. 5 December, 1915.

At first I had the same doubt as to whether any notice at all should be taken of these representations,[1] but, upon reflection, I hardly see how we can ignore them.

The letter you have drafted is admirable throughout, and I hope it will be sent.   Faithfully Yours,   W.W.

WWTLI (RSB Coll., DLC).
[1] See RL to WW, Dec. 3, 1915 (third letter of that date).

My dear Mr. Secretary,   The White House. 5 December, 1915.

I am glad the Danish Minister gave you an opportunity to be so frank with him, and I hope he realizes how entirely friendly to Denmark the frankness was. It would appear from the enclosed message from the Danish Minister of Foreign Affairs that he does.

I hope that you will do as you suggest, namely, first ascertain just what is meant by the occupation of Greenland and, should that matter be satisfactorily cleared up, proceed at once to the negociation of a treaty for the purchase of the Danish West Indies. The opportunity has apparently come, and we may be able to relieve the Danish Government of a considerable embarrassment.   Faithfully Yours,   W.W.

WWTLI (SDR, RG 59, 711.5914/49½, DNA).

My dear Mr. Secretary,   The White House. 5 December, 1915.

No doubt you are right that there is not sufficient evidence of acts here to base a demand for Albert's recall upon; but do you not think that there is evidence enough of his exercise of authority and of his control of the evidently large sums of money which are being spent in the country for purposes of non-neutral activity and outrages against our peace? Since he is attached to the German Embassy we do not need evidence enough to convict to justify us in saying that he is *persona non grata*.

Faithfully Yours, W.W.

WWTLI (SDR, RG 59, 701.6211/323½, DNA).

My dear Mr. Secretary, The White House. 5 December, 1915.

I read this letter *after* writing my annotation on the evidence you sent me with regard to Albert.

There is a great deal of weight in what you say about the assistance Albert has been able, and willing, to render our trade in many particulars; but my feeling is so strong that his is the directing and the most dangerous mind in all these unhappy intrigues which are now so deeply exciting the resentment of this country that I should like to find sufficient ground to ask his recall.

In view of what Gerard says in his despatch of yesterday,[1] it is plainly wise to move with circumspection in this case and not add it to[o] brashly to the others; but Albert is, I am convinced, the king pin.

Faithfully Yours, W.W.

WWTLI (SDR, RG 59, 701.6211/327½, DNA).

[1] J. W. Gerard to RL, Dec. 3, 1915, T telegram (SDR, RG 59, 701.6211/321, DNA). Gerard reported Von Jagow's belief that the publication of a demand to recall Von Papen and Boy-Ed would "cause great feeling in Germany" and that such a demand ought not to be made without a bill of particulars of the acts that had made the diplomats *personae non gratae*. Gerard urged delay of the publication and assured Lansing that the recall would be made when proofs or details were presented.

To Edith Gittings Reid

Dearest Friend, The White House. 5 December, 1915.

Thank you with all my heart for your letter of the other day, asking to see me. You may be sure I would have replied to it sooner had it been possible for me to fix a time. Congressmen are rushing upon me from every quarter and it is hard to say when, if at all, I can have a moment of my own.

My first idea, of course, was to run over and see you, but it has seemed literally impossible to work that out. Congress meets to-morrow; Tuesday I muss [must] address it; Wednesday I am to entertain the Democratic National Committee at lunch. Would it be possible for you and Mr. Reid to come over and take lunch with us on Thursday? We could have a little talk after lunch.

I shall hope for it, and look forward to seeing you again with the deepest pleasure.

In haste, with love from us all,

Your devoted friend,   Woodrow Wilson

WWTLS (WC, NjP).

From Edward Wright Sheldon

My dear Mr. President: [New York] December 5th, 1915.

It is an altogether delightful memory, your dinner for '79 last Tuesday. The gracious hospitality, the impressive national setting, the fine spirit of the gathering and the touching personal note that prevailed make the memory of the evening inspiring and enduring. It was a noble tribute to you and one that seemed a worthy response to your great generosity. The men rose to the occasion most gratifyingly, and never appeared to better advantage. I only trust that the entertainment did not mean undue fatigue to you.

I wish that we might sometimes meet informally and recall by-gone days and draw pictures of the future. But I fear that this must be postponed until that distant time when your public burdens are lightened.

Yours sincerely,   Edward W. Sheldon.

ALS (WP, DLC).

Remarks to a Group of Women[1]

[Dec. 6, 1915]

Miss Martin,[2] and ladies: I did not come here anticipating the necessity of making an address of any kind. As you have just heard, I hope it is true that I am not a man set stiffly beyond the possibility of learning. I hope that I shall continue to be a learner as long as I live.

I can only say to you this afternoon that nothing could be more impressive than the presentation of such a request in such numbers and backed by such influences as undoubtedly stand back of you. Unhappily, it is too late for me to consider what is to go into my message, because that went out to the newspapers at least a week ago; and I have the habit—perhaps the habit of the teacher—of confining my utterances to one subject at a time, for fear that two subjects might compete with one another for prominence. I have felt obliged, in the present posture of affairs, to devote my message to one subject, and am, therefore, sorry to

say that it is too late to take under consideration your request that
I embody this in my message. All I can say with regard to what
you are urging at present is this:

I hope I shall always have an open mind, and I shall certainly
take the greatest pleasure in conferring in the most serious way
with my colleagues at the other end of the city with regard to
what is the right thing to do at this time concerning this great
matter. I am always restrained, as some of you will remember,
by the consciousness that I must speak for others as well as for
myself so long as I occupy my present office, and, therefore, I
do not like to speak for others until I consult others and see
what I am justified in saying.

This visit of yours will remain in my mind not only as a delightful compliment, but also as a very impressive thing which
undoubtedly will make it necessary for all of us to consider very
carefully what it is right for us to do.

T MS (WP, DLC).
  1 Wilson received Sara Bard Field and Frances Joliffe, envoys from the Woman Voters' Convention held in San Francisco in September 1915, and a committee of three hundred women who were attending the first national convention
of the Congressional Union for Woman Suffrage, the suffrage organization which
favored an all-out campaign for passage of a federal amendment. The envoys
presented petitions favoring a federal amendment signed by half a million
voters.
  2 Anne Henrietta Martin, full-time suffragist and head of the successful
campaign for Nevada's equal suffrage law in 1914. Miss Martin opened
this meeting with Wilson by reminding him that the group were not only suf-
fragists, but also voters. She told him: "Speak to your party and as its leader
impress upon Congress the importance of passing the suffrage amendment."
See The Suffragist, Dec. 11, 1915.

To Margaret Randolph Axson Elliott

The White House Dec 6 1915

Cannot you and Ed come to my wedding on December 18th
Would have written but date was not definitely decided on till
few days ago   Do try to come   Edith and I want you so much
and rest of family long to see you   Love from all
                                        Woodrow Wilson

T telegram (WC, NjP).

An Annual Message on the State of the Union

[Dec. 7, 1915]

Gentlemen of the Congress: Since I last had the privilege of
addressing you on the state of the Union the war of nations on
the other side of the sea, which had then only begun to disclose

its portentous proportions, has extended its threatening and sinister scope until it has swept within its flame some portion of every quarter of the globe, not excepting our own hemisphere, has altered the whole face of international affairs, and now presents a prospect of reorganization and reconstruction such as statesmen and peoples have never been called upon to attempt before.

We have stood apart, studiously neutral. It was our manifest duty to do so. Not only did we have no part or interest in the policies which seem to have brought the conflict on; it was necessary, if a universal catastrophe was to be avoided, that a limit should be set to the sweep of destructive war and that some part of the great family of nations should keep the processes of peace alive, if only to prevent collective economic ruin and the breakdown throughout the world of the industries by which its populations are fed and sustained. It was manifestly the duty of the self-governed nations of this hemisphere to redress, if possible, the balance of economic loss and confusion in the other, if they could do nothing more. In the day of readjustment and recuperation we earnestly hope and believe that they can be of infinite service.

In this neutrality, to which they were bidden not only by their separate life and their habitual detachment from the politics of Europe but also by a clear perception of international duty, the states of America have become conscious of a new and more vital community of interest and moral partnership in affairs, more clearly conscious of the many common sympathies and interests and duties which bid them stand together.

There was a time in the early days of our own great nation and of the republics fighting their way to independence in Central and South America when the government of the United States looked upon itself as in some sort the guardian of the republics to the south of her as against any encroachments or efforts at political control from the other side of the water; felt it its duty to play the part even without invitation from them; and I think that we can claim that the task was undertaken with a true and disinterested enthusiasm for the freedom of the Americas and the unmolested self-government of her independent peoples. But it was always difficult to maintain such a rôle without offence to the pride of the peoples whose freedom of action we sought to protect, and without provoking serious misconceptions of our motives, and every thoughtful man of affairs must welcome the altered circumstances of the new day in whose light we now stand, when there is no claim of guardianship or thought of wards

but, instead, a full and honourable association as of partners between ourselves and our neighbours, in the interest of all America, north and south. Our concern for the independence and prosperity of the states of Central and South America is not altered.
We retain unabated the spirit that has inspired us throughout
the whole life of our government and which was so frankly put
into words by President Monroe. We still mean always to make
a common cause of national independence and of political liberty
in America. But that purpose is now better understood so far
as it concerns ourselves. It is known not to be a selfish purpose.
It is known to have in it no thought of taking advantage of any
government in this hemisphere or playing its political fortunes
for our own benefit. All the governments of America stand, so
far as we are concerned, upon a footing of genuine equality and
unquestioned independence.

We have been put to the test in the case of Mexico, and we
have stood the test. Whether we have benefited Mexico by the
course we have pursued remains to be seen. Her fortunes are
in her own hands. But we have at least proved that we will not
take advantage of her in her distress and undertake to impose
upon her an order and government of our own choosing. Liberty
is often a fierce and intractable thing, to which no bounds can
be set, and to which no bounds of a few men's choosing ought
ever to be set. Every American who has drunk at the true foun-
tains of principle and tradition must subscribe without reservation to the high doctrine of the Virginia Bill of Rights, which
in the great days in which our government was set up was everywhere amongst us accepted as the creed of free men. That doctrine is, "That government is, or ought to be, instituted for the
common benefit, protection, and security of the people, nation,
or community"; that "of all the various modes and forms of government, that is the best which is capable of producing the greatest degree of happiness and safety, and is most effectually secured against the danger of maladministration; and that, when
any government shall be found inadequate or contrary to these
purposes, a majority of the community hath an indubitable, in-
alienable, and indefeasible right to reform, alter, or abolish it,
in such manner as shall be judged most conducive to the public
weal." We have unhesitatingly applied that heroic principle to
the case of Mexico, and now hopefully await the rebirth of the
troubled Republic, which had so much of which to purge itself
and so little sympathy from any outside quarter in the radical
but necessary process. We will aid and befriend Mexico, but we
will not coerce her; and our course with regard to her ought to

be sufficient proof to all America that we seek no political suzerainty or selfish control.

The moral is, that the states of America are not hostile rivals but coöperating friends, and that their growing sense of community of interest, alike in matters political and in matters economic, is likely to give them a new significance as factors in international affairs and in the political history of the world. It presents them as in a very deep and true sense a unit in world affairs, spiritual partners, standing together because thinking together, quick with common sympathies and common ideals. Separated they are subject to all the cross currents of the confused politics of a world of hostile rivalries; united in spirit and purpose they cannot be disappointed of their peaceful destiny.

This is Pan-Americanism. It has none of the spirit of empire in it. It is the embodiment, the effectual embodiment, of the spirit of law and independence and liberty and mutual service.

A very notable body of men recently met in the City of Washington, at the invitation and as the guests of this Government, whose deliberations are likely to be looked back to as marking a memorable turning point in the history of America. They were representative spokesmen of the several independent states of this hemisphere and were assembled to discuss the financial and commercial relations of the republics of the two continents which nature and political fortune have so intimately linked together. I earnestly recommend to your perusal the reports of their proceedings and of the actions of their committees.[1] You will get from them, I think, a fresh conception of the ease and intelligence and advantage with which Americans of both continents may draw together in practical coöperation and of what the material foundations of this hopeful partnership of interest must consist,—of how we should build them and of how necessary it is that we should hasten their building.

There is, I venture to point out, an especial significance just now attaching to this whole matter of drawing the Americas together in bonds of honourable partnership and mutual advantage because of the economic readjustments which the world must inevitably witness within the next generation, when peace shall have at last resumed its healthful tasks. In the performance of these tasks I believe the Americas to be destined to play their parts together. I am interested to fix your attention on this prospect now because unless you take it within your view and permit the full significance of it to command your thought I cannot find the right light in which to set forth the particular matter that

---

[1] *Proceedings of the First Pan American Financial Conference . . . Washington, May 24 to 29, 1915* (Washington, 1915).

lies at the very front of my whole thought as I address you to-day. I mean national defense.

No one who really comprehends the spirit of the great people for whom we are appointed to speak can fail to perceive that their passion is for peace, their genius best displayed in the practice of the arts of peace. Great democracies are not belligerent. They do not seek or desire war. Their thought is of individual liberty and of the free labour that supports life and the uncensored thought that quickens it. Conquest and dominion are not in our reckoning, or agreeable to our principles. But just because we demand unmolested development and the undisturbed government of our own lives upon our own principles of right and liberty, we resent, from whatever quarter it may come, the aggression we ourselves will not practice. We insist upon security in prosecuting our self-chosen lines of national development. We do more than that. We demand it also for others. We do not confine our enthusiasm for individual liberty and free national development to the incidents and movements of affairs which affect only ourselves. We feel it wherever there is a people that tries to walk in these difficult paths of independence and right. From the first we have made common cause with all partisans of liberty on this side the sea, and have deemed it as important that our neighbours should be free from all outside domination as that we ourselves should be; have set America aside as a whole for the uses of independent nations and political freemen.

Out of such thoughts grow all our policies. We regard war merely as a means of asserting the rights of a people against aggression. And we are as fiercely jealous of coercive or dictatorial power within our own nation as of aggression from without. We will not maintain a standing army except for uses which are as necessary in times of peace as in times of war; and we shall always see to it that our military peace establishment is no larger than is actually and continuously needed for the uses of days in which no enemies move against us. But we do believe in a body of free citizens ready and sufficient to take care of themselves and of the governments which they have set up to serve them. In our constitutions themselves we have commanded that "the right of the people to keep and bear arms shall not be infringed," and our confidence has been that our safety in times of danger would lie in the rising of the nation to take care of itself, as the farmers rose at Lexington.

But war has never been a mere matter of men and guns. It is a thing of disciplined might. If our citizens are ever to fight effectively upon a sudden summons, they must know how modern fighting is done, and what to do when the summons comes to render themselves immediately available and immediately effective. And the government must be their servant in this matter, must supply them with the training they need to take care of themselves and of it. The military arm of their government, which they will not allow to direct them, they may properly use to serve them and make their independence secure,—and not their own independence merely but the rights also of those with whom they have made common cause, should they also be put in jeopardy. They must be fitted to play the great rôle in the world, and particularly in this hemisphere, for which they are qualified by principle and by chastened ambition to play.

It is with these ideals in mind that the plans of the Department of War for more adequate national defense were conceived which will be laid before you, and which I urge you to sanction and put into effect as soon as they can be properly scrutinized and discussed. They seem to me the essential first steps, and they seem to me for the present sufficient.

They contemplate an increase of the standing force of the regular army from its present strength of five thousand and twenty-three officers and one hundred and two thousand nine hundred and eighty-five enlisted men of all services to a strength of seven thousand one hundred and thirty-six officers and one hundred and thirty-four thousand seven hundred and seven enlisted men, or 141,843, all told, all services, rank and file, by the addition of fifty-two companies of coast artillery, fifteen companies of engineers, ten regiments of infantry, four regiments of field artillery, and four aero squadrons, besides seven hundred and fifty officers required for a great variety of extra service, especially the all important duty of training the citizen force of which I shall presently speak, seven hundred and ninety-two non-commissioned officers for service in drill, recruiting and the like, and the necessary quota of enlisted men for the Quartermaster Corps, the Hospital Corps, the Ordnance Department, and other similar auxiliary services. These are the additions necessary to render the army adequate for its present duties, duties which it has to perform not only upon our own continental coasts and borders and at our interior army posts, but also in the Philippines, in the Hawaiian Islands, at the Isthmus, and in Porto Rico.

By way of making the country ready to assert some part of its real power promptly and upon a larger scale, should occasion arise, the plan also contemplates supplementing the army by a force of four hundred thousand disciplined citizens, raised in increments of one hundred and thirty-three thousand a year throughout a period of three years. This it is proposed to do by a process of enlistment under which the serviceable men of the country would be asked to bind themselves to serve with the colors for purposes of training for short periods throughout three years, and to come to the colors at call at any time throughout an additional "furlough" period of three years. This force of four hundred thousand men would be provided with personal accoutrements as fast as enlisted and their equipment for the field made ready to be supplied at any time. They would be assembled for training at stated intervals at convenient places in association with suitable units of the regular army. Their period of annual training would not necessarily exceed two months in the year.

It would depend upon the patriotic feeling of the younger men of the country whether they responded to such a call to service or not. It would depend upon the patriotic spirit of the employers of the country whether they made it possible for the younger men in their employ to respond under favorable conditions or not. I, for one, do not doubt the patriotic devotion either of our young men or of those who give them employment,—those for whose benefit and protection they would in fact enlist. I would look forward to the success of such an experiment with entire confidence.

At least so much by way of preparation for defense seems to me to be absolutely imperative now. We cannot do less.

The programme which will be laid before you by the Secretary of the Navy is similarly conceived. It involves only a shortening of the time within which plans long matured shall be carried out; but it does make definite and explicit a programme which has heretofore been only implicit, held in the minds of the Committees on Naval Affairs and disclosed in the debates of the two Houses but nowhere formulated or formally adopted. It seems to me very clear that it will be to the advantage of the country for the Congress to adopt a comprehensive plan for putting the navy upon a final footing of strength and efficiency and to press that plan to completion within the next five years. We have always looked to the navy of the country as our first and chief line of defense; we have always seen it to be our manifest course of prudence to be strong on the seas. Year by year we have been creating a navy which now ranks very high indeed among the navies of the maritime nations. We should now definitely determine how we shall complete what we have begun, and how soon.

The programme to be laid before you contemplates the construction within five years of ten battleships, six battle cruisers, ten scout cruisers, fifty destroyers, fifteen fleet submarines, eighty-five coast submarines, four gunboats, one hospital ship, two ammunition ships, two fuel oil ships, and one repair ship. It is proposed that of this number we shall the first year provide for the construction of two battle ships, two battle cruisers, three scout cruisers, fifteen destroyers, five fleet submarines, twenty-five coast submarines, two gunboats, and one hospital ship; the second year, two battleships, one scout cruiser, ten destroyers, four fleet submarines, fifteen coast submarines, one gun boat, and one fuel oil ship; the third year, two battle ships, one battle cruiser, two scout cruisers, five destroyers, two fleet submarines, and fifteen coast submarines; the fourth year, two battle ships, two battle cruisers, two scout cruisers, ten destroyers, two fleet submarines, fifteen coast submarines, one ammunition ship, and one fuel oil ship; and the fifth year, two battle ships, one battle cruiser, two scout cruisers, ten destroyers, two fleet submarines, fifteen coast submarines, one gunboat, one ammunition ship, and one repair ship.

The Secretary of the Navy is asking also for the immediate addition to the personnel of the navy of seven thousand five hundred sailors, twenty-five hundred apprentice seamen, and fifteen hundred marines. This increase would be sufficient to care for the ships which are to be completed within the fiscal year 1917 and also for the number of men which must be put in training to man the ships which will be completed early in 1918. It is also necessary that the number of midshipmen at the Naval academy at Annapolis should be increased by at least three hundred in order that the force of officers should be more rapidly added to; and authority is asked to appoint, for engineering duties only, approved graduates of engineering colleges, and for service in the aviation corps a certain number of men taken from civil life.

If this full programme should be carried out we should have built or building in 1921, according to the estimates of survival and standards of classification followed by the General Board of the Department, an effective navy consisting of twenty-seven battleships, of the first line, six battle cruisers, twenty-five battleships of the second line, ten armored cruisers, thirteen scout cruisers, five first class cruisers, three second class cruisers, ten third class cruisers, one hundred and eight de[s]troyers, eighteen fleet submarines, one hundred and fifty-seven coast submarines, six monitors, twenty gunboats, four supply ships, fifteen fuel ships, four transports, three tenders to torpedo vessels, eight vessels of special types, and two ammunition ships. This would be a navy fitted to our needs and worthy of our traditions.

But armies and instruments of war are only part of what has

to be considered if we are to consider the supreme matter of national self-sufficiency and security in all its aspects. There are other great matters which will be thrust upon our attention whether we will or not. There is, for example, a very pressing question of trade and shipping involved in this great problem of national adequacy. It is necessary for many weighty reasons of national efficiency and development that we should have a great merchant marine. The great merchant fleet we once used to make us rich, that great body of sturdy sailors who used to carry our flag into every sea, and who were the pride and often the bulwark of the nation, we have almost driven out of existence by inexcusable neglect and indifference and by a hopelessly blind and provincial policy of so-called economic protection. It is high time we repaired our mistake and resumed our commercial independence on the seas.

For it is a question of independence. If other nations go to war or seek to hamper each other's commerce, our merchants, it seems, are at their mercy, to do with as they please. We must use their ships, and use them as they determine. We have not ships enough of our own. We cannot handle our own commerce on the seas. Our independence is provincial, and is only on land and within our own borders. We are not likely to be permitted to use even the ships of other nations in rivalry of their own trade, and are without means to extend our commerce even where the doors are wide open and our goods desired. Such a situation is not to be endured. It is of capital importance not only that the United States should be its own carrier on the seas and enjoy the economic independence which only an adequate merchant marine would give it, but also that the American hemisphere as a whole should enjoy a like independence and self-sufficiency, if it is not to be drawn into the tangle of European affairs. Without such independence the whole question of our political unity and self-determination is very seriously clouded and complicated indeed.

Moreover, we can develop no true or effective American policy without ships of our own,—not ships of war, but ships of peace, carrying goods and carrying much more: creating friendships and rendering indispensable services to all interests on this side the water. They must move constantly back and forth between the Americas. They are the only shuttles that can weave the delicate fabric of sympathy, comprehension, confidence, and mutual dependence in which we wish to clothe our policy of America for Americans.

The task of building up an adequate merchant marine for

America private capital must ultimately undertake and achieve, as it has undertaken and achieved every other like task amongst us in the past, with admirable enterprise, intelligence, and vigor; and it seems to me a manifest dictate of wisdom that we should promptly remove every legal obstacle that may stand in the way of this much to be desired revival of our old independence and should facilitate in every possible way the building, purchase, and American registration of ships. But capital cannot accomplish this great task of a sudden. It must embark upon it by degrees, as the opportunities of trade develop. Something must be done at once; done to open routes and develop opportunities where they are as yet undeveloped; done to open the arteries of trade where the currents have not yet learned to run,—especially between the two American continents, where they are, singularly enough, yet to be created and quickened; and it is evident that only the government can undertake such beginnings and assume the initial financial risks. When the risk has passed and private capital begins to find its way in sufficient abundance into these new channels, the government may withdraw. But it cannot omit to begin. It should take the first steps, and should take them at once. Our goods must not lie piled up at our ports and stored upon side tracks in freight cars which are daily needed on the road; must not be left without means of transport to any foreign quarter. We must not await the permission of foreign ship-owners and foreign governments to send them where we will.

With a view to meeting these pressing necessities of our commerce and availing ourselves at the earliest possible moment of the present unparalleled opportunity of linking the two Americas together in bonds of mutual interest and service, an opportunity which may never return again if we miss it now, proposals will be made to the present Congress for the purchase or construction of ships to be owned and directed by the government similar to those made to the last Congress, but modified in some essential particulars. I recommend these proposals to you for your prompt acceptance with the more confidence because every month that has elapsed since the former proposals were made has made the necessity for such action more and more manifestly imperative. That need was then foreseen; it is now acutely felt and everywhere realized by those for whom trade is waiting but who can find no conveyance for their goods. I am not so much interested in the particulars of the programme as I am in taking immediate advantage of the great opportunity which awaits us if we will but act in this emergency. In this matter, as in all others, a spirit of common counsel should prevail, and out of it should come an early solution of this pressing problem.

There is another matter which seems to me to be very intimately associated with the question of national safety and preparation for defense. That is our policy towards the Philippines and the people of Porto Rico. Our treatment of them and their attitude towards us are manifestly of the first consequence in the development of our duties in the world and in getting a free hand to perform those duties. We must be free from every unnecessary burden or embarrassment; and there is no better way to be clear of embarrassment than to fulfil our promises and promote the interests of those dependent on us to the utmost. Bills for the alteration and reform of the government of the Philippines and for rendering fuller political justice to the people of Porto Rico were submitted to the sixty-third Congress. They will be submitted also to you. I need not particularize their details. You are most of you already familiar with them. But I do recommend them to your early adoption with the sincere conviction that there are few measures you could adopt which would more serviceably clear the way for the great policies by which we wish to make good, now and always, our right to lead in enterprises of peace and good will and economic and political freedom.

The plans for the armed forces of the nation which I have outlined, and for the general policy of adequate preparation for mobilization and defense, involve of course very large additional expenditures of money,—expenditures which will considerably exceed the estimated revenues of the government. It is made my duty by law, whenever the estimates of expenditure exceed the estimates of revenue, to call the attention of the Congress to the fact and suggest any means of meeting the deficiency that it may be wise or possible for me to suggest. I am ready to believe that it would be my duty to do so in any case; and I feel particularly bound to speak of the matter when it appears that the deficiency will arise directly out of the adoption by the Congress of measures which I myself urge it to adopt. Allow me, therefore, to speak briefly of the present state of the Treasury and of the fiscal problems which the next year will probably disclose.

On the thirtieth of June last there was an available balance in the general fund of the Treasury of $104,170,105.78. The total estimated receipts for the year 1916, on the assumption that the emergency revenue measure passed by the last Congress will not be extended beyond its present limit, the thirty-first of December, 1915, and that the present duty of one cent per pound on sugar will be discontinued after the first of May, 1916, will be $670,-365,500. The balance of June last and these estimated revenues come, therefore, to a grand total of $774,535,605.78. The total estimated disbursements for the present fiscal year, including twenty-five millions for the Panama Canal, twelve millions for probable deficiency appropriations, and fifty thousand dollars for miscellaneous debt redemptions, will be $753,891,000; and the balance in the general fund of the Treasury will be reduced to $20,644,605.78. The emergency revenue act, if continued beyond its present time limitation, would produce, during the half year then remaining, about forty-one millions. The duty of one cent per pound on sugar, if continued, would produce during the two months of the fiscal year remaining after the first of May, about fifteen millions. These two sums, amounting together to fifty-six millions, if added to the revenues of the second half of the fiscal year, would yield the Treasury at the end of the year an available balance of $76,644,605.78.

The additional revenues required to carry out the programme of military and naval preparation of which I have spoken, would, as at present estimated, be for the fiscal year 1917, $93,800,000. Those figures, taken with the figures for the present fiscal year which I have already given, disclose our financial problem for the year 1917. Assuming that the taxes imposed by the emergency revenue act and the present duty on sugar are to be discontinued, and that the balance at the close of the present fiscal year will be only $20,644,605.78, that the disbursements for the Panama Canal will again be about twenty-five millions, and that the additional expenditures for the army and navy are authorized by the Congress, the deficit in the general fund of the Treasury on the thirtieth of June, 1917, will be nearly two hundred and thirty-five millions. To this sum at least fifty millions should be added to represent a safe working balance for the Treasury, and twelve millions to include the usual deficiency estimates in 1917; and these additions would make a total deficit of some two hundred and ninety-seven millions. If the present taxes should be continued throughout this year and the next, however, there would be a balance in the Treasury of some seventy-six and a half millions at the end of the present fiscal year, and a deficit at the end of the next year of only some fifty millions, or, reckoning in sixty-two millions for deficiency appropriations and a safe Treasury balance at the end of the year, a total deficit of some one hundred and twelve millions. The obvious moral of the figures is that it is a plain counsel of prudence to continue all of the present taxes or their equivalents, and confine ourselves to the problem of providing one hundred and twelve millions of new revenue rather than two hundred and ninety-seven millions.

How shall we obtain the new revenue? We are frequently reminded that there are many millions of bonds which the

Treasury is authorized under existing law to sell to reimburse the sums paid out of current revenues for the construction of the Panama Canal; and it is true that bonds to the amount of approximately $222,000,000 are now available for that purpose. Prior to 1913 $134,631,980 of these bonds had actually been sold to recoup the expenditures at the Isthmus; and now constitute a considerable item of the public debt. But I, for one, do not believe that the people of this country approve of postponing the payment of their bills. Borrowing money is short-sighted finance. It can be justified only when permanent things are to be accomplished which many generations will certainly benefit by and which it seems hardly fair that a single generation should pay for. The objects we are now proposing to spend money for cannot be so classified, except in the sense that everything wisely done may be said to be done in the interest of posterity as well as in our own. It seems to me a clear dictate of prudent statesmanship and frank finance that in what we are now, I hope, about to undertake we should pay as we go. The people of the country are entitled to know just what burdens of taxation they are to carry, and to know from the outset, now. The new bills should be paid by internal taxation.

To what sources, then, shall we turn? This is so peculiarly a question which the gentlemen of the House of Representatives are expected under the Constitution to propose an answer to that you will hardly expect me to do more than discuss it in very general terms. We should be following an almost universal example of modern governments if we were to draw the greater part or even the whole of the revenues we need from the income taxes. By somewhat lowering the present limits of exemption and the figure at which the surtax shall begin to be imposed, and by increasing, step by step throughout the present graduation, the surtax itself, the income taxes as at present apportioned would yield sums sufficient to balance the books of the Treasury at the end of the fiscal year 1917 without anywhere making the burden unreasonably or oppressively heavy. The precise reckonings are fully and accurately set out in the report of the Secretary of the Treasury which will be immediately laid before you.

And there are many additional sources of revenue which can justly be resorted to without hampering the industries of the country or putting any too great charge upon individual expenditure. A tax of one cent per gallon on gasoline and naptha would yield, at the present estimated production, $10,000,000; a tax of fifty cents per horse power on automobiles and internal explosion engines, $15,000,000; a stamp tax on bank cheques, probably $18,000,000; a tax of twenty-five cents per ton on pig iron, $10,000,000; a tax of twenty-five cents per ton on fabricated iron and steel, probably $10,000,000. In a country of great industries like this it ought to be easy to distribute the burdens of taxation without making them anywhere bear too heavily or too exclusively upon any one set of persons or undertakings. What is clear is, that the industry of this generation should pay the bills of this generation.

I have spoken to you to-day, Gentlemen, upon a single theme, the thorough preparation of the nation to care for its own security and to make sure of entire freedom to play the impartial rôle in this hemisphere and in the world which we all believe to have been providentially assigned to it. I have had in my mind no thought of any immediate or particular danger arising out of our relations with other nations. We are at peace with all the nations of the world, and there is reason to hope that no question in controversy between this and other Governments will lead to any serious breach of amicable relations, grave as some differences of attitude and policy have been and may yet turn out to be. I am sorry to say that the gravest threats against our national peace and safety have been uttered within our own borders. There are citizens of the United States, I blush to admit, born under other flags but welcomed under our generous naturalization laws to the full freedom and opportunity of America, who have poured the poison of disloyalty into the very arteries of our national life; who have sought to bring the authority and good name of our Government into contempt, to destroy our industries wherever they thought it effective for their vindictive purposes to strike at them, and to debase our politics to the uses of foreign intrigue. Their number is not great as compared with the whole number of those sturdy hosts by which our nation has been enriched in recent generations out of virile foreign stocks; but it is great enough to have brought deep disgrace upon us and to have made it necessary that we should promptly make use of processes of law by which we may be purged of their corrupt distempers. America never witnessed anything like this before. It never dreamed it possible that men sworn into its own citizenship, men drawn out of great free stocks such as supplied some of the best and strongest elements of that little, but how heroic, nation that in a high day of old staked its very life to free itself from every entanglement that had darkened the fortunes of the older nations and set up a new standard here,—that men of such origins and such free choices of allegiance would ever turn in malign reaction against the Government and people who had welcomed and nurtured them and seek to make this proud country once more a hotbed of European passion. A little while ago such a thing would have seemed incredible. Because it was incredible we made no preparation for it. We would have been almost ashamed to prepare for it, as if we were suspicious of ourselves, our own comrades and neighbors! But the ugly and incredible thing has actually come about and we are without adequate federal laws to deal with it. I urge you to enact such laws at the earliest possible moment and feel that in doing so I am urging you to do nothing less than save the honor and self-respect of the nation. Such creatures of passion, disloyalty, and anarchy must be crushed out. They are not many, but they are infinitely malignant, and the hand of our power should close over them at once. They have formed plots to destroy property, they have entered into conspiracies against the neutrality of the Government, they have sought to pry into every confidential transaction of the Government in order to serve interests alien to our own. It is possible to deal with these things very effectually. I need not suggest the terms in which they may be dealt with.

I wish that it could be said that only a few men, misled by mistaken sentiments of allegiance to the governments under which they were born, had been guilty of disturbing the self-possession and misrepresenting the temper and principles of the country during these days of terrible war, when it would seem that every man who was truly an American would instinctively make it his duty and his pride to keep the scales of judgment even and prove himself a partisan of no nation but his own. But it cannot. There are some men among us, and many resident abroad who, though born and bred in the United States and calling themselves Americans, have so forgotten themselves and their honor as citizens as to put their passionate sympathy with one or the other side in the great European conflict above their regard for the peace and dignity of the United States. They also preach and practice disloyalty. No laws, I suppose, can reach corruptions of the mind and heart; but I should not speak of others without also speaking of these and expressing the even deeper humiliation and scorn which every self-possessed and thoughtfully patriotic American must feel when he thinks of them and of the discredit they are daily bringing upon us.

While we speak of the preparation of the nation to make sure of her security and her effective power we must not fall into the patent error of supposing that her real strength comes from armaments and mere safeguards of written law. It comes, of course, from her people, their energy, their success in their undertakings, their free opportunity to use the natural resources of our great home land and of the lands outside our continental borders which look to us for protection, for encouragement, and for assistance in their development; from the organization and freedom and vitality of our economic life. The domestic questions which engaged the attention of the last Congress are more vital to the nation in this its time of test than at any other time. We cannot adequately make ready for any trial of our strength unless we wisely and promptly direct the force of our laws into these all-important fields of domestic action. A matter which it seems to me we should have very much at heart is the creation of the right instrumentalities by which to mobilize our economic resources in any time of national necessity. I take it for granted that I do not need your authority to call into systematic consultation with the directing officers of the army and navy men of recognized leadership and ability from among our citizens who are thoroughly familiar, for example, with the transportation facilities of the country and therefore competent to advise how they may be coördinated when the need arises, those who can suggest the best way in which to bring about prompt coöperation among the manufacturers of the country, should it be necessary, and those who could assist to bring the technical skill of the country to the aid of the Government in the solution of particular problems of defense. I only hope that if I should find it feasible to constitute such an advisory body the Congress would be willing to vote the small sum of money that would be needed to defray the expenses that would probably be necessary to give it the clerical and administrative machinery with which to do serviceable work.

What is more important is, that the industries and resources of the country should be available and ready for mobilization. It is the more imperatively necessary, therefore, that we should promptly devise means for doing what we have not yet done: that we should give intelligent federal aid and stimulation to industrial and vocational education, as we have long done in the large field of our agricultural industry; that, at the same time that we safeguard and conserve the natural resources of the country we should put them at the disposal of those who will use them promptly and intelligently, as was sought to be done in the admirable bills submitted to the last Congress from its committees on the public lands, bills which I earnestly recommend in principle to your consideration; that we should put into early operation some provision for rural credits which will add to the extensive borrowing facilities already afforded the farmer by the

Reserve Bank Act adequate instrumentalities by which long credits may be obtained on land mortgages; and that we should study more carefully than they have hitherto been studied the right adaptation of our economic arrangements to changing conditions.

Many conditions about which we have repeatedly legislated are being altered from decade to decade, it is evident, under our very eyes, and are likely to change even more rapidly and more radically in the days immediately ahead of us, when peace has returned to the world and the nations of Europe once more take up their tasks of commerce and industry with the energy of those who must bestir themselves to build anew. Just what these changes will be no one can certainly foresee or confidently predict. There are no calculable, because no stable, elements in the problem. The most we can do is to make certain that we have the necessary instrumentalities of information constantly at our service so that we may be sure that we know exactly what we are dealing with when we come to act, if it should be necessary to act at all. We must first certainly know what it is that we are seeking to adapt ourselves to. I may ask the privilege of addressing you more at length on this important matter a little later in your session.

In the meantime may I make this suggestion? The transportation problem is an exceedingly serious and pressing one in this country. There has from time to time of late been reason to fear that our railroads would not much longer be able to cope with it successfully, as at present equipped and coördinated. I suggest that it would be wise to provide for a commission of inquiry to ascertain by a thorough canvass of the whole question whether our laws as at present framed and administered are as serviceable as they might be in the solution of the problem. It is obviously a problem that lies at the very foundation of our efficiency as a people. Such an inquiry ought to draw out every circumstance and opinion worth considering and we need to know all sides of the matter if we mean to do anything in the field of federal legislation.

No one, I am sure, would wish to take any backward step. The regulation of the railways of the country by federal commission has had admirable results and has fully justified the hopes and expectations of those by whom the policy of regulation was originally proposed. The question is not what should we undo? It is, whether there is anything else we can do that would supply us with effective means, in the very process of regulation, for bettering the conditions under which the railroads are operated and for making them more useful servants of the country as a whole. It seems to me that it might be the part of wisdom, therefore before further legislation in this field is attempted, to look at the whole problem of coordination and efficiency in the full light of a fresh assessment of circumstance and opinion, as a guide to dealing with the several parts of it.

For what we are seeking now, what in my mind is the single thought of this message, is national efficiency and security. We serve a great nation. We should serve it in the spirit of its peculiar genius. It is the genius of common men for self-government, industry, justice, liberty and peace. We should see to it that it lacks no instrument, no facility or vigor of law, to make it sufficient to play its part with energy, safety, and assured success. In this we are no partisans but heralds and prophets of a new age.[2]

Printed reading copy (WP, DLC).
  [2] There is a WWT outline, a WWsh undated draft, and a WWT draft (with the composition date of Nov. 29, 1915) in WP, DLC. The printer scrupulously reproduced Wilson's variant spellings and capitalizations.

To Edward Wright Sheldon

My dear Ed: The White House December 7, 1915

Your letter about the dinner has given me the deepest pleasure. How sincerely and earnestly I share with you the wish that we might sometimes get together for informal chat to recall the old days and forecast those that are to come, and I am not going to give up the hope that that will be possible even before I lay down the duties of the Presidency. It was tantalizing to get only a little glimpse of you the other night and not have a real talk, but we shall hope for more fortunate days when the world has quieted a bit and the country returned to its normal pace again.   Affectionately yours,   Woodrow Wilson

TLS (photostat in RSB Coll., DLC).

From Edward Mandell House

Dear Governor: New York. December 7th, 1915.

I have had several conferences with Sir Horace Plunkett during the last few days. I have not gotten much of value from him, although I have been able to give him a sympathetic insight into the situation here which he, in turn, communicated to some of his friends in the Government at home.[1]

He feels that the great danger to the Allies is the pressure the

Central Powers are bringing upon the nearby neutrals to join them. If they succeed in any considerable degree, he thinks the final result doubtful.

There is a general belief among the Allies that if we made clear our attitude in the controversy, it would at least relieve this danger and perhaps have the effect of bringing some of the neutrals on their side.

I feel sure it would be best to refrain from decisive action until the wearing down process has continued for some months longer. The danger in this of course lies in the possibility that Sir Horace speaks of in regard to the nearby neutrals, and also in the possibility of decisive success by the Allies. I do not look for this latter by force of arms, or indeed in any other way for a long while. Yet it might come through internal disorder in Germany. In the first instance it would make our task much more difficult, and in the other instance, we would forever lose the good will of everybody.

If you think it would be profitable for me to come to Washington to discuss these things with you and to decide more definitely concerning my proposed trip, please let me know and I will run over for a day at any time you designate.

Affectionately yours,   E. M. House

TLS (WP, DLC).

[1] House talked with Plunkett on December 3, 6, and 7. Plunkett's diary (bound diary, Horace Plunkett Foundation, London) entries recording these conversations follow: "Event of the day, long conference with Col House. He told me his (& Wilson's) whole mind upon the war. They are determined to see the allies through but they cannot go further than public opn. will support them. Those who in England & the U. S. were trying to bring them into the war were really evoking reactions which kept them out. Bernsdorff had been with House only yesterday and had stated that he recognized the U. S. was drifting toward the allies. Wilson was going to open his 'campaign'—this is a bad complication—at once. The note will be a sort of 'Amerika ueber Alles'—an attempt to get a consciously united nation taking its own line without any dictation or interference from outside.

"The chief trouble in the Anglo-American situation was the temperament of Sir Cecil Spring Rice. He is the slave of his nerves & all the State Department—Lansing, Polk, & Phillips he named—found him impossible to negotiate with. The President, Lansing, & House wd. like me to be appointed ambassador! It would be the end of me as it is the most unhealthy post in the ambassadorial service. It is of course an absurd idea in many other ways. I know no foreign languages, have no wife or plate & its not my job. But it is a delightfully American idea!

"House seemed to think a severance of diplomatic relns. with Austria might come out of the Ancona affair. The only question was whether the ship was running away. If Bernsdorff were the only link with the Central European powers the situation wd. be immensely simplified. That link could be used or snapped as occasion required.

"House still believes America will make the terms of peace even if she does not participate in the war." (Dec. 3, 1915.)

"I went to lunch with House where I met Capt [Guy] Gaunt R.N. our naval attaché. I had a straight talk about the relations of U. S. & G Britain. House declared that (1) The U. S. means to see the allies through if necessary (2) that the U.S. wd. take action in its own way & at its own time. I feel strongly that Wilson means to come in when he has made his position at home unassailable." (Dec. 6, 1915.)

"Another long talk with House. Unless he is a liar—and I am absolutely satisfied he is the embodiment of truth—the President is seeking to break off diplomatic relations with Austria over the Ancona outrage & then to have a single
diplomatic link (the German) with the Central powers. House talks as if the only
question about this link is not whether but when it shall be snapped. I have
insisted all through that the only hope of a lasting peace is one agreed to by
the U. S. & B. Empire." (Dec. 7, 1915.)

An After-Luncheon Talk at the White House
to the Members of the Democratic National Committee

8 December, 1915

The advantage, gentlemen, of being at your own table is that
you can make a speech without being called on. But I am not
really intending to make a speech today. I made my speech yesterday. This is a family party, and I wanted to say how sincerely
I appreciate the opportunity of seeing you face to face and having at least a few minutes with you, in order that we may not
be mere names to one another, but real individuals.

One of the great difficulties that I have experienced is in
dividing the twenty-four hours up into as many divisions as there
are persons as I want to see. A great deal is said about the isolation of the President, but I think it is the limited number of
hours in the twenty-four that causes the apparent isolation. I
would appreciate it very much if you gentlemen would regard
this as an intimation—this manner as an intimation—of the way
in which I would like you to treat me. I would like you to treat
me as a member of your household, as I would wish to treat you
as a member of mine. In earnest of that, I have sought to get you
around this table in order that you might have something of
that feeling.[1]

And I wanted to say just a word or two about what we are
all most deeply interested in. That is the success of the Democratic party. The Democratic party not only has a great niche
in this country, but it has an infinitely difficult niche. For example, the forces that makes for publicity are not on our side.
The facilities of publicity are not on our side. We have to do
something very dramatic and very striking to be talked about at
all. It is absolutely necessary that the impression we make on
the country, therefore, should be the impression of momentum;
that we aren't depending upon the accidental occasions of publicity, but rather depending upon the great force of the American
people themselves and of everything that they stand for. The

[1] There were fifty-three persons present at the luncheon. They were seated
around a round table in the East Room. There were no place cards, and no
aides were present.

only thing that renders a task like mine endurable is the knowledge that I am at least attempting to interpret the morals and purposes of this people.

Now, in my judgment, without intending to express a partisan opinion, that has not been the spirit of the leaders of the Republican party. They have been consciously allied, let me say conscientiously allied, if you will, with certain dominant forces in the country under the illusion that those dominant forces were the forces that best understood the main material interests of the country. As I so often expressed it in the last campaign, they believe that those who have the biggest material stake in the business of the country are the only ones fitted to be trustees. That, in the minds of many men, many men whom I know and respect, is a sincere opinion. It isn't an effort to do the country a harm; it is a real conviction. Now, we have—I know most of us have—a passionate conviction to the other effect—that nobody is fit to constitute himself a trustee for any great people; that the only persons fitted for that task or qualified by circumstance are the persons whom the people have chosen to be their representatives and spokesmen for the time being, and that the processes of choice ought to be just as free as possible.

Now, everything that we have tried to do has had that thought at its center. Take the great thing, perhaps the greatest and most serviceable thing we have done for the businessmen of the country—the establishment of the Federal Reserve System. The idea of that is that the bankers of the country, however conscientious and gifted they may be, are not fitted to say what the processes of credit in the country should be, and that the access to credit should be universal; that not the bankers should pick out the men who are to have credit, but the men who are to have credit should pick out themselves by deserving credit and showing that they have the goods by standing back of the credit.

With such a mission, with such a conviction, it seems to me we ought to go into the next campaign with absolute enthusiasm. We aren't talking now about what we would like to do if we were the party in power. We are the party in power, and we can talk about what we have done. There is no boasting about it, about showing the record of what we have accomplished. And I think we can challenge anybody to deny that that record has back of it this single purpose: We may not in all respects have intelligently served that purpose, but that that purpose lies back of it is indisputable. Therefore, I, for my part, look forward to the next campaign with a great deal of confidence and enthusiasm, because, when we put it up to the other side that it is a case of

"put up or shut up," they haven't anything to put up and will
have to shut up. I mean they haven't any rival policies, any
policies worthy to rival ours, through which to challenge the
confidence of the American people. They are desperately cling-
ing to the one issue of the tariff, and nobody on either side of
the house can prove anything about the tariff now. The thing
isn't working, because commerce isn't working. You can't prove
anything one way or the other. We can prove that the Under-
wood-Simmons tariff bill produced the revenue, and more than
the revenue, it was calculated to produce, so long as it had a
chance to produce it, during the months preceding the war. But
that is all that anybody can prove. And anybody who stands up
now and says that he can predict what is going to follow this
war sufficiently to suggest what the tariff policy should be is
talking through his hat, and everybody knows he is talking
through his hat. He is talking in ignorance, that the man on the
street can see to be ignorance. If the party that we have to fight
is reduced to this single issue, which is at present a blind alley,
then I say let's keep them in the blind alley and get out at the
other end.

There is nothing else they can fight on, and, therefore, our
thoughts should constantly be, it seems to me, not to let anything
interfere with the momentum of this enthusiasm and success.
We ought to sink everything, if there is anything to sink, that
would interfere with the solidarity and trimphant force of the
party. We are not partisans of men, we are partisans of ideas.
I don't believe that it is entirely because I was born and bred
a Democrat that I believe the ideas to be on the Democratic side,
but ever since I have been able to think, the ideas that gave
some kind of flutter of imagination to the mind I always found
to be on the Democratic side—the belief in common men, the
belief in humanity, the belief in those visions that were dreamed
so sincerely by the men who set this government up, the confidence in such things as I quoted yesterday from the Virginia
Bill of Rights.

Why, I have been in companies where it seemed as if I were the
only man who really believed, down in his heart, that a people
had the right to do anything with their government that they
damned pleased to do, and that it was nobody else's business
what they did with it. That is what I believe. If the Mexicans
want to raise hell, let them raise hell. We have got nothing to do
with it. It is their government, it is their hell. And after they
have raised enough of it, it will sit so badly on their stomachs
that they will want something else. They will get down to hard

pan and make a government that will stay put, but unless you let them have it out, they won't have a government that will stay put. If you let outside members, if you let the benevolent gentlemen in the United States who have money invested down there, tell them what kind of government they should have, it isn't going to stay put, and it ought not to stay put. Such gentlemen, no matter what their investments are, haven't the right to tell the Mexicans what sort of government they ought to live under.

I have had a very interesting experience about Mexico. For example, I learned the truth about Mexico by hearing a multitude of liars talk about it. You know, an interesting thing about the truth is that it matches, whereas lies don't, they depend so much upon invention. If I tell you a long story, I can't tell you enough to keep out the truth. I must fill in with the truth, just as a sort of background. So, if you hear liars enough on the same subject, you will find to a certain extent they are all telling the same story—that is, the part they didn't invent, that is, the part that is so. If you hear liars enough, you are aware of what is going on. And I have heard so much tall lying about Mexico since I came into office that it has all become familiar to me. Some gentlemen came in to see me about Mexico not long ago, and I anticipated what they were going to say. I knew it all by heart. They went out wondering whether I was in earnest or not. I was earnest in this, that I was on to them.

Now, I passionately believe in these things, and I am ready to fight for them. Unless we are passionate believers in these things and are ready to fight for them, we aren't genuine dyed-in-the-wool Democrats. If we have that kind of enthusiasm, no kind of material enthusiasm can stand against us. It makes no difference how much money is spent on the other side if our hearts are in it. If the people believe we believe in it, we have got anybody on the run that stands against us.

I wanted to say these things to you, gentlemen, in an informal fashion without sticking to parliamentary language. This is one of the few occasions when I can say it. On other occasions, I am on dress parade. I have to speak parliamentary language and be exceedingly courteous to the other side. There are certain things that it is natural for the carnal man to do which is not becoming in the President of the United States, and my office is sometimes a great burden to me in the matter of vocabulary, because there are some things I would like to say which can't be said in parliamentary terms. And I wanted you to get acquainted with my own feeling in this matter and wanted you to feel that this is a family party, and I hope it is only a beginning of family intercourse. I am told that it will be unconstitutional to adjourn without having (I think it was a toast).

T MS (C. L. Swem Coll., NjP).

Remarks to the American National Red Cross[1]

December 8, 1915.

Ladies and gentlemen: It is always with satisfaction that I reflect that I have the honor for the time being at any rate of being at the head of this great society. I believe that more and more, as the experience of the world discloses the necessities of mercy, the invaluable services of this association are more and more realized. It is very delightful that one of the great international institutions of the world should be an institution of mercy and of sympathy, and that, wherever it goes, its symbol should be recognized as a symbol without partisanship—as a symbol of fraternity, a symbol of impartial humanity.

In recent months, of course, the opportunities of the Red Cross have been extraordinary. It has not had as abundant resources as some of us wished it might have, but, nevertheless, the benevolence of the world has been poured out to it in a very generous fashion, and the work which it has been able to accomplish in these months of stress and agony has been a very noble work and a very extended work indeed. I feel it a very solemn privilege to be associated with its work, even though not in an active fashion, and stand always ready to assist it in every way that it is possible for me to assist it, either personally or officially.

This afternoon my privilege is the very simple one of presiding for a time at this session and sharing with you the pleasure of hearing the program of the afternoon carried out.

T MS (WP, DLC).

[1] At the organization's annual meeting in Washington. Wilson, who presided at the afternoon session, shared the platform with William Howard Taft and introduced Dr. Richard Strong, who reported on the campaign against typhus in Serbia.

To Josephus Daniels

Confidential.

My dear Mr. Secretary: The White House December 8, 1915

I take the liberty of enclosing a very important confidential memorandum from the Secretary of State[1] upon which I would like your advice. It seems to me of the highest importance that we should do something of the sort suggested in this memorandum and I would be very much obliged if you would before giving me your opinion consult with the Secretary of State about the whole matter at your early convenience.

I am writing also to the Secretary of the Treasury, the Secretary of War, the Secretary of Commerce, the Attorney General, and the Postmaster General.

The matter seems to me of pressing importance.

Cordially and faithfully yours,   Woodrow Wilson

TLS (J. Daniels Papers, DLC).
¹ Printed as Enclosure in RL to WW, Nov. 20, 1915 (first letter of that date).

From Seth Low

Sir: New York, N. Y. December 8th, 1915.

Referring to the letter of your Colorado Coal Commission to you, dated March 5th, 1915,¹ in which we reported progress up to that date and informed you that it was our purpose to visit Colorado later in the year, I have now the pleasure to say that your Commission proposes to leave for Colorado on December 26th, for the purpose of acquainting itself on the spot with conditions as they now exist. The Commission believes that the intense feeling growing out of the recent strike has quieted down at least so far to permit the Commission to obtain a reasonably accurate impression as to the operation of the new Colorado law creating a State Industrial Commission; as to the working of the plan recently put into operation by the Colorado Fuel and Iron Company;² and as to the relations at present existing between the miners and operators of the State at large. If circumstances permit the Commission to be useful in any way, it will naturally do everything in its power to comply with your instructions. Upon its return it will submit to you a report embodying its findings, and any recommendations that may seem to be called for.

I have the honor to be,   Very respectfully,   Seth Low.

TLS (WP, DLC).
¹ Printed as an Addendum in this volume.
² About this plan, which supplanted unionism with employee representation at company expense, see Ben M. Selekman and Mary Van Kleeck, *Employes' Representation in Coal Mines: A Study of the Industrial Representation Plan of the Colorado Fuel and Iron Company* (New York, 1924); and R. MacGregor Dawson, *William Lyon Mackenzie King: A Political Biography, 1874-1923* (Toronto, 1958), pp. 242-47. King was the author of the plan. See also Raymond B. Fosdick, *John D. Rockefeller, Jr.: A Portrait* (New York, 1956), pp. 154-63.

From William Gibbs McAdoo

Dear Mr. President: Washington December 9, 1915.

I have given a great deal of thought to the question of the Post-mastership in the Cities of New York and Brooklyn, and while I do not, of course, wish to even seem to be trenching upon the jurisdiction of the Postmaster General, I nevertheless have been given permission by him to express my views on these matters. Moreover, I am obliged to do so because so many of my friends in New York City have been pressing these matters upon my attention and it is impossible for me to avoid them.

I think it would be a mistake not to appoint a Democrat to succeed Mr. Morgan, the present Postmaster.[1] While I have high regard for him, personally and officially, I think that the Democrats of New York would be greatly disappointed if he should be reappointed. They feel—and I think justly—that this important place should be filled by a Democrat and that there are numerous Democrats of the requisite character and ability for the position. Politically speaking, it would be a very great mistake, in my opinion, not to appoint a Democrat. Mr. Roosevelt appointed Mr. Wilcox,[2] a lawyer, and not very well known publicly at that time, and after Mr. Wilcox' resignation, Mr. Morgan, another Republican, was appointed. The Republicans have always appointed a Republican Postmaster at New York when they have been in power.

Mr. Morgan's term expires December 14, 1915. His successor ought to be named on that date, if Mr. Morgan himself is not reappointed. We ought to show no indecision or vacillation.

His successor should be a man of standing, character and proven ability. Among all the men whose names I have heard mentioned, I think that Mr. John Z. Lowe, whom you appointed last March Collector of Internal Revenue in the most important District of the City of New York, is the most available and desirable man. Mr. Lowe is a lawyer of ability, is a man of standing in the community, has proven his ability as an administrative officer in this most important Internal Revenue collection district, and has shown great tact and discretion in the discharge of his difficult duties. He is a brother-in-law of Judge Samuel Seabury, an Associate Justice of the Court of Appeals of New York, and this, by the way, is one of the objections which I understand Mr. Murphy might urge against him. Judge Seabury is likely to be a candidate for Governor of New York. He is a strong man and it is very likely that he will be nominated. If he is, I feel confident that he can be elected. I understand that Mr.

Murphy thinks that Mr. Lowe's appointment might contribute to Judge Seabury's success. Whether there is any ground for this or not I am unable to say, but I do not think it is a sufficient objection to Mr. Lowe. Mr. Lowe is much better known than Mr. Wilcox was when President Roosevelt appointed him Postmaster at New York, and moreover, Mr. Lowe has behind him a record of efficient administration of a very difficult office, which Mr. Wilcox did not have when he was appointed.

Some of the New York Congressmen have told me that if Mr. Lowe should be named they would consider it a very satisfactory appointment, although on the whole they would prefer to see some member of the organization chosen. Mr. Lowe is not a member of the organization but he has not antagonized it.

If Mr. Lowe should be chosen I would suggest that ex-Congressman Henry M. Goldfogle be appointed Collector of Internal Revenue to succeed him. Mr. Goldfogle is a lawyer and has the requisite ability for this position. He is an organization man and I think his appointment would be very pleasing to the Democratic organization in New York.

As to Brooklyn: I think that the present Assistant Postmaster, Mr. Cleary,[3] ought to be appointed. The Democratic Congressmen in Brooklyn (including Congressman Fitzgerald, I understand), as well as our most important friends there, are very earnest in their advocacy of Mr. Cleary. I understand that he is in all respects qualified for the place, and it seems a pity, in view of the political fight ahead of us, not to select the man whom all factions in Brooklyn seem to favor. While I would not advise the appointment of an incompetent or unfit man in any circumstances, I think it highly desirable to choose a man who is acceptable to all factions if he has the requisite ability and character. Secretary Redfield tells me that he favors Mr. Burton,[4] who is now serving under a temporary appointment. Mr. Burton may be a very good man for all I know, but certainly he is no more competent, if as competent, for the work than the present Assistant Postmaster, Mr. Cleary, and he brings absolutely no political strength.

If the Postmaster General should concur in these views, I think we shall have a very happy solution of these problems.[5]

Faithfully yours,   W G McAdoo

TLS (WP, DLC).

[1] Edward M. Morgan, a career postal employee, was appointed postmaster of New York City in September 1907 and served until March 1917.

[2] William Russell Wilcox, lawyer, served as postmaster of New York City from 1905-1907, as chairman (for New York City) of the State Public Utilities Commission from 1907-1913, and became chairman of the Republican National Committee in 1916.

[3] Peter J. Cleary became assistant postmaster of Brooklyn in June 1915 and held the position until his retirement, except for one year as acting postmaster of Brooklyn in 1923.

[4] Walter C. Burton, former state senator and member of the New York State Civil Service Commission, was appointed postmaster of Brooklyn in July 1916 and held the position until his death in 1923.

[5] The postmastership of New York City finally went in March 1917 to Thomas Gedney Patten, defeated in his bid for a fourth term in Congress in November 1916.

From Edith Bolling Galt

My own precious One: [Washington] Dec. ninth 1915

While you are talking to me about Mrs. Reed,[1] and my other hand is in your own dear one, I am sending this little message of inexpressable love to greet you tomorrow morning when you are so many miles away.

It can't be any thing but just a message, for I had so much rather talk to you than write. But nothing either written or spoken can ever tell you how completely you make the world for me, or how I shall miss you these next two days.

I am so infinitely proud of you, and feel so exalted above other women in having your love that I feel I must do some wonderful thing in the world to prove my wish to serve you.

Don't be blue Precious. We are not *really* far apart. And Saturday will soon be here. And then *no more journeys*!!!

With all my love.   Your own,   Edith

ALS (WP, DLC).

[1] That is, Edith Gittings Reid, who had lunch with Wilson at the White House on December 9.

From the Diary of Colonel House

December 10, 1915.

Sidney Brooks came to tell of his visit to Washington, especially as to his interview with the President which he described as being delightful in every way.[1] It lasted thirty-five minutes. Brooks told of the British Ambassador's state of mind which, taken together with the letter I have today from Sir Horace Plunkett, who is stopping at the Embassy, is illuminating. The manner in which he tried to block Brooks is typical of his actions whenever prominent Englishmen come to this country. It was clear to Brooks that if it had not been for me, he would not have [been] able to have gotten anywhere and his visit to Washington would have been a failure. Spring-Rice had warned the State Department, as he had me, that Brooks had no official connection whatever with the Foreign Office. He did this so thoroughly that he frightened them and they asked me for advice as to their treatment of Brooks. Brooks tells me that when Sir Horace Plunkett appeared, he evidently smoothed Spring-Rice down and he became more pleasant.

1 Brooks saw Wilson at the White House on December 9.

To Edith Bolling Galt

Columbus Ohio Dec. 10 [1915]

Arrived well and fit easy journey fine nights rest love to all

W.

T telegram (WP, DLC).

A Luncheon Address to the Chamber of Commerce of Columbus, Ohio[1]

December 10, 1915.

Mr. President,[2] gentlemen of the Columbus Chamber of Commerce: I want, first, to express my very deep gratitude to you for the cordial manner in which you have greeted me and my sense of privilege in standing here before you to speak about some of the things in which we are mutually interested.

You, gentlemen, are perhaps more interested in those matters of policy which affect the business of the country than in any others; and yet it has never seemed to me possible to separate the business of a country from its essential spirit and the life of its people. The mistake that some men have made has been in supposing that business was one thing and life another, whereas they are inseparable in their principles and in their expression.

I must say that, in looking back upon the past, there is something about the history of business in this country which is not wholly satisfactory. It is interesting to remember that, in the early years of the republic, we felt ourselves very more a part of the general world than we have felt since then. Down to the War of 1812, the seas were full of American ships. American enterprise was everywhere expressed in American commerce when we were a little nation. And yet, now that we are a great nation, the seas are almost bare of our ships, and we trade with other countries at the convenience of the carriers of other nations. The truth is that, after the War of 1812, we seem deliberately to have chosen

1 In the Masonic Temple.
2 William P. Tracy. The Editors are unable to identify him further.

to be provincial, to shut ourselves in upon ourselves, exploit our own resources for our own benefit rather than for the benefit of the rest of the world. And we did not return to address ourselves to foreign commerce until our domestic development had so nearly burst its jacket that there was no straitjacket in which it could be confined. Now, American industry in recent years has been crying for an outlet into the currents of the world. There were some American minds, some American businessmen, and not a few, who were not built upon the provincial type, who did find their way into foreign markets and made the usual American peaceful conquest in those foreign markets. But others seemed deliberately to refrain, or not to know that there were opportunities to be availed of.

Until the recent banking act, you couldn't find, so far as I am informed, a branch of an American bank anywhere outside of the United States, whereas other nations of the world were doing their banking business on foreign shores through the instrumentality of their own bankers. I was told at a meeting of the American Bankers' Association that much of the foreign banking business—the business in foreign exchange—had to be done in our ports by branches of Canadian banks established among ourselves. Being literalists, we interpreted the National Banking Act to mean, since it did not say that the national banks could engage in this business, that they could not engage in it, and some of the natural, some of the necessary, functions of banking were not performed by American bankers. I refer to this merely as an evidence of what I take leave to call our provincialism.

Moreover, during this period this very interesting thing happened—that American businessmen were so interested to be protected against the competition of other businessmen in other countries that they proceeded by organization to protect themselves against each other and engaged in the politics of organization rather than in the statesmanship of enterprise. For your organization for the purpose of preventing successful competition is not morally any higher than running politics upon the basis of organization rather than upon the basis of statesmanship and achievement. Organization is necessary to politics, and it is necessary to business. But the object of organization ought not to be exclusion; it ought to be efficiency. The only legitimate object of organization is efficiency. It can never be legitimate when it is intended for hostile competitive purposes. I have never entertained the slightest jealousy of those processes of organization which led to greater and greater competency, but I have always been jealous of those processes of organization which were intended in the spirit of exclusion and monopoly. Because the spirit of exclusion and monopoly is not the American spirit. The American spirit is a spirit of opportunity and of equal opportunity, and of admitting every man to the race who can stand the pace.

So I say that we have reason to look back upon the past of American business with some dissatisfaction. But I, for my part, look forward to the future of American business with the greatest confidence. American business has altered its point of view, and, in proportion as it has altered its point of view, it has gained in power and in momentum. I have sometimes heard exhortations to the effect that politics ought not to be injected into business. It is just as important that you should not inject business into politics. It is even more important that you should not inject business into politics because, so far as the business of this country is concerned, there ought not to be any politics.

I, gentlemen, am a Democrat, as you probably have heard, and I am a militant Democrat, but it is because I believe that the principles of Democracy will be of more service to the country than any other kind of principles. Not because I believe Democrats are better than Republicans; it is because I think Republicans are mistaken and Democrats right, and I hope and believe that I hold that conviction in no narrow partisan spirit. I find that I am one of the few men of my acquaintance who absolutely believe every word, for example, of the Virginia Bill of Rights. Most men use them for Fourth of July purposes, and use them very handsomely, but I stand before you and tell you that I believe them. For example, the Virginia Bill of Rights—I cite that because it was one of the first bills of rights, and the others were largely modeled upon it or run along the same lines—the Virginia Bill of Rights says that, when a government proves unsuitable to the life of the people under it—I am not quoting the language but the meaning—they have a right to alter or abolish it in any way that they please. When things were perhaps more debatable than they are now about our immediate neighbor to the south of us, I do not know how many men came to me and suggested that the government of Mexico should be altered as we thought that it ought to be altered. But, being a subscriber to the doctrine of the Virginia Bill of Rights, I could not agree with them. The Mexicans may not know what to do with their government, but that is none of our business; and so long as I have the power to prevent it, nobody shall "butt in" to alter it for them. That is what I mean by being a Democrat built on the original plan of the bills of rights.

Now, those bills of rights say some things that are very pertinent to business. They assert the absolute equality of right on the part of individuals to access to opportunity. That is the reason I am opposed to monopoly; not because monopoly does not produce some excellent results of a kind, but because it is intended to shut out a lot of people who ought not to be shut out. And I believe that democracy is the only thing that vitalizes a whole people instead of vitalizing only some of the people of the country. I am not fit to be the trustee of prosperity of this country; neither are you. Neither is any group of men fit to be the trustees for the economic guidance of this country. I believe in the common man. I believe the genius of America to be that the common man should be consulted as to how he is governed and should be given the same opportunity with every other man under his government. I believe that that spirit is the spirit of the average businessman in America. I am sure that it is the spirit of the average businessman in America, because, although it is a current theory that the President of the United States is a very much secluded person, a good many people talk to him, I assure you, and he takes particular pains to know what the people are talking about who do not talk directly to him. Nobody who has been bred in the atmosphere of American societies from one end of this continent to the other can mistake the spirit of the average man, and I am for the average man. The country consists of him. He is the backbone of the country. The man who is above the average uses him and ought to respect his tools, ought to respect his instruments, ought to respect the veins through which the very lifeblood of the country flows.

With regard to the future of business in this country, no man can speak with confidence, because it happens that the distressing events of the months since the great European war began have put America in a peculiar relation to the rest of the world. It looks as if we would have to be the reserve force of the world in respect of financial and economic power. It looks as if in the days of reconstruction and recuperation, which are ahead of Europe, we would have to do many of the things, many of the most important things, which hitherto have been done through European instrumentalities. No man can say just how these matters are going to shape themselves, but every man can see that the opportunity of America is going to be unparalleled, and that the resources of America must be put at the service of the world as they never were put at its service before. Therefore, it is imperative that no impediments should be put in the way of commerce with the rest of the world. You cannot sell unless you buy.

Commerce is only an exalted kind of barter. The bartering may not be direct, but, directly or indirectly, it is an exchange of commodities and the payment of the balances, and, therefore, there must be no impediments to the free flow of the currents of commerce back and forth between the United States, upon which the world will in part depend, and the other countries which she must supply and serve.

And for the first time, gentlemen, it happens—I believe providentially—that the businessmen of America have an instrumentality in the new banking law such as they never had before for the ebb and flow and free course of the natural processes of credit. For the first time we are not bound up in an inelastic currency. Our credit is current, and that current will run through all the channels of commerce in every part of the world.

A gentleman present here today told me that he had done what I trust it is not his habit to do; he said he had been looking up an old speech of mine and that, when I addressed the American Bankers' Association in Denver some years ago,[3] I said that I had been called upon a little while before to speak to the bankers of New York on the elasticity of the currency, and that I had replied that I spoke upon it with the more freedom because I knew nothing about it. Being a professor at that time, on a salary, I was not in a position to know anything of the elasticity of the currency. I hope that he is ready to believe that, in the time that has intervened, I have taken pains to find out something about the elasticity of the currency, for I was an enthusiastic supporter of the bill which finally established the Federal Reserve System, and I think that I understand it. At any rate, gentlemen, jesting apart, it does furnish the businessmen of this country with an instrument such credit never possessed before.

Credit is a very spontaneous thing. Its excursions ought not to be personally conducted. There have been times in this country when the expeditions of credit were personally conducted. I could name some of the agencies where guides were provided. But if you are starting an enterprise in one part of the country, you do not want any guides; you rather resent guidance from another part of the country. And there were times when there were limited circles in the eastern portion of our great country who thought they knew more about business in the other parts of the country than the people who lived in those parts of the country. I always doubted them. I now know that they did not.

The vision of a democracy that I have is this—that you must not be presumptuous enough to determine beforehand where the

<hr>

[3] His address is printed at Sept. 30, 1908, Vol. 18.

vitality is going to come from. The beauty of a democracy is that you never can tell when a youngster is born what he is going to do with himself, and that no matter how humbly he is born, no matter where he is born, no matter what circumstances hamper him at the outset, he has got a chance to master the minds and lead the imaginations of the whole country. That is the beauty of democracy—that you do not beforehand pretend to pick out the vital leaders, but they pick themselves out. The men who are going to lead you and dominate you pick themselves out and elect themselves by an electoral process over which legislation can have no control whatever. I like to think of the youngsters now playing somewhere, perhaps in a gutter, who are sometime or other going to stand up and speak the voice of America for all the world to hear.

So I want you to share with me this vision of the future of American business—of a cosmopolitan spirit, of a spirit of enterprise out of which the old timidity has gone. For you will have to admit, gentlemen, that American businessmen have been timid. They have constantly run to Washington and said, "It looks like rain; for God's sake, give us shelter." You do not need Washington. There is genius enough in this country to master the enterprise of the world, and it ought not to ask odds of anybody. I would like to have the thrilling pride of realizing that there was nobody in America who was afraid to match wits with the world. When I move about this country, I feel, as you do, the vitality of the thing that is going on in it—the quick origination of minds when they meet new circumstances, the readiness with which Americans adapt themselves to new circumstances. That is the spirit of conquest.

I originally, for example, belonged to a stock which has never failed to feel at home anywhere as soon as it got there. I mean the Scotch Irish. The Scotch Irish have taken leave to belong the minute they landed, and presently a good deal else has belonged to them besides themselves, and I like to picture that as also typical of America. Whom would you pick out among the early Americans as the typical American? You know that, for more than a hundred years after the settlement of this country, for nearly a hundred years after the establishment of the Union, there was always a frontier on this continent, and the typical American was the man who did not need any assistance from anywhere or anybody, but who went out into a new country, made his own home for himself, established his own government, arranged everything to suit himself, and then occasionally went back to his old home, rich and powerful and contented.

That was the typical American. There was a certain community somewhere, in what used to be the frontier back in Jackson's day, who sent a pitiful plea to Washington begging that they would hurry up and give them a territorial form of government, because they did not have any government; they happened to be beyond the bounds of the governments theretofore set up. Jackson sent them a very proper reproof. He said that they were the first Americans he had heard of who did not know how to set up a government for themselves and take care of themselves. The characteristic American community for a long time was the frontier community made on the spot, and made according to the local pattern. So that when I hear Americans begging to be assisted by authority, I wonder where they were born. I wonder how long they have breathed the air of America. I wonder where their papers of spiritual naturalization are.

America now may make peaceful conquest of the world. And I say that with all the greater confidence, gentlemen, because I believe, and hope that the belief does not spring merely from the hope, that, when the present great conflict in Europe is over, the world is going to wear a different aspect. I do not believe that there is going to be any patched-up peace. I believe that thoughtful men of every country and of every sort will insist that when we get peace again we shall have guarantees that it will endure and that the instrumentalities of justice will be exalted above the instrumentalities of force. I believe that the spirit which has hitherto reigned in the hearts of Americans, and in like people everywhere in the world, will assert itself once for all in international affairs, and that, if America preserves her poise, preserves her self-possession, preserves her attitude of friendliness towards all the world, she may have the privilege, whether in one form or another, of being the mediating influence by which these things may be induced.

I am not now speaking of governmental mediation. I have not that in mind at all. I mean the spiritual mediation. I mean the recognition of the world that here is a country that has always wanted things done that way, and whose merchants, when they carry their goods, will carry their ideas along with them, and that this spirit of give and take, this spirit of success only by having better goods and better brains and better training will, through their influence, spread the more rapidly to the ends of the world. That is what I mean by the mediating influence which I think American commerce will exert.

So I challenge you, and men like you throughout the United States, to apply your minds to your business as if you were building up for the world a great Constitution of the United States, as if you were going out in the spirit of service and achievement— the kind of achievement that comes only through service, the kind of achievement which is statesmanship, the statesmanship of those arrangements which are most serviceable to the world. As you do this, the American spirit, whether it be labeled so or not, will have its conquest far and wide. And when we come back from our long voyage of trade, we will not feel that we have left strangers behind us, but that we have left friends behind us, and have come home to sit by the fireside and speak of the common kinship of all mankind.

T MS (WP, DLC).

From Frank Mason North and Others

Columbus, Ohio,
Honored and dear Friend: December 10, 1915.

We deem it a high privilege to present to you on this evening of the day of your visit to the City of Columbus, Ohio, to be present among other engagements at the meeting of the Executive Committee of the Federal Council of the Churches of Christ in America, the following resolution adopted by the Executive Committee at its sessions this afternoon. The resolution reads:

"The Executive Committee of the Federal Council, as these sessions at Columbus, Ohio, draw to a close, place on record their appreciation, first of all, of the presence with the Executive Committee of Woodrow Wilson, the President of the United States. We tender to him hearty thanks that amid the multitudinous cares of state he has taken opportunity thus to express his deep interest in the welfare of the Christian churches of our country. The guidance and blessing of God are invoked for him in his most responsible position as Chief Magistrate."

In behalf of the Executive Committee

Frank Mason North   Chairman
Charles S. Macfarland   General Secretary
Shailer Mathews   Committee
Eugene R Hendrix
Wm. H. Roberts

TLS (WP, DLC).

An Address to the Federal Council of Churches in Columbus

[Dec. 10, 1915]

Mr. Chairman,[1] ladies and gentlemen: I feel an unaffected diffidence in coming into this conference without having participated in its deliberations. I wish that I might have been here to learn the many things that I am sure have been learned by those who have attended these conferences. I feel confident that nothing that I say about the rural church will be new to you. I want you to understand that I am here simply because I wished to show my profound interest in the subject which you have been considering and not because I thought I had anything original to contribute to your thought.

I think, as we have witnessed the processes of our civilization in recent years, we have more and more realized how our cities were tending to draw the vitality from the countryside, how much less our life centered upon country districts and how much more upon crowded cities. There was a time when America was characteristically rural, when practically all her strength was drawn from quiet countrysides, where life ran upon established lines and where men and women and children were familiar with each other in a long established neighborliness. But our rural districts are not now just what they used to be and have partaken in recent years of something of the fluidity that has characterized our general life. So that we have, again and again, been called upon, from one point of view or another, to study the revitalization of the countryside. There was a time, no longer ago than the youth of my own father, for example, when pastors found some of their most vital work in the country churches. I remember my dear father used to ride from church to church in a thickly populated country region and minister to several churches with a sense of ministering to the most vital interests of the part of the country in which he lived. After all, the most vitalizing thing in the world is Christianity. The world has advanced, advanced in what we regard as real civilization, not by material but by spiritual means, and one nation is distinguished from another nation by its ideals, not by its possessions; by what it believes in, by what it lives by; by what it intends; by the visions which its young men dream and the achievements which its men of maturity attempt. So that each nation exalts, when it writes its poetry or writes its memoirs, the character of

[1] Wilson referred either to Gifford Pinchot, chairman of the Commission on the Church and Country Life, or to Frank Mason North, chairman of the executive committee of the Federal Council of Churches.

its people and of those who spring from the loins of its people.

There is an old antithesis upon which I do not care to dwell, because there is not a great deal to be got from dwelling on it, between life and doctrine. There is no real antithesis. A man lives as he believes he ought to live, or as he believes that it is to his advantage to live. He lives upon a doctrine, upon a principle, upon an idea, sometimes a very low principle, sometimes a very exalted principle. I used to be told, when I was a youth, that some of the old casuists reduced all sin to egotism, and I have thought, as I watched the career of some individuals, that the analysis had some vital point to it. An egotist is a man who has got the whole perspective of life wrong. He conceives of himself as the center of affairs. He conceives of himself as the center of affairs even as affects the providence of God. He has not related himself to the great forces which dominate him with the rest of us, and, therefore, has set up a little kingdom all his own in which he reigns with unhonored sovereignty. So there are some men who set up the principle of individual advantage as the principle, the doctrine, of their life, and live by that, and live generally a life that leads to all sorts of shipwreck. Whatever our doctrine be, our life is conformed to it.

But what I want to speak of is not the contrast between doctrine and life, but the translation of doctrine into life. After all, Christianity is not important to us because it is a valid body of conceptions regarding God and man, but because it is a vital body of conceptions which can be translated into life for us— life in this world and a life still greater in the next. Except as Christianity changes and inspires life, it has failed of its mission. That is what Christ came into the world for, to save our spirits, and you cannot have your spirit altered without having your life altered.

When I think of the rural church, therefore, I wonder how far the rural church is vitalizing the lives of the communities in which it exists. We have had a great deal to say recently, and it has been very profitably said, about the school as a social center, by which is meant the schoolhouse as a social center; about making the schoolhouse, which in the daytime is used for the children, a place which their parents may use in the evenings and the other disengaged times for the meetings of the community, where they are privileged to come together and talk about anything that is of community interest, and talk about it with the utmost freedom. Some people have been opposed to it because there are some things that they do not want talked about. Some boards of education have been opposed to it because they realized that it might not be well for the board of education to be talked about. Talk is a very dangerous thing. Community comparisons of views are a very dangerous thing to the men who are doing wrong thinking. But I, for my part, believe in making the schoolhouse the social center—the place that the community can use for any kind of coordinating that it wants to do in its life. But I believe that where the schoolhouse is inadequate, and even where it is adequate, that the most vital social center should be the church itself, and that, not by way of organizing the church for social service—that is not my topic tonight; that is another topic—but of making the community realize that that congregation, and particularly that pastor, is interested in everything that is important for that community, and that the members of that church are ready to cooperate and the pastor ready to lend his time and his energy to the kind of organization which is necessary outside the church as well as in, for the benefit of the community.

It seems to me that the country pastor has an unparalleled opportunity to be a country leader, to make everybody realize that he, as the representative of Christ, believes himself related to everything human, to everything human that has as its object the uplift and instruction and inspiration of the community or the betterment of any of its conditions; and that, if any pastor will make it felt throughout the community that that is his spirit, and that his interest, and that he is ready to draw his elders or his deacons or his vestrymen with him as active agents in the betterment of the community, the church will begin to have a dominating influence in the community such as it has lost for the time being and we must find the means to regain.

For example, in a farming community one of the things that the Department of Agriculture at Washington is trying to do is to show the farmers of the country the easiest and best methods of cooperation with regard to marketing their crops, learning how to handle their crops in a cooperative fashion, so that they can get the best service from the railroads; learning how to find the prevailing market prices in the accessible market, so as to know where it will be best and most profitable to send their farm products and to draw them together into cooperative association with these objects in view. The church ought to lend its hand to that. The pastor ought to say, "If you want somebody to look after this for you, I will give part of my time, and I will find other men in my congregation who will help you in the work and help you without charging you anything for it. We want you to realize that this church is interested in the lives of the people of this community and that it will lend itself to any legitimate project that advances the life and interest of this community."

Let the rural church find that and then discover, as it will discover, that men begin to swing their thoughts to those deeper meanings of the church in which we wish to draw their attention, that this is a spiritual brotherhood, that the pastor and his associates are interested in them because they are interested in the souls of men and the prosperity of men as it lies deep in their hearts. There are a great many ways by which leadership can be exercised. The church has too much depended upon individual example. "So let your light shine before men" has been interpreted to mean "Put your individual self on a candle stick and shine." Now, the trouble is that some people cannot find a candle stick, but the greater trouble is that they are a very poor candle, and the light is very dim. It does not dispel much of the darkness for me, individually, to sit on top of a candle stick, but if I can lend such little contribution of spiritual force as I have to my neighbor and to my comrade and to my friend, and we can draw a circle of friends together and unite our spiritual forces, then we have something more than example: we have cooperation.

Cooperation, ladies and gentlemen, is the vital principle of social life; not organization merely. I think I know something about organization. I can make an organization, but it is one thing to have an organization and another thing to fill it with life. And then it is a very important matter what sort of life you fill it with. If the object of the organization is what the object of some business organizations is and the object of many political organizations is—to absorb the life of the community and run the community for its own benefit—then there is nothing profitable in it. But if the object of the organization is to afford a mechanism by which the whole community can cooperatively use its life, then there is a great deal in it. An organization without the spirit of cooperation is dead and may be dangerous. The vital principle is cooperation, and organization is secondary. I have been a member of one or two churches that were admirably organized and were accomplishing nothing. You know some people dearly love organization. They dearly love to sit in a chair and preside. They pride themselves upon their knowledge of parliamentary practice. They love to concoct and write minutes. They love to appoint committees. They boast of the number of committees that their organization has, and they like the power and the social influence of distributing their friends among the committees. And then, when the committees are formed, there is nothing to commit to them.

This is a nation which loves to go through the motions of public meeting, whether there is anything particularly important to consider or not. It is an interesting thing to me how the American is born knowing how to conduct a public meeting. I remember that, when I was a lad, I belonged to an organization which at that time seemed to me very important, which was known as the Lightfoot Baseball Club. Our clubroom was a corner, an unoccupied corner, of the loft of my father's barn, the part that the hay had not encroached upon, and I distinctly remember how we used to conduct orderly meetings of the club in that corner of the loft. I had never seen a public meeting, and I do not believe any of the other lads with whom I was associated had ever seen a public meeting, but we somehow knew how to conduct one. We knew how to make motions and second them; we knew that a motion could not have more than two amendments offered at the same time, and we knew the order in which the amendments had to be put, the second amendment before the first. How we knew it I do not know. We were born that way, I suppose! But nothing very important happened at those meetings, and I have been present at some church organization meetings at which nothing more important happened than happened with the Lightfoot Baseball Club. I remember distinctly that my delight and interest was in the meetings, not in what they were for—just the sense of belonging to an organization and doing something with the organization, it did not very much matter what. Some churches are organized that way. They are exceedingly active about nothing. Now, why not lend that organizing instinct, that acting instinct, to the real things that are happening in the community, whether they have anything to do with the church or not?

We look back to the time of the early settlements in this country and remember that in old New England the church and the school were the two sources of the life of the community. Everything centered in them. Everything emanated from them. The school fed the church, and the church ran the community. It sometimes did not run it very liberally, and I, for my part, would not wish to see any church run any community. But I do wish to see every church assist the community in which it is established to run itself, to show that the spirit of Christianity is the spirit of assistance, of counsel, of vitalization, of intense interest in everything that affects the lives of men and women and children. So that I am hoping that the outcome of these conferences, of all that we say and do about this very important matter, may be to remind the church that it is put into this world, not only to serve the individual soul, but to serve society also. And it has got to go to work on society in one sense with a greater sense of exigency of the thing than in the case of the individual, because you have got to save society in this world, not in the next. I hope that our society is not going to exist in the next. It needs amendment in several particulars, I venture to say, and I hope that the society in the next world will be amended in those particulars —I will not mention them. But we have nothing to do with society in the next world. We may have something to do with the individual soul in the next world by getting it started straight for the next world, but we have got nothing to do with the organization of society in the next world. We have got to save society, so far as it is saved, by the instrumentality of Christianity in this world. It is a job, therefore, that you have got to undertake immediately and work at all the time, and it is the business of the church.

Legislation cannot save society. Legislation cannot even rectify society. The law that will work is merely the summing up in legislative form of the moral judgment that the community has already reached. Law records how far society has got, and there have got to be instrumentalities preceding the law that gets society up to that point where it will be ready to record. Try the experiment. Enact a law that is the moral judgment of a very small minority of the community, and it will not work. Most people will not understand it and, if they do understand, they will resent it, and whether they understand it and resent it or not, they will not obey it. Law is a record of achievement. It is not a process of regeneration. Our wills have to be regenerated and our purposes rectified before we are in a position to enact laws that record those moral achievements. And that is the business, primarily, it seems to me, of the Christian.

There are a great many arguments about Christianity. There are a great many things which we spiritually assert which we cannot prove in the ordinary, scientific, sense of the word "prove." But there are some things which we can show. The proof of Christianity is written in the biography of the saints, and by the saints I do not mean the technical saints—those whom the church or the world has picked out to label saints, for they are not very numerable—but the people whose lives, whose individual lives, have been transformed by Christianity. It is the only force in the world that I have ever heard of that does actually transform the life, and the proof of that transformation is to be found all over the Christian world and is multiplied and repeated as Christianity gains fresh territory in the heathen world. Men begin suddenly to erect great spiritual standards over the little personal standards which they theretofore professed and will walk smiling to the stake in order that their souls may be true to themselves. There is nothing else that does that. There is something that is analogous to it, and that is patriotism. Men will go into the fire of battle and freely give their lives for something greater than themselves—their duty to their country. And there is a pretty fine analogy between patriotism and Christianity. It is the devotion of the spirit to something greater and nobler than itself. These are the transforming influences. All the transforming influences in the world are unselfish. There is not a single selfish force in the world that is not touched with sinister power, and the church is the only embodiment of the things that are entirely unselfish—the principles of self-sacrifice and devotion. Surely this is the instrumentality by which rural communities may be transformed and led to the things that are great. And surely there is nothing in the rural community in which the rural church ought not to be the leader and in which it ought not to be the vital actual center.

That is the simple message that I came to utter tonight, and, as I began by saying, I dare say it is no new message, I dare say it has been repeatedly said in this conference. I merely wanted to add my testimony to the validity and power of that conception. Because, ladies and gentlemen, we are in the world to do something more than look after ourselves.

The reason that I am proud to be an American is because America was given birth to by such conceptions as these—that its object in the world, its only reason for existence as a government, was to show men the paths of liberty and of mutual serviceability, to lift the common man out of the paths, out of the slough of discouragement and even despair; set his feet upon firm ground; tell him, "Here is the high road upon which you are as much entitled to walk as we are, and we will see that there is a free field and no favor, and that, as your moral qualities are and your physical powers, so will your success be. We will not let any man make you afraid, and we will not let any man do you an injustice."

Those are the ideals of America. We have not always lived up to them. No community has always lived up to them. But we are dignified by the fact that those are the things we live for and sail by. America is great in the world, not as she is a successful government merely, but as she is the successful embodiment of a great ideal of unselfish citizenship. That is what makes the world feel America draw it like a lodestone. That is the reason that the ships that cross the sea have so many hopeful eyes lifted from their humbler quarters towards the shores of the new world. That is the reason why men, after they have been for a little while in America and go back for a visit to the old country, have a new light in their faces—the light that has kindled there in the country where they have seen some of their objectives fulfilled. That is the light that shines from America. God grant that it may always shine and that, in many a humble hearth in quiet country churches, the flames may be lighted by which this great light is kept alive.

T MS (WP, DLC).

To Edith Bolling Galt

Columbus Ohio Dec 10 15

Day passed off very successfully without great fatigue well and fit love   W

T telegram (WP, DLC).

From Thomas Watt Gregory

My dear Mr. President: Washington December 10, 1915.

I acknowledge receipt of yours of the 8th enclosing the confidential memorandum from the Secretary of State about which you ask my advice.

I think the idea the Secretary of State has in mind is an excellent one, but see no necessity for an executive order; in fact, I think it would be much better to arrange for this without any special publicity.

As I was leaving Washington on an important matter the afternoon of the day I received your note, I arranged a conference at once with the Secretaries of State, of the Treasury, of War and the Postmaster General, and I think we got the matter into fairly good working shape. I have delegated a man from my Department to confer with Counsellor Polk, of the State Department, and one representative each from the Treasury and Post Office Departments, and these men are to meet at 2 o'clock tomorrow and work out the details.

All the members of the Cabinet referred to approved the plan, and I believe much good will be accomplished.

If you feel that you need any further advice from me on this subject, I will be delighted to respond.

Faithfully yours,   T. W. Gregory

TLS (WP, DLC).

From William Nesbitt Chambers[1]

Dear Mr. President: Chatham, N. J. Dec. 10, 1915.

You may or you may not remember me as a member of the Class of '76 at Princeton University. It is a long call back to that time. Many men who knew you then and have followed your work since have no little family pride in the splendid work you are doing—guiding the affairs of the country at this time when men's souls are being tried as by fire. May the good hand of the Lord be upon you to steady and strengthen your heart and hands and continue the grace of wisdom for all the problems you have to consider.

I have just arrived from Adana, Turkey. We were a party of 12 missionaries, large and small. Through the good offices of Ambassador Morganthau at Constantinople and Consul Nathan[2] at Mersine we were allowed to leave the country through the port of Mersine on the U.S.S. Des Moines. On behalf of the party I desire to express our gratitude and our appreciation of the favor rendered us and the very great kindness shown us by Capt. Blakely[3] and the other officers and men of the Des Moines.

I had the privilege of conducting a Sabbath service on board— a novel and startling thing to me. I stood with one hand on a great gun, and in the other was the Gospel—the one made for the destruction of men and the other revealed for their life and peace. I could satisfy myself only with the thought that the world needs them both. In the hands of such men as yourself the one would be used to restrain evil and the other to develop righteousness and good-will to men.

This leads me to say that the Armenian situation in Turkey is so appalling in its awful cruelty and relentless extermination of that people that one could wish that such a power as the United States should become so strong on land and sea that such a government as Turkey would never dare to commit such a horrible crime. Would that your influence could be exerted in some way to stay the spoiler and rescue the miserable remnant. By spring, if present conditions continue, they will be as the people of Moab, as described in Is. 16:14, "and the remnant shall be very small and of no account."

                    Yours very sincerely,   Wm. N. Chambers

TLS (WP, DLC).
  [1] Princeton 1876, missionary in Turkey for the American Board of Commissioners for Foreign Missions since 1879.
  [2] Edward Isaac Nathan.
  [3] Commander John Russell Young Blakely, U.S.N.

From William Gibbs McAdoo

PERSONAL.

Dear Mr. President: Washington December 10, 1915.

In my letter of yesterday, which was written hastily, I assumed that there was no question about Mr. Cleary having the requisite qualifications for Postmaster in Brooklyn. I thought that Mr. Burleson's objections to him were based on other grounds. He tells me today that Mr. Cleary is not, in his opinion, a competent man for the place and that this judgment is formed upon Mr. Cleary's record in the Department. I simply want to make clear to you that my recommendation of Mr. Cleary was based upon the other assumption and upon the fact that his appointment would be acceptable to so many elements of the party in Brooklyn.   Faithfully yours,   W G McAdoo

TLS (WP, DLC).

From Samuel Gompers

Sir: Washington, D. C. Dec. 10, 1915.

Through the courtesy of Hon. William B. Wilson, Secretary of the Department of Labor, I have been advised that conforming to your convenience, on Wednesday morning, December 15, 1915, at ten o'clock, you will afford Secretary Wilson, Mr. Andrew Furuseth, President of the Seamen's Union, and the undersigned, an opportunity of an interview for the purpose of presenting to you a souvenir of appreciation of your assistance in the enactment and the signing of the Seamen's law. I am quite confident that when you see the pictorial history of the effort to secure that law, and the artistic workmanship of the frame, you will appreciate both to the fullest.

Of course the presentation will occupy but a few minutes of your time, but there are two other matters which at the interview on Wednesday I should like to have the opportunity of presenting to you for your consideration. You know that I shall ask no more time than you can devote to these matters, nor attempt to impose upon your courtesy. If for any reason you cannot give the time, say about fifteen minutes, to the consideration of these matters, a day or two later, if convenient to you will be entirely agreeable to me. I do believe, however, that the matters should be brought to your attention as soon as your time and convenience admit. At least one of these matters has reference to a question in which you are greatly interested, and in which I should find it a pleasure to aid.[1]

I have the honor to remain,

Yours very respectfully,   Saml. Gompers.

TLS (WP, DLC).
[1] Wilson's reply to this request is missing. Wilson received Gompers and Furuseth on December 15.

Remarks to the Gridiron Club

December 11, 1915.

Mr. President[1] and gentlemen: I have only once or twice had the pleasure of dining with the Gridiron Club. It has always been very delightful to me to take part, when I was privileged to do so, in the very entertaining program of your evening. I believe, however, that it is not my own thought, but what is really in your own hearts, that has led me to feel throughout that there underlay all the fun making a very serious vein of thought and intention, and this evening that feeling has been stronger upon me than usual. There has been jest, there has been thrust, there has been sarcastic implication, but through it all there has run a serious idea, which I take it is the idea of the present moment among the American people.

Some of the things that Mr. Cannon[2] said tonight made my thoughts run back and reminded me of many of the elements that have gone to make up our present temperament. He spoke of the mixture of blood that had taken place on the banks of the Wabash. He spoke of those old days when the nation was in the making, when the stream of impulse was running westward, when the nation was being compounded, when all her energy was bent upon building up her own communities and spreading her own polity from coast to coast; of those days when, perhaps, individuals stood up more prominently in their personal force than they do in our own day, when they took a flavor from the individual initiative which was necessary in that time, and when all the world waited to see what was going to be made out of America. And then my thought came on to the present time, when America has almost been made. Her bloods are not yet entirely mixed and united, but she has built, and built strongly and solidly, from coast to coast. And there is no longer any cen-

[1] Edgar Callender Snyder, of the *Omaha Bee*.
[2] Representative Joseph Gurney Cannon, Republican of Illinois, former Speaker of the House of Representatives.

tering of our thought upon merely domestic enterprises. We now stand to make or mar our character among the nations of the world.

It is interesting how America has seemed to choose a century as its dramatic unit. It used one century to settle the country; it used another century to determine what national influence should predominate; it took another century to build a nation; and now it is facing a third century, questioning itself as to its purpose—what is to be done with this nation upon the arena of the world's affairs. And we are the responsible actors in this act of the drama. I wonder if we realize the full responsibility that is upon us?

I know what that last song meant. I happen to be President, but that song would have been sung no matter who was President. It means that America is now ready to follow responsible leaders of her own choosing, and that it wishes to be led in some direction in particular and not to drift. And the responsibility that rests upon me is not so much, so far as I have the power, to choose the course which I individually might prefer, as to do my best to interpret the spirit and purpose of the country for which for the time being I speak. I must listen and try to interpret; I must remember and try to reproduce. Now, the spirit of America is a very subtle thing, and no man can be sure that he can reproduce it. But I am quite sure of several traits that belong to us and that we wish to express and strengthen. One is that we are not afraid either of our own destiny or of anything that anybody else can do to us. America is characterized by the spirit of self-confidence and, in the best sense of the word, self-sufficiency. But America is also characterized, though upon the surface it may not seem so, by an abhorrence of extremes. America does not like the extreme radical, and it cannot continue to grow if it submits to the extreme conservative. Reaction is out of the question. America can never turn back and never will turn back, but the pace at which she advances she wishes to be a well-considered and moderate pace. She wants progress, but she wants ordered progress; she wants well-considered progress. She wants to drive down stakes that represent the point which her thought has reached, and she will never pull those stakes up again.

Now, the question of preparation, which has been the note of the evening, is a question of how we shall express that spirit of America—of self-confidence—and with all moderation. There is one extreme that America wishes always to avoid. She does not want to be ruled by the spirit of any class or by any dominant idea. She does not want to be ruled by the spirit of a military class; she does not want to be ruled by the spirit of a lawyer class. Legalism is the enemy of progress, and militarism is the end of progress. There cannot be any progress when the professionalism of the soldier dominates in a national polity, and God forbid that we should have combined the professionalism of the soldier with the legalism of the lawyer. That would be a crust which we never could break. America wants to express her own strength rather than the strength of a profession. She wants to feel that she is ready to do for herself what she will not let any class of her citizens do for her. That, permit me to say, is the spirit in which the program of preparation which has been proposed is conceived. Whether it is an adequate program to express that spirit, I admit, is a debatable question. I have never heard of a program which was not debatable.

The things that are not debatable, gentlemen, it seems to me, are principles. I cannot tell you how much time I waste hearing men expound principles to me, whereas, the only question I want them to expound to me is how we are going adequately to put those principles into operation. America is a practical nation. It is agreed upon its principles, and the only thing we can differ upon is the method of putting those principles into practical operation. We want a nation sufficient for self-defense, and yet we do not want a nation which submits to the military spirit. If there is any better program than the one proposed, let somebody suggest it, for it has now come to a case of "put up or shut up!" But, above all things else, America is impatient when it comes to a national question, and particularly a national question of such vital importance as this, of any factional spirit whatever. Look at what we are witnessing in the world, gentlemen. Look at the combination of parties and the disappearance of party lines in Great Britain and France and Germany and Italy. And because we happen not to be engaged in this terrible struggle, shall we omit to do the same handsome thing and combine all counsels in order that the nation may be served?

Why, gentlemen, the equipoise of the world in a way depends upon us. It is one thing, and a comparatively easy thing, to combine parties to conduct a war, but it is a more difficult and a more handsome thing to combine parties in order to preserve and glorify peace. For there is only one thing to do in the case of war, and that is to concentrate all energies upon the fighting; whereas, there are many things, and delicate and difficult things, to do in peace, and the combining of the counsels of peace is the act, not merely of military strategy, but of statesmanlike accomplishment.

My hope and ambition for America is that, in the months immediately ahead, she shall exhibit to the world an example of combined and amicable counsel for the best fortunes of America and of the world such as no other nation ever exhibited. I, for my part, can testify that, in the things I have been permitted to propose, I have no conscious partisan feeling whatever, and I challenge all men of all parties to come to the assistance of the nation with their unprejudiced counsel. For this is the thing, the only thing, which will make America what she boasts—that she has always been the leader of the world along the paths of liberty and of peace.

May I take advantage of this opportunity to say a word or two to the members of this club as representing the great fraternity of the press? There is one thing that is particularly dangerous just now, gentlemen, and that is to publish conjectural versions of what is going on in the foreign relations of this country. Nothing could be more dangerous than that. We are at peace with all nations. I hope and believe that there is no pending question which need disturb that feeling. But there are many difficulties which may be thrown in the way by speculative accounts of what is being said and done and what is to be expected, and I should hope that the gentlemen of the press would seek to learn from the Secretary of State, if they will be so gracious, what it is wisest for them to say and not to say. The Secretary playfully outlined some of the things that you do after your interviews with him, and I know from my own conferences with him that his feeling for the representatives of the press is my own—the feeling of the greatest cordiality and confidence. But you do some very dangerous things sometimes: in saying, for example, in a case, such as he cited, that a message has been received which has not been received, and the reasons the Secretary did not say anything which were the reasons which you yourselves give. Those things are immediately transmitted to foreign nations and constitute part of the transaction thereafter, because they constitute part of the mental atmosphere in which the foreign mind acts and the foreign government responds.

I am uttering this counsel and making this request with the greatest seriousness of purpose, because we can manage American affairs by common counsel, but our common counsel will not determine what other nations are going to do. Whenever we make a move, the next move is not up to us, but it is up to some other government, and we ought to be very careful how we set the stage for what they are going to do. This is a concrete example, gentlemen, if I may say so, of the sort of spirit which should prevail in America. Things are not easy. If you could read the dispatches which I hourly read, you would see how infinitely complicated the threads of the foreign pattern are, how many influences are at work which do not appear upon the surface, how many things there are which it is best not to talk about, how many things there are which bid us suspend judgment and wait until the next move is made. And I adjure every man who feels his responsibility as an American citizen to reflect upon these things and not make it more difficult than it inevitably is to keep the balance even in our transactions with foreign countries.

I believe that I have caught, tonight, gentlemen, the real spirit of this gathering and that the spirit of this gathering is, as I have said, the spirit of the country. Patriotism, gentlemen, is not a mere sentiment. Anybody can feel warm about the heart, who has any heart at all, when he thinks of his country and all it means to him and the dear people that live in it and the responsibilities that rest upon him. But that is not patriotism. That is the effect of patriotism, it may be. Patriotism is a deeply grounded principle of action which bids every man subordinate his own interests to the interests of the common weal and to act upon that, though it be to the point of utter sacrifice of himself and everything that is involved.

I have sometimes thought that there is a sense in which patriotism in its redeeming quality resembles Christianity. Christianity makes a man forget himself and square everything that he does with a great love and a great principle, and so does patriotism. It makes him forget himself and square every thought and action with something infinitely greater than himself. I believe, and you believe, that the interests of America are coincident with the interests of the world, and that, if we can make America lead the way of example along the paths of peace and regeneration for herself, we shall enable her to lead the whole world along those paths of promise and achievement. So, gentlemen, I believe that we should go away from here tonight feeling that we have renewed our pledge to each other to think of America before we think of ourselves and before we think of anything else.

I read a very interesting essay once called, "Christmas, Its Unfinished Business."[3] The writer commented upon the peace congresses and upon their comparative futility, and he speculated why it was that war often seemed more handsome than

[3] See the address printed at Sept. 10, 1912, n. 3, Vol. 25.

peace; why it was that a family would hang the dead lad's musket up over the mantelpiece but would not hang his yardstick up over it. And he found, as everybody will find who analyzes the matter, that the reason was this—that that musket represented utter self-sacrifice and the yardstick did not, and that peace would come to the world when peace was as handsome as war in this—that every man would devote his spirit to the service of something else other than his personal self-interest.

Peace will come to the world when we love our fellow men better than we love ourselves. And, for my part, the love of my fellow men translates itself in action into my belief in the capacity of America to set the example of freedom and of liberty. I believe that, individually, we are of little efficacy, but that, united as Americans, we may make conquest of the spirit of the world, and that that spirit, turning to us as in those first days of hope when the republic was set up, will see that there burns in the East, as in the West, a light that shines around the world, kindled at the hearths of American homes and burning in the imaginations of those who lead the American nation.

T MS (WP, DLC).

From Washington Gladden

Dear Mr President: Columbus, Ohio. Dec 11 1915

I want to express to you my sense of the value of the service which you rendered to the country and the church by both of your addresses yesterday. Especially grateful am I for your testimony last evening, which brought to a grand close a meeting which I hope will be epochal. It is a great thing for the church and for the country and for the world to have one who stands where you do speak as you did last night. And the best of it was that you knew what it was that you were trying to commend.

I have not troubled you much with questions or counsels, but I am going to venture to ask you to give a few minutes to the little pamphlet which I enclose.[1] It is not often that your policy fails of my hearty approval; but here is a matter in which I wish I might have a hearing.

I wish I could tell you how much in love I am with that little family at Williamstown. Now and then I come across people who capture me right away, and they got me! I wish they belonged to me, but I'm not covetous.

Yours faithfully   Washington Gladden

ALS (WP, DLC).

¹ Washington Gladden, *A Plea for Pacifism* (Columbus, Ohio, 1915). Only the first page survives in WP, DLC; a revised version appeared in *The Nation*, CIII (Aug. 3, 1916), Supplement, 2. Gladden declared himself a pacifist and opposed preparedness as an inevitable step toward war.

From William Gibbs McAdoo

CONFIDENTIAL.

Dear Mr. President: Washington December 11, 1915.

It is extremely important for you to invite Senator Clarke to see you immediately about the shipping bill. He has been made again chairman of the Committee on Commerce of the Senate and I am afraid that he may think that the Secretary of Commerce, Judge Alexander, Senator Fletcher and myself are ignoring him in having consultations about the bill.¹ As you know, we have been merely trying to prepare a tentative draft as a basis for discussion. Senator Simmons spoke to me about this matter yesterday and thinks that in view of some unfortunate publications which have appeared in the papers that you ought to ask the Senator to come in to see you at once and give him a copy of the bill, with the suggestion that it has been put into form merely as a basis for discussion, and ask him to consider it and give you his views and suggestions.²

I think it would also be well if you would send for Mr. Kitchin in like manner.³

The situation is a little sensitive for the reasons I have stated and prompt action on your part may prevent an unfortunate contretemps. I enclose three copies of the bill,⁴ one for yourself and one each for Senator Clarke and Mr. Kitchin.

Cordially yours,   W G McAdoo

TLS (WP, DLC).

¹ McAdoo and Redfield had prepared a draft of a new shipping bill in early November. Redfield had asked Wilson to send the draft to Fletcher and Alexander for their criticisms. W. C. Redfield to WW, Nov. 5, 1915, TLS (WP, DLC). Wilson replied as follows: "Thank you for your letter of November fifth with the enclosures, which I herewith return. I am glad that such progress is being made towards a recasting of the bill for [the] Merchant Marine. My own feeling is that it is a measure for which we are bound to fight because so much of vital importance depends upon it." WW to W. C. Redfield, Nov. 9, 1915, TLS (Letterpress Books, WP, DLC).
² Wilson saw Clarke on December 14.
³ Wilson apparently was unable to arrange for a meeting with Kitchin.
⁴ "A BILL To establish a United States Shipping Board for the purpose of encouraging, developing and creating a naval auxiliary and merchant marine to meet the requirements of the commerce of the United States with foreign countries and with its territories and possessions, and for other purposes," redraft of Dec. 10, 1915, T MS (WP, DLC). The bill empowered the shipping board to purchase and construct vessels, to rent or sell its vessels to private shipping firms, to regulate all corporations engaged in interstate or international commerce to by ship, to set rates for such commerce, and to license all shipping firms. If the board's commissioners judged it necessary, they could establish

corporations to purchase, construct, sell, and rent ships. The bill further provided that vessels sold or leased through the shipping board might be taken, at a fair price set by the board, by the United States "absolutely or temporarily for use as transports, naval auxiliaries, or any naval or military purpose."

From Frederick Bicknell Lynch

My dear Mr President: New York Dec. 11th 1915

I think Jos. Johnson[1] should be appointed postmaster at New York. He is the best man mentioned for the place. As fire commissioner under Mayor Gaynor he gave the city excellent service and was very popular with the men—reduced the fire loss forty per cent by eliminating the incentive for fires, over insurance, and improved the service while decreasing the cost. He is popular with the retail and wholesale trade and his appointment would not be seriously criticized by anyone. Politically it would be strong. He belongs to the organization but has been independent also   He is an American—not Irish, German or Jewish.

Sincerely Yours   Fred B Lynch

ALS (WP, DLC).

[1] A former newspaper correspondent, fire commissioner from 1912 to 1914, and chief of the transit bureau of the New York Public Service Commission in 1915.

From Edward Mandell House, with Enclosure

Dear Governor: New York City. December 12th, 1915.

I am enclosing you a copy of a letter which has just come from Lord Bryce.

I am glad you saw Sidney Brooks. He has done excellent work, the fruits of which are already apparent.

In answering Lord Bryce I suggested that a trip over here now would be useful. I have a feeling that Spring-Rice does not send reports home that truthfully portray the situation here, not only as regards the public but the Administration. Therefore the more people who visit here like Bryce, Plunkett and Brooks who know America and have the confidence of their people at home, the better.

I wrote Sir Edward Grey the other day suggesting that it might be well if he would send Mr. Drummond,[1] his Secretary, over for a short stay in order to get a more intimate view of things here than he could get by letter.

Drummond is acting in the same capacity as Sir William Tyrrell formerly did, but is perhaps an abler man. I recalled to Sir Edward the good Sir William did in clearing up the misunderstanding between the two governments in regard to Mexico which could not have been done through the regular channel.

If you do not approve this suggestion let me know and I can arrange it otherwise.

Bertron told me Saturday in confidence, but for your information, that Vanderlip and Wm. R. Grace[2] had formed a company and had purchased the remaining seven ships of the Pacific Mail and would ply them between South America and the United States. Vanderlip wished you to know this.

Unless you desire me to go to Europe before, I am thinking of going to Texas in the early part of January for a few weeks. I shall not do this though if there is anything of importance to hold me here that you think I can do.

Your speeches in Columbus have added much to the joy of your friends. Even the opposition find it difficult to criticize what you said.

At Dudley's suggestion, I am seeing Senator O'Gorman today. Dudley thinks that by a little patting on the back, the Senator will fall into line and do anything you desire. I am willing to make the effort for we must weld all our forces together for the coming campaign.

Governor Glynn was with me yesterday. He is disgruntled, but if a postmaster can be appointed at Hudson, New York, to his liking, he too, will fall into line. I will discuss this with Burleson later.   Devotedly yours,   E. M. House

TLS (WP, DLC).
  1 [James] Eric Drummond.
  2 The American International Corp., organized in November 1915 to encourage American investments in the Orient and South America, purchased the merchant fleet of the Pacific Mail Steamship Co. and contracted with W. R. Grace and Co. to manage the ships. The plan became public knowledge on December 13. See also the *New York Times*, Dec. 12 and 14, 1915.

E N C L O S U R E

James Viscount Bryce to Edward Mandell House

Private.

Forrest Row, Sussex, England.
Dear Colonel House: November 26th, 1915.

As you asked me to send you a line when anything occurred to me that it might be worth your while to know regarding views and feelings entertained here, I write this to say that there is not the slightest change in British sentiment regarding the duty and necessity of prosecuting the war with the utmost vigour, and listening to no suggestions for negotiations with the German Government.

We know that they would not listen to any terms we could propose, at the best, the evacuation of Belgium with ample compensation to her for all she has suffered, and also, of course, the evacuation of Northern France and Luxemburg.

She on the other hand would insist on indemnities, for without them bankruptcy stares her in the face. So there is nothing for it but to fight on.

We hear that Jane Addams (who ought to have known better after her journey around Europe) and other women and some men of the extreme Pacifist type, are trying to engender a movement for mediation. They might spare themselves the trouble. We are not in the least discouraged by the Balkan difficulties, bad as they are, and the Armenian massacres, which the German Government could have stopped, have heightened our indignation against them as well as against the Turks, whose rule over Christians must be extinguished, once for all.

Is there any chance of our seeing you again soon on this side? It would be a great pleasure.

I am greatly relieved at what seems a favorable turn of events in Mexico.

With our very kind regards to Mrs. House,

Sincerely yours,   James Bryce.

TCL (WP, DLC).

To Seth Low

My dear Mr. Low: The White House December 13, 1915

I am very much interested and pleased to know that the Colorado Coal Commission expects to visit Colorado immediately after Christmas. I agree with the view of the Commission that this is a favorable time to make the visit, and I shall look forward to its report with the greatest interest.

Cordially and sincerely yours,   Woodrow Wilson

TLS (S. Low Papers, NNC).

To Jane Addams

The White House
My dear Miss Addams: December 13, 1915

I hope you realize how the hearts of all your friends have gone out to you in your illness[1] and how anxious we are to hear that you are making steady and rapid progress towards a recovery. These are just a few lines to express my warm sympathy and my own hopes for your prompt restoration to health.

Cordially and sincerely yours,   Woodrow Wilson

TLS (J. Addams Papers, PSC-Hi).
[1] Jane Addams entered the hospital on November 30 with what was later diagnosed as tuberculosis of the kidney. Her illness received considerable, and sometimes skeptical, comment because it prevented her from sailing on the Ford peace ship.

To William Nesbitt Chambers

[The White House]
My dear Mr. Chambers: December 13, 1915

I have your letter of December tenth and have read it with the greatest interest. I am heartily glad to learn that you are safely out of Turkey and thank you sincerely for the personal part of your letter.

The situation with regard to the Armenians is indeed nothing less than appalling. You may be sure that we have been doing everything that is diplomatically possible to check the terrible business.

In haste, with much regard,

Sincerely yours,   Woodrow Wilson

TLS (Letterpress Books, WP, DLC).

From Robert Lansing, with Enclosure

PERSONAL AND CONFIDENTIAL:

My dear Mr. President: Washington December 13, 1915

I enclose copy of a confidential telegram which I have just received from Mr. Egan, at Copenhagen.

The amount which Denmark asks as consideration for the transfer of the Danish West Indies seems to me excessive. I should like, however, your views as to what would be, in your opinion, a proper consideration. Evidently the Danish Government is willing to sell if they can get their price.

Faithfully yours,   Robert Lansing.

TLS (WP, DLC).

ENCLOSURE

Copenhagen, December 12, 1915.

CONFIDENTIAL. Referring to the Department's instruction number two fifty-four and to my telegram number 191, December 3, 4 p.m.

The Minister for Foreign Affairs after consultation with his colleagues named thirty million dollars as selling price. I said this was too enormous and with the additional expense of the Panama Canal and the present war it seemed to me that Congress would hardly consent to it. I had to admit however that I had no means of estimating the military value of the islands. He answered that we were not considering the commercial value of the islands but their military value. He cited the case of Helgoland which the British Government would now be glad to get back at any cost. In case of not impossible international difficulties no price that our Government could afford to pay would be too great. He added that I was right in considering the sum very great but he said that it must be great in order to impress the popular imagination and to carry the project through the Landsthing. He had little fear of the Lower House if popular opinion could be impressed as to be almost unanimous. Denmark wanted money very badly but less than this amount would not be of great use in the present difficulties of the Government. The King[1] would naturally be against a project which would make his Kingdom smaller during his reign. To placate him he hoped that my Government would consent to have Denmark assume the ownership of Cape York already de facto Danish and the rest of Greenland. Full report by mail.

The sum seems to me really enormous; I had expected an offer of about twenty millions. There is no doubt in my mind that Germany will eventually have Denmark which it already considers its northern province. Now that Germany is fully occupied our chance of getting these islands at all is at its best. It seems to me the acquisition of these islands ought to be part of our preparedness for future difficulties.

American Minister, Copenhagen.

T telegram (WP, DLC).
[1] Christian X.

A Memorandum by Robert Lansing

MEMORANDUM OF CONVERSATION WITH BARON ZWIEDINEK
AUSTRIAN CHARGÉ
DECEMBER 13, 1915.

The Chargé called upon me, having made an appointment by telephone, to discuss the ANCONA note. He asked me in the first place whether I had read the dispatch which he had sent to his Government on Saturday night. I told him that I had and I thought it fairly represented the substance of our conversation. I said to him what while I realized the spirit of Austria in the conduct of the war that I did not wish his Government to think for a moment that our position was less firm than it was; that there could be only one thing for Austria to do and that was to comply with our demands.

He said to me—"But suppose the facts are not as you stated them on the information which you had." I said—"That, of course, may make some difference in the matter, although I do not conceive they could vary enough to change our position."

He said to me if the Austrian Government then should say that they would investigate the matter and that if they found the facts substantially as stated they would comply with our three demands would that be acceptable to this Government? I replied to him that that seemed a reasonable proposition, if it was a full and frank acceptance of the demands.

He then said it was very difficult for him to communicate with his Government. I said I appreciated that and in order that he might advise his Government fully in the matter that I would be willing to forward through our Ambassador at Vienna a cipher message for him.[1]   Robert Lansing.

TS memorandum (WP, DLC).

[1] Zwiedinek reported on this conversation (in English as deciphered) as follows: "Lansing said that note although very firm and determined does not intend to offend but *has to be* taken as strong appeal to our sense of chivalry and self-respect not to endorse an action by which duty of due consideration for safety of travellers evidently neglected. Life of travellers demands ample consideration even if it would sometimes become necessary to *let* steamer go. Lansing and administration would be painfully surprised if Austria Hungary would defend an act which contrary to *our* proud tradition and against laws of humanity which America absolutely determined to defend whereas cooperation and severe punishment of commander would produce here on the contrary *all over* country *excellent* effect of which we could be proud.

"I believe that situation demands very serious and prompt attention." J. H. von Bernstorff to the Foreign Office, quoting E. Zwiedinek to S. Burián, Dec. 13, 1915, T telegram (Der Weltkrieg, No. 18a, Unterseebootkrieg gegen England, ganz geheim, vol. 15, p. 44, GFO-Ar).

From William Joel Stone

Dear Mr. President: [Washington] December 13, 1915.

I intended to call at your office this morning to ascertain whether your engagements are such as to enable you to give me an audience during the week; but I have a slight attack of Grippe and my doctor thinks it would be imprudent for me to leave my residence today. What I desire to see you about relates to our foreign affairs. There are features of this business which I wish to discuss with you. I want to know more definitely what your policy is. I want to know this for several reasons, and partly that I may better understand the circumstances which concern my own attitude. Within the last few days several Democratic Senators have talked with me about our diplomacy with respect to the European Powers, and they appear to be quite seriously disturbed. Senators seek me for information about foreign affairs because of my connection with the Senate Committee having jurisdiction over subjects coming before the Senate with relation to foreign affairs, but I know nothing that is not generally known through the Press and am as much confused as those who come to me. I feel obliged to say that the situation in the Senate as I see it is not reassuring.

I have an engagement with you for Wednesday about a pardon case. I apprehend that your time for some days in the immediate future is pretty well covered by engagements, but I am sending this note merely to advise you of my earnest wish to have a good long talk with you as soon as possible.[1]

Very sincerely yours,   Wm. J. Stone

TLS (WP, DLC).

[1] Wilson had a brief conference with Stone on December 15. He undoubtedly asked Stone to talk to Lansing, preparatory to the long conversation about foreign affairs that he would have with the Senator after he, Wilson, had returned from his wedding trip. Wilson conferred with Stone for at least an hour and a half during the morning of January 6. About Lansing's conference with Stone, see RL to WW, Dec. 21, 1915 (first letter of that date).

From William Phillips

My dear Mr. President: Washington December 13, 1915.

The French Ambassador, acting as Dean of the Diplomatic Corps and also in his individual capacity, called upon me a day or two ago to say that various Ambassadors and Ministers had asked him what would be proper for them to do to express their congratulations on the occasion of your marriage on the 18th instant; adding that naturally they would not wish to do anything which was not entirely agreeable to you.

I took the liberty of saying that I thought that nothing would be expected of them as a Diplomatic Corps, but that I preferred to make inquiries in regard to the form which their individual congratulations should properly take. In this connection Mr Jusserand mentioned flowers.

I should be very grateful if you would kindly indicate the nature of the reply which I can make, and at the same time forgive me for bothering you with such an inquiry.

With assurances of respect, etc., I am, my dear Mr. President,
Faithfully yours, William Phillips.

TLS (WP, DLC).

To Edward Mandell House

The White House Dec 14, 1915

Could you possibly make it convenient to come down tonight and spend tomorrow with me   Forgive the request I have not had an open day before.   Woodrow Wilson

T telegram (E. M. House Papers, CtY).

To Washington Gladden

The White House
December 14, 1915

My dear Doctor Gladden:

Your gracious letter of December eleventh gratified me very deeply and I want to thank you for it with all my heart. I do not know anyone whose approbation is more cheering to me than yours.

Of course, I will read the pamphlet. I always question again my own judgment when men like you differ from me, and I hope with all my heart that sooner or later I can square my conduct with the things that you approve.

Cordially and sincerely yours, Woodrow Wilson

TLS (W. Gladden Papers, OHi).

To Joseph Patrick Tumulty

Dear Tumulty: [The White House, Dec. 14, 1915]

I am perfectly willing that Miss Gibson[1] should quote me as saying the following:

"I have been deeply touched by the good wishes so generously expressed by many thousands of my fellow-citizens in connection with my marriage. Those good wishes have been extended in such good taste and with such genuine feeling that they have given me a fresh appreciation of the fine feeling of the people of this country towards those whom they have trusted and who are trying to serve them."[2]   The President.

TL (WP, DLC).
    [1] Mrs. Idah McGlone Gibson, journalist, at this time employed by the Scripps Newspapers. Idah M. Gibson to JPT, Dec. 9, 1915, TLS (WP, DLC).
    [2] Tumulty quoted Wilson's comment in JPT to Idah M. Gibson, Dec. 14, 1915, T telegram (WP, DLC).

From Charles Stedman Macfarland

My dear Mr. President: New York December 14, 1915.

Although you have already received a copy of the resolutions adopted by our Executive Committee at Columbus, I want to add a personal word of gratitude.

I do not think you can realize the great help that it was to the Federal Council and all its great interests to have you present with us at the meeting in Columbus.

Indeed, the spirit expressed by the resolution of the Federal Council just previous to your inauguration[1] has since that time been deepened among the leaders of our churches, and I believe that their sense of confidence in you has constantly increased.

But all I meant to say is that I am personally very grateful for the help you rendered us by your visit to Columbus.

I have sent Mr. Tumulty the various letters which I carry to Europe, and have asked him to call your attention to them, as I felt that you might like to be informed as to the nature of my mission.[2]

I earnestly hope that it may be conducted in such a manner that it will not in any way embarrass our national interests, and, indeed, that it may prove a moral and spiritual help in relation to the great task with which it is concerned.

Sincerely and gratefully yours,   Charles S. Macfarland

TLS (WP, DLC).
    [1] Printed at March 5, 1913, Vol. 27.
    [2] These letters are missing. The Federal Council of Churches was sending Macfarland to Europe on a "mission of fraternity and good will" to the churches and Christians of the belligerent and neutral nations. He was to inquire into the prospects for peace and for Christian cooperation in the reconstruction of postwar Europe. He sailed on December 14 and returned in late January after visiting the Netherlands, Germany, Switzerland, France, and England. In Holland, Germany, and France, he spoke with political leaders as well as churchmen. In his autobiography, Macfarland writes that he had conferred with Wilson about the trip on December 10 during the President's brief visit to Columbus. See Charles Stedman Macfarland, *Across the Years* (New York, 1936), pp. 101-12.

Joseph Patrick Tumulty to Horace Herbert Clark

Dear Sir: [The White House] December 14, 1915

The pressure of affairs has prevented the President from writing to you and he asks me to say that he is sorry to have delayed in sending you this message:

He will be very glad to have you refer to him about any transaction which you and he have had with each other, since his personal knowledge of you is of course limited to that.

I am returning to you herewith the testimonial from Mr. George L. Dickinson.

Very truly yours,   [J. P. Tumulty]

CCL (WP, DLC).

James Watson Gerard to Robert Lansing

Berlin via Copenhagen December 14, 1915.

Von Jagow has written me confidentially that Rintelen was sent to America on suggestion of Melville Rice to buy entire product Du Pont factory and that if he attempted more he exceeded his instructions.   Gerard, Berlin.

T telegram (WP, DLC).

Robert Lansing to Count Johann Heinrich von Bernstorff

My dear Mr. Ambassador: [Washington] December 15, 1915.

I have been hoping to hear from you in regard to the LUSITANIA affair. I feel that continued delay in reaching an agreement in this matter may precipitate a situation which both of us would seriously regret. I trust that you can give me an indication as to the attitude of your Government upon the formula which we considered sometime ago.

I am, my dear Mr. Ambassador,

Very sincerely yours,   Robert Lansing

CCL (SDR, RG 59, 763.72/2327½A, DNA).

From the Diary of Colonel House

Washington, December 15, 1915.

I arrived at the White House in time to shave and dress for breakfast with the President at eight. We immediately began to talk over pending matters. I shall not attempt to give in detail the conversation.

After breakfast we went to the study and remained together for an hour. The President had telephoned to Lansing to come to the White House at ten in order to confer with me and later with the President also. The President wished me to discuss foreign affairs with Lansing and give him my views, particularly, concerning the controversy with Austria and Germany.

I found the President not quite as belligerent as he was the last time we were together. He seemed to think we would be able to keep out of the war. His general idea is that if the Allies were not able to defeat Germany alone, they could scarcely do so with the help of the United States because it would take too long for us to get in a state of preparedness. It would therefore be a useless sacrifice on our part to go in.

I called his attention to the necessity of our having the Allies on our side for the reason we would have to undertake the task alone when Germany was ready to deal with us. He admits this, and yet I cannot quite get him up to the point where he is willing to take action. By action, I mean not to declare war, but to let the Allies know we are definitely on their side and that it is not our intention to permit Germany to win if the strength of this country can prevent [it]. The last time we talked he was quite ready to take this stand, but he has visibly weakened. I am wondering whether it is not the influence of Congressmen and Senators upon him. They know so little of what is happening and think merely in local terms. Their views therefore are not valuable in a situation like this. They are more interested in their home patronage and domestic measures. They come to Washington filled with the provincial ideas of their constituents, believing that America is invulnerable and invincible.

The President and I discussed in detail the advisability of my going to Europe at this time and the purpose of the mission. I thought I might defer the visit until later, but he thought I should go immediately. His reasoning is that Great Britain is so inadequately represented here that it is essential that we get in better communication with them, and he does not believe this can be arranged unless I go in person. I suggested as an alternative, having Lord Bryce or some other representative Englishman come over. He did not think this would be nearly as advantageous to this country as if I should go to England and carry our point of view directly to that Government. He thought if Grey sent someone over, it would perhaps put us in better touch with Grey, but we would still lack an intimate touch with Asquith, Balfour,

Lloyd George, Kitchener and others whom I know and who are as influential as Grey.

We discussed the British Ambassador's irritability and his inclination to fraternize with the opposition to the Government. I let him know of the Ambassador's intimation to Sidney Brooks that in dealing with me as a private citizen, he might get into trouble over the Logan Act of 1795[1] (?). This angered the President, as I knew it would, and he declared that Spring-Rice was not only incompetent, but also a mischief maker and that if they did not recall him, he would send him home. He authorized me to make it very clear to the British Government that he was rapidly becoming *persona non grata* and that our method of communications were becoming seriously blocked because of the Ambassador and our lack of confidence in him.

I do not like to handle this disagreeable matter, for my personal relations with the Ambassador are of the most cordial character, and yet I feel it is essential that something be done.

I called the President's attention to the impossibility of doing things quickly in London. Matters that he and I would settle in a day would easily occupy a week or perhaps two there. I asked him to remember the slowness of the British mind as exhibited even in such a crisis as this war. They have been a year and a half getting thoroughly awakened to the situation. The President wondered if I could not facilitate matters somewhat by going to France earlier than anticipated and getting them to help push.

As to Germany, he thought circumstances should determine whether I should visit there. We decided that unless I was invited, I should not go. The excuse for my going on the trip at all was discussed at some length. Since I last talked with him about it a new and better reason has occurred to me and the President accepted it as being the one to use. That is "it is thought inadvisable to bring home any of our Ambassadors from the belligerent countries at this time, and in order that they may have a more intimate knowledge of our position regarding pending international questions, at the President's request, I am undertaking the journey."

He asked me to write what I had in mind to give out to the press and send it to him tomorrow for him to look over and make any suggestions that seemed pertinent.

When ten o'clock came the President had to leave for the Executive Offices to meet an appointment. Immediately after-

[1] Enacted in 1799, it prohibited private citizens from purporting to conduct foreign relations on behalf of the United States Government.

ward, Secretary Lansing came and we sat in the President's study upstairs and conferred for an hour. Lansing agreed with me that delay in my visit is desirable. He thinks we have come to an impasse with both Austria and Germany and it may lead to a breakage of diplomatic relations, in which event, questions with the Allies will become automatically settled. His view and mine are the same, but I do not like to present my thoughts upon this subject strongly to the President for fear he may think I do not wish to go. As a matter of fact, it is the breaking up of our plans for the winter. Loulie is not well and I dread the trip at this time. I do not feel able to leave our apartment without renting it, and that in itself, involves no end of annoyange [annoyance]. However, such matters are trivial and not to be thought of in connection with so important work.

Lansing and I went into the question of relations with Great Britain and he expressed himself even more strongly than the President regarding the British Ambassador. He declares he can do nothing through him or with him and it is imperative that he be removed.

I spoke to him about our Ambassador to Russia, Mayre [Marye], and of his unfitness for the post, and urged him to make a change there as soon he thought it feasible He said the Government was being seriously embarrassed every day because of Mayre's inability to negotiate the questions arising between the two countries and because of the same lack of ability in the Russian Ambassador in Washington. Both Mayre and Bachmeteff[2] are hopelessly incompetent.

Lansing made a suggestion which I heartily approved and which is likely to be carried out. The most important matter pending between Russia and the United States is a commercial treaty, and Lansing thought he might follow precedent and appoint a special ambassador to undertake these negotiations. I had already spoken to the President of the desirability of ridding the service of Mayre and had suggested John Garrett, formerly Minister to Argentine, as a suitable successor.

Lansing and I discussed South American affairs, the coming Pan American Conference, January 6th,[3] and the progress of the

[2] George Bakhméteff.

[3] The "January 6th" referred to the day that Wilson was scheduled to address the Second Pan American Scientific Congress in Washington. The congress, planned in 1908 at a similar gathering in Santiago, Chile, solicited papers on such topics as anthropology, engineering, international and public law, mining and metallurgy, public health, and commerce, in order to bring together leaders of scientific thought and public opinion throughout the Americas. See Second Pan American Scientific Congress, *The Final Act and Interpretative Commentary Thereon* (Washington, 1916), and Second Pan American Scientific Congress, *The Report of the Secretary General* (Washington, 1917).

convention between us and the South and Central American Republics. We also discussed the desirability of having Ambassador Fletcher come at once to his proposed new duties in Mexico. Lansing promised to wire Carranza today asking whether Fletcher would be *persona grata* and if his reply is favorable, Fletcher's name will be sent to the Senate.

At this juncture, the President returned to join the conference. We brought up again the advisability of my going abroad now or later. Lansing argued as he had to me, that it had better be later, but the President insisted that it should be now. He is evidently not satisfied with existing conditions, particularly in regard to our relations with the Allies, and he thinks I may materially strengthen our position by this trip. Both the President and Lansing thought my excuse for going abroad a good one and that it would do away with any mystery, and would also save the faces of our Ambassadors, which of course, is important. In making this excuse I have minimized to the public the importance of my mission, but I much prefer this to having the sensibilities of our representatives abroad hurt.

I asked the President to again read me what Gerard had sent in regard to his interview with the Kaiser.[4] He went to the safe and got it out and read it to Lansing and me. They both criticised Gerard seriously for not sending the full text of his conversation. However, I asked them if he had not epitomized it all in the few lines he had sent and whether if he had written a volume he could have made it more pregnant. The upshot of what Gerard wrote was that the Kaiser said "he would attend to America when this war was over; that President Wilson's attitude regarding Germany eliminated him from any possibility of mediator. When the war was ended, he, the Kaiser, would make peace with the King of England and the Czar of Russia, just the three of them."

We had to laugh at this characteristic, egotistic, picture which the Kaiser had drawn of himself.

Lansing left and the President and I took up various semi-important subjects, such as the Postmaster of New York and other domestic affairs. The President had another engagement at the Executive Offices and left me. I took a walk and dropped in on the Attorney General for a half hour. He showed me a letter the President had written him on his birthday which had

---

4 This letter has never been found. Gerard, in J. W. Gerard to EMH, Nov. 2, 1915, TLS (E. M. House Papers, CtY), refers to "a *very important piece of paper*, which of course must be kept secret in the inner circles," which he was sending to the President. Gerard, in J. W. Gerard to EMH, Nov. 23, 1915, TLS, *ibid.*, again referred to "the slip of paper I sent the President three weeks ago, containing about four lines, *but the most important news I have ever sent.*"

gratified him beyond measure. It showed real friendship and made Gregory feel that his work was well worth while.

I discussed with him in general terms the British Ambassador's reference to the Logan Act. He read it carefully and declared there was nothing in it. The President, Lansing and I had taken up this matter in some detail and it was agreed, at my suggestion, that it would be best for me to be appointed a special agent of the State Department so there could be no question regarding this Act. Gregory also thought this would be advisable.

I returned to the White House and asked William Phillips and Frank Polk to come over in succession. I talked with them about departmental affairs, about my trip abroad, and some of the details in connection thereto. Phillips asked my advice as to the removal of our Consul General to Egypt.[5] I advised it, although I suggested that he look into the political aspect of it before doing so. The man is thoroughly unfit, as I happened to know before Phillips was apprised of it.

No one excepting the family was with us at lunch and the conversation was quite general. Margaret desired me to convert her father to her belief that it was desirable for Congress to legislate regarding Woman's Suffrage. I expressed myself as favorable to Womans Suffrage, but thought it inadvisable for her father to act as she desired. After lunch the President showed me some of the presents which had come for Mrs. Galt. He also showed me a diamond brooch he had gotten her for a wedding present.

Grayson and I went into a half hour session relating to family and household matters. I seem to be the receptacle for everything and everybody when I am in Washington. It is tiresome, though in a way, gratifying.

McAdoo came in. I advised him for the hundredth time to leave patronage matters alone, and I especially advised him to keep out of the New York Postmaster controversy. He promised he would do so, but I am certain he will not. He seemed depressed. He thinks Tumulty is working against him all the time and the President is listening to Tumulty, which indeed, is more or less true. He is also depressed over his finances, and seems to think his efforts are not sufficiently appreciated to warrant his continuation in office. I tried to reassure him, but with what success I do not know. He promised to leave patronage questions alone, but I believe it is quite impossible for him to do so. We talked of the shipping bill in some detail and he assured me it would pass.

5 Olney Arnold.

Secretary Lane followed McAdoo and while he was with me Tumulty dropped in and later Burleson. I had them all in the Green Room. The matters discussed were of passing importance and related entirely to administration affairs and of the coming campaign.

The President and I dined alone and talked of affairs in general and of a lighter character. After dinner we went to see Mrs. Galt. She was alone and the three of us sat for a half hour in intimate personal conversation. She expressed regret that we were going to Europe and also that I was not to be at the wedding. She said it did not seem right, but I made it clear that it would be an impossibility on account of the hurt feelings it would engender. They showed me where they would stand Saturday at the wedding and went into the details of the ceremony.

I left the President and went to call on the McAdoos. I returned to the White House to await the President's return. We had a few moment's conversation only, as it was after eleven o'clock and time for me to take my train for New York.

It was agreed that the President should write me a letter of marque in addition to my being appointed special agent. It was further agreed that no one abroad should know that I was a special agent, for we both thought it would minimize my influence. We are using it simply for a protection in the event of trouble with the Senate. There is some evidence that the opposition in the Senate wish to make an issue of me if it can be done, and if they attempt it, it will be along the lines of my acting for the Government without having any legal authority to do so.

My visit to Washington was satisfactory, for the President, notwithstanding his approaching marriage, devoted as much of the day to me as was necessary to formulate our plans.

To Frederick Bicknell Lynch

My dear Mr. Lynch: [The White House] December 16, 1915

Thank you for your note about Joseph Johnson and the New York postmastership. It is an appointment which is giving me a great deal of serious thought and perplexity, and your testimony about Johnson is very valuable to me.

Cordially and faithfully yours, Woodrow Wilson

TLS (Letterpress Book, WP, DLC).

From Edward Mandell House, with Enclosures

Dear Governor: New York. December 16th, 1915.

This is Sir Edward Grey's message which came by cable to the White House yesterday.

I am also enclosing a suggestion to be given out concerning my proposed trip. Please cor[r]ect and return.

Bernstorff was in this morning. He plead very strongly against sending a sharp note to Berlin. He thought if given time he could get an apology and indemnity for the Lusitania. He does not believe it can be done at once.

The Reichstag dissolves Saturday. After that, he thinks something can be accomplished without danger to his Government. Popular opinion, he believes, will not sustain such an apology as will satisfy us. But he believes it may be given out later in a way that his public will not get it in its full form.

He is inclined to believe Austria will meet our requirements in the Ancona.

I spoke to him in regard to my trip telling him it might not extend beyond London, but that would depend upon his Government. He has not heard from Berlin concerning the matter about which he wrote, but is expecting an answer any day.

He declared I would be welcome in Germany if anyone would be upon such a mission.

He maintains that there are no plots instigated by Germans brewing here, and that we would find it out sooner or later. He thinks this belief is the main cause of friction and is causing your determination to sever relations.

I let him know that there was a feeling among Americans that if Germany was successful, she would finally quarrel with us, with or without provocation, and if this feeling could be overcome, and it could be by the elimination of militarism, the feeling would immediately die out. He admitted this.

I so much enjoyed being with you yesterday and catching the little glimpse of dear Mrs. Galt.

Affectionately yours,   E. M. House

TLS (WP, DLC).

E N C L O S U R E   I

Much obliged for your telegram December 11th.[1] We will try to act in the spirit of it.   [Edward Grey]

[1] EMH to E. Grey, Dec. 10, 1915, T telegram (E. M. House Papers, CtY). House urged the British government to follow more liberal policies concerning

American shipping in the Far East; to confer broader powers upon Sir Richard Crawford, British trade adviser in Washington; to permit the release of American-owned goods now held at Rotterdam; to follow a liberal policy toward British ships under American charter; and to make concessions regarding goods in Germany manufactured under running contracts with American importers. All this, House said, would have "an enormous effect on public opinion at the present moment." House undoubtedly showed Wilson this telegram on December 15.

ENCLOSURE II

I am going to Europe at the request of the President and Secretary Lansing for the purpose of taking information to some of our Ambassadors in order that they may have a more intimate knowledge of this Government's attitude regarding certain phases of pending international questions, and in order to obtain from them their point of view.

It is thought inadvisable to bring home at this time any of our Ambassadors from the belligerent countries and it has been found impossible to convey or to obtain by cable or correspondence quite the correct atmosphere.

I hope to return within six or eight weeks.

December 16th, 1915.

T MSS (WP, DLC).

ENCLOSURE III

From Dudley Field Malone

Dear Mr. President   [New York] Dec. 16, 15

The appointment of Johnson would be unfit and unworthy of your nomination. Of this I know I can convince you in three minutes.

Will be in Washington at the Shoreham to-morrow Friday but will not come near you in your last *busy* day unless you send for me.

You know I wish you and the wonderful lady all the blessing of God.   Yours as ever   D.F.M.

Dudley happened in and wrote this.   E.M.H.

ALI (WP, DLC).

To Edward Mandell House, with Enclosure

Dear Friend,   The White House. 17 December, 1915.

After thinking of many more formal kinds of letter, I have concluded that the enclosed is the best kind. I hope that you will think so, but if you do not let me know and I will change it.

We are in the midst of the rush of the final arrangements, but have time always to think, and think always with deep affection and gratitude, of you.

Our love to Mrs. House,

Your grateful friend,   Woodrow Wilson

WWTLS (E. M. House Papers, CtY).

ENCLOSURE

To Edward Mandell House

My dear Friend,   The White House 17 December, 1915

I am deeply obliged to you for generously consenting to go once more to Europe and speak as my trusted and confidential friend to those in authority there who should know, and know at first hand, what our attitude and purpose are in this time of war and world-wide disturbance.

You need no instructions. You know what is in my mind and how to interpret it, and will, I am sure, be able to make it plain to those with whom you may have the privilege of conferring.

Cordially and faithfully Yours,   Woodrow Wilson

ALS (E. M. House Papers, CtY).

From Robert Lansing, with Enclosure

PERSONAL AND CONFIDENTIAL.

My dear Mr. President: Washington December 17, 1915.

I send you herewith the text of the Austrian reply in the ANCONA case. My own view is that it is a special pleading consisting of technicalities and quibbles. I believe it would be a mistake to reply to it in detail and that the best course is to send a short and firm note, avoiding argument of legal points and discussion of facts. We can rest the whole case on the Admiralty's admission that the vessel was torpedoed while she was standing still and while people were on board. It seems to me that it would be most unwise to elaborate in our reply.

I realize that such a course may invite serious consequences and yet I do not see how we can consistently recede from our position or enter into any correspondence, such as the Austrian Government appears to be desirous of doing.

I will prepare at once a draft reply, possibly I can send it to you tonight, for I think our answer should go within two or three days.   Faithfully yours,   Robert Lansing

TLS (SDR, RG 59, 865.857 An 2/71, DNA).

ENCLOSURE

Vienna (via Berne) December 15, 1915.

1027. Department's 1011; December 6, 6 P.M. Following note received from Minister for Foreign Affairs noon today:

In reply to the much esteemed note number 4167 which his excellency, Mr. Frederic Courtland Penfield, Ambassador Extraordinary and Plenipotentiary of the United States of America, directed to him in the name of the American Government under date of the ninth instant in the matter of the sinking of the Italian steamer ANCONA, the undersigned, preliminary to a thorough, meritorious treatment of the demand, has the honor to observe that the sharpness with which the Government of the United States considers it necessary to blame the commanding officer of the submarine concerned in the affair and the firmness in which the demands addressed to the Imperial and Royal Government appear to be expressed might well have warranted the expectation that the Government of the United States should precisely specify the actual circumstances of the affair upon which it bases its case. As is not difficult to perceive, the presentation of the facts in the case in the aforesaid note leaves room for many doubts and even if this presentation were correct in all points and the most rigorous legal conception were applied to the judgment of the case, it does not in any way sufficiently warrant attaching blame to the commanding officer of the war vessel or to the Imperial and Royal Government.

The Government of the United States has also failed to designate the persons upon whose testimony it relies and to whom it apparently believes it may attribute a higher degree of credibility than to the commander of the Imperial and Royal fleet. The note also fails to give any information whatsoever as to the number, names, and more precise fate of the American citizens who were on board of the said steamer at the critical moment.

However, in view of the fact that the Washington cabinet has now made a positive statement to the effect that citizens of the United States of America came to grief in the incident in question, the Imperial and Royal Government is in principle ready to enter into an exchange of views in the affair with the

Government of the United States. It must, however, in the first place, raise the question why that Government failed to give juridical reasons for the demands set forth in its note with reference to the special circumstances of the incriminating events upon which it itself lays stress, and why in lieu thereof it refused [referred] to an exchange of correspondence which it has conducted with another government in other cases. The Imperial and Royal Government is the less able to follow the Washington cabinet on this unusual path, since it by no means possesses authentic knowledge of all of the pertinent correspondence of the Government of the United States, nor is it of the opinion that such knowledge might be sufficient for it in the present case, which, in so far as it is informed, is in essential points of another nature than the case or cases to which the Government of the United States seems to allude. The Imperial and Royal Government may therefore leave it to the Washington cabinet to formulate the particular points of law against which the commanding officer of the submarine is alleged to have offended on the occasion of the sinking of the ANCONA.

The Government of the United States has also seen fit to refer to the attitude which the Berlin cabinet assumed in the above mentioned correspondence. The Imperial and Royal Government finds in the much esteemed note no indication whatever of the intent with which this reference was made. Should however the Government of the United States thereby have intended to express an opinion to the effect that a prejudice [precedent] of whatever nature existed for the Imperial and Royal Government with respect to the juridical consideration of the affair in question this Government must, in order to preclude possible misunderstandings, declare that as a matter of course it reserves to itself full freedom of maintaining its own legal views in the discussion of the case of the ANCONA.

In having the honor to have recourse to the kindness of his excellency the Ambassador of the United States of America with the most respectful request to be good enough to communicate the foregoing to the American Government and on this occasion to state that the Imperial and Royal Government, in no less degree than the American Government and under all circumstances, most sincerely deplores the fate of the innocent victims of the incident in question, the undersigned at the same time avails himself of this opportunity to renew the expression of his most distinguished consideration to his excellency the Ambassador.   Signed,   Burian. Penfield.

T telegram (SDR, RG 59, 865.857 An 2/71, DNA).

A Proclamation

[Dec. 18, 1915]

Whereas, I have received from the Senate of the United States a resolution, passed Dec. 17, 1915, reading as follows:

"Whereas, The attention of the people of the United States has been from time to time directed to the appalling situation in Poland, where practically the entire population today is homeless, and where men, women, and children are perishing by the thousands for lack of shelter, clothing, and food, and

"Whereas, The people of the United States have demonstrated their sympathy for the suffering people on all sides in the great European war by their splendid and successful charitable work in Belgium, Serbia, and other places, and feeling that the American people would quickly respond to an appeal for help in Poland, once the tragedy of the situation there is brought home to them,

"Be it resolved, That, appreciating the suffering of that stricken people, it is suggested that the President of the United States set aside a day in the forthcoming holiday season upon which day a direct appeal to the sympathy of all American citizens shall be made and an opportunity shall be given for all to contribute to a much-needed holiday for relief in Poland.["]

And whereas I feel confident that the people of the United States during this holiday season will be moved to aid a people stricken by war, famine, and disease,

Now, therefore, I, Woodrow Wilson, President of the United States, in compliance with the suggestion of the Senate thereof, do appoint and proclaim Jan. 1, 1916, as a day upon which the people of the United States may make such contributions as they feel disposed for the aid of the stricken Polish people.

Contributions may be addressed to the American Red Cross, Washington, D. C., which will care for their proper distribution.

In witness whereof, I have hereunto set my hand and caused the seal of the United States to be affixed.

WOODROW WILSON.

Done at the City of Washington, this 18th day of December, in the year of our Lord one thousand nine hundred and fifteen, and of the independence of the United States the one hundred and fortieth.

By the President.   ROBERT LANSING,
                                      Secretary of State.

Printed in the *New York Times*, Dec. 21, 1915.

To Robert Lansing, with Enclosures

Dear Mr. Secretary   The White House 18 December,1915

Here is the note with my alterations—which, as you will see, are alterations of form only.

Thank you for its prompt preparation. Please do not hesitate to communicate with me at the Hot Springs, West Virginia.

In haste,

Cordially and sincerely Yours,   Woodrow Wilson

ALS (RSB Coll., DLC).

E N C L O S U R E   I[1]

You are instructed to address a note to the Austro-Hungarian Minister of Foreign Affairs, textually as follows:

Quote: The Government of the United States has received the note of your Excellency relative to the sinking of the ANCONA, which was delivered at Vienna on December fifteenth, nineteenfifteen, and transmitted to Washington, and has given the note ⟨very⟩ *immediate and* careful consideration.

Quote: The admission in the report of the Austro-Hungarian Admiralty which was transmitted to this Government by the Austro-Hungarian Chargé d'Affaires at Washington that the ANCONA was torpedoed after her engines had stopped and when passengers were still on board is a sufficient fact alone to condemn the officer responsible for the sinking of the vessel as having wilfully violated the recognized law of nations and those humane principles which a belligerent should observe in the conduct of hostile operations. The details of the sinking of the vessel; the witnesses corroborating the Admiralty's report; the number of Americans killed and injured, are not essential to the establishment of the guilt of the commander. The fact is that citizens of the United States were killed, injured, or put in jeopardy by the commander's lawless act.

Quote: The rules of international law and the principles of humanity, which were so grossly violated by the commander of the submarine, have been too generally recognized and too manifest from the standpoint of right and justice to admit of debate. The Government of the United States therefore has no other course but to hold the Austro-Hungarian Government responsible for the admitted conduct of the commander of the submarine. As this Government holds these views as to the illegality of the act and the responsibility therefor, the Imperial and Royal Government must realize that the Government of the United States cannot further discuss the admitted circumstances of the case or the established law and principle violated by the commander. The Government of the United States can only repeat the demands which it made in its note of December sixth, nineteen-fifteen, sincerely hoping that with the foregoing explanation of its position the Imperial and Royal Government will perceive the justice of those demands and comply with them in the same spirit of frankness and regard for good relations with which they were made. Unquote

T MS (SDR, RG 59, 865.857 An 2/71, DNA).
    ¹ Words in angle brackets in this document deleted by Wilson; words in italics added by him.

ENCLOSURE II

Suggested substitute:
First paragraph the same.
(Second paragraph) On (insert the date) Baron Zwiedenek, the Chargé d'Affaires of the Imperial and Royal Government at Washington, transmitted to the Secretary of State a report of the Austro-Hungarian Admiralty with regard to the sinking of the steamship ANCONA in which it was admitted that the vessel was torpedoed after her engines had been stopped and when passengers were still on board. This admission alone is, in the view of the Government of the United States, sufficient to fix upon the commander of the submarine which fired the torpedo the responsibility for having wilfully violated the recognized law of nations and entirely disregarded those humane principles which every belligerent should observe in the conduct of war at sea. In view of these admitted circumstances the Government of the United States feels justified in holding that the details of the sinking, the weight and character of the additional testimony corroborating the Admiralty's report, and the number of Americans killed or injured are in no way essential matters of discussion. The culpability of the commander is in any case established, and the undisputed fact is that citizens of the United States were killed, injured, or put in jeopardy by his lawless act.

    The rules of international law and the principles of humanity which were so wilfully violated by the commander of the submarine have been so long and so universally recognized and are so manifest from the standpoint of right and justice that the Government of the United States does not feel called upon to debate them and does not understand that the Imperial and Royal Government questions or disputes them.

The Government of the United States therefore finds no other course open to it but to hold the Imperial and Royal Government responsible for the act of its naval commander and to renew the definite but respectful demands made in its communication of the sixth of December, 1915. It sincerely hopes that the foregoing statement of its position will enable the Imperial and Royal Government to perceive the justice of those demands and to comply with them in the same spirit of concern for the good relations now existing between the United States and Austria-Hungary which prompted the Government of the United States to make them.[1]

WWT MS (SDR, RG 59, 865.857 An 2/71, DNA).

[1] Wilson's "suggested substitute," with a few changes by Lansing, was sent as RL to F. C. Penfield, Dec. 19, 1915, T telegram (SDR, RG 59, 865.857 An 2/71, DNA); printed in FR-WWS 1915, pp. 647-48.

To Claude Kitchin

[The White House] December 18, 1915

I did not have a chance before leaving to congratulate you most heartily on your admirable speech of Friday.[1] We all admire it extremely.   Woodrow Wilson

T telegram (Letterpress Books, WP, DLC).

[1] Speaking, actually on Thursday, December 16, in the House of Representatives about renewing the War Revenue bill, Kitchin had elicited "rebel yells" from fellow Democrats during his lengthy attack on Republican tariff policies. Republicans had charged that the revenue bill had nothing to do with the war but was part of a Democratic plan to repeal the free sugar clause of the Underwood tariff. "The trouble with the Republicans," Kitchin said, "is that these taxes are going direct into the Treasury, where they belong. A Republican hates to see anything go into the Treasury. . . . He had rather put these taxes into the pockets of the tariff-protected barons." New York Times, Dec. 17, 1915.

To Edith Bolling Wilson

18 Dec. '15

With tender love to the loveliest lady in the world.   W.[1]

ALI (WP, DLC).

[1] A note accompanying his wedding present to Mrs. Galt.

An Announcement

[Dec. 18, 1915]

Mr. Woodrow Wilson
and
Mrs. Norman Galt
née Edith Bolling
announce their marriage
on Saturday the eighteenth of December
nineteen hundred and fifteen
Washington, D. C.[1]

Printed announcement (WC, NjP).

[1] The wedding took place in Mrs. Galt's house on Twentieth Street at 8:30 P.M. in the presence of thirty-eight relatives and close friends. The Rev. Herbert Scott Smith of St. Margaret's Church performed the Episcopal marriage ceremony, and the Rev. James H. Taylor of Central Presbyterian Church delivered the benediction. There were no attendants, and Mrs. Bolling gave her daughter away. Ike Hoover had taken charge of elaborate floral arrangements in the house, including an "altar" constructed of ferns, Scotch heather, orchids, and American Beauty roses. Guests were served supper after the ceremony. See Irwin Hood Hoover, *Forty-Two Years in the White House* (Boston and New York, 1934), pp. 70-75; *Washington Post*, Dec. 19, 1915; and *New York Times*, Dec. 19, 1915.

From William Jennings Bryan

Miami, Florida
My Dear Mr President   Dec 18 1915 9 P.M.

At this hour when, according to the afternoon paper, the wedding ceremony is being performed I beg to extend on behalf of Mrs Bryan & myself congratulations and good wishes. Length of days and happiness to you & Mrs Wilson   With assurances of respect I am, my dear Mr President,

Very truly yours   W. J. Bryan

ALS (WP, DLC).

Edith Bolling Wilson to Sallie White Bolling

My dearest Mother: Hot Springs, Virginia Dec. 19, 1915

We have just finished lunch and while we are waiting for the coffee I am starting a line to you to say here we are, safe and sound and deeply happy.

We were too early for our train when we left the house, so we went for a ride and then round about to the long bridge and over the river to Alexandria, where we had planned to take the train.

We were just about on time there but the train was a few minutes late as they ran it in 2 sections and ours was the last section.

We waited in the machine about 20 minutes guarded by a *big* squad of Secret Service men. We had done the unexpected: There was no crowd. When our car came along we got off quietly chaperoned by the faithful Hoover, and the journey was begun. We found Otey[1] and Brooks serving a welcome to us as we got in the car with a dainty little supper of chicken salad, nuts, candy & toast, and fruit, on the table the centre of which Otey had put my orchids. So we got our coats off & sat down for a little talk over the salad. We both had a good night & got up to find we were over a half hour late so breakfasted in the car and arrived here at 8:45. Found Robertson[2] & the big car waiting for us at the station, and only about 50 people gathered.

It is only a few blocks to the Hotel where we have the most charming rooms—2 bed rooms, 2 baths, dining room, and charming living room (where I am now writing) all filled with Beauty roses and carnations. Then we have 2 furnished porches, which I am afraid it will be too cold to enjoy.

We are all unpacked, have had hot baths and *Woodrow* is now dictating a letter to Mr. Swem. So I am talking to you. The weather is cold but radiant, and so are we. I feel much rested and am picturing all you dear ones together today and do hope your cold is much better. Give fondest love to each one and say this is to them too, as I can't send so many letters. Hope Mr. Hoover sent you the flowers (the 2 big baskets) & that you were able to get the cake I asked you to send for me. Will you call Susie & tell her Otey & I are OK, & I will send her a line soon. Woodrow sends his love with mine and says we are as happy as children off on a holiday. Tell Bert I have the yellow garter for her. Love to your precious self,   always   Edith

I put Father's book in my bureau drawer for fear something would happen to it. Ask Randolph to keep the other one for us.

E.B.W.

ALS (WP, DLC).
[1] Probably a new maid.
[2] Actually, Francis Robinson.

From Domicio da Gama

Private and personal

My dear Mr. President,   Washington December 20th, 1915

The Ambassadors and Ministers of the Republics of Central and South America, wishing to give you a joint and public manifestation of their deep appreciation of your many kindnesses and constant and special courtesy to them, have thought of offering you and Mrs. Wilson a *soirée* at the Pan American Building on a date that they would ask you to choose, between the tenth and the 21st of next month, if possible. Coming soon after the Scientific Congress and within the first month of your marriage, this feast would show to Mrs. Wilson and the Americans how highly and fondly we the other Americans care for her husband and their President.

I was charged by my colleagues to tender you this invitation, which I do in a doubtful English but with a very genuine heart.

Anticipating a favorable answer, I beg to remain, Mr. President,   Yours very respectfully   D. da Gama

ALS (WP, DLC).

From Claude Kitchin

Dear Mr. President: Scotland Neck, N. C. Dec 20/15

I certainly do thank you for, and appreciate your wire of congratulations on my speech in the House last Thursday. Your words are most gratifying and encouraging.

I am,   Very sincerely,   Claude Kitchin

ALS (WP, DLC).

From David Starr Jordan

Stanford University
My dear Sir: California December 20, 1915.

Since the interview you kindly granted me in November, a wholly unexpected change has come over the plan for "Continuous Mediation."

While I have much sympathy with the purposes of Frau Schwimmer and much respect for Mr. Ford, I could not see my way at all to joining the expedition. If there is anything I can do for the welfare of Europe, it must be reached in a very different way.   Very truly yours,   David Starr Jordan

TLS (WP, DLC).

From Lucy Marshall Smith and Mary Randolph Smith

Dear Mr. Wilson,   [New Orleans, c. Dec. 20, 1915]

This is the very best setting New Orleans has for the moonstone. We know you prefer an excellent heart to a fine exterior, only we wanted both as none to[o] good to send with our loving

congratulations and hearty good wishes to the best of friends.[1]
With love for Edith and "may hourly joys attend you tomorrow and tomorrow and tomorrow."

Lucy and Mary Smith.

ALS (WP, DLC).
  [1] The Smiths were sending Wilson, as a Christmas present, Wilkie Collins,
The Moonstone (London, 1868; many later edns.) See WW to Lucy M. and Mary
R. Smith, Dec. 27, 1915. This book is in the Wilson Library, DLC.

From Robert Lansing

PERSONAL AND PRIVATE:

My dear Mr. President: [Washington] December 21, 1915.

I had a long conversation this afternoon with Senator Stone
in regard to our relations with the belligerent countries, and I
am disturbed at his attitude. He clearly indicated after we had
talked awhile that he thought that we were bearing too severely
upon the Teutonic Allies and were not pressing Great Britain as
strongly as we should in insisting upon observance of our trade
rights. When I suggested that loss of life seemed to me to require
more drastic treatment than loss of property, he replied that they
both involved *rights*. I said to him that the right of life was an
inherent right, the loss of which could never be indemnified, but
that the right of property was a legal right, which could be fully
remedied by an indemnity. I could see, however, that this in no
way satisfied him, for he then referred to German Babies dying
because Great Britain would not allow us to send them con-
densed milk, and followed it up with dyes, potash, etc., etc.

This seems to me a serious matter, for, while I believe the
Senator will not oppose the policies of the Administration, I do
not think he will support them whole-heartedly or enthusiastically. This is especially unfortunate with Senator Lodge radically pro-Ally at the head of the minority of the committee, and
ready to take advantage of a situation which offers possibilities
of political advantage.

Probably Senator Stone is influenced by the fact that he has
a considerable German constituancy, which he wishes to keep in
good humor, but whatever the reason, his ideas of our neutral
duty will make it difficult for him to deal with our foreign affairs
in a way that will strongly support the Administration and carry
through its policies.

I hope that you will find it possible as soon as you return to
Washington to ask Senator Stone to come and see you and see if
something cannot be done to change his attitude, as it will other-

wise make the situation one which will be hard to handle. I do not think the case one which permits much delay.

Faithfully yours,   Robert Lansing

CCL (SDR, RG 59, 763.72/2337A, DNA).

From Robert Lansing, with Enclosure

Dear Mr. President: Washington December 21, 1915.

I enclose to you herewith a copy of a memorandum presented by the Colombian Minister under instructions from his Government, in which he emphasizes the importance which Colombia attaches to the prompt ratification of the Treaty of April 6, 1914, now before the United States Senate.

Faithfully yours,   Robert Lansing

TLS (SDR, RG 59, 711.21/329½A, DNA).

E N C L O S U R E

LEGACIÓN DE COLOMBIA.
Washington, D. C.

Memorandum.

Presented to His Excellency Robert Lansing Secretary of State of the United States by the undersigned Envoy Extraordinary and Minister Plenipotentiary of the Republic of Colombia, by order of his Government.

Deeply concerned over the successful outcome of the Treaty of the 6th of April, 1914, between the Republic of Colombia and the United States of America, my Government believes it to be its duty to omit no word or act or lawful means to urge this agreement upon the Government of the United States and upon the enlightened opinion of those who influence American policies. This being the case, I take the liberty, pursuant to instructions from my Government, to lay before Your Excellency a synopsis of the grounds on which the Republic of Colombia bases its hope that this settlement will receive the approval of the American Senate, thus according that measure of reparation which the most elementary justice decrees as due to Colombia for the loss of the Isthmus—the most important portion of her territory—for the loss of her eminent domain over the Canal and her ownership of the Panama Railroad, and for the violation of her sovereignty and rights of property which the United States solemnly guaranteed by the treaty of 1846.

That the Treaty of the 6th of April, 1914, deserves and demands the approval of the Senate of the United States is self-evident.

In the first place the Treaty under consideration was entered into on the spontaneous initiative of the Government of the United States. Not only the preceding Administration but also that of His Excellency President Wilson made clear to Colombia their desire to settle once and for all the pending controversy and to legalize the United States' title to the Canal and to the Panama Railroad. It was this initiative—most highly commendable in itself—which led the Government of Colombia to suspend its efforts to arrive at a solution of the existing differences by arbitration.

In the second place the treaty is a matter of the most elementary justice, not solely by reason of the recognition of the rights of Colombia implied by the aforementioned initiative of the United States, but also by reason of the taking of the Isthmus of Panama, to which Mr. Roosevelt has since confessed, and which his own Administration sought to repair, admitting that the material and moral losses inflicted upon Colombia were susceptible of reparation, by the convention signed by Señor Cortes,[1] the then Colombian Minister, and Mr. Root, the Secretary of State of the United States in Mr. Roosevelt's Administration.

In the third place, if the treaty of the 6th of April, 1914, is not carried into effect as proposed by the United States (toward which practical result my Government naturally looks; albeit, in order to meet the wishes of the United States, it was forced to overcome strong opposition both in the Congress and among the people of Colombia) then the acts of Mr. Roosevelt, instead of remaining exclusively his acts and the acts of his Administration, would be openly and solidaridly endorsed and ratified by the Government and people of the United States who would thus set their seal of approval *ex post facto* upon the said acts, and deny that just reparation which today is admittedly due to Colombia.

In the fourth place the indefinite shelving of the Treaty of the 6th of April, 1914, would perforce lead to a situation, as abnormal as could well be, in regard to the friendship and relations of the two countries. A people and a Government which —obedient to the highest dictates of a spirit of conciliation—have determined, in the face of grievous injury, to persist in their friendship towards the United States would be placed in a most humiliating and difficult position, would be deprived of their rights, discouraged in their affections, and would see their trustful abnegation requited with unmerited scorn.

In the fifth place, this same hypothesis—which the Government of Colombia would fain believe impossible—is entirely incompatible with the development of commercial relations between the United States and a country whose broad and favoured soil is ready to welcome the commercial and financial expansion of the richest nation in the world; a nation whose greatness will inccease [increase] from year to year so long as it follows the paths of righteousness and seeks to advance hand in hand with its sister republics of the great American continent.

In the sixth place the supposition that the Treaty might not meet with the approval of the Senate of the United States would aggravate, to the greater injury of Colombia, a permanent condition of overwhelming difficulty and disadvantage. As a matter of fact the transit over the Panama railroad and through the Panama canal is most onerous and uncertain and must remain so unless the existing controversy is settled and the rights of Colombia are recognized. This is a matter of special importance to those Departments of the Republic situated on the Pacific coast. The inhabitants of this region are fired today by the hope of important agricultural developments which might be realized in the immediate future; yet they are in fact hampered in their progress and well-being by the difficulties inherent to the existing international situation, and this state of things will go from bad to worse if the Treaty does not receive the approval of the United States Senate, as Colombia has been led to expect.

In the seventh place, the establishment of relations with the so-called Republic of Panama—a Department the independence of which Colombia can never recognize except under the conditions laid down in this treaty—calls for prompt ratification of the agreement, as, under existing conditions, relations with Panama are out of the question. This makes for continual miscarriages in civil, Criminal and commercial affairs. Extradition is impossible even for murder, counterfeiting and other felonies. There is no diplomatic or consular representation between Colombia and her segregated Department, no exchange of legal process exists, and the administration of justice instead of promoting better relations is frequently the object of grave contentions.

In voicing its concern over the successful outcome of the Treaty of the 6th of April, 1914, the ratification of which has been so long delayed by the Senate of the United States, my Government wishes to record its full faith in the determination of the United States to set its Seal upon this Treaty which will be a monument of Justice to inspire all the nations of Latin-America with confidence in the high aims and ideals of the

United States and will bind them closer to the country of George Washington.   Julio Betancourt.

T MS (SDR, RG 59, 711.21/329½A, DNA).
   1 Enrique Cortés.

From Robert Lansing, with Enclosures

PERSONAL AND PRIVATE:

My Dear Mr. President: Washington December 21, 1915.

I enclose for your information a conversation which I had today with Baron Zwiedinek, as I assume you desire to keep in close touch with anything that deals with the ANCONA case.

Faithfully yours,   Robert Lansing.

TLS (SDR, RG 59, 865.857 An 2/94½, DNA).

E N C L O S U R E   I

MEMORANDUM OF CONVERSATION WITH BARON ZWIEDINEK, AUSTRIAN CHARGÉ, DECEMBER 21, 1915.

Baron Zwiedinek called and said he had received two telegrams from his Government which he desired to communicate to me. He then read the telegrams, copies of which are annexed. In commenting on them he said he felt very hopeful that his Government would be able to find a satisfactory way to meet the desires of the United States; that he knew they were anxious to preserve friendly relations. I said to him that he must realize that we had taken a position from which we could not recede. He said he knew that; that he thought it was possible that the Austrian Government would be willing to acknowledge that our attitude as to the principle involved should be accepted and that he thought that the difficulty would lie in our demand for the punishment of the commander. I told him it seemed to me that the Commander not only was bound by his instructions, but also by the law and principles of humanity, and that if he violated these he was as guilty as if he had violated his instructions. He replied that if his Government had held a different view as to the principle involved which they now held [hold] and had issued instructions in accordance with their former view, that the Commander would certainly not be to blame for following such instructions.

To this I said: "Either the Commander is guilty, or your Government is guilty. If your Government desires to take the responsibility they should frankly say so, exonerating the Commander, but they should assume his guilt." He replied that that was a very difficult thing for a Government to do. I said I realized that but it seemed to me the only alternative and if it did assume such responsibility it would be necessary for the Austrian Government to apologize, in addition to denouncing the act and offering to indemnify the sufferers.

He said that he would take the matter up immediately with his Government and hoped that they could reach a satisfactory conclusion. He also said that he was very sorry that they had not received his telegrams before they answered our first note, because he thought it would have made a difference in the tone of their reply.

He also asked me what I thought of the advisability of the Austrian Government recalling Consul General von Nuber, as he realized that his presence caused the present newspaper attacks upon him. I told him I thought it would be a way to remove one of the difficulties which we had to face in order to preserve good relations, and doubtless it would be expedient to have him recalled. He said he realized that even if the facts were not proven against von Nuber, which he knew they could not do, at the same time if he was under suspicion he would not be useful as a Consular officer and that he thought he would advise his Government to recall him.   Robert Lansing

TS memorandum (SDR, RG 59, 865.857 An 2/94½, DNA).

ENCLOSURE II

Handed me by Austrian Chargé, Dec. 21/15 RL

Berlin Via Sayville, NY Dec 20 1915

For Baron Zwiedinek we thoroughly appreciate the interpretation given by Mr. Lansing to the American note on the Ancona case and trust that an accurate knowledge of the entire conditions under which the sinking of steamer took place will corroborate the secretary of State in his opinion on the chivalrous spirit of our navy a detailed statement we are preparing and for which any details which Mr. Lansing could place before us would be most valuable will contain authentical and important information about the behaviour both of the commander of the submarine and of the crew of the Ancona we hope it will show Mr. Lansing that his idea about the spirit of our navy has not been erroneous and that the officer commanding the submarine did everything in his power to combine the necessities of warfare with the duties of humanity.   Foreign Secretary Burian.

E N C L O S U R E   I I I

Handed me by Austrian Chargé, Dec 21/15 RL

Berlin, Via Sayville, NY. Dec 20th 15.

Statim[1] for Baron Zwiedinek Washington you should tell the Secretary of State that always anxious to insure the practice of firm principles of humanity and wishing to conform to the averred rules of international lane law [sic] we quite agree with the United States government that all consequences to be drawn from the Ancona case depend on the quiestio facti[2] viz on authentical and exact information how the sinking of the steamer took place a statement containing this information and based on reports of the Austro Hungarian admiralty will be handed over to Mr. Penfield in a few days in answer to his letter of the 1 inst.

Foreign Secretary Burian.

TC telegrams (SDR, RG 59, 865.857 An 2/94½, DNA).
[1] Latin for urgent.
[2] That is, the facts as they stand.

From Edward Mandell House

Dear Governor: New York. December 21st, 1915.

The Evening Post has a sensational article by David Lawrence concerning my trip.[1]

It became necessary therefore for me to give out the statement I sent you. I wanted Lansing to give it out, but this premature publication by the Post, made it seem best to do otherwise.

Sir Cecil was here the other day. He remained with me an hour and a half and I have never seen him more amiable and reasonable. He was almost affectionate in his manner. In his note asking for an appointment he closed by saying, "With much love." He is a queer Sir Cecil. He wished to know if he was doing anything wrong, or everything to please the State Department. It was rather a staggering question and I had to tell him that some of his methods might be improved upon. He promised to do better.

I am enclosing you a check for $1000.00 which the Gerards sent Mrs. House to buy a wedding gift.

I hope you are having a restful and happy time and I am thinking of you both with deep affection.

Your devoted friend,   E. M. House

TLS (WP, DLC).
[1] D. Lawrence, "Col. House to Go Again to Europe," New York *Evening Post*, Dec. 21, 1915. Lawrence reported House's intention to leave within a fortnight for Europe to "canvass the prospects for peace" and to make clear to belligerent governments that unofficial visitors, such as the Ford peace party or

William Jennings Bryan, did not represent Wilson. House's mission may not uncover new peace moves, Lawrence speculated, but it could put Wilson "in a better position to meet the thousands upon thousands of appeals that he gets . . . to call a conference of neutrals or take the initiative in eliciting the terms of peace that each of the belligerents wants."

From Edward Mandell House, with Enclosure

Dear Governor: [New York] December 22nd, 1915.

Bernstorff has just been in. He has heard from his Government. They would like for me to come directly to Berlin to discuss peace upon the general terms of military and naval disarmament.

Bernstorff understands that I must go to London first and he will so inform his Government. Their feeling was that it would be better to come to Berlin first. In my opinion this would not do.

In the conversation which Bernstorff repeated to his Government, I said I believed if they would consent to a plan which embraced general disarmament, you would be willing to throw the weight of this Government into the scales, and demand that the war cease. That we were not concerned regarding territorial questions or indemnity, but we were concerned regarding the larger questions which involved not only the belligerents, but the neutrals also.

The Allies will take care of the territorial and indemnity questions and we need not go into that at this time. If we start with such discussions it would involve us in controversies that would be needless and footless.

I believe we ought to move with circumspection and not permit the German Government to lead us into an attitude that would place us in a disagreeable position with the Allies. It is possible they will undertake this. I am always suspicious of their diplomacy. However, knowing this in advance, I feel we can avoid any pitfalls. But we cannot be, I think, too cautious.

It will be of great value if you will write me now and then, when you have time, and in such a way that I may show the letter to some member of each government where I should happen to be. Your messages last year to Poincare and Delcasse[1] did no end of good. They were indirect and therefore all the more appreciated. It is hard to estimate the effect of flattery and politeness upon Europeans, and this may be said of the British and Germans as well as of the Latin races. They value such things far beyond our conception.

In this connection, Bernstorff told me that the Ancona matter might have been settled with Austria had a different form of note been written. That they were very proud and deeply resented the stern tone of the note. He told me, too, he was sure the Lusitania controversy would be satisfactorily settled. But he was afraid the Ancona note would cause a rupture of diplomatic relations with Austria.

Bernstorff intimated that he did not quite trust Gerard where I was concerned. I insisted that his Government communicate with me at London through Gerard so as to confirm Bernstorff's assertion that I would be welcome. He was willing to do this, but intimated his belief that Gerard last year did not promptly and accurately transmit the German Government's views regarding my visit. You will remember the unaccountable delay.

I do not believe it would be wise to go to Berlin without direct assurances other than from Bernstorff.

Will you not write me immediately upon receipt of this your impressions as to what to say in London and what to say in Berlin and how far I shall go. It looks as if at last we were getting somewhere.

Unless you write promptly I shall not get your letter as we are sailing on the Rotterdam on the morning of the 28th.

I am, with deep affection,

Your devoted,   E. M. House

If you write so that the letter reaches me X'mas or Sunday, please put a special delivery stamp on it, otherwise I will not get it until Monday.

P.S. I am enclosing a cablegram which has just come from Sir Edward Grey.

I had Woolley look into the National Movie Association Dinner at which they desire you to speak. He reported yesterday that you would receive another invitation directly from the President, and he believed it advisable for you to accept. The other invitation which you said you did not receive, you must have overlooked for Tumulty replied that you could not accept.

TLS (WP, DLC).
[1] WW to EMH, April 15, 1915, Vol. 32.

ENCLOSURE

December 22nd, 1915.

Your letter of December 7th and decision received.[1] I understand from Spring-Rice that you have decided to come here. Very glad and am much looking forward to seeing you again and discussing matters.   (E. Grey)

TC telegram (WP, DLC).

1 EMH to E. Grey, Dec. 7, 1915, CCL (E. M. House Papers, CtY):

"I have not replied to your letter of November 11th for the reason I hoped to receive another after you had gotten my cable saying I referred to the fourth paragraph of your letter of September 22.

"Things are moving rapidly here—much more so than appears on the surface. There have been several occurrances recently of far reaching importance, but of which I feel it unwise to write.

"The President and I have considered the advisability of my going to London in order that we might have a more intimate understanding. There are reasons for and against this.

"You are quite wrong in thinking that we have any desire to lessen the effectiveness of England's sea power at this time. It is the one reassuring potential element in the war. We all believe that England has made a mistake in not immediately letting through the purchases made in Germany prior to March 1st. It would ease the situation in every direction and would help us to help you. Delay in these not important matters have caused what friction there is.

"I have asked Sir Horace Plunkett to send an important message to you and Mr. Balfour which will go by this mail. I would appreciate it if this is not repeated to anyone for the time being. It has great possibilities for harm if it should get beyond you two. I gave it to Sir Horace to send as a matter of safety and because I trust him entirely.

"My mind is not now running towards peace, even upon the broad lines spoken of before. What is most needful at present is a better working understanding with you and how this is to be brought about is uppermost in our thoughts. The machinery we are using is not altogether satisfactory. Just why I cannot explain here, and perhaps it may be necessary for me to see you in person.

"It is one of the ironies of Fate that when our people are feeling closer to yours than ever before, the feeling with you is drifting away from us. This, however, is explanable and inevitable and will not last.

"We are all living under great strain, but I hope we may be able to see things clearly so that the problems that confront us may be solved for the good of mankind.

From William Cox Redfield

My dear Mr. President: Washington December 22, 1915.

I hand you communication on the subject of a tariff commission sent me December 18 by Prof. F. W. Taussig of Harvard University.[1] I venture to think it worthy of your careful reading. I trust you may find time to read it since it bears upon a matter of so much current importance.

There are three considerations which I think should be carefully reviewed before the decision is made to establish a tariff commission in the form at least in which it has appeared in our Cabinet discussions. These are considerations which affect, first, the quality of the work to be done under the change; second, the permanent political expediency of the change; third, the effect of the change upon the public appreciation of the Government Departments and on our own estimate of their work.

Let me discuss them in reverse order. Any act which depreciates the Government Departments as regards the quality of their work and the public estimate of it is of doubtful wisdom. It is the reverse of the policy which Prof. Taussig urges and which I approve. Statements of fact made by the responsible officers of the Government Departments ought to be, and I think are, taken at their par by the public, except such part of it as for partisan purposes may want something else done. The evidence of this in the case under discussion is the fact that there are no criticisms of the work done under the present method but only the expressed fear lest somebody who has not yet arisen may at some time say that the reports are partisan. Such a statement the reports themselves ought to and do answer. To change the method on the avowed ground that departmental work errs through its partisan character is a confession of weakness I should not care to make and which I think untrue.

I do not sympathize with the viewpoint expressed by some of my colleagues that the normal attitude of the head of a Department toward its work is to develop it for party advantage. This conception seems to me wrong except only so far as party advantage may normally come out of doing the work in the best way, which means in a way to serve all the people without regard to a party. I think this is the spirit in which our departmental work is much of it done, and I can see no reason why a statement of commercial fact done in this spirit should not be taken at par just as a statement of scientific fact is. There is no reason why the report on the hosiery industry should not be taken with the same weight as a report upon the cotton crop or upon coal mines or any other subject. I think in fact they are so taken and that the charge of partisanship is made for purely political purposes and is without serious weight.

Will the political expediency of the moment if met produce a lasting result? The Tariff Board[2] was a failure in large part because its results were done in a hurry, although over two years were spent upon the three reports they got out and over eight times the money which has been at the disposal of the present force. The reports, though under the supervision of a board supposed to know its job, showed in many details the lack of the technical manufacturer's training. In an address before the House of Representatives I tore the report into shreds, showing that the able men who composed the board did not have the knowledge of the technique of industry so as to know what they were about in many respects.

The public will expect something definite from the change. What is it to be? Will the Federal Trade Commission, charged with its new powers, continue the studies now making or will they not? It takes many months, sometimes years, to thoroughly study an industry. Neither Congress nor the public comprehend this. They will want, as President Taft wanted from his Tariff Board, statements of fact quicker than they can be made and digested. It seems to me certain that there will be dissatisfaction with the speed with which the reports can be made and with the character of the reports when made. Work of this kind is of such a nature that it can not be hurried and no definite limit can be set for it. When the field work is done months of study are requisite in the office, and nothing is more destructive of the character of the work than to have it pressed by the demand of some committee or public body. If, however, men are in charge of the work who do not understand its essential nature, they will normally accede to these requests which are destructive of quality and their work will show it. I should, to be candid, look forward to the time when, freed from official cares, it might become my duty as a manufacturer to criticise the work of such a commission arising from the very causes which I now foresee and state. It has taken two and a half years for me, with the aid of able assistants, to develop a professional force to its present high level. I think it certain that force will deteriorate under the leadership of any commission not composed of men technically familiar with the subject and giving to it but a portion of their time. It seems to me inevitable that the result must be disappointment on the part of Congress and the public and that the reaction is sure.

I have already covered incidentally the question of the quality of the work. I think the essential fact at the bottom of the present agitation is ignorance. Men do not know what is being done and talk as if there was nothing being done. There is a vague idea that the tariff can be gotten out of politics, a matter which Prof. Taussig clearly treats in the inclosed. The tariff being a matter of fiscal policy must always be a political matter. To my thought the present condition calls for an enlightenment of the ignorance which prevails, for an assertion of the possibility and the fact of truth telling as regards the facts of industry on the part of a great Government Department, for meeting the present vague and ignorant demand with the truth as to what exists and has existed, the comparison, for example, of the work now done with that which the Tariff Board did and with that which no board save one of highly trained experts can be expected to do.

In closing let me say that while of course I shall accept with good will whatever action may be deemed necessary, I think it my duty to present these considerations and to express my belief that the facts when fully known and understood not only do not warrant yielding to the cry for a tariff commission but point rather to an extension under departmental auspices of the work now going on.

Let me say finally, in order to clear myself of any suspicion of departmental feeling in the matter that I would willingly approve the transfer of the present work to another Department if that should be deemed desirable.

Yours very truly,   William C. Redfield

TLS (WP, DLC).

¹ F. W. Taussig, "A Tariff Commission," T MS (WP, DLC). Taussig began his memorandum with comments on the things that a tariff commission could not accomplish. Most important, such a commission could not determine the general tariff policy of the United States. That decision belonged to Congress and the voters. A commission could, however, encourage more careful preparation of tariff legislation. Taussig then reviewed various types of commissions. An independent and permanent body would be "a constant *incentive to change*," because it could justify its continued existence only by recommending revisions. An independent body, modeled on the ill-fated Tariff Board of 1909-1912, should be temporary and empowered to "make inquiries, secure a body of accurate information, be prepared to make recommendations *for a given situation.*" Taussig favored the creation of a permanent bureau in an executive department to carry on research and make recommendations concerning the administration of the tariff laws. However, he warned that such a subordinate bureau might not attract the most qualified people.

² Article 718, Section 2, of the Payne-Aldrich Tariff Act of 1909 provided for a staff, to be appointed by the President, empowered only to secure information relating to the application of minimum and maximum rates and the administration of the customs laws. Broadly interpreted, this section became the basis for Taft's Tariff Board, which assumed broader investigative powers than those specifically assigned to it.

To Helen Woodrow Bones

My dear Helen: Hot Springs, Virginia December 23, 1915

Edith and I have conferred about this and she is generously willing to have any date set that is free within the time indicated by the Brazilian Minister and this letter of Mr. Phillips'. Would you be generous enough to have a little conference with Mr. Phillips and arrange the matter?

Edith joins me in dearest love to all. We are having a fine free time and you may expect us to come back in great shape.

Affectionately yours,   [Woodrow Wilson]

CCL (WP, DLC).

From Margaret Woodrow Wilson

Darling Father,   The White House [c. Dec. 23, 1915]

It was dear of you to write to me and I just loved your letter.¹ I am so glad that you are having a rest and such a happy rest.

We miss you and Edith sorely, but we have to think of your happiness.

What a fine escape you made!

We shall think of you often on Christmas day.

Good night, dearest Father. I love you, and oh I'm so glad that you are happy.   Your devoted daughter,   Margaret.

ALS (WC, NjP).
  [1] It is missing.

To Edward Mandell House

My dear Friend,   Hot Springs, Va., 24 December, 1915.

Your letters of December twenty-first and twenty-second have reached me here, the former enclosing Mrs. House's cheque for one thousand dollars, the Gerard's wedding gift, or, rather for the purchase of the Gerard's wedding gift. Thank you for both the letters.

I was deeply annoyed by the Evening Post's performance. David Lawrence is a nuisance. He has written me a long letter of explanation in which he says that he had learned that Mr. Bry[a]n intended to sail on the twenty-eighth and that he reasoned that it would be best to tell about your trip first, for fear there might be surmised to be some connection between Mr. Bryan's arrand and your own.[1]

Sir Cecil is certainly a most puzzling and incalculable person. It is very important that some less childish man should take his place.

I do not know that Bernstorff is much more satisfactory. I feel, with you, that it is necessary to get corroboration of his representations from the other side before we can act with confidence on them. What you tell me of your latest conversation with him about peace is, nevertheless, most interesting. It makes me feel, as you evidently do, that it is possible that we are on the eve of some real opportunity. I pray it may turn out to be so! At any rate, it is the more clear that you are starting on your present errand at just the right juncture.

You ask me for instructions as to what attitude and tone you are to take at the several capitals. I feel that you do not need any. Your own letters (for example, this one in which you report your conversation with Bernstorff) exactly echo my own views and purposes. I agree with you that we have nothing to do with local settlements,—territorial questions, indemnities, and the like,—but are concerned only in the future peace of the world and the guarantees to be given for that. The only possible guarantees, that is, the only guarantees that any rational man could accept, are (a) military and naval disarmament and (b) a league of nations to secure each nation against aggression and maintain the absolute freedom of the seas. If either party to the present war will let us say to the other that they are willing to discuss peace on such terms, it will clearly be our duty to use our utmost moral force to oblige the other to parley, and I do not see how they could stand in the opinion of the world if they refused.

The errand upon which you are primarily bound you understand as fully and intimately as I do, and the demand in the Senate for further, immediate, and imperative pressure on England and her allies makes the necessity for it the more pressing. About the possibilities in the direction of peace you need no further intimation than that given above. If any particular question arises I know that you will cable me fully, and I shall of course reply at the earliest possible moment.

I am sure that you know how fully my heart goes with you and how deeply grateful I am for the incomparable and inestimable services you are rendering the country and me, your friend. Mrs. Wilson joins me in most affectionate messages to you both. We are having a heavenly time, and I am sure that I am being daily rendered more fit for the winter's work. I shall miss you and your counsel about domestic matters very sorely and very constantly, but the greater must be preferred to the less.

Please give my most respectful and sincere regards to Sir Edward Grey and to the other troubled and responsible men with whom you will confer in England, France, and Germany. It would make me very happy to cooperate with them in any way for the peace of the world and a perfect understanding between them and this country.

With all my heart,

Your devoted friend,   Woodrow Wilson

WWTLS (E. M. House Papers, CtY).
¹ D. Lawrence to WW, Dec. 22, 1915, TLS (WP, DLC).

Two Letters to Robert Lansing

Hot Springs, Va.,
My dear Mr. Secretary,   24 December, 1915.

This is indeed not a little disturbing, but I think it comes from other querters than the Senator's own personal thinking. It makes House's errand all the more pressing and opportune. I shall have a talk with the Senator at the earliest possible moment after my return and shall try my best to make the situation as a whole so clear to him that he will take our view of it.

With much regard,

Cordially and faithfully Yours,   Woodrow Wilson

WWTLS (SDR, RG 59, 763.72/2337½, DNA).

My dear Mr. Secretary,   Hot Springs, Va.,
                                          24 December, 1915.

I am not sure whether I am encouraged or not by this, but I am clear that you said the right things to the Baron and that it was very wise to make him see the position of the United States without any penumbra about the edges of the statement.

Cordially and faithfully Yours,   Woodrow Wilson

WWTLS (SDR, RG 59, 865.857 An 2/95½, DNA).

From Robert Lansing, with Enclosure

My dear Mr. President: Washington December 24, 1915.

The Austrian Chargé has just called and handed me a telegram which he received from his Government yesterday. I enclose you a copy.

Wishing you and Mrs. Wilson a very happy Christmas believe me, my dear Mr. President,

Faithfully yours,   Robert Lansing

TLS (SDR, RG 59, 865.857 An 2/95½A, DNA).

E N C L O S U R E

Handed me by Austrian Chargé, Dec 24/15. RL

Berlin via Sayville NY. Dec. 23, 1915.

For Baron Zwiedinek   American note handed over to me 21 inst   tell Secretary of State that the answer we are preparing shall be guided by the same concern for good relations between both countries as mentioned by Federal Government   in consequence of the Christmas holidays our answer cannot be expected before next week.   Foreign Burian.

TC telegram (SDR, RG 59, 865.857 An 2/95½A, DNA).

From Josephus Daniels

My Dear Friend: Washington. Dec. 24, 1915.

The love and greetings on this Christmas time go out to you and Mrs. Wilson from the whole Daniels family. We hope that the day will bring cheer to you both and that happiness will crown every day of the New Year.

With affectionate regards,
                    Your sincere friend,   Josephus Daniels

ALS (WP, DLC).

From Brand Whitlock

Dear Mr President: New York. 24 December 1915

I have postponed my felicitations only because I felt that it would perhaps be kinder not to intrude at a moment when you had sought seclusion, but on this Christmas Eve I may indulge my desire to extend to you my respectful and sincere congratulations and to express to you my wish sincere and cordial and, may I be so bold as to add, my affectionate wishes for your happiness. And I know that you will permit me to include in the wish your charming Lady, and to ask you to present my most humble duties and to make my compliments. May all joy be yours and hers, and may the world treat you both as well as—well, as well as you would be treated if I, for instance, were the world, for I think I am sensible of the vast debt the whole world owes you in a time when the world so greatly needs such devoted and unselfish services as you have so splendidly, and are so splendidly giving it.

When I had the pleasure of being received by you in Washington you did me the honor to ask me to tell you when we were to leave for my return to my post. We are booked to sail on the Rotterdam, of the Holland-America line, next Tuesday, the 28th December. My little visit home has done me much good, and I am really impatient to return to my duties. It has meant much to me to see America again, and much to see you, who so ideally represent it.

I am, my dear Mr. President, with great respect and admiration, and ever high regard.
                    Your devoted   Brand Whitlock

ALS (WP, DLC).

From Ignace Jan Paderewski[1]

New York, Dec. 24, 1915.

In behalf of stricken Polan[d] I beg of your excellency to accept with the homage of deepest respect the expression of most profound gratitude for your truly magnamious action.

Paderewski.

T telegram (WP, DLC).
[1] Ignace Jan Paderewski (1860-1941), Polish pianist, composer, and statesman. He had been on an extensive speaking and concert tour of the United States since February 1915 in order to raise funds for Polish refugees displaced by the war, and to create interest among Americans in the future of a unified and free Polish nation. The standard biography is Charles Phillips, *Paderewski, the Story of a Modern Immortal* (New York, 1934).

To Edward Mandell House

Hot Sprgs Va Dec 25th, 1915.

Your two grateful friends join in sending Mrs. House and you their most affectionate Christmas greetings.   W.W.

T telegram (E. M. House Papers, CtY).

To Robert Lansing

Hot Springs, Va.,
My dear Mr. Secretary,   26 December, 1915.

This is encouraging as to the spirit of the Austro-Hungarian government, but I fear they are preparing to contest the facts with us, and the inferences to be drawn from them.

Faithfully Yours,   Woodrow Wilson

WWTLS (SDR, RG 59, 865.857 An 2/96½, DNA).

From Edward Mandell House

Dear Governor: New York. December 26, 1915.

Your letter of December 24th came to me last night.

I think we agree entirely. I merely wanted to know whether you had changed your mind at all after Bernstorff's communication.

Another straw blew our way yesterday afternoon and is, I think, significant. The Belgian Minister of Finance,[1] who is in America for a short stay, asked for an interview. He desires me to see King Albert and obtain his views at first hand in regard to peace overtures. He said King Albert was not quixotic, that he was a sensible practical man and I would find his views not altogether in harmony with those of the governments in London and Paris.

I asked if Belgium was willing to waive an indemnity. He did not reply to this directly, but said what they desired most was the preservation of their nationality.

He desired the conference with King Albert to be kept confidential. I explained the impossibility of this, letting him know that my movements would be known to both the British and French as long as I was in their territory.

He then thought since Whitlock had not conferred with the Belgian Government for more than a year, I might use that as an excuse for seeing the King. I was non-committal excepting that I would have to be frank with both London and Paris regarding the conference, but I would hold in confidence what he had told me concerning King Albert's views.

It was agreed finally that in the event I thought it advisable, to have the conference, I should let King Albert know when I arrived at Boulogne and he would send his motor to take me for the five hour trip to his headquarters.[2]

The doubt in my mind is not concerning the British and French Governments, for that can easily be gotten over, since they would attribute such a conference to an entirely different purpose, but what I fear is its effect upon the German Government should it become known to them.

I feel we have already gotten the advantage that would accrue from a conference with the King, excepting it would be absolute confirmation.

The Minister knows I am to repeat to you our conversation, but he begs that it be held in strictest confidence between the two of us. He doubtless felt it was an indiscretion to say so much to me, but he evidently thought the good outweighed the evil.

I am sure I need not tell you how deeply I appreciate your confidence, your friendship and affection. It makes me eager to serve and to try to justify it all.

Affectionately yours,   E. M. House

TLS (WP, DLC).
[1] Alois, Burgrave van de Vyvere.
[2] At La Panne. House visited him on February 8, 1916.

To Margaret Randolph Axson Elliott

Dearest Madge,   Hot Springs, Va., 26 December, 1915.

I am sure you will understand why I have not written sooner in reply to your dear letter of the ninth.[1] The combination of public business and getting married has been a quite overwhelming one, as you may imagine; and I know that you will forgive what I cannot help being ashamed of. For it was an exceedingly sweet letter, my dear Sister, and made our hearts very warm. We were sorrier than I can tell you that you and Edward could not be at our wedding, perfectly as we understood the reason. It was a very simple, very dignified, and very pretty wedding and I have been exceedingly, perfectly happy ever since. Edith is a very wonderful person, really and truly, as you will find out for yourself someday; and it is very delightful to learn that it will probably be necessary in the near future for you to come East on some unavoidable errands and that that day may be near at hand. Do make it as soon as possible and come direct to us.

We are having a perfect honeymoon here. We start back to Washington on the fifth of January, and then the winter's swirl will begin with a vengeance; but in the meantime we are as quiet and far away here, in all seeming, as if we had nothing to do with the great world.

Edith joins me in warm love to you both. We are quite well and hearty.

Your loving brother,   Woodrow Wilson

May I add just a word Madge dear to send our Xmas greetings and thank you for the card received this morning telling of your Season's thought of us.

May the New Year be rich in blessing to you both and bring you soon to see us is the affectionate wish of yours,

Edith.

WWTLS (WC, NjP)
1 Margaret R. A. Elliott to WW, Dec. 9, 1915, ALS (WP, DLC).

From Jessie Woodrow Wilson Sayre

Dearest Father,   The White House Dec. 26, 1915

We had a very Happy Christmas, though, of course, we missed our dear ones at Hot Springs and in Williamstown unutterably. Josephine[1] was her own dear self and the center of fun; and the oval room remains a magnet still because we all want to watch her play with her new things every moment. Uncle Stock and she are inseparable, and he seems in the best of spirits. He almost made a special trip from Middletown to see my baby but had to give it up when he found that he could only arrive when the boy was asleep and must leave before he awoke!

I hope your Christmas was all that you could desire, full of peace and rest and happiness. Edith's dear letter made me very happy as her letters always do; and Uncle Stock was quite touched by his. Indeed she has brought great happiness to us all this Christmas tide and we are full of gratitude to her.

Frank sends his love with mine and his thanks for the wonderful gift you sent us, dear generous Father! How can we thank you enough for all you have done for us, but most of all for the love you shower upon us.

Ever devotedly your daughter   Jessie.

ALS (WC, NjP).

¹ Annie Wilson Howe Cothran's daughter.

To Robert Lansing

Hot Springs, Va.,

My dear Mr. Secretary,   27 December, 1915.

Thank you for this. I think I appreciate, as I know you do, the importance of an early confirmation, or, rather, ratification, of the treaty with Colombia. I hope with all my heart that that most desirable comsummation may be brought about.

Cordially and sincerely Yours,   Woodrow Wilson

WWTLS (SDR, RG 59, 711.21/330½, DNA).

To Robert Lansing, with Enclosure

My dear Mr. Secretary,   Hot Springs, 27 December, 1915.

I have read this with misgivings. We certainly do not wish to be drawn into a correspondence with the Austro-Hungarian government; but, if they propose arbitration, how can we refuse to consider that? To do so would be contrary to all our traditions and would place us in a very difficult pos[i]tion to justify in the opinion of the rest of the world, do you not think so?

Faithfully Yours,   Woodrow Wilson

WWTLS (SDR, RG 59, 865.857 An 2/97½, DNA).

E N C L O S U R E

Vienna, via Berne. December 24, 1915.

1049. From informal conversation with a responsible official of the Ministry of Foreign Affairs I am inclined to anticipate that the Austro-Hungarian reply to our last ANCONA note will again contend that the American demands are based on inaccurate and insufficient evidence. Feeling in responsible quarters opposed to rupture of diplomatic relations. Should a settlement through diplomatic channels prove impossible it is probable that suggestion will be made that the dispute be submitted to arbitration. In an interview published today the Hungarian Premier, Tisza,[1] says that the dispute must be amicably settled in a few days satisfactory to both parties which can only be accomplished through correspondence between the two governments. Article by jurist, Dr. Lammasch,[2] was excluded from the Freie Presse of the nineteenth by the Government but appearing in both morning and evening editions today may indicate views of the Government undergoing change. He says that the sources of our information are open to question especially since our contentions are in such sharp conflict with Austro-Hungarian Admiralty's report. He recalls the Dogger Bank incident[3] between Great Britain and Russia and suggests that the present difficulty with the United States be settled by recourse to a similar arbitral board. Ministry of Foreign Affairs informally advise me that their reply to our last note will be delivered early next week.

Penfield.

T telegram (SDR, RG 59, 865.857 An 2/88, DNA).

[1] Count István (Stephen) Tisza.

[2] Heinrich Lammasch, professor of international law, University of Vienna, and member of the Permanent Court of Arbitration at The Hague.

[3] In October 1904, the Russian Baltic Fleet opened fire on a flotilla of British fishing boats in the North Sea, thinking them Japanese torpedo boats. An international commission of arbitration required Russia to apologize to Great Britain and to compensate the fishermen.

To John Barrett

Hot Springs Va Dec 27/15

Please present my warmest greetings to the delegates to the Pan-American Scientific Congress and extend to them on my behalf a most cordial welcome. It seems to me to be of the happiest omen that the attendance upon this congress should be so large and the interest in its proceedings so great. I hope that the greatest success will attend every activity of the congress and that the intimate intercourse of thought which it produces will bind America still closer together throughout both continents alike in sympathy and in purpose   Woodrow Wilson

T telegram (J. Barrett Papers, DLC).

To Domicio da Gama

Hot Springs, Virginia,
My dear Mr. Ambassador: December 27, 1915

The invitation conveyed by your letter of December twentieth on behalf of the Ambassadors and Ministers of the Republics of Central and South America gave Mrs. Wilson and me the greatest gratification, and I have sent word to the White House requesting that a date be selected and that you be apprised, inasmuch as here the programme of our winter's engagements is not accessible to me. I hope that before this reaches you, you will have received the information.

Let me repeat that the invitation gives us peculiar gratification. It is very delightful that the representatives of the Republics of this hemisphere should have so gracious and generous a thought of our pleasure and we shall look forward to the occasion with anticipations of the greatest enjoyment.

Pray convey to the Ambassadors and Ministers and accept for yourself the very warm expression of our regard.

Cordially and sincerely yours,   [Woodrow Wilson]

CCL (WP, DLC).

To James Paul Clarke

Hot Springs, Virginia,
My dear Senator: December 27, 1915

When I last saw you[1] I did not have at hand a copy of the tentative draft of a shipping bill which the Secretary of the Treasury and the Secretary of Commerce collaborated on with my approval and, indeed, at my request, but the copy has since come into my hands and my interest in the matter is so deep and earnest that I venture to send it to you for your consideration.

Of course, you will understand that like all such drafts it is for the purpose merely of making a very definite suggestion, and suggestions of this kind can be made definite only when thrown into the form of an Act of Congress.

I very much appreciated your generous attitude in our recent conversation and I am sure that you will read this result of our conference with an entirely open mind.

Cordially and sincerely yours,   [Woodrow Wilson]

CCL (WP, DLC).
  [1] That is, on December 14.

To William Phillips

Hot Springs, Virginia,
December 27, 1915

My dear Mr. Phillips:

I am ashamed that you should have had to wait all this time for a reply to your letter of December thirteenth conveying the question of the French Ambassador acting as Dean of the Diplomatic Corps as to what would be the most acceptable form in which they could convey their congratulations to Mrs. Wilson and myself on the event of our marriage. I dare say the question has answered itself by this time. Our own feeling is that a simple letter signed by the various members of the Diplomatic Corps jointly would be a very delightful souvenir. If that suggestion meets with your approval and does not come too late, I would be very glad to have you hand it on to M. Jusserand.

With all the best wishes of the season,
Cordially and sincerely yours,   [Woodrow Wilson]

CCL (Letterpress Books, WP, DLC).

To Edward Mandell House

Hot Springs Va Dec 27th, 1915.

Our loving thoughts will follow you across the sea and in all your generous labors on the other side   The good wishes that go with you from us are too many and too deep to express.

Woodrow Wilson.

T telegram (E. M. House Papers, CtY).

From Joseph Patrick Tumulty

Dear Governor: The White House December 27, 1915

This note, brief though it is, is freighted with birthday greetings and congratulations! The past year has been a happy one for you, but my hope is that the year to come will bring you even greater happiness and joy, and that your every effort for the advancement of our country will meet with success. How much you have accomplished! And what a privilege it has been to stand at your right hand!

With a wealth of good wishes to you and to Mrs. Wilson, in which Mrs. Tumulty and the children join with one accord, believe me, always,   Affectionately yours,   Tumulty

TLS (WP, DLC).

Two Letters from Edward Mandell House

Dear Governor: New York. December 27th, 1915.

The only worry I leave behind is the New York situation.

Dudley, Frank Polk and I have been working on it during the last few days and I think things will shape up properly. It is essential, I believe, for you to talk with Dudley before you do anything in New York affairs, otherwise they may become hopelessly involved again. He will tell you when he sees you what has been done, and explain the end to which we have been working.

In this connection we both think if you would drop a little note to Senator O'Gorman giving some evidence of appreciation for the statement which he made the other day concerning your re-election and your defence program, it would help out wonderfully. Affectionately yours, E. M. House

Dear Governor: New York. December 27th, 1915.

In view of the letter you send me from Gerard today in which he criticized the London Embassy,[1] I am wondering whether it came through your office in Washington unsealed.

Gregory writes that Burleson tells him that there will be a resolution offered in Congress asking whether or not I received compensation upon my last trip abroad, and whether I will receive any this time and how much.

I have never accepted compensation while trying to serve either my State or the National Government, and I never accepted expense money until my last trip abroad when you so kindly insisted upon it.

Lansing spoke of compensation, but I wrote him I would accept nothing further than my expenses. I would not take that, but my income is something less than $20,000. and the unusual cost incident to a trip of this nature, makes it almost necessary.

I dislike to trouble you with such matters and at such a time and do so merely because I am leaving tomorrow. Affectionately yours, E. M. House

TLS (WP, DLC).
[1] It is missing in both the Wilson and House Papers.

From William Cox Redfield

My dear Mr. President [Washington] Decr 27, 1915

It is a privilege to write you a note of remembrance on your birthday to come tomorrow and one free from every suspicion of being official. This then is just a word of goodwill and affection from one friend to another. It expresses, feebly enough, my appreciation of what the last year has been in strain and in care, in taking anxious thought for the morrow. I rejoice that in some ways the clouds are breaking and especially I am glad for the rich measure of personal happiness that has come to you. With God overhead, with the loving support of your associates, with happiness at home, you may face the future with a quiet mind.

Sincerely   William C. Redfield

ALS (WP, DLC).

To Lucy Marshall Smith and Mary Randolph Smith

Dear, dear Friends,   Hot Springs, Va., 27 December, 1915.

How generous you are to us! The presents you sent Edith are singularly beautiful (if I may assume to be a judge) and your thought of us never flags. Now comes this copy of the MOON-STONE, which I shall devour with all my relish of a detective plot and which will at every page remind me of your affectionate remembrance of my preferences and my pleasures. Thank you with all my heart!

I cannot tell you how often or with what deep affection we think of you. You are so truly irresistible that you have made Edith feel about you both as we all do, and she shares our thoughts of you both with a zest equal to our own. Come back to us just as soon as you can, and make us happy in your conpanionship again, please.

We are having a heavenly time here. Edith reveals new charms and still deeper loveliness to me every day and I shall go back to Washington feeling complete and strong for whatever may betide. I am indeed blessed beyond my (or any other man's) deserts. We do not do anything that needs to be described. There is little to do here but walk and ride and play golf and loaf and spice it all with a little work, not to forget that there *are* duties as well as pleasures in the world. Every day we feel fresher and fitter (Edith was very tired, of course, with the last distracting rush of things, when she got here) and our dear native State is giving us most hospitable weather and refreshment.

We send you our most loving greetings and for the New Year the hope that everything that is good and desirable may come to you.   Your devoted friend,

You dear "Smith Sisters," I have you on my dressing table where I see your charming, beaming, little figures every morning first thing, and I only wish your real selves were as accessible.

Thank you with all my heart for this new and sweet thought of me.

We are having such a delicious holiday that I grudge each day as it passes. And we think, and speak of you many, many times. May 1916 bring you both its greatest happiness and add to ours by bringing *you* to us.   Fondly   Edith

WWTL (photostat in RSB Coll., DLC).

To Robert Russa Moton

                                Hot Springs, Virginia
My dear Principal Moton: December 28, 1915

I am sure I am giving voice to the feeling of the vast majority of those interested in education in this country, and particularly in the education of the Negro, when I express my gratification at your election as Principal of Tuskegee Institute.[1] I have known something of the special work you have been trying to do for the people of your race and of the spirit in which you have undertaken it, and I believe that your selection as the head of Tuskegee Institute means the promotion there of the best, most practical, and most hopeful ideals for the development of the negro people. I take pleasure in extending to you my sincere congratulation.

                    Very truly yours,   [Woodrow Wilson]

CCL (Letterpress Books, WP, DLC).
    [1] Moton's election as Booker T. Washington's successor had been announced on December 20.

To William Cox Redfield

                                Hot Springs, Virginia
My dear Mr. Secretary: December 28, 1915

Your letter of December twenty-seventh makes my heart very warm and I thank you for it very cordially and sincerely. It has the spirit of true friendship in it and you may be sure that there goes back to you and yours from me, not the mere greetings of the season, but the warm good wishes of a sincere and grateful friend.

        Cordially and faithfully yours,   Woodrow Wilson

TLS (W. C. Redfield Papers, DLC).

To Joseph Patrick Tumulty

My dear Tumulty: Hot Springs, Virginia December 28, 1915

I deeply and truly appreciated your generous birthday letter. I think you know and have always known how highly I value my association with you, and that you should judge me as generously as you do and have towards me the feelings which you so warmly express gives me deep and lasting joy.

My thoughts go out to you all in the most cordial good wishes at this change from year to year, and this letter carries with it the warmest and sincerest greetings of
                    Your affectionate friend,   Woodrow Wilson

TLS (J. P. Tumulty Papers, DLC).

To William Jennings Bryan

                                          Hot Springs, Virginia
My dear Mr. Bryan: December 28, 1915

It was certainly very gracious of you and Mrs. Bryan to think of us in the hour of our happiness and I want to thank you most sincerely for the generous message you sent us under the date of December eighteenth. May I not send to Mrs. Bryan and you in return my very best wishes for the New Year?
          Cordially and sincerely yours,   [Woodrow Wilson]

CCL (Letterpress Books, WP, DLC).

From Robert Lansing and Others

                          Washington DC 325 PM Dec 28, 1915

Our heartiest greetings   warm congratulations upon passing into another year under conditions so promising for a long life of happiness
          Lansing, McAdoo   Daniels   Gregory   Burleson,
          Garrison, Lane   Houston   Redfield, Wilson

T telegram (WP, DLC).

From Robert Lansing, with Enclosures

PERSONAL AND CONFIDENTIAL:

My dear Mr. President: Washington December 28, 1915.

I enclose for your information a memorandum of an interview which I had yesterday with the Danish Minister. My own belief is that Denmark will come to the figure of $20,000,000 and that it will be possible to negotiate a treaty of cession with that amount as a consideration. I will advise you in case I hear further from the Danish Minister or from Mr. Egan.

Faithfully yours   Robert Lansing.

TLS (SDR, RG 59, 711.5914/53½, DNA).

ENCLOSURE I

MEMORANDUM OF AN INTERVIEW WITH THE DANISH MINISTER.
December 27th, 1915.

The Danish Minister called on me this afternoon and stated that he had received word from his Government that they had made an offer to negotiate for the sale of the Danish West Indies on the basis of a hundred million kroner which, the Minister said, equal $27,000,000. I told Mr. Brun that this Government would consider such an amount too great a consideration for the Islands—that we were not good bargainers, and when I suggested that $20,000,000 might form a basis for negotiation I had stated the maximum sum which this Government was willing to consider—that he must understand, being here in America, the difficulties at the present time which the Government was having in raising sufficient funds for carrying out a policy of preparedness and that he must know that any such sum as $27,000,000 would, in all probability, be disapproved by Congress; that I hoped, therefore, he would explain this fully to his Government and I thought when they understood the situation they would be willing to modify their figures.

The Minister also spoke to me about the desire of his Government to obtain from this Government an agreement by protocol that it would not object to the extension of Danish occupation of Greenland. I told him that the Danish West Indies and Greenland should be combined in one negotiation; that Denmark had something which we desired, and that evidently we had something which Denmark desired; that it seemed to me it would be possibly the most advisable way to incorporate the two subjects in one treaty rather than to have a treaty of cession of the Danish West Indies and a protocol relating to Greenland. The Minister said he had no objection to adopting this course.

He also left with me a memorandum relative to Greenland which embodied instructions which he had received from his Government.

The Minister left with the understanding that he would communicate fully to his Government the views which had been expressed by me.   Robert Lansing.

TS memorandum (SDR, RG 59, 711.5914/53½, DNA).

E N C L O S U R E   I I

Handed to me by Danish Minister Dec. 27/15. RL
                    Memorandum.
                                    December 27, 1915.

In the conversation which the undersigned had the honor of having on November 10th with the Secretary of State, relative to the Danish West India Islands, Mr. Brun mentioned to Mr. Lansing the intentions and wishes of the Danish Government with regard to Greenland stating that Danish explorers had travelled over and had charted almost all of the uninhabited parts of Greenland and that, in consideration of Danish feelings on the subject and of the interests of the Eskimoes, it was desirable that the Danish Government should extend its care by the suzerainty of the state to include the whole of Greenland.

The undersigned wishes to add to this information the fact that Danish mission work and Danish commerce have already been extended to the Eskimoes at Cape York, and he is now by a cablegram from his Government dated December 24th further instructed to say that the Danish Government would very much desire to receive the binding promise of the American Government that no objection would be raised to the said extension of the care and suzerainty of Denmark to the whole of Greenland.

The Danish Government thinks that this promise should be given by a protocol or similar act simultaneously with the arrangement regarding the Danish West India Islands.
                                              C Brün

TC memorandum (SDR, RG 59, 711.5914/53½, DNA).

From Robert Lansing

PERSONAL AND CONFIDENTIAL:

My dear Mr. President: Washington December 28, 1915.

As a matter of precaution I think that we should consider what action should be taken in case Austria fails to meet our demands or refuses to do so.

The severance of diplomatic relations, under normal conditions, would not be considered an act of war but merely an expression of disfavor. Under present conditions, however, I feel convinced that that course would be looked upon as hostile by Austria, and would result in war.

If my surmise is correct and war is the inevitable consequence of breaking off relations, should the Government take that action without consulting Congress, the war-making power?

I know from information which has been received from various quarters that the conduct of the Administration, if war results from the stand we have taken in the ANCONA case, will be attacked on the ground that Congress alone has power to declare war and that the Executive exceeds his power if he brings about a situation which must eventuate in war. Perhaps this would be an unjustifiable criticism, and yet there seems to be a measure of reason in it on account of the constitutional provision. In fact I am not at all certain in my own mind that it is not a sound position.

It might be avoided by laying the papers in the case before Congress with an address dealing with the situation and showing that, while the dignity of the United States precludes continued relations with Austria, the Administration realizes that the severance of relations would in all probability bring about a state of war, and that, therefore, in view of the power conferred on Congress, the papers are presented to it before such action is taken in order to obtain its approval and to avoid any charge of infringement upon the constitutional rights of the Legislative by the Executive.

I do not say that I consider this the best course to pursue, but it has the merit of placing the responsibility where it legally belongs, although the conduct of the negotiations created a situation which seems to offer no other solution than the breaking off of diplomatic relations.

In submitting the foregoing I do so only because it seems to me that possibly the future action should be considered carefully and a decision reached before the time arrives to act.

Faithfully yours,   Robert Lansing.

TLS (WP, DLC).

From Felexiana Shepherd Baker Woodrow

My dear Tommy: Columbia, S. C., Dec. 28, 1915.

This is just a line to let you know how deeply I sympathise with you in your happiness.

I have felt so much for you in your terrible loneliness, and now I feel sure you will have a real home.

"Whoso findeth a Wife findeth a good thing."

"A prudent Wife is from the Lord."

Of course, I take it for granted, that in this, as in all things else, you have acted wisely.

May you have many happy returns of this day, with long years of usefulness, and the enjoyment of the delights of a true home.

With love to your Wife,   Affectionately,   "Aunt Felie."

HwCL (received from James Woodrow).

Alvey Augustus Adee to Joseph Patrick Tumulty

Sir: Washington December 28, 1915.

The American Minister at Berne has requested the Department to inform the President and Colonel House that the Swiss Secretary of State, Federal Councillor Hoffmann,[1] in reply to an interpellation on December 23rd in the Swiss Parliament as to the intention of the Swiss Government relative to intervention in favor of peace, submitted a written declaration to the effect that the Swiss people desire to express their ardent sympathy towards their neighbors in the war now raging in Europe, and their sincere desire for the attainment of peace, but that the Swiss Government does not consider it proper to attempt to intervene in favor of peace until the belligerent states themselves have manifested their desire for such a result. Mr. Hoffmann further stated that all overtures in favor of peace at this time would be considered by the belligerent nations as indiscreet and even unfriendly acts, and would do harm instead of advancing the cause of peace. It was further stated that the Federal Council would follow with care the course of (?). The Swiss Government will be happy if in the future it can contribute towards the securing of peace without departing from its neutrality.

I am, Sir,

Your obedient servant, For the Secretary of State: Alvey A. Adee

TLS (WP, DLC).

[1] Arthur Hoffmann, member of the Swiss Federal Council and its president in 1914; at this time he was serving as Minister of Foreign Affairs.

Four Letters to Robert Lansing

Hot Springs, Virginia
My dear Mr. Secretary: December 29, 1915

I do not know when I have been more gratified than by the telegram of congratulation and good wishes which I received yesterday signed by yourself and the other members of the Cabinet. May I not express to you and through you to our colleagues my grateful appreciation? Any man ought to be strong and ought to thank God and take courage who has such friends and whose colleagues support him in such unstinted and affectionate fashion.

Cordially and sincerely yours,   Woodrow Wilson

TLS (SDR, RG 59, 811.001 W 69/162, DNA).

Hot Springs, Va.,
My dear Mr. Secretary,   29 December, 1915.

I have your letter of yesterday about our relations with Au[s]tria-Hungary.

What new elements in the case make you feel now, what, I remember, you did not feel at the outset of this matter, that a breach of diplomatic relations would *probably*, rather than possibly, mean war? I do not now recall any new influences that have recently come into the field, and I would very much like to know what has made this impression on your mind.

You may of course be right. All along there has been reason to fear that such might be the outcome. And I quite agree with you that we ought to think our course out very frankly and carefully, blinking nothing.

I do not think that it would be wise in any case to lay the matter publicly before Congress. The most that I could do would be to consult with the leaders on the hill. To lay the matter publicly before Congress would in effect be to announce that we expected war and might be the means of hastening it.

There are some wise and experienced men on the Senate Committee on Foreign Relations and it is quite possible that we might get useful guidance from them. For myself I do not doubt the constitutional powers of the Executive in this connection; but power is a different matter from wise policy.

Your answer to some of the questions I raised or suggested in my last brief note to you on the news from Vienna will necessarily form a part and a very fundamental part of our discussion of the whole situation. If the Imperial and Royal Government thinks that it can put a very different face upon the ANCONA case by representations which it thinks us bound in fairness to it to consider, how can we refuse to discuss the matter with them until all the world is convinced that rock bottom has been reached?

Cordially and faithfully Yours,   Woodrow Wilson

WWTLS (SDR, RG 59, 865.857 An 2/110½, DNA).

Hot Springs, Va.,
My dear Mr. Secretary,   29 December, 1915.

Thank you very much for these memoranda. I think the tack you took with the Danish Minister a very serviceable one, and feel that, on the whole, the negotiations look quite promising.

Cordially and faithfully Yours,   Woodrow Wilson

WWTLS (SDR, RG 59, 711.5914/54½, DNA).

Hot Springs, Va.,
My dear Mr. Secretary,   29 December, 1915.

Thank you very much for letting me read these letters from our Ambassador at Rome.[1] His letters are singularly lacking in definiteness of impression, and yet, taken as wholes, they do serve to give one something of the atmosphere of the court at which he is living and of the politics that is stirring Europe just now.

I do not think he states the feeling of animosity towards the United States with entire accuracy or with a full knowledge of all the elements involved; but I fear that in the main he is right.

Cordially and faithfully Yours,   Woodrow Wilson

WWTLS (SDR, RG 59, 763.72/2340½, DNA).
[1] T. N. Page to RL, Dec. 4, 1915, TLS (SDR, RG 59, 763.72/2325½, DNA), and T. N. Page to RL, Dec. 4, 1915, TLS (SDR, RG 59, 763.72/2326½, DNA).

To Brand Whitlock

Hot Springs, Virginia
My dear Mr. Whitlock: December 29, 1915

Your generous and charming letter written on Christmas eve did not reach me in time for me to answer it before you sailed, but I am going to send this message of deep appreciation and of Godspeed tardily after you. It was a real pleasure to see you when you were here and to get again the impression of sincerity and genuineness and true insight which I have always got of you when I have had the privilege of coming into direct personal contact with you, and you may be sure that my warmest best wishes go with you as you return to the post in which you have done such signal services to justice and to humanity and have brought so much honor upon your country. May God speed you in everything.

Mrs. Wilson joins me in the most cordial messages of good will for the New Year.

Cordially and faithfully yours,   [Woodrow Wilson]

CCL (Letterpress Books, WP, DLC).

To Jessie Woodrow Wilson Sayre

My darling Jessie,   Hot Springs, Va, 29 December, 1915.

No message received yesterday gave me deeper pleasure than yours and Frank's,[1] bless your hearts. I love you both with all my heart, and your love for me makes me deeply happy.

I hope that you get the best news from Francis. You were wise to leave him where he will get just the care and the food he is used to, but I know how hard it has been for you to be separated from him. Next Christmas he can come himself without risk, and then we shall have a higher time than ever.

These are blessed days for Edith and me. She is beyond all measure lovely and delightful and we dread to see these blis[s]ful days of quiet and seclusion come to an end. We wish so much that you and Frank could stay until we get back on the sixth!

With dearest love to all from us both,

Your devoted Father,   Woodrow Wilson

WWTLS (photostat in RSB Coll., DLC).
[1] Jessie W. W. Sayre and F. B. Sayre to WW, Dec. 28, 1915, T telegram (WP, DLC).

To Sallie White Bolling

Dearest Mother,   Hot Springs Virginia 29 December, 1915

It was *very* sweet of you to think of my birthday and send me the pretty card that came yesterday. I hope you know how entirely you have won my affection and how truly I have made you my own mother in my heart and this card made me very warm about the heart because it made me feel as if you accepted me as one of your own. My adorable sweetheart and wife joins me in dearest love to you all, and I am proud to subscribe myself

Your loving son, Woodrow Wilson

ALS (WP, DLC).

To Josephus Daniels

My dear Daniels: Hot Springs, Virginia December 30, 1915

Your letter of December twenty-fourth bearing the affectionate greetings of the Daniels family has touched and delighted us very much indeed and Mrs. Wilson joins me in thanking you with thanks that come from the heart. It is delightful to have such friends and to feel the warmth and genuineness of their friendship.

We join also in sending you our warmest best wishes for the New Year.   Affectionately yours, Woodrow Wilson

TLS (J. Daniels Papers, DLC).

To Jessie Kennedy Dyer

My dear Jessie: Hot Springs, Virginia December 30, 1915

It was delightful to receive your letter of the twenty-seventh[1] and to know that you all had a happy Christmas and are all well. You may be sure that in the midst of all my duties I lose not the least bit of my affectionate interest in you and your welfare, and I wish with all my heart that I might have a glimpse of you in your home. We send you the most cordial and affectionate greetings for the New Year.

This is just a little message of affection but it is a message of very genuine affection.

Faithfully yours, Woodrow Wilson

TLS (Letterpress Books, WP, DLC).
1 It is missing.

From Robert Lansing, with Enclosure

My dear Mr. President: Washington December 30, 1915.

I enclose a copy of a telegram which has just been received from Vienna under date of the 29th. I assume that by tomorrow or next day we will receive the full text of the note.

From the summary given by Mr. Penfield it would seem as if the ANCONA case offered possibilities of solution.

Faithfully yours,   Robert Lansing.

TLS (SDR, RG 59, 865.857 An 2/95, DNA).

E N C L O S U R E

Vienna, Via Berne, Dec. 29, 1915.

1063. CONFIDENTIAL. Austro Hungarian answer to second ANCONA note received at four thirty this afternoon. It is communication upwards of three thousand words. Will require all night to translate and encipher.

Note is practical compliance with our demands. It acknowledges culpability of submarine commander who it states has been punished. Will pay indemnities under certain conditions, but specifically leaves question of future conduct of submarine warfare for further discussion. Reciprocal desire for maintenance of good relations is expressed.[1]   Penfield

T telegram (SDR, RG 59, 865.857 An 2/95, DNA).
    [1] F. C. Penfield to RL, Dec. 29, 1915, T telegram (WP, DLC); printed in FR-WWS 1915, pp. 655-58. Penfield summarized its contents very well, omitting only the description of *Ancona*'s encounter with the submarine.

From Robert Lansing

PERSONAL AND PRIVATE:

My dear Mr. President: Washington December 30, 1915.

In regard to the Pan American Treaty—I have seen, in addition to the Ambassadors, nine of the ministers, and given them copies of the four articles. They all express personal delight at the Treaty and feel sure that their governments will be glad to enter into such a convention. I have still the representatives of three other countries to see, and hope to do so tomorrow.

The number of persons who know of this plan makes the possibility of secrecy very difficult, in fact, some of the papers have already got hold of the fact that there is some plan on foot for a Pan American Agreement, or conference in line with the address which I made on Monday.[1] I have, since being questioned by one of the reporters on the subject, notified all the Ambassadors and Ministers to be kind enough to keep the matter secret. I had already told them that the matter was confidential when I gave them the memorandum, but I am afraid that they have showed it to some of their fellow-countrymen who are here attending the Scientific Congress and so a considerable number are undoubtedly in possession of the fact that we are attempting to unite the Americas in an agreement of some sort. I thought I would tell you this so that you will understand if you see anything in the papers on the subject.

Yesterday Ambassador Suárez said to me that he was in hopes of receiving from his Government an acceptance of the plan and that he was most desirous to obtain it and felt sure if a little time was given he could do so. His change of attitude is certainly interesting.   Faithfully yours,   Robert Lansing.

TLS (SDR, RG 59, 710.11/215½A, DNA).
 1 To the Second Pan American Scientific Congress. Lansing had defined Pan-Americanism as an international policy of the Americas, based upon geographical isolation, similar political institutions, and common conceptions of human rights. Without mentioning the negotiations for a treaty, he alluded to the need for mutual security among the American nations and to growing cooperation in politics, commerce, and intellectual life. See Second Pan American Scientific Congress, *Report of the Secretary General*, pp. 55-59.

Two Letters to Robert Lansing

Hot Springs, Va.,
My dear Mr. Secretary,   31 December, 1915.

   This does indeed afford us something more than a ray of hope for a satisfactory settlement, and my mind is, at any rate for the time being, much relieved.
          Faithfully Yours,   Woodrow Wilson

WWTLS (SDR, RG 59, 865.857 An 2/111½, DNA).

Hot Springs, Va.,
My dear Mr. Secretary,   31 December, 1915.

   It was no doubt inevitable, as we indeed anticipated, that this should leak. It is embarrassing, however, if only because we shall now have to explain the matter prematurely (?) to members of the Senate Committee.

   I told Senator Stone, as I believe you know, some time ago what was afoot, and I am sure that it met with his entire approval. I suggest that you seek an interview with him, apprise him of the whole situation, and seek his advice.
          Faithfully Yours,   Woodrow Wilson

WWTLS (SDR, RG 59, 710.11/216½, DNA).

To Harry Freidenwald[1]

Hot Springs, Virginia December 31, 1915

Will you not express to the meeting which is being planned for Sunday evening to collect funds for the relief of Jews stricken by the war in Europe my profound sympathy with the object of the meeting and my sincere hope that there will be a great outpouring for the relief of these distressed people?[2]

Woodrow Wilson.

T telegram, WP, DLC).

[1] Ophthalmologist and chairman of the Baltimore committee of the American Jewish Relief Committee.

[2] Tumulty had informed Wilson of the meeting earlier on the same day, explaining that a similar meeting in New York, to which Thomas R. Marshall had sent a message, had raised $8,000. "This movement has the backing of all the prominent Jews of the country," Tumulty added. "The cause is most commendable. Do you think it wise or advisable to send a telegram . . . expressing sympathy with the movement. . . . The suggestion has come to me through friends connected with the Baltimore Sun." JPT to WW, Dec. 31, 1915, T telegram (WP, DLC).

To Felexiana Shepherd Baker Woodrow

Dear Aunt Felie,   Hot Springs, Va., 31 December, 1915.

Please do not think this a dictated letter. This little writing machine has for a very long time been practically the only pen I use.

Your birthday greeting gave me a great deal of pleasure, and your messages to Edith and me have made our hearts very warm. I hope with all my heart that you will have a chance to know her. You will then know for certain that I never did a better or happier thing than to gain her.

We are both well and exceedingly happy and join in sending you all the warmest and best wishes of the season.

Affectionately Yours,   Woodrow Wilson

WWTLS (received from James Woodrow).

From Walter Hines Page

Dear Mr. President: London, Dec. 31, 1915

My Christmas guess, of no particular value but as good as anybody else's, is that the war will end next Summer or Autumn —sooner only if some decisive military event give the Germans a good excuse to make terms. We live in a censored world here —in a sort of fog; but there are too many signs of impending German disaster to doubt its coming: this in spite of the extraor-

dinary series of bad failures by the Allies—the Dardanelles
failure, the Balkan failure, two military failures in France when
the German line was actually broken. These failures have
singularly little effect on the English whose slow stupidity one
curses with the more vehemence and whose cool endurance one
admires with the more confidence the more one sees of them. The
up[s]hot of it is they are invincible, but they bungle their work
so that a victory is far, far more costly than it ought to be. They
think that the all-around changes they have just made in their
military commands are great improvements. I can form no
opinion about that; but anybody can see that some sort of
changes was desirable.

There is great dissatisfaction, too, with the Government; but
there's no way to change it except by the voluntary resignation
of the Ministers. The Prime Minister will not resign (his ec-
centric wife said the other day that "nobody but God could put
Herbert out"); and Sir Edward Grey's resignation will not be
accepted by him. It is against these two that the fiercest criticism continues to beat—against Asquith because the war doesn't go
forward fast enough and because he doesn't seem to deal frankly
with the people, and against Grey for the diplomatic failure to
secure the Balkan States to the Allies. There was undoubtedly a
lack of imagination in the early stages of the war, when Turkey
and all the Balkan States might possibly have been won over to
the Allied side. But during those months the English were thinking chiefly of keeping the Germans out of Calais and of holding
the German line in France till the Russians shd. threaten—Berlin!
The story goes about now that the Turks offered to permit the
British to go through the Dardanelles for the payment of a sum
that is small in comparison with what the Dardanelles failure
cost. The answer they got was that the English do not do things in
that way. The navy and army regard Sir Edward Grey, who is
supposed to be responsible for this answer, as a visionary statesman—"too much of a gentleman," as old Lord Fisher said of Mr.
Balfour.

Of course we who are onlookers here have long ago passed the
place where we can be surprised by any event; but unless new
and disastrous things happen in the Balkans or beyond, I have
good hope that Sir Edward will not be driven out of office till
the war end. He will then go because his eyes demand rest. Else
he may go blind. I lay stress on this because his continuing in
office is of prime importance to us. He sees more nearly eye-to-
eye with us than (I think) any other member of the Cabinet.
He has to yield to his associates, who reflect and represent British

opinion about the uses of sea-power; and especially does he have
to yield to the military and naval group and to the lawyer group.
But he has softened many a blow. The diplomatic corps here
share my estimate of him. Within the last few days allied and
neutral diplomats alike have expressed to me the greatest alarm
lest he shd. resign in disgust at the criticism of him wh. comes
from half the points of the compass. I don't think the diplomats
now in service command great weight or brains: I fear that one
has a tendency to lessen his list of great men as he sees them at
close range. But, as nearly as I can judge, the group in London
make a higher average by a good deal than the group at any
other capital. Imperiali,[1] the Italian Ambassador, dined with me
three nights ago and I cd. get him to talk about nothing else
than Sir Edward. Merry del Val,[2] the Spanaird, gave me a call
lasting a whole working morning, to express his alarm. The
Dutch Minister[3] danced all around the room muttering his fear:
"God knows we have a hard enough time now. But, with Curzon,
who can tell what we shd. suffer?" And it's Curzon they talk
about for the Foreign Office if a change shd. be made. In their
Oxford days Spring Rice wrote some doggerel

I am George Edward Curzon

Ah—a *very* superior purzon—etc.

And Curzon has never lived this down—has, in fact, tried to live
up to it. He talks to you in the tones of a vice-regal phonograph.
Those of us who have so far fought thro' this war have long ago
got past the least trace of awe of noble lords, or vice-regents,
or royalty; but you don't want—for steady intercourse—to deal
with a fellow who has an air of ordering all mundane things:
you're afraid you'll be tempted some day to say what you think
of him, wh. wdn't. be diplomatic. In India Curzon quarreled with
Kitchener—wh. I secretly hold to his credit. For nobody seems
able to work with Kitchener. For 20 years he ordered savages
and dependent nations about, and his colleagues find him what
we Americans call a stuffed prophet. The people believe him
great and the Government use him as an effective dummy. His
name raised a great army, Lord Derby[4] actually doing the work.
Thus, you see, we live not in an ordered world, but in a world of
ragged hopes and fears. I fancy that History, in one of her
vagaries, will set down these plausibilities for facts—that Asquith
was England's greatest Prime Minister and that Grey failed in the

[1] Marquis Guglielmo Imperiali.

[2] Alfonso Merry del Val y Zulueta.

[3] Jonkheer Reneke de Marees van Swinderen.

[4] Edward George Villiers Stanley, Earl of Derby, Director-General of Recruiting.

great war as Secretary for Foreign Affairs—both wide of the truth.

I've heard nothing lately about the British reply to our long note. I know they are looking up facts for a reply, and I'll ask when I see Sir Edward next—in a day or two. But I think I have written you that I do not expect any important concession to our demands. The navy party has public opinion squarely behind it: they are going to do all they can to starve out Germany and settle the bill with neutrals after the war. There isn't much feeling against us on the score of our protests against British action. Feeling flares up when provoked by any event; but nobody has time or feelings to spare from the demands of the war. Then, too, so long as the *Lusitania* controversy is unsettled, our Notes and protests are regarded by the public, I will not say by the Government, as formal. Austria is no longer thought of by the British as an independent power—only a German satrapy, like Turkey or Bulgaria. Consequently the English conception of the *Ancona* controversy is that it is an incident. Only Germany is regarded as a real power here. Any Englishman who speaks quite frankly will say something like this: "We caught and destroyed between 70 and 80 German submarines so that their activity off the English and Irish coast had to be discontinued. The American controversy gave them a convenient way to 'come down.' Rather than confess an English victory they pretended to give in to the American Government. Of course the American Government had to accept their 'come down'; but of course also it wasn't worth the breath it took to utter it. The real test is the *Lusitania*: will they disavow that?"

Such is the public feeling here as the year ends. Men take only a languid interest in everything but the war. The eternal wrangle about the Government's inefficiency goes on all the time. You may look out the window anywhere at any time of day and see recruits drilling in the streets and convalescent wounded taking an outing. God knows how many hospitals there are in London and all over the Kingdom or how many maimed lie in them. On Christmas day I saw 1000 in one hospital—cheerful fellows in the main singing Christmas songs.

Meantime at the Embassy we have a very full day's work every day—now fortunately routine business in the main, but an enormous volume of it. The Government is as courteous as ever; but everybody in the Government is worked to death. A dense cloud of weariness hangs over all London. Every day or two some man breaks down and has to go off or to give up. Administrative work has its casualties. There are no idle people here—men or women—of any class. Nobody reads a book. The newspapers are meagre. The theatres have mere diversions—"funny shows" chiefly. Social activity is reduced to a minimum. *Punch* is unutterably dull. Thank Heaven for sleep! and a London winter is foggy and heavy-eyed.

At this place in my letter I had an interesting interruption. Harold Fowler, the young fellow whom I brought over with me as my private secretary, resigned a year ago, and in spite of all that I cd. do, went into the English army. He has been in France for six months—for the last three months in command of an *18*-inch gun just back of the trenches. He is as much of a real man as any young fellow I have ever known. I made him a member of my family and he lived with me. Having 10 days' leave, he is in London. He came into my library just at the end of the last page; and I've found out more from him than from a dozen or two high officers back from the front. The Englishman has remarkable endurance. He has no nerves. Cornered he will fight as a tiger. He doesn't mind dying and he dies heroically. But, with all these qualities, he is such a stupid ass than [that] you wish to brain him with the butt of your gun. He is unorganizable. You can't make a fighting machine of him. He loses twice as many men on every move as he need lose. Man for man, he is worth 5 Germans—alone. In an army every German is worth 5 Englishmen. This sort of fighting, therefore, *can* be carried on for years and years. Fowler sometimes thinks it may. Both sides lack initiative. Both sides have Old-World faults. The Australians, New Zealanders, and Canadians (being Englishmen set free) are by far the best soldiers in this war. This American youth is like them. When he was appointed on the General's staff, he begged & begged to command a gun till he got it. He's there to do the effective work—not for safety. There's little chance, I fear, that he will come out whole—or come out at all. When he goes, he'll be gone forever. Kipling said when his boy went off: "I'll never see him again," and now he's dead.

This estimate of the English by Fowler is startlingly accurate. They lack knack. Else they'd end the job quickly. They lack knack at all *new* tasks. That's the trouble with their Government in war time. They manage their finances and their navy incomparably—two tasks they've done for centuries—continuously done. I came near writing that they muddle everything else: I think they do.

A very well-informed Dane from Copenhagen—an under-Secretary in one Department of his government—told me last night after dinner and cigars, that he often fears that the English will drive the Danes into the war on the German side by this stupidity about preventing Danish trade—in spite of the fact that every 3 Danes out of 4 are pro-British. I am told his judgment may be twisted by the trade-troubles that he has to handle. But he said that he knew the Germans were building 24 gigantic submarines. When they are ready they will come out for ships to & from the U. S. much further out at sea than the scene of the *Lusitania* & *Arabic* attacks and consequently further from danger of British attack.*

Well, my poor letter is dwindling down to mere gossip, and it's the dullest week of the year in London. Let me add my most hearty good wishes to you & Mrs. Wilson for the New Year and for all New Years. We keep in our trenches here with good spirits and unwearying efforts; and contrary to the predictions of wiser men, I still hope that the war will end in 1916. Yet I confess I fear the wiser men who say 1917 or 1918 may guess better than I.   Sincerely Yours   Walter H. Page

* Just as I am about to seal this, private information comes from Liverpool that German submarines have sunk several British ships in the Irish sea during the past week.

ALS (WP, DLC).

A Memorandum by Robert Lansing, with Enclosure

MEMORANDUM OF CONVERSATION WITH GERMAN AMBASSADOR.
December 31st, 1915.

The German Ambassador called upon me and handed me the *annexed paper*,[1] which is the substance of a telegram which he had received from Berlin. He said that this did not complete his instructions in the matter as the telegram said—"to be continued."

The Ambassador said that he appreciated this was going over the ground which we had traversed many times, but he thought that while his Government suggested arbitration he had received an intimation that they would like to know the reasons why we were unwilling to submit the case to arbitration. He added that he believed that his Government, if a fairly good case could be made out against arbitration, would follow the course which had been adopted apparently by Austria in their ANCONA case.

I answered him that we had discussed the illegality of retaliatory measures by a belligerent and that so far as the legal point of view was concerned I could not see that there was anything to arbitrate. In addition to this I called his attention to the next to the last paragraph in the German reply in the FRYE case, dated November 29, 1915, wherein they specifically stated that persons on board a vessel about to be sunk should be placed in safety.[2] The Ambassador seemed surprised at this statement of his Government and said—"Have they gone as far as that?" I said—"Yes, that is their language and of course it applies as well to belligerent merchant ships as to neutral merchant ships engaged in contraband trade because the only legal ground for sinking a neutral vessel would be its temporary belligerent character."

He said he would communicate with his Government at once in regard to the matter and see if they would not follow out a course which they had so plainly set forth as to the illegality of retaliatory measures, and as to the duties imposed upon the commander of a submarine in sinking a merchant vessel.

He said he was hopeful that we could reach an agreement along these lines.   Robert Lansing

TS memorandum (SDR, RG 59, 763.72/2339½, DNA).
    [1] Wilson's emphasis.
    [2] It is printed as Enclosure IV with RL to WW, Jan. 7, 1916 (second letter of that date).

ENCLOSURE

Handed me by German Amb. Dec. 31/15 RL
The substance of a telegram recd from Berlin.

The German submarine war against England's commerce at sea, as announced on February 4, 1915, is conducted in retaliation of England's inhuman war against Germany's commercial and industrial life. It is an acknowledged rule of international law that retaliation may be employed against acts committed in contravention of the law of nations. Germany is enacting such a retaliation, for it is England's endeavor to cut off all imports from Germany by preventing even legal commerce of the neutrals with her and thereby subjecting the German population to starvation. In answer to these acts Germany is making efforts to destroy England's commerce at sea, at least as far as it is carried on by enemy vessels.

The question whether neutral interests may in any way be injured by retaliatory measures should, in this instance, be answered in the affirmative. The neutrals by allowing the crippling of their commerce with Germany contrary to international law which is an established fact, cannot object to the retaliatory steps of Germany for reasons of neutrality. Besides, the German measures, announced in time, are such that neutrals easily could have avoided harmful consequences by not using enemy vessels

employed in commerce with England. If Germany has notwithstanding limited her submarine warfare, this was done in view
of her long standing friendship with the United States and in
the expectation that the steps taken by the American Government in the meantime aiming at the restoration of the freedom
of the seas would be successful.

As Germany cannot see a violation of international law in her
course of action she does not consider herself obliged to pay
indemnity for damages caused by it, although she sincerely
regrets the death of American citizens who were passengers on
board the Lusitania. In view of the amicable relations between
our two countries the German Government is however ready to
have differences of opinion settled through international arbitration—a way always warmly recommended by the United States—
and therefore to submit to the Court of Arbitration at the Hague
the question, whether and to which extent Germany is obliged
to pay indemnity for the death of American citizens caused by
the sinking of the Lusitania. The sentence of the Court should
in no way be taken as deciding the question whether or not the
German submarine war is justified according to international
law, but it would be a means to settle definitively the regrettable
Lusitania incident.

T MS (SDR, RG 59, 763.72/2339½, DNA).

From Joseph Patrick Tumulty

The White House, January 2, 1916.

In view of critical situation here arising out of PERSIA case[1]
think it would be unwise for you to prolong your vacation. Hope
you will pardon this suggestion. Regards.   Tumulty.

T telegram (WP, DLC).
[1] News reached Washington on January 1 that a torpedo had struck and
sunk the British liner, *Persia*, off the coast of Crete on December 30, killing,
among others, two Americans. See Link, *Confusions and Crises*, pp. 76-78.

To Joseph Patrick Tumulty

Hot Springs, Virginia, January 2, 1916.

Am consulting the Secretary of State by wire. Will come if he
thinks the case in a shape to be handled at once.

Woodrow Wilson.

T telegram (WP, DLC).

To Robert Lansing

[Hot Springs, Va., Jan. 2, 1916]

Are we sufficiently informed as to the facts in the case of the Persia to form a judgment and plan for a course of action? I would very much like your candid advice as to whether you think it best that I should return to Washington at once. I would suggest a message like the following to Penfield Quote: Having just received the reply of the Austro-Hungarian government in the matter of the ANCONA and having formed a most favourable impression of the friendly and reasonable attitude of that government and of the probability of an amicable and satisfactory settlement, we are the more deeply disturbed by the news that reaches us of the destruction of the steamship PERSIA. Please make immediate inquiry at the Foreign Office concerning the facts and express the grave solicitude of this government and seek assurances of early and very serious action on the part of the A[u]stro-Hungarian government in this case in the spirit and upon the principles as frankly set forth in its last note to us concerning the ANCONA—Unquote.[1]   Wilson.

WWT telegram (WP, DLC).
[1] This was sent as RL to F. C. Penfield, Jan. 3, 1916, printed in *FR-WWS 1916*, pp. 143-44.

A Letter and a Telegram from Robert Lansing

PERSONAL AND PRIVATE:

My dear Mr. President: Washington January 2, 1916.

The enclosed copies of telegrams[1] telling of the sinking of the British steamship PERSIA on December 30th about three hundred miles northwest of Alexandria do not, in my opinion, seriously affect the ANCONA case, since the evidence of torpedoing is inconclusive, the nationality of the submarine, if one was the cause, is unknown, and it is stated that the PERSIA carried an armament.

The fact that the vessel was carrying a 4.7 gun raises a question which, it seems to me, we ought to settle.

Three or four days ago I forwarded to the Italian Ambassador at his request the statement in regard to armed merchant vessels, which we issued in September, 1914.[2] I had discussed the question some four or five weeks before with Mr. Barclay of the British Embassy and told him that, in view of the development of submarines as commerce destroyers, which had been unknown when our statement was issued, I felt that the arming of merchant vessels with any gun, of sufficient calibre to attack a submarine, would make it very difficult, if not impossible, to insist that a submarine should expose itself to attack by coming to the surface and hailing a vessel so armed; and that, while the armament might be termed "defensive," it was capable of being used offensively against a submarine and so, I thought, that a merchant ship carrying a gun or guns would have to be considered and treated as a vessel of war if it entered our ports.

In view of this opinion, which I believe I stated to you orally some time ago, I wrote the Italian Ambassador a letter enclosing the statement of September, 1914, explaining the change of view which the new conditions had forced upon us. I enclose a copy of that letter with our printed statement as to the status of armed merchant vessels.[3]

Since we issued the statement of September, 1914, formally, it appears to me advisable to issue a new statement setting forth the new conditions resulting from the successful employment of submarines in interrupting and destroying commercial vessels, the impossibility of a submarine's communicating with an armed merchant ship without exposing itself to the gravest danger of being sunk by gunfire because of its weakness defensively, the unreasonableness of requiring a submarine to run the danger of being almost certainly destroyed by giving warning to a vessel carrying an armament, and that, therefore, merchant vessels should refrain from mounting guns large enough to sink a submarine, and that, if they do, they become vessels of war and liable to treatment as such by both belligerents and neutrals.

The chief difficulty with the situation seems to me to lie in this: If some merchant vessels carry arms and others do not, how can a submarine determine this fact without exposing itself to great risk of being sunk? Unless the Entente Allies positively agree not to arm any of their merchant vessels and notify the Central Powers to that effect, is there not strong reason why a submarine should not warn a vessel before launching an attack?

You will recall the case of the BARALONG where a German submarine was bombarding a vessel from which the crew had escaped in boats, when a tramp steamer approached flying the American flag. The submarine remained on the surface and awaited the steamer, which on nearing the submarine lowered the American flag, hoisted the British colors, and with a gun mounted on the stern (a defensive armament according to our early definition) opened fire and sank the German vessel killing all the crew.[4] The British Government would urge that this was merely a *ruse de guerre* and entirely allowable, and so it would have been under old conditions, but under the new conditions it presents a strong argument in favor of submarine attack without warning.

Not only, therefore, should we, in my judgment, rewrite our statement as to the status of armed merchant vessels but show that if any vessel of that class is armed, all merchant vessels are in danger of sudden attack without warning. As to the use of the American flag on any merchant ship converted into an armed vessel it might be well also to make representations to the British Government.

In view of the sinking of the PERSIA it would seem to be opportune and advisable to act in this matter, if it is decided to act, as expeditiously as possible.

                    Faithfully yours,   Robert Lansing.

TLS (WP, DLC).

¹ R. P. Skinner to RL, Jan. 1, 1916, received 9 A.M. and 12 noon, T telegrams (WP, DLC). Skinner, the American Consul General at London, reported, first, that *Persia* had sunk and that, among its passengers, was Robert N. McNeely, American Consul at Aden. In his second telegram, he added the names of two other American passengers and the information that four boatloads of passengers had escaped.

² Printed in *FR-WWS 1914*, pp. 611-12.

³ It is RL to Count Vincenzo Macchi di Cellere, Dec. 31, 1915, CCL (SDR, RG 59, 763.72111/3509g, DNA):

"In accordance with your request, I am inclosing memorandum issued by the Department on September 19, 1914, which defined the general rules this Government then felt should be followed in cases involving the status of armed merchant vessels visiting American ports.

"Since this memorandum was drawn up the situation has been changed by the use of submarines as commerce destroyers, and for that reason this Government feels that these rules should be modified, as a small caliber gun on a merchant ship is just as effective for purposes of attack against the submarine as the large caliber gun. Therefore, the presence of any gun on a merchant ship of a belligerent nationality could well create presumption that the armament was for offensive purposes, thereby causing this Government to treat the ship as a ship of war."

⁴ In addition, see RL to WW, Aug. 30, 1915, n. 1, printed as an Enclosure with WW to EBG, Aug. 30, 1915 (third letter of that date), Vol. 34.

Private.   Washington, D. C. January 3, 1915 [1916]

Press reports indicate sinking of two more vessels in the Mediterranean without warning. These with the sinking of the Persia will cause, I believe, popular excitement which may manifest itself in Congress. I should say, therefore, that it would be well if you could return at once to Washington. Personally, I am very much alarmed over the seriousness of the situation.

                    Robert Lansing.

T telegram (WP, DLC).

To Joseph Patrick Tumulty

Hot Springs, Va., 6:00 p.m. January 3, 1916.

Please consult Secretary of State and if he approves request Senator Stone to meet me tomorrow morning at the White House at ten bringing with him such other Senators as he thinks it wise and best to bring.[1]   Woodrow Wilson.

T telegram (WP, DLC).

[1] Wilson met with Senator Stone and Representative Henry D. Flood at the White House on the morning of January 4. According to the *New York Times*, Flood and Stone informed Wilson that some senators were threatening to precipitate a discussion of the sinking of merchant ships, and Wilson replied that the administration was doing its best to meet the situation. After his appointment with the President, Stone postponed the scheduled meeting of the Senate Foreign Relations Committee because the facts on the *Persia* case were not complete and some committee members were absent. *New York Times*, Jan. 5, 1916.

From Margaret Woodrow Wilson

My beloved Father,   [Philadelphia, c. Jan. 3, 1916]

I love the beautiful letters you have sent me during your holiday, and I have wanted to answer them before this. You would forgive me, or rather you would understand my not writing, (you would forgive in any case) if you knew how great a rush I have been in since Christmas. Everybody including Tom, Dick and Harry (Harry Shipman) has been in Washington at some congress or other during the holidays.

Thank you so much for your generous present to me, darling Father. I am going to get something personal and lasting with it, that will always remind me of you and your love. I don't think any girl in the world ever had a more loving or generous Father than I.

Please thank Edith for her dear letter to me. The dear lady! We, Helen and I, are waiting eagerly for her to come home to us, and it goes without saying that we are homesick for you.

I am writing this from Dr. Kyle's[1] home because I have come to see him about a little difficulty with my voice, which no one not even Mr David notices when I sing, but which hampers me all the same. I'll tell you all about it when I see you. It's too long a story to tell you now.

I can't tell you how much I love you, most wonderful Father. Thank you for the dear *dear* letters and the big checque.

Give my love to sweet Edith.

Ever your devoted,   Margaret.

ALS (WC, NjP).

[1] David Braden Kyle, M.D., specialist in diseases of the ear, nose, throat, and chest, and Professor of Laryngology at Jefferson Medical College.

A Memorandum by Joseph Patrick Tumulty

Washington, D. C. January 4, 1916.

About ten minutes to ten o'clock this morning I had a very interesting conversation with the President at the White House, my purpose being to bring to him the atmosphere of Washington and the country as far as I could ascertain with reference to the sinking of the PERSIA by a submarine. The other purpose of my visit was to warn him that Senator Stone might induce him to make some admission with reference to his attitude which might embarrass the President in the future.

The President looked very well after his trip and seemed to be in a fine mood although it was plainly evident that the PERSIA affair rested heavily upon him. My attitude toward this matter was for action, and action all along the line. This did not seem to meet with a very hearty response from the President. He informed me that it would not be the thing for us to take action against any government without our government being in possession of all the facts. I replied that that was my attitude, but I thought there should be action and vigorous action as soon as all the facts were ascertained. He agreed with me in this. When I began to tell him about the attitude of the country and the feeling in the country that there was a lack of leadership, he stiffened up in his chair and said, "Tumulty, you may as well understand my position right now. If my re-election as President depends upon my getting into war, I don't want to be President. I have been away and I have had lots of time to think about this war and the effect of our country getting into it, and I have made up my mind that I am more interested in the opinion that the country will have of me ten years from now than the opinion it may be willing to express today. Of course, I understand that the country wants action, and I intend to stand by the record I have made in all these cases, and take whatever action may be necessary, but I will not be rushed into war, no matter if every damned congressman and senator stands up on his hind legs and proclaims me a coward." He continued, speaking of the severance of diplomatic relations, "You must know that when I consider this matter, I can only consider it as the forerunner of war. I believe that the sober-minded people of this country will applaud any efforts I may make without the loss of our honor to keep this country out of war." He said that if we took any precipitate action right now, it might prevent Austria from coming across in generous fashion.

T MS (WP, DLC).

From Robert Lansing, with Enclosure

PERSONAL AND PRIVATE:

My dear Mr. President: Washington January 4, 1916.

I enclose translation of a cipher message in private code received from Ambassador Page at London. I do not feel that I have an adequate vocabulary to comment upon it.

Faithfully yours,   Robert Lansing

TLS (WP, DLC).

ENCLOSURE

London, January 3, 6 p.m.

3500 Personal and Confidential for the information of the Secretary and the President only.

The Washington correspondents of the most important London papers report that the last Austrian note on the ANCONA would have been acceptable if the PERSIA had not been sunk. This opinion, the sinking of the PERSIA, and the [lack of][1] a settlement [of the] LUSITANIA provoke unfavorable comment on the Administration in every London newspaper today. Following are a few speculate (specimen) comments:

The Morning Post says "We have long ago relinquished all expectation that neutral nations would effectually intervene in respect of repeated outrages of the law of nations," and "at the same time it must be said that their position in this regard is singularly inconsistent with their pleadings addressed to the allied belligerents that they may be allowed to trade with the enemy."

The TIMES says "The Germans and Austrians can have no objection against engaging in further diplomatic correspondence with President Wilson to any extent and to congratulating each other upon the 'refreshing and delightfully pungent irony' with which they answer the 'clumsy tone' of his efforts. Why after all the Germans may argue should the killing of a single American in the PERSIA do more than that of a hundred Americans in the LUSITANIA and of the many Americans killed in other ships."

The DAILY TELEGRAPH says: "The interchange of notes has now plainly reached and passed the point of farce and no spirited nation can long endure that condition of affairs."

The STANDARD says: "If President Wilson thinks it worth while to continue arglebargling[2] with the governments of Germany and Austria when the crimes of the YSAKA MARU the VILLE DE LA

CIOTAT and the PERSIA have been committed while the note promising redress for that of the ANCONA—with the tongue of course in the cheek—was on its way to him, that is his concern." And the STANDARD says of the Austrian note: "If the United States will accept this it will accept anything."

The PALL MALL GAZETTE says "Berlin and Vienna we dare say are quite prepared to work upon a commercial tariff in their slaughter of American citizens so long as Washington is content to put a price upon them, and to declare the honor of the United States satisfied by a receipt upon the 'butcher's bill'." and "The proverbial fly upon the wheel does as much to influence locomotion as the diplomatic pen can effect in the restraint of German deviltry." and "It is for the American people to decide whether their national prestige and dignity can be assuaged upon this mercantile basis. But we cannot forget that when President Wilson took up his pen upon the destruction of the LUSITANIA he announced himself with considerable emphasis as the champion of reason, justice and humanity upon the high seas. After half a year's correspondence with the Central Empires he must be painfully conscious of the entire futility of his performances in that capacity."

The WESTMINISTER GAZETTE says: "The German warlords apparently take a cynical pleasure in apologizing to the American Government one day and proving to their own people the next day that their apology was humbug."

Public opinion both official and unofficial is expressed by these newspaper comments with far greater restraint than it is expressed in private conversations. Ridicule of the Administration runs the programs of the theaters; it inspires hundreds of [cartoons]; it is a staple of conversation at private dinners and in the Clubs. The serious class of Englishmen including the best friends of the United States feel that the Administration's reliance on notes has reduced our Government to a third or fourth rate power. There is even talk of spheres of German influence in the United States as in China.

No Government could fall lower in English opinion than we shall fall if more notes are sent to Austria or to Germany. The only way to keep any shred of English respect is the immediate dismissal without more parleying of every German and Austrian official at Washington. Nobody here believes that such an act would provoke war.

I can do no real service by mincing matters. [My previous telegrams] and letters have been purposely restrained as this one. We have now come to the parting of the ways. If English respect be worth preserving at all, it can be preserved only by immediate action. Any other course than immediate [severing] of diplomatic relations with both Germany and Austria will deepen the English opinion into a conviction [that the administration was insincere] when it sent the LUSITANIA notes and that its notes and protests need not be taken seriously on any subject.

And English opinion is allied opinion. The Italian Ambassador said to me: "What has happened? The United States of today is not the United States of fifteen years ago when I lived in [Washington."] French officers and members of the Government who come here express themselves even more strongly than do the British.

The English newspapers today publish translations of ridicule of the United States from German papers.

Steamers to the United States are still held up at Liverpool presumably because of submarine activity in the Irish Sea.

Amambassador London.

T telegram (WP, DLC).
¹ Corrections from a typed copy enclosed in WHP to WW, Feb. 23, 1916, ALS (WP, DLC).
² Disputing about.

From William Cox Redfield

My dear Mr. President: Washington January 4, 1916.

Some days ago I handed you copy of a proposed anti-dumping bill, approved by myself and by the Federal Trade Commission,¹ for your consideration as to its form and as to the wisdom of causing it to be introduced as early in the session as practicable. May I now present certain considerations bearing on this matter.

Some anti-dumping legislation is necessary in order to allay serious anxiety now existing in some portions of the business world, and with cause (see pp. 40 and 41 of my Annual Report), to permit a large and earlier investment in new American industries (for example, dyestuffs) which are definitely threatened with attempted destruction by means on the part of foreign producers that would not be tolerated in our own country, and to give assurance of our intention when just cause shall exist to support legitimate American industries, who ask no special privileges but only assurance that they shall not be destroyed by Government-aided foreign monopolies combined for that purpose.

Two different systems are in use for providing the security suggested, one in Canada, one in Australia. The Canadian sys-

tem is that of special tariffs. The Australian system is in substance to declare the so-called "dumping" of the suggested kind
an offense.

A tariff will not serve the purpose. There is reason to believe
that the combined German dyestuff makers, for example, could
afford to absorb and would in fact absorb a duty as high as 50
per cent over a period of several years, and having absorbed
would still deliberately undersell any American producer for the
purpose of driving the American industry out of business. I have
been told by a representative of the German industries that the
German verein would not permit the growth of an American dyestuff industry. Their method is simple. They would secure
reduced rates from Government-owned railways and Govern-
ment-influenced steamship lines. I know of a case where a special
rate was given a German manufacturer on a German railway
for the purpose of securing export business which was reduced
45 per cent from the regular rate. They would enhance prices to
other nations and to their own peoples, and if there were any
loss it would be distributed among the entire industry. The value
of the American market is such they could well afford to do this
for two years or more if they might control our markets thereafter. American dyestuff manufacturers have frankly stated to
me that they ask no tariff protection as that is commonly understood. They are willing to work under the Underwood tariff,
and even to undertake the manufacture of such dyestuffs as are
on the free list, for example, indigo. They do feel, and in my
judgment rightly, that we ought to prohibit the deliberate
destruction of their industry on the part of a foreign monopoly
backed by its Government.

Furthermore, the foreign monopoly named has after many
years of searching scientific study developed its processes and
perfected its methods, and time is required for the new American industry to do this same work. The American manufacturers
express no doubt of their ability to compete on even terms with
the foreign producers so soon as they have had time to develop
the necessary processes and actually get their goods upon the
market. They are now producing certainly four times and probably six times as much as they were at the beginning of 1915.

I take the dyestuff manufacture as an example but there are
others. We have begun making chemical porcelain, filter paper,
blue print paper, and other articles heretofore solely made
abroad. Each of these industries is threatened in a like manner.

I have no fixed ideas that I wish to urge. The bill submitted
to you seems the simplest and most effective way. The tariff

method proposed by an amendment to the Underwood law does not seem to me effective. I think the manufacturers feel so too. We ought, however, to do something effective because it is right, because both equity and patriotism call for it. To be frank, I think we should be seriously handicapped in the fall campaign if we failed to do something definite on this important subject at this session.   Yours very truly,   William C. Redfield

TLS (WP, DLC).

1 It is missing. Redfield had, however, suggested similar legislation in his annual report. He proposed to make it "unlawful to sell or purchase articles of foreign origin or manufacture where the prices to be paid are materially below the current rates for such articles in the country of production or from which shipment is made, in case such prices substantially lessen competition on the part of the American producers or tend to create a monopoly in American markets in favor of the foreign producer, and that it be made unlawful for any person to buy, sell, or contract for the sale of articles of foreign origin, or to fix a price for same or to make a rebate upon such price, conditioned upon the purchaser thereof not using or dealing in wares produced or sold by the competitors of the manufacturer or seller, where the effect is to substantially lessen competition in the production in the United States of such articles, or tends to create a monopoly in the sale of such articles in American markets in favor of a foreign producer." U. S. Department of Commerce, *Report of the Secretary of Commerce, 1915* (Washington, 1916), p. 43.

From Albert Sidney Burleson, with Enclosures

My dear Mr. President: Washington January 4, 1916.

I enclose herewith a letter which I have this moment received from Mr. Marbury.

I regret very much that conditions have developed which necessitate the shortening of your well deserved vacation.
          Faithfully yours, A. S. Burleson

E N C L O S U R E   I

William Luke Marbury to Albert Sidney Burleson

My dear General: Baltimore January 3rd, 1916.

My friend Mr. Charles H. Grasty has just been showing me a letter which he has written to the President.

I am so heartily in accord with the views expressed in that letter, and am so anxious to make sure that it reaches the President without delay, that I have induced Mr. Grasty to let me send it to you by a special messenger, and I now want to ask you to do me the favor to personally present it to the President, if possible, before the next meeting of the Cabinet to consider the war situation.

I don't want to add anything to the views expressed in Mr. Grasty's letter further than to say that I am profoundly convinced that the present situation of this Country as the richest country on earth, the most defenseless and without a single friend among the nations, is one full of peril and it ought not to be permitted to continue.

It would require many years to provide ourselves with the military and naval force necessary to make us safe from attack. It would probably require but a few minutes interchange of views between our Government and the Governments of the Allies to insure an arrangement which would make us safe for all times.

I am going to try to see you personally tomorrow.

Sincerely yours,   W L Marbury

E N C L O S U R E   I I

From Charles Henry Grasty

Dear Mr. President: Baltimore, Jan. 3rd, 1916.

When I went to Europe about a year ago, you were good enough to indicate in a letter to me that suggestions in respect to the war situation would be acceptable.

Of the eighteen months war period, I have spent a year in Europe and six months in America, the last two or three months in a tour of the west and northwest. I think I know something of conditions abroad and sentiment at home.

As regards the situation abroad the vital fact of the hour is that the enmity which is growing up in the hearts of the people of England and France against the United States, leaves us without a single friend. I will not go into the question as to whether there are any adequate grounds for the existence of such enmity, but I know that it does exist to an extent of which the American people have no idea whatever. And in my opinion we stand in imminent danger of European attack after the war.

The chances of getting through Congress and carrying out in time to do any good a program of preparedness adequate to protect us from that danger are so slim as to be negligible.

I believe that duty and self-preservation call for immediate action by our Government along the following lines:

1—Compel Austria and Germany immediately to settle the Persia, Ancona and Lusitania cases, precisely as indicated in our notes, every "i" to be dotted and every "t" crossed.

2—Either of them failing to comply, or after compliance a

repetition of the outrages occurring, take the first step toward war.

3—Conclude arrangements with the Allies based on the precedent condition of their acceptance of the Monroe Doctrine and their future co-operation in its maintenance; the United States, to cut off all supplies from Germany direct or through neutrals; put her financial and industrial resources at the disposal of the Allies and give naval assistance if needed.

I have the honor to remain,

Most sincerely, Charles H Grasty

TLS (WP, DLC).

To Joseph Patrick Tumulty

Dear Tumulty: [The White House, Jan. 5, 1916]

I warmly appreciate this and hope that you will say so to Mr. Miranda, but I feel that so long as I am President it would not be proper for me to seem to be trying to exploit my views in a money-making way.[1] The President.

TL (WP, DLC).

[1] Thomas N. Miranda, business manager of the B. S. Moss Motion Picture Corp. and assistant general manager of the New York News Service. He sought permission to hire a competent screenwriter for a motion picture based on Wilson's *When A Man Comes to Himself.* T. N. Miranda to JPT, Dec. 31, 1915, TLS (WP, DLC).

To Endicott Peabody[1]

My dear Dr. Peabody, The White House 5 January, 1916.

It was a pleasure to catch a glimpse of you at the Hot Springs, and I am only sorry that I did not have a chance to have a talk with you about Groton. My interest in the School has always been very great and my association with its 'Boys,' old and young, very delightful and I wish for you and for all who work for the School a New Year of unbroken and happy good fortune.

Cordially and sincerely Yours, Woodrow Wilson

ALS (MHi).

[1] Founder and headmaster of Groton School.

To Albert Sidney Burleson

My dear Burleson: The White House January 5, 1916

Thank you sincerely for your letter of yesterday with its enclosures, the letter from Mr. Marbury and the letter from Mr.

Grasty. I have read both with close attention and am very much impressed by their contents.

In haste   Affectionately yours,   Woodrow Wilson

TLS (A. S. Burleson Papers, DLC).

To Charles Henry Grasty

Personal.

My dear Mr. Grasty: The White House January 5, 1916

I have your letter of January third and have read it with profound interest. No one could help being impressed by the view which it presents and I am sincerely obliged to you for writing to me so frankly.

Cordially and sincerely yours,   Woodrow Wilson

TLS (R. S. Baker Coll., DLC).

From Robert Lansing

PERSONAL AND CONFIDENTIAL:

My dear Mr. President: Washington January 5, 1916.

The Danish Minister left with me this noon a paraphrase of a cablegram which he had received yesterday from his Government—a copy of which is herewith enclosed.[1]

You will perceive that the Danish Government continues to insist upon their previously stated consideration for the Danish West Indies, namely, 100,000,000 kroner, which is equivalent to $27,000,000. I would like your views in regard to the matter. I confess that the amount seems to me large. At the same time I believe the purchase of the Islands would meet with general approval in view of the public opinion of the country in regard to national defense. I should dislike very much to see the negotiations fail, or the treaty if negotiated, fail on account of the amount agreed upon as the purchase price.

Do you think it would be well for you to take the matter up with Senator Stone, or any other Senators, in order to find out their opinion as to what the temper of the Senate would be in case we made a treaty on the basis of $27,000,000?

Faithfully yours, Robert Lansing

TLS (SDR, RG 59, 711.5914/55½, DNA).
[1] C. Brün, "Paraphrase of Cablegram received on January 4th, 1916 from the Danish Minister of Foreign Affairs," HwS MS (SDR, RG 59, 711.5914/55½, DNA). De Scavenius explained that Denmark asked thirty million dollars for the Danish West Indies in order to "render opposition difficult" and to cover the

great costs of protecting Denmark's neutrality in the war. He doubted that the difference between twenty and thirty million dollars would be important to the United States in light of the sums proposed for preparedness, but he thought that his country could accept an offer of $27,000,000.

Two Letters from Robert Latham Owen

My dear Mr. President: [Washington] January 5, 1916.

I wish to strongly urge upon your attention the importance of putting upon the Supreme Bench, in place of the Late Justice Lamar,[1] a man who has demonstrated his complete sympathy with the Progressive view, and shown himself to regard the interests of human beings as superior to the interests of property holding.

I feel very strongly on this matter, and hope you will not lose sight of this vital distinction in making your nomination. We have not on the bench a single progressive man, in my point of view.   Yours, very respectfully,   Robt. L. Owen

[1] Joseph Rucker Lamar had died on January 2.

My dear Mr. President: [Washington] January 5, 1916

I wish to call your attention very expressly to the importance of making the Corrupt Practices Act[1] introduced by Senator Kern an Administration measure. I believe unless this is done and this Act put into effect, the Democrats may expect another Mark Hanna campaign, with the possibility of infinite harm to the Nation.

I venture to remind you that while you received an overwhelming electoral vote, nevertheless, out of the 15,000,000 votes you only received 6,293,000 while the men who believed in the protective tariff principle received over 7,600,000 and the socialist vote increased nearly a half million from 1908 to 1912.

It is of the greatest importance, in my opinion, to prevent the Republicans coming together and using the protective tariff issue to the disadvantage of the Democratic Party. As a matter of Party expediency, I think we should pass a bill providing for a non-partisan, permanent tariff commission, with a maximum and minimum schedule, within which there should be a mobility of the tariff, with authority vested in the President to make reciprocal arrangements for the purpose of enlarging our foreign commerce and for the further purpose of enabling the President to raise the rate, where necessary, to enlarge our revenue, in such instances where it can be done without injury to American commerce, and further, to enable the President to safe-guard American enterprise against unfair practices from abroad, such as the shipment of goods into this country for sale at a price under the normal cost of production.

By having expert men of a high class to ascertain the facts, and the changing facts, bearing upon the question of the cost of production at home and abroad, the President would be adequately and properly advised, and I am willing to trust any President that the people of the United States would ever elect.

But, as a matter of Party expediency, such a tariff commission would conciliate two millions or three millions of progressive men who would be glad to support the Democratic Party except for their obcession on the protective tariff principle.

I demonstrated from the fourteen schedules in my speech on the tariff in 1908, the utter fallacy of the claim that a high protective tariff was necessary, based upon the labor cost, by showing that the total labor cost did not approximate in any case the tariff rates fixed or proposed.

I wish to speak to you with regard to this at your early convenience.   Very respectfully,   Robt. L. Owen

TLS (WP, DLC).
  [1] One of many bills introduced in the Senate and House to revise, amend, and codify laws concerning publicity for contributions and expenditures made to influence the election of senators, representatives, the Vice-President, and the President, and the amount of money to be spent in campaigns for each office.

From Benjamin Ryan Tillman

Dear Mr. President: Washington. January 5, 1916.

While the matter is fresh on my mind I am writing to remind you of a promise you made in the Navy Department to help me press through Congress the Bill I introduced for the construction of an Armor Plant.[1]

The Senate Naval Committee has just had a meeting, or rather an attempted meeting; for we did not get a quorum. The Republicans are lined up against anything being done. Senator Penrose wants hearings, the meaning of which you know. The Democrats as usual were, many of them, absent. This is a vice of all the committees I serve on. The Democrats are indifferent, and seem to be unconscious of their duty; and are unwilling to learn the value of promptitude in attending committee meetings. The Republicans are always present.

If you have any idea as to how you could expedite matters, and let us get the Bill on the Calendar both in the Senate and the House, please put them into affect at once. Otherwise, with the immense building program looming ahead of us, the Government will be unmercifully robbed; and money is too scarce in the Treasury and the necessity for new taxation too evident to allow this if we Democrats can help it.

Please help me if you can.

Very sincerely yours,   B. R. Tillman

TLS (WP, DLC).

¹ Tillman had introduced a bill appropriating $11,000,000 to construct a government-owned plant to manufacture armor plate for the navy's ships. An opponent of the so-called Armor Trust since 1896, he had fought to lower the prices charged by Bethlehem Steel Co. and Carnegie, Phipps and Co., the two producers, and had long agitated for governmental competition with their monopoly. See Francis Butler Simkins, *Pitchfork Ben Tillman: South Carolinian* (Baton Rouge, La., 1944), pp. 347-52 and 512-13; and Link, *Confusions and Crises*, pp. 335-36.

From Walter Hines Page

Dear Mr. President: London, Jan. 5, 1915 [1916]

I wish—an impossible thing, of course—that some sort of guidance could be given to the American correspondents of the English newspapers. Almost every day they telegraph about the visits of the Austrian chargé or the German ambassador to the State Dp't to assure Mr. Lansing that their governments will of course make a satisfactory explanation of the latest torpedo-act in the Mediterranean or to "take one further step in reaching a satisfactory understanding about the *Lusitania*." They usually go on to say also that more Notes are in preparation to Germany or to Austria. The impression made upon the European mind is that the German and Austrian officials in Washington are leading the Administration on to endless discussion, endless Notes, endless hesitation. Nobody in Europe regards their pledges or promises worth anything at all: the *Arabic* follows the *Lusitania*, the *Hesperian* follows the *Arabic*. The *Persia* follows the *Ancona*. "Still conferences and Notes continue," these people say, "proving that the American government, which took so proper and high a stand in the *Lusitania* Notes, is paralysed—in a word, is hoodwinked and 'worked' by the Germans." And so long as these diplomatic representatives are permitted to remain in the United States, "to explain," "to parley" and to declare that the destruction of American lives and property is disavowed by their governments, and to send their dispatches in neutral bags &c. &c. &c., atrocities on sea and land will of course continue; and they feel that our Government by keeping these German and Austrian representatives in Washington condones and encourages them and their Governments.

This is a temperate and even restrained statement of the English feeling and (as far as I can make out) of the whole European feeling.

It has been said here that every important journal published in neutral or allied European countries, daily, weekly, or monthly, which deals with public affairs, has expressed a loss of respect for the U. S. Gov't and that most of them make continuous severe criticisms (with surprise and regret) of our failure by action to live up to the level of our *Lusitania* notes. I had (judiciously) two American journalists, resident here—men of judgment and character—to inquire how true this declaration is. After talking with neutral and allied journalists here and with men whose business it is to read the journals of the continent, they reported that this declaration is substantially true—that the whole European press (outside Germany & its allies) uses the same tone towards our Government that the English press uses—of disappointment verging on contempt, and many of them explain our keeping diplomatic intercourse with Germany by saying that we are afraid of the German vote, or of civil war, or that the peace-at-any-price people really rule the U. S. and have paralysed our power to act —even to cut off diplomatic relations with governments that have insulted and defied us.

Another (similar) declaration is that practically all men of public influence in England and in the European allied and neutral countries have publicly or privately expressed themselves to the same effect. The report that I have about that is less definite than about the newspapers, for, of course, no one can say just what proportion of men of public influence have so expressed themselves; but the number who have so expressed themselves is overwhelming.

In this Kingdom, where I can myself form some opinion, more or less accurate, and where I can check or verify my opinion by various methods—I am afraid, as I have frequently already reported, that the generation now living will never wholly regain the respect for our Gov't that it had a year ago. I will give you three little indications of this feeling: it wd. be easy to write down hundreds of them:

(1) The governing class: Austen Chamberlain told Mrs. Page a few nights ago that for sentimental reasons only he wd. be gratified to see the U. S. in the war along with the Allies, but that merely sentimental reasons were not a sufficient reason for war —by no means; that he felt most grateful for the sympathetic attitude of the large mass of American people, that he had no right to expect anything from our Government whose neutral position

was entirely proper. Then he added, "But what I can't for the life of me understand is your Government's failure to express its disapproval of the German utter disregard of its *Lusitania* Notes. After 8 months, it has done nothing but write more Notes. My love for America, I must confess, is offended at this inaction and—puzzled. I can't understand it. You will pardon me, I am sure."

(2) "Middle class" opinion: A common nickname for Americans in the financial and newspaper districts of London is "Tooprouds."

(3) The Man in the Street: At one of the moving-picture shows in a large theatre a little while ago they filled in an interval by throwing on the screen the picture of the monarch, or head of state, and of the flag of each of the principal nations. When the American picture appeared, there was such hissing and groaning as caused the managers hastily to move that picture off the screen.

Some time ago I wrote House of some such incidents and expressions as these;[1] and he wrote me that they were only part & parcel of the continuous British criticism of their own Government—in other words, a part of the passing hysteria of war.[2] This remark shows how House was living in an atmosphere of illusion. As the matter stands to-day our Government has sunk lower, as regards British and European opinion, than it has ever before been in our time, not as a part of the hysteria of war but as a result of this process of reasoning, whether it be right or wrong:

We said that we shd. hold the Germans to strict accountability on account of the *Lusitania.* We have not settled that yet and we still allow the German ambassador to discuss it after the *Hesperian* and other such acts showed that his *Arabic* pledge was worthless. The *Lusitania* grows larger and larger in European memory and imagination. It looks as if it wd. become the great type of war atrocities & barbarities. I have seen pictures of the drowned women & children used even on Christmas cards. And there is documentary proof in our hands that the warning, wh. was really an advance announcement, of that disaster was paid for by the German ambassador and charged to his Government. It is the *Lusitania* that has caused European opinion to regard our foreign policy as weak. It is not the wish for us to go to war. No such general wish exists.

I do not know, Mr. President, who else, if anybody, puts these facts before you with this complete frankness. But I can do no less and do my duty.

No Englishman, but two quite intimate friends, has spoken to me about our Gov't for months. But I detect all the time a tone of pity & grief in their studied courtesy and in their avoidance of the subject. And they talk to every other American in the Kingdom. It is often made unpleasant for Americans in the clubs and in the pursuit of their regular business and occupations; and it is always our inaction about the *Lusitania*. Our controversy with the British Gov't causes little feeling and that is a sort of echo of the *Lusitania*. They feel that we haven't lived up to our promises and professions.

That is the whole story.

Believe me yours always heartily,   Walter H. Page

The dismissal of Dumba and of the attachés has had little more effect on opinion here than the dismissal of the Turkish ambassador. Sending these was regarded as merely kicking the dogs of the man who had stolen our sheep.

ALS (WP, DLC).
  1 WHP to EMH, July 21, 1915, ALS (E. M. House Papers, CtY).
  2 EMH to WHP, Aug. 4, 1915, printed as an Enclosure with EMH to WW, Aug. 4, 1915, Vol. 34.

From Robert Lansing

My dear Mr. President: [Washington] January 6, 1916.

Since I communicated with you this morning I have had an opportunity to look over some of the newspapers and I find a general idea prevails that the plan of a Pan American Treaty involves the guarantee of republican forms of government.

It seems to me it would be well, therefore, if possible, for you to make clear tonight that the plan does not contemplate a guaranty of republican forms of government, but removes from the benefit of the guaranty of territory and independence a nation which abandons the republican form. The guaranty of a republican form would, of course, be a direct interference with the internal affairs of a country and entirely contrary to the views which we have expressed and the course which we have followed in regard to the sovereign right of a people to decide their domestic questions without outside interference.

I make this suggestion in view of the opposition which may be aroused, not only in this country, but in other American republics, if it is thought that there is any plan to coerce the people of a sovereign state in the conduct of their internal affairs.

                Faithfully yours,   [Robert Lansing]

CCL (SDR, RG 59, 710.11/224A, DNA).

John Barrett to Joseph Patrick Tumulty

Washington, D.C.
Dear Mr. Tumulty: Thursday AM [Jan. 6, 1916]

With reference to the President's address tonight which will be the climax of our great Pan American Congress & in which the Latin American delegates are expectantly interested, is it possible that the President might wish to see me for a few moments today to help put him in close touch with the drift & thought of the Congress?

If so, please telephone me at Branch 155, Main 4420, the New Willard, where, during the Congress, I have my headquarters.[1]

Is it not possible to have an advance of the President's speech for the press & to be *translated* into Spanish & ready to cable to South America today or tonight,—for the papers all over South America are asking me for it.

If not, please arrange that it be typewritten immediately after delivery & let one of my men, who will be in close touch with the official stenographer, get a copy as soon as possible to translate & put on the cable.

Please also say to the President that *there will be no other speaker* except the Chilean Ambassador, who is President of the Congress & will introduce the President.

We hope to begin promptly at nine & have urged the delegates to be on hand before the President arrives.

Hastily Yours,   John Barrett

ALS (WP, DLC).
[1] Wilson wrote "Thanks!" on this letter, but there is no evidence that he met Barrett before delivering his address to the congress.

An Outline of an Address

PAN-AMERICAN SCIENTIFIC CONGRESS.
Washington, 6 January, 1916.

Salutation and felicitation. Sexperiences of the Sessions.

This drawing together of the Americas long dreamed of. It is delightful to see it becoming a reality on the solid foundation of a realization of common needs, common principles, common purposes.

The international language of science, as well as the universal language of commerce, a most suitable vehicle in which to express this intellectual and practical community of interest.

But our thought cannot pause at the artificial frontiers of these fields. It must of necessity go on to certain very practical and far-reaching inferences. Science and commerce and the practical arts of life can thrive only in the air of peace and an ordered political life among the nations. They are of necessity silent amidst war and revolution.

The recent Pan-American financial conference made us very conscious of all this. Governments must cooperate and laws agree if financiers and merchants are to have successful intercourse with one another and render one another acceptable service. And this Congress, devoted though it is to the discussion of questions which seem to have no direct or immediate relation to politics, has developed a consciousness of the same thing.

While events move statesmen, unless they be asleep or indifferent, must think and act; and the statesmen of the two Americas have been thinking and preparing for action by a very candid and practical interchange of views.

They have seen that underneath and back of all their community of interest in the general fields of thought and action there necessarily lay a political community of interest, and that that interest would best express itself in definite guarantees of peace and amity that would make the intercourse of the states of this hemisphere the intercourse of friends and equals.

The Monroe Doctrine the United States proclaimed on her own single authority and has been always ready to maintain on her own single responsibility. But that doctrine demanded nothing more than that the governments on the other side of the water should never attempt to extend their political systems to this side of the water. It did not di[s]close the attitude of the United States with regard to the exercise of her own power on this side the sea; and if the states of the Americas have not hitherto established more cordial intimacies, it has no doubt been very largely because of fears and suspicions on that score.

This is the field that is clearing up now. More and more within the last few years the statesmen of the two continents have been drawn together in close and confidential conference, and their thought has taken this practical turn, that they must guarantee not only the safety of the Americas as against foreign aggression but also their domestic peace and security.

This they can, and I believe will, do by exchanging mutual guarantees of political independence and territorial integrity; by hastening the friendly settlement of all pending boundary disputes; by a joint adoption of the principle and practice of impartial inquiry and arbitration in respect of all matters in dispute among themselves; and by binding themselves to prevent the fitting out from the territory of any one of them of armed expeditions hostile to the established government of any neighbour state, and to prohibit the exportation of materials of war from one American republic to another to supply armed insurgents there.

These are actions of self-restraint and of mutual justice and respect. They are based upon a recognition of absolute equality of right and of political privilege among the states of America. They are guarantees of peace because they are guarantees against all selfish aggression and guarantees of actual community of political ideal and political purpose.

They are what the world has long striven towards and desired. God grant that America may have the high privilege of realizing them first among the nations of the world!

WWT MS (WP, DLC).

An Address to the Pan American Scientific Congress

[[Jan. 6, 1916]]

Mr. Ambassador, ladies, and gentlemen: It was a matter of sincere regret with me that I was not in the city to extend the greetings of the government to this distinguished body, and I am very happy that I have returned in time at least to extend to it my felicitations upon the unusual interest and success of its proceedings. I wish that it might have been my good fortune to be present at the sessions and instructed by the papers that were read. I have become somewhat inured to scientific papers in the course of a long experience, but I have never ceased to be instructed and to enjoy them. The sessions of this congress have been looked forward to with the greatest interest throughout this country, because there is no more certain evidence of intellectual life than the desire of men of all nations to share their thoughts with one another.

I have been told so much about the proceedings of this congress that I feel that I can congratulate you upon the increasing sense of comradeship and intimate intercourse which has marked its sessions from day to day. And it is a very happy circumstance in our view that this, perhaps the most vital and successful of the meetings of this congress, should have occurred in the capital of our own country, because we should wish to regard this as the universal place where ideas worthwhile are exchanged and shared. The drawing together of the Americas, ladies and gentlemen, has long been dreamed of and desired.

It is a matter of peculiar gratification, therefore, to see this great thing happen; to see the Americas drawing together, and not drawing together upon any insubstantial foundation of mere sentiment.

After all, even friendship must be based upon a perception of common sympathies, of common interests, of common ideals, and of common purposes. Men cannot be friends unless they intend the same things, and the Americas have more and more realized that in all essential particulars they intend the same thing with regard to their thought and their life and their activities. To be privileged, therefore, to see this drawing together in friendship and communion based upon these solid foundations affords everyone who looks on with open eyes peculiar satisfaction and joy. And it has seemed to me that the language of science, the language of impersonal thought, the language of those who think, not along the lines of individual interest, but along what are intended to be the direct and searching lines of truth itself, was a very fortunate language in which to express this community of interest and of sympathy. Science affords an international language, just as commerce also affords a universal language, because in each instance there is a universal purpose, a universal general plan of action. And it is a pleasing thought to those who have had something to do with scholarship that scholars have had a great deal to do with sowing the seeds of friendship between nation and nation. Truth recognizes no national boundaries. Truth permits no racial prejudices. And when men come to know each other and to recognize equal intellectual strength and equal intellectual sincerity and a common intellectual purpose, some of the best foundations of friendship are already laid.

But, ladies and gentlemen, our thought cannot pause at the artificial boundaries of the fields of science and of commerce. All boundaries that divide life into sections and interests are artificial, because life is all of a piece. You cannot treat part of it without by implication and indirection treating all of it, and the field of science is not to be distinguished from the field of life any more than the field of commerce is to be distinguished from the general field of life. No one who reflects upon the progress of science or the spread of the arts of peace, or the extension and perfection of any of the practical arts of life, can fail to see that there is only one atmosphere that these things can breathe, and that is an atmosphere of mutual confidence and of peace and of ordered political life among the nations. Amidst war and revolution even the voice of science must for the most part be silent, and revolution tears up the very roots of everything that makes life go steadily forward and the light grow from generation to generation. For nothing stirs passion like political disturbance, and passion is the enemy of truth.

These things were realized with peculiar vividness and said with unusual eloquence in a recent conference held in this city for the purpose of considering the financial relations between the two continents of America, because it was perceived that financiers can do nothing without the cooperation of governments, and that, if merchants would deal with one another, laws must agree with one another—that you cannot make laws vary without making them contradict, and that amidst contradictory laws the easy flow of commercial intercourse is impossible, and that, therefore, a financial congress naturally led to all the inferences of politics. For politics I conceive to be nothing more than the science of the ordered progress of society along the lines of greatest usefulness and convenience to itself. I have never, in my own mind, admitted the distinction between the other departments of life and politics. Some people devote themselves so exclusively to politics that they forget there is any other part of life, and, so soon as they do, they become that thing which is described as a "mere politician." Statesmanship begins where these connections, so unhappily lost, are re-established. The statesman stands in the midst of life to interpret life in political action.

The conference to which I have referred marked the consciousness of the two Americas that, economically, they are very dependent upon one another, that they have a great deal that it is very desirable they should exchange and share with one another, that they have kept unnaturally and unfortunately separated and apart when they had a manifest and obvious community of interest. And the object of that conference was to ascertain the practical means by which the commercial and practical intercourse of the two continents could be quickened and facilitated. And where events move, statesmen, if they be not indifferent or be not asleep, must think and act. For my own part, I congratulate myself upon living in a time when these things, always susceptible of intellectual demonstration, have begun to be very widely and universally appreciated and when the statesmen of the two American continents have more and more come into candid, trustful, mutual conference, comparing views as to the practical and friendly way of helping one another and of setting forward every handsome enterprise on this side the Atlantic.

But these gentlemen have not conferred without realizing that back of all the material community of interest of which I have spoken there lies and must lie a community of political interest. I have been told a very interesting fact—I hope it is true—that, while this congress has been discussing science, it has been, in spite of itself, led into the feeling that behind the science there was some inference with regard to politics, and that if the Americas were to be united in thought, they must in some degree sympathetically be united in action. What these statesmen, who have been conferring from month to month in Washington have come to realize is, that, back of the community of material interest, there is a community of political interest.

I hope I can make clear to you in what sense I use those words. I do not mean a mere partnership in the things that are expedient. I mean what I was trying to indicate a few moments ago—that you cannot separate politics from these things, that you cannot have real intercourse of any kind amidst political jealousies, which is only another way of saying that you cannot commune unless you are friends, and that friendship is based upon your political relations with each other perhaps more than upon any other kind of relationships between nations. If nations are politically suspicious of one another, all their intercourse is embarrassed. That is the reason I take it, if it be true, as I hope it is, that your thoughts, even during this congress, though the questions you are called to consider are apparently so foreign to politics, have again and again been drawn back to the political inferences. The object of American statesmanship on the two continents is to see to it that American friendship is founded on a rock.

The Monroe Doctrine was proclaimed by the United States on her own authority. It always has been maintained and always will be maintained upon her own responsibility. But the Monroe Doctrine demanded merely that European governments should not attempt to extend their political systems to this side of the Atlantic. It did not disclose the use which the United States intended to make of her power on this side of the Atlantic. It was a hand held up in warning, but there was no promise in it of what America was going to do with the implied and partial protectorate which she apparently was trying to set up on this side of the water. And I believe you will sustain me in the statement that it has been fears and suspicions on this score which have hitherto prevented the greater intimacy and confidence and trust between the Americas. The states of America have not been certain what the United States would do with her power. That doubt

must be removed. And latterly there has been a very frank interchange of views between the authorities in Washington and
those who represented the other states of this hemisphere, an
interchange of views cheering and hopeful, because based upon
an increasingly sure appreciation of the spirit in which they were
undertaken. These gentlemen have seen that, if America is to
come into her own, into her legitimate own, in a world of peace
and order, she must establish the foundations of amity so that
no one will hereafter doubt them.

I hope and I believe that this can be accomplished. These conferences have enabled me to foresee how it will be accomplished.
It will be accomplished, in the first place, by the states of America uniting in guaranteeing to each other, absolutely, political
independence and territorial integrity. In the second place, and
as a necessary corollary to that, guaranteeing the agreement to
settle all pending boundary disputes as soon as possible and by
amicable process—by agreeing that all disputes among themselves, should they unhappily arise, will be handled by patient,
impartial investigation and settled by arbitration; and the agreement necessary to the peace of the Americas, that no state of
either continent will permit revolutionary expeditions against
another state to be fitted out on its territory, and that they will
prohibit the exportation of the munitions of war for the purpose
of supplying revolutionists against neighboring governments.

You see what our thought is, gentlemen—not only the international peace of America, but the domestic peace of America. If
American states are constantly in ferment, if any of them are
constantly in ferment, there will be a standing threat to their
relations with one another. It is just as much to our interest to
assist each other to the orderly processes within our own borders as it is to orderly processes in our controversies with one another. These are very practical suggestions which have sprung up
in the minds of thoughtful men, and I, for my part, believe that
they are going to lead the way to something that America has
prayed for for many a generation. For they are based, in the
first place, so far as the stronger states are concerned, upon the
handsome principle of self-restraint and respect for the rights of
everybody. They are based upon the principles of absolute
political equality among the states, equality of right, not equality
of indulgence. They are based, in short, upon the solid, eternal
foundations of justice and humanity. No man can turn away
from these things without turning away from the hope of the
world. These are things, ladies and gentlemen, for which the

world has hoped and waited with prayerful heart. God grant that it may be given to America to lift this light on high for the illumination of the world.

Printed in *Address of President Wilson at the Pan American Scientific Congress* . . . (Washington, 1916); with corrections from a reading of the CLSsh notes (C. L. Swem Coll., NjP).

To Benjamin Ryan Tillman

My dear Senator: The White House January 6, 1916

I have your letter of January fifth. I remember very well my promise to help all I could with the bill for the construction of an armor plant and I stand ready to redeem my promise, but you must be my guide as to how I can help. If you will tell me what you think the best way, I shall be very glad indeed to adopt it. Do you think I had better see Senator Kern and other members of the Steering Committee?

When I get an opportunity you may be sure I will speak to Senators about this for it is a matter which I have very much at heart and I hope you can give me serviceable tips.

Cordially and faithfully yours,   Woodrow Wilson

TLS (B. R. Tillman Papers, ScCleU).

From Robert Lansing

My dear Mr. President: Washington January 6, 1916.

I am very much obliged to you for letting me see Mr. Grasty's letter, which I have read with interest and return to you herewith.   Faithfully yours,   Robert Lansing

TLS (WP, DLC).

To Edward Mandell House[1]

Washington, January 7, 1916. 6 p.m.

No. 1. Second ANCONA note from Austria made splendid impression. Sinking of PERSIA caused note to be forgotten and created utmost indignation. Strong feeling that something must be done by Administration but as there is no evidence as to how ship was sunk no plan of action settled on yet. *German and Austrian Governments deny knowledge.* Austrian representative here much disturbed and assures us that his Government would repudiate act if it is found to have been Austrian submarine. Senate has begun discussion of foreign affairs. Strong feeling expressed because of English attitude but no embargo can pass nor is any action by Congress probable unless with President's approval. Republicans standing by President. Protest sent to England on seizure of mails on neutral ships.[2] Still great complaint of interference with our trade by Great Britain.   Lansing.

T telegram (SDR, RG 59, 865.857 An 2/112½A, DNA).
  [1] Lansing's addition printed in italics.
  [2] RL to WHP, Jan. 4, 1916, *FR-WWS 1916*, pp. 591-92.

To Robert Lansing

My dear Mr. Secretary,   The White House. 7 January, 1916.
   The acquisition of the Danish West Indies seems to me of sufficient importance to justify us in negotiating on the basis of twenty-seven millions. I think it would be a mistake to break off at this evidently opportune time on a question of money, within reasonable bounds.
   I take it, from your letter, that your own judgment is the same.
                          Faithfully Yours,   W.W.

WWTLI (SDR, RG 59, 711.5914/56½, DNA).

Two Letters to Robert Latham Owen

My dear Senator: [The White House] January 7, 1916
   I warmly sympathize with the views expressed in your letter of January fifth about the sort of man who should be appointed to the vacant seat on the Supreme Court, and I hope with all my heart I can find just such a man.
               Cordially and sincerely yours,   Woodrow Wilson

My dear Senator: [The White House] January 7, 1916
   I would be very much obliged if you would let me see a copy of the Corrupt Practices Act which you have introduced. I think you know how deeply I am interested in this whole question and I want to cooperate in every way possible.
               Cordially and sincerely yours,   Woodrow Wilson

TLS (Letterpress Books, WP, DLC).

From Robert Lansing, with Enclosure

My dear Mr. President: [Washington] January 7, 1916.

I have been thinking over, as I know you have, some means of placing submarine warfare on a basis which will prevent the horrors which have characterized it in the past.

I think that I appreciate the German point of view in regard to the danger to a submarine in attacking an armed merchant vessel, and have prepared a memorandum on the subject, which I enclose.

If the argument has merit the method of reaching a settlement on a basis which would safeguard human life would seem to be an agreement by Germany and Austria not to torpedo enemy vessels without putting the people on board in safety, provided they did not continue to flee, in consideration of an agreement by the Entente Powers not to permit their merchant ships to carry an armament.

I am sure the Teutonic Powers would agree to this, and I cannot see how the Entente Powers could reasonably object to such an arrangement, particularly in view of the fact that there is no case recorded to my knowledge of a submarine being destroyed by gunfire from a merchant vessel.

This plan would be practically a *modus vivendi* and could be made reciprocal on account of the activities of British submarines in the Baltic.

Would you advise my attempting to obtain such agreements?

Faithfully yours,   Robert Lansing

TLS (Lansing Letterpress Book, SDR, RG 59, DNA).

E N C L O S U R E

January 7, 1916

MEMORANDUM ON ARMED MERCHANT VESSELS AND SUBMARINE WARFARE.

The arming of merchant vessels is allowable when the armament is of a character which can be only used defensively.

When the statement as to the Status of Armed Merchant Vessels was issued in September, 1914, by the Department of State, the assertions contained as to the limitation of armament, which would give it a defensive character, was based on the use of naval ships in intercepting private commercial vessels. It was predicated manifestly on the defensive strength of ships of war, otherwise there would be no necessity to consider any restriction upon the armament carried by a merchant vessel.

Since the statement was issued the submarine has become a practical and successful agent in the capture and destruction of vessels of commerce, and, as a result, the principle on which the arming of merchant ships is declared to be allowable, should be applied to the new conditions created by this instrument of naval warfare.

Comparison of the defensive strength of naval vessels operating on the surface and submarines shows that the latter are almost defenseless in construction, their only means of protection from an enemy being their power to submerge. A merchant ship carrying a small calibre gun could destroy with one shot a submarine provided it came to the surface within range. Thus an armament, though falling within the limitations of defensive armament as previously defined, may be used effectively against a submarine. If it can be so used, it would appear to lose its defensive character.

The rule of visit, which is the only means of protecting private vessels engaged in commerce from being suddenly attacked and is the only means of putting in force the rule that the people on board shall be put in safety before a vessel is sunk, could hardly be required justly of a submarine, if the observation of the rule compels the submarine to expose itself to almost certain destruction by coming to the surface and offering itself as a target to a gun mounted on the merchant ship which it is required to hail and order to "lie to."

If it is admitted that a submarine may be employed in intercepting enemy's commerce and that in doing this it must hail vessels and put the passengers and crews in places of safety, it would appear to be a reasonable requirement that all merchant vessels should be without armament of any sort since a gun of whatever calibre and wherever mounted could be used offensively against a submarine on the surface with good prospect of destroying it.

A merchant vessel, therefore, carrying an armament should be treated by a belligerent or a neutral as an armed ship of the enemy and not possess the immunities attaching to private commercial vessels of belligerent nationality as now set forth in the rules of international law.

T memorandum (SDR, RG 59, 763.72/2351½, DNA).

From Robert Lansing, with Enclosures

PERSONAL AND CONFIDENTIAL:

My dear Mr. President: Washington January 7, 1916.

The German Ambassador has just called upon me and stated that he was instructed by his Government to say, in the first place, that they had heard through the press reports of the sinking of the PERSIA and that they had no information whatsoever in regard to it.

He then handed me a communication which he was also instructed to deliver, setting forth the attitude of the German Goverment in regard to submarine warfare in the Mediterranean. At his request I am making public this statement.

The Ambassador then handed me a communication in regard to the LUSITANIA case, which he said his Government wished to be considered confidential unless it was satisfactory to this Government, when it could be embodied in a more formal document. I enclose the communication, together with one marked "strictly confidential" relating to arbitration of questions of fact in connection with submarine warfare.

I have not studied the proposed reply of Germany in regard to the LUSITANIA with sufficient care to express a final opinion. There is lacking any recognition of liability since the indemnity which they proposed to pay is, in fact, on the basis of comity and not on the basis of right—at least that is my view at present. If in any way the agreement to pay the indemnity can be construed into a recognition of liability it would seem as if a final settlement of the case was very near.

I also enclose for your information an extract from the reply of the German Government in the FRYE case, which has a direct bearing on submarine warfare in general and must be read, I think, with these other communications. In view of that declaration I do not see why the German Government is not willing to definitely admit liability in the LUSITANIA case.

The German Ambassador desires that the reply in the FRYE case should be made public and, as I could see no reason to withhold it, I agreed to do so.

I hope that I may soon receive your views in regard to the communication relative to the LUSITANIA as I think the negotiation, if it is to be continued, should be pressed to speedy settlement.   Faithfully yours,   Robert Lansing

TLS (SDR, RG 59, 841.857 L 97/124½, DNA).

E N C L O S U R E   I

Lusitania Case.

Confidentially communicated, January 7/16, by German Ambassador.

The German submarine war against England's commerce at sea, as announced on February 4, 1915, is conducted in retaliation of England's inhuman war against Germany's commercial and industrial life. It is an acknowledged rule of international law that retaliation may be employed against acts committed in contravention of the law of nations. Germany is enacting such a retaliation, for it is England's endeavor to cut off all imports from Germany by preventing even legal commerce of the neutrals with her and thereby subjecting the German population to starvation.

In answer to these acts Germany is making efforts to destroy England's commerce at sea, at least as far as it is carried on by enemy vessels.

The question whether neutral interests may in any way be injured by retaliatory measures should, in this instance, be answered in the affirmative. The neutrals by allowing the crippling of their commerce with Germany contrary to international law which is an established fact cannot object to the retaliatory steps of Germany for reasons of neutrality. Besides, the German measures, announced in time, are such that neutrals easily could have avoided harmful consequences by not using enemy vessels employed in commerce with England. If Germany has notwithstanding limited her submarine warfare, this was done in view of her long standing friendship with the United States and in the expectation that the steps taken by the American Government in the meantime aiming at the restoration of the freedom of the seas would be successful.

The German Government, on the other hand, recognizes from the course which the negotiations so far have taken, the difficulty to reconcile in principle the American and the German point of view, as the interests and legal aspects of the neutrals and belligerents naturally do not agree in this point and as the illegality of the English course of procedure can hardly be regonized [recognized] in the United States as fully as it is in Germany. A perpetuation of this difference of opinion, however, would not tend to further the amicable relations between the United States and Germany which have never been disturbed and the continuation of which is so sincerely desired by both Governments. Actuated by this spirit the Imperial Government again expresses its deep regret at the death of American citizens caused by the sinking of the Lusitania and, in order to settle this question amicably, declares its readiness to pay indemnity for the losses inflicted.

E N C L O S U R E   I I

Handed me by German Amb. Jany 7/16 RL

Strictly confidential!

Upon request of the American Government the German Government is prepared in cases in which American interests are concerned, to have the questions of fact cleared up by an International Commission of Investigation in accordance with Section III of the Hague Arbitration Convention of October 18, 1907.

E N C L O S U R E   I I I

FOR THE PRESS.

January 7, 1916.

The German Ambassador today left at the Department of State under instructions from his Government the following communication:

1.) German submarines in the Mediterranean had, from the beginning, orders to conduct cruiser warfare against enemy merchant vessels only in accordance with general principles of international law, and in particular measures of reprisal, as applied in the war zone around the British Isles, were to be excluded.

2.) German submarines are therefore permitted to destroy enemy merchant vessels in the Mediterranean—i.e. passenger as well as freight ships as far as they do not try to escape or offer resistance—only after passengers and crews have been accorded safety.

3.) All cases of destruction of enemy merchant ships in the Mediterranean in which German submarines are concerned are made the subject of official investigation and, besides, submitted to regular prize court proceedings. In so far as American interests are concerned, the German Government will communicate the result to the American Government. Thus also in the "Persia" case if the circumstances should call for it.

4.) If Commanders of German submarines should not have obeyed the orders given to them, they will be punished; furthermore, the German Government will make reparation for damage caused by death of or injuries to American citizens.

E N C L O S U R E   I V

Extract from German note on FRYE case—11/29/1915

"Until the decision of the Permanent Court of Arbitration, the German Naval Forces will sink only such American vessels as are loaded with absolute contraband, when the preconditions provided by the Declaration of London are present. In this the German Government quite shares the view of the American Government that all possible care must be taken for the security of the crew and passengers of a vessel to be sunk. Consequently, the persons found on board of a vessel may not be ordered into her life-boats except when the general conditions, that is to say, the weather, the condition of the sea, and the neighborhood of the coasts afford absolute certainty that the boats will reach the nearest port. For the rest the German Government begs to point out that in cases where German naval forces have sunk neutral vessels for carrying contraband, no loss of life has yet occurred."

T MSS (SDR, RG 59, 841.857 L 97/124½, DNA).

A Telegram and a Letter from Edward Mandell House

[London, Jan. 7, 1916]

[Arrived yesterday.][1] Have had conference[s] with Sir Edward Grey and Balfour separately. The three of us will meet Monday to try to formulate some plan which I can submit to you and which they can recommend to their colleagues. Their minds run parallel with ours but I doubt their colleagues. Sir Edward Grey is now in favour of the freedom of the seas provided it includes the elimination of militarism, and further provided we will join in general court [covenant] to sustain it. Your action concerning LUSITANIA and PERSIA will have bearing on what can be done. Sir Edward Grey and Balfour understand but their colleagues are doubtful as to your intentions regarding a vigourous foreign policy. It would help [in] the conference Monday if you could cable me some assurance of your willingness to cooperate in a policy seeking to bring about and maintain permanent peace among civilized nations.

WWT decode of T telegram (WP, DLC).
¹ Text in brackets in this and following telegrams between Wilson and House from copies in the House Papers, CtY.

Dear Governor: London, January 7, 1916.

We arrived in London yesterday morning and during the day I had a conference with both Sir Edward Grey and Mr. Balfour, besides seeing several important editors like St Loe Strachey of the Spectator.

I have made engagements to meet everyone whom I had planned to see and am hoping to get to France within two weeks.

Page has shown me copies of his cablegrams and letters to you. There may be that feeling he describes in England, but it does not show itself in my presence.

I was with Sir Edward for an hour and a half yesterday and dined with Balfour, and the three of us are to lunch together Monday. When Sir Edward asked me what members of the Cabinet I wished to meet at lunch I suggested that he have only Balfour since we were the only three that spoke your language.

I told him if we failed to come to a better understanding with England and failed to help solve the problems brought about by this war properly, it would be because his government and people could not follow you to the heights you would go.

Having Page's expression of their opinion in mind I gave him what seemed to me to be the spirit of America. I asked him not to be misled by the motives which actuated New York, Chicago and some of the commercial centers, but to accept my word that we were not a people driven mad by money. On the contrary, I thought that no nation in the world had such lofty ideals and would be so willing to make sacrifices for them.

I recalled the fact that our population was made up of idealists that had left Europe for a larger freedom and this spirit was as strong now as it had been at any time in our existence.

I talked to him about our shipping troubles at some length and urged him to make matters easier for you. He explained the difficulties he encountered which he felt sure you did not fully realize. I will not go into an explanation of this now.

I touched lightly upon Spring-Rice and sowed the seeds for a further discussion.

He admits that things have gone badly for the Allies, but declares that England was never more resolute than now and that the outcome will be successful. I find all with whom I have talked so far of the same opinion. Their confidence seems greater now than it did when I was here before.

Sir Edward showed me a despatch from Lansing concerning the note. I do not think he liked its tone. It was rather peremptory.[1]

I am writing with some haste in order to catch an early boat.

Affectionately yours,   E. M. House

TLS (WP, DLC).

[1] RL to C. A. Spring Rice, Jan. 5, 1916, TLS (FO 115/2024, p. 8, PRO): "As the Department has received no reply from your Government to its note of October 21st in regard to British measures believed by this Government to restrict its legitimate trade with belligerent and neutral countries of Europe, I have to ask whether you will be kind enough to inquire of your Government when we may expect to receive its formal answer. As you know, the matter will probably come up for discussion in the Congress and I hope the reply of your Government, acceding to our contentions which seemed to me perfectly well founded, will shortly be received in order that the situation may be speedily relieved."

From Mary Randolph Smith

Dear Mr Wilson   New Orleans [c. Jan. 7, 1916]

The little card, announcing that we were to have the Littell & the Century *too*, from our very best & dearest friend, was greeted with joy & added a great pleasure to the day.

It *is* so nice to be thought of by those we love & our Christmas needed a bright note or two for Lucy had been so stubbornly wretch[ed] for two weeks.

She got up on Christmas day—too soon alas!—& has'nt been well since. I am very anxious to take her to the piney woods where it is good & dry, for we are having such a lot of dampness & fog.

Our half blind friend enjoys having the Littell read to him & so it gives us double pleasure.

The joint letter from you & darling Edith made us so happy in giving us the feeling that you were really having a rest & a beautiful time

What a pity that it had to be cut short by the laying of this new dreadful burden on your shoulders!

I hope you will soon get rid of it all as you have done with Mexico!

Ben's[1] temporary job has come to an end & we are again distressed about him. He says they were very nice to him & told him that Congress had'nt appropriated sufficient funds to go on with & that they might need him again some time. Poor boy! He certainly has had a long, hard time.

Stockton delighted us with a little visit on his way to Houston & told us all about the wedding & all you best beloved people.

We long to be with you & can hardly wait for the time to come which will unite us again.

Dear love to Edith & to all the precious family, with many thanks from us both.

                    Always faithfully   Mary R. Smith

ALS (WP, DLC).
  ¹ Benjamin M. King, who had been living in the Smith home for at least two years.

From Robert Latham Owen

My dear Mr. President: [Washington] January 8, 1916.

I have directed sent you immediately a proposed Corrupt Practices Act which Senator Kern introduced at my instance. I regard it as of vital importance to your success and the success of the Democratic Party next Fall.

                    Yours, faithfully,   Robt. L. Owen

TLS (WP, DLC).

From Benjamin Ryan Tillman

Dear Mr. President: [Washington] January 8, 1916.

You asked me to "guide you how you can best help in pressing the armor plant bill through Congress." I suggest this: See Congressman Padgett, Chairman of the Naval Committee of the House, and urge prompt action at that end of some one of the bills now pending there for the same purpose.¹ If they get such a bill on the House Calendar—or pass it would better, though I don't expect that just yet—they could substitute the Senate bill for the House bill, and thus have it become a law just as soon as you sign it.

I will do my utmost at this end to get the bill on the Senate Calendar, and pass it too, sometime this next week, if such a thing be possible. You can, of course, help me in the Senate by asking Senator Kern, and others of your loyal friends who are Senators, to assist as much as possible.² In other words, we want "team work," both in the Committees and in the Chamber. The House has the advantage of us, inasmuch as its Committee on Rules can shut off debate whenever it is desirable, while the Senate itself has no such rule.

I congratulate you upon your analysis and eloquent presentation of your view—which I also had and wrote you—for uniting all the Americas. I am sure you will have struck a cord that vibrates from the Great Lakes to Cape Horn, and great good will come of the policy hereafter.

With the compliments of the Season, I am

Very respectfully,   B. R. Tillman

TLS (WP, DLC).
¹ Wilson saw Padgett on January 12.
² The Executive Office and White House diaries do not record a meeting between Wilson and Kern about this time.

To Edward Mandell House

[The White House] 9 January, 1916.

Your cab[l]e of yesterday received. Would be glad if you would convey my assurance that I shall be willing and glad when the opportunity comes to cooperate in a policy seeking to bring about and maintain permanent peace among civilized nations.

Wilson.

WWT telegram (WP, DLC).

Two Letters to Robert Lansing

My dear Mr. Secretary,   The White House. 10 January, 1916.

This seems to me reasonable, and thoroughly worth trying.¹

Faithfully Yours,   W.W.

WWTLI (SDR, RG 59, 763.72/2352½, DNA).
¹ See RL to WW (with its Enclosure), Jan. 7, 1916 (first letter of that date).

My dear Mr. Secretary,   The White House. 10 January, 1916.

I have tried hard to find something in this note about the LUSITANIA out of which a satisfactory answer to our demands could be made, but must admit that I have failed. It is a concession of grace, and not at all of right.

And yet I do not see that it would be essentially out of tune with it if the Imperial Government were to say that, even while it was arguing and without abatement insisting on the necessity for retaliation and even the right to retaliate, it was not willing to make that necessity an excuse for abreviating the rights of neutrals or for unnecessarily imperiling the lives of non-combatants, and that, therefore, while wishing to make very plain the imperative grounds for its recent policy, it was ready to recognize very frankly the justice of the contentions of the United States with regard to the rights of American citizens and assume the responsibility which she (the Imp. Gov.) had incurred by the incidental ignoring of those rights on the occasion referred to.

She could in this wise put Great Britain more obviously in the wrong as compared with herself, by showing that she, in contrast with Great Britain, was willing to make good for the damage done neutrals.

I understand you had a conference with Bernstorff to-day. Do you think from the present aspect of the situation that a suggestion such as I have outlined would set the settlement a step forward, or not?   Faithfully Yours,   W.W.

WWTLI (SDR, RG 59, 841.857 L 97/125½, DNA).

To Samuel Gompers

Personal and Confidential.

My dear Mr. Gompers: The White House January 10, 1916

I have read with the greatest interest the action of the Executive Council of the American Federation of Labor with regard to the Seaman's Act.[1] I want to say that I am in entire sympathy with their support of the Act itself. I think that only a fair trial of the Act is necessary to convince thoughtful and observant men of its justice and practicability.

          Cordially and sincerely yours,   Woodrow Wilson

TLS (photostat in RSB Coll., DLC).
[1] S. Gompers to WW, Jan. 7, 1916, TLS (WP, DLC), enclosing "RESOLUTION ADOPTED BY SAN FRANCISCO CONVENTION AMERICAN FEDERATION OF LABOR, NOVEMBER 8-22, 1915" and "EXCERPT FROM REPORT OF EXECUTIVE COUNCIL OF AMERICAN FEDERATION OF LABOR TO SAN FRANCISCO CONVENTION. NOVEMBER 8-22, 1915," T MSS (WP, DLC). The American Federation of Labor convention said that it stood "unalterably opposed" to the repeal of the Seamen's Act "or any attempt to impair the safety of travel at sea or renew the bonds under which seamen have been compelled to labor." It also cited the care taken in passing the bill, the importance of "freedom for the seamen," and the increase in tonnage of the American merchant marine despite opposition to the bill. The executive council reported to the convention on the efforts of the United States Chamber of Commerce for repeal of the act or for subsidies to equalize American and foreign shipping costs.

From Edward Mandell House

[London, Jan. 10, 1916]

Your cable of yesterday received and was very [welcome]. The conference today was entirely satisfactory. We are to meet again Saturday to continue discussion. So far there is no disagreement between us. This may come however when concrete proposals are made. My plan is to come to a tentative agreement with them before going to the Continent on the twentieth and let them bring their colleagues into line before I return. They have agreed to undertake this.

EBWhw decode of T telegram (WP, DLC).

From William Gibbs McAdoo

PERSONAL.

Dear Mr. President:　　　　　Washington January 10, 1916.

I hand you herewith two copies of the last revision of the proposed shipping bill.[1] It is dated January 10th. This is the result of a long conference I had with Judge Alexander and Senator Fletcher on Friday, last, at which Mr. Thurman,[2] Solicitor for the Department of Commerce, was present. I think the bill is now in such form that we can safely ask Senator Clarke to offer it in the Senate and Judge Alexander to offer it in the House. I would respectfully suggest that you immediately request Senator Clarke and Judge Alexander to meet you for a conference on this subject, with a view to securing their cooperation and getting them to introduce the bill without further delay, provided, of course, that you approve the bill yourself. If you care to have any explanation of the bill, I shall be happy to run over it with you any time that you may designate. I think it is most important to get a bill introduced at the earliest possible moment. After you have talked with Senator Clarke and Judge Alexander (I think it would be much better if you would have them come together than separately), I think it would be advisable to get in touch with Congressman Kitchin and Senator Simmons, Chairmen, respectively, of the Ways and Means Committee of the House and the Finance Committee of the Senate. Will you kindly let me know what course you are going to take in this matter?

Faithfully yours,　　W G McAdoo

TLS (WP, DLC).

[1] "A BILL To establish a United States Shipping Board for the purpose of encouraging, developing and creating a naval auxiliary and naval reserve and a merchant marine to meet the requirements of the commerce of the United States with its territories and possessions, and with foreign countries, and for other purposes," Jan. 10, 1916, T MS (WP, DLC). This draft differed only slightly from that described in WGM to WW, Dec. 11, 1915, n. 1. Among the changes were the inclusion of coastwise ships among those that might be purchased from the shipping board; greater emphasis on the requirement that all ships purchased from the board be registered in the United States; limits on the transfer of titles to ships purchased from the board; a procedure for retiring old ships belonging to the board; and a requirement that the United States own a majority of the stock of any corporation established by the board. Alexander introduced this bill with minor changes on January 31, 1916. It was H.R. 10500, 64th Cong., 1st sess.

[2] Albert L. Thurman.

From Dudley Field Malone

Dear Mr. President: Port of New York January 10, 1916.

Will you consider it a very great intrusion in matters not under my jurisdiction if I ask you please not to finally decide on the nomination of a postmaster here in New York before you give me a chance to tell you what this New York situation is; on which, you may have heard from Colonel House, I have been working so hard for months and which seems now to have reached a point of real success for the State and National Campaign before us.

Anything done in New York at the present time in the way of appointments may collide with these large plans which are so important to you. I know this is a most unusual request and I know you will not think it is egotism on my part to make it; but I have been worrying for months, and working so quietly with Colonel House to get things in shape here in the State of New York, that I know you will not want anything to interfere with the plans that have been made. If you will just send me a wire, I will come to Washington immediately upon the receipt of a message from you and come quietly. I am sending this letter to you by Doctor Grayson in order that you may get it at once and in order that it may not pass through any other hands.

I have just returned from Buffalo, where I spoke, with Myron T. Herrick, to twelve hundred of the most representative business men I have ever seen gathered together. They came from all parts of New York State. There was a unanimous opinion, among Democrats and Republicans alike, that it would be a most generous and magnificent thing, and pleasing to the entire country, if you could see your way clear to offer Mr. Taft the vacancy on the Supreme Court Bench. I consulted the Democratic politicians in Buffalo, like William J. Connors, Norman E. Mack, the Collector of Customs there, Mr. George Bleistein,[1] and many others, —just privately to get their view as to what they would think of this nomination,—and they all said at once that they thought it would be the strongest, finest thing you could do in the circumstance. I also think, Mr. President, that it would be a fine political stroke, because of Mr. Taft's generous treatment of you, your policies and your administration. Mr. Lane would be my first choice, but if you do not wish to take anybody out of your Cabinet, I feel that the appointment of Mr. Taft would produce the most desirable results for you and your administration.

Please give my warmest remembrance to Mrs. Wilson, to Margaret, Miss Bones, and the family, and believe me to be,
          Yours most faithfully,   Dudley Field Malone

TLS (WP, DLC).
1 They were William James Conners, president of the Magnus Beck Brewing Co. and proprietor and publisher of both the *Buffalo Enquirer* and the *Buffalo Courier*; Norman Edward Mack, editor and publisher of the *Buffalo Daily Times* and New York member of the National Democratic Committee since 1900; and George Bleistein, former owner of the *Buffalo Courier*, president of the Courier Co., and Collector of Customs in Buffalo.

From Alexander Walters

My Dear Sir: New York City, N.Y., Jan., 10, 1916.

I thank you most heartily for permitting me to speak with you this morning about the appointment of The Recorder of Deeds. After leaving the White House the idea Occured to me that it might be a good thing to see the Senators who have declared themselves opposed to the Confirmation of colored men who are nominated by yourself for office.

If you have not any objection, I would like to take up with the Senators the matter of Confirmation of colored men for it would greatly handicap us in the Fall Campaign and would be all the Republicans would want to use against us to be able to say for a certainty that Democratic Senators will not confirm colored men.[1] We will not insist on the nomination of a colored man for the Recorder of Deeds but we do think, that a similar office carrying about the same salary should be given us. I am of the opinion that with the National Conventions and the election of Congressman and of Presidents in this year that they would fail to confirm a colored man to a prominent position.

It seems to me that it would ruin the Colored Democratic Organization to surrender on the point of Confirmation. It is the principle that we are contending for. To surrender would destroy our chances of building up the Colored Democratic Organization.

Thanking you for past favors, I remain

Most Respectfully,   Alexander Walters

TLS (WP, DLC).
1 "I would be obliged if you would say for me to Bishop Walters that I see no objection to his consulting with the Senators as he suggests." WW to JPT, TL, n.d. (WP, DLC).

Alexander Walters to Joseph Patrick Tumulty

Cumberland, Md., Jan. 10, 1916.

Letter sent the President to-day was read and signed as I was taking the train for Montgomery, Ala. I did not notice mistakes until I read my copy in the train. Before the word FAIL put NOT and make it read WOULD NOT FAIL TO CONFIRM. Sorry

I did not have time to read carefully the letter before I signed
it.   A.

T telegram (WP, DLC).

To Edward Mandell House

[The White House, Jan. 11, 1916]
It now looks as if our several difficulties with Germany would
be presently adjusted. So soon as they are the demand here especially from the Senate will be imperative that we force England
to make at least equal concessions to our unanswerable claims of
right. This is just at hand.¹ I send this for your information and
guidance.²   W.

WWhw telegram (WP, DLC).
¹ House decoded this sentence: "This is just." T decode of WW to EMH,
Jan. 12, 1916, T telegram (E. M. House Papers, CtY).
² Lansing telegraphed to House on the same day: "LUSITANIA case progressing.
Satisfactory settlement probable. Germany apparently believes if case settled
it will leave only matters with Great Britain unsettled and some action will
be necessary." RL to EMH, Jan. 11, 1916, T telegram (SDR, RG 59, 841.857
L 97/126½A, DNA).

To Samuel Gompers

My dear Mr. Gompers: [The White House] January 11, 1916
Your letter of January seventh I have read with the deepest
interest, and you may be sure shall give the most serious and
friendly consideration to the objections you urge.¹
        Cordially and sincerely yours,   Woodrow Wilson

TLS (Letterpress Books, WP, DLC).
¹ It is missing; however, a note on a cross reference sheet says that it was a
letter protesting against the appointment of William Howard Taft to the Supreme
Court.

To James Duval Phelan

My dear Senator: The White House January 11, 1916
You may be sure that my heart and my judgment of Mr. Lane
responds to the suggestion of your letter of January tenth,¹ but
how in the world could I spare him as Secretary of the Interior?
    In haste
        Cordially and sincerely yours,   Woodrow Wilson

TLS (CSt).
¹ It was sent to the Attorney General.

From Robert Lansing, with Enclosures

PERSONAL AND PRIVATE:

My dear Mr. President:　　　[Washington] January 11, 1916.

I have your comment upon the proposed reply of the German Government in the LUSITANIA case. With your views I entirely agree.

Yesterday I had an interview with Count von Bernstorff, of which I enclose a memorandum which was made immediately after I talked with him. You will perceive that I took very much the line of approach which you suggest in your letter.

Faithfully yours,　Robert Lansing

CCL (SDR, RG 59, 841.857 L 97/1261½, DNA).

ENCLOSURE I

MEMORANDUM OF CONVERSATION WITH
THE GERMAN AMBASSADOR.

January 10, 1916.

The German Ambassador called this morning and read me a wireless dispatch which he had received from his Government, a copy of which he handed me, upon the understanding that it would be treated as strictly confidential.

After I had made a few comments on the dispatch I referred directly to the LUSITANIA case and said that I feared that the proposed note, copy of which he had given me, would not be satisfactory; that the question of indemnity was only important so far as it was an admission of liability; and that as I read his draft of the note the indemnity was given as an act of grace and not because Germany was liable for illegal conduct. I told him that I thought it was necessary that Germany should admit liability frankly as that would amount to a disavowal, and disavowal in some form we must have.

He replied that they had great difficulty on account of Great Britain's continuance of her illegal blockade and that the German public, and many in the Government were not willing to abandon the policy of reprisals.

I told him that I did not see that that was at all necessary; that while there might be justification for retaliation against Great Britain, that retaliation was necessarily illegal conduct in a strict sense and that all it was necessary to do was to admit that it was illegal and that insofar as neutrals were concerned it imposed liability on the German Government. I said to him that

that was the same course we were taking with regard to Great Britain—that Great Britain's interruption of trade to Germany was admittedly retaliatory and that it, therefore, was illegal and so far as neutrals were concerned it imposed liability on Great Britain; and that I could not see how we could treat the matter differently with the two Governments.

He told me he would at once communicate these views to his Government in the hope that a course might be found which would meet our views.[1]   Robert Lansing

TS memorandum (SDR, RG 59, 841.857 L 97/126½, DNA).
    [1] Bernstorff reported at length on this conversation in J. H. von Bernstorff to the Foreign Office, received Jan. 13, 1916, T telegram (Der Weltkrieg, Unterseebootkrieg gegen England, No. 18a, ganz geheim, Vol. 16, n.p., GFO-Ar). However, he did not mention Lansing's essential point—admission of German liability that would amount to a disavowal—and suggested only a redrafting of the third counterproposal by deletion of its second paragraph.

E N C L O S U R E   I I

Handed me by German Amb. Jany 10/16 RL *Strictly Confidential* Copy.

We have modified submarine war, waged in retaliation against illegal English Starvation policy, to meet American Wishes. Result was that submarine war lost considerably in efficiency. This was done in consideration of valued friendly relations which Germany desires continued with America. In return we expected that U. S. Government would contend with us for freedom of seas and obtain from England reestablishment of legitimate neutral trade with Germany. The United States on November fifth sent note to England to which apparently no reply has been made, at any rate no concessions obtained from England. Instead, British Government recently published White Paper enumerating all measures which tend to cut off Germany from legitimate commerce and to control neutrals. American Note which was very much to the point exposed the illegality of these measures.

Since August last and, even before Germany modified submarine war, if incidents happened they were regrettable mistakes for which due reparation has been made. Germany showed good will by making concessions seriously affecting efficiency of submarine war. England has conceded nothing but instead boasts of more and more success in strangling Germany. We therefore may expect and should be grateful if America at last takes energetic steps to establish real freedom of seas.

T MS (SDR, RG 59, 841.857 L 97/126½, DNA).

From Edward Mandell House

Dear Governor: London, January 11, 1916.

I am seeing as many people as can be crowded into the waking hours and shall continue to do so until we leave on the twentieth. Soldiers, sailors, politicians and editors are on my list.

Our friend, A. G. Gardiner, was with me for an hour and a half yesterday. I gave him more time than to others because I wanted to increase, if possible, his already high opinion of you.

These efforts have been merely to create a better and more favorable understanding of your purposes. But my real effort has been directed at Grey and Balfour. I did not think it wise to discuss intimate affairs with all the Cabinet, and these two were chosen because of my confidence in them which I know you share. It seemed better to place the responsibility directly on them.

The general line of my argument was that you had arranged a closer union of the Americas so if it was thought best not to enter a world wide sphere, we could safely lead an isolated life of our own. If this were decided upon, I told them, we would increase our army and navy and remain within our own hemisphere.

On the other hand, I explained, you believed that in order to fully justify our existence as a great nation, it might be necessary to bring to bear all our power in behalf of peace and the maintenance of it.

They wanted to know how far you would be willing to enter into an agreement concerning European affairs. I thought you would not be willing to do this at all, but you would be willing to come to an agreement with the civilized world upon the broad questions touching the interests and future of every nation. Such questions, for instance, as the general elimination, so far as practicable, of militarism and navalism.

We did not define, to the satisfaction of any of us, what would constitute a solution of these two fundamental questions. We agreed to think it our [out] and to have another conference Saturday. This delay, of course, is the British of it, but in questions involving such issues, the postponement is not unreasonable.

Balfour made the remark that he would see what concessions his colleagues would be willing to make to American opinion. I asked him to please not put it in that way since we did not consider they were making any concessions whatever to us, but it was quite the other way round. We were willing to consider some means by which we could serve civilization, but if we did, it, we felt it would be at a sacrifice of our traditional policy and entailed some danger which does not now confront us.

I also told them that unless they were willing to approach the matter in an unselfish spirit, there was no need to attempt it at all.

They are so confident of ultimate success that I endeavored to shake it somewhat, and I think I did. I asked if it were not within the bounds of possibility that Germany would push Russia further back in the spring and summer giving her an excuse to make a separate peace upon terms which might be more favorable than if the Allies were victorious. If this were done, Germany might throw her entire weight on the western front, and without seeking to strike France a mortal blow, offer her equally favorable terms. This [They] admitted this possibility.

Germany, I told them, considered she had but one antagonist, and before going under would be willing to promise Russia a free hand towards warm sea ports both to the south and west. She could return to France Alsace and Lorraine and could restore Belgium with the exception of Antwerp and the mouth of the Rhine. This would leave her with the Austrian Empire practically a part of the German Empire and would secure a free hand in Asia Minor, Egypt, India and parts of Africa, as her ultimate goal.

Under such conditions British sea power, I thought, would not last three months, not because it might be defeated at sea, but because all nations would protest against the restrictions of trade.

They did not think to turn this argument against us, which they might have done, by saying that if such things happened, the democracies of the world would of necessity, be compelled to become autocracies for self preservation. So I let it go as our thought of their danger and of our willingness to contribute to the welfare of civilization, as we understand it.

Affectionately yours,   E. M. House

TLS (WP, DLC).

Gilbert Monell Hitchcock to Joseph Patrick Tumulty

My dear Mr. Tumulty: Washington, D. C. January 11, 1916.

Please call the President's attention to the enclosed amendment which Senator Clarke, of Arkansas, proposes to offer to the Philippine bill.[1] This amendment is likely to have the support of some Senators on both sides of the Senate especially on the democratic side. I would like an opportunity of discussing

it with the President within the next two or three days if possible.
This amendment may present rather a serious complication.

Yours truly,   G M Hitchcock

TLS (WP, DLC).

¹ A proposed amendment to S. 381, 64th Cong., 1st sess., printed copy (WP, DLC), which reads: "The President is hereby authorized and directed to withdraw and surrender all the supervision, jurisdiction, control, or sovereignty now possessed or exercised by the United States in or over the people and territory of the said Philippines, and he shall on behalf of the United States fully recognize the independence thereof as a separate and self-governing nation and the sovereignty and control over the same of the government instituted by the people thereof. This transfer of possession, sovereignty, and governmental control shall be completed and become absolute within two years from the date of the approval of this Act, under the terms and in the manner hereinafter prescribed. For the purpose of a complete and prompt compliance with this direction, the President is hereby invested with full power and authority to make such orders and regulations and to enter into such negotiations with the authorities of said Philippines or others as may be necessary to finally settle and adjust all property rights and other relations as between the United States and the said Philippines, and to cause to be acknowledged, respected, and safeguarded all of the personal and property rights of citizens or corporations of the United States resident or engaged in business in said Philippines or having property interests therein. In any such settlement or adjustment so made in respect to the rights and property of the United States as against the said Philippines the President shall reserve or acquire such lands and rights and privileges appurtenant thereto as may, in his judgment, be required by the United States for naval bases and coaling stations within the territory of said Philippines.

"Immediately upon the passage of the Act, the President shall invite the cooperation of the principal nations interested in the affairs of that part of the world in which the Philippines are located, in the form of a treaty or other character of binding agreement, whereby the cooperating nations shall mutually pledge themselves to recognize and respect the sovereignty and independence of the said Philippines, and likewise mutually obligating themselves, equally and not one primarily nor to any greater extent than another, to maintain as against external force the sovereignty of said Philippines for the period of five years from the taking effect of such treaty or agreement. If any of the nations so invited to join in such undertaking shall decline to do so, then the President shall include as parties to such convention or agreement such nations as may be willing to join therein and to assume such obligations; and if none are willing to so unite therein, then the President is authorized to give such guaranty on behalf of the United States alone."

This was to be inserted at the end of the Jones bill.

To Joseph Patrick Tumulty

[The White House, c. Jan. 12, 1916]

I will be very glad to see the Senator on this subject¹ at the earliest opening in my calendar.²   W.W.

ALI (WP, DLC).

¹ That is, Senator Hitchcock, on the Clarke amendment.
² Wilson met with Hitchcock at the White House on January 17.

From Lindley Miller Garrison[1]

My dear Mr. President: Washington. January 12, 1916.

In my judgment we are facing a critical juncture with respect to the military part of the national defense program.

I am convinced that unless the situation is dealt with promptly and effectively, we can indulge in no reasonable expectation of any acceptable result.

So far as the military part of national defense is concerned, there can be no honest or worthy solution which does not result in national forces under the exclusive control and authority of the national government. Any other solution is illusory and not real, is apparent and not substantial.

There is a perfectly legitimate field of discussion and debate as to the means of obtaining these national forces. The proportion thereof that should be regular standing army, that should be organized reserves of the regular standing army, or should be drawn from the body of citizens for shorter periods of national service than those in the regular standing army, are all legitimate and proper matters for consideration, analysis and discussion.

But there is absolutely no dissent, from the military standpoint, from the conclusion that the only measure of national defense that possesses any virtue is one which produces national forces. From the beginning of the Government to this time, excepting during periods of actual war, the acknowledged weakness and defect of the situation arose out of the lack of any system producing these federal forces. The situation was rendered worse by the presence of State troops, raised, officered, trained and governed by the States, that were assumed to be a military reliance for the Nation, when, in fact, they are not and can never be made to be. Under the Constitution of the United States, these State troops must always be governed, officered and trained by the respective States.

The very first line of cleavage, therefore, which must be encountered and dealt with by the student of the situation is between reliance upon a system of State troops, forever subject to Constitutional limitations which render them absolutely insecure as a reliance for the Nation, or reliance upon national forces raised, officered, trained and controlled by the national authorities. Upon this subject there does not exist, and there cannot legitimately exist, any difference of opinion among those who are unbiased and who believe in real national security and defense.

[1] Italicization in the following letter by Tumulty.

The policy recommended to you and adopted by you, squarely placed the Nation upon the sure foundation of national forces. If that policy is made effective by legislation, there will be secured to this country for the first time a real, stable foundation for the military part of its national defense. If, however, instead thereof a policy is adopted based upon the State troops as the main reliance of this country for its military arm, not only has no advance been made from the deplorable and inexcusable situation in which we have so long been, but an effective block has been placed across the pathway toward a proper settlement. The adoption of such a policy would serve to delude the people into believing that the subject had been settled and therefore required no further consideration upon their part. It would therefore, in my judgment, be infinitely worse than an entire failure of all legislative enactment upon the subject. The latter would at least leave it open for future settlement.

I of course am not advised as to the statements of intention made by Mr. Hay to you in the conversations held with you prior to your message to Congress at the opening of the present session. I have always felt, and have so expressed myself to you, that the situation in the Congress was such that unless you personally exerted the power of your leadership, you would not obtain any worthy results in this matter.

Mr. Hay has now made open declaration of his intention. He announces that he does not intend to press for the enactment of the military policy advocated in your message. With respect to the regular army, he does not purpose giving us the organizations asked for, and imperatively necessary if the federal volunteers (so-called Continental Army) are to be properly trained; he purposes adding a few thousand men to the enlisted strength of the army in its present organization, the adding of a few regiments of field artillery to the existing organizations of the regular army, the entire abandonment of the idea of a federal force of national volunteers, and the passing of a bill granting direct federal pay to the enlisted men and officers of the State troops.

In my judgment, the effect of the enactment of Mr. Hay's program would be to set back the whole cause of legitimate, honest national defense in an entirely unjustifiable and inexcusable way. It would be, in my judgment, a betrayal of the trust of the people in this regard. It would be illusory and apparent without any reality or substance.

There is, unfortunately, very little knowledge and very little intense personal interest in any of the Members of the House concerning military affairs. Apart from the power that always

resides in every Chairman of Committee, Mr. Hay has the additional power of dealing with a subject concerning which the rest
of the House has no knowledge and about which it has never
concerned itself. In this particular instance his proposal of set-
tling this matter by voting money to the enlisted men and officers
of the State troops appeals to the direct personal, political interest of the Members. In these circumstances it seems to me to
be perfectly clear that unless you interpose your position as
leader of the country on this great subject, the result will be
the lamentable one which I have just described.

It seems to me equally imperative that this interposition should
be immediate. If this proposed program of Mr. Hay is accepted
by the Committee and by public opinion, and by the House, as a
real solution of this vital matter, any position subsequently taken
will be negligible so far as substantial, actual results are concerned.

The issue must be plainly and clearly drawn. It has nothing
whatever to do with the numbers of men to be raised or with the
means of raising them, as Mr. Hay would have it appear that it
has. It is between two absolutely different systems, one of which
is based upon the Nation undertaking upon its own responsibility
the raising and management of the national troops; and the
other of which leaves us in the position that we have always
been in since the institution of the Government,—to rely upon the
States doing this thing for the Nation,—a situation in which the
Nation is relying upon a military force that it does not raise, that
it does not officer, that it does not train, and that it does not
control. A mere statement of the situation shows that the two
different proposals are as wide apart as any two proposals upon
any subject possibly can be.

Mr. Hay's proposal to include a draft or compulsory provision
so that at the outbreak of war the Nation could bring under its
control these State troops, utterly fails to meet the essential objections to the perpetuation of the militia system. The difficulty to
be dealt with does not arise out of the Government not being
able to take over these troops in the event of war, but arises out
of its inability, under the Constitution, to have the essential unity
of responsibility, authority and control in the raising, officering,
training and governing of its military forces.

If the public obtains the impression that Mr. Hay's solution
is merely another means of accomplishing the same end as your
proposed policy, they will accept the same and rest content that
their desires have been properly met. If, on the other hand, they
are clearly and unmistakably advised that to adopt the policy

suggested by Mr. Hay is to make a mockery of all that was worthy and virtuous in the proposal of a proper military policy, and that it is a delusion to consider such a solution as a real reliance or security, then there is hope that we can obtain results commensurate with the necessities of the case and with a self-respecting consideration and treatment thereof.

I cannot, therefore, too strongly urge upon you my view of the imperative necessity of your seeking an occasion at the earliest possible moment to declare yourself with respect to the matter, and in doing so, to make it clear beyond peradventure that nothing excepting national forces, raised by the Nation and subject to its exclusive authority, responsibility and control, is any real settlement of this issue.

Sincerely yours, Lindley M. Garrison

TLS (WP, DLC).

To James Paul Clarke

My dear Senator: [The White House] January 13, 1916

May I not take the liberty of handing you the enclosed[1] as a substitute for the bill you were kind enough to let me send you the other day as a formulated suggestion? I think that this draft is improved in many particulars.

I am so deeply concerned about this whole matter that I know you will pardon my begging you to give it your most serious consideration.

Cordially and sincerely yours, Woodrow Wilson

TLS (Letterpress Books, WP, DLC).
[1] The new draft of the shipping bill, about which see WGM to WW, Jan. 10, 1916, n. 1.

From Edward Mandell House

Dear Governor: No. 4. London, January 13, 1916.

Your cable concerning our shipping troubles has come.

I wish I might be with you today to tell you of conditions here. Page had Sir Edward Grey and Lord Robert Cecil[1] to lunch and we discussed these matters at length.[2] Lord Robert told me, and Sir Edward confirmed it, that if he acceded to your request, his resignation would be demanded at once. Personally, he is perfectly willing to do anything. He even goes so far as to suggest that it might come to the complete abandonment of the blockade, in which case Germany would perhaps win.

He does not believe there can be half way measures. It has to be rigid, or not at all.

In regard to the parcel post, both Sir Edward and Lord Robert said that something like three tons of rubber had gone from the United States to Sweden and from Sweden to Germany in that way and upon a single boat. They have an entire distrust of Germany. They do not believe she will play the game fairly. They believe she is now using the Red Cross to serve her purposes and are declaring that the babies of Germany are dying for lack of milk, only to create a feeling against England and to get food supplies in.

Sir Edward intimated that he, himself, would be willing, if Germany would abandon her blockade against both passenger and merchant ships, to permit food stuffs to go into neutral ports without question. This is what I proposed last year to which he consented, but which Germany refused.

He considers that Germany is violating neutrality laws just as much by sinking neutral ships destined to neutral ports as Great Britain is in carrying such ships into port and preventing the cargoes from reaching their destination.

I have presented our side of the argument to nearly every member of the Cabinet. I have given them the state of public feeling in America and have told them of the danger which the Allies run in doing these things and in creating adverse opinion against them. They know your position now as well as I know it, and they appreciate it.

The Chancellor of the Exchequer[3] told me yesterday that England would be forever grateful for the position you have taken in the war. I made the assertion that Germany would have won during this past summer, had it not been for America. He admitted it and said there was not an intelligent man in England that did not know it, and those of the Government knew it better than anyone else.

I am giving you the situation as it actually is so you can use your own judgment as to how to proceed.

France is even more determined than England to keep up the blockade in all its severity, and will not listen to any loosening of it that England proposes. She does not want to base it upon law, but prefers to let it be a matter of retaliation. I told Sir Edward that our people would not acquiesce in this and he should talk them out of such a position.

It is necessary for me to move with some circumspection regarding these question[s] that properly belong to Page's duties, but I take some chances trusting that I may not offend. Page has been exceedingly cordial and pleasant and has done what he could. He does not know, of course, the purpose of my visit or what I am discussing with Grey and Balfour.

Among the many editors I have talked to is Robert Donald of the Chronicle. The Chronicle now has perhaps the largest circulation of any paper in England. Donald promised yesterday to write a leader concerning you. It will probably appear after I leave, but he will arrange to have Page forward it to you.

I believe I have gotten enough sentiment in influential quarters favorable to the position you have taken to bring public opinion in England entirely around. It is not advisable, however, to use it at this time but it may be later and then I think it can be done.

I have had two conferences with Bryce. I talk to him more freely than to anyone excepting Grey and Balfour. I wish he could be in America for he would sense the situation there better than anyone else. I told him in the strictest confidence something of our difficulties with Sir Cecil and asked his advice. He thought it would be exceedingly unwise for me to take the matter up here. He believes if I do, it will probably destroy my influence, which he was good enough to think of more importance than Sir Cecil's recall.

I believe we had better leave the matter in abeyance until I return, for if done now, it may interfere with some of the plans we have in mind.   Affectionately yours,   E. M. House

TLS (WC, DLC).

1 Rt. Hon. Lord Edgar Algernon Robert Gascoyne-Cecil, at this time parliamentary undersecretary for foreign affairs.

2 Grey's report of this conversation (E. Grey to C. A. Spring Rice, Jan. 12, 1916, TLS [C. A. Spring Rice Papers, FO 800/242, PRO]) reads as follows:

"When lunching at the American Embassy to-day to meet Colonel House, and talking with Mr. Page and Colonel House alone after lunch, I explained the difficulty of our giving way about the blockade of Germany.

"I told them that we had drafted a reply, which, like their own Note, was based on legal grounds, following in fact the lines of their Note. But I was sorely tempted to reply from the human point of view, explaining that, if we were limited to the right of search on the high seas, and not allowed to interfere with any goods said to be going into the 'common stock' of a neutral country, such a wide door would be open to German evasion of our action that we might just as well give up altogether the attempt to prevent any goods, even the most absolute contraband, from reaching Germany in any quantities through neutral countries. I should then ask the United States to say plainly whether this was what they desired and intended.

"Mr. Page asked why I had not done this.

"I said because it was risky to take this sort of unusual line.

"Colonel House thought that the effect might be embarrassing.

"I said that I should probably have added an observation that the United States, I understood, wished to be impartial, but they complained when we brought goods into port, and either submitted them to a Prize Court,—where the whole matter could be argued, and compensation claimed if we were wrong,—or, after the necessary delay for investigation, sent them on to the neutral country if we were satisfied that they were really destined for it: against this the United States protested; while, on the other hand, Germany, on the high seas near our coast, sank neutral merchant vessels with all their cargo on board, even when destined to a neutral port, sending ship's papers, goods, and all documentary evidence to the bottom of the sea, and went on doing this month after month without any protest from the United States: for the United States protests to Germany seemed to be confined to attacks on passengers, and did not deal with the question of the cargo of ships. This was not equal treatment.

"Both Mr. Page and Colonel House considered that this would be a reasonable criticism for me to make.

"I observed that the United States might of course reply to this by asking whether, if they induced Germany to forgo attacking merchant vessels of every description with submarines, in view of the fact that the submarines could not bring them into port, we would give up the blockade, which had been instituted subsequently to the announcement of Germany's submarine policy.

"They asked me what answer we should make in such a case.

"I replied that I could not say what the opinion of the Government here would be, or what would be the opinion of our Allies, whom we should have to consult. It would, of course, be open to the United States to take up the question with Germany, and, if they succeeded, we should no doubt have to give an answer."

Irwin Laughlin made notes of the meeting immediately afterwards. (Hw copy of memorandum, Jan. 12, 1916, tipped into Charles Seymour, *The Intimate Papers of Colonel House* [2 vols., London, 1926], II, 124 A-D. This volume is in WC, NjP.) Laughlin's account follows:

"Luncheon at Embassy today; Sir Edward Grey, Lord Robert Cecil, Mr. House, the Ambassador and myself.

"Mr. House, on being questioned by the Ambassador, stated carefully to Sir E. Grey, twice over—the second time in reply to Sir E. Grey who said 'Now I want to get that exactly right'—that 'the United States wanted the British government to do what would enable the United States to do what was necessary for the Allies to win the war.' On being asked by Sir E. Grey what the United States *would actually do* Mr. House said, after some hesitation, that the United States would 'continue to do what it had been doing,' and then referred the question (with a gesture of desperation) to the Ambassador as being more 'au courant' with matters in hand. The Ambassador did not make any definite answer and the conversation then became vague on this point. Mr. House had previously said, in amplification of his statement, that this represented not only the feeling of the people of the United States, but of 'all of the Cabinet but one,' whom he did not name, and of the President as well.

"Sir E. Grey asked Mr. House whether the United States wanted the British Government to ease the blockade of Germany and to let foodstuffs in. Mr. House replied definitely and without qualification in the negative.

"House had been fencing with Grey and suggesting—always vaguely—that the United States was sympathetic to the cause of the Allies and was willing to help if the British Government would act in such a way as to make this possible; and this led to the direct questions put by both the Ambassador and Sir E. Grey as to exactly what it was that the United States wanted the British Government to do."

3 Reginald McKenna.

To Robert Latham Owen

My dear Senator: [The White House] January 14, 1916

Thank you for sending me a copy of the proposed Corrupt Practices Act introduced by Senator Kern at your instance. I have read the bill and want to say that it meets with my entire approval. I hope most sincerely that it may be possible to pass it at an early date.

                Cordially and sincerely yours,   Woodrow Wilson

TLS (Letterpress Books, WP, DLC).

To William Gibbs McAdoo

My dear Mac: The White House January 14, 1916

I sent a copy of the revised shipping bill to Senator Clarke yesterday, as I promised, and have now at last had time to read the
bill carefully myself. It seems to me excellent, simply and clearly
drawn and just as safe against legitimate criticism as it could
possibly be made.

Always   Faithfully yours,   Woodrow Wilson

TLS (W. G. McAdoo Papers, DLC).

From William Gibbs McAdoo, with Enclosure

Dear Governor,   [Washington] Jany 14/16

The attached memorandum is submitted for your consideration and for such weight as you think it is worth.

Affy Yours   WGM

ALI (WP, DLC).

E N C L O S U R E

Confidential MEMORANDUM:

The Republican leaders are most anxious to make the tariff
an issue in the coming campaign. In the Spring of 1915 they
made consistent and persistent attacks upon the Democratic
tariff act, alleging that the business depression existing at that
time was due wholly to its enactment and Democratic incom-
petency, when, as a matter of fact, the chief cause of the depression was the European war. When prosperity began to return and
became a fixed and very obvious fact, in the Fall of 1915 they
changed their line of attack and said that the European war was
responsible for the return of prosperity; that the quality of this
prosperity was unsatisfactory and that in any event it was
ephemeral and would disappear as soon as the war ended; that
American manufacturers would then begin to feel the deadly effects of the Underwood tariff law because it would permit
European nations to "dump" such extraordinary quantities of
their manufactured products upon the American market, at any
sort of prices, that the home manufacturer would be seriously
hurt, if not destroyed by this competition.

In October last I made a trip through the Central West and
Northwest, speaking in the following places: Indianapolis,

Indiana; St. Louis and Kansas City, Missouri; Reno, Nevada; San Francisco, Portland, Seattle, Billings and Helena, Montana; Fargo, North Dakota; Madison, Wisconsin, and Chicago, Illinois. In almost every one of the large cities I visited I found that there had been a carefully cultivated sentiment, amounting to a genuine fear, on the part of manufacturers and many business men, that this country is in jeopardy from a possible invasion of its markets by manufacturers and merchants of Europe after peace is restored.

It is by this skilful appeal to the fears of the manufacturers and business men of America that the Republicans hope to make the tariff an issue, and it is through such fears that they hope to induce the business interests of the country to support the Republicans in the next campaign. In nearly every speech I made I took occasion to give the reasons for what I believe to be a perfectly groundless and foolish fear. I have not the least belief in the possibility that there can be such a volume of dumping upon American markets after the close of the European war as to affect our domestic situation in the slightest degree. On the contrary, I believe that the chief industrial nations of Europe now engaged in that great conflict will be unable to restore their industrial efficiency and productivity for a long time. I doubt if they can for many years create the number of skilled workmen required to replace those who have been killed in war. Even when normal conditions are restored in Europe, the burden of debt which each one of the belligerent nations must carry, will greatly increase the cost of production in their mills and factories. As against this, American manufacturers are improving their methods, turning out their product at lower cost through constantly increasing efficiency, and are extending and strengthening their hold upon the foreign markets accessible to them, so that they will be in an infinitely stronger position after the European war than they have ever been before. We shall be better prepared to meet world competition in the future than ever before in our history.

The proposals of the Secretary of Commerce for the enactment of "Anti-Dumping" legislation are, I think, most unfortunate. They can not be justified on any other ground than that advanced by the Republican orators who are trying needlessly to alarm the country. The fact that a Democratic Cabinet member is supporting the Republican view of this question and is urging it in speeches and letters, whereas other Democratic members of the Cabinet are stoutly contesting this view, is producing, I think, a most unfortunate situation. Prominent Democratic members of the Senate and the House deplore the position taken by the Secretary of Commerce. They have expressed themselves to me very strongly about this matter. They have no fear of Republican propaganda of this kind, but they think that Democratic support of Republican alarmists' theories makes the situation difficult and does infinite harm.

Permit me to say that when the Underwood tariff bill was under discussion I proposed an anti-dumping provision, patterned on the Canadian law, which was incorporated in the bill as it passed the House. This provision was stricken out in the Senate, and the conferees of the two Houses supported the Senate's view and the Underwood bill was passed without the anti-dumping clause. I supported the provision at that time because I thought that it would do no harm to insert it in the bill and that it would deprive the Republicans and the alarmists of the country of any ground for claiming that the industries of the country were imperilled by any possible danger of this kind.

Certainly at the time the Simmons-Underwood tariff bill was under discussion a large number at least of influential Democrats in both Houses of the Congress were opposed to the anti-dumping clause. Doubtless they are still opposed to such a clause, believing that it is merely an entering wedge for reopening the entire tariff subject. Whether such a measure, if advocated, would command the support of the Democrats in both Houses of Congress I am not prepared to say, but in any event I am profoundly convinced that the injection of this subject, and its advocacy as a Democratic measure, will be extremely hurtful from every point of view. The principal injury will result from strengthening the fears and apprehensions of the business interests of the country, which will have a tendency to check the prosperity of the country now so well under way and fast becoming so deeply rooted.

Unless you are going to adopt this anti-dumping measure as a policy of the Administration, I am satisfied that it ought to be dropped as quickly as possible; but if the matter is to be considered at all, it should be considered as a part of a tariff commission program and not as a separate matter, and that it would be better, even in that case, to confine action to an investigation by such a commission of the "dumping" problem and not go beyond that.

T MS (WP, DLC).

From Cleveland Hoadley Dodge

My dear Mr. President: New York January 14, 1916.

I happen to know more about the Mexican situation, and am more deeply interested, than most of the people who are howling against your policy in the present emergency. I want you to know that, aside from any personal feeling towards you, I most heartily approve of the wise course which you are pursuing in relation to the horrible tragedy which has recently taken place in Chihuahua.[1] Many of the men who are criticising you so severely are sincere but entirely ignorant, and, on the other hand, most of the criticism comes from those who wish to make partisan capital out of this unfortunate affair. It is most unfortunate that this should have happened just at the time when we all hoped that the Mexican situation was pretty well settled, but I feel confident that you are doing just right, and I am sure that the sober sense of the bulk of the American people, as usual, is back of you.

I was much impressed last Sunday with what Halsey told me regarding the attitude of all the American missionaries in Mexico who almost without a dissenting voice have expressed their approval of Carranza, and their confidence that he eventually will solve the serious difficulties which confront him.

Again assuring you of my hearty endorsement,

Very sincerely yours,   Cleveland H. Dodge

TLS (WP, DLC).

[1] A band of *Villistas*, under the leadership of Colonel Pablo López, had robbed and murdered seventeen Americans at Santa Ysabel, near Chihuahua City, Mexico, on January 10, 1916. The victims, connected with the American-owned La Cusi Mining Co., were on their way to reopen one of the company's mines. Pressure for American intervention to punish the murderers rose even among the administration's allies in Congress. However, Wilson and Lansing reiterated the State Department's warning against Americans traveling in Mexico —a warning ignored by the murdered men—and reminded Congress and the public that the responsibility to punish the murderers lay with the Carranza government, not with the United States. Indeed, Wilson, on January 13, told a number of senators and others who called at the White House that he deeply deplored the crime and that the administration would take every step in its power to see that the murderers were punished. However, he reiterated that he was firmly opposed to any form of armed intervention and regretted that the Americans had not heeded the specific warnings given to them to stay out of dangerous territories. *New York Times*, Jan. 14, 1916; New York *World*, Jan. 14, 1916. See also Link, *Confusions and Crises*, pp. 201-203.

A Memorandum by Joseph Patrick Tumulty, with Enclosure

MEMORANDUM FOR THE PRESIDENT   January 15, 1916.

These facts should be borne in mind in the President's reply to the Secretary of War's letter of the twelfth of January:

On page one, the Secretary of War admits that "there is a perfectly legitimate field of discussion and debate as to the means of obtaining these national forces. The proportion thereof that should be regular standing army, that should be organized reserves of the regular standing army, or should be drawn from the body of citizens for shorter periods of national service than those in the regular standing army, are all legitimate and proper matters for consideration, analysis and discussion." With this admission of the Secretary of War that these questions are a legitimate field of discussion, it is probable that he will base his resignation on the fact that the President has acknowledged the truth of this argument and has conceded to the Committee of which Mr. Hay is the chairman, the privilege of debating this matter. The President should emphasize that the only understanding he had with Mr. Hay was this: that he hoped that the Committee on Military Affairs would produce a plan as good, if not better, than the one the Secretary of War had proposed; that if the Committee did not, the President would unhesitatingly and unswervingly adhere to the Garrison programme.

The President is just as much interested in the defence programme as the Secretary of War or anybody else but has been embarrassed by the unyielding attitude of those who have had to do with it, and have simply taken the position that unless the plan they proposed was accepted, they wouldn't "play ball." The President could not take this position and make any headway in Congress. Emphasize this fact,—that there shall be no yielding on the part of the Executive on this defence programme. The Democratic majority in Congress must provide adequate defence for the nation or by its failure admit its own impotency as a party; that the President intends vigorously to push this programme and, if necessary, will appeal to the country for support. Call attention to the fact that Congress has only been in session a short while, that neither Mr. Garrison nor the President has any right to anticipate antagonism from the Committee whose hearings are yet incomplete. Call the Secretary of War's attention to the fact that the President will exercise his power of leadership to the utmost when that exercise shall become necessary. The President does not agree with the Secretary of War that there is very little knowledge on the part of any member of the House concerning military affairs. Call attention of the Secretary of War to the fact than even if the programme which came to the President's desk did not meet with his approval, he would have the power of veto, and go to the country. In the last analysis in this vital matter, the responsibility rests entirely with the President and it is his intention to discharge it to the best of his ability; that responsibility shall be discharged, and without fear or favor.

Since writing the above, the attached letter of the fourteenth instant has been received from the Secretary of War.

T memorandum (WP, DLC).

E N C L O S U R E

From Lindley Miller Garrison[1]

My dear Mr. President: Washington. January 14, 1916.

What you said to-day by way of response to my letter of the 12th requires me to make my position perfectly clear to you.

You stated that Mr. Hay told you that your proposal of Federal volunteers could not be procured, and that the same end for which you were striving could be procured by other means—by utilizing the State troops as the basis of the policy and making appropriations of pay to the States conditioned on Federal control of the State troops.

You stated to him that you were not interested in any particular program or means of accomplishing the purpose of securing the men, and would accept his proposal if it accomplished that purpose.

Since the policy that was recommended to you and adopted by you discarded as absolutely impossible a military system based upon State troops, and asserted that the only possible basis for a military policy was National forces, it is entirely clear that the proposals are diametrically opposed to each other and are irreconcilable.

Those who are conscientiously convinced that nothing but National forces can properly be the basis of a policy of national defense, cannot possibly accept a policy based upon State forces. It not only does not in itself offer an acceptable solution, but acts to prevent any proper solution.

If those who are thus convinced are faced with the necessity of declaring their position on the matter, they can only show their sincerity and good faith by declining to admit the possibility of compromise with respect to this essential, fundamental principle.

I am thus convinced.

I feel that we are challenged by the existing situation to declare ourselves promptly, openly and unequivocally, or be charged properly with lack of sincerity and good faith.

We cannot hope to see our program, based on this essential principle, succeed if we admit the possibility of compromise with respect to it.

Yours is the ultimate responsibility; yours is the final determination as to the manner in which the situation shall be faced and treated. I fully realize this and I do not desire to cause you the slightest embarrassment on my account; if, therefore, my withdrawal from the situation would relieve you, you should not hesitate for a moment on that account.

Sincerely yours, Lindley M. Garrison

TLS (WP, DLC).
¹ Italicization in the following letter by Tumulty.

To Joseph Patrick Tumulty, with Enclosure

Dear Tumulty,   The White House. 15 January, 1916.

Here is a draft of a letter to the Sec'y of War. What do you thing [think] of it?   W.W.

WWTLI (WP, DLC).

ENCLOSURE

The White House.
My dear Mr. Secretary,   15 January, 1916.

I am very much obliged to you for your letters of January twelfth and January fourteenth. They make your views with regard to adequate measures of preparation for national defence sharply clear. I am sure that I already understood just what your views were, but I am glad to have them restated in this succin[c]t and striking way. You believe, as I do, that the chief thing necessary is, that we should have a trained citizen reserve and that the training, organization, and control of that reserve should be under immediate federal direction.

But apparently I have not succeeded in making my own position equally clear to you, though I feel sure that I have made it perfectly clear to Mr. Hay. It is that I am not irrevocably or dogmatically committed to any one plan of providing the nation with such a reserve, and am cordially willing to discuss alternative proposals.

Any other position on my part would indicate an attitude towards the Committee on Military Affairs of the House of Representatives which I should in no circumstances feel at liberty to assume. It would never be proper or possible for me to say to any committee of the House of Representatives that so far as my participation in legislation was concerned they would have to take my plan or none.

I do not share your opinion that the members of the House who are charged with the duty of dealing with military affairs are ignorant of them or of the military necessities of the nation. On the contrary, I have found them well informed and actuated by a most intelligent appreciation of the grave responsibilities imposed upon them. I am sure that Mr. Hay and his colleagues are ready to act with a full sense of all that is involved in this great matter both for the country and for the national parties which they represent.

My own duty towards them is perfectly plain. I must welcome a frank interchange of views and a patient and thorough comparison of all the methods proposed for obtaining the objects we all have in view. So far as my own participation in final legislative action is concerned, no one will expect me to acquiesce in any proposal that I regard as inadequate or illusory. If, as the outcome of a free interchange of views, my own judgment and that of the Committee should prove to be irreconcilably different and a bill should be presented to me which I could not accept as accomplishing the essential things sought, it would manifestly be my duty to veto it and go to the country on the merits. But there is no reason to anticipate or fear such a result, unless we should ourselves take at the outset the position that only the plans of the Department are to be considered; and that position, it seems to me, would be wholly unjustifiable. The Committee and the Congress will expect me to be as frank with them as I hope they will be with me, and will of course hold me justified in fighting for my own matured opinion.

I have had a delightfully frank conference with Mr. Hay. I have said to him that I was perfectly willing to consider any plan that would give us a national reserve under unmistakable national control, and would support any such scheme if convinced of its adequacy and wise policy. More he has not asked or desired.[1]

WWTL (WP, DLC).

[1] There is an undated WWsh draft of this letter in WP, DLC. This letter was sent as WW to LMG, Jan. 17, 1916, TCL (WP, DLC).

From Walter Hines Page

[London] January 15, 1916, 2 p.m.

3585. Confidential for the Secretary and the President. To be deciphered in the Secretary's office.

I make the following inquiry for my personal information. Members of the British Cabinet privately and unofficially say that the British *submarine blockade* of Germany in the Baltic is now effective. Suppose the British Government were to declare a strict blockade of Germany analagous to and in the terms of the United States blockade of the Confederate States, including the doctrine of continuous voyage, would the Administration regard this declaration more favorably than it regards the Order in Council of March 11?

I shall not use your answer in any way except as a general guide to my personal and informal conversations and in no way to indicate that you have expressed any opinion.

Amembassy, London.

T telegram (SDR, RG 59, 763.72112/2190½, DNA).

From Charles Richard Crane

Madison, Wis., Jan. 15, 1916.

Please continue your Mexican policy. The Cuban war was a disgrace. The President was forced into it by ambitious politicians and an unscrupulous press. We gained nothing which we would not soon have gained through diplomacy. If we had settled the matter by diplomacy we should not now have the burdensome Phillippine responsibility; the only thing achieved by our course was *one* political reputation and we do not need to repeat our error, even to reinforce that reputation.

Charles Crane.

T telegram (WP, DLC).

A Telegram and a Letter from Edward Mandell House

[London, Jan. 15, 1916]

I have something of importance to communicate by letter leaving next Wednesday steamer. Would suggest not sending any note to England concerning shipping troubles until it arrives. It is equally *utmost importance* to continue relations with Germany and Austria until then. There seems to be some daylight ahead if fortune favors us.

EBWhw decode of T telegram (WP, DLC).

Dear Governor: *No. 5.* London, January 15, 1916.

The other night Page had to meet me at dinner Lloyd George, McKenna, Chamberlain and Lord Reading. It was a hopeless company to try any conversation with that was worth while. He could not have brought together members of the Cabinet that were more distrustful of one another. Reading took me aside and said that Lloyd George wished to see me alone with him and asked me to dine with them last night.

George did not know the purpose of my visit, nor that I had talked with Grey and Balfour, although he must have some inkling of it.

We agreed that the war could only be ended by your intervention. We discussed other mediums, none of which were satisfactory. George thought intervention should not come until around the 1st of September, therefore we settled tentatively upon that date.

We both believe it will be apparent by then that no decisive victory can be had by either side. He believes the Allies will have a great advantage during the summer which will more than off-set the advantage Germany now holds, and will make the time propitious for your intervention. Neither of us believe the belligerents can make peace proposals to one another, and if they are made, they would not be accepted.

We believe public opinion in the belligerent countries would force the governments to accept your mediation. George goes even further than I had thought and says that you can dictate terms of peace, and he does not believe any agreement is possible without such dictation.

He thinks, for instance, you could say to Germany, Belgium and France must be evacuated and Alsace and Lorraine be restored to France. That you could say to Russia, Poland must be made an independent power, taking the component parts from Russia, Germany and Austria.

Militarism, too, would go by your demand. Germany, he thinks, could get compensation in Asia Minor.

I find George, Bryce and other English statesmen with whom I have talked, insistent that Turkey be eliminated and Germany and Russia take over certain parts of it.

George said there was one thing England would never consent to even discuss and that was the German idea of the freedom of the seas. I let him talk for some moments telling why they would not do this. I then told him it was not a German proposal, but was made by me in Berlin last year with your approval, and that the Germans had adopted it as their own, somewhat to our embarrassment.

I made a short argument in behalf of the proposal, and he admitted it was debatable and might be done. Lord Reading, who was present and who said nothing at the moment, called this morning to say he did not believe that English public opinion would countenance its discussion. I convinced him, too, that it was debatable.

I did not talk to George as freely as I have to Grey and Balfour, although very much to the same purpose. We thought it wise to confine any tentative agreement which might be had to Grey, Balfour, Asquith, George and Reading, and not take in the entire Cabinet. Reading was included simply because he was present and because he is George's confidant.

George and Grey believe if we can come to some understanding concerning intervention, we can adjust our shipping troubles. That is why I cabled you today asking that no more notes be sent until this letter arrives, and also suggesting that nothing be done to rupture our relations with the Central Powers. The whole plan rests upon our being able to deal with all the belligerents.

George thinks, and so do I, that it would enormously strengthen your hand in intervening, for you to put through as large a military and naval program as possible. Not that it would be finally carried out, but because of the power it would give you. He believes unless you do this your intervention might fail.

During the conversation he said that no man had ever lived with such an opportunity, and that if the world went on for untold centuries, history would record this as the greatest individual act of which it had record.

I hope and pray you will not let anything interfere with this plan. It can be done, but only by making it paramount and not allowing the lesser things to confuse it.

He said, at one time, that this peace should be a peace to make friends and not enemies, meaning that when the war is over, Germany and England should have no differences such as were left after the Franco-Prussian War.

He brought up many of the difficulties that would be encountered, such as the islands of the Pacific taken by Australia and New Zealand, the South African Colonies, the Bagdad Railway, etc. etc. We both thought compromises could be reached with you sitting as arbiter.

My thought was that England might give Germany a freer

hand in Asia and look to Africa as her sphere of influence. That in my opinion, India could not be held more than a half or a century longer, and that if I were guiding the destinies of England, I would concentrate on Africa, Australia and her other colonies outside of Asia.

I am seeing Grey and Balfour this afternoon and I will write you again.

My plan now is to go to Paris on the 20th, leaving there on the 23rd and remaining in Berlin until the 30th or 31st, returning to Paris or going to Italy at that time. It is not essential that I go to Italy excepting it seems well to have a closer connection there. When I return here, it will take about ten days before I can sail for home.   Affectionately yours,   E. M. House

TLS (WP, DLC).

From Charles William Eliot

Dear Mr. President: Cambridge, Mass. 15 January 1916.

First, may I be allowed to congratulate you on the successful working out of the principal policies and measures of your Administration. You have done fundamental things and they have promptly succeeded. Now that you have thoroughly committed the American people to the doctrine of nonintervention by force with foreign Governments on behalf of American capitalists, or American workmen, who have chosen to undertake risky adventures in foreign parts, and have hence effectively promoted a genuine Pan-American Union in the interests of political liberty, free commercial intercourse, and sympathetic fellowship, might you not frame and head a declaration on the part of all the American Republics that American sympathies go heartily with the Republic of France in its efforts to resist invasion of its territory, and to uphold the cause of the free Governments and the small independent States of Europe?

Such a declaration would not be inconsistent with our legal attitude of strict neutrality, and would give hearty satisfaction to innumerable Americans who feel that the legal attitude of their Government does not adequately express the moral sympathies or the hopes of the American people, as they watch from far this portentous struggle between democracy and autocracy.

I am, with the highest regard,

Sincerely yours,   [C. W. Eliot]

CCL (C. W. Eliot Papers, MH-Ar).

From Walter Lanfersiek[1]

Dear Sir: Chicago, Ill. Jan 15, 1916

Under date of January 11, 1916, I am in receipt of an acknowledgment from the Department of State of my letter of December 27, 1915.[2]

The Executive Committee of the Socialist Party has asked you to receive a committee representing more than a million voters of the United States, and upon a matter of vital interest to the nation. I would respectfully call to your attention that this request is not answered by the acknowledgment of the Department of State.

Trusting that you will give this matter your further consideration, and that I shall have a favorable reply fixing a date for the desired interview,[3] I am

Very respectfully yours,   Walter Lanfersiek

TLS (WP, DLC).

[1] Executive secretary of the Socialist party.

[2] W. Lanfersiek to WW, Dec. 27, 1915, TLS (WP, DLC), requesting an appointment with Wilson for the executive committee of the Socialist party. Tumulty referred the letter to the State Department for acknowledgement. The committee wanted to endorse H. J. Res. 38, calling upon Wilson to convene a congress of neutral nations. Representative Meyer London, Socialist of New York City, had introduced the resolution on December 6.

[3] Wilson met the Socialist party delegation on January 25 at the White House.

From Edward Mandell House

Dear Governor: No. 6   London, January 16, 1916.

I had another session with Grey and Balfour yesterday, but it was inconclusive.

I find Balfour argumentative and lacking in decision. He and I did most of the talking with Sir Edward coming in every now and then to support my position. It would be a calamity if anything should happen to prevent Sir Edward's continuance in the Government until peace is made. And yet if we push them too hard upon the question of neutral trade, he is likely to go.

The feeling is becoming more and more set and the country is demanding that the Government stand firm. I enclose you an article from the Mail which is characteristic of others that appear daily.[1]

Grey, Balfour and George say if they could tell the country that there was a chance of bringing about a tentative understanding with us, the people would yield to almost any demand we might make. But the opinion is firmly fixed that America will do nothing, and that England must fight the battle alone with the only weapon that has so far proved effective.

Nearly every American here, and this includes our entire Embassy I think, would be glad to see us come into the war on the side of the Allies. This feeling is shared, of course, by many Englishmen and by nearly all the French, although one is constantly told that this is not desired.

I believe I have convinced those to whom I have been able to talk freely, that it is best for all concerned for us to keep out, conserving our strength so at the proper moment, we may lead them out of their troubles.

I am more and more certain that it would be a mistake from every viewpoint for us to come in, although we should be ready to throw our weight at the right time in the right direction for the good of humanity. We are growing stronger as they grow weaker, consequently our power is increasing in double ratio.

I am sure that our policy should be to have no serious friction with the Allies over the blockade, and to keep upon such terms with Germany that our diplomatic relations may be maintained. If you can do this, and I would do it in spite of all the protests at home and abroad, you will find yourself the potential factor in concluding peace. It does not matter how much you are reviled now if the end justifies your course. The criticism, both in Europe and America comes from ignorance and from partisan feeling and can be swept aside by your final action.

Affectionately yours,   E. M. House

P.S. Of course I do not mean to advise that diplomatic relations should not be immediately broken if the Central Powers sink another passenger ship without warning. If this were not done, it would discredit us everywhere, and greatly minimize your influence.

TLS (WP, DLC).

1 "The Sham Blockade: How to Turn It into a Reality," London *Daily Mail*, Jan. 15, 1916, clipping (WP, DLC). It proposed that the Admiralty take charge of blockade policy and that the Allies declare a blockade of the entire German coast and extend the contraband list to include "all articles that may be of service to Germany," as well as all goods of German origin. American legal precedents would then support British policy, and Britain could reply to neutral criticism that it was "impossible for us to sacrifice vital legal rights for the sake of neutral Powers."

Baron Oscar von der Lancken Wakenitz[1] to Count Adolf von Montgelas[2]

Brüssel, den 16.Januar 1916.

pp. Alsbald nach Rückkehr des Gesandten Brand-Whitlock hatte ich mit ihm eine lange freundschaftliche Unterhaltung. pp.

Aus der Unterhaltung allgemeiner Art mit dem Gesandten Brand-Whitlock möchte ich noch folgendes erwähnen.

Whitlock ist bekanntlich ein alter persönlicher Freund und Schützling Wilsons. Er hatte mit diesem jetzt eine vertraute Aussprache und versicherte mir, daß Wilson, der der richtige Typus des magisterhaften deutschen Professors sei, in seiner Politik im Grunde kein eingeschworener Deutschenfeind sei. Nach Whitlocks Überzeugung hält Wilson die Vernichtung oder auch nur eine schwere politische Schwächung Deutschlands nicht im amerikanischen Interesse gelegen und zwar aus dem einfachen Grunde, weil das wichtigste Ziel der amerikanischen Politik ebenso wie für uns "freedom of the sea" sei. Ein relatives Wohlwollen Wilsons für Deutschland folge auch aus seiner persönlichen Bewunderung für die deutsche Philosophie und Literatur. Ein solches Volk, habe Wilson gesagt, müsse seinen Aufstieg behalten.

In der Munitionsfrage habe Wilson nicht anders gekonnt, da ihm die gesetzliche Handhabe zum Verbot fehlte. Außerdem habe ihm die Überlegung geleitet, daß auch Amerika einmal in einem größeren Krieg Munition von Übersee beziehen müßte.

Sehr beschäftigte Wilson die Frage, wann seine Friedensvermittlung einzusetzen haben werde. Denn daß er den Frieden zu vermitteln haben werde, das scheint dem Präsidenten nach Whitlocks Äußerungen ganz selbstverständlich zu sein. Nach einer eingehenden Besprechung der sich bietenden Möglichkeiten seien Wilson und er (Whitlock) allerdings zum Ergebnis gekommen, daß jetzt noch kein Faktum vorliege, das auch nur von fern die Brücke zum Frieden bilden könnte. Whitlock selbst ist überzeugt, daß wir bei Wilson zum gegebenen Zeitpunkt wohlwollende Bereitschaft finden würden. Schon allein aus dieser Absicht der Friedensvermittlung sei Wilson nicht gewillt gewesen, Amerika in den Krieg verwickeln zu lassen.

Über das Verhalten des Londoner Botschafters Page in der Cavell-Sache seien Wilson und Lansing sehr aufgebracht gewesen und hätten den Botschafter am liebsten sofort abberufen. Page habe dann tüchtig den Kopf gewaschen erhalten. Die Mission des Obersten House habe ebenfalls den Zweck, Page klar zu machen, daß er ein neutraler Vertreter sei.

Whitlock selbst halte ich für einen zwar schwachen, aber ehrlichen und ziemlich offenen Menschen. Er erzählte mir, daß man ihm während seines Urlaubs ½ Million Dollar angeboten habe, wenn er von seinem Posten zurücktrete und in Amerika Vorträge über die Deutschen in Belgien halte. Er hätte nur zuzugreifen brauchen. Da er kein begüterter Mann ist, bedeutet das für ihn gewiß ein Opfer. Aber er sucht seinen Lohn offenbar in anderer Richtung: Aus Andeutungen darf ich schließen, daß er für die Friedenspläne Wilsons der Mittelsmann zwischen diesem und uns sein möchte, und daß auch bei Wilson die Absicht besteht, den ihm völlig ergebenen und gefügigen Mann für diese Zwecke zu benutzen, sobald dem Präsidenten die Zeit dafür gekommen erscheint. gez: Lancken

TCL (Der Weltkrieg No. 2, Vermittlungsaktionen, geheim, vol. 15, pp. 86-87, GFO-Ar).

[1] Head of the political department for the governor-general of Belgium.
[2] Expert on American affairs in the German Foreign Office.

TRANSLATION

Brussels, January 16, 1916

. . . Immediately after the return of Minister Brand Whitlock, I had a long, friendly talk with him. . . .

From the general conversation with Minister Brand Whitlock, I would like to mention the following:

Whitlock, as is well known, is an old personal friend and protégé of Wilson's. He has had a confidential talk with him recently, and he assured me that Wilson, who was the ideal type of the schoolmasterly German professor, was at bottom no sworn enemy of Germany in his policy. Whitlock is convinced that Wilson believes that the destruction or even merely a severe political weakening of Germany was not in the American interest—namely, for the simple reason that the most important aim of American policy is, as it is for us, the "freedom of the seas." A relatively benevolent attitude toward Germany on Wilson's part was also the result of his personal admiration for German philosophy and literature. Such a people, Wilson had said, had to be allowed to maintain their high level of achievement.

As far as the munitions question is concerned, Wilson could not have acted otherwise, because he lacked the legal authority to prohibit it [the export of arms]. Moreover, he had been guided by the consideration that, at some time, America, too, might have to procure munitions from overseas during a great war.

Wilson has been very taken up with the question as to when his peace mediation should begin. For, according to Whitlock's remarks, it was self-evident to the President that *he* would have to mediate the peace. After a detailed discussion of the possibilities that presented themselves, however, Wilson and he (Whitlock) had come to the conclusion that at present there was still no circumstance available that could even remotely constitute a bridge toward peace. Whitlock himself is convinced that, at the appropriate time, we shall find Wilson favorably disposed toward it. If for no other reason than this hope to mediate in the cause of peace, Wilson has not been willing to permit America to become involved in the war.

Wilson and Lansing have both been very upset about the behavior of Ambassador Page in London in the Cavell matter and would have preferred to recall the Ambassador immediately. Subsequently, Page had been brought roundly to task. Colonel House's mission, likewise, has the purpose of making it clear to Page that he should be a neutral representative.

I consider Whitlock himself a weak but honest and rather open-minded man. He told me that, during his leave, he had been offered half a million dollars if he would resign his post and lecture in America about the Germans in Belgium. All that he would have had to do would have been to grab the opportunity. As he is no wealthy man, this certainly meant a sacrifice for him. But he is apparently looking for his reward along other lines: From certain indications I may conclude that he wants to be the middleman between Wilson and us in carrying out the former's peace plans; and that Wilson, too, intends to use this pliable man, who is wholly devoted to him, for this purpose, as soon as the President thinks that the time for it has come.

Signed: Lancken

To Robert Lansing

My dear Mr. Secretary,   The White House. 17 January, 1916.

I have just had a cable from House in which he says that he is to mail me a letter by the steamer which leaves England on Wednesday next which will contain something of importance which leads him to beg that we will send no note to England about shipping troubles until we see it and which renders it also of the greatest importance that nothing should break our relations with Germany and Austria until we have been made acquainted with it. He adds that there seems to be some daylight ahead "if fortune favours us." I can only guess what he may mean by the last phrase.

I thought it important that you should have this at once.

Faithfully Yours,   W.W.

WWTLI (R. Lansing Papers, NjP).

To Seth Low

My dear Mr. Low: The White House January 17, 1916

Thank you sincerely for your letter of January twelfth.[1] I am very much pleased and cheered by what you tell me of the work of the Colorado Coal Commission and shall look forward to the report with the greatest interest. May I not thank you very sincerely?   Faithfully yours,   Woodrow Wilson

TLS (S. Low Papers, NNC).

[1] S. Low to WW, Jan. 12, 1916, TLS (WP, DLC). Low reported that he had returned from Colorado and that he had found the coal operators cooperative and respectful of the President's commission. As soon as the other members of the commission had returned, they would submit a report to Wilson.

To Cleveland Hoadley Dodge

My dear Cleve: The White House January 17, 1916

Your letter of January fourteenth came when my heart was pretty sad about the Mexican situation. It acted, therefore, like a ray of light in a dark place and I thank you for it with all my heart as well as with all my mind. Your approval in a matter which I am sure you understand to the utmost reassures me immensely.   Affectionately yours,   Woodrow Wilson

TLS (WC, NjP).

From Joseph Patrick Tumulty

Dear Governor: The White House January 17, 1916.

I cannot impress upon you too forcibly the importance of an appeal to the country at this time on the question of preparedness. No matter what the character of the information is that you are receiving, I get it from all sources that there is no enthusiasm on the "hill" for preparedness, and that the country itself is indifferent because of the apparent inability of the country to grasp the importance of this question. This indifference arises out of two things: first, the attitude of the pacifists whose feelings have been nurtured by the preachings of Mr. Bryan; second, and those in the country who believe in preparedness but who are frightened because of the talk of militarism as outlined by Mr. Roosevelt.

The great bulk of the people are looking for leadership; they do not wish to follow Mr. Bryan; they are reluctant to follow Mr. Roosevelt except in sheer desperation, and they are waiting for you. I believe they are yearning at this time for leadership.

Now is the time when impressions are being made and the impression abroad in the country is that we are drifting and that there is an utter lack of leadership. The American people are a sentimental people and even on a question as deep and as vital as national defence, they ask for "entertainment and guidance." What is needed now, even from a political standpoint, is an appeal to the country.

The situation which confronts you now is just such a one as we had to cope with in the famous Smith-Martine fight. If you will recall the visit you paid me at my law office in Jersey City immediately after the election, you will be reminded that you made the statement that some of your friends advised you to allow the matter to drift, that Martine was incompetent and that the State would resent your interference. I remember very distinctly what my advice to you then was. I said that the State was yearning for leadership, that it felt that the decent people who needed to be aroused as a matter of honesty, were in favor of Martine, and I further made the statement to you that unless you led, some one else would take the leadership, very much to your injury and prestige. You were advised that if we had a meeting in Hudson County, there would not be a corporal's guard in attendance. The enthusiastic meetings in Newark and Jersey City showed the interest of the people and how quick they accepted your leadership, with the result that Smith was overwhelmingly defeated. There is no doubt how the body of the American people feel on this question. Certainly they need no convincing in view of the criticism you are receiving because of your attitude in Mexico— that you are a man who deeply desires peace.

You can therefore with much greater reason address them on this question, and address them with great force and earnestness. I am afraid if you delay in this matter, it will be too late because our enemies are busy and active. If some unfortunate thing should arise in international affairs or in Mexico within the next few weeks and an announcement come then that you were to make an appeal to the country, it would be looked upon as an anti-climax and an attempt upon your part to retrieve yourself. Now is the psychological moment to make your plea for national defence and incidentally to discuss Mexico and our foreign relations. The only argument against big armament is that the commander-in-chief of the army and the navy would abuse the power with which the people entrusted him. Your patience and watchful waiting in Mexico is a conclusive answer to this argument. In other words, you must ask the country to accept your leadership or the leadership of others who can't lead. Your voice is the only responsible voice in America that can speak with certainty and calmness as to the need for these things. Your position is that of trustee.

The popular argument against preparedness is that we are not threatened from any quarter and therefore this programme of preparedness is not necessary. Our answer to that should be that while there is no direct threat from any nation, we cannot always be certain because of our present position as a nation; that circumstances developing after the European war may in some way threaten the sovereignty of America. In other words, what is needed now is punch all along the line and a frank exposition of this whole matter. You might in some diplomatic way hint in a speech that you had a responsibility as trustee of the nation and leader of your party. If your trusteeship and leadership are to be repudiated, you wish the country to know who is responsible. I look at it in this way: If your leadership in this matter is rejected, the Democratic party may as well go out of the business of government. Our all is staked upon a successful issue in this matter. You can therefore afford to be most emphatic in stating what your attitude is.

I beg to call your attention to the following editorial from the New York Times of the 16th of January:

"Too many of the Senators and Representatives seem to be thinking less of the national honor than of political advantage. There is no doubt of the will of a large majority of the people, but it lacks articulate expression of a sufficiently forcible character to stimulate the national legislators to action. The burden of inspiring the American public to an unmistakable utterance of its will in the matter of defense rests upon the President. He must personally get in contact with the people, explain the situation to them, make their duty plain. They will not fail to respond. Unless the large personal popularity of the Chief Executive is exerted and his eloquence and logic are employed to induce the people to overcome the apathetic indifference or unreasonable hostility to preparedness exhibited in Congress, we cannot hope that the matter will be settled before adjournment. The Military and Naval Committees of the House of Representatives, where the bills must originate, are wasting their time."

J. P. Tumulty

TLS (WP, DLC).

From Robert Lansing, with Enclosure

My dear Mr. President: Washington January 17, 1916.

I enclose for your consideration the draft of a letter to the British Ambassador dealing with the submarine question, and suggesting a method by which future loss of life on merchant vessels might be avoided.

My first inclination was to send letters to the German Ambassador and Austrian Chargé, but two reasons prevented; first, I was convinced that the German and Austrian Governments would assent to the proposal as it only required them to conform to the rules of international law, while it required their enemies to modify a present practice which might be construed into the relinquishment of a legal right; and, second, if Germany and Austria acceded promptly to the suggestion, any demur by Great Britain, France, Italy or Belgium would, if it became known (as it would undoubtedly through the German or Austrian Embassies), arouse adverse criticism in the press of this country and excite public resentment against the Entente Powers, which appears to be increasing from day to day.

By adopting this method of approach the proposal can be kept secret if it is refused by the Entente Governments and if it is considered inexpedient to make it public.

Faithfully yours, Robert Lansing

TLS (SDR, RG 59, 763.72/2352½A, DNA).

ENCLOSURE

Draft.

My Dear Mr. Ambassador:

It is a matter of the deepest interest to my Government to bring to an end, if possible, the dangers to life which attend the use of submarines as at present employed in destroying enemy commerce on the high seas, since on any merchant vessel of belligerent nationality there may be citizens of the United States who have taken passage or are members of the crew, in the exercise of their recognized rights as neutrals. I assume that Your Excellency's Government are equally solicitous to protect their nationals from the exceptional hazards which are presented by their passage on a merchant vessel through those portions of the high seas in which undersea craft of their enemy are operating.

While I am fully alive to the appalling loss of life among noncombatants, regardless of age or sex, which has resulted from the present method of destroying merchant vessels without removing the persons on board to places of safety, and while I view that practice as contrary to those humane principles which should control belligerents in the conduct of their naval operations, I do not feel that a belligerent should be deprived of the proper use of submarines in the interruption of enemy commerce since these instruments of war have proven their effectiveness in this particular branch of warfare on the high seas.

In order to bring submarine warfare within the general rules of international law and the principles of humanity without destroying its efficiency in the destruction of commerce, I believe that a formula may be found which, though it may require slight modifications of the practice generally followed by nations prior to the employment of submarines, will appeal to the sense of justice and fairness of all the belligerents in the present war.

Your Excellency will understand that in seeking a formula or rule of this nature I approach it of necessity from the point of view of a neutral, but I believe that it will be equally efficacious in preserving the lives of all non-combatants on merchant vessels of belligerent nationality.

My comments on this subject are predicated on the following propositions:

1. A non-combatant has a right to traverse the high seas in a merchant vessel entitled to fly a belligerent flag and to rely upon the observance of the rules of international law and principles of humanity if the vessel is approached by a naval vessel of another belligerent.

2. A merchant vessel of enemy nationality should not be attacked without being ordered to stop.

3. An enemy merchant vessel, when ordered to do so by a belligerent submarine, should immediately stop.

4. Such vessel should not be attacked after being ordered to stop unless it attempts to flee or to resist, and in case it ceases to flee or resist, the attack should discontinue.

5. In the event that it is impossible to place a prize crew on board of an enemy merchant vessel or convoy it into port, the vessel may be sunk, provided the crew and passengers have been removed to a place of safety.

In complying with the foregoing propositions which, in my opinion, embody the principal rules, the strict observance of which will insure the life of a non-combatant on a merchant vessel which is intercepted by a submarine, I am not unmindful of the obstacles which would be met by undersea craft as commerce destroyers.

Prior to the year 1915 belligerent operations against enemy commerce on the high seas had been conducted with cruisers carrying heavy armaments. Under these conditions International Law appeared to permit a merchant vessel to carry an armament for defensive purposes without losing its character as a private commercial vessel. This right seems to have been predicated on the superior defensive strength of ships of war, and the limitation of armament to have been dependent on the fact that it could not be used effectively in offense against enemy naval vessels, while it could defend the merchantman against the generally inferior armament of piratical ships and privateers.

The use of the submarine, however, has changed these relations. Comparison of the defensive strength of a cruiser and a submarine shows that the latter, relying for protection on its power to submerge, is almost defenseless in point of construction. Even a merchant ship carrying a small calibre gun would be able to use it effectively for offense against a submarine. Moreover, pirates and sea-rovers have been swept from the main trade channels of the seas, and privateering has been abolished. Consequently, the placing of guns on merchantmen at the present day of submarine warfare, can be explained only on the ground of a purpose to render merchantmen superior in force to submarines and to prevent warning and visit and search by them. Any armament, therefore, on a merchant vessel would seem to have the character of an offensive armament.

If a submarine is required to stop and search a merchant vessel on the high seas and, in case it is found that she is of enemy character, and that conditions necessitate her destruction, to remove to a place of safety all persons on board, it would not seem just or reasonable that the submarine should be compelled, while complying with these requirements, to expose itself to almost certain destruction by the guns on board the merchant vessel.

It would, therefore, appear to be a reasonable and reciprocally just arrangement if it could be agreed by the opposing belligerents that submarines should be caused to adhere strictly to the rules of international law in the matter of stopping and searching merchant vessels, determining their belligerent nationality, and removing the crews and passengers to places of safety before sinking the vessels as prizes of war, and that merchant vessels of belligerent nationality should be prohibited and prevented from carrying any armament whatsoever.

In presenting this formula as a basis for conditional declarations by the belligerent governments, I do so in the full conviction that your Government will consider primarily the humane purpose of saving the lives of innocent people rather than the insistence upon a doubtful legal right which may be denied, on account of new conditions.

I would be pleased if you would be good enough to bring this suggestion to the attention of your Government and inform me of their views upon the subject and whether they would be willing to make such a declaration conditioned upon their enemies making a similar declaration.

A communication similar to this one has been addressed to the Ambassadors of France and Italy and the Minister of Belgium at this capital.

I should add that my Government is impressed with the reasonableness of the argument that a merchant vessel carrying an armament of any sort, in view of the character of submarine warfare and the defensive weakness of undersea craft, should be held to be an auxilliary cruiser and so treated by a neutral as well as by a belligerent government, and is seriously considering instructing its officials accordingly.

T MS (SDR, RG 59, 763.72/2352½A, DNA).

To Robert Lansing

My dear Mr. Secretary,   The White House. 17 January, 1916.

This draft has my entire approval. I hope that you will send it to the Governments you have indicated to me;[1] and I most sincerely hope that they will feel that we are right in our argument and suggestion and will be willing to cooperate with us in attaining the object we have in view, an object which they must surely wish to accomplish as earnestly as we do, and which this seems in the circumstances the only feasible way of reaching.

Faithfully Yours,   W.W.

WWTLI (SDR, RG 59, 763.72/2353½, DNA).
[1] Lansing's so-called *modus vivendi* was embodied in RL to C. A. Spring Rice, Jan. 18, 1916, TLS (FO 115/2017, pp. 42-49, PRO); printed in *FR-WWS 1916*, pp. 146-48. Spring Rice sent a summary to London: C. A. Spring Rice to E. Grey, Jan. 21, 1916, Hw telegram (FO 115/2017, p. 50, PRO).

From Edward Mandell House

Dear Governor: No. 7.   London, January 17, 1916.

After I leave here on the 20th there will not be an opportunity to write you freely again until my return since they seldom send a pouch from Paris, and I would hesitate to say [send] anything in the pouch from Berlin.

Sir Edward thinks a trip to Italy would be of no use whatever at this time and advised me not to make it. This will enable me to take the Rotterdam, sailing from here February 19th. I feel that it is important to get back and tell you of conditions over here.

I heard that the King was feeling somewhat dissatisfied with your position. I therefore arranged to see him and after an hour's conversation, I left him in the happiest frame of mind and just as cordial as ever.

A member of the Household of the King of Belgium who is here tells me that the King is expecting me to have a conference with him at his headquarters before I return. I shall arrange to motor there from Paris upon my return from Berlin.

I leave here the 20th for Paris. Remain there two days leaving there for Berlin on the 23rd. After a week in Berlin I will return to Paris for a week and will then come here.

Jusserand intimated that his government would prefer seeing me after I returned from Berlin rather than before, and I have arranged my trip accordingly.

I expect to be in England again on the 10th or 11th of February, and should be able to wind up everything here by the 19th.

I am sending this for your information.

Affectionately yours,   E. M. House

I am lunching with Asquith today, and am dining tonight to meet the Archbishop of Canterbury[1] and Lord Stamfordham.[2]

TLS (WP, DLC).
  [1] The Most Rev. Randall Thomas Davidson.
  [2] Arthur John Bigge, Baron Stamfordham, was private secretary to the King.

To James Hay

My dear Mr. Hay: The White House January 18, 1916

I feel we are under a sort of obligation to each other to keep one another posted and, therefore, I venture to write you a few lines as to a recent interchange of views on my part with the Secretary of War. I want you to know just what I said to him about my position with regard to the way in which the programme for preparation is to be handled.

I told him that I entirely agreed with him that we should have a trained citizen reserve and that the training, organization and control of that reserve should be under immediate federal control. I added that I did not consider myself irrevocably or dogmatically committed to any one plan of providing the nation with such a reserve, that I was cordially willing to discuss alternative proposals; that I did not feel that I was at liberty to take any other attitude towards the Committee on Military Affairs, for I felt that it would never be possible or proper for me to say to any committee of the House that so far as my participation in legislation was concerned they would have to take my plan or none.

I told him, as I told you, that I welcomed a frank interchange of views and a patient and thorough comparison of all the methods proposed of obtaining the objects we have in view. I assured him that so far as my own participation in final legislative action was concerned I was sure no one, least of all yourself, would expect me to acquiesce in any proposal that I regarded as inadequate or illusory, but that there was in my opinion no reason to anticipate or fear such a result. I told him that I had had a delightfully frank conference with you and that I had said to you that I was perfectly willing to consider any plan which would give us a national reserve under unmistakable national control, and that I would support any such scheme if convinced of its adequacy and wise policy and that that was all that you had asked or desired.

Frankly, as I told you, I do not believe that such a reserve can be supplied through the National Guard because of the apparently insuperable constitutional obstacles to a direct control of training and organization by the National Government. I feel certain that the country will demand of us imperatively a genuine nationalization of the reserve forces which we are about to create. But it would, of course, be ridiculous for me to say that I would not consider methods which men thoroughly acquainted with the subject matter felt ready to propose. I wish with all my heart that the Committee could see its way to a direct and immediate acceptance of the plan for a Continental Army and I believe that it will ultimately find that it must turn in that direction.

Cordially and sincerely yours,   Woodrow Wilson

TLS (J. Hay Papers, DLC).

To Charles William Eliot

My dear Doctor Eliot: The White House January 18, 1916

Thank you sincerely for your letter of January fifteenth. What you say about the principal policies and measures of this administration reassures and strengthens me very much indeed.

I feel the force of what you say about the Republic of France and yet I cannot help feeling that it would hardly be consistent with the policy of detachment from the European struggle which I have hitherto so sedulously sought to maintain if I were to express a sympathy which, after all, would go to the very merits of the present struggle.

With warmest regard,

Cordially and sincerely yours,   Woodrow Wilson

TLS (C. W. Eliot Papers, MH-Ar).

To Carter Glass

My dear Glass: The White House January 18, 1916

It goes mighty hard to say that I cannot respond affirmatively to the very attractive invitation which you participated in extending to me to visit Lynchburg,[1] but I want frankly to tell you just why it seems to me impossible. I do not think that the Congress quite realizes the genuine demand of the country for an adequate plan of preparation for national defence. I feel that it is my duty to explain this matter to the country and summon its support and that I ought to devote my whole energy without turning aside to the business of this session in which I want to be of assistance in every possible and legitimate way.

In such circumstances, it seems clearly impossible for me to prepare anything that I would be willing to utter on such an occasion as that which is being planned for in Lynchburg. Will you not be generous enough to explain this to the gentlemen who were so kind and courteous to see me the other day with you and urge this invitation upon me?

Cordially and faithfully yours,   Woodrow Wilson

TLS (C. Glass Papers, ViU).
[1] Glass and a group from Lynchburg had called on Wilson on January 17.

To Robert Lansing

My dear Mr. Secretary,   The White House. 19 January, 1916.

Here is a paper which Mr. Aredondo handed Senator Stone with the request that he see that it reached my hands.[1] Senator Stone handed it to me this morning.

The information which it contains, if true is very important indeed, and I hope that it will be possible to follow it up at once. A representation to Guatemala of a very direct and explicit kind ought to be sufficient to put a stop to mischief there by carrying the plain intimation that we should regard such things as a direct offence against the peace and dignity of the United States; and the other matters it ought to be possible, with the clues furnished, for our secret service to follow up very effectively. I hope that it will be feasible to make an immediate investigation.

Faithfully Yours, W.W.

WWTLI (SDR, RG 59, 812.00/17171½, DNA).
1 Untitled memorandum, T MS (SDR, RG 59, 812.00/17171½, DNA), describing the work of Felix Díaz's agents in the United States to raise money and arms for an attack on Salina Cruz in early February. Arms and ammunition were to be shipped to Guatemala from New Orleans before the end of January.

To William Gibbs McAdoo

My dear Mac: The White House January 19, 1916

I have your memorandum about the "dumping" business. There is a great deal of force, of course, in what you say. At the same time, there is another side to the matter which I want to talk over with you as soon as may be.

In haste Affectionately yours, Woodrow Wilson

TLS (W. G. McAdoo Papers, DLC).

To Thomas Watt Gregory

The White House
My dear Mr. Attorney General: January 19, 1916

I must confess that I am always uneasy when I find myself differing from you in judgment, but I do think that in the case presented by Senator Stone regarding the respite for Marion W. Rose, recently convicted in the United States Court for the Western District of Missouri of conspiracy to defraud the United States, the circumstances are sufficiently extraordinary to justify a respite of forty days. I would be very much obliged if you would have an arrangement made for this, and beg that you will accept my apologies for a difference of judgment.

Always Faithfully yours, Woodrow Wilson

TLS (T. W. Gregory Papers, DLC).

From James Hay

Washington, D.C.
My dear Mr. President: January 19th 1916.

I appreciate very much your consideration in writing to me and letting me know your thoughts and impressions about the perplexing problems which we have to solve. I am sure that only in this way can we reach a conclusion which will be satisfactory to the country and to ourselves.

The Committee is now engaged in hearing all persons who can give it information. The legislation so far as the Committee is concerned has not reached the formative stage. Until it has reached such a stage I have thought it best not to advocate any one of the plans proposed.

I am free to confess that the National Guard seems to me now the best medium through which to obtain our ends. The constitutional obstacles to a direct control of training and organizing the National Guard can in my judgment be easily overcome.

But if after the evidence is all in, the continental army plan shall seem best I will certainly advocate it.

I will consider it a privilege if I may from time to time consult you.   Very sincerely yours,   [James Hay]

CCL (J. Hay Papers, DLC).

From John Purroy Mitchel

New York, Jan. 19, 1916.

I feel that I would fail in my duty toward you, and toward this city, did I not protest to you as vigorously as I can against the appointment of Joseph Johnson, as postmaster of New York. Being conspicuously unfit and ineligible, his appointment would occasion for you a material loss of public confidence in this city. In view of his activities and slanderous attacks, during the Mayoralty campaign and since, his appointment would be publicly construed as unfriendly to the fusion administration.

John Purroy Mitchel.

T telegram (WP, DLC).

From Horace Herbert Clark, with Enclosure

My dear Mr. President: Washington, D.C., Jany 19 1916.

If you not mind the suggestion, would not this be satisfactory in reference to the letter, and efface to a considerable degree the appearance of being second hand. In case it is necessary for you to answer an inquiry it might be stated that while I am not personally known to you except through the agency of one business transaction, yet I have been highly endorsed by friends of yours.

Very truly yours   H. H. Clark

P.S. I am enclosing a brief outline of the benefits which would accrue to the present owners[1]

ALS (WP, DLC).

¹ Wilson immediately had McAdoo send his former secretary, Kenyon B. Conger of New York, to Los Angeles to investigate Mrs. Hulbert's business affairs. Mrs. Hulbert later wrote (*The Story of Mrs. Peck* [New York, 1933], pp. 250-51), that Conger said to her: "Those two boys in Washington are worried about you." When she asked who they were, he replied, "Why—the President and Mr. McAdoo."

Conger reported to McAdoo (K. B. Conger to WGM, Feb. 10, 1916, TLS [WP, DLC]) in great detail. He wrote that Clark was of somewhat dubious character, and that Mrs. Hulbert and Allen S. Hulbert had entered into a three-year contract under which Clark would manage their business affairs upon terms highly disadvantageous to the Hulberts. Conger warned them to keep a sharp eye on Clark, be sure that he held his expenses to a minimum, and to deny him access to their additional funds and assets. Conger praised Allen highly for his industry and determination to succeed. Wilson reimbursed McAdoo for Conger's expenses in WW to WGM, Feb. 24, 1916, TLS (W. G. McAdoo Papers, DLC). This letter is the last one in the Wilson or other collections concerning Mrs. Hulbert and her affairs until WW to Mary A. Hulbert (draft), Nov. 1, 1916.

E N C L O S U R E

In event of this transaction being brought to a successful issue, the benefits accruing to the friends in question may be stated in these terms: For the planted thirty acres they will receive $15,000. in cash and a syndicate ownership of 45 acres of planted and fully improved land, the market value of which, based on the present selling price of orange groves, which are as yet not yielding, would be $1,500. per acre. This they would own free and clear. Even if the transaction should progress no further than this outline, it would place them in a position of independence. With a little time and the help I have suggested there is absolutely no question as to making it a success.

Hw MS (WP, DLC).

Robert Lansing to Edward Mandell House

Washington, January 19, 1916. 6 p.m.

No. 3. German Foreign Office apparently has come to no decision on LUSITANIA. Strongly urged to meet our views by some of their people on ground that such action would in the end cause public sentiment to turn against England. Favorable action seems probable. British Ambassador thinks his country can make no further material concessions and expects a deadlock. Draft of English note in answer to our note to England now in hands of France for revision. In view of probable settlement with Germany resentment in Congress centering on England. Mexican situation causing trouble in Congress.   Lansing.

T telegram (SDR, RG 59, 841.857 L 97/127½A, DNA).

To John Purroy Mitchel

My dear Mr. Mayor: The White House January 20, 1916

I received your telegram about the appointment of Mr. Johnson. The case puzzles and balks my judgment in an unusual degree and I am warmly obliged to you for your frankness.

Cordially and sincerely yours,   Woodrow Wilson

TLS (J. P. Mitchel Papers, DLC).

From Robert Lansing

PRIVATE AND CONFIDENTIAL:

My dear Mr. President: Washington January 20, 1916.

In connection with the paper of Mr. Arredondo, which was handed you by Senator Stone in relation to a revolution in the southern states of Mexico, headed by Felix Diaz, I beg to say that the Government has the case, I think, very well in hand. Agents of the Department of Justice have been in New Orleans watching Larrea[1] and the Chief of the Secret Service informs me that no arms or ammunition can get out of the southern ports or even out of New York, for Guatemala, without his knowledge, and that he knows of nothing which confirms Mr. Arredondo's statement. Mr. Bielaski also informs me that Felix Diaz is today in New York; also that the story originated, he thinks, from an inquiry of one of his Agents in New Orleans as to whether such a revolution was planned, and that the person of whom the inquiry was made gave out the report and is not desirous of finding out where Diaz is, so that he can not be connected with the supposed revolution.

The Department of Justice is today sending out telegrams to its Agents in regard to the Arredondo statement, and this Department is endeavoring to have Captain Martin,[2] Military Attaché at Guatemala, take a trip along the Guatemala border and ascertain if there are any foundation at all for the frequent rumors of revolutionary movements there. The Department is also sending a telegram to the legation at Guatemala to assist Captain Martin to investigate, discreetly, the rumors.

I believe that everything has been done during the past two months that could be done to run down the truth and to prevent any possible uprusing [uprising] along the Guatemalan border of Mexico.   Faithfully yours,   Robert Lansing.

TLS (WP, DLC).
1 Gonzalo Larrea.
2 Walter F. Martin.

To Morris Sheppard

My dear Senator: [The White House] January 21, 1916

Ordinarily, as you evidently feel yourself, I should have no objection to the publication of any letter of mine,[1] but just at the present juncture I am afraid the publication of my letter of July twenty-eighth, 1915, to you in regard to the cotton situation[2] might do some harm because of its very unfavorable references to Great Britain. It is hardly right for me to make such declarations public with regard to matters which I am attempting to handle diplomatically, but might it not be possible for some friend of yours to show the letter to the editor[3] so that his mouth might be closed as to the nonsense of your having anything to conceal?

With the warmest regard,
          Cordially and faithfully yours,   Woodrow Wilson

TLS (Letterpress Books, WP, DLC).
  [1] Wilson was replying to M. Sheppard to WW, Jan. 17, 1916, TLS (WP, DLC).
  [2] Printed at that date in Vol. 34.
  [3] Sheppard had written that he wanted to send Wilson's letter to the editor of an agricultural publication who had attached "some significance to my failure to give it out."

From Charles William Eliot

Private

Dear Mr. President: Cambridge, Mass. 21 January 1916.

I heartily agree with the statement you make in your note to me of the eighteenth, that a candid expression of the sympathy which naturally exists between Pan-America and the Republic of France under her present awful afflictions would not be consistent with the policy of detachment from the European struggle which you have heretofore sought to maintain. It is because of that clear inconsistency that I venture to urge upon you a new departure.

The attitude of detachment from the moral issues of the war was at first a natural accompaniment of the neutral attitude of the United States. In the early months of the war there was often doubt about the actual facts of Germany's military and naval action. You repeatedly waited to ascertain the facts, before protesting against violations of international treaties and conventions; and when the facts were ascertained, protesting seemed ineffective or too late.

Again, the motives and intentions of Germany were not completely obvious during the first six months of the war, as they are now. For a time one could even accept the allegation that Germany believed that she was fighting a defensive war. Furthermore, during the first year of the war it was possible to hope that the Government of the United States by abstaining from expressing any opinion about the moral aspects of the war and its effects on political liberty throughout the world and on the liberties of small nations in particular, might later come to exert a strong influence in favor of peace with justice, as an umpire or conciliator, when the war ceased. The events of the last six months have destroyed that hope or prospect. That argument against expressing the real sentiments of the American people concerning the causes of this war and its objects no longer has any force. Everybody now sees that a strong neutral Power which claims and urges the commercial rights of neutrals during a bitter war, inevitably comes to be disliked and distrusted by both parties to the combat.

The whole civilized world now sees clearly that the objects of Germany and Austria-Hungary in starting the long-prepared war were enlargement of territory and the opening of new routes for their commerce and trade; and all the world now sees that the German method of carrying on war is thoroughly barbarous —military necessity being treated as a sufficient reason for violation of treaties, widespread devastation, and sweeping massacres of non-combatants.

Under these new conditions, cannot the American Republics join in a frank expression of their opinions and hopes concerning the war, addressed to the one Republic which is engaged in desperate resistance to the fierce attacks of the Central monarchies?

I believe that such a statement as you would write might contribute much to bringing the war to a close, and to showing the way to prevent such wars in the future. Moreover, it would greatly relieve the minds of many Americans who do not find the attitude of "detachment from the European struggle" a worthy interpretation of the moral rights and duties of the American Republics, in face of the present tremendous attacks on the American theories of political liberty and the American ideals of public justice and mercy.

You would naturally base such a statement on international and humanitarian grounds, rather than upon any national interests; but I cannot help thinking that you would incidentally reinforce in the minds of our people, the national policies you have consistently advocated—including your present advocacy of a measure of national preparedness against attack.

I cannot conceive of any other act which would so greatly strengthen the moral influence of the President of the United States, or more brightly illumine your own career.

I am, with the highest regard

Sincerely yours,   Charles W. Eliot

TLS (WP, DLC).

From Jessie Kennedy Dyer

My dear Uncle Woodrow: Camden, Ark., Jan. 21, '16.

Your letter came some days ago and I assure you was greatly appreciated. You were certainly prompt in replying, and it made me feel mighty good to get such a dear letter from you.

A week ago to-day I was pleasantly surprised by receiving a little box of wedding cake. Thank you many, many times for it, but most of all for thinking of me.

We are having some *real winter* weather now and all have had bad colds but are getting better now. Hope all of you are well and enjoying all the good things of this life. Give our love to all the folks.

With a big share of love & good wishes for you from

Your loving Niece   Jessie K. Dyer.

ALS (WP, DLC).

To Joseph Patrick Tumulty

U.S.S. MAYFLOWER,
Via Navy Department Radio [Jan. 22, 1916]

Please send me by wireless the documents Senator Clarke will send to the office today.   Woodrow Wilson

T telegram (WP, DLC).

Constantin Brün to Robert Lansing

Washington, D. C.
Dear Mr. Secretary of State,   Jan. 22, 1916.

In accordance with our conversation on January 19th, I at once cabled to the Danish Government suggesting that they should agree to a sum of 25 (twenty five) Million Dollars being named as a base for the negociation and consideration of a treaty for the transfer of the Danish West India Islands to the sovereignty of the United States.

I am today in receipt of a cablegram from the Danish Minister of Foreign Affairs authorizing me to agree to the said proposition.

The Minister adds that he will now expect to receive a draft of the treaty to be negociated between you and myself, and he also submits to you that for reasons which I believe are obvious it is desirable that the matter should be proceeded with as speedily as possible.

Believe me, dear Mr. Lansing,

Yours very sincerely   C. Brün.

ALS (SDR, RG 59, 711.5914/57½, DNA).

To Joseph Patrick Tumulty

U.S.S. MAYFLOWER, Via Radio,
Navy Department, January 23, 1916.

Please say to Senator Clarke, of Ark., that the amendment[1] as he has worked it out is satisfactory to me. If the Senate thinks it necessary to take definite action at this time the amendment in this shape is excellently worked out and safeguarded.

Woodrow Wilson.

T telegram (WP, DLC).

[1] An amendment (WP, DLC) by adding handwritten and typed text to the printed amendment to S. 381, about which see G. M. Hitchcock to JPT, Jan. 11, 1916, n. 1. The second sentence of the first paragraph read: "This transfer of possession, sovereignty, and governmental control shall be completed and become absolute not less than two years nor more [than] four years from the date of the approval of this Act, under the terms and in the manner hereinafter prescribed; PROVIDED, That if the President shall, at the expiration of the said period of four years, find that the condition of the internal or external affairs of said Philippines is such as to warrant him in so doing, he is hereby further authorized, by proclamation duly made and published, to extend the said time to and including the date of the final adjournment of the session of Congress which shall convene next after the expiration of the said period, to the end that the Congress may in its discretion further consider the situation in the said Philippines; but any such extension of time by the President shall not otherwise delay or nullify the operative force of this act, unless the Congress shall hereafter so direct."

The first sentence of the second paragraph, stating the obligation to protect Philippine sovereignty against external threats, was amended to eliminate the five-year maximum on the obligation. The final sentence was extended to read: ". . . and if none are willing to so unite therein, then the President is authorized to give such guaranty on behalf of the United States alone, for the period of five years from and after the expiration of said period of four years, or any extension thereof, and pending the existence of such separate guaranty by the United States, the United States shall be entitled to retain and exercise such control and supervision in the said Philippines as may be necessary to enforce order therein and to avoid external complications."

To Claude Kitchin

My dear Mr. Kitchin: The White House January 24, 1916

In common, I dare say, with everyone who wishes to be thoughtful of the future economic prosperity and development of the country, I have been thinking a great deal recently about what it would be wise to do to provide the Government with the necessary data to furnish a sound basis for the policy which should be pursued in the years immediately ahead of us, years which will no doubt be full of many changes which it is at present impossible even for the most prescient to forecast, and the more I have thought about the matter the plainer it has become to me that we ought to have some such instrumentality as would be supplied by a tariff board.

I am convinced, as I suppose every disinterested person must be, that it would be a mistake to provide for such a board with the idea of serving any particular theory of fiscal policy. What we would need would be above all things else a board as much as possible free from any strong prepossession in favor of any political policy and capable of looking at the whole economic situation of the country with a dispassionate and disinterested scrutiny. I believe that we could obtain such a board if the proper legislation were enacted and it is quite clear to me what the field of its inquiry and its activities should be. It should, it seems to me, investigate the administrative and fiscal effects of the customs laws now in force or hereafter enacted; the relations between the rates of duty on raw materials and those on finished or half finished products; the effects of *ad valorem* and specific duties and of those which are a compound of specific and *ad valorem*; the arrangement of schedules of duties and the classification of the articles in the several schedules; the provisions of law and the rules and regulations of the Treasury Department regarding entry, appraisement, invoices and collection; and in general the working of the customs tariff laws in economic effect and administrative method.

It could and should also secure facts which would be very useful to the administrative officers of the Government, to the Congress, and to the public at large, through investigations of the revenue derived for customs duties and the articles subject to duty, the cost of collection thereof, and the revenue collected from customs duties at the several ports of entry; and it should be directed to investigate and throw light from every possible angle on the tariff relations between the United States and foreign countries; the rates of duty imposed on American products in foreign countries; the existence and effects of discriminating duties, commercial treaties and preferential provisions; the effects of export bounties and preferential transportation rates; and the effects of any special or discriminating duties that may be levied by the United States. It might in this connection furnish the State Department with very valuable information regarding treaty and tariff relations between the United States and foreign countries.

It might further be of great assistance to the Congress and to the public and to American industry by investigating the industrial effects of proposed or existing duties on products which compete with products of American industry; the conditions of competition between American and foreign producers, including all the essential facts surrounding the production of commodities at home and abroad; the volume of importation compared with domestic production; the nature and causes of the advantages and disadvantages of American as compared with foreign producers; and the possibility of establishing new industries or of expanding industries already in existence through scientific and practical processes in such a manner as substantially to promote the prosperity of the United States.

I think it would be very useful and, indeed, necessary to require the board to act in conjunction with all appropriate agencies already in existence in the several departments of the Government and even with appropriate agencies outside of the existing departments, in order to avoid so far as possible duplications of work and to make all sources of official information available to the same end.

If broadly enough empowered, such a board might be very helpful in securing the facts on which to base an opinion as to unfair methods and circumstances of competition between foreign and domestic enterprises and as to the possibilities and dangers of the unfair "dumping" of foreign products upon the American market and the steps requisite and adequate to control and prevent it. It might in this field, as well as in others, secure very valuable information for the guidance of American consuls, and for the use of the Board of General Appraisers and other Treasury officials.

I have gone into these particulars because I felt that they would make clearer than I could make it in general phrases my idea of the field of unpartisan[1] inquiry within which such a commission could render a useful and perhaps indispensable service to the country, and I am taking the liberty of bringing the matter to your attention just at this time because I hope that it will be

possible for the Committee of Ways and Means of the House
of Representatives to take this question up immediately with a
view of formulating some policy and action concerning it. I feel
confident that you will agree with me that the situation of the
whole world in the matter of economic development is so unusual and our own interest in the changes probably impending
so vital that I am justified in pressing this great topic upon the
consideration of the Committee at this time.

  With warmest regards,

        Cordially and sincerely yours,   Woodrow Wilson[2]

TLS (C. Kitchin Papers, NcU).
  [1] Wilson dictated "nonpartisan."
  [2] The second, third, fourth, fifth, and sixth paragraphs of this letter were
paraphrases of portions of an undated and unsigned T memorandum, "*Tariff
Commission*" (WP, DLC). David F. Houston later wrote (*Eight Years with
Wilson's Cabinet* [2 vols., Garden City, N.Y., 1926], I, 197) that he was the
author of the memorandum.

To James Hay

My dear Mr. Hay: The White House January 24, 1916

  Thank you very much for your letter of January twentieth. It
is written in the same frank spirit of counsel that has characterized you throughout our conferences about the important matters
which now confront us and makes me more confident than ever
that after a frank interchange of views we shall agree upon the
thing that is best, all things considered.

  As you know, my judgment moves decidedly in one direction,
while apparently yours is, for the present at least, moving in another, but that does not at all impair my confidence that we can
do what the country will demand of us.

        Cordially and sincerely yours,   Woodrow Wilson

TLS (J. Hay Papers, DLC).

From Robert Lansing, with Enclosures

PERSONAL AND CONFIDENTIAL.

My dear Mr. President: Washington January 24, 1916.

  I received late Saturday night a letter from Count Bernstorff
enclosing two drafts of memoranda in the LUSITANIA case.
Copies of these papers I am sending you.

  Neither of the drafts seems to me to be at all satisfactory.
There is no acknowledgement of the illegality of the sinking of
the LUSITANIA and no admission of liability for the indemnity of-

fered. The proposed memoranda are no improvement over the last one which the Ambassador submitted. They come no nearer meeting our demands. The offer of indemnity is based on good will; it is an act of grace and not a matter of right.

I shall not see the Ambassador until I have your opinion of this last effort to settle the controversy, but, when I do, I am disposed to tell him very frankly that further conversations will be useless as they do not appear to bring us any nearer together, and that there seems to be no other course but to make a formal demand upon the German Government for admission of illegal conduct by the submarine commander and of liability for the lives of citizens of the United States destroyed by the sinking of the vessel.

It does not seem to me to be in accord with the dignity of this Government to continue these informal negotiations which have become purely dilatory and offer no possible middle ground for an agreement.

Of course if we take this step and Germany fails to comply with our demands it will mean that we will have to send Bernstorff home or announce that we will do so unless full satisfaction is given within a definite time. While I dislike this course I see no alternative. We have delayed bringing this matter to a direct issue as long as we can. I had hoped a satisfactory settlement through delay.[1] With more or less justice there has been increasingly severe public criticism of the policy pursued by the Government. If I felt that all would come right in the end I would be indifferent to public comment, but in view of these drafts of memoranda I am convinced that further delay will accomplish no good purpose and will only add to the belief that we are not insisting on compliance as we should.

It is possible that a demand, which the German Government understands to be inflexible, will accomplish more than our informal negotiations have accomplished. I do not think that they want a diplomatic break, and, if they are convinced that compliance is the only way to avoid it, they may submit. In any event I see no other course which we can honorably take.

I would like to see you as early today as possible or else talk with you over the telephone, in order that I may arrange an interview with Count Bernstorff as he requests.

Faithfully yours,   Robert Lansing.

TLS (SDR, RG 59, 841.857 L 97/128½, DNA).
[1] Thus in the text.

ENCLOSURE   I

Confidential!

Washington, D. C.,

My dear Mr. Secretary,   January 22, 1916.

I beg to thank you for your note of January 21st by which you kindly transmitted to me a cipher message from the German Foreign Office concerning the LUSITANIA case.

As it is too late to trouble you this afternoon I beg to submit to you confidentially the two enclosed drafts of memoranda, which are both based on the instructions I received to-day. I sincerely hope that one of the two will prove satisfactory to you and that we may at last settle this old case.

I should be very much obliged to you, if you would kindly let me know by telephone when I may have the pleasure of discussing the matter with you on Monday.

Believe me, my dear Mr. Lansing,

Very sincerely yours,   J. Bernstorff

TLS (SDR, RG 59, 841.857 L 97/128½, DNA).

ENCLOSURE   II

The German submarine war against England's commerce at sea, as announced on February 4, 1915, is conducted in retaliation of England's inhuman war against Germany's commercial and industrial life. It is an acknowledged rule of international law that retaliation may be employed against acts committed in contravention of the law of nations. Germany is enacting such a retaliation, for it is England's endeavor to cut off all imports from Germany by preventing even legal commerce of the neutrals with her and thereby subjecting the German population to starvation. In answer to these acts Germany is making efforts to destroy Emgland's [England's] commerce at sea, at least as far as it is carried on by enemy vessels. If Germany has notwithstanding limited her submarine warfare this was done in view of her long standing friendship with the United States and in the expectation that the steps taken by the American Government in the meantime aiming at the restoration of the freedom of the seas would be successful.

The German Government, on the other hand, recognizes from the course which the negotiations so far have taken the difficulty to reconcile in principle the American and the German point of view, as the interests and legal aspects of the neutrals and belligerents naturally do not agree in this point and as the illegality of the English course of procedure can hardly be recognized in the United States as fully as it is in Germany. A perpetuation of this difference of opinion, however, would not tend to further the amicable relations between the United States and Germany which have never been disturbed and the continuation of which is so sincerely desired by both Governments. Actuated by this spirit the Imperial Government again expresses its deep regret at the death of American citizens caused by the sinking of the Lusitania and, in order to settle this question amicably, declares its readiness to pay indemnity for the losses inflicted.

ENCLOSURE III

The attack on the Lusitania formed part of the reprisals enacted by the Imperial Government against Great Britain on account of her illegal starvation policy. According to the German opinion such reprisals were amply justified by the inhuman British warfare. At that time the Imperial Government had not yet issued the instructions which now regulate the German submarine warfare and according to which the Arabic case was settled. These instructions were issued with regard to the friendship of many years' standing between Germany and the United States and in expectation that the steps the American Government has undertaken in the meantime to reestablish the freedom of the seas would be successful. Even before these instructions were issued it was, however, not the intention of the Imperial Government that our reprisals should lead to the loss of the lives of noncombattants. My Government has, therefore, on previous occasions expressed its deep regret that American lives should have been lost on the Lusitania.

As for the question whether the Imperial Government is obliged to grant an indemnity in this case, it appears from the negotiations which have hitherto taken place that a further accentuation of the difference of opinion which has arisen on this point would not [have] been apt to promote the friendly relations between Germany and the United States which both Governments have at heart and which so far have never been troubled. In a spirit of friendship and conciliation, therefore, the Imperial Government in order to settle definitely the Lusitania incident, declare themselves willing to grant an indemnity for the lives of American citizens which were lost by the sinking of the boat.

T MSS (SDR, RG 59, 841.857 L 97/128½, DNA).

To Robert Lansing

My dear Mr. Secretary,   The White House. 24 January, 1916.

I do not see wherein this memorandum differs from that previously submitted and which we declared unsatisfactory. I entirely agree with you that we cannot accept it as a recognition of our rights. It is only a concession as of grace.

You will remember the despatch I sent you from House, in which he asks that we take no steps against Germany until we receive the letter which he was to send by a steamer leaving England last Wednesday, the nineteenth of January. I have not the least idea what that letter contains, but I do not think that it would be prudent to take any step towards a diplomatic break before we know what is in it.

I hope, therefore, that you will until then only see Bernstorff and let him know that the reply he has submitted is not satisfactory and seems to close conversations unless his government can see its way to a change of attitude, and then feel your way for a few days. House's letter ought to reach by the twenty-seventh. I assume it will come in the pouch from London.

Or would it be practicable and wise to put Bernstorff off until then?   Faithfully Yours,   W.W.

WWTLI (SDR, RG 59, 841.857 L 97/129½, DNA).

From Robert Lansing, with Enclosure

PERSONAL AND CONFIDENTIAL:

My dear Mr. President: Washington January 24, 1916.

I enclose a confidential telegram received from Ambassador Page at London, which was decoded yesterday. The telegram was in the private cipher and is more or less garbled—however, I think that it is sufficiently clear in expressing Mr. Page's view as to the present situation.

I give more weight to the telegram because he had, at the time of sending it, had the advantage of consultation with Colonel House. Possibly you have received from Colonel House telegrams which will throw light on Mr. Page's point of view and also that of the British Government. I hope that you will have had this called to your attention before determining what course we should take with regard to Germany.

Faithfully yours,   Robert Lansing.

TLS (SDR, RG 59, 763.72112/220¾, DNA).

ENCLOSURE[1]

London January 22, 1916.

3622. CONFIDENTIAL to the Secretary and the President Only. (Private Cipher)

Great Britain's Allies, especially France, strongly insist on ⟨Great Britain's Allies⟩ tightening the economic pressure on Germany. Public opinion here also has become earnestly aroused and demands an absolute blockade. The Government cannot long resist this demand for the country is convinced that a ⟨beginning (#)⟩ *decisive* victory depends on it. If the war end as a draw Europe will remain under a burden of armaments and there can be no hope of a ⟨continuing⟩ *continuous* peace. The Allies believe that ⟨(#) may accept it⟩ *the question may* largely rest with us whether the war shall end as a draw. If we so object to a blockade as to cause an indecisive peace Ally opinion will hold us responsible for the burdens of armaments and the political complications that will follow.

The following information which comes to me indirectly from an official source illustrates my meaning: Japan has forced ⟨(# # #)⟩ *the tentative consent of some of the Allies to her* acquiring and retaining certain large advantages and privileges after the war ends. She wishes to set up a sort of Monroe Doctrine behind which it is feared she would exploit China and dominate the Pacific. England withholds her consent and has provoked an angry attitude by Japan who wishes to secure her spoils and privileges while England is helplessly engaged in the ⟨(group incomplete)⟩ *war with* Germany. The British Government is disgusted and distrustful of Japan but it is for the moment helpless. England's final attitude to Japan must depend largely on the ⟨(expeditionary?)⟩ *feeling* at the end of the war between England and the United States. If the United States should oppose the blockade ⟨(#)⟩ *of Germany* and the war should end as a draw Japan will be able to extort her full demands because England will need her navy indefinitely on this side of the world. If the United States acquiesce in the blockade and the war ends with German defeat, both England and the United States will be in the way of Japan's aggressions and ⟨that will be an invitation.⟩ *Japan will be checkmated.* The only hope therefore of a permanent peace lies in such a decisive defeat of Germany as will prevent a new era of armament and a new set of dangerous complications both in Europe and in the Pacific; and a decisive ⟨(# #)⟩ *defeat* may depend on the degree of active sympathy we show by our attitude to the forthcoming blockade.

Our attitude to the blockade therefore will have far reaching results for us and for the whole world. Permanent peace ⟨(#)⟩ *depends on the* active sympathy of the two great English-speaking nations. There is ⟨(no?) occasion for⟩ *no other* practical and enduring basis of it. Besides nothing else can long save us from war. We are the larger in white population and potentially the stronger of these nations (and) permanent peace cannot come without our active sympathy with the smaller empire which ⟨(it)⟩ is now spending ⟨its subjects (#)⟩ *itself to withstand* the assault *of* military monarchy on free government. If we accept the forthcoming blockade as England ⟨acceded to⟩ *accepted* our weaker blockade against the Confederacy we shall save the world from the aggressive ambitions both of Germany and of Japan. If we insist *on* technical objections in order to build up a code of naval and marine law one or both the aggressive military monarchies will smash our legal structure in their assault on democratic civilization.

Events are pushing us to the necessity of a ⟨share of⟩ *sharp* decision. It may be a silent ⟨(#)⟩ *decision* but it must be clear. We should already have been drawn into this conflict but for England's complete naval supremacy over Germany. If the German navy had the seas we should have been goaded into war. The only course that can insure peace for us in the future in the world-wide conflict between military monarchy and free government is such a direction of events as will bring an active sympathy between the British Empire and the United States. The forthcoming blockade will give probably the last tactical opportunity for such an active sympathy.

For these reasons this seems the critical moment of this war for us; a moment that demands a constructive and decisive suggestion. If you have such a suggestion, however tentative, that I may privately use it may secure a permanent peace after this war ends and change the course of history for a century.

I write this ⟨profuse⟩ *profound* conviction having in mind only our own interests, our own security, and our own duty to our democratic ideals. This is our only practical lead ⟨toward⟩ *to insure* a lasting peace ⟨our representation⟩.

Amembassy London.

T telegram (SDR, RG 59, 763.72112/2200¾, DNA).

1 The following telegram has been corrected from a copy received from the embassy in London, which bears the same file number. Garbled words and omissions are in angle brackets; the corrected text is in italics.

To Robert Lansing

My dear Mr. Secretary,   The White House. 24 January, 1916.

This is very obscure, but I think I gather the sense of it.

I doubt if we can assume that it has any admixture or colour of House's views in it. I think it is all Page.

It of course has some force in it and deserves to be thought over on its own merits. Indeed, the arguments it urges are evident enough and of considerable weight.

In any case we ought to wait until we get House's letter to which I refer in the mem. attached to your letter about the latest communication from Bernstorff.

Faithfully Yours,   W.W.

WWTLI (SDR, RG 59, 763.72112/2201½, DNA).

From Robert Lansing, with Enclosure

PERSONAL AND CONFIDENTIAL:

My dear Mr. President: [Washington] January 24, 1916.

I send you herewith a telegram, of which I assume you have received a flimsy, in relation to Chile's attitude in regard to the Pan American Treaty. I also send a communication which I have just received from the Brazilian Ambassador, which indicates that influences are at work to defeat the purposes of the treaty. DaGama assured me over two months ago, that there was no doubt but that his Government would endorse the principle of the treaty, as he had been assured by it to that effect. I do not know what influences are at work but I have my suspicions.

I think the Chilean objection is directed to the Third Article proposed, which embodies the principle of the Bryan Peace Treaties and makes arbitration compulsory.

Please return these documents for the files, after reading.

Faithfully yours,   Robert Lansing

CCL (SDR, RG 59, 710.11/230, DNA).

ENCLOSURE

STRICTLY CONFIDENTIAL.

Santiago, January 21, 1916.

The President's proposed Pan American treaty has been submitted to the Chilean Senate Committee on Foreign Affairs in secret session, and it has been decided that it is unacceptable in its present form, especially the provisions relating to the arbitration of territorial controversies. Chile has always opposed compulsory arbitration on account of Tacna-Arica question. Suarez has been instructed. Active telegraphic interchanges have been carried on between Chile and Brazil and Muller has promised not to proceed further in the negotiations unless treaty so framed as to obviate Chilean objections. I am informed confidentially that the Argentine Minister of Foreign Affairs when in Santiago last May told the then Minister for Foreign Affairs of Chile, Mr. Lira,[1] that the President's plan was not highly regarded in the Argentine. This does not harmonize with Naon's recent conversations with me. There is a suspicion that Naon has gone farther than his Government or that Argentine would be glad to have Brazil and Chile bear the onus of rejecting treaty. Both Brazilian and Chilean governments are now sounding Argentine Government as to how far it will support Chile. At the suggestion of Muller, Ecuador has also been informed of Chilean attitude but without suggestion of any line of policy. I would ask that the source of this information be treated with utmost reserve, especially as regards representatives of countries mentioned.

[Henry Prather Fletcher]

T telegram (SDR, RG 59, 710.11/230, DNA).
[1] José María Valderrama Lira.

To Philip H. Chadbourn[1]

[The White House]
My dear Mr. Chadbourn: January 24, 1916

I was deeply touched by the gifts which you brought me the other day from various persons and associations in Belgium. They constitute so spontaneous an expressions[2] of gratitude for what citizens of the United States have been able to do for the relief of those who have suffered disaster from the war that they affect me almost as poignantly as human voices would, and I hope that you will have some opportunity to express to those from whom the gifts came the profound feeling of appreciation they produced in me. I am sure that what America has been able to do for the Belgians it did from the heart, and it is very delightful even in the midst of the terrible circumstances of this war to think of such evidences of disinterested international friendship between the two peoples.

May I not express to you also my warm appreciation of your own gift, the interesting medal recently struck off in Belgium depicting America receiving the homage and thanks of Belgium? This will always be one of my most interesting possessions.

Cordially and sincerely yours,   Woodrow Wilson

TLS (Letterpress Books, WP, DLC).
  1 Chadbourn served with the Commission for Relief in Belgium from February to December 1915, when he returned to live in New York. He met Wilson at the White House on January 19.
  2 Wilson dictated "expression."

To Araminta Cooper Kern

My dear Mrs. Kern: [The White House] January 24, 1916

Thank you with all my heart for your letter.[1] It has given me very deep pleasure and Mrs. Wilson joins me in sending you our warmest regards, notwithstanding that she has not had the pleasure that I have had of meeting you and realizing what a genuine and delightful friend you are. I wish most sincerely that she had the advantage of having you at hand that we might have the pleasure of having you share the season's activities with us, but I realize the strength and importance of the reasons that keep you in Indianapolis. I am only sorry that the Senator must be left lonely.

It is fine to hear how well the boys are doing in school and I hope that you will give them my warmest regards and best wishes.

You need have no fear that the jingoes will force or even hurry me into anything. I think I know them and know how small an element in the country they represent.

Cordially and sincerely yours,   Woodrow Wilson

TLS (Letterpress Books, WP, DLC).
  1 It is missing.

From Robert Lansing, with Enclosure

PERSONAL AND STRICTLY CONFIDENTIAL:

My dear Mr. President: Washington January 25, 1916.

I enclose a memorandum of a conference with the German Ambassador, which took place this afternoon. In accordance with our understanding this morning you will see that I have delayed matters in a measure and, at the same time, have practically broken off our informal conversations—though I am to see him tomorrow morning.

Faithfully yours,   Robert Lansing.

TLS (WP, DLC).

ENCLOSURE

MEMORANDUM OF CONFERENCE WITH THE GERMAN AMBASSADOR
IN REGARD TO THE LUSITANIA CASE, JAN. 25, 1916.

I said to the Ambassador that I had considered very carefully
the two memoranda which he had sent me Saturday night, and
that I regretted to say that neither of them was at all satisfactory;
that I could not see any material change from the memorandum
which he had previously submitted on the subject. He replied
that he thought they differed in the fact that they left out the
portion which related to a warning of American citizens. I told
him I considered that non-essential; that the essential ommission
was the frank admission on the part of Germany that the sinking
of the LUSITANIA, being an act of reprisal, was an illegal act; and
that while it might be justified in regard to enemies, it could
not be justified in regard to neutrals; that their rights were
violated and that the violation of rights imposed upon the German Government the liability of which the outward manifestation was the payment of a reasonable indemnity.

The Ambassador said that they had offered to pay the indemnity and he thought it might be concluded from that they recognized that a right had been invaded, and that, therefore, there
was liability.

I told him I did not read the memoranda in that way; that the
language indicated that the payment of an indemnity would be
an act of grace on the part of Germany, growing out of her
desire to preserve the friendship of the United States; that when
Italians were massacred by a mob in New Orleans the United
States had paid a considerable indemnity but had denied obligation to do so and, therefore, had denied liability for the wrong.[1]

The Ambassador asked me what I desired him to do. I said that
in view of the circumstances I could see no good reason for continuing our informal conversations on the subject, unless his
Government frankly admitted the illegality of the submarine
commander's conduct and also admitted liability for the American lives lost. He replied that he was convinced his Government
would not be willing to consent to such admissions in view of
the fact that it would be turning black into white, as they had
always denied the wrong and the liability. I answered him that he
evidently, then, had reached the same conclusion—that further
informal negotiations would be useless.

The Ambassador seemed greatly perturbed and sat for several
moments considering the situation. He finally said: "And what

would be your course in case my Government will not accede to these terms, which seem harsh?"

I replied: "I see no other course, Mr. Ambassador, except to break off diplomatic relations."

The Ambassador said: "I do not see how the matter could stop with the breaking off of diplomatic relations. It would go further than that."

I replied: "Doubtless you are correct in this view. I have given the matter most earnest consideration and have discussed it with the President, and I can assure you we do not hesitate to assume responsibility for what may occur in case your Government refuses to accede to our just demands. You know that we have striven to arrange this controversy amicably and for that reason I submitted to you a formula which I thought would, to an extent at least, harmonize the attitude of your Government with mine. I feel that we have gone as far as we can in accordance with the dignity and honor of the United States."

The Ambassador took the copies of the memorandum which he had been holding in his hand and started to make certain changes in them. I said to him that I thought it would be as well if he would take them to the Embassy and prepare a memorandum meeting our views, with the understanding that it might be possible to induce his Government to adopt it, and that I would see him tomorrow morning at 11:45. He replied that he would do so, but that he doubted very much if his Government could be induced to admit the wrong conduct of the submarine commander; or that it was liable for the death of the Americans on board the LUSITANIA.   Robert Lansing.

TS memorandum (WP, DLC).
[1] See n. 6 to remarks at a press conference, April 11, 1913, Vol. 27.

To Robert Lansing

My dear Mr. Secretary,   The White House. 25 January, 1916.

Do you not think that it would be wise to post Gerard pretty fully in this matter. I think that House ought to know the full facts, but I do not like to go over Gerard's head and tell House and not him. House, according to this despacth,[1] will be in Berlin to-day and it is of the utmost importance, of course, that he be fully posted. It might be well to instruct Gerard specifically to tell House everything, though I suppose he would do so in any case.
                    Faithfully Yours,   W.W.

WWTLI (SDR, RG 59, 763.72/2355¾, DNA).
[1] EMH to WW, Jan. 15, 1916.

From Joseph Patrick Tumulty

Dear Governor: The White House January 25, 1916.

Claude Kitchin is coming here today to oppose the idea of a Tariff Commission. He will tell you that he has made two speeches against it. I think the idea set out in your letter is excellent and will win favor throughout the country; but I am afraid that you will again be charged with inconsistency for the reason that in some of your speeches in the last campaign, you opposed the idea of a Tariff Commission.

When you have seen Kitchin, you will of course consider what he has to say and hold the matter in abeyance for a few days. Then I would write him a letter containing these ideas:

First; Re-affirming what you said in your letter of the 24th of January.

Second; Tell him that you appreciate the motives which actuate him and that you are glad to have his frank opinion.

Third; Explain in the frankest possible way the reasons for your change of heart in this matter, but give the reason, namely, economic changes that are bound to spring out of the war. Call his attention to what you said in your Message. (See excerpt attached.)[1]

Fourth; That Congress has so much to do at the present time that it is impossible to collect all the data necessary upon which to base honest and correct re-adjustments of the tariff law.

If you do not write a letter of this kind, I am afraid you will be charged with inconsistency.   Tumulty

TLS (WP, DLC).

[1] It is missing; however, Wilson embodied it in his letter to Kitchin of January 26.

From Edward Mandell House

Dear Governor: Paris, January 25, 1916.

I am enclosing you the editorial which Robert Donald has written for the Chronicle about which I wrote some days ago.[1]

He has repeated almost verbatim the lecture I gave him and because of the Chronicle's influence, I am sure it will do good. It makes me confident that when we really undertake to direct a campaign of education, it can be done. It has not seemed to me wise at this particular time, but there will come a day when it will be necessary to do this, and I have no doubt but that it can be done effectively.

Sharp tells me, and I believe it to be largely true, that the anti Administration feeling, both in France and in England, is the result of alienated Americans such as you castigated so thoroughly in your address before Congress. Men like Robert Bacon[2] ferry across the Atlantic at short intervals giving out interviews here and there, and condemning you and everything you stand for.

I am only staying here two days and am making no attempt to see anyone. I shall do so upon my return. There may be the feeling against us that so many Americans speak of, but I have not come in touch with it. I have been treated more courteously as your representative upon this trip than at any time before. Everything has been done that was possible for my convenience and comfort.

I am enclosing you translations of some articles that have appeared in the Paris papers of today and which may interest you in as much as they indicate a friendly feeling.[3]

It is pleasant to talk with Sharp if for no other reason that he is so thoroughly American and loyal to you and all you represent.

I sincerely hope that it will be possible for you to keep out of any controversy in regard to the blockade until I can talk with you. I think it is of the greatest importance that we find a way out that is satisfactory to our people and to the Allies.

Affectionately yours,   E. M. House

TLS (WP, DLC); P. S. omitted.

[1] "President Wilson's Policy," London *Daily Chronicle*, Jan. 21, 1916, clipping (WP, DLC). Donald chastized the British press for having the impertinence to advise Wilson to enter the war and described sympathetically the dilemmas of American neutrality. It was important to preserve Anglo-American friendship because it would be "a large part of the future of the world." Wilson, he went on, had satisfied neither side in the war. The Germans hated America as much as Britain, and Americans had good reason to resent British commercial policy as well as German outrages. Wilson faced further domestic difficulties as a result of his neutrality. He had alienated German Americans, Bryan Democrats, and the monied interests. Because American newspapers opposed Wilson, Britons lost sight of the true Wilson—the "standard-bearer of a great movement," the spokesman for the "mass of the sane public opinion," and the champion of the "maintenance of treaty obligations and international law."

[2] Assistant Secretary of State, 1905-1909, and Acting Secretary, 1906 and 1909, Ambassador to France, 1909-12. He was an ardent Francophile and a prominent proponent of preparedness.

[3] "Colonel House's Journey, Extract from 'Le Temps' of January 23rd, 1916," T MS; "The Mission of Colonel House, Le Figaro . . . January 22nd, 1916," T MS; "Col. House's Mission, La Libre Parole, January 24, 1916," T MS; "The House Mission in Paris, Le Gaulois . . . January 23rd, 1916," T MS; "Special Cable to the Chicago Daily News, January 24, 1916," T MS; all in WP, DLC. Each of the articles repeated the official version of the purpose of House's trip to Europe—to acquaint American ambassadors with Wilson's thinking about the war. All stressed the importance of the impressions that House would

take back. They all credited House with a perfect balance between diplomatic tact and authority and welcomed him as further evidence that Americans felt greater affinity with the Allies than with Germans. The extracts from *Le Temps*, inspired by Jules Cambon, according to House, dealt extensively with America's mounting impatience with Germany and her allies. The cable to the *Chicago Daily News*, prepared by A. H. Frazier of the American embassy, simply summarized French coverage of House's brief stop in Paris.

From George Thomas Marye

Sir: Petrograd, 25 January, 1916

I herewith submit my resignation as Ambassador to Russia to which high office you did me the distinguished honor to appoint me. The severity of the winter in Petrograd I find trying to my health.

I have the honor to be, Sir,
          Your obedient Servant   George Thomas Marye

ALS (WP, DLC).

To Claude Kitchin

My dear Mr. Kitchin: The White House January 26, 1916

Our conversation yesterday made me realize that in my letter of the twenty-fourth I had not set forth as I should have set them forth my reasons for changing my mind on the question of creating a tariff board, for I must frankly admit that I have changed my mind since I last spoke on that subject.

I have changed my mind because all the circumstances of the world have changed and it seems to me that in view of the extraordinary and far-reaching changes which the European war has brought about it is absolutely necessary that we should have a competent instrument of inquiry along the whole line of the many questions which affect our foreign commerce.

I have had in this change of mind no thought whatever of a change of attitude towards the so-called protection question. That is neither here nor there. A commission such as I have suggested would have nothing to do with theories of policy. They would deal only with facts and the facts which they would seek ought to be the actual facts of industry and of the conditions of economic exchange prevailing in the world, so that legislation of every kind that touched these matters might be guided by the circumstances disclosed in its inquiries.

I dare say you feel as I do, that it would be folly at this time, or until all the altered conditions are clearly understood, to attempt to deal with questions of foreign commerce by legislation, and yet having dealt directly and clearly with the whole question of unfair competition within our own borders, it is clear that as soon as we know the facts we ought to deal with unfair methods of competition as between our own nation and others, and this is only one of the many things that we would probably wish to deal with. The other matters I have attempted to indicate in my previous letter to you. I am glad to supplement that letter by this explicit statement of the considerations which have been most influential with me.

You will remember that in my last message to Congress I foreshadowed just the considerations which were operating in my mind in this matter. The passage to which I refer was this:

"Many conditions about which we have repeatedly legislated are being altered from decade to decade, it is evident, under our very eyes, and are likely to change even more rapidly and more radically in the days immediately ahead of us, when peace has returned to the world and the nations of Europe once more take up their tasks of commerce and industry with the energy of those who must bestir themselves to build anew. Just what these changes will be no one can certainly foresee or confidently predict. There are no calculable, because no stable, elements in the problem. The most we can do is to make certain that we have the necessary instrumentalities of information constantly at our service so that we may be sure that we know exactly what we are dealing with when we come to act, if it should be necessary to act at all. We must first certainly know what it is that we are seeking to adapt ourselves to. I may ask the privilege of addressing you more at length on this important matter a little later in your session."

I need hardly say that I appreciate very fully the motives by which you are yourself actuated and it is, therefore, with the greater confidence that I lay the whole matter thus fully before you. Congress has so much to do at the present time that it is clearly impossible that it should be able to collect all the data which such a commission would gather, and I feel that it would presently find such a commission indispensable to it.

    Cordially and sincerely yours,   Woodrow Wilson

TLS (C. Kitchin Papers, NcU).

A Memorandum by Robert Lansing, with Enclosure

MEMORANDUM OF CONVERSATION WITH GERMAN AMBASSADOR ON THE LUSITANIA CASE, JANUARY 26, 1916.

The German Ambassador called at 11:45 this morning and handed me a memorandum which he proposed to communicate to his Government for their approval. In the memorandum was the admission of liability of the German Government for the lives of American citizens lost on the LUSITANIA but no admission of the illegality of the act of the submarine commander in sinking the vessel.

After reading the memorandum I told the Ambassador that I did not think it would be satisfactory but that I would submit it to the President if he so desired. He asked me in what particulars I would have it changed. I told him in the particular as to the admission of illegality so far as neutrals were concerned. He then made several changes in the memorandum and after we went over them together he dictated them to Mr. Sweet.[1] The result was the annexed memorandum which the Ambassador will send today to Berlin for the approval of his Government

Over the telephone I read the proposed memorandum to the President who said that he thought if Bernstorff could obtain that our demands would have been fully met.

I then telephoned the German Ambassador that the President considered the memorandum satisfactory and that I hoped he could secure it.   Robert Lansing.

TS memorandum (SDR, RG 59, 841.857 L 97/131½, DNA).
[1] Richard C. Sweet, clerk to the Secretary of State.

ENCLOSURE

January 26, 1916.

The German submarine war against England's commerce at sea, as announced on February 4, 1915, is conducted in retaliation of England's inhuman war against Germany's commercial and industrial life. It is generally recognized as justifiable that retaliation may be employed against acts committed in contravention of the law of nations. Germany is enacting such retaliation because it is England's endeavor to cut off all imports from Germany by preventing even legal commerce of neutrals with her and thereby subjecting the German population to starvation. In answer to these acts Germany is making efforts to destroy England's commerce at sea, at least as far as it is carried on by enemy vessels. If Germany has notwithstanding limited her submarine warfare this was done in view of her long-standing friendship with the United States and in view of the fact that the sinking of the LUSITANIA caused the death of citizens of the United States. Thereby the German retaliation affected neutrals, which was not the intention as retaliation becomes an illegal act if applied to other than enemy subjects.

The Imperial Government, having, subsequent to the event, issued to its naval officers the new instructions which are now prevailing, expresses profound regret that citizens of the United States suffered by the sinking of the LUSITANIA and, recognizing the illegality of causing their death, and admitting liability therefor, offers to make reparation for the lives of the citizens of the United States who were lost by the payment of a suitable indemnity.

In the note of the American Government, July 21, concerning the LUSITANIA incident, the Government of the United States invited the practical cooperation of the Imperial German Government in contending for the principle of the freedom of the seas, and added that this great object could, in some way be accomplished before the present war ends. The Imperial Government will at all times gladly cooperate with the Government of the United States for the purpose of accomplishing this common great object. [1]

T MS (SDR, RG 59, 841.857 L 97/131½, DNA).
[1] Bernstorff sent this draft over the State Department wire (it arrived in Berlin on January 28), saying that the Washington administration regarded it as an ultimatum, that Wilson had accepted the draft, and that a break in relations would ensue if the German government rejected it. Bernstorff added that he had just talked with the Swedish Minister, W. A. F. Ekengren, who in turn had just talked with Lansing. Lansing had said that he feared an imminent break with Germany, which would propel the United States into the war, and that Wilson definitely would not recede from his demands and that the decision for peace or war was now in the hands of the German government. J. H. von Bernstorff to the Foreign Office, received Jan. 28, 1916, T telegram (Der Weltkrieg, Der Unterseebootkrieg gegen England No. 18a, ganz geheim, Vol. 17, n.p., GFO-Ar).

Robert Lansing to James Watson Gerard

Washington, January 26, 1916. 5 PM

No. 2645 STRICTLY CONFIDENTIAL FOR THE AMBASSADOR AND COLONEL HOUSE:

On the 22d the German Ambassador submitted two tentative drafts of a memorandum in the LUSITANIA case by which the German Government repeated its regret that Americans were killed by the justifiable retaliatory act of its submarine commander and offered, out of regard for the friendship of the two countries, to pay an indemnity.

On the twenty-fifth I had an interview with Count von Bernstorff and told him that both drafts were unsatisfactory; that the act of the submarine commander, being retaliatory, was admittedly illegal and though it might be justified against an enemy it could not be justified against neutrals. I told him that this Government would be satisfied with nothing less than an admission of the wrongful conduct of the submarine commander and an admission of liability for the lives of American citizens lost by his act. He replied that he was sure his Government could not go as far as that as they had denied liability. He asked me what would be our course in case Germany could not meet our demands. I replied that I saw no other course except to break off diplomatic relations, to which he answered that he thought it would go further than that in case we followed that course. I told him that was probably correct but that I had discussed the matter fully with the President and that we would not hesitate to assume responsibility for the consequences. He stated that he would think the matter over and see me again today.

At noon today the German Ambassador called and after discussing the matter he submitted the following memorandum which he is sending to his Government for their approval.

(Here insert attached memorandum (Blue))

If the German Government can agree to the above memorandum I believe that the LUSITANIA case will be satisfactorily ended. The memorandum was read to the President and received his approval.   Lansing.

T telegram (SDR, RG 59, 763.72/13402B, DNA).

From Robert Latham Owen

My dear Mr. President: [Washington] January 26, 1916.

I had fully intended coming with Senator Hollis and Mr. Lever to meet you in regard to the question affecting rural credits, but find that I shall be compelled to be out of the city at that time.

I am in sympathy with the point of view presented by Senator Hollis, and I hope that you may see your way clear to acquiesce in his proposal, for which I believe he will give you sound reasons.[1]   Respectfully,   Robt. L. Owen

TLS (WP, DLC).

[1] Senator Henry F. Hollis and Representative A. F. Lever had drafted a rural credits bill which they intended to discuss with Wilson and Secretary Houston on January 28. The bill created a system of federal land banks to lend money on a long-term basis to farmers organized into credit cooperatives against the security of their land. The banks would raise their initial capital, $500,000 per bank, by the sale of tax-exempt stock; the federal government would purchase any stock not sold to private firms or individuals within ninety days. The

federal government would also supply annually up to $6,000,000 at 2 per cent interest if the banks did not raise sufficient money. At the White House meeting, Houston objected to federal underwriting, and Lever suggested a compromise of $3,000,000 as the amount of annual support. Wilson stunned everyone by replying that this amount might be too modest, and the Hollis-Lever bill became an administration measure. See Link, *Confusions and Crises*, pp. 345-48.

From Robert Lansing, with Enclosures

PERSONAL AND CONFIDENTIAL:

My Dear Mr. President: Washington January 27, 1916.

The British Ambassador called upon me this morning and handed me the enclosed paper which is the substance of a telegram received by him from Sir Edward Grey in regard to our proposition as to a *modus vivendi* in connection with submarine warfare. I also enclose a telegram upon the same subject, deciphered late yesterday, received from Ambassador Page at London.

It seems to me that the British Government expected us to denounce submarine warfare as inhuman and to deny the right to use submarines in attacking commercial vessels; and that these statements by Sir Edward Grey evidence his great disappointment that we have failed to be the instrument to save British commerce from attack by Germany.[1]

I must say that I am very considerably disturbed as to Mr. Page's attitude on all subjects which in any way affect the policies of Great Britain. He certainly is influenced very strongly by the atmosphere in which he is and I frequently doubt whether he urges the cases involving American rights with the force and vigor which he should as American Ambassador.

In regard to the submarine matter I think there is nothing to be done until we have heard from the Allies of Great Britain but I presume in view of these telegrams that they will be opposed to any arrangement. I do not think it is necessary for us to act immediately upon such refusal but we should consider what course we are going to take in regard to Americans traveling on vessels carrying arms, which can be used offensively against submarines. I doubt whether we can insist that vessels so armed can be considered other than as auxiliary cruisers of the respective navies of the Allies.

I would be very much gratified if you could give me your views on this subject.

Faithfully yours,   Robert Lansing.

TLS (WP, DLC).
[1] Spring Rice's report of this conversation is C. A. Spring Rice to E. Grey, Jan. 27, 1916, HwC telegram (FO 115/2017, pp. 68-69, PRO).

E N C L O S U R E   I

Handed me by British Amb. Jany 27/16 RL

Strictly confidential and unofficial being telegram from Sir Edward Grey. Not to go on files. RL

Letter will have to be considered in consultation with French Govt. and other Allies affected.

Meanwhile I regard letter as described by you with most painful surprise: it had seemed to me incredible that upshot of controversy about German submarine warfare would be that United States Government would propose to justify and legalise wholesale sinking of merchant vessels by German submarines and to deprive British vessels of the chance of defence which United States Government have hitherto recognised as legitimate.

Defensive armament of merchant vessels does not render them superior in force to submarines: it does not enable them to take the offensive against submarines when guns are placed in the stern: it gives no protection against torpedoes. It enables merchant vessel to defend itself when pursued by a submarine and attacked by gunfire. This is precisely parallel to defence against pursuit by an armed cruiser which United States Government previously allowed.

At the outset of the war it was generally recognised (1). that merchant vessels and their cargoes should be brought into a Prize Court and should not be sunk unless in very exceptional circumstances.

(2). That defensive armament of merchant vessels was legitimate and United States Government made regulations accordingly.

United States Government now propose that sinking of merchant vessels shall be the rule and not the exception and that no chance of defense shall be allowed.

Both rules are thus altered to the direct advantage of Germany and the disadvantage of all the allies who own merchant shipping.

Furthermore this is proposed by the United States when they have already presented in a note certain demands which if conceded would make it impossible for Great Britain and the Allies to prevent free export and import from or to Germany of all goods of any description whether contraband or not through neutral countries thus preventing us from applying to present conditions the principles applied by the United States Government itself in the Civil War. New methods of warfare are to be conceded to Germany while the Allies are to be deprived of previously recognised means of pressure or even defense.

I cannot adequately express the disappointment and dismay with which such an attitude on the part of the United States will be viewed here.

It confronts us with a most serious situation which must of course be considered in consultation with our Allies.

It would be desirable that the United States Government should define what is meant by removing passengers and crew to a place of safety. Would this condition be satisfied by placing them in open boats on the high seas? I understand that at one time the United States Government held it would not thus be satisfied. And if not, what would be the minimum required to satisfy the condition? And what would happen if Germany disregarded the conditions of the United States Government, and other governments had, by denying the use of their ports, compelled British and allied merchant vessels to go without any means of defense? The United States Government can always bring pressure to bear on the allies: it is only by direct action that United States Government could enforce conditions on Germany. Would United States Government be prepared to take such action?

You should send this telegram privately to Secretary of State, and if desired leave him a copy of it but privately and unofficially as without consultation with the allies and without knowing what answer of United States Government would be to questions asked above I cannot give an official reply on behalf of His Majesty's Government.[1]

T MS (WP, DLC).
[1] The original of this telegram is E. Grey to C. A. Spring Rice, Jan. 25, 1916, T telegram (FO 115/2017, pp. 60-62, PRO).

E N C L O S U R E   I I

London January 25, 1916.

3648. CONFIDENTIAL FOR THE SECRETARY AND THE PRESIDENT ONLY.

Sir Edward Grey sent for me this afternoon to talk about the Administration's proposals about submarine warfare and about forbidding any merchantman from carrying a gun astern for defensive use. I was obliged to tell him that I knew nothing about such proposals. He seemed disappointed (#) he showed me a telegram on the subject from Spring-Rice not omitting Sir Edward's telegram of today in reply.

I have only once before seen Sir Edward so grave and disappointed and that was when he informed me that the British had sent the German Government an ultimatum. After he discovered that I had not been informed of the subject he seemed disposed to say little. He did say however that he indulged the hope that the Department had not foreseen the results of the proposal which was wholly in favor of the gentlemen [Germans] theoretically and practically (#) wholly against the allies. Then he asked me for House's address because as I gathered he had talked with him at my table so frankly and freely about the relations of our two Governments that he thought he ought to inform House that he (#) then know that this proposal would (an?) [had] come. He spoke as one speaks of a great calamity. He said that he would not mention the subject in his speech in the House of Commons tomorrow because the announcement that such a proposal had been made by the United States would cause a storm that would drive every other subject out of the mind of the House and of the country. He is the best friend that we have in the Government and his surprise and dismay are overwhelming.

Sir Edward is too courteous as to expose himself but the Government and British opinion will regard this change by us of an accepted practice made while the war is in progress as a complete German victory over us in the submarine controversy engendered bitterness against us will be intense in the Allied countries and such influence as we might have had with the Allied Governments will be lost. If this proposal be persisted in the Administration will forfeit the confidence (group incomplete) good will of England and France. Can we gain enormously by it to offset this loss? (#) [I hope that you] will reread my confidential telegram of the 22d instant.

It has been rumored here in well-informed circles for several weeks and I believe it is true that the British Government have been constructing extra munition works in England and Canada which can on short notice be manned and used to make as many munitions as the United States now supplies. The reason given for this expensive preparation is the fear of Bernstorff's success in his efforts to cause the Administration to embarrass the Allies. If necessary orders placed in the United States could now be stopped within a month without diminishing the total supply. If no merchantman may carry a defensive gun into an American port (#) change may precipitate a cutting off of American orders not from any wish to cut them off but from fear that other embarrassing acts by us may follow.   Page.

Amembassy London.

T telegram (WP, DLC).

From Charles Richard Crane

Dear Mr President   [New York] January 27 1916

Among others you are considering for the Supreme Court I hope is Mr Brandeis. Outside of a small and hopelessly irreconcilable group in Boston—to which Dr Eliot does not belong—I believe the appointment of Mr Brandeis would be a most popular one throughout the United States and give the best possible encouragement to the progressives both inside and outside of the party.

President Eliot has just been visiting me here and I am sure that you have not a warmer nor wiser supporter and, when the time comes, I believe he will say so in a way that will count. I know that he has a well defined picture that he is preparing to paint of you and your great service to the country and the world.

With cordial greetings,

Always sincerely and devotedly   Charles R. Crane

ALS (WP, DLC).

ADDENDA

Two Letters to James Richard Nugent

My dear Mr. Nugent: Princeton, N. J. November 14, 1910

I am just getting my head a little above the flood of letters and telegrams that came rushing upon me, and in this, which is almost the first letter I have voluntarily sent since the election, I want to express to you the deep appreciation I feel for the way in which you managed the campaign, and particularly of the generous and thoughtful care you bestowed upon my comfort and convenience. You have won, I need hardly tell you, my genuine friendship and I trust I may have more than one opportunity to express to you in person how warmly I feel about it all.

I wonder if you could give me the address of the chief stenographer who went about with us? I want to get from him, if possible, copies of all my speeches so as to revise them, because I find such a general demand that they should be published, if not entirely, at any rate substantially at length.[1]

Cordially and sincerely yours,   Woodrow Wilson

[1] See J. R. Nugent to WW, Nov. 15, 1910, Vol. 22.

My dear Mr. Nugent: Princeton, N. J. December 9th 1910

I write you just a line to ask if you will not be kind enough to give me the name and address of the stenographer who was in charge of reporting my speeches. I would like, if possible, to get from him a complete file of them. I sincerely hope that you are keeping well. I should like at as early an opportunity as possible to have a talk with you.[1]

Very sincerely yours,   Woodrow Wilson

TLS (NjHi).
[1] See J. R. Nugent to WW, Dec. 10, 1910, Vol. 22.

From Robert Lansing, with Enclosure

Dear Mr. President: Washington October 20, 1914.

I enclose you a copy of a memorandum which was left me to-day by the Russian Ambassador.

This is very much like the proposal Mr. Straight made the other day in regard to French Treasury notes, concerning which I spoke to you.[1] Of course I can see that these proposed obligations of the Russian Treasury amount practically to promissory notes, which could be used in paying for supplies purchased in this country.

This proposition seems different to me from a war loan, so far as its form is concerned, but there is no doubt it is a loan or a series of loans to the Russian Government.

I told the Russian Ambassador that I would present this memorandum to you for your consideration.[2]

Very sincerely yours,   Robert Lansing

TLS (SDR, RG 59, 861.51/74½, DNA).
[1] See RL to WW, Oct. 23, 1914, and a memorandum by Robert Lansing, Oct. 23, 1914, Vol. 31.
[2] Wilson returned Lansing's letter and its enclosure with an attached hand-written note (same file number as above) which read: "Covered by our conversation W.W." Lansing's memorandum, cited in n. 1 above, is a record of their conversation.

E N C L O S U R E

[Handed to me by the Russian
Ambassador, Oct. 20, 1914, 4 P.M.
Robert Lansing]

In consequence of the present situation in Europe our manufacturers are compelled to purchase large quantities of goods in the UNITED STATES. The American manufacturers do not sell goods in any other way than cash American Port (F.O.B.). In endeavour to help our manufacturers in the matter of payments for the purchased goods and not having sufficient funds in the UNITED STATES our Government would like to issue SHORT TERM OBLIGATIONS of the IMPERIAL RUSSIAN TREASURY (to be issued in dollars). The amount of the issue and the interest rate are to be determined as soon as the Federal Government will declare themselves favourably (not to have any objections to the issue).

It is understood that this issue will help both sides, American manufacturers as well as Russian manufacturers.

T MS (SDR, RG 59, 861.51/74½, DNA).

From Seth Low and Others

Sir: New York, N. Y., March 5, 1915.

Your Colorado Coal Commission begs leave to submit herewith a report of progress to date.

Upon receipt of your letter of instructions, dated December 21, 1914,[1] the commission addressed a letter to the Hon. George A. Carlson, governor-elect of Colorado, handing him a copy of your letter of instructions to the commission, and offering to him our good offices in any way in which we could be of service. The letter of the commission was addressed to the governor-elect of Colorado rather than to the then governor, with the idea of emphasizing the fact that this commission was appointed not to take any action with reference to the past but in order to be of service if possible in bringing about better conditions in the coal mining industry of Colorado in the future. Immediately after his inauguration on January 12, 1915, Gov. Carlson acknowledged the receipt of the commission's letter and welcomed its cooperation in all mutually agreeable ways.

At the same time Gov. Carlson transmitted to the commission so much of his message as dealt with industrial relations, calling our attention to the fact that the legislature was likely to pass a law creating an industrial commission and providing for a system of workmen's compensation. The governor also said that he felt safe in pledging to your commission the cooperation of the industrial commission of Colorado when appointed. Subsequently Gov. Carlson forwarded to the commission a copy of the bill dealing with these subjects as introduced. Through the National Civic Federation, of which Mr. Low is president, Colorado has secured the services of competent experts for the detailed study of this measure. Your commission, through its chairman, has kept in touch with this proposed legislation and is satisfied if the bill becomes a law substantially in the form approved by the experts consulted by the Colorado Legislature the State of Colorado will be in the front rank of States having good legislation for diminishing accidents among workingmen; for the payment of suitable compensation in cases of industrial accident; for the regulation of conditions affecting the health of workingmen in industry; for official mediation and voluntary arbitration in case of industrial disputes.

Subsequently, your commission sent a letter to all of the coal operators in Colorado, 132 in number, inclosing a copy of your instructions to the commission and tendering our good offices.

From 71 of the operators, producing 61 per cent of the coal mined in Colorado, your commission has received a joint reply to its letter. These 71 operators say explicitly that no useful purpose can be served by your commission going to Colorado, and the temper in which they write says, even more eloquently than their words, that with them "the dead past" has not yet "buried its dead."

From the Colorado Fuel & Iron Co., and from several of the

smaller operators, your commission has received letters conceived in a very different spirit. We have recently had the opportunity to confer with Mr. Welborn, the president of the
Colorado Fuel & Iron Co., and with a group of the New York
directors, including Mr. John D. Rockefeller, jr. The attitude of
the Colorado Fuel & Iron Co., as stated by these gentlemen, is
frankly to cooperate with this commission. They explained to
your commission in great detail the efforts that company is making to get into closer relations with its employees and to provide
a means for the joint consideration of grievances and for their
correction. The company does not speak of its plan as a thing
complete in itself; but it hopes that it will prove to be the first step
in a movement which will bring about increasingly good results.
These gentlemen, however, while not opposing an early visit
of your commission to Colorado, are clearly of the opinion, like
the 71 operators who signed the joint letter, that a visit of this
commission to Colorado at present would be untimely. They point
out, as the others do, that the new legislation now under consideration in Colorado will have an important bearing on the conditions to prevail after its passage, and that for this reason,
among others, a visit from this commission at the present time
might easily tend to postpone the normal development of better
conditions. While this commission has nothing to do with the
controversies of the past, it is called upon to work with conditions
created by the past. For the time being nothing seems to be so
essential for Colorado as the opportunity which time gives to
learn and to apply the lessons which the recent past must have
taught.

After careful deliberation, therefore, upon every aspect of the
question, your commission is persuaded that it can accomplish
more by waiting until next autumn before going to Colorado than
by going now. We have already secured the cooperation of the
governor of Colorado, of the Colorado Fuel & Iron Co., and of
several of the smaller operators; and we believe that time will
enlarge the area of cooperation, not only through the force of
public opinion but also, as we hope, by the demonstrated usefulness of cooperation. Time will also serve to show whether the new
steps taken by the Colorado Fuel & Iron Co. are in the right direction, and generally whether the new State legislation is adequate
and how it is working. For all of these reasons we think a later
visit to Colorado will be more useful than one made now. We
have reason to believe that this opinion is shared in labor circles.
Your commission in reaching this decision does not forget that it
was appointed to do everything in its power to advance the wel-

fare of the miner as well as of the operator. The commission indeed is profoundly convinced that the welfare of one is inextricably bound up with the welfare of the other. It is clear, however, that a commission without legal authority and which therefore must depend for anything that it can accomplish either upon the willing cooperation of all parties or upon the force of public opinion must be so considerate in its approach to the subject as to disarm even prejudice if that be possible. For the work which you have committed to this commission we are convinced that time will be a friendly element in bringing about the desired results. While, however, your commission has postponed its visit to Colorado for reasons stated, we assure you that we shall keep in close touch with the situation, and shall be ready at any moment to meet as best we may any new development.

Very respectfully,   Seth Low.

Chas. W. Mills.

Patrick Gilday.

PCL (S. Low Papers, NNC).
  1 WW to S. Low, Dec. 21, 1914, Vol. 31.

From Edward Mandell House

Dear Governor: New York. November 14th, 1915.

You told me to remind you to write a line to Walker W. Vick, 61 Broadway, New York, so you could appoint a time when he might come to Washington and have a short interview with you.

He was very pleased when I told him you would do this. I hate to make such a suggestion, but in this instance I believe it is important.

The friends of Poland are greatly distressed that nothing worth while has been done for her. They say that Belgium is a garden-spot compared with Poland, and this, I believe, is true.

Padewreski [Paderewski] and other Poles very much desire for this Government to take some action, and I see in today's papers that Germany is now willing to allow something to be done as in Belgium.[1] Before this they took an entirely different attitude.

It would be particularly pleasing to the millions of Poles in America if something could be done. The Relief Committee headed by Mr. Taft and other prominent citizens, have done nothing and 30,000 letters sent out to leading banks and corporations brought less than $8000. Do you think it worth while to take hold of the matter? If so I will be glad to try and think up some plan along the line of the Belgian Relief Commission.

Padewreski told me a day or two ago that there was scarcely a Polish child left under eight years of age and that history holds no greater tragedy than what has befallen Poland in this war.

Affectionately yours,   E. M. House

TLS (WP, DLC).
[1] The New York *Evening Post*, Nov. 13, 1915, reported that Dr. Vernon C. Kellogg, director of the Commission for the Relief of Belgium, had arrived in Berlin on November 13 after a trip through Poland, taken at the instance of the German government, to study the problem of the relief of Poland.

INDEX

NOTE ON THE INDEX

THE alphabetically arranged analytical table of contents at the front of the volume eliminates duplication, in both contents and index, of references to certain documents, such as letters. Letters are listed in the contents alphabetically by name, and chronologically within each name by page. The subject matter of all letters is, of course, indexed. The Editorial Notes and Wilson's writings are listed in the contents chronologically by page. In addition, the subject matter of both categories is indexed. The index covers all references to books and articles mentioned in text or notes. Footnotes are indexed. Page references to footnotes which place a comma between the page number and "n" cite both text and footnote, thus: "624,n3." On the other hand, absence of the comma indicates reference to the footnote only, thus: "55n2"—the page number denoting where the footnote appears.

The index supplies the fullest known form of names and, for the Wilson and Axson families, relationships as far down as cousins. Persons referred to by nicknames or shortened forms of names can be identified by reference to entries for these forms of the names.

All entries consisting of page numbers only and which refer to concepts, issues, and opinions (such as democracy, the tariff, the money trust, leadership, and labor problems), are references to Wilson speeches and writings. Page references that follow the symbol Δ in such entries refer to the opinions and comments of others who are identified.

In this index, we have omitted, under WOODROW WILSON, the entries, "Press Conferences," and "Public and Political Addresses and Statements." These are fully listed in the Table of Contents. We will follow this practice in future volumes.

N.B. In the entries for Woodrow Wilson and Edith Bolling Galt, we have not attempted to note their expressions of love for one another. Except for the first letters that they exchanged, all of the letters between Wilson and Mrs. Galt were love letters. The letters are of course indexed for subjects, names, events, and so on.

Volumes 13 and 26 are cumulative contents-index volumes covering Volumes 1-25.

INDEX

A. Jaeckel and Co., 272n2

ABC powers: see Argentina; Brazil; Chile

Across the Years (Macfarland), 354n2

Acuña, Jesús, 95

Adamson water power bill, 232

Adana, Turkey, 337

Addams, Jane, 196, 199, 200,n1, 348-49,n1; on preparedness, 134-35, 158

Address of President Wilson at the Pan American Scientific Congress, 446n

Adee, Alvey Augustus, 405

Africa, 466, 486

agricultural appropriation bill (March 1915), 97

Agriculture Committee (House of Reps.), 97

Agriculture, Department of, 232, 238n4

Agriculture and Forestry Committee (Senate), 97

Alaska, 232, 233

Alaska coal leasing bill, 231-32,n1

Albert I (of Belgium), 391-92,n2, 499

Albert, Heinrich Friedrich, 264n1, 281, 282, 282-83, 290-91

Alexander, Joshua Willis, 345,n1, 459,n1

Alfonso XIII (of Spain), 88n4, 130, 144, 176

Allen, Anjenett Holcomb (Mrs. Charles Sterling), mother of Mrs. Hulbert, 237

Allen, William Vincent, 153,n1

Alsace, 71n3, 466, 484

Altrude: see Gordon, Alice Gertrude

American Association for Labor Legislation, 184n1

American Bankers' Association, 322, 325

American Board of Commissioners for Foreign Missions, 337n1

American Federation of Labor, 184; and Hillstrom case, 206-207, 211, 214; and Seamen's Act, 458,n1

American International Corp., 347n2

American Jewish Relief Committee, 412n1

American Labor Legislation Review, 184n1

American Note (*New Statesman*), 223,n1

American Peace Society, 195n1

American Red Cross, 120, 243-44, 316,n1, 367, 472

American Revolution, 47-48

American Women's War Hospital (Paignton, England), 77n2

Ancona incident: see Austria-Hungary and the United States

Andrews, John Bertram, 184,n1

Annapolis: see United States Naval Academy

anti-dumping legislation, 502, 511; Redfield on, 427-29; Owen on, 434; McAdoo on, 476

Antwerp, Belgium, 74, 466

Arabic incident: see Germany and the United States

Archibald, James Francis Jewell, 277n1

Argentina, 54-55, 254, 520; see also Pan-American Pact

Arlington Memorial Amphitheater, 11n1

Armenians: plight of, 3, 104-105, 119, 337, 348, 349

armor trust, 434n1, 446, 456

Armstrong, Hamilton Fish, 152,n1, 182

Army (U.S.): see United States Army

Arnold, Frances Bunsen Trevenen, 110,n2

Arnold, Olney, 360,n5

Arredondo, Eliseo, 93, 94, 95, 101, 103, 501, 505

Asia Minor, 466, 484

Asquith, Emma Alice Margaret (Margot) Tennant (Mrs. Herbert Henry), 413

Asquith, Herbert Henry, 74, 356, 413, 414, 485, 499

Auchincloss, Gordon, 44, 178,n1

Auchincloss, Janet House (Mrs. Gordon), 44; appendectomy, 118, 127, 137, 152, 155

Australia, 427, 428, 486

Austria-Hungary, 131, 484, 507

Austria-Hungary and the United States: *Ancona* sinking, comments and negotiations concerning, 192,n1, 208-209, 222, 234, 235-37,n2, 244, 245, 282, 286-88,n2, 310n1, 351,n1, 362, 364-66, 368-70, 378-80, 381-82, 389, 391, 394-95, 403-404, 406-407, 410, 411, 415, 420, 425, 426, 430-31, 446-47; talk of U.S. severance of diplomatic relations, 260, 404, 406-407, 426-27, 435; and recall of Von Nuber, 265, 276-77,n1, 379; and *Persia* sinking, 420, 446-47; and armed merchant vessels and submarine warfare, 448-49, 495; House urges continuance of diplomatic relations, 483, 491

Axson, Stockton (Isaac Stockton Keith Axson II), brother of EAW, 393, 394, 455; drafts engagement announcement for WW and EBG, 16-17, 33-34

B. S. Moss Motion Picture Corp., 431n1

Bachmann, Gustav, 131n1

Bacon, Robert, 525,n2

Baker, Newton Diehl, 134, 193

Bakhméteff, George, 358,n2, 536-37

Balfour, Arthur James, 3, 4,n1, 5, 9, 279, 356, 382n1, 413; on armed

WOODROW WILSON

and Hillstrom case, 58, 69, 73, 73-74, 84, 210; to spend summer at Jersey shore, 58-59,n1, 72, 103, 127, 155; on his typing and typewriter, 70, 412; and Countess de Belleville and Louise Thuliez case, 88,n1,2,3,4; concern over leak in State Department, 91; Davidson College yearbook dedicated to, 95-96, 107; and campaign of 1916, 103, 176, 239, 313-14, 347, 424; sent *Princetonian* issues from his managing editor days, 152, 182; returns to Princeton to vote, 159-60,n1; arrival in New York, 175; annoyed by article in *Washington Times*, 235,n2, 273; appeal for aid to Red Cross, 243-44; fete planned by South American diplomats for WW and EBW, 372-73, 386, 396; receives gifts from Belgian association, 520-21

APPEARANCE

200; He was looking exceedingly fit; no lines of care, but well filled cheeks, of good healthy color and a fine clear eye through the glistening pince-nez, 280

APPOINTMENTS

House's ideas on change in Chile, 64; to Liberia, 68,n1; suggestions for